UNIVERSITY OF
GLOUCESTERSHIRE

NORMAL LOAN

NORMAL LOAN

The Sunday Times – Culture

REBUILDING THE MATRIX

SCIENCE AND FAITH

IN THE 21ST CENTURY

DENIS ALEXANDER

A LION BOOK

Published by
Lion Publishing plc
Mayfield House, 256 Banbury Road,
Oxford OX2 7DH, England
www.lion-publishing.co.uk
ISBN 0 7459 5116 3

First hardback edition 2001
First paperback edition 2002
10 9 8 7 6 5 4 3 2 1 0

Acknowledgments
Scripture quotations taken from the *Holy Bible,
New International Version*, copyright © 1973,
1978, 1984 by International Bible Society.
Used by permission of Hodder & Stoughton
Limited. All rights reserved. 'NIV' is a registered
trademark of International Bible Society. UK
trademark number 1448790.

A catalogue record for this book is available
from the British Library

Typeset in Photina
Printed and bound in Finland

Contents

Acknowledgments

This book has been written in odd moments during a busy research career spanning two continents. I must therefore first acknowledge my publishers for their patience and faith in believing that the manuscript would eventually be completed. They have been exemplary in maintaining contact and making encouraging noises at those times (all too frequent) when the author had not produced anything for a long time. An earlier title for the book was *Science and Faith at the End of the 20th Century*, but unfortunately the century did not prove long enough.

Kind friends have read early drafts of particular chapters and made many useful comments and corrections. In particular I would like to thank Professor Tom Blundell (Biochemistry Department, University of Cambridge), Tom Chapman (geologist and associate pastor, Eden Chapel, Cambridge), Dr John Coffey (History Department, University of Leicester), Dr Jonathan Doye (Chemistry Department, University of Cambridge), Professor John Polkinghorne (ex-president, Queens' College, Cambridge) and Professor Bob White (Earth Sciences Department, University of Cambridge) for their helpful suggestions. I should also hasten to add that the mention of these names does not imply that these individuals agree with every point made in the book, and in most cases they have read through specific sections relating to their specialities rather than the complete manuscript. The errors that remain are entirely my responsibility.

Last, but by no means least, I would like to thank my wife Tina, together with Chris, Helen and Sheona, for their love, support and understanding during the years in which I have been writing *Rebuilding the Matrix*.

Introduction

The scientific enterprise is full of experts on specialist areas but woefully short of people with a unified worldview. This state of affairs can only inhibit progress, and could threaten political and financial support for research.

Nature **Commentary, 14 August 1997, p. 619**

Contemporary Western societies are profoundly ambivalent about science. On the one hand, science is invested with exaggerated expectations and inflated hopes. The vision is for a high-tech universe whose powers we manipulate to serve our own ends. At the other extreme, a vigorous anti-science lobby perceives science to be the source of all our current woes. Scientists are viewed as dangerous meddlers, wresting secrets from nature that are best left well alone, playing God as they pry into the sequence of the human genome and uncover the fundamental forces that hold the universe together.

The rapid advances in science that are predicted for the 21st century, particularly in the biological sciences, will certainly bring increasing pressure to bear on our notions of human identity and value. Scientific advances are continually throwing up questions which science itself is poorly equipped to address. We will need to draw on all the resources we can lay our hands on if we are to maintain human justice, dignity and worth in the face of scientific disciplines, such as neuroscience and the new genetics, which increasingly lay bare our own biological constitutions. It is for this reason that a significant proportion of science funding is now routinely being made available to ethicists, philosophers and theologians – in order to tackle the ever more pressing moral and ethical questions raised by scientific advances. Without serious public understanding, discussion and debate there is a real danger that science will continue to appear threatening and dehumanizing to many people.

In this context it is a matter for regret that science is often associated in popular culture – and even within some segments of the scientific community – with hostility to religious faith. In the rosy optimistic glow which marked the end of the 19th century many thought that, as science and education spread, religious belief would decline automatically. Now, more than a century later, we know that this expectation was mistaken. For good or for ill, religious belief continues to exert a dominant influence over the great majority of the world's population: 87 per cent of the population at the start of the 21st century consider themselves to be 'part of a religion'.[1] While in some technologically advanced areas of the world, such as Europe, the late 20th century saw a decline in commitment to institutional religion, in the USA, by any criteria the nation which currently leads the world in science, the reverse happened and religion boomed. All the evidence suggests that both science and religion are with us for a very long time to come. Yet, rather than drawing on the resources of religion to affirm human values, a small but vocal group of scientists has insisted on using science as a weapon for attacking religious belief. At the same time, and at the opposite extreme, creationists have carried out a vigorous campaign to ban the teaching of evolution in American schools. The result has been an unnecessary polarization between science and religion in which more moderate voices have often been drowned out by the media attention given to extremist positions.

This book is an attempt to address this issue from the perspective of a working scientist who is tired of the rhetoric of the extremists and who wishes to present the views of that silent majority of scientists who, though the pressures of their professional lives rarely allow them time to contribute to the debate, would nevertheless dissociate themselves from such extremes.

I have tried to write a multidisciplinary overview of the subject covering a wide range of topics, although my own bent towards the biological sciences will be apparent. There seem to be many highly specialized works on the market, focusing on particular aspects of the debate, but not so many books that can introduce the general reader to a broad overview. I am very aware of the kind of apology which Erwin Schrödinger (1887–1961) wrote in his introduction to *What is Life* in 1944: 'A scientist is supposed to have a complete and thorough knowledge, at first hand, of some subjects, and therefore is usually expected not to write on any topic of which he is not a master.'[2] Drawing on so many different disciplines is a dangerous business for the non-specialist and I apologize in advance to those whose specialized fields have been distilled down to alarmingly condensed summaries. This book utilizes the resources of sociologists, historians of science, philosophers, scientists and theologians, and it is therefore inevitable that the broad brush will distort the picture on occasion. Nevertheless, sufficient references are provided, I hope, for those who wish to follow up individual topics in greater detail and obtain a more nuanced view. In order not to overburden the text with citations I have, in some chapters, bunched them into groups of references on which I have been dependent for a particular section.

I have largely allowed those hostile to religious belief to set the agenda, and the book assumes no particular religious commitment on the part of its reader nor, for that matter, any specialist scientific background. The greatest space has been given to topics such as evolution and evolutionary psychology (sociobiology), which are often perceived as inimical to faith. I myself write from a Christian perspective because Christianity is the religion I know most about, and it is also the one which has been most involved in the emergence of modern science since the 17th century. I have made no attempt to incorporate the beliefs of other world religions into the discussion; if I had the book would have increased in length several-fold. However, I have spent fifteen years of my career lecturing and carrying out scientific research (latterly in human genetics) in the Middle East and am therefore well aware of the substantial contributions made to the history of science by Islamic scholars. In fact the first drafts of the earlier chapters were written in West Beirut, the rigours of the Lebanese civil war ensuring that many evenings were spent at home, allowing time for writing. I have left some allusions to this violent environment in the text because of their usefulness as illustrations. They remain as vestiges of past evolutionary stages of earlier sections of the book.

Most chapters can, I hope, be read as stand-alone essays so that topics can be browsed according to inclination. Nevertheless, there is a unifying thread of argument through the book as a whole, which is best summarized by giving some idea of the questions addressed by each chapter.

Chapter 1 sets the scene by asking how we come to adopt the overarching paradigms within which we carry out our thinking about science, faith and the relationship between them.

Chapter 2 provides a vivid example from the 19th century – when racism was integrated into the scientific worldview – of how science can be misused for ideological purposes.

Chapter 3 then goes on to address the question as to whether science has had a secularizing effect on society and considers the popular view that there is a 'conflict' between science and religion.

The following four chapters proceed to delve into history to determine where the idea of conflict between science and religion may have come from.

Chapter 4 tracks the emergence of modern science out of Greek natural philosophy, with a particular focus on the way in which a Judeo-Christian worldview promoted the arrival of an empirical and utilitarian stance towards the acquisition of scientific knowledge.

Chapter 5 discusses some of the early tensions which occurred between religion and science, using the examples of Galileo and the church, the supposed hostility of Protestants to Copernicus, the role of the Bible, and the emphasis by the early modern scientists on generating mechanical explanations for things.

Chapter 6 recounts the way in which the success of science led to its increasing use in support of conflicting ideologies after 1700, the French Philosophes, the English Nonconformists and the early geological controversies providing some highly contrasting examples.

Chapter 7 looks at the life of Darwin, the introduction of his theory of evolution and the very mixed reactions that this stimulated. It then examines how the idea of conflict between science and religion, in Britain at least, was not due to this ground-breaking theory, as is often thought, but was a by-product of the professionalization of science that occurred during the latter part of the 19th century.

Having surveyed some sociological and historical factors that have influenced science–faith interactions over the centuries, the remainder of the book turns to the contemporary scene and asks what kind of relationship between these two domains of human interest and experience is appropriate for the 21st century. This takes us immediately to the heart of the matter: the nature of scientific and religious knowledge and the ways in which they interrelate, a subject which occupies chapter 8.

The topic of chapter 9, creation and evolution, provides an opportunity to illustrate some important distinctions between the types of questions addressed by science and those addressed by religion. The argument of this chapter will provide no comfort to creationists nor to those who view evolutionary theory as a tool to promote particular ideologies.

Chapter 10 picks up some of these themes in greater detail, considering some of the reasons why evolution has been supposed to have religious significance. Topics such as the role of chance, the origin of life and the concept of 'nature red in tooth and claw' are all given an airing – but the chapter concludes that the biological theory of evolution is essentially devoid of any religious significance.

A further evolutionary theme is critically assessed in chapter 11: the idea that morality can be extracted from biology by arguments based on evolutionary psychology (sociobiology).

Chapter 12 focuses on the extent to which knowledge about God can be inferred from the material structure of the universe, considering some of the pros and cons of the 'anthropic principle', particularly as it relates to physics and cosmology, and the question of multiple universes.

That old bugbear of the science–faith debate – miracles – is given a fresh examination in chapter 13, and David Hume's famous arguments against miracles are worked through in the light of more recent understandings of the nature of scientific knowledge.

Finally chapter 14 spells out in detail why 'rebuilding the matrix' – restoring the theistic paradigm that gave birth to modern science – has more chance of generating a truly humanizing science than other paradigms.

Some definitions may be useful. 'Science' is a notoriously difficult word to define. It derives from the Latin *scientia*, meaning 'knowledge', and entered the English language in the Middle Ages. At that time it was synonymous with 'knowledge'. However, it soon came to refer to an accurate and systematized body of knowledge. I use the word in this book to refer specifically to modern science, that powerful mixture of theorizing, observation and testing by experiment that came to be known as the 'empirical method'. This emerged in Europe from the 17th century onward, eventually giving rise in the 19th century to a professional class known as 'scientists'. The word 'science' in this modern sense only came into common usage during the 19th century, and even then was synonymous for many years with the term 'natural philosophy', a 'natural philosopher' being a person of science. In its contemporary sense we can define science as 'an intellectual endeavour to explain the workings of the physical world, informed by empirical investigation and carried out by a community trained in specialized techniques'. In general I have tried to use the term 'natural philosophy' for science before the 19th century and the term 'science' thereafter.

The term 'scientist' is more recent and was invented by a Victorian vicar called William Whewell. He lived in the earlier part of the 19th century before specialization became the vogue, and was seemingly good at nearly everything. Apart from publishing numerous papers on topics ranging from maths, geology and theology to education, philosophy and the movement of the tides, he also wrote and translated poetry and Plato. Besides this, Whewell was Master of Trinity College, Cambridge, and successively held chairs there in both mineralogy and moral philosophy, as well as inventing numerous scientific words that have become part of our language, like 'physicist', 'anode', 'cathode' and so on. Whewell introduced the word 'scientist' in the *Quarterly Review* for March 1834, almost as a joke, but later as a more serious suggestion.[3] Though the word found an immediate home in America, it took about sixty years for the term to become well accepted in Britain. Many 'scientists' were happier to be called 'natural philosophers' or 'naturalists', partly because they found the word ugly (though not as ugly as 'physicist'), and partly because they remained under the mistaken impression that it was one of those new and vulgar expressions recently imported from America.

I have already used the words 'religion' and 'faith' without definition. I take the word 'religion' to refer to organized systems of belief in God as practised by communities and not just by individuals. However, the purpose of this book is to range more widely than organized systems of religious belief, and so I have tended to use the word 'faith' where appropriate, particularly to incorporate personal systems of belief.

Chapter 1

Why Do We Believe
What We Do Believe?
Where Do Our Beliefs
About Science and Faith
Come From?

Nullus quippe credit aliquid, nisi prius cogitaverit esse credendum.
No one, indeed, believes anything unless he previously knows it to
be believable.
Augustine, *De Praedestinatione Sanctorum*, 2:5

Issues of science and religion are important to our civilisation –
far too significant to be left to either the devoutly religious
physicist or the scoffing atheistic biologist. People holding
different beliefs and forms of expertise need to work together in
an open, non-confrontational environment accepting both science and
religion as valid aspects of human experience. It is a challenge
facing the coming millennium.
Geoffrey Cantor, *Nature* 403, 2000, p. 831.

Most books about science and faith start with the assumption that the
relationship between the two is essentially dependent on historical and/or
intellectual debate, and that people adopt their views about them by a process of
rational argument. Professor X (usually a biologist these days) writes a
bestselling book which claims that science renders faith in God unnecessary,
whereas Professor Y (more often a cosmologist or physicist) writes another book
which states that recent scientific advances have rendered faith in God more
plausible than it was a few years ago. You read both books, so the assumption
goes, and then make up your own mind, in the process acquiring a different set
of beliefs about science, faith and how they relate.

The roles of historical and rational argument cannot, of course, be underestimated, and much of this book depends on the validity of such argumentation. There would be little point in writing books which present a viewpoint unless there was some chance that the occasional reader would be persuaded to change their views after reading them. Later chapters in this book will argue for the need to justify our belief systems on precisely such rational grounds. Nevertheless, sociological insights suggest that the adoption of many of our beliefs occurs, in the first instance, not by rational argument at all, and least of all by evidence, but by a very different set of social processes.

Scientists are generally wary of sociologists, and often downright hostile. The reasons for such hostility are not difficult to unravel. Sociologists who study science sometimes give the impression that the acquisition of scientific knowledge can be explained in purely sociological terms. Thus it appears that the main determinants of scientific theories are not the properties of the universe around us, but rather the power wielded by a certain school of scientists, or their ideological concerns, or economic forces which control scientific programmes. According to such sociological accounts, scientific knowledge is just one more type of human construct which has no more claim to our assent than any other form of knowledge. Not surprisingly, scientists become rather huffy when they read such material, for virtually all scientists believe that, in carrying out their research, they are gradually generating better descriptions of the physical world that, while certainly incomplete, over time correspond more and more closely to reality. Those descriptions are certainly not complete, but they are improving. Scientists point out that, while it is quite clear from the history of science that all kinds of economic, political and religious factors have played important roles in determining the direction of science, and even the content of some scientific theories, nevertheless, ultimately, scientific knowledge does provide reliable 'maps' of the world around us. Science is not merely a social construct. That conviction led to what the press came to dub the 'Science Wars' during the late 1990s, a series of debates and confrontations between sociologists and scientists, more vocal in the USA than in Europe, which revolved around the extent to which scientific knowledge could be explained in sociological terms (see more on the 'Science Wars' in chapter 8).

But the excesses of certain sociologists should not cause us to throw the baby out with the bathwater. Sociological analysis is often helpful in understanding not only (with the benefit of hindsight) why a research programme has developed in a particular direction, but also the wider question of why people hold certain beliefs, such as those about science, religion and the relationship between them.

Passionate beliefs and tacit beliefs

It is sometimes thought that the beliefs which are held most strongly by societies are those which are expounded with great passion. But a moment's thought will show that this is not the case. Passionate beliefs tend to be minority beliefs. The smaller your voice, the louder you need to shout in order to make yourself heard. The *really* strong beliefs in societies are those which are tacitly maintained. The strength of the belief is in direct proportion to the degree to which discussion of it is felt to be unnecessary. The assumption that the belief is true runs so deep that to unearth it and critically discuss it would be like digging up the foundations of the Tower of London to show that the stones underneath were really as big as everyone knew they must be anyway.

How do we come to accept such deeply held assumptions? Most of them are simply 'given' to us as the earliest data of our lives. At the beginning we are presented with a language in which everything is already labelled. Language is not a matter for discussion, only something to be learned. Yet language is not a neutral medium to express meanings about objects and concepts that exist in the world around us. Words are loaded in different directions by connotations that derive from their use against the background of a particular history and/or geography. The word 'wicked' to my generation means something quite different from its meaning for my students.

Along with the essential labelling provided by language comes the assignment of meaning and value to the social roles of those in our immediate environment. At the same time there is a further labelling of what behaviour is acceptable and what is unacceptable, of the friends with whom it is 'right' that we mix, and the kind of 'personal biography' which society around us expects us to have in the future. This early construction of our social world by significant people in our lives is an essential part of living in a human society. 'The world of childhood is massively and indubitably real.'[1] Without the 'givens' of childhood there would be no real hope of progressing into adulthood in a normal way. It is in childhood that we are given our 'database' which will certainly be modified, but never totally erased, as we progress through life. The acquisition of such a database is labelled 'acculturalization' by sociologists – 'the social processes by which we are constituted in and by culture, learning how to "go on" as knowledgeable agents... centred on the family, peer groups, education, media and work organizations'.[2] We are socialized not merely by ideas, but by the way ideas are structured, related to authority and made relevant to our particular needs and interests.

Together with language and the assignment of social roles comes extensive labelling of a different kind. This is that enormous baggage of beliefs and opinions we unconsciously absorb by a kind of osmosis from our environment.

14

Snatches of conversation on a telephone and the drone of a newsreader's voice; frowns of disapproval at a critical moment or a smile of welcome at another; the sneering voice when a certain person is mentioned; the titles of books lying around the house or, perhaps, the absence of any books at all – all these and thousands more 'bits' of environmental input help to shape our most deeply held assumptions about life, ourselves, society, science, politics, religion or whatever.

The media play a critical role in this osmotic process on a global scale. There are more than 850 million television sets in more than 160 countries watched by 2.5 billion people every day.[3] Britons read 28 million newspapers and watch an average of 3.5 hours of television daily.[4] Surveys have shown that 58 per cent of the British population rely on TV as their principal source of news and 68 per cent believe that TV news reporting is the most objective available.[5] In the USA, the typical family keeps at least one TV set switched on more than seven hours daily, and two-thirds of the American public get all their news from TV.[6] The average American child sees more than 20,000 commercials on TV per year, and, by the time he or she reaches the age of eleven, will already have watched 8,000 televised murders and about 100,000 lesser acts of brutality.

There is a continuing and active debate within the field of cultural studies as to whether the dominating effects of this saturating barrage of media exposure are homogenizing or diversifying. The answer is clearly both, depending on who is watching what where and in what context. Homogenization of cultures means the process of bringing belief systems more in line with certain common denominators, whereas diversification occurs when TV programmes tend to break down the hegemony of the dominant culture. Within a particular country the forces of homogenization certainly appear overwhelming. Once again, it is the tacit assumptions that are the most powerful in their socializing force. For example, commercial TV by its very structure assumes the correctness of capitalism. There would be little point in advertising were it not for the existence of choice and the operation of market forces. In turn, certain assumptions are built into advertising: an increase in the quality and number of your consumer goods will bring you greater happiness; authoritative scientific statements ('tested in laboratory X') are nearly always made by males; desirable bodies are invariably sleek and cellulite-free; personal security comes not by changing social structures but by the purchase by the individual of the 'correct' foods, medicines and medical-insurance plans. Advertising can be used quite easily to convert products into brand names so that the brand name becomes the name for the product, and sometimes even the process of using it ('I'm going to hoover my house today'). In the USA, Bayer aspirin is generally held to be better than other forms of aspirin, because adverts have been telling the American public so for as long as they can remember, even though all aspirin is chemically identical whatever its commercial source. Advertising can also be used to manipulate a company image until it has very little connection with reality. Dow Chemical, the company that once scorched Vietnam with napalm and the defoliant Agent Orange, now presents calendar-picture-style country scenes in its TV adverts in the USA with the claim that the company is 'protecting wildlife'.

What is absent from the TV screen may be as powerful in shaping public attitudes as what is present. In a study analysing television coverage of developing countries over a three-month period, published in 2000 by the British Department for International Development, it was reported that there was no coverage of 67 of the total 137 developing countries. Of the 70 countries mentioned, 16 were covered only in the context of reporting visits from Westerners, wildlife events, sport or the fact that a round-the-world balloon had travelled over them. Most coverage concentrated on conflict, war or terrorism, with little explanation of background. Ironically, TV ratings wars in one's own country result in the global village being made less accessible to the viewing audience. The unbalanced and limited reporting that does occur often reinforces negative stereotypes of violent countries far away which are beyond redemption.

Television is particularly powerful in validating assumptions about national identity and character. National ceremonies and historic moments receive extensive coverage; in the United Kingdom royal marriages and funerals act as a focus to unite national sentiments. Foreign news coverage generally assumes that the overseas actions of the government presently in power are correct. During the Gulf War of the 1990s the media played a key role in obtaining public consent for Western military intervention. The press were at all times accompanied by military personnel and were taken to chosen sites in limited 'pools'. During the first six months of TV coverage of the war in the USA, out of the 2,885 minutes of news analysed on major TV channels, only 29 minutes, or about 1 per cent, dealt with popular opposition to the military intervention.[7] During the NATO bombardment of Kosovo in 1999 the media in NATO countries were similarly supportive overall of government actions. It is not for nothing that TV stations are vigorously guarded by the military when countries pass through times of revolution. Media control is a key factor in social control.

The media analyst Douglas Kellner comments that:

> Ideology mobilizes sentiment, affection, and belief to induce consent to certain dominant core assumptions about social life (such as the value of individualism, freedom, the family, the nation, success, and so on). These core assumptions, the 'common sense' of a society, are deployed by groups, whereby, for example, groups and forces in struggle tend to

deploy discourses of democracy, freedom, and individualism which they inflect according to their own ideological agendas and purposes.[8]

The role of the media in homogenizing cultures is made easier by the non-reflective way in which the viewing public looks to TV for entertainment, escape and as a source of news. To quote Kellner again, this time commenting on his experience of teaching media studies in a Californian environment in which media saturation of his students is extraordinarily high, 'It has been my experience in over 25 years of teaching that students and others are not naturally media literate, or critical of their own culture, and should be provided with methods and tools of critique to empower them against the manipulating force of existing society and culture.'[9] Among these manipulating forces are not only tacit 'common-sense beliefs' about the economic and social structure of society, and national identity, but also the dominant assumptions in society about race, gender and class. TV 'is an agency of the established order and as such serves primarily to extend and maintain rather than alter, threaten or weaken conventional conceptions, beliefs, and behaviours... its chief cultural function is to spread and stabilize social patterns'.[10]

In contrast to the culturally homogenizing role of the media when maintained within national boundaries it can also subvert the accepted social order if transferred to a quite different context. Satellite dishes have been declared illegal in Saudi Arabia, Egypt, Bahrain and Iran, with the head of the Iranian Majlis (parliament) committee on Islamic arts and guidance declaring, 'This is a way of curbing the cultural assault... we showed the world that we are against foreign culture.'[11] The head of the Majlis committee is surely correct. Television is global in its circulation of similar narrative forms around the world, through soap operas, news, sport, quiz shows, music videos and blockbuster movies. The American TV and film industry is by far the largest contributor to this worldwide circulation of cultural assumptions, with its lion's share of 75 per cent of the worldwide TV-programme exports.[12] Countries which permit satellite dishes have little hope of their societies ever being quite the same again.

Belief systems and pluralism

Transition to adulthood is supposed to be marked by critical examination of the 'givens' we have received during childhood. The most fundamental 'givens' cannot, of course, be rejected, otherwise we could no longer be acting members of society, but there is an enormous mass of inherited assumptions that do not come into that category. What do we do with them? In practice, often very little. A remarkably high proportion of them are carried on into adult life and, very likely, will soon be shaping the primary socializing patterns of our own children. Barry Barnes expresses it like this:

> For most people, whatever their way of life, the beliefs they accept and utilize are held unselfconsciously, and are rarely reflected upon. Moreover, when reflection does occur, it tends merely to depict these beliefs as natural representations of 'how things are'. Critical, analytical examination of beliefs, their origins, functions, and claims to validity, is the province of specialized, academic roles in modern societies, and is a phenomenon of little general significance. The 'Western layman' lives in a taken-for-granted world: solid, objective and intelligible; on the whole he thinks with his beliefs, but not about them.[13]

Thankfully this picture is not the whole truth, because we could probably all cite without difficulty certain beliefs and convictions that we came to hold after a definite period of reading, discussion and thought about the matter. Many of these convictions may be closely linked to our profession or major activities in life, since our very preparation for them and involvement in them forces us to think through the issues they raise. Yet, if we were to do a survey of all our various beliefs and opinions, we might be surprised to find that those which we hold due to careful consideration are in a minority.

One experience which forces reflection, or at least some kind of reaction, commonly occurs when people go and live in a completely different culture from their own. Suddenly, their familiar assumptions are challenged. Many of the fixed points of life simply disappear. Even their own cultural 'signals' for various forms of politeness are now found to carry quite different meanings, leading to hopeless tangles in communication. The result for some is culture shock: vehement criticism of all the negative aspects of the 'new culture' and a retreat into a local community of foreigners who share one's own cultural presuppositions and among whom one can, therefore, be truly 'at home'. There are no people as English as the English abroad (and of course the same could be said of other nationalities), and the reasons are not too difficult to find. One way to maintain identity in a 'threateningly foreign culture' is to live in a subculture in which the familiarities of home are emphasized. This provides a continuously comforting stream of validation for 'what we all know to be true really'. Armies are only too aware of the need to provide their forces overseas with an environment in which they can feel at home. When I lived in Turkey I experienced several times the curious sensation of visiting the grounds of US military bases. The effect is rather like going through the back of the wardrobe and coming out in Narnia (the mythical land invented by C.S. Lewis in *The Lion, the Witch and the Wardrobe*), except that this 'Narnia' is full of American houses, cars, drugstores, supermarkets, baseball courts, traffic signs and movies. It is, indeed, like walking into 'little America'. A totally enclosed value system with its own cultural rules floats like a moored battleship in a sea of moderately secularized Islamic society.

This example of passing through a gate into 'another world' is not as far from our own experience as we might think. So far we have emphasized the homogenizing effects of our early socializing experiences and of popular culture, which combine to prepare us to operate with a certain national identity and language within a given society. But over this deep layer of shared national assumptions lies a second layer of cultural practices, lifestyles and belief systems that tends to vary a great deal between different subsets of people living in contemporary Western societies. The deep layer is like the ocean depths, the second layer more like the changing character of the ocean waves above.

Pre-industrial peoples are usually equally cohesive in both these layers of cultural belief and practice, so holding a worldview and social norms that act like glue to keep society together. Community is valued over individualism. Customs and values are shared by all members of the society. Not all will have the same lifestyle, since that depends on wealth and class, but social roles are generally accepted and well defined. Even post-industrial societies can maintain high levels of cohesiveness for lengthy periods. Such has happened in Japan, where the level of social conformity remains much higher than in Western countries, and in recently industrialized Middle Eastern countries such as Turkey. But, with time, social homogeneity tends to be undermined by the forces of modernization, a process already noticeable in both Japan and Turkey, where traditional social norms are being steadily subverted, particularly in the big cities such as Tokyo and Istanbul.

Modern Western societies are marked by their pluralism, now accentuated even further by the cultural forces operating under the rubric of postmodernity. Large institutions and corporations, faceless bureaucracies, tiny religious sects, ecofeminists, green activists and genetic engineers – all these can coexist within the same country, validating their own subcultures and belief systems. Tribes of subcultures wax and wane, depending on the interests of the moment. We all tend to gravitate to the subculture where we feel most 'at home', and passing through other subcultures in our pluralistic societies can be inconvenient at the very least, and at other times positively unnerving. The very symbols which are so reassuringly familiar in our own milieu may be just those which alienate the visitor. The sight of white lab coats, a jumble of power packs and electrophoresis equipment, rows of chemical reagents and PhD students running around, eager to carry out the next experiment, fills me with the greatest delight. I can feel my muscles positively relaxing and my brain clearing as I hear the whine of high-speed centrifuges, the steady roar of cell-culture hoods and the whirring of printers as they churn out reams of precious data. Yet, in my honest moments, I have to admit that not everyone feels comfortable in what to me is such a homely scientific research environment. And, on my part, I find it a disturbing experience to pass through big company offices where endless secretaries are sending interminable e-mails to everybody else (with n copies), and am positively terrified at the thought of landing up in a highly emotional religious revival meeting and being expected to tune my emotions 'correctly' to the religious vibes which are being propagated.

The desire to feel 'at home' is a very strong human drive: at home in our jobs, at home in our families, at home within ourselves and, ultimately, at home in some sense in the universe. When I worked at the American University Hospital in West Beirut during the Lebanese civil war there was some very fierce fighting between two rival militias outside our own physical home. For six hours we lay flat on our faces in the corridor, deafened by the shattering explosions of rocket-propelled grenades hitting a building opposite our own, the silence after each landing being broken by the sound of falling glass and the hiss of air escaping from the destroyed tyres of burning cars. I was actually trying to read (with considerable scepticism, I should add) a newly arrived research paper published by the *Journal of the Society for Psychical Research* on 'out-of-body experiences' which, under the circumstances, seemed highly suitable reading for the occasion, but gave up the attempt on realizing that I had read the same page eight times and absorbed nothing. The sheer mind-shattering noise of modern explosives overpowers the brain and disrupts all normal patterns of thought. Yet, once a ceasefire was declared and the fighting was over, the drive to recreate the 'normal' world again was very strong. Burnt-out cars were dragged away, the glass was swept up and the windows were mended; the marks of war were gradually erased. As soon as the sniping stopped, I picked up my racket as usual and headed for the tennis courts. There was a great amount of social visiting as people talked through what had happened on their street. Apart from actual death or wounding, the greatest trauma was always destruction of the home by fire or a direct hit. I know people who lost three homes during the Lebanese civil war, yet they would still go on building and creating a new one, not just for shelter, but also because being truly 'at home' is the only way to stay sane in the midst of anarchy and violence.

The French sociologist Pierre Bourdieu has emphasized the notion of *habitus* to signify 'a system of socially learned cultural predispositions and activities that differentiate people by their lifestyles'.[14] We naturally gravitate towards people who share a similar *habitus* to our own. The act of leaving the comfort zone of our own *habitus* to spend time in the *habitus* of others can itself be a discomforting experience. Just as we may go through 'culture shock' by visiting another country, as the assumptions of our familiar worldview are challenged,

20

or as our *habitus* is disrupted by war or revolution, so in a less dramatic but no less powerful way can the apparent veracity of our beliefs and cultural practices be eroded by continual exposure to subcultures within society in which those beliefs are either ignored as irrelevant or perhaps ridiculed for their stupidity. The aspiring biochemist with his or her eyes set on a life of research to create a new line of genetically engineered super-cows, having a milk output double that of their competitors, may find it difficult to keep to the 'true path' if he or she lives in a commune of anti-GM-food, cow-respecting Hindus.

Paradigms and paradigm shifts

How can we maintain a belief system in the midst of such pluralism? In particular, how can the worldviews by which people run their lives (however dimly articulated their precepts) be maintained in the face of data that suggest they could just be false? The worldviews that determine the overall direction of our lives are not unlike the paradigms which, Thomas Kuhn has claimed, characterize the workings of a scientific community.[15] Kuhn has defined a paradigm as 'what the members of a scientific community, and they alone, share... it is their possession of a common paradigm that constitutes a scientific community of a group of otherwise disparate people'.[16] For Kuhn 'normal science' is the science that scientists do most of the time within the framework of their paradigm – that overarching set of beliefs held in common which enables them to communicate with each other and do experiments, the results of which will only be readily interpretable on the grounds that the paradigm is true. Major advances in different branches of science, claims Kuhn, have occurred through a succession of 'revolutions' whereby data which do not fit with the established paradigm gradually accumulate. At first there are vigorous attempts to absorb this information into the accepted pattern, but eventually the day comes when the paradigm can no longer stand the burden of its inner contradictions, and a new paradigm is established that makes sense of the new data in a more satisfactory way. This 'revolution' in paradigm shifts then makes way for a new period of 'normal science'.

Whether Kuhn's model provides a valid description of the historical development of scientific theories is a topic outside our present scope. In reality historians of science often find that the really big disagreements in research fields have not been at the points of major transition, but during the times of so-called 'normal science'. But, for our present purposes, it is intriguing to note that while the 'paradigm' language may have lost plausibility in historical studies, scientists have widely adopted the paradigm concept into their discourse. For example, in my own field of immunology, it is common in review articles to read of 'competing paradigms' within a particular research area. Kuhn's model has even been used by scientists to comfort themselves during a particular time of crisis in their field, since the crisis itself holds out the hope of an imminent return to normality. This could possibly be an interesting example of a sociological theory that becomes self-validating by helping to generate the right conditions for its own fulfilment. For example, the field of astronomy was thrown into a crisis some years ago by the realization that most of the material content of the universe – so-called 'dark matter' – remained unidentified. When a field of scientific research specializing in observing things in the universe has operated for a considerable time within the paradigm that most things have been discovered, only for someone to suddenly find that, in reality, most things have escaped attention, this is, by any criteria, a difficult situation to handle.[17] The search for dark matter in the universe continues, with some degree of success.

By analogy with its use in the scientific context, we can also use the 'paradigm' concept to refer to that worldview which forms the general framework (consciously or unconsciously) whereby we run our lives. More strictly we probably operate our lives using a subset of paradigms, each one having varying relevance depending on the matter in hand. But lurking behind the subset is a Paradigm with a capital 'P', that framework of reference within which the other paradigms operate, or at least should do if we have an interest in our beliefs being at least moderately consistent with each other. Such Paradigms are invariably metaphysical in nature, that is, they go well beyond anything of which science is able to inform us. They wrap themselves around the 'second layer' of cultural practices, lifestyles and belief systems mentioned above, and give them coherence and a certain sense of direction. If somebody believes that nothing exists, by definition, beyond what they can experience with their own sense organs, then clearly this is a Paradigm which is likely to affect many other aspects of their lives. On the other hand, a person who holds that there is some spiritual force residing in nature which makes it sacred in some ultimate sense has a Paradigm which is liable at least to set the tone of their subset of paradigms. Another person who operates within the Paradigm that there is a God who has brought the universe into being, and who has particular intentions for their life, will run their life in a different direction yet again.

The analogy between such a personal Paradigm and the Kuhnian paradigm held by a scientific community is a useful one although, like any other analogy, we must beware of pressing it too far. Just as a scientific community can absorb an enormous amount of new data under the umbrella of its paradigm during a period of 'normal science', so we are all experts at incorporating new data into the framework of our personal Paradigms. Most of the input from daily life is unconsciously pigeon-holed into compartments of our minds that have had much practice in the art, and material that does not seem to fit can be readily rationalized away. This process of absorption into a pre-established worldview helps to explain why two people brought up in similar environments can nevertheless each end up with a set of firmly held beliefs so different that one can hardly communicate a concept that the other will understand, let alone appreciate. They have simply developed different pigeon-holes.

What we see depends upon the colour of the spectacles with which we view it. While one person sees in evolution a cosmic process leading to some ultimate point involving human perfectibility, another may see a struggle for survival that can be used to validate his or her views on a free-market economy, while for a third evolution may represent the ultimate argument for the non-existence of God. Such is the flexibility of the human mind that different Paradigms may absorb the same theories and data with ease, like an amoeba invaginating its food, until later they are regurgitated in a barely recognizable form as validations of the Paradigm's own enduring truthfulness.

Consigning ugly facts to limbo is something that we all do. For example, a heavy taboo on the subject of death is currently operating in Western industrialized societies, almost as weighty (so popular mythology would have it) as the taboo on the subject of sex that was supposed to characterize the 19th century. Perhaps the fact of death is simply too threatening to the personal Paradigms of a large segment of the population. While the god of personal health and vitality may be carefully nurtured with the help of science, technology and health foods in this life, modern societies have been left with no answer for the unthinkable void beyond. So, on the whole, it seems sensible that nice people do not even mention the subject. Death is placed, along with troublesome minorities and faraway injustices, in the wasteland of the unmentionable.

Paradigms with a small 'p' can be no less powerful in validating all kinds of beliefs which are widely held by societies, albeit less extensive in their scope than the 'grand metaphysical Paradigms' with a capital 'P' which act as integration points for the overall direction of our lives. As an example of the power of a small 'p' paradigm, consider the fact that most people reading this book will be of the opinion that Europeans in medieval times generally believed that the earth was flat, and that belief in a round earth only became disseminated after the work of early astronomers such as Copernicus and Galileo. It is a well-known story that the sailors who sailed with Columbus on his epic voyages westward across the Atlantic were afraid to sail due to the possibility that they might fall off the edge of the flat earth. I have to admit that I believed this paradigmatic account concerning the convictions of medieval people until quite recently. The paradigm was enforced by occasional jocular allusions to 'flat-earth societies' in the press, and by the use of the term 'flat-earther' as a form of abuse referring to someone totally obdurate in their beliefs in the face of all evidence to the contrary. What was the point in using such terms unless they referred to people in a past age, such as the sailors on Columbus' ships, who did indeed believe that the earth was flat? The 'flat-earth' paradigm fits well with the general conception that pre-scientific people in medieval times were really quite ignorant about the world. In Joseph Chiari's play, *Christopher Columbus*, the following dialogue is put into the mouths of Columbus and a Prior:

> Columbus: The earth is not flat, Father, it's round!
> The Prior: Don't say that!
> Columbus: It's the truth; it's not a mill pond strewn with islands, it's a sphere.
> The Prior: Don't, don't say that; it's blasphemy.[18]

The problem with the 'flat-earth' paradigm is that it is certainly false. Historians have been telling us for some time that the commonly held belief that people in medieval times thought the earth was flat is without historical foundation. As long ago as the early 1930s the historian Cecil Jane wrote that:

> By the middle of the 15th century, the sphericity of the globe was
> accepted as a fact by all, or at the very least by almost all, educated men
> throughout Western Europe. There is no foundation for the assertion,
> which was once credited, that in Spain a contrary view was maintained
> by orthodox theologians and supported by religious prejudice.[19]

And an eminent contemporary historian of science, David Lindberg, reminds us that:

> In the usual story, theoretical dogma regarding a flat earth had to be
> overcome by empirical evidence for its sphericity. The truth is that the
> sphericity of the earth was a central feature of theoretical dogma as it came
> down to the Middle Ages – so central that no amount of contrary theoretical
> or empirical argumentation could conceivably have dislodged it.[20]

Lindberg is here referring, of course, to the dominant Aristotelian worldview bequeathed to the Middle Ages by the Greek philosophers, who pictured the universe as based on a spherical earth surrounded by the sun, moon, planets and stars which revolved around the earth on concentric spheres. 'After the fifth century BC no Greek writer of any repute' thought of the earth as anything but round. The only exceptions were the atomists Leucippus and Democritus, who seem to have imagined the earth as a flat disc surrounded by air.[21]

One of the people Columbus consulted very carefully before embarking on his voyage was the theologian and philosopher Pierre d'Ailly (1350–1420), who discussed the earth's geography and structure in some detail. Without obstacles (such as mountains), D'Ailly wrote, a person could walk round the globe in a few years. We know that Columbus consulted D'Ailly avidly because his own copy of D'Ailly's writings is heavily annotated.[22] Many other great medieval thinkers wrote extensively on the sphericity of the earth. Bede (c. 673–735), the great historian and natural scientist of the early Middle Ages, affirmed that the earth is at the centre of a spherical cosmos, and can be called a perfect sphere because the surface irregularities of mountains and valleys are so small in comparison with the vast size of the universe. Jean Buridan (c. 1300–58) and Nicolas Oresme (c. 1320–82) even discussed the rotation of the earthly sphere. No educated person at the time of Columbus could possibly have escaped a worldview based on the earth as a globe.

So how did the popular mythology become established that people in medieval times thought the earth was flat? The historian Jeffrey Russell has carried out a detailed investigation of this question and has uncovered two main sources. First, the American historical novelist Washington Irving (1783–1859) wrote a book, published in 1828, entitled the *History of the Life and Voyages of Christopher Columbus*, which he spent three years in Spain composing. But although Irving clearly did consult some historical documents, he also deliberately mingled fiction with what he regarded as a historical reconstruction in his 'biography' of Columbus.[23] Into his account was introduced a dramatic confrontation between Columbus and the foolish clergymen at the 'council of Salamanca', which forms the basis for the episode in Joseph Chiari's play, cited above. Columbus was 'a simple mariner, standing forth in the midst of an imposing array of professors, friars and dignitaries of the church; maintaining his theory with natural eloquence, and, as it were, pleading the cause of the new world'. Waxing eloquent, Irving goes on to describe how Columbus' conviction that the earth was round was 'assailed by monastic bigotry... with citations from the Bible... To these were added expositions of various saints... A mathematical demonstration was allowed no weight, if it appeared to clash with a text of scripture, or a commentary of one of the fathers.'

But the episode is pure fabrication. There never was such a council at Salamanca. All philosophers and theologians of the era knew the earth was round. Neither do any biblical texts suggest otherwise. Columbus was not afraid of falling off the edge of a flat earth, nor were his sailors. Irving not only let his imagination run riot, but used his sources carelessly and his work is peppered with other errors. His book now is viewed by historians as an interesting period piece, a work of the imagination, not of serious history. Nevertheless, it was not long before Irving's purple prose was being incorporated into school textbooks, quoted and re-quoted, without any attempt to determine the accuracy of his sources. Later Irving's *Life of Washington* displayed similar tendencies, attributing to the first US president a fictitious genealogy.

By 1873 Irving's fictitious 'council at Salamanca' had found its way into John Draper's book, *The History of the Conflict Between Religion and Science*, an immensely influential work, which in the USA had fifty printings in as many years, and in Britain twenty-one printings in fifteen years. Drawing on Irving's account, Draper had Columbus being attacked at Salamanca by fanatical pedants led by the alleged 'Grand Cardinal of Spain' hurling arguments at Columbus drawn from the early church fathers. Irving's work was a convenient source for someone looking for ammunition to fuel his thesis that science and religion were at loggerheads. Draper's book represented the first attempt by an influential figure to declare explicitly that science and religion were at war. As Jeffrey Russell comments, 'It fixed in the educated mind that "science" stood for freedom and progress against the superstition and repression of "religion".'[24] Draper's work was widely translated into other languages.

The birth of the 'conflict thesis' between science and religion in late-Victorian England is a topic to which we shall return in later chapters. For the moment it is worth noting the way in which, like a mutant gene, historical errors can be passed down the generations via a lineage of carriers that can be traced and identified. The genetic disease porphyria is rare in Europe, but is carried by 30,000 Afrikaners. In Johannesburg there are more carriers of this disease than in the whole of Holland, yet all descend from a single member of the small founding population that originally emigrated from Holland. Because porphyria is so common in one family line it is sometimes called Van Roojen disease in South Africa today.[25] In a similar way the 'flat-earth error' was passed down through popular books until it gradually spread and became the generally accepted view of what people in a previous era believed.

The second historical source of the error is to be found in the writings of Antoine-Jean Letronne (1787–1848), a member of the French National Institute (which had replaced the earlier Royal Academy of Sciences that was closed down following the French Revolution). Although Letronne's contemporaries in the institute were well aware of the medieval belief that the earth was a globe, as is evident from their writings, Letronne himself chose to argue the opposite. Such a view fitted much better with his thesis that the advance of scientific discoveries had swept away the ignorant beliefs of the theologians. The writings of Letronne, just like those of Irving, were quickly taken up by others, who again did not bother to check the accuracy of their sources, so contributing to the wider dissemination of the flat-earth error.

Why does the error continue to be so pervasive? Russell argues that such fallacies take on a life of their own, eventually making a 'cycle of myths' which reinforce one another.

The cycle becomes so embedded in our thought that it helps to form our worldview in ways that make it impervious to evidence. We are so convinced that medieval people *must* have been ignorant enough to think the world flat that when the evidence is thrown in front of us we avoid it, as we might when driving, swerving around an obstacle in the road.[26]

Such is the power of paradigms.

Paradigms, science and faith

If educated society can hold to such bizarre and mutant paradigms of historical belief, can it also be wrong about its image of science and scientists, or its notion of faith, or, in particular, about the relationship between the two?

Scientists are rather sensitive about their public image, mainly because its portrayal in the media during the past century has often been less than flattering.[27] Mr Spock, the ice-cold rationalist of the starship *Enterprise*, from the American TV series *Star Trek*, gives an impression of one of the more common media images of the scientist – in this case an emotionless half-human with a utilitarian moral sense who is there to solve complicated problems. Such media stereotypes are not atypical. The hero scientist was prominent in the 19th- and early-20th-century writings of Jules Verne, Sir Arthur Conan Doyle and H.G. Wells, and more recently in the Indiana Jones film trilogy of the 1980s. Here, the fearless adventurer in the physical and intellectual world, guided by an open-minded rationality, sets to work to put the world to rights. It is in some ways a comforting image for the scientist, but hardly one to give an accurate picture of the daily grind of scientific research, nor one that adequately reflects the sheer diversity of the scientific community. The absent-minded-professor image also lives on in the media – the classic nerd whose good intentions are subverted by unexpected outcomes with disturbing or bizarre consequences. The scientists think they know how to control things, but then something escapes or goes wrong, or the environment kicks back and the world is threatened. Such Hollywood themes are familiar ones.

But the literary creation which has been most potent and lingered longest in the Western psyche is undoubtedly the *Frankenstein* image generated by Mary Shelley (1797–1851). 'What terrified me will terrify others,' wrote Shelley of the nightmare that allegedly provided the inspiration for *Frankenstein*, her Gothic horror story of 1818. The depiction of the mad scientist operating outside any civilized constraints continues to frighten and the *Frankenstein* imagery is still frequently used by the tabloid press to proclaim the dangers of cloning, or genetically engineered foods, or whatever else might be the current scientific or technological bugbear. Francis Crick's emotive phrase for molecular biology as an exploration of 'the borderline between the living and the dead', with its echo of Frankenstein's words, did little to dispel the potency of the *Frankenstein* mythology. One-third of all horror movies have a scientist as the villain. The popular press often tends to portray scientists in a sinister light, and the reporting of science is frequently distorted, and sometimes completely mythical. 'First Cloned Human Embryo', proclaimed the front-page headlines of an issue of *The Daily Mail*, accompanied by a picture of a '12-day-old male human embryo consisting of 400 cells'.[28] The story was quickly picked up by the media in other parts of Europe. 'They've Really Done It: They've Taken Themselves for God!' proclaimed the German tabloid *Bild Zeitung* the following day.[29] Only later on was the real situation revealed by more sober newspapers, like *Libération* in France, which explained that there was no human embryo and the picture was actually of a culture of human embryonic stem cells, with as much similarity to a human embryo as bark has to the whole tree. Cloning, the sequencing of the human genome and the accelerating applications of biotechnology during the course of the 21st century are likely to provide the media industry with a rich vein of *Frankenstein* material for many years to come. A recent cartoon from *The Guardian* shows a figure parting his manly chest like a model in an anatomy textbook to reveal a bar code representing his DNA analysis – the ultimate identity index. Media images like these will continue to shape the public's scientific imagination more powerfully than any amount of rational argument.

It has to be said, however, that public perceptions of science vary considerably between countries. At the close of the 20th century, support for science in the USA was running at an all-time high: a poll found that 70 per cent of Americans say they are interested in science and technology, the highest number ever recorded.[30] This number was up from 61 per cent in 1992 and 67 per cent in 1995, and exceeded the 68 per cent who said they were interested in economic policy. By contrast, the public in European countries and in Japan generally have a much higher level of concern about the possible dangers of science and technology, typified by a vigorous campaign against genetically modified foods, far greater (so far) than anything seen in the USA.

But, irrespective of the varying views about science in different countries, the general public commonly operates within the paradigm that scientists are overly rational and cold-blooded creatures in white coats who value detached logic over human empathy, problem-solving over passion, objective knowledge over personal experience, and who are driven more by obsessive curiosity than by any particular moral concerns. Personal observation of a typical research laboratory for a few weeks might quickly dispel such stereotypes, but, as with the assumption that people in medieval times believed in a flat earth, entrenched beliefs are not always that easy to dislodge.

Images of faith suffer just as much from media and public stereotyping as images of science, and again it is such stereotypes feeding into the public psyche that generate the paradigms colouring people's views of the world around them. 'Faith' on TV, in Britain at least, is often portrayed as belonging to the spooky and the unusual, those aspects of the universe that science apparently cannot explain. The baffled scientist is brought in to scratch his head and admit that all these strange goings-on and bumps in the night are quite beyond rational explanation. When scientific discoveries are tackled in serious TV documentaries, as they sometimes are very effectively, the science is presented as objective and rational. By contrast, the media image of 'faith' is more often touchy-feely, and belongs to the realm of the emotions more than to the realm of reason. When Professor Susan Greenfield presented her British TV series on the brain in the year 2000, she made much of the fact that spiritual experiences are encompassed within the brain and can be reduced to the firing of neurons. Implied in her presentation was the assumption that religion is primarily about feelings locked up in our heads, rather than reflections of a rational external reality. But what Professor Greenfield omitted to emphasize was that *all* our human experiences, including those as we carry out our investigations of the brain, involve the firing of neurons. The picture provided to the viewer was that neuronal firing when it involved science was rational, whereas neuronal firing that involved religious belief was irrational, though quite how one could so readily distinguish between these two sets of neuronal firing events was never made clear.

Typical TV programmes may portray people with faith favourably for holding personal convictions, but any idea that those convictions might have validity outside their own personal worldview is treated with suspicion. Science provides universal knowledge which is valid for anyone, whereas faith provides personal knowledge that has no necessary validity beyond the individual's subjective experience. That such images have powerful effects on the general population is supported by the 52 per cent of university students in a recent survey who agreed with the statement, 'Scientific thinking is based on evidence, religion is based just on faith,' and by the 49 per cent who affirmed that 'Science is about objective facts, religion is about feelings and subjectivity.'[31]

Many people with faith would disown such stereotypes as vigorously as scientists might disown the sinister images that the media so often bestow upon them. The objection could be made that a particular faith, for example in a God who made the universe, might be based on evidence which goes well beyond science, but which is not necessarily irrational. Furthermore, objective arguments might be put forward to support the case for a rational faith in God. The similarities and differences between scientific and religious belief systems will be discussed further in later chapters. But for the moment we may note that the idea that faith can be supported by serious rational argument is not frequently encountered in the media; for the media, faith is the personal experience, the irrational blind leap in the dark, or the weird and wonderful, and evidence which threatens the stereotype tends to be marginalized or downplayed.

Publicly conveyed images of the relationship between science and faith are likewise heavily influenced by the stereotypic treatment that each tends to receive. The most popular media portrayal remains one of conflict (the 'conflict thesis'). According to this popular mythology, people in earlier times tended to be very religious and described the natural world around them largely in religious terms. However, with the advent of modern science, the natural world became much better understood, and so scientific explanations tended to replace religious ones. Naturally the church was upset by such developments and did its best to stifle the new knowledge, but with time the new science conquered the intellectual life of the Western world, leaving the theologians with little to do except carry out a rearguard action in which they occasionally snipe at recent scientific advances.

It is doubtful that any contemporary philosopher or historian of science, irrespective of their own personal beliefs, would subscribe to such a 'just-so story', and in academic circles such mythological accounts have largely been discarded. Nevertheless, in popular culture such scenarios linger on. The idea that science and religion are in conflict is kept alive by the misguided attempts of American school boards to ban the teaching of evolution on one hand, and by the occasional polemic against religion by a scientist on the other. In the survey of the opinions of university students in Britain, already cited above, 72 per cent of respondents agreed that 'There has been continual conflict between science and religion throughout history,' but only 34 per cent agreed that 'Few major scientists have been religious by the standards of their times.' The conflict thesis is alive and well and lives on in classroom teaching, in TV studios and in popular journalism. Like stereotyped images of scientists in film and other media, and like the belief that medieval people thought the world was flat, the conflict thesis has become a widely accepted paradigm, not thought about or analysed as much as simply accepted as 'what everyone knows to be the case'. And when the odd piece of contrary data appears, we swerve around it like an obstacle in the road.

The widespread acceptance of the conflict thesis by at least some sections of the scientific community may be likened to other periods during the history of science when ideological beliefs, which most people now would maintain are quite false, were then provided with strong scientific validation. The most notorious example is provided by the well-documented way in which scientists used their findings to support racism during the 19th and earlier half of the

20th centuries, the subject of the next chapter. Scientists are proud of their objectivity, but in this case the science turned out to be bogus and the selective use of evidence was driven by social and political concerns. Clearly the adoption of the conflict thesis is quite different in its implications from the espousal of racism, and on this point the analogy does not hold, but earlier scientific support for racist ideas does provide a potent example of the way in which the scientific community can validate a paradigm which eventually turns out to be quite unsupported by the evidence.

Chapter 2

Science and Savages
An Example from History – the Ideological Use of Science to Support Racism

The Negroes of Africa have received from nature no intelligence that rises above the foolish. Hume invites anyone to quote a single example of a Negro who has exhibited talents.
Immanuel Kant

The brains of the bushman... leads towards the brain of the simiadare (monkeys). This implies a connection between want of intelligence and structural assimilation. Each race of Man has its place, like the inferior animals.
Charles Lyell

In general, the brain is larger in mature adults than in the elderly, in men than in women, in eminent men than in men of mediocre talent, in superior races than in inferior races.
Paul Broca

A savage was unable to live with civilized man as an equal, since civilization's complex associations could not be comprehended by his inferior brain whose capacity was geared to a far simpler framework of association.
Herbert Spencer

It is always a shock to delve into fairly recent history and discover that our immediate ancestors believed things very firmly that, to us, seem not only unbelievable, but also naive and dangerous. Should the world last another 100 years, people in the 22nd century will no doubt view some of our cherished assumptions with the same incredulity. Beliefs that appear so obviously true during one period of time or in one culture may seem quite bizarre at another period of time or in a different culture. Yet the distance in time or space between the milieu in which the belief is obvious and the milieu in which it appears bizarre may be relatively small. For two different cultures it may be only a few hours' flight, and for historical periods merely the lifetime of a single person.

I once had a great-aunt who lived to the ripe old age of 104. She managed to outlive two husbands and pass on her genes to numerous offspring. During her last few years of life she used to keep a small bottle of rum under her chair ('for medicinal purposes only, my dear'), available for a quick swig in case she 'had a turn'. As she cheerfully chatted about the experiences of her teenage years, one's mind would be stretched back into history: here was a person who had seen Gladstone and Disraeli, who remembered waving at Queen Victoria and crying about the casualties of the Crimean War. Talk about 'ancient history' or 'early antiquity' can be misleading. Certain events and beliefs are closer than we realize. In a sense the 19th century, only one long lifespan away, is so close that when its beliefs seem radically different from our own, the contrast is all the more stark than for earlier centuries. For no topic is this more true than views about race.[1]

Today it is fashionable to believe in racial equality. It is one of those 'obvious' beliefs which is legislated by the state, preached on by the media and propagated by a great array of institutions in society. This is not to say that it is practised on the streets with any degree of consistency, nor that either active or covert racists do not exist in considerable numbers in most societies. But the *idea* of racial equality is widely accepted and forms an expected part of the public statements made by political, scientific and religious leaders. This was not the case 100 years ago. In the 19th century the idea that there were 'superior' and 'inferior' races was so widely accepted that, for the great majority of people, it would hardly be considered a topic for discussion. The only points for debate were the extent of the inferiority and the possible biological reasons for it. The belief in inferior races was validated by a constant barrage of supporting evidence. This created such an all-encompassing canopy that few people ever felt the need to consider any other paradigm. As with any efficient paradigm, the concept of racial inequality was able to absorb and 'make sense' of an immensely wide range of data.

The 18th-century legacy

In many respects, 19th-century thought belongs more to the 20th century than to the 18th century, but views about race are an exception. Indeed, some 18th-century views on the subject are very mild when compared with the rabid commentaries of the 19th, though many of the best-known philosophers of the 18th century could hardly be described as egalitarian. For example, David Hume (1711–76), who held a number of political posts, including the stewardship of the English Colonial Office in 1766, wrote, in his *Essays Moral and Political*, that 'there is some Reason to think, that all the Nations, which live beyond the polar Circles, betwixt the Tropics, are inferior to the rest of the Species, and are utterly incapable of all the higher Attainments of the human Mind'.

Immanuel Kant (1724–1804), one of the greatest philosophers in the history of Western thought, wrote on the question of race in several books and essays, supporting Hume in his opinions:

The Negroes of Africa have received from nature no intelligence that rises above the foolish. Hume invites anyone to quote a single example of a Negro who has exhibited talents. He asserts that among the hundreds of thousands of blacks who have been seduced away from their own home countries, although very many of them have been set free, yet not a single one has ever been found that has performed anything great whether in art or in science or in any other laudable subject; but among the whites people constantly rise up from the lowest rabble and acquire esteem through their superior gifts. The difference between these two races of man is thus a substantial one: it appears to be just as great in respect of the faculties of the mind as in colour.

François Voltaire (1694–1778), like many writers of his time, was much struck with the physical appearance and speech of the Hottentots, or Nama, their preferred name – the native people of South Africa and Namibia. In his fictitious *Lettres d'Amabed*, written by an Indian of Benares to Shastasid, Amabed writes from the Cape of Good Hope: 'I am convinced that these people cannot have the same origin as ourselves. Our chaplain claims that the Hottentots, Negroes and Portuguese are descended from the same father. The idea is certainly ridiculous.'

18th-century biologists were generally more constrained in their comments than the philosophers. However, Carolus Linnaeus (1707–78), the great Swedish taxonomist whose *Systema naturae* was seen by later anthropologists as a major foundation stone of their field, defined four families of man according to skin colour. *Homo americanus* was described as 'reddish, choleric, obstinate, contented and regulated by customs'; *Homo asiaticus* as 'sallow, grave, dignified, avaricious and ruled by opinions'; and *Homo afer* as 'black, phlegmatic, cunning, lazy, lustful, careless and governed by caprice'. Considering the home country of the classifier, it is perhaps not surprising to find that *Homo europaeus* was defined as 'white, fickle, sanguine, blue-eyed, gentle and governed by laws'. These and similar definitions became embedded in both anthropological literature and popular publications for more than 150 years.

A new and distinctive contribution of the 19th century to the question of race was the way in which scientific research consistently supported the idea of inferior peoples. As the scientific community became both professionalized and specialized during the course of the century, so its public voice on racial issues became more influential. This was not at all because scientists as a class were particularly racist. Far from it, they were, according to what seemed very reasonable at the time, models of objectivity with a keen desire to find the 'true facts'. What is so striking is the way in which the 'facts' they found fitted in so readily with the 'inferior-race paradigm' which had been inherited from the 18th century. Such a paradigm also encompassed, rather comfortingly, the economic necessities arising from 19th-century European colonial expansion, with its consequent harnessing of local native populations as a cheap labour force. 'Scientific proof' of the natives' inferiority, in some cases even casting doubt on whether they came from the same human stock, was welcome news to industrialists and politicians who might otherwise have experienced a twinge of conscience over the plight of millions of native workers in the colonies, upon whose labours their profits depended.

The Monogenists and Polygenists

Discussion on race in the earlier part of the 19th century was dominated by the controversy between the Monogenists and the Polygenists. The Monogenists believed humankind was descended from a single genetic stock and that, therefore, there was a single human species. Differences were the result of environmental pressures acting over many generations of varied breeding patterns, and the characteristics so acquired were seen as being inherited by the offspring. Within the Monogenist viewpoint, which was supported by the biblical insistence that the whole of humankind was indeed descended from an original pair, there was a wide variety of opinions. But what is remarkable is that the Monogenist theory, which is of course known to be true today and which might have been expected to establish the principle of racial equality, was in fact frequently used to maintain precisely the opposite. So Georges Cuvier (1769–1832), the famous French founder of palaeontology and modern comparative anatomy, referred to native Africans as 'the most degraded of human races, his form approaches that of a beast and his intelligence is nowhere great enough to arrive at regular government'. Another Monogenist of a rather different school, Charles Lyell (1797–1875), founder of modern geology, wrote that 'the brains of the bushman... leads towards the brain of the simiadare (monkeys). This implies a connection between want of intelligence and structural assimilation. Each race of Man has its place, like the inferior animals.'

The way in which Monogenist arguments on the inheritance of acquired characteristics could be used to support the idea of inferior races is also seen very clearly in the writings of Armand de Quatrefages (1810–92). While discussing the superiority of whites to Negroes, De Quatrefages wrote, 'Does it follow that, because all the races of dogs belong to one and the same species, they all have the same aptitudes? Will a hunter choose indifferently a setter, or a bloodhound to use as a pointer or in the chase? Will he consider the street cur as of equal value with either of these pure breeds? Certainly not. Now we must never forget that, while superior to animals and different to them in many respects, man is equally subject to all the general laws of animal nature.'

The Polygenists believed that there were several human species which had separate origins, and again there were several varied forms of this theory. Polygeny was particularly strong in the USA in the decades before the Civil War, and was used to support the idea that Negroes and American Indians were of quite separate stock in comparison with whites. One of the leading spokesmen for the theory was Louis Agassiz (1807–73), a Swiss naturalist and disciple of Cuvier who emigrated to the USA in the 1840s and became a professor at Harvard. Agassiz was an enthusiastic scientist and a great fund-raiser, doing much to establish American biology during the 19th century. Yet, at the same time, he was one of the few established biologists to hold out against Darwin's theory of evolution, and was converted from monogenic to polygenic views after arriving in the States, apparently as a result of pressure by friends and also the intense personal revulsion he experienced on first meeting Negroes. Though counting himself an opponent of slavery, Agassiz believed that Negroes were a separate race, and that Adam and Eve were precursors of the Caucasian race only, and he saw himself as an objective scientist proposing political theories 'in light of the biological facts':

There are upon earth different races of men, inhabiting different parts of its surface, which have different physical characteristics; and this fact... presses upon us the obligation to settle the relative rank among these races, the relative value of the characters peculiar to each, in a scientific point of view... As philosophers it is our duty to look it in the face.

The 'biological facts' which Agassiz espoused went little beyond the cultural stereotypes already widely accepted among Caucasians: 'The indomitable, courageous, proud Indian – in how very different a light he stands by the side of the submissive, obsequious, imitative Negro, or by the side of the tricky, cunning, and cowardly Mongolian! Are not these facts indications that different races do not rank upon one level in nature.' From biological facts to political theory was a very short step for Agassiz: 'It seems to us to be mock-philanthropy and mock-philosophy to assume that all races have the same abilities, enjoy the same powers and show the same natural dispositions, and that in consequence of this equality they are entitled to the same position in human society.'

Agassiz was a religious man who opposed the theory of evolution on religious grounds. But, just to show how dangerous it is to try to extract historical patterns from individual examples, Asa Gray (1810–88), Professor of Natural History at Harvard for thirty-one years, a man more convinced in his traditional Christian belief than Agassiz, was an ardent supporter of Darwin's theory of evolution, so much so that Darwin confided in him about his theory two years before the *Origin of Species* was published in 1859. At the same time Gray was a Monogenist who was against slavery and welcomed the fact that Darwin's theory, applied to man, 'makes the Negro and the Hottentot our blood-relations'.

Brain and skull collecting

If Agassiz's polygenism seems to have been rooted largely in his personal foibles, then there were many others who sought to put the whole theory on a much sounder mathematical footing. Samuel Morton was a distinguished scientist and physician from Philadelphia who made a collection of more than 1,000 human skulls. His purpose in this seemingly ghoulish pursuit was strictly scientific: he wished to test the hypothesis that races could be ranked by the size of their brains as measured by the volume of the cranial cavities. Morton's conclusions, published in three major works, were repeatedly reprinted during the 19th century as 'hard data' on the differences of mental prowess between human races and matched, as Stephen J. Gould remarks, 'every good Yankee's prejudice – whites on top, Indians in the middle and blacks on the bottom; and, among whites, Teutons and Anglo-Saxons on top, Jews in the middle and Hindus on the bottom'. As a bonus, by obtaining skulls from Egyptian pyramids, Morton showed that whites had *always* had the advantage over blacks.

In France, Paul Broca (1820–80), founder of the Anthropological Society of Paris, was carrying out similar work on human brains. Like Morton, Broca was a Polygenist and held that Adam and Eve were precursors of the Jewish race only, other races of man coexisting with the Adamite family. Broca was a scientist who expressed his views rather clearly:

In general, the brain is larger in mature adults than in the elderly, in men than in women, in eminent men than in men of mediocre talent, in superior races than in inferior races... Other things being equal, there is a remarkable relationship between the development of intelligence and the volume of the brain... a prognathous [forward-jutting] face, more or less

37

black colour of the skin, woolly hair and intellectual and social inferiority, are often associated, while more or less white skin, straight hair and an orthognathous [straight] face, are the ordinary development of the highest groups in the human series... A group with black skin, woolly hair and a prognathous face has never been able to raise itself spontaneously to civilization...

Such facts were not pleasing to everyone, but, as Broca himself remarked, 'There is no faith, however respectable, no interest, however legitimate, which must not accommodate itself to the progress of human knowledge and bend before truth.'

One of Broca's specialities was to collect the brains of famous people in order to check their weight. Indeed, as Stephen J. Gould remarks, for a while the collecting of brains became quite a cottage industry, and different centres vied for the privilege of weighing the famous brains of those recently deceased. Great was the joy when Georges Cuvier's brain was dissected on the morning of Tuesday, 15 May 1832, and found to weigh in at a massive 1,830 grams, more than 400 grams above average. But, as time went on, some embarrassing anomalies emerged. For example, Louis Pierre Gratiolet (1815–65), who claimed that the size of the brain bore no relationship to its degree of intelligence (which of course it does not), found that German brains were, on average, 100 grams heavier than French brains. This was clearly not a finding that could be accepted lying down, and Broca was soon able to work through the relevant data and cut the German advantage down to a mere thirty-two grams on average. After some further elimination of data from individuals who had died by violence or execution, the average brain weight for Germans fell below that of the French, and so the day was saved for France.

Similar anomalies came about, including the finding that 'inferior' yellow people scored very well, having heavier brains than 'the most civilized people of Europe'. Since Broca knew that Europeans were the 'highest race', he concluded such discoveries could clearly not be very meaningful, and so he dutifully explained them away. The finding that West African blacks had an average cranial capacity of about 100 cubic centimetres less than the European races, however, was accepted as valid data. The brain of the great mathematician, K.F. Gauss, was 1,492 grams, only slightly larger than average, but fortunately it was found to be much more convoluted than the brain of a Papuan native, and so, yet again, the paradigm of racial inferiority absorbed the new facts with effortless ease.

Ironically, Broca's own brain was later discovered to be only slightly above average at 1,424 grams, while poor Franz Josef Gall, one of the founders of phrenology, had a meagre brain weight of only 1,198 grams. The famous author Anatole France only just managed to scrape across the 1,000 gram barrier at 1,017 grams.

While the rest of Europe was busy weighing brains, the British were involved in other kinds of measurements. Francis Galton (1822–1911), a cousin of Charles Darwin and founder of modern statistics, was a passionate measurer of almost everything. At one time he managed to construct a 'beauty map' of the British Isles by classifying the women he passed in the streets as attractive, indifferent or repellent. It emerged that London ranked highest for beauty, Aberdeen lowest. Like so many other scientists of his time, Galton's views on race were shaped more by his own travels than by any empirical data that he was able to gather, and his own social background did not encourage egalitarian views:

It is in the most unqualified manner that I object to pretensions of natural equality. The experiences of the nursery, the school, the university, and of professional careers, are a chain of proofs to the contrary... in whatever way we may test ability, we arrive at equally enormous intellectual differences.

Galton decided to solve the ethnic problem with mathematics, and his attempts were a precursor of the Intelligence Quotient (IQ) measurements of the 20th century. Galton used fourteen grades in his study of human intellect, seven on each side of the mean. Small letters from 'g' to 'a' denoted the less intelligent side, whereas capital letters from 'A' to 'G' denoted the more intelligent side. So 'g' was equivalent to an imbecile, whereas 'G' represented an eminent person. 'X' was reserved for a very small group of illustrious persons, 'x' being a complete imbecile. Galton estimated that the mean intellect differed for each population, and so the range from small 'x' to capital 'X' was larger or smaller depending upon the subjects being measured. For example, a slightly less-than-average Australian was placed on the same level by Galton as a very illustrious dog.

Galton's arguments had a strong influence on his cousin Darwin, who, after reading Galton's book, *Hereditary Genius*, wrote, 'You have made a convert of an opponent in one sense, for I have always maintained that, excepting fools, men did not differ much in intellect, only in zeal and hard work.'

Race and evolution

Darwin's own theory of evolution had profound implications for concepts of race in the late 19th century. As with any powerful new idea, this biological theory was press-ganged to support a wide variety of ideologies, many of them mutually exclusive. However, Darwin himself never interpreted his theory in an overtly racist way. Though startled by the wild appearance of the first 'wild savages' that he observed in South America during his voyage on the *Beagle*,[2] Darwin did not waver from his Monogenist position, and his few specific remarks on race are moderate indeed compared with those of some of his admirers.

Herbert Spencer (1820–1903) did much to popularize Darwinism, his writing being more warmly received in America than in Europe. 'Probably no philosopher', wrote editor Henry Holt, 'ever had such a vogue as Spencer had from 1870 to 1890.' From the mid-1860s until 1903, the sales of Spencer's works in America totalled 370,000 volumes, not counting unauthorized editions, and ranged in subject from biology and psychology to sociology and ethics. Spencer thought that people's cultural life developed according to the same evolutionary principles observable in the biological world, a somewhat diffuse philosophy that later came to be known as 'social Darwinism'. A central part of Spencer's thesis was that different races were going through different stages of 'cultural evolution' or development, and so one had to take such 'facts' into account when assessing the level of understanding of a given group of people. Thus Australians were considered by Spencer to have no power of concentration or integration of separate ideas, and Negro children in America, who were educated with white children, did not 'correspondingly advance in learning – their intellects being apparently incapable of being cultured beyond a particular point'. In fact Spencer believed that a long history of evolutionary struggle bequeathed a physically larger brain to succeeding generations, which was of greater quality due to its store of accumulated experiences. For example, the European inherited some thirty cubic inches of brain more than the lowly Papuan, which helped to explain the presence of men such as Newton and Shakespeare in England, but the inability of Papuans to 'count up to the number of their fingers'. The savage, for Spencer, gave Caucasians a unique opportunity to study the history of their own race, since they themselves had passed the same point along the evolutionary path at some remote time in the past. So, as John S. Haller puts it, Spencer believed 'a savage was unable to live with civilized man as an equal, since civilization's complex associations could not be comprehended by his inferior brain whose capacity was geared to a far simpler framework of association'.

Spencer's disciple John Fiske (1842–1901) went all over America giving public lectures and disseminating the ideas of cultural evolution. As Fiske once remarked, 'the difference in volume of brain between the highest and lowest men is at least six times as great as the difference between the highest and the lowest ape', so it was clearly a waste of time to spend money on educating the savage masses. They were simply not ready for it. Even for those races which succeeded in going beyond the condition of savagery, Fiske noted that they had 'been arrested in an immobile type of civilization, as in China, in ancient Egypt, and in the East generally'.

Neither Darwin himself, nor his 'British bulldog' Thomas Henry Huxley (1825–95), a fervent supporter of his theory, had time for Spencer's views on cultural evolution, and Darwin noted in his autobiography, surely correctly, that Spencer was a particularly egotistical man. But it is significant that neither Darwin nor Huxley criticized Spencer's views on race as such – the concept of racial inferiority was so widely accepted at the time that it was not something which would arouse comment.

One common thread that ran through many of the racial ideas of the period was that of 'recapitulation', the notion that animal development mimicks the major stages of evolution. This theory grew out of the incompleteness of the fossil record and the resulting lack of a satisfactory tree explaining the entire process of evolution. The German zoologist Ernst Haeckel, therefore, suggested that the tree of life could be deduced from the embryological development of higher forms, summarizing this concept in the immortal phrase 'ontogeny recapitulates phylogeny', 'ontogeny' meaning the growth of individuals and 'phylogeny' referring to the evolutionary history of lineages. In place of studying fossils, one could actually read the evolutionary record of an individual by looking at the stages in their growth from an embryo, each stage representing an adult ancestral form in the same order. So the gill slits of an early human embryo represented those of an ancestral adult fish, and the temporary tail at a later embryonic stage revealed a reptilian ancestor.

Haeckel was one of Darwin's greatest popularizers, and such is the power of ideas that his theory of recapitulation soon found itself percolating into several other disciplines, not least the psychoanalytical theories of Freud and Jung. Haeckel left no one in any doubt as to how he viewed evolution as an ideological weapon:

> Evolution and progress stand on the one side, marshalled under the
> bright banner of science; on the other side, marshalled under the black
> flag of hierarchy, stand spiritual servitude and falsehood, want of reason
> and barbarism, superstition and retrogression... evolution is the heavy
> artillery in the struggle for truth; whole ranks of dualistic sophisms fall
> before [it]... as before the chain shot of artillery.

Haeckel (who considered that the 'Indogermanic race has far outstripped all other races of men in mental development'), along with many others, used the theory of recapitulation to affirm what everyone knew to be true: the racial superiority of Northern European whites. Herbert Spencer remarked that 'the

41

intellectual traits of the uncivilized... are traits recurring in the children of the civilized', while America's leading psychologist of his time, G. Stanley Hall (1844–1924), stated that 'most savages in most respects are children, or, because of sexual maturity, more properly, adolescents of adult size'. The application of the same ideas to colonialism was a natural extension, and when Benjamin Kidd was justifying colonial expansion into Africa he wrote, in 1898, that we are 'dealing with peoples who represent the same state in the history of the development of the race that the child does in the history of the development of the individual. The tropics will not, therefore, be developed by the natives themselves.' School boards in America recommended the 'Song of Hiawatha' for primary schoolchildren on the grounds that they would identify with it, since they were passing through the savage stage of their ancestral past.[3]

Race and anthropology

One of the more bizarre applications of recapitulation arose in the field of criminal anthropology. In 1876 an Italian physician named Cesare Lombroso introduced the idea that criminals were essentially apes living in human societies who, because they had not advanced along the normal evolutionary path, were like throwbacks to our ancestral past. Their criminal behaviour was, therefore, equated with their animal state, animal behaviour itself being viewed by Lombroso as criminal. Lombroso made an intensive study of the anatomy of criminals and noted many signs which demonstrated their primitive status: 'The apish features of born criminals include relatively long arms, prehensile feet with mobile big toes, low and narrow forehead, large ears, thick skull, large and prognathous jaw, copious hair on the male chest, and diminished sensitivity to pain.'

Lombroso's theories, which were widely influential in Europe and elsewhere at the end of the 19th century, included the important point that the similarities between apes and savages 'explained' the criminal behaviour of both. As Lombroso expressed it, criminals 'speak differently because they feel differently: they speak like savages, because they are true savages in the midst of our brilliant European civilization'. From such a theory it was but a short step to calls for reforms of legal codes and penal practices. Lombroso suggested that various physical and social characteristics could identify a criminal in early life so that he could be exiled from society before causing any harm. It was pointless to expect reform in an individual so obviously criminal by nature:

> The fact that there exist such things as born criminals, organically fitted for evil, atavistic reproductions, not simply of savage men but even of the

fiercest animals, far from making us more compassionate towards them, as has been maintained, steels us against all pity.

As Gould has pointed out, leaders of this new school of criminal anthropology were no neo-Nazi types but 'enlightened socialists and social democrats' who viewed their theory as 'the spearhead for a rational, scientific society based on human realities'. The genetic determination of criminal action, Lombroso argued, is simply the law of nature and of evolution: 'We are governed by silent laws which never cease to operate and which rule society with more authority than the laws described on our statute books. Crime appears to be a natural phenomenon... like birth or death.'

It cannot be overemphasized that such views did not appear at all extremist in the context of 19th-century attitudes towards racial questions. Though there was of course criticism of the ideas of Lombroso and others of his ilk, such critiques were over matters of detail, and did not touch the core assumption of racial inferiority. On this subject society spoke with an almost monolithic voice, so that the consensus of scientific, religious, medical and political authorities flowed together in one powerfully authenticating stream. Thus, commenting on the views of American physicians concerning the Negroes, Haller writes that 'physicians were generally agreed on the condition of the Negro in the late 19th century, arguments to the contrary were *simply not to be found* in the transactions and journals of the medical societies' [my italics]. Someone consulting the *Encyclopaedia Britannica* (ninth edition) would find that 'the premature closing of cranial sutures and lateral pressure of the frontal bone necessarily limited Negro development to the lower functions of life'.

Frederick Hoffman was a statistician who worked for the Prudential Insurance Company in America and who published articles in both medical and statistical journals. In 1896 the American Economic Association published Hoffman's 300-page enquiry entitled *Race Traits and Tendencies of the American Negro*. This fascinating document, which summarizes a century's active research in the field, comments that, after thirty years of freedom, Negro and Caucasian were 'further apart than ever in their political and social relations'. Hoffman cited 'indisputable evidence' of physicians and statisticians that the Negro showed 'the least power of resistance in the struggle for life', but presented the lack of suicides among Negroes as an instance of their inferior psychological state. He concluded that philanthropy was highly unsuccessful in raising the Negro to the 'state of the Caucasian' and called for a halt to the 'modern attempts of superior races to lift inferior races to their own elevated position', since the result was almost criminal in its interference with the natural order of racial struggle among nations and peoples.

Saddest of all was the fact that the 19th-century paradigm of racial inferiority was so powerful and all-inclusive that even some black intellectuals accepted both the evolutionary framework that science had apparently given them and the fate that awaited them in what they were told was to be their unsuccessful struggle for survival.[4]

The power of the racist paradigm

Why should we look in such sickening detail at a 19th-century view which now only a tiny minority would accept? Quite apart from the important point that today an incipient racism is once again apparent in various biological theories, including measurements of intelligence[5] and some of the more extreme claims of sociobiology, it is a useful exercise to take a hard look at recent history and try to mentally soak ourselves (for a while) in the same barrage of data that people were receiving then, so that we can begin to feel, at least to a small extent, how they could have been so persuaded about a belief which we now hold to be so abhorrent. Only in this way will we be able to understand how we ourselves may now, quite easily, hold beliefs that are mistaken, but which we would probably defend with great vigour, simply because alternative views have never been available to us.

How did blacks and other 'inferior races' break out of the bind which 'natural laws' had apparently placed them in? How did the monolithic 19th-century belief in racial inferiority give way so dramatically to the more egalitarian views which are espoused, if not practised, more than a century later? To examine this paradigm shift is fascinating, but well beyond the scope of this book. As it happens, both religion and science had crucial roles to play. However, it was not until news of the flames of the gas chambers at Auschwitz and Dachau spread around the world that people finally reacted in horrified revulsion to the logical conclusions of what the 19th century had accepted as being so true that it was virtually beyond discussion.

It is a sign of the power of successful and all-embracing paradigms that they render different theories unbelievable. Alternatives to a prevailing view can only gain a hearing when they are at least assigned the status of 'genuinely possible'. But, as long as the old paradigm continues to soak up and make sense of new data, it will continue to reign supreme, and the question of the need for an alternative will not even arise.

The scientists' task is to operate within the accepted paradigm of their chosen speciality as practised by the scientific community. But, when the foundations are shaken and the old landmarks begin to crumble, there is a critical phase during which they are asked to believe the unbelievable – to believe, in fact, what no one has ever believed before: a new paradigm, a new map which will include upon its contours not only the old data, but all the new data as well. That is one way in which science advances, and scientists who hold very static views on issues of science and faith, for example those whose thinking has been shaped so far by the 'conflict thesis', or who think scientific knowledge is the only kind that means anything, might do well to consider the way in which their own research field progresses by creating new paradigms to encompass new data. Such reflections may themselves provide an important clue as to how ideas on a larger canvas may be related in ways which, at the moment, appear strictly unbelievable.

Chapter 3

God's Funeral, Science Triumphant?
Science, Faith and Secularization

[By] the twenty-first century, religious believers are likely to be found only in small sects, huddled together to resist a worldwide secular culture.

Peter Berger, *New York Times*, 1968

The assumption that we live in a secularized world is false. The world today, with some exceptions... is as furiously religious as it ever was, and in some places more so than ever. This means that a whole body of literature written by historians and social scientists... loosely labeled as 'secularization theory', was essentially mistaken.

Peter Berger, *The National Interest*, 1996

I believe in a bit of Scientology, Catholicism, Judaism and the Eastern philosophies. I take a bit of each, I am a hybrid.

Nicole Kidman, 2001

The argument so far is that many of our beliefs are absorbed imperceptibly as a result of our upbringing, from the media and from our general cultural milieu. These beliefs feed into the Paradigms which act as the overarching ordering principles of our lives and, at the same time, support a broad array of more focused paradigms that hold sway over specific sub-domains of our beliefs, profoundly influencing the way we interpret the world around us. Of course some of our paradigms have been worked out for ourselves following a period of considered reflection and thought, but the number we have simply absorbed from our environment without much thought remains surprisingly high. The paradigm that people in medieval times believed in a flat earth, as well as racist beliefs in the 19th century, have been provided as examples of the way in which paradigms can be 'passively absorbed'. It has also been suggested that beliefs about science, about faith, and about the relationship between them, are often adopted by a process of passive adoption rather than as a result of a considered investigation. As a result, models such as the 'conflict thesis' understanding of the relation between science and faith remain widely disseminated in popular culture, and therefore frequently become absorbed as a paradigmatic view.

Nothing has been said so far as to whether the conflict thesis, or any other view, may or may not as a matter of fact provide a valid description of historical and contemporary interactions between science and faith. For the moment our focus is on the way such paradigmatic beliefs are nurtured and maintained, and the question of their truth claims will be considered in detail in later chapters.

One of the ways in which paradigms are comfortably maintained is by living in an environment in which the majority of people believe the same, creating what Peter Berger refers to as 'plausibility structures'. The comfort zone is generated not necessarily by any conscious espousal of the paradigm by that community, but simply by the assumption that it's true. Discomfort occurs only when the paradigm is challenged by moving into a different environment, or by exposure to counter-evidence. It is the argument of this chapter that, contrary to common belief, science has made little if any contribution to the secularization of Western society, but that secularization, at least in Western Europe, has generated an environment in which the 'conflict thesis' is nurtured and rarely challenged in popular culture.

The secularization debate

The secularization debate is a minefield and those who enter it should tread gingerly. This is not to say that some reasonably well based conclusions cannot be drawn once the topic has been thoroughly discussed, but it's a subject on which the sociologists and historians frequently disagree, so some caution is called for.

As with many topics, definitions matter a lot in the secularization debate. Secularization, for example, is not the same as secularism. Secularism is the ideological espousal of non-religious views of the world, morality, society, and so on. Secularization theory is a research programme that aims to describe how, as a matter of fact, religious beliefs, institutions and structures in societies have changed over a period of time. Beliefs about secularization should therefore be verifiable independently of the personal beliefs of the sociologist or the historian though, as with any field of study, the possibility of personal bias may never be totally absent. The 'secularization story' that emerges depends entirely on how secularization itself is defined.

Three types of 'secularization story' have been told over the past few decades. The first emphasizes the 'social differentiation' that has occurred during the past few centuries of European history in which the functions of Church and State have been largely separated. It is then maintained that these historical developments have had particular implications for the social significance of religion. A second 'secularization story' has focused more on the religious beliefs and practices of individuals within society, rather than on institutions, whereas a third emphasis in the secularization debate has drawn attention to the way in which Western societies have changed in such a way that religious beliefs are thought to have become privatized. Clearly all of these various strands have the potential to be closely linked, but which emphasis is chosen as a starting point for an understanding of secularization makes a profound difference to the story that finally emerges.

A complete discussion of these various strands is clearly beyond the scope of a single chapter. The aim here is more modest: to unpack in a little more detail these three main emphases of the secularization debate, and then to focus in on the particular question of whether science has played a role in secularization in *any* of its varied guises. Finally we shall consider the question as to whether secularization has made it easier to believe in certain kinds of relationship between science and faith.

Secularization as social differentiation

The word 'secularization' comes from the Latin *saeculum* meaning 'age', a term used in medieval times to refer to the world in contrast to the church. For centuries the word was utilized in a non-polemical way, the 'secular clergy' of the Middle Ages being those serving ordinary parishes in contrast to those in religious orders. Secularization (*secularizatio*) was the word in the 16th century which described the process whereby monasteries and land were transferred from ecclesiastical to civil control. From this time the word came to designate the transfer or relocation of persons, things and functions from their traditional location in the religious sphere to the secular spheres.[1]

This largely neutral use of the term continued until the 1860s, when 'secularization' began to incorporate the more emotive concept of anticlericalism, together with an espousal of overtly this-worldly ('secular') attitudes. For the first time expressions such as the 'secularization of art' or the 'secularization of politics' came into general usage, meaning the freeing of these areas of life from their theological origins or bias. It took another 100 years before sociologists had processed out many (though not all) of the term's 19th-century polemical overtones, eventually giving the word secularization its more modern descriptive meaning of 'that process whereby religious thinking, practice and institutions lose social significance'.[2]

Durkheim expressed the process in a thesis that contributed greatly to the 'orthodox model' of secularization expounded back in the 1960s and 1970s: 'political, economic and scientific functions gradually free themselves from religious control, establish themselves separately and take on a more and openly temporal character'.[3] According to this view, as industrialization and capitalism develop, so there is a gradual pulling apart of church and state. 'At the beginning', there is a powerful validation of religious belief, because religion is inextricably intertwined with daily social life. The ruling monarch is also ruler of the church. The ecclesiastical powers are the ultimate powers in society because they control the courts, the use of land, the economic life of the people and the very moral fabric of society. Whether you are rich or poor, whether you work much or little, whether you live by just gain or unjust gain, the result is the same: in such a society you are faced continually with the physical presence of a religious power and authority which controls the institutional operation of that society. As an 'ideal type' of such a society, church control of many parts of 12th-century Europe is often taken as a base line, and the 'secularization story' then becomes the way in which church and state are gradually 'dissected out' over the intervening centuries.

One of the ways social differentiation happens during this process is by the development of specialized roles and institutions to handle specific functions previously handled by the church.[4] For example, institutions arise to provide education, health care, welfare and social control, all of which were once in the domain of religious institutions. It has been suggested that the fragmentation involved in this process itself subverts any notion of a grand moral order giving coherence to the various social functions, as was the case when all were unified under church control.

Another form of social differentiation that, it has been claimed, underlies the secularization of societies is the transition of populations from rural agrarian communities into urbanized conglomerates in industrialized cities. In the 'old days' the village church was the centre of community life but industrialization broke up communities by the need to increase the mobility of the work force. The fragmentation of rural communities, in this view, led to a reduction in the social influence of religion.

The understanding of secularization as 'that process whereby religious thinking, practice and institutions lose social significance' at least has the advantage that it can be measured to some extent, and attempts can be made to link the process to specific historical events that may have contributed to the process. It is indeed a historical fact that the social functions of the church have largely been taken over by the state in Western European countries over the few preceding centuries. The loss of the social significance of religion inherent in such a process is therefore not particularly surprising.

There are, however, major problems with this 'orthodox secularization model', which will emerge even more acutely as we consider religious beliefs within society and the putative privatization of religion. One major problem is that the model is remarkably ethnocentric since it only pertains to Western European countries, and even within this area the pattern of secularization differs markedly between countries. It is no accident that the model has been developed by sociologists and historians within the only geographical area, namely Western Europe, in which the model most likely has some validity. Neither is it a coincidence that the model has been attacked most stringently by those outside Western Europe. For example, the USA has never had a state church and therefore the social differentiation inherent in the secularization model based on the history of Western Europe does not apply. More than that, the founding fathers ensured a stringent separation between church and state in the USA, the precise location of the separation line providing a focus for a continuing debate. Despite, or perhaps because of, this very different history, religion in the USA is booming in ways that will be considered further below.

The idea that religion, taken as a worldwide phenomenon, is losing its social significance, lacks empirical support. Jose Casanova has drawn attention to the powerful social influence of religion during the 1980s in a case study focusing on Spain, Poland, Brazil and the USA, concluding that 'During the entire decade of the 1980s it was hard to find any serious political conflict anywhere in the world that did not show behind it the not-so-hidden hand of religion.'[5] Religions maintain a dominant social influence in the daily life and culture of the majority of the world's population. The idea, so popular in the earlier part of the 20th century, that modernization would necessarily be associated with a decline in the social influence of religion, has not come to pass. Peter Berger was one of the most influential proponents of the 'orthodox secularization model' back in the 1960s and 1970s[6], but more recently has distanced himself from his earlier beliefs, commenting:

> The assumption that we live in a secularized world is false: The world today, with some exceptions... is as furiously religious as it ever was, and in some places more so than ever. This means that a whole body of literature written by historians and social scientists over the course of the 1950s and '60s, loosely labeled as 'secularization theory', was essentially mistaken.[7]

Berger goes on to suggest that 'The key idea of secularization theory is simple and can be traced to the Enlightenment: Modernization necessarily leads to a decline of religion, both in society and in the minds of individuals. It is precisely this key idea that has turned out to be wrong.' Two American professors of sociology, Rodney Stark and Roger Finke, have likewise launched a robust critique of the traditional secularization thesis in their book *Acts of Faith:*

Explaining the Human Side of Religion, concluding that 'After nearly three centuries of utterly failed prophesies and misrepresentations of both present and past, it seems time to carry the secularization doctrine to the graveyard of failed theories, and there to whisper, *Requiescat in pace* [Rest in peace].'[8]

No one is in any doubt that 'secularization as social differentiation' is a useful concept that draws our attention to processes that have in fact occurred during the course of European history. But, as Casanova reminds us, the confusion comes when this historical account of secularization is conflated 'with the alleged and anticipated consequences which those processes were supposed to have upon religion'.[9] What at least seems quite clear is that those consequences have varied greatly within individual European countries – the social function of religion is currently quite different in, for example, Northern Ireland and Poland in comparison with England and Sweden. As far as the global picture is concerned, the 'orthodox model' of secularization theory appears to have little general validity. The history of the relationships between religions and states have followed such different patterns that the construction of any kind of generalization becomes highly problematic. The idea that developing countries will inevitably pass through a process of secularization akin to that experienced in Europe is ethnocentric and poorly supported by the data. Secularization is a profoundly contingent process, conditional upon a set of local variables.

Secularization as a decline in religious belief

Secularization is not the transition from a golden 'age of faith' to an age of no faith, for the simple reason that there never has been 'an age of faith'. There have, of course, been periods in the history of Western Europe when the social role of religion was considerably greater than it is at present, but the popular idea that the mass of people in past centuries were innately religious and centred their lives around godly concerns in contrast to their godless modern counterparts is mistaken. There is always a temptation in studies of secularization to take a period of a country's history when religious observance was rather high and then to take this as a baseline in order to chart a decline in religious belief. But real history is usually more ambiguous and does not lend itself to neat hyperbolic curves.

As we have seen, it was in the latter half of the 19th century that the idea of 'secularization' began to attract popular attention in Europe. Does that mean that the previous era represented an 'age of faith'? The available data hardly support such a thesis. Take almost any century of European history and you will find examples of large segments of the population, of varying class, for whom religious belief meant very little. Humbert of Rome (1200–77) reported that in the Italy of his day 'the poor rarely go to church, rarely to sermons; so that they know little of what pertains to their salvation'.[10] Keith Thomas has charted in considerable detail the religious practices of the British over the period 1600 to

1900.[11] In the Elizabethan period 'a substantial proportion of the population regarded organized religion with an attitude which varied from cold indifference to frank hostility',[12] and at that time 'the attraction of non-religious systems of belief was enhanced by the fact that the hold of orthodox religion upon the British people had never been complete. Indeed it is problematical as to whether certain sections of the population at this time had any religion at all.'[13] In 1606 Nicholas Bound observed that people certainly knew more about Robin Hood than they did about stories in the Bible, which were 'as strange unto them as any news that you can tell them'.[14] In 1672, Sir Charles Wolseley wrote that 'irreligion in its practice hath been the companion of every age, but its open and public defense seems to be peculiar to this'. Montesquieu reported from England in 1731 that 'There is no religion in England... if religion is spoken of everyone laughs.'

Church attendance statistics provide the most common data for attempts by historians and sociologists to track changing levels of commitment to religious belief. Although it would not be too difficult to demonstrate that the correlation between the two is by no means absolute, particularly during periods (unlike the present) when church attendance carried certain social rewards, it seems reasonable to accept that church attendance figures provide at least a rough guide to religious commitment. Even if we ignore any notion of a previous golden 'age of faith', there are sufficient data to show that in the 20th century, at least, church membership was in decline in Western Europe. In mainland Britain, for example, religious adherence grew significantly over the course of the last sixty years of the 19th century, a time of growth and professionalization of the sciences, peaking in 1904–05 at a level of about 50 per cent of the population who demonstrated either membership or adherence to a church. After 1905 church adherence went into gentle decline for the first half of the 20th century, a decline that became steep only after the 1950s[15], reaching a level of about 14 per cent of the adult population, together with a further 2.5 per cent attached to other major world religions, by the end of the century.[16] In stark contrast to this pattern, church adherence in the USA rose steadily from about 33 per cent of the population in 1890 to more than 60 per cent by 1970, thereafter remaining at a level of 50 per cent or higher for the remainder of the century.[17] Therefore the country that is currently the world leader in terms of its contribution to the scientific enterprise, possessing a culture which is most 'modern' in terms of its production and use of technology, also has one of the highest levels of (voluntary) religious commitment of any country of the world. As Finke concludes, following an extensive analysis of 'an unsecular America':

> The historical evidence on religion in the USA does not support the
> traditional model of secularization... modernization did not usher in a new
> era of secularization in America. Instead, the evidence displays the vitality

of religious organizations and the continuing commitment of individuals. Rather than declining, church adherence rates have shown a rapid increase in the 19th century and remarkable stability throughout the 20th.[18]

The lack of any neat correlation between 'modernization' and a decline in religious commitment is mirrored by a similar failure to demonstrate convincingly that either urbanization or industrialization – two other 'markers' of modernity – are necessarily associated with religious decline. In fact data have been presented suggesting precisely the reverse, namely, that throughout most periods of church growth in both Britain and the USA urbanization was proceeding rapidly but that church growth slowed down when urbanization was also slowing down and stagnating.[19] Any simple correlation between urbanization and secularization is likewise questioned by a study contrasting religion observance in the metropolitan centres of London, New York and Berlin at a time when the populations in all three centres were greatly influenced by the effects of industrialization.[20]

A problem with the use of church adherence statistics as a measure of religious belief is that they reflect only commitment to institutional religion, excluding the religious beliefs of individuals. If secularization is 'that process whereby religious thinking, practice and institutions lose social significance', then the beliefs of individuals can readily be excluded from consideration by definition, since privatized religion is less likely to have social impact. Such a tidy solution ignores, however, the fact that individual beliefs do have social consequences even when they remain unexpressed via any institutional commitment. For example, if many individuals in society believe that nature is in some sense sacred and inviolable, and that it is therefore wrong to manipulate the natural world artificially, then they may well oppose the sale of genetically modified foods, campaign against the use of animals in research and promote organic farming, all activities that have significant social and economic consequences.

It is interesting to note that as people severed their links with institutional religion in Western Europe during the latter half of the 20th century, rather than turning to atheism they tended instead to generate their own mix-and-match package of personal religious belief, drawing heavily on the resources provided by New Age thinking. Secularization appears to involve not a decline in faith per se, but rather a multiplication of faiths. The prime effect of modernization is not the decline of religion but the growth of religious and ideological plurality. Despite current church adherence of only 13 per cent (and regular attendance at around 7 per cent), about 70 per cent of the British population have a stated belief in God (compared with 94 per cent in the USA). The fragmentation of religious belief has made it more difficult to draw a clear line differentiating 'religion' from 'personal philosophy', but the exotic flowering

ontaining strong religious elements has certainly drawn
ation. As the tide of institutional religion has gone down, so
native religious belief have washed up to take its place. In
nurch attendance is only 2 per cent, but the 1990 World
reported that 81 per cent of Icelanders express a confidence in
life after death, 88 per cent say they believe humans have a soul and 40 per cent
believe in reincarnation. 'Believing without belonging' is a common European
phenomenon. In the UK more than 500 new religious movements had
established themselves by the 1990s. The actress Nicole Kidman reflects this
trend when she commented, 'I believe in a bit of Scientology, Catholicism,
Judaism and the Eastern philosophies. I take a bit of each, I am a hybrid.'

In one survey of personal values in Britain, 60 per cent of the sample saw
themselves as 'religious persons', half regularly felt the need for prayer,
meditation or contemplation, and one in five reported having had a profound
religious experience.[21] Polls also consistently report high levels of belief in
horoscopes, out-of-the-body experiences, extrasensory perception and alien
visitors from outer space.[22] Whereas even the most liberal definition of religion
might exclude some of these beliefs as 'religious', they do at least illustrate the
way in which private belief systems do not readily become 'secular domains'
even following a lengthy process of public secularization.

Two general conclusions may therefore be drawn from this brief survey of
'Secularization as a decline in religious belief'. The first is that modernity, as
expressed by industrialization and urbanization, is not necessarily associated
with a decline in religious adherence, but may in some cases correlate with
increased adherence. Second, even in Western Europe, where the traditional
secularization model appears to have some validity,[23] the secularization of
society is not invariably followed by an increased secularity of personal belief.

Secularization as the privatization of religion

The privatization of religion is an explicit component of the traditional
secularization model. As religious institutions hand over their roles within
societies to the state, so religious belief becomes internalized, thereby losing its
social significance. We have already challenged this view by observing that
private religious beliefs can have social consequences, even if not mediated via
religious institutions. Furthermore, religious institutions have continued to play
seminal roles during the course of European history even as the process of
secularization has been continuing. Which of the militant secularists who were
dominant in Berlin during the late 19th century, a time when church
attendance was about 5 per cent, would have predicted in 1889 that the
Protestant Church, 'said by friends and enemies alike to be on its last legs in
Berlin, would a century later play a vital role in a revolution in that city'?[24]

Similarly, the social role of the Catholic Church in Poland, a highly industrialized and urbanized society, became dominant in the people's struggle against communism as expressed in the Solidarity movement during the closing decades of the 20th century.[25] Nevertheless, such outstanding examples should not detract from the fact that in most places in Western Europe over the past few decades, for most of the population much of the time religion has indeed become largely a matter of private belief, rarely discussed in polite conversation and even more rarely acted upon in a way that might engender any social impact. As with other aspects of the orthodox model, however, it should not be concluded that the model has any universal validity with respect to the privatization of religion, any more than it does in its other aspects. Casanova claims that from a global perspective it is precisely the *deprivatization* of religion in many parts of the world that has been so characteristic of modern religion.[26]

Science and secularization

There is relatively little discussion of the role of science per se in the secularization literature. This in itself is of interest as there is a common perception that science has in some way contributed to the process of secularization.[27] As religious explanations of the natural world became less convincing and were replaced by scientific explanations, so the story goes, science became the dominant intellectual force in society, thereby exerting a secularizing influence. There are a number of difficulties with such an account, several of which will emerge during the course of the next few chapters as we examine the historical relationship between science and religious belief.

One problem faced by writers on secularization theory is to determine in what sense 'science' might be invoked as a contributor to secularization. We have already defined science as 'an intellectual endeavour to explain the workings of the physical world, informed by empirical investigation and carried out by a community trained in specialized techniques'. Its task is to produce testable ideas. In its modern version, complete with experimentation, scientific journals and societies, science has been with us only since the 17th century. In contrast, 'technology' refers to the practical arts with their goal of the production of usable objects and is therefore as old as the earliest human artefacts. Only in the last two centuries has science had a dramatic impact on technology. Should the writer on secularization therefore draw attention to the influence of 'science' in its strictest sense? The problem with this strategy is that the interactions between science and religious belief have often been mutually beneficial, and from the 17th to the 19th centuries the social role of science in supporting religion was widely maintained. Numerous examples have also been provided of the ways in which the religious commitments of scientists directly influenced the direction of their research or even the content of their scientific theories.[28]

Should secularization theorists instead draw attention to the potentially secularizing influence of technology? The ground here is no less shaky. As already noted, it has often been during times of industrial expansion and urbanization, when technology has been disseminated more widely through societies than in previous eras, that church adherence has shown an increase. A study by the National Science Foundation (1998) reported that 70 per cent of Americans say they are interested in science and technology, the highest proportion ever recorded, increased from 61 per cent in 1992 and 67 per cent in 1995.[29] Americans generally are vastly more positive about the overall impact of science and technology than people in Europe or Japan. Using a list of questions to generate an 'index of scientific promise' as a measure of positive attitudes, and an 'index of scientific reservation' to measure negative ones, the study revealed a 'confidence ratio' between the two indices of 1.9 for the USA, compared with European values in the range 1.1–1.3. So if we compare Europe with the USA, it is apparent that a high level of religious adherence in the USA correlates with a high level of approval of technology, whereas in Europe low religious adherence correlates with a lower approval rating for technology. To extract a cause–effect relationship between these two parameters is clearly contentious; although this does not exclude the possibility that such a relationship exists, for the moment it is simply worth noting that the correlation provides no support for the idea that technology is an inherently secularizing force.

McLeod came to similar conclusions based on his comparison of the levels of religious adherence in New York, Berlin and London:

> Reference... to the effects of industrialization, or of the rise of science, does not get us very far towards explaining the differences between these three cities... In particular, generalized explanations of this kind usually imply that the most 'modern' sectors of the population, those most conversant with modern science, technology, and business methods, and those enjoying the benefits offered by an industrial economy, are those most likely to reject religion, whereas most of the evidence for 19th-century Europe suggests that such rejection was most common in the working class, and particularly the poorer working class.[30]

A safer strategy is to point out that science has frequently been used as an icon in support of political or social campaigns, and it is with this iconoclastic function that we find science being used as a battering-ram, or even as a substitute religion, to lessen the social significance of institutionalized religion. The use of science, or 'natural philosophy' as it was then called, by the Philosophes of 18th-century France, to undermine the power of the church and its priesthood, provides a convincing example (see chapter 6). The new mechanical science espoused by Isaac Newton was promoted by Newton himself in England as further evidence for the wonders of God in creation, but by the time his science had crossed the channel it became radicalized and was used by writers such as Voltaire to attack traditional religious beliefs.[31] A further example is the political use of science by socialists in late-19th-century Germany. The churches of the time were largely anti-socialist and so were seen by working class Berliners as a major obstacle to their aspirations. Darwinism, materialism and a faith in science were all invoked to combat the 'reactionary churches'. This stance was often mingled with the writings of German classical writers such as Goethe and Schiller which became the 'basis for a secular faith, built round such values as freedom, the endless pursuit of knowledge, and reverence for nature'.[32] In England during this same period an ideological use of science was made for rather different goals by 'Darwin's bulldog' T.H. Huxley who attacked the power of the church in the name of science with the specific aim of obtaining for the emerging profession of science the kind of financial rewards and intellectual kudos that the church then possessed (see chapter 7).

Arguably, then, it is not science per se which has proved to be a force for secularization, nor technology its handmaiden, but rather the various transformations of science that have been brought about by campaigners eager to use the prestige of its success and intellectual status to achieve certain secularizing goals. That such ideological uses of science are by no means over is well illustrated by the anti-religious crusades of writers such as Richard Dawkins and Peter Atkins in our own day, who combine entertaining and deservedly popular accounts of science with the claim that scientific knowledge is subversive to religious belief. Daniel Dennett even thinks that Darwinism is a 'universal acid' which seeps through the beliefs of society, gradually aligning them with his own naturalistic presuppositions.[33] To what extent such ideological uses of science may or may not be justified is the subject of future chapters. What seems clear is that it is possible to attach either religious, secular or overtly political 'overtones' to science, for example by the repeated presentation of science in particular contexts, until the science itself becomes transformed as a carrier of a particular message that is not necessarily intrinsic to the science itself, but imposed from outside by the personal agenda of the communicator.

Religious commitment in the scientific community

A rather different approach to the question of whether science may exert a secularizing influence is to examine the religious beliefs of the scientists themselves. If the pursuit of a scientific career is in some way inimical to religious belief, then it might be expected that a negative correlation should be found between the practice of science and personal faith. Some limited data are available on this question from both the 19th and 20th centuries.

The Victorian era was famous for its doubters. It was the high level of religious practice of their era which made such well publicized doubting so visible and so interesting. But when prominent Victorians doubted, it was very rarely because of Science. Rather, as Chadwick points out, the late-19th-century critique of Christianity 'owed its force... not at all to the science of the 19th century. Its basis was ethical, its instrument the ethical criticisms of the 18th century. It attacked Christian churches not in the name of knowledge but in the name of justice and freedom.'[34] In surveying the entire course of this period of British history, Chadwick could find only three scientists who showed signs, in the course of their intellectual development, of being led away from religion at least partly by their scientific beliefs.[35] These conclusions are borne out by the study of Susan Budd in which she read through the biographies of 150 members of the secular movement dating from 1850 to 1950 and found that as far as she could ascertain from this material, ideas from geology, evolution and science in general were influential in only three cases of loss of religious faith.[36]

Francis Galton, the founder of modern statistics, decided in 1873 to apply his new methods to the 'causes which operate to create scientific men' including their heredity and religious background. In the published report of his survey (*English Men of Science: Their Nature and Nurture*) Galton clearly expected 'dogmatism' to have more of a deterrent effect than his answers showed: 'One would have thought that the anathemas from the pulpit against most new scientific discoveries... must have deterred many.' The evidence did not bear out his expectations. Out of the 126 replies from scientists that he received (all men!), 7 out of 10 reported that they were members of one of the established churches, and the remaining 38 of the sample either professed no church membership, or qualified the concept of 'established church' with further information. In answer to the direct enquiry, 'Has the religious creed in your youth had a deterrent effect on the freedom of your researches?' seven out of eight respondents said, 'No'. Galton's survey can clearly be criticized on methodological grounds, not least because it depended on returns from a mailed questionnaire rather than on a truly random sample. But it was a pioneering kind of approach in its field, and perhaps the most interesting observation for our present study is that Galton was expecting to find a hostility to religion among scientists which he did not find, an illustration of the mismatch that can so easily develop between perception and reality.

Given the current American passion for polling their citizens on every kind of topic, it is perhaps not surprising that the USA provides most of the available contemporary data to address the question of scientists' religious beliefs. In some ways it is an advantage to obtain data from a country where religious belief is exceptionally high: as in Victorian Britain, any deficit of religious belief within any segment of the population should be readily detectable against such a high background.

The results overall suggest that the level of religious belief among American scientists is comparable with that found in the general population. For example, the 1969 Carnegie Commission survey of over 60,000 college professors in the USA, approximately one-fourth of all the college faculty in the USA, showed that 55 per cent of those involved in the physical and life sciences described themselves as religious, and about 43 per cent as attending church regularly.[37] Intriguingly, this survey also revealed a clear inverse correlation between the degree of religious commitment and the 'hardness' of the science involved: whereas the 'hard sciences' such as the physical and life sciences scored 55 per cent of 'religious persons', this figure was 33 per cent for psychology and 29 per cent for anthropology. Why are the most irreligious persons found in the least scientific disciplines? Similarly Lemert in 1979 reported that in a survey of religious beliefs among scientists in the USA, 63 per cent of those in the physical sciences look favourably upon religion, concluding that any simplistic equation of science with secularity is false.[38] More recently (1997) the results of a survey were published which had been carried out by two historians, Edward Larson and Larry Witham, with the aim of repeating as closely as possible a survey originally carried out by the psychologist James Leuba published in 1916. Leuba had circulated 1,000 questionnaires to randomly selected names from the 1910 edition of *American Men of Science*. From these he received about a 70 per cent response. The first question in Leuba's questionnaire gave respondents the option of ticking the following affirmation: 'I believe in a God in intellectual and affective communication with humankind, i.e. a God to whom one may pray in expectation of receiving an answer. By "answer" I mean more than the subjective, psychological effect of prayer.' 41.8 per cent of Leuba's respondents agreed with this statement, 41.5 per cent agreed with 'I do not believe in a God as defined above' and 16.7 per cent agreed that 'I have no definite belief regarding this question.'[39] Leuba predicted that the level of disbelief would increase with the continued spread of education. To test his prediction, Larson and Witham sent a replica of Leuba's questionnaire (in 1996) to 1,000 randomly picked names from the current edition of *American Men and Women of Science*, this time drawing a 60 per cent response rate. Of these, 39.3 per cent declared themselves to be believers in a personal God who answers prayer, 46.3 per cent expressed disbelief, while 14.5 per cent remained agnostic.[40] What is of course striking about these data are their close similarity to Leuba's results from

1916, suggesting that close to a century of scientific and technological advance has had little effect on the level of personal religious belief among the American scientific community taken as a whole. Leuba's prediction of a decline in belief with the advance of education has not therefore come to pass.

The publication in *Nature* of Larson and Witham's survey led to considerable interest in the national press, leading to diametrically opposed headlines describing precisely the same results. Whereas *Nature* published the results under the heading 'Scientists are still keeping the faith', a stance followed by *The Times* with its title 'US scientists retain belief in God, survey discovers', the *Daily Telegraph* chose a potentially more worrying headline for its readership: 'Disbelief proves to be a constant among scientists'.[41] The amusing contrast brings out a serious point: in the secularization debate it is often perceptions that are sociologically more powerful than reality. The perception that religious belief is in terminal decline in any given community or society is very likely to have an autocatalytic effect by promoting precisely what is perceived to be already happening. Beliefs that lack social validation or that appear not to have a future are generally not popular beliefs. The reverse is also the case. A society or community in which there is an increase in religious belief will also tend to engender an autocatalytic effect in the promotion of more belief for precisely the same reasons. When Horace Mann carried out his famous religious census of 1851 and found that 'only' 36 per cent of the British population were in church on a given Sunday, he saw this as a sign of 'spiritual destitution', whereas publication of a similar figure today would be taken as a sign of religious revival. In contemporary British society 'only' one in ten of the population attend a place of worship. This is clearly a decline from 1851. On the other hand, there is no other single voluntary social practice which involves anywhere near 10 per cent of the British population, including popular spectator sports such as football. From this perspective churchgoing is currently the most popular British leisure past-time. For good or ill 'spin' makes an enormous difference to the way in which information is disseminated and absorbed.

An example of how difficult the interpretation of statistics can be comes from a further analysis by Larson and Witham of the religious beliefs of American scientists, this time focusing on that elite echelon of scientists who are members of the National Academy of Sciences (NAS). Again publishing their results in *Nature*,[42] this time under a heading slanted in an opposite direction to that previously used ('Leading scientists still reject God'), the authors report their findings based on the same questionnaire used by Leuba, but this time sent only to members of the NAS. Of these only 7 per cent expressed belief in a personal God, whereas 72.2 per cent affirmed disbelief and 20.8 per cent agnosticism. The difference in level of belief in the 'elite scientist' group (7 per cent) as compared with the 'average scientist' group (39.3 per cent) is clearly striking, but the question remains: what does this difference mean? In the absence of any comparative data about the level of belief and disbelief among the top echelons of other American professional groups, such as lawyers, historians, novelists and accountants, it is impossible to determine whether a low level of belief is specifically the characteristic of successful scientists, or whether it is the average property of any group of individuals who reach the top of their profession. The data could mean that very intelligent scientists find that faith is incompatible with science and act accordingly. Or it could mean that highly successful scientists, like successful people from other professions, are very busy people who do not have time for religious practice. Or it could mean that successful scientists are a particularly arrogant subset of people and since arrogance is incompatible with personal belief in God, faith is thereby excluded. Many other possible interpretations come to mind which do not involve the relationship between science and faith. I do not have any particular prejudice as to which of these interpretations (if any) may be correct, but only wish to point out the difficulty of knowing what the numbers mean as they stand.

It would be of great interest to compare the beliefs about religion held by American scientists with their counterparts in other countries of the world. Unfortunately the data from other countries are sparse. Anecdotal data from Britain suggests that the level of religious belief among scientists is as high as, possibly higher, than the level in the population taken as a whole. However, firm data to support this claim are lacking. Some limited anecdotal and statistical data are also available,[43] suggesting that the sciences are proportionally more highly represented than the arts among the Christian sstudent population in Britain, indicating that some 'selection pressure' may be in operation whereby Christians are drawn to study science and/or scientists are more likely to become Christians while at university.

Overall we may conclude from this brief survey that there is little support for the suggestion that science has promoted secularization, although various transformations of science have been used at different times to promote secularizing trends in society. There is also currently no evidence from the scanty data available to support the notion that science has a secularizing influence within the scientific community. The chapters that follow will provide further material relevant to both these points.

Does secularization make any difference?

Despite the various qualifications already outlined, we have accepted that the orthodox secularization model has validity within the boundaries of Western Europe, while at the same time rejecting the idea that the model is necessarily applicable to other regions of the world with their very different histories. The idea, popular in the earlier secularization literature, that other more religious parts of the world would eventually 'catch up' with Europe, by mimicking its secularization history, shows little signs of happening. Intrinsic to this idea was the notion that technology was a force for modernity and therefore secularization and that as Western technology spread round the world, so it would automatically act as a secularizing influence. But we have already noted that this supposed linkage is suspect and remains poorly supported by the data.

Secularization theory appears to reflect the self-confidence of an earlier generation of European historians who assumed that history operates as a straight line, with themselves as the end-point. There is now a greater awareness that secularization is not an inexorable by-product of modernity but a contingent process shaped by the particular political, cultural and economic factors in a given society.

Most Western European societies may be secularized, in the sense that there has been a decline in the social function of religion in comparison with previous eras, but this does not of course mean that the process of secularization has proceeded as far as is possible. In Britain a state church remains with the sovereign as its titular head, and its pronouncements are duly reported by the press. Baptisms and marriages in churches remain common features of daily social life. The largest national holidays remain dominated by the religious calendar. At times of national or local crisis or mourning, people flock into churches as a central unifying focus for socially expressed concern. Religious discourse remains common as a form of public debate, discourse which has received renewed attention due to the moral and ethical challenges raised by the rapid advances in science itself. Even vociferous public opponents of religious belief provide evidence, ironically, for the incompleteness of the secularization process. A truly secularized society is one in which there is a complete silence about God and religious concerns in any kind of public context, where the social significance of religion has declined to 'absolute zero'. Vigorous public debate, the publication of books, broadcasts on radio and TV, all ensure that the silence is nowhere near zero.

Nevertheless the silence is substantially greater than a century ago when religious concerns played a greater public role in the functioning of society. Does that make a difference? There are many ways of answering that question, but the answer that concerns us here brings us back to the paradigms which, it was suggested, play overarching roles in ordering our belief systems. It is much more comfortable to maintain a paradigm when it is shared by the majority of people around us, particularly by those whom sociologists label our 'significant others', the people who play the most influential social roles in influencing our beliefs. Paradigms are nurtured by constant affirmation, or by the unspoken assumption that they are correct, and conversely can more easily wither when starved of social support. So it is quite easy to maintain the paradigm, for example, that historically science has always been at loggerheads with religion, or that there is some innate hostility between science and faith, for the simple reason that in a secular society there is, for most of the time, a deafening silence about alternatives. At the same time, comments by teachers at school, the assumptions of the media, chats with colleagues in the pub, and the occasional publicity given to a book by a scientist attacking religion, can all provide the kind of social nutrition which ensures that the paradigm will be maintained without discomfort. Furthermore, science itself can be transformed by constant repetition in an ideological context until the perception of science itself changes and it becomes a 'carrier of secularization'. At this point science ceases to be merely an activity carried out by the scientific community, the results of which are published in scientific journals but, in addition, becomes encrusted with various philosophical barnacles that are not intrinsic to the scientific enterprise itself.

The point of crisis for paradigms comes when we begin to analyse them dispassionately and the consequent accumulation of opposing data reaches such a combined weight that it brings them crashing to the ground. Investigating paradigms objectively can be a dangerous pastime, particularly one's own. The remainder of this book will be committed to the argument that: first, the paradigms concerning science and religion that are most often comfortably maintained in secularized societies are factually wrong; and, second, that the use of the various transformations of science as ideological tools for either secularizing or religious purposes represents an abuse of science.

Chapter 4

The Bridge to Disenchantment
The Roots of Modern Science (1) — From the Greeks to the Scientific Revolution

Let no man upon a weak conceit of sobriety or an ill-applied moderation
think or maintain, that a man can search too far, or be too well
studied in the book of God's word, or in the book of God's works,
divinity or philosophy; but rather let men endeavor an endless progress
or proficience in both; only let men beware... that they do not unwisely
mingle or confound these learnings together.
Sir Francis Bacon, 1605

The greatest souls are capable of the greatest vices as well as of the
greatest virtues; and those who walk slowly can, if they follow the
right path, go much further than those who run rapidly in the wrong
direction.
René Descartes, *Discourse on Method*, 1637

But as the two great books, of Nature and of Scripture, have the
same author; so the study of the latter does not at all hinder an
inquisitive man's delight in the study of the former.
Robert Boyle, *The Excellence of Theology*, 1665

If we hope to understand what it means to inhabit the world of
modern science, we cannot afford to be ignorant of the itinerary
that brought us to it... The historian's task is not to grade the past
but to understand it.
David Lindberg, 1992

Once upon a time the ancient Ionian Greek thinkers, such as Thales of Miletus, and

Democritus of Abdera, laid the foundations of modern science by attempting to understand the world without invoking the intervention of the gods. This pioneering thinking was obscured by a series of superstitious philosophers, such as Pythagoras, Plato and Aristotle, who imbued the natural world with all kinds of mystical beliefs. Harnessed to the dogmatism of the church, such beliefs later kept Europe in a long dark age which continued until the rediscovery of the free thinking Ionian philosophers during the Renaissance. This led to the founding of the mechanistic philosophy with its emphasis on sceptical enquiry, objectivity and the experimental method. Naturally, such a movement led to repeated clashes with theologians, who tried to hold back the new knowledge because it threatened their cherished beliefs. However, in the end science triumphed by overthrowing the obscurantism of religion and other mystical systems of thought until it reached the pinnacle of its prestige and explanatory power at the present time. Small pockets of superstition still remain, but these will gradually die out as the influence of science continues to spread.

Parodied in this exaggerated form, such a triumphalist account has all the trappings of mythology. Indeed, I know of no recent historian of science who would seriously contemplate such a scheme. Am I then creating men of straw, only to knock them down? The answer is, that although such an outline forms no part of the current academic study of the history of science, something very close to this mythology lives on in TV studios, in the minds of those who wish to utilize science as a carrier of a secular ethos, and therefore in the thinking of a considerable sector of the public. Scientists themselves are still sometimes guilty of propagating such 'Whiggish' views of the history of science, the epithet 'Whiggish' originating from Herbert Butterfield's classic book, the *Whig Interpretation of History* (1931), in which Butterfield criticized those English historians allied with the Whig party who had rewritten history as a story of how their nation had gradually approached their own political ideals:

> The sin in historical composition... is to abstract events from their context and set them up in implied comparison with the present day, and then to pretend that by this 'the facts' are being allowed to 'speak for themselves'. It is to imagine that history as such... can give us judgments of value – to assume that this ideal or that person can be proved to have been wrong by the mere lapse of time.

The late Carl Sagan's popular TV series *Cosmos*, viewed back in the 1970s by 140 million people (three per cent of the human population at the time), remains a classic example of a 'Whiggish' rewriting of the history of science. In *Cosmos* Sagan selected various aspects of the roots of science that appeared to him to be 'modern', and then charted the stepping stones of modernity through the centuries until he finally arrived at 'truly modern science'. Such an approach is particularly tempting to scientists when they write on the history of science since, naturally, they are interested in tracing the particular paths which have given their profession its current characteristics.

But, as Lindberg points out, 'the historian's task is not to grade the past but to understand it'.[1] Brooke and Cantor also warn us against the dangers of 'imposing master-narratives on historical data': the tendency, for example, by scientists to select only the historical triumphs of science and to ignore the failures. Or the proposal that there is some overarching scheme that will reconcile the historical relationship between science and religion into one single coherent model.[2]

It is clear that only a fool or a knave would attempt to write the history of science in a few short chapters. In an attempt to be neither, I shall start by displaying my hand openly and saying that I have no intention nor hope of attempting such a goal. My aim is much more limited in scope: to give a brief and selective overview of some of the interactions between science and faith during the emergence of the scientific enterprise. My agenda is influenced by the assumption that many of my scientific colleagues hold about these interactions, namely, that they have been characterized by a mutual and unremitting antagonism, a perspective that has come to be known as the 'conflict thesis'. My aim is not to replace this thesis by some alternative that will then provide the 'metanarrative' within which all such interactions should be subsumed. The goal of the next few chapters is more modest: to point out that the 'conflict thesis' is grossly inadequate as a way of describing the historical relationship between science and faith, to listen to what the early 'natural philosophers' themselves stated about this question, and to examine some of those moments in history when science and religious belief have indeed come into conflict. The account that follows should therefore be accepted for what it is, a narrowly selective slice out of a very big and complex cake. Extensive references are provided for those who wish to delve deeper.[3]

In history, as in science, there are many times when it is wise to keep one's options open – the results remain too tentative to draw firm conclusions. On the other hand, fear of being branded 'Whiggish' should not detract from the important task of making judicious interpretations where the data allow. There is no point in holding back from the interpretative exercise when the data start to point strongly in a particular direction. As Evans comments in his robust defence of the objectivity of history, 'The first pre-requisite of the serious historical researcher must be the ability to jettison dearly held interpretations in the face of the recalcitrance of the evidence.'[4]

In the discussion that follows the comments made in the Introduction should be remembered that the term 'scientist' is a recent invention which was not widely used until the late 19th century and 'science' (*scientia* in Latin) referred for many centuries to any system of belief characterized by intellectual rigour, whether or not it had anything to do with nature. For example, in the Middle Ages it was common to refer to theology as a science. We shall therefore use the more general term 'natural philosopher' which was in widespread use up to the 19th century to describe those who investigated nature. 'Science' will be used as a synonym for 'natural philosophy'; although the connotations of these terms are somewhat different, 'science' has the advantage of brevity.

Greek Roots

Modern science began with *both* the rediscovery *and* the subsequent overthrow of Greek science. Though the overthrow was certainly not a total one, yet it is difficult to see how modern science could have developed without the radical reassessment of the foundations of Greek science which took place during the years 1500 to 1700.[5] The various Greek philosophers may be pictured as the currents of a broad stream, with many tributaries flowing throughout history, in the process being churned up as if in a rapids, so that the faster flowing water beyond contains some totally new currents as well as certain vital elements of the old. What are those 'vital elements'? We may list them as logic, mathematics and, to some degree, experimentation. All three of these elements are present in the thinking of the oldest Ionian sophists ('wise men') of the Eastern Greek school. They thrived on the western seaboard of what is now Turkey during the 6th and 5th centuries BC.

As a successful man of affairs and widely travelled business man, it was Thales of Miletus (624–565 BC) who first harnessed the geometry that he learned from the Egyptians in a systematic way in order to tackle practical problems, such as determining the distance from the shore to a ship at sea. His pupil, Anaximander (611–547 BC) concentrated on geography, making maps and introducing useful instruments such as the sundial to the Ionian colonies. Yet for Thales and Anaximander, as for all the Ionian philosophers, their 'science' was never perceived as being separate from their philosophy. The ultimate goal of their thinking was always the same: to find some formula or principle that would express the true essence of the world which they observed. For Thales that ultimate principle was 'water', by which he meant a dynamic essence, without shape or colour, that united all things by flowing continuously between earth, sky and throughout the living world. Anaximenes (c. 570 BC), also from Miletus, extended the ideas of Thales by seeing 'air' (*pneuma*) or 'breath' as the essence of all things, rather than the 'water' of Thales. 'As our soul, being air, sustains us, so *pneuma* and air pervade the whole world.' The universe itself was therefore seen as being, in a sense, alive.

Pythagoras

At the same time that the Ionian philosophers were flourishing on the western coast of Turkey, across the Ionian sea, in the Dorian colonies that dotted what is now Sicily and the southern tip of Italy, Greek philosophy was taking a rather different direction. Pythagoras, who settled in Croton around 530 BC, has been both pilloried (Bertrand Russell: Pythagoras 'founded a religion of which the main tenets were the transmigration of souls and the sinfulness of eating beans') and hero-worshipped (Arthur Koestler: 'Pythagoras was... the founder of Science, as the word is understood today'), though the truth is probably somewhere between these extremes. Details of the life of Pythagoras himself are shrouded in mystery, and a knowledge of both his teachings and of the Brotherhood that he founded have come to us as reported by other Greek philosophers in the centuries following his death, the very term *philosophos* (philosopher) having been introduced into the Greek language by the Pythagoreans.

The central tenet of the Pythagoreans was that numbers have a separate, objective existence outside our minds. It was Pythagoras who first used the word 'cosmos' to refer to an ordered universe and the key to the cosmos was seen as being the mathematical harmonies by which it was characterized. So the musical scale was found to be expressed by simple numerical ratios, the pitch of a note being dependent on the length of the string which produces it. In Aristotle's interpretation, the Pythagoreans

> regarded numbers as the elements of all things, and the whole heaven as
> a musical and numerical scale. The very arrangement of the heavens
> they collected and fitted into their scheme. Thus, as ten was thought to be
> perfect and comprise in itself the whole nature of numbers, they said that
> the bodies which moved in the heavens were ten in number; but since the
> visible heavenly bodies are but nine, they invented a counter-earth.

Just as ten was the perfect number so, for the Pythagoreans, the sphere was the perfect figure. They therefore maintained that the earth as well as the planets were spheres, although there is no evidence that this belief followed from any observations on their part.

The Brotherhood was a religious order in which Pythagoras himself appears to have achieved semi-divine status. At the end of his life he was banned from Croton and his disciples were either killed or exiled. Yet the Pythagorean passion for seeing mathematical harmony in the order of the cosmos lived on, later having a profound influence on Plato, and on through Plato to Kepler and the scientific revolution of the 17th century in Europe.

The 'mysticism' of Pythagoras is sometimes contrasted with the 'rationalism' of the Ionians. Yet although the philosophy of the Ionians was never embodied in the kind of political and religious community which characterized the Pythagoreans, yet they were one with the followers of Pythagoras in seeing their 'science' as but a handmaiden of their philosophy, a philosophy that had as its central quest a description of the ultimate sources of harmony in a universe in which matter itself pulsated with life. Right at the beginning of our story we can already discern the type of creative interactions between 'religion' and 'science' that were to continue on through the centuries.

The Atomists

This seeking after the final reality of all that exists was no less the goal of Leucippus (c. 475 BC) and his better known pupil Democritus (c. 470–400 BC), founders of the Atomist school of philosophy in the Ionian colonies. For the Atomists, that 'final reality' was to be found in the twin elements of solid atoms and the void between them. In their philosophy, the void had as much primary reality as the atoms. The atoms themselves were eternal, indivisible, and had a confused motion in all directions, which was also eternal. The visible world was made of 'entanglements' of atoms. Exactly how they moved and entangled was governed by 'necessity'. Whereas for us the idea of necessity implies a connection between events ('the door slammed shut, blowing the papers off the desk'), for the Greeks, a necessity was an internal cause of behaviour inherent in matter itself. So whereas for us it is 'obvious' to ask the question about a falling stone: 'What are the causes of it falling?' for the Atomists the question was radically different: 'What is it in the nature of a stone which makes it fall?' So the 'necessity' inherent in fire caused it to fly upward, whereas the 'necessity' in the nature of the stone caused it to fall towards the earth.

It takes a considerable mental effort to try to think ourselves into a totally different worldview. But, even though we will never be more than partially successful in the attempt, the effort is vital if we are to avoid a complete misinterpretation of the thought of another age. Though the Atomists have frequently been looked to as the forerunners of a purely materialistic philosophy, in reality they were not so far from Thales and Anaximenes, with their 'ultimate principles' of Water and Air, as might first appear, nor even from the 'ultimate reality' of numbers as espoused by Pythagoras. In Democritus it is not that we have no 'god' ('ultimate reality'), but rather that we have a 'god' pulverized into millions of particles in which each atom, governed by necessity, takes on autonomous and god-like qualities. So although Democritus did not see the world as a living organism, yet 'soul' was seen by him as consisting of especially small, round atoms (the word *atom* is Greek for 'indivisible'), with each individual soul being dispersed at death and its particles scattered throughout the universe. 'Soul and mind pervade the universe and are breathed in by us from it'. Furthermore, the gods of Greek mythology that appeared to men were seen by Democritus as being active and personal, breaking in on people's lives from the air around, but subject to the laws governing every other atomic compound in the world, and so destined for eventual decay and incorporation back into the 'atomic whirl' which makes up the universe.

The ideas of the Atomists were later revived by Epicurus, and during the 1st century BC found a champion in the Roman Lucretius, who used them to attack religion. There is therefore a certain irony in the observation that the most recent proponent of the spirit, if not the letter, of Democritus, was the late theologian Teilhard de Chardin, who saw human consciousness as being due to 'some sort of psyche in every corpuscle' of the human body. The soul atoms plus necessity of Democritus appear not very distant in properties from the psychic corpuscles of De Chardin.

By the middle of the 5th century BC the philosophers of Athens had begun to overshadow both the Eastern and Western schools of Greek thought. The Ionian Anaxagorus came to Athens in 464 BC, full of enthusiasm and new ideas, and there spent thirty years of his life. His philosophy had a profound influence on both Plato and Aristotle and therefore forms one of the important tributaries of the river of Greek thought which flowed into Europe during later centuries.

Anaxagorus

'All things were together, then Mind (*nous*) came and set them in order.' According to Diogenes, this was the opening of Anaxagorus' first book of his one and only treatise, the *Physica*. Mind was seen by Anaxagorus as being conscious and intelligent, and completely separate from the world of 'things'. There are no limits on its knowledge and judgment. Mind is ultimately responsible for all movement of matter, and introduces rational order into matter by means of circular motion. A portion of Mind is actually *in* living things, and is therefore identical with the *psyche* or animating principle which gives life to organic matter. Anaxagorus never gave the title 'god' to Mind but it is clear that he thought of Mind as being divine. He later withdrew from Athens due to opposition against his 'atheism', though in the context of the times this involved the accusation that he disbelieved in the divinity of the sun, which Anaxagorus insisted on calling an 'incandescent stone'. (On coming across the epithet of 'atheist', it is always worthwhile to check what such a title means in its cultural and historical context. Some centuries after Anaxagorus, the early Christians were labelled 'atheists', since they disbelieved in the divinity of the Roman emperor.)

Anaxagorus was firmly in the Ionian tradition in maintaining that the order of the cosmos can be traced to some ultimate principle but, unlike the earlier Ionians, whose 'Water', 'Fire' or 'Atoms plus Void' pervaded the universe as part of its very being, in Anaxagorus we find a clear distinction between 'things' and 'Mind', a dualism which was developed at much greater length by Plato and Aristotle. Both of these thinkers acknowledge their debt to Anaxagorus, though complain that he failed to make full use of the concept of Mind, bringing it in as the prime cause of order, but then leaving 'Mind' out of his actual descriptions of eclipses, meteors, rainbows and other phenomena. The echoes of their complaint are still with us, and form a recurring theme in discussions of science and faith down the centuries.

Plato and Aristotle

'Everyone by nature is a disciple either of Plato or of Aristotle.' Though the alternatives may not be quite that stark, the fact that this assertion is repeated so often is at least a reminder of the immense influence on European history of these two giants of Greek philosophy.

Plato (427–348/7 BC) was a wealthy Athenian aristocrat who, inspired by the teaching of Socrates, made it his life's aim to work out the principles of a perfect State which would allow people to live the ideal life. The 'ideal life' in Plato's vision was restricted to a small minority of ruler–philosophers and guardians, and his *Republic* makes chilling reading when viewed against a backcloth of 20th century totalitarian regimes. For example, it was Plato who first prescribed the death penalty for unrepentant impiety. Plato's political idealism was underpinned by a philosophical idealism in which absolute reality was viewed as a series of Ideas. These Ideas lay behind the whole of the perceived world that, since it was in a constant state of flux, could never be properly described by the senses. So the Idea of something in our minds was more real, for Plato, than the physical representation of that Idea that we see with our eyes. The soporific Burmese cat which lolls languidly upon my lap as I write, with the occasional annoying flick of its tail in order to scatter pens and papers off the desk, is thus less truly an entity than the Platonic Idea of Cat.

In Plato's philosophy, change is associated with degeneration, whereas Ideas are changeless, and therefore perfect. The story of creation reads more like devolution than evolution: out of pure Goodness ('god') comes the World of Reality consisting of perfect Ideas, then the World of Appearance which is its shadow, and only after that do we find man, and finally the animals, which 'came from men who were wholly unconversant with philosophy and had never gazed on the heavens'.

Given the low status of man (the observer) and the constant change taking place in the observed world around us, it is hardly surprising that true knowledge, in Plato's philosophy, cannot be obtained via the senses, since 'if we would have true knowledge of anything, we must be quit of the body... While in company with the body, the soul cannot have true knowledge.' Plato did not dismiss the value of the senses altogether, but did see mathematics as most closely approximating Ideal Forms. 'Let none who has not learnt geometry enter here' was inscribed over the entrance to his school, the Academy, and Plato showed respect to a science only to the extent to which it could be expressed in mathematics. It was due to this primacy of mathematics that Plato followed Pythagorus in saying that the shape of the world *must* be a perfect sphere, and that all motion *must* take place in perfect circles at uniform speed. This passion for circularity was destined to dominate astronomy for the next 2,000 years.

Another idea which was to have a great influence was Plato's emphasis on deduction: a long series of consequences were rationally deduced from an initial proposition, and if these consequences appeared to conform with reality, then the proposition was accepted as plausible. Similar deductive methods were also expounded by Archimedes and Euclid. Though important for deriving mathematical theorems, the method of deduction also tended to downgrade evidence derived from the senses.

Plato's picture of the universe as a living entity, with a soul penetrating its body, was hardly central to his teaching, yet this idea was picked up and amplified by later thinkers and became one of the main tributaries of Greek thought flowing into Europe. A major channel for such Platonic ideas was the movement that arose in Alexandria early in the 3rd century AD and which became known as neoplatonism. In neoplatonic philosophy, the 'Idea' of Plato became almost personified. The Idea rules over matter as the soul rules over the body. When matter breaks away from the Idea, then it tends towards chaos. Matter itself, therefore, tends to be seen as evil, or leading to disorder. The soul's aim should be to free itself from the dangers of matter, and hope instead for union with the divine soul of the universe.

Neoplatonic doctrine passed into Christianity through the work of St Augustine (AD 354–430) who, on his own admission, borrowed heavily from neoplatonic sources. Suspicious of all knowledge obtained by the direct use of the senses, Augustine ignored or rejected those early Greek thinkers who had begun the first gropings towards understanding the world around them. 'When people study the operations of nature which lie beyond our grasp,' wrote Augustine, they merely give reign to a 'diseased craving' and a 'lust for experimenting and knowing'. In place of the earthy materialism of Hebrew culture, with its biblical insistence that God's world was made to be enjoyed by responsible stewards, and that 'all created things were to be received with thanksgiving', Augustine shrank from the world, and in doing so left a legacy of Christianity to the Latin West which was a distorted version of the faith of the early church. Cast in a neoplatonic mould, Augustine's *Confessions* and *City of God* dominated the medieval church, giving the impression in the process that there was little profit to be had from investigations of the natural world.

That other great giant of Greek philosophy, Aristotle (384–322 BC), became a pupil of Plato at the age of seventeen in Athens. After Plato died, Aristotle went to live in Lesbos, an island off the coast of Asia Minor. In 342 Aristotle became tutor to Prince Alexander of Macedon, but returned as a public teacher to Athens four years later when Alexander started out on his great tour of world conquest.

Aristotle was a brilliant zoologist and his striking personal observations of the natural world come in refreshing contrast to the rather arid idealism of his master. Aristotle recorded the life and breeding habits of about 542 species of animal, made embryological investigations of the developing chick, gave a detailed account of the habits and development of octopuses, and, for the first time, introduced diagrams in order to illustrate anatomy. In Aristotle's great work entitled *On the Parts of Animals* he wrote:

> But of a truth every realm of nature is marvellous. It is told that strangers, visiting Heraclitus and finding him by the kitchen fire, hesitated to enter. 'Come in, come in', he cried, 'the gods are here too'. So should we venture on a study of every kind of creature, without horror, for each and all will reveal something that is natural and therefore beautiful. *Absence of haphazard and conduciveness of all things to an end* are ever to be found in nature's works, and her manner of generating and combining in ever-changing variety is of the highest form of the Beautiful [my italics].

There is something very appealing in Aristotle's fascination for the natural world, for it is this driving curiosity, coupled with an eye for detail, that are essential qualities of a scientist in any age.

Aristotle developed the ideas of earlier Greek thinkers in seeing everything that existed as having its own *physis* or physical nature, which thereby determined its 'natural' place in the hierarchical order of the universe. Natural motion occurred when something was out of place and was in process of returning to its 'correct' location. So stones would fall towards earth because that was where they 'belonged', just as fire would burn upward in order to join the celestial fires. It was in the nature of a bird to fly, or a fish to swim. Indeed, that was the reason for their very existence, and Aristotle saw 'everything that nature makes' as being a 'means to an end'. He was thus a teleologist (*telos* is Greek for 'end' or 'aim'), a tradition that was vigorously continued by Galen of Pergamum (AD 131–201), whose extensive writings on biology and medicine were translated into Latin, Syriac, Arabic and Hebrew, dominating the intellectual world on these subjects from the 3rd to the 16th centuries. As Galen wrote:

It was the Creator's infinite wisdom which selected the best means to attain His beneficent ends, and it is a proof of His omnipotence that He created every good thing according to His design, and thereby fulfilled His will.

For Aristotle and Galen true knowledge was always causal knowledge. This understanding of the natural world in terms of final causes rather than the immediate causes required to explain the phenomena in question dominated medieval philosophy and theology long after Aristotle and Galen, and has contributed to discussions of science and faith ever since. The rather murky debate between so-called 'creationists' and 'evolutionists', which we shall consider further in chapters 9 and 10, arguably owes more to Aristotle than to the early chapters of Genesis, and the spirit of Aristotle hangs more heavily over books like Richard Dawkins' *The Blind Watchmaker* than even that of William Paley (of whom more in chapters 7 and 10).

It was the comprehensive nature of Aristotle's system that made it such a compelling worldview. My own unreflecting use of the word 'nature' in the sentence just written illustrates just how far Aristotelian concepts of 'nature' and 'natural' have become embedded in the English language. Aristotle broadly divided the universe into an earthly domain and a heavenly domain, with quite different rules ordering what went on in these two areas. As far as the earthly order was concerned, Aristotle envisaged everything as belonging to a great 'ladder of nature', with inanimate matter at the bottom of the pile, followed by plants and up through the various animals to man. Each species was for ever fixed in this hierarchy, according to its particular *physis*. Just as plants and animals have their own forms, so any kind of natural motion on earth also had its own *physis* in that it tended to be in straight lines, whereas unnatural motion required some force to be applied from outside.

In contrast to the earthly domain, Aristotle saw the heavenly order as consisting firstly of a series of spheres of pure 'elemental nature' – the most dense sphere was an 'earthy exhalation' – then came water, air and fire. The heavenly bodies were arranged in a series of (invisible) concentric spheres, with the earth at the centre, and were made out of an absolutely pure 'fifth element' or 'quintessence'. (I was delighted to see this Aristotelian word in modern garb in *The Guardian* newspaper recently: 'Once the *quintessential* symbol of women as flesh and only flesh, Miss World is now something altogether more subtle' [my italics]). The boundary of the universe was formed by the outermost sphere, whose divine harmony caused the circular revolution of the whole celestial system.

Beyond the edge of the universe was Aristotle's god, the Unmoved Mover who, like a giant flicking an onion, kept the whole complex series of spheres moving rather ponderously around the immovable earth. Since both *physis* and matter itself are eternal in Aristotle's system, there is no concept of creation. Instead

'Nature makes everything to a certain purpose', nature itself is seen as semi-divine. The closer things become to the highest form of all, the more they become divine, and so the heavenly bodies pulsate with divine life.

Alexandria

Aristotle died in 322 BC, but as the intellectual life of the Greek speaking world gradually shifted from Athens to Alexandria, following its founding by Alexander the Great in 331 BC, it was Alexander's former tutor Aristotle who became the model philosopher for a city dominated by the great 'temple of the Muses' (the origin of our word 'museum'), with its library of 400,000 books. The astronomer Ptolemy was active in Alexandria around the middle of the 2nd century, and summed up Greek maths and astronomy in his work *The Great Astronomer*, which was given the name *Almagest* by the Arabs (by prefixing the Arabic definite article *al* to the Greek *megiste*, meaning 'great'). The *Almagest* is the most complete work of Greek astronomy that we have.

A striking characteristic of the intellectual life of Alexandria during this period was its pluralism and openness to new ideas. The temper of life is summarized nicely by Gregory Thaumaturgus, a student of a Christian teacher of Alexandria called Origen (c. AD 186–254), when describing Origen's teaching methods and attitudes to non-Christian philosophies:

> He required us to study philosophy by reading all the existing writings of the ancients, both philosophers and religious poets, taking every care not to put aside or reject any... For us there was nothing forbidden, nothing hidden, nothing inaccessible. We were allowed to learn every doctrine, non-Greek and Greek, both spiritual and secular, both divine and human; with the utmost freedom we went into everything and examined it thoroughly, taking our fill of and enjoying the pleasures of the soul.

A similar attitude to natural philosophy is seen in the work of Johannes Philoponus, an Alexandrian Christian of the first half of the 6th century, who held a chair in philosophy in the academy, and who was one of the last great ancient commentators on Aristotle. Philoponus used his extensive knowledge of Aristotle to launch a major attack on his philosophy, and anticipated the 17th-century natural philosophers by using the biblical theology of creation to challenge Aristotle's philosophy of the eternity of the heavens. Since that which is created has a beginning and an end, and so must be subject to change, how could the heavens be perfect? Furthermore, Philoponus observed that the stars, far from following eternally identical paths over a long period of time, in fact trace out paths that are not concentric, so casting further doubt on the Aristotelian dichotomy between the celestial and terrestrial regions.

Despite the work of outstanding thinkers such as Philoponus, Alexandria was already in decline by the end of the 4th century. Greek science was dispersed, some of it to lie in forgotten papyri, locked away in desert monastery libraries, some to accumulate in cities like Jerusalem and Byzantium. Apart from two of his logical works, Aristotle's writings were lost to the view of the Western world along with most of the major works of Greek science. Instead, it was the form of neoplatonism that Augustine brought into Christianity which dominated the Western world until the 12th century. Some rudimentary concepts of Greek science filtered down along this neoplatonic stream, but in forms that would hardly have been recognized by their original proponents.

The bridge

The story of how the ancient texts of Greek science were gradually translated and filtered into Europe is a familiar one. Preserved by the Muslim world, transcribed texts, some of them very poor, began to be translated from Arabic into medieval Latin from the late 10th century, and translation became a major scholarly activity from the 12th century onward. There were two main centres for translation: Sicily and Spain. In Toledo there was a 'Translators' College' in which texts in Arabic were read out in Spanish and translated directly into Latin. Gerard of Cremona (c. 1114–87) translated no fewer than seventy to eighty works, possibly with the aid of helpers. The transmission of many of the texts had been a long and tortuous process. For example, some of Aristotle's works, such as *Physics*, passed from Greek into Syriac, then to Arabic, next to Hebrew, and finally from Hebrew into Latin. It was hardly surprising that certain elements of the original Aristotle were lost in the process, but by the 13th century his writings became available in the original Greek and the quality of translation improved.

The appearance of Greek texts in Latin was a fairly haphazard process and the order of translation bore little resemblance to the chronology of authorship. So the works of Aristotle (4th century BC) became available over the same period as Ptolemy's *Almagest* (2nd century AD), which was translated from Arabic into Latin in 1175, and as Euclid's *Elements* (c. 300 BC), which were rediscovered in an Arabic translation by an English monk called Adelard of Bath in AD 1120. Greek thought also passed directly into Europe via Arab philosophers, such as Averroes (1126–98), who perhaps did more than any other person to familiarize the intellectual circles of Europe with the ideas of Aristotle.

Our minds are so geared to viewing what is modern as being intrinsically better, in contrast to those things which are 'old and irrelevant', that it is difficult to think our way back into the mindset of medieval 'science' (an attitude dubbed 'chronological snobbery' by C.S. Lewis). For us, the translation of an ancient text would be of great potential historical significance, but we would be unlikely to look to it as a source of scientific information. For the medieval world it was the reverse: the authoritarian structure of society involved a framework of thinking in which the ancients were looked to as the supreme authorities in matters of philosophy, and 'science' was therefore the analysis and illustration of what the great philosophers taught. As Peter Harrison comments: 'For the scholastics, nature existed primarily in books, and if from time to time they were to add glosses to the authorities on the basis of their own observations of the world, they nonetheless saw as their main task the preservation and transmission of a world which had already been observed by great minds in the past.' Nevertheless it should not be imagined that the waves of Greek philosophy that flooded into medieval Europe were merely passively accepted – quite the reverse; new translations became the objects of passionate debate, and Greek science was not accepted wholesale but instead fused with medieval theology.

William of Conches (d. after 1154), at one stage a member of the Plantagenet household and a tutor of the future King Henry II, developed his elaborate cosmology and physics based on platonic sources at least partly derived from new translations. But his science was expounded within a Christian framework in which it was perfectly correct to 'inquire into the natural causes of things'. In his *Philosophy of the World* William of Conches expresses his frustration with those who are too quick to utilize divine intervention as an explanation for natural events: 'However, we say that the cause of everything is to be sought.' Finding natural explanations for things in no way detracts from God's role as creator since 'I take nothing away from God; all things that are in the world were made by God, except evil; but he made other things through the operation of nature, which is the instrument of divine operation.'[6] By such strategies platonic science was brought within the framework of Christian theology.

The 12th century also saw the first attempts by scholars in Europe to debate Aristotelian science, but it was not until a century later that the Dominican friar, St Thomas Aquinas (c. 1224–74), carried out a programme on a much larger scale in which the teaching of Aristotle was fused with medieval theology to form a system which came to be known as 'scholasticism' by later philosophers. Thus was continued the long process whereby the church, like an amoeba, tended to invaginate and absorb great globules of philosophy that were often incompatible with its basic tenets, in the process Christianizing them sufficiently to remove any threat to the social order, but at the same time giving their acceptance a weight of authority and respectability that they would never have otherwise obtained. Never mind that Aristotle believed that matter was eternal: his system was Christianized by tagging a creation and an ending of the universe on at either end, the static Aristotelian worldview in the middle remaining essentially unchanged. Never mind that Aristotle's 'Unmoved Mover' was remote from the God of Christianity: Aquinas proceeded to base his 'First Proof' of the existence of God entirely on Aristotle's physics; since everything that moves needs something else to move it, if you press the regression back far enough, there must be an entity to start the movement off in the first place, this entity being the 'Unmoved Mover' or 'God'. This rather unsatisfactory argument was dealt with as it deserved by William of Ockham in the 14th century. Although Aquinas was probably thinking in terms of logical hierarchies rather than a 'first cause' in a temporal sense, Aristotelian echoes are distinctly discernible in those who today look for God at the very edge of the known universe at the moment of the Big Bang.

Aristotle's static universe provided an appropriate framework for the social hierarchies of medieval Europe. Thomas Aquinas not only managed to absorb Aristotle into his great *Summa Theologica*, but also a neoplatonic forgery known as the *Celestial Hierarchy* by the so-called Dionysius the Areopagite, at the time widely accepted as a genuine work. The result was a fusion of Aristotelian physics, neoplatonic speculations and medieval theology whereby the hierarchy of society was reflected in the very order of the universe. Just as popes, archbishops, bishops, emperors, kings and earls all had their rightful place in the social structure, so there were celestial hierarchies with various ranks of angels and archangels having specific duties depending on which particular Aristotelian crystalline sphere they found themselves. This social and celestial order had its counterpart in man's own physical body, in which the higher noble organs, such as the heart and lungs, were separated by the diaphragm from the lowly organs of the belly.

It is intriguing to consider some of the emphases in Greek philosophy which passed into Europe by translation from the 12th to 15th centuries. Some of these streams of thought were immensely beneficial for the birth of the scientific movement. Other streams proved sterile, and it was only as they were displaced by the competing theologies and philosophies of the 16th- and 17th-century natural philosophers that modern science became possible. As Steven Shapin remarks: 'Nothing so marked out the "new science" of the 17th century as its proponents' reiterated claims that it was new.'

Logic and mathematics

One great ability bequeathed by the Greeks was the habit of thinking in a logical and orderly manner. As A.N. Whitehead put it, 'Galileo owes more to Aristotle than appears on the surface of his Dialogues: he owes to him his clear head and his analytic mind.' The endless scholastic debates of early medieval Europe were not sterile through lack of logic or intelligence, but through operating within a worldview in which appeals to authority were the ultimate arbiters of truth in every sphere of life.

Together with logic, the Greeks bestowed upon Europe the platonic passion for mathematics, which was to have such a profound effect upon the scientific revolution. Whereas after Aquinas it was the structure of Aristotle's universe that dominated the thinking of medieval Europe, yet Plato and Pythagorus continued to inspire philosophers to look at nature through mathematical eyes. The Florentine scholar Marsilio Ficino (1433–99) played a leading role in trying to unite platonic and biblical ideas, translating Plato's *Works* into Latin in order to make them more accessible. Nicholas Copernicus (1473–1543), a key transitional figure in the scientific revolution, objected to Ptolemy's astronomy, not so much on the basis of new observations as on its mathematical inelegance, and was thoroughly within the Greek intellectual tradition in being content to make calculations based on the observations of others, rather than making any of his own. The thinking of Copernicus was dominated by the heavenly pattern of circularity, and his decision to place the sun instead of the earth at the centre of the universe seems to have been influenced by his admiration for the mathematical cult of Pythagorus, as impressed upon European readers through the 'Hermetic writings'. This collection of writings was supposed to have been written by an ancient Egyptian figure, known as Hermes Trismegistus ('thrice blessed Hermes'), who claimed to have written down the wisdom of the Egyptians during the time of Moses. The writings became available to the West after the fall of Constantinople in 1453 and were rapidly translated from the Greek, soon to obtain a wide readership. Here, or so it was widely believed at the time, was a revelation about the physical world as valid as the revelation that had been given to Moses about the moral world. It was left to the great classical scholar Isaac Casaubon (1559–1614) to reveal that 'Hermes Trismegistus' had never existed and that his 'wisdom' had in fact been composed by various neoplatonic writers of the 2nd century AD. But, in the meantime, 'Hermes Trismegistus' continued to act as a powerful validator of neoplatonic ideas to the Western world, emphasizing that the secrets of the cosmos had been written in a mathematical language that could be discerned, for example, in musical harmonies. As Hugh Kearney comments, 'In this tradition, the pursuit of mathematics was not a secular activity. It was akin to religious contemplation', and 'to men with imagination, the message of neoplatonism offered a heaven-sent escape route from the rationalism of academic Aristotelianism'.

The mathematical vision of the harmony of the spheres is seen most vividly in the writings of another of the great founders of modern astronomy, Johannes Kepler (1571–1630), one of the few astronomers of his time to speak out strongly in support of Copernicus. Kepler was born into one of the oldest

Protestant families in Weil, a small town in south-west Germany. After studying at Tübingen he wrote his first major work, the *Mysterium Cosmographicum*, published at the age of twenty-five, in which he attempted to show that the orbits inscribed by the six planets (including the earth as a planet) in the system of Copernicus corresponded to the five perfect solids of Euclid. Kepler's later works are no less saturated with this mathematical vision of the harmony of God's universe, a vision that, coupled to the observational data of the stars painstakingly gathered by Tycho Brahe, was to lay the foundations of modern astronomy. Twenty years after writing the *Mysterium*, Kepler described how 'I feel carried away and possessed by an unutterable rapture over the divine spectacle of the heavenly harmony', and in his *Harmonice Mundi* (1619) Kepler pictures each planet as having its own musical scale that was determined by its speed, the musical climax being a chord sounded by all six planets. 'The motions of the heavens', Kepler wrote, 'are nothing else but a perennial concert made up of rational (unheard) music.' Astronomers are 'the priests of God, called to interpret the Book of Nature', and the key to that interpretation is mathematics:

> Why waste words? Geometry existed before the Creation, is co-eternal with the mind of God, *is God himself...* geometry provided God with a model for the Creation and was implanted into man, together with God's own likeness – and not merely conveyed to his mind through the eyes.

As Kearney writes, 'Mathematics held an overwhelming appeal for almost all the original minds of the 17th century.' Yet, as the century proceeds, mathematics seems to have become much more a tool, less a cosmic passion, than in the effusive outpourings of a Copernicus or a Kepler. Thus, Galileo (1564–1642) was less in the neoplatonic tradition typified by the hermetic writings, much more in the mechanical tradition of Archimedes. He accepted Copernicanism not because of any mystical feelings for the sun, but because of a mechanical analogy derived from his astronomical observations. Yet Galileo's rejection of some of the more florid aspects of neoplatonism should not detract from the fact that mathematics was absolutely central to his science:

> Philosophy is written in this grand book the universe, which stands continually open to our gaze. But the book cannot be understood unless one first learns to comprehend the language and read the letters in which it is composed. It is written in the language of mathematics... without which it is humanly impossible to understand a single word of it...

René Descartes (1596–1650) and Isaac Newton (1642–1727) are just two more of the giants of the 17th century's scientific revolution who, in their very different ways, emphasized the primacy of mathematics. Again, for both of them, their mathematical visions of the universe were set firmly within theological frameworks, God, for Descartes, being like an ingenious engineer, whereas Newton saw also in creation the work of the divine artist.

Should nature be investigated?

In tracing the immensely positive legacy of mathematics from the Greek world into the scientific revolution of the 17th century, we have already crossed not one but many bridges. In the world of Kepler, Galileo and Newton, it is assumed that the universe is a fascinating place, waiting to be explored, analysed and understood. Underlying this assumption is the conviction that the universe *can* and *should* be understood, and that the world reflects a rational and divinely appointed order which contains no corners too dark or too sacred for human beings to investigate. In these assumptions we are already very far from the attitudes of much Greek philosophy. As already noted, platonic thought did not encourage experimentation since an object was nothing more than a realization of its form, and matter was the source of its inability to realize that form perfectly. So the only way to understand the actual world was by an intellectual comprehension of the forms of things not, as seems so 'obvious' to us now, by obtaining actual sensory data concerning matter itself.

As well, nature was generally perceived by the Greeks as divine, pulsating with 'empathies' and 'sympathies', to be feared, rather than probed. According to Plato, the very cosmos is a living creature. In Greek mythology Salmoneus, who tried to mimic storms, was struck down for his pains by the 'Almighty Father', and Prometheus, who stole fire from the gods, was duly punished by the Lord of Heaven. Any attempt to compete with nature was seen by the Greeks as *hubris* (impiety), and liable to failure, if not outright punishment. Early attempts at mechanics were viewed with some suspicion, since they appeared to be working against nature by, for example, lifting heavy burdens by small forces. As Reijer Hooykaas points out, the word *machina* meant 'an instrument', but was also used to signify craftiness, and Pappus in the 3rd century AD wrote that people who used mechanical devices were also known as 'wonder workers' and presumably gained their power over nature by magic. Similarly, the alchemy of the Middle Ages was seen as an attempt to wrest secrets from 'Mother Nature' by changing the 'form' of lead into the 'form' of gold, in the process arousing both the fascination and the fear of societies convinced that the feats of nature could be surpassed only by magic. Roger Bacon, who spent a large fortune on his personal research during the 13th century in a period otherwise dominated largely by theoretical philosophizing, felt that such 'natural magic' was quite acceptable, but was still imprisoned as a sorcerer because it was felt that any attempt to equal nature was both impious and audacious. Through the Renaissance period the term '*experimentum*' included both the practice of witchcraft as well as that of scientific experimentation.

Quite apart from the continuing influence of Greek views about nature, given the absolute dominance of natural events over the daily lives of people in the Middle Ages, it is hardly surprising that 'Mother Nature' was held in such awe and fear. Death, disease, hunger, pestilence and war were common facts of everyday life, no less for those caught up in the early scientific movement than for anyone else. When the astronomer Johannes Kepler, writing in 1597, reviewed the fortunes of his grandfather's twelve children, his account makes dismal reading but is not atypical for the period. The first three children had died in infancy. The fourth was Kepler's father, who started a tavern in 1577, had his face lacerated in 1578 when a jar of hard gunpowder exploded nearby, and finally went into exile and died. Kepler also records that the fifth child 'is dead, the mother of many children, poisoned they think, in the year 1581'. The sixth was also dead, the seventh 'was vicious and disliked by his fellow townsmen... wandered in extreme poverty through France and Italy... died in the end of dropsy after many earlier illnesses'. The seventh, Katharine, was 'intelligent and skilful but married most unfortunately, lived sumptuously, squandered her goods, now a beggar'; numbers nine through twelve were all dead. The natural philosopher Conrad Gesner died of the plague in 1567, together with about 3,700 of the 6,000 inhabitants of Zurich. The malevolence of uncontrolled nature was an ever present reality.

The demythologizing of nature

How was the fatalism which so readily accompanied such natural calamities overcome? Why was it that, gradually up to 1550, but then with increasing determination, natural philosophers began to probe the secrets of the universe without fear of *hubris*? An important factor in this transition appears to have been the 'demythologizing of nature' which came about not through the secularization of the scientific enterprise, but through a wide dissemination of the Christian doctrine of creation.

For the 21st-century secular scientist, used to spending his days generating and assessing data, in whose scientific journals the word 'god' hardly receives a mention from one year to the next, it is quite a surprise to peruse the voluminous writings of the 17th-century founders of modern science and find that, whether Catholic or Protestant, Italian, French, Dutch, German or British, all are unanimous in their conviction that a study of God's 'book of Nature' is both a duty and a delight. This defining paradigm did much to set the tone of 17th-century science.

Johannes Kepler, writing the dedication of *Mysterium Cosmographicum*, presents a theological rationalization for the study of the universe: 'the magnificent temple of God... the Book of Nature, which is so highly esteemed in the Holy Scriptures'. The investigation of Nature was not to be carried out *only* because this benefited humankind but because of its inherent fascination. The universe was Kepler's Mount Everest, the very presence of which demanded its conquest:

> For has not the all-merciful Creator... given every creature all it needs, and beauty and pleasure beyond in over-flowing measure?... we do not ask for what useful purpose birds do sing, for song is their pleasure since they were created for singing. Similarly we ought not to ask why the human mind troubles to fathom the secrets of the heavens. Our Creator has added mind to our senses not simply so that man might earn his daily keep – many kinds of creatures possessing unreasoning souls can do this much more skilfully – but also so that from the existence of the things which we behold with our eyes, we might delve into the causes of their being and becoming, *even if this might serve no further useful purpose* [my italics].

Such a proclamation should strike a chord in the mind of any scientist committed to basic research, for whom the quest for understanding is both its own justification and its own reward. Later on, when Galileo wrote his book the *Sidereal Message* reporting on the startling new discoveries made with his telescope, Kepler wrote an enthusiastic response which he sent as a long letter to Galileo:

> I yearned to discuss with you, most accomplished Galileo, in a highly agreeable kind of discourse, the many undisclosed treasures of Jehovah the Creator, which He reveals to us one after another. For who is permitted to remain silent at the news of such developments? Who is not filled with a surging love of God, pouring itself copiously forth through tongue and pen?

Scientific discovery, for Kepler, led directly to worship, an instinctive response to the sheer wonder and excitement of uncovering the 'treasures of the Creator'. But nature itself, for all its wonders, was never itself to be worshipped. As Kepler writes:

> My aim is to show that the heavenly machine is not a kind of divine, live being, but a kind of clockwork.

Kepler himself remained a transitional figure in the watershed between the old organismic concepts of the universe and the new ideas of a mechanistic universe, ordered and maintained by a divine clockmaker. In contrast Galileo could be vehemently polemical in his critique of the Aristotelian universe and his language is largely devoid of the 'empathies' and 'sympathies' that were routinely 'packaged' along with a belief in an animate universe. No less than Kepler, and often with greater theological clarity, did Galileo see himself as studying the very works of God, convinced that the 'book of Nature' and the 'book of God's Word', the Bible, spoke with a single voice:

> For the holy Bible and the phenomena of nature proceed alike from the divine Word, the former as the dictate of the Holy Ghost and the latter as the observant executrix of God's commands.
>
> A hundred passages of holy Scripture... teach us that the glory and greatness of Almighty God are marvelously discerned in all his works and divinely read in the open book of heaven.

What is so striking in this quotation is that, for Galileo, heaven was an *open* book, revealed physically by the power of the telescope, but also liberated theologically from the strictures of the static Aristotelian worldview:

> Sarsi says he does not wish to be numbered among those who affront the sages by disbelieving and contradicting them. I say I do not wish to be counted as an ignoramus and an ungrateful person toward nature and toward God; for if they have given me my senses and my reason, why should I defer such great gifts to the errors of some man.

The intellectual exploration of nature, for Galileo, rested on two unshakeable truths. The first was the value of the observer as a creature made by God to understand the works of His creation:

> When I consider what marvellous things and how many of them men have understood... I recognize and understand only too clearly that the human mind is a work of God's and one of the most excellent.

The second truth was Galileo's conviction that God, as the great 'mathematician', had made a universe that was intelligible by the human mind, so that investigating 'the true constitution of the universe' was 'the most important and most admirable problem that there is... and the greatness and nobility of this problem entitles it to be placed foremost among all questions capable of theoretical solution'. It was his belief in the rationality of God and the coherence of God's creation that made Galileo so convinced 'that the same God who has endowed us with senses, reason and intellect' could not have intended for us 'to forgo their use and by some other means to give us knowledge which we can attain by them. He would not require us to deny sense and reason in physical matters which are set before our eyes and minds by direct experience or necessary demonstrations.'

After perusing the theological writings of Galileo, which are many, it is much easier to accept the words of A.N. Whitehead, written some three centuries later as he pondered on the particular 'tone of thought' that led to the emergence of modern science in 17th-century Europe, and nowhere else:

> It must come from the medieval insistence on the rationality of God, conceived as with the personal energy of Jehovah and with the rationality of a Greek philosopher... My explanation is that the faith in the possibility of science, generated antecedently to the development of modern scientific theory, is an unconscious derivative from medieval theology.

Joseph Needham, an authority on the history of Chinese science and technology, echoed Whitehead's view when he commented that one of the reasons that China failed to develop modern science was because it 'lacked the idea of (divine) creation'. And after reading what Galileo himself wrote, the attempts in later centuries to try and build a mythology of the 'atheistic free-thinking Galileo versus the obscurantism of religion' into the conflict thesis seem mildly ludicrous. Certainly, Galileo clashed with the medieval Church, as we describe below in greater detail, but it was a clash which sprang directly from the roots of his own faith, and which was opposed to the church's defence of Aristotelian cosmology, not to religious belief as such.

Francis Bacon

Whereas the theological comments of natural philosophers like the German Kepler and the Italian Galileo flowed naturally from the context of their scientific discoveries, for the Englishman Francis Bacon (1561–1626), the onslaught against the negative influences of the Greek philosophers was carried out as a literary campaign. Bacon, who entered Trinity College, Cambridge, at the age of thirteen, later became Lord High Chancellor and, like many popularizers of science who themselves carry out few experiments, has sometimes suffered a bad press. Or perhaps a rather haughty manner did not endear himself to his critics. As William Harvey, famous for his discoveries on the circulation of the blood, rather snidely remarked at the time, 'He writes philosophy (i.e. science) like a Lord Chancellor.' Yet, whatever Bacon's weaknesses may have been, his campaign for a new scientific method that would replace that of Aristotle clearly exerted an important influence on the natural philosophers of his time – and was one of the inspirations which led to the founding of the Royal Society, whose early members clearly held themselves to be his disciples. There is, therefore, general agreement with Bacon's own claim that he was the one who 'rang the bell which called the wits together', the 'wits' being the Fellows of the Royal Society.

For the purposes of our present discussion, Bacon's interest lies in the use of his considerable literary gifts to criticize the thought of the ancients in the name of a biblical theology. Bacon chose *Novum Organum* as the title of his principal work on the scientific method, indicating that his method was to replace that discussed in the *Organon*, a medieval compilation of Aristotle's writings. The front page of his *Great Instauration* (1620) depicts a ship passing between two pillars, bearing the inscription *plus ultra* (still further). This was a direct reference to the two pillars of Hercules, the ancient symbols of *non ultra* (no further), which Bacon saw as representing the fear of the ancient world to progress further than the wisdom already laid down by the great sages. Bacon exhorts his readers to 'discard these preposterous philosophies which have... led experience captive, and triumphed over the works of God; and to approach with humility and veneration to unroll the volume of creation'. As Bacon observed, 'many have not only considered it to be impossible but also as something impious to try to efface the bounds nature seems to put to her works', but it was 'heathen arrogance, not the Holy Scripture, which endowed the skies with the prerogative of being incorruptible'. Far from pillars beyond which no mortal could pass without fear of retribution from 'Mother Nature', Bacon used passage after passage from the Bible to convince his readership that 'no parcel of the world is denied to man's inquiry and invention'. Aristotle's philosophy, argued Bacon, made not only science but also faith in God impossible as well:

> When he [Aristotle] had made nature pregnant with final causes, laying
> it down that 'Nature does nothing in vain, and always effects her will
> when free from impediments', and many other things of the same kind
> [he] had no further need of a God.[7]

So, said Bacon, 'There [is] but one course left... to try the whole thing anew upon a better plan, and to commence a total reconstruction of sciences, arts, and all human knowledge, raised upon the proper foundations.'

What is so striking about the writings of the natural philosophers of this period is their abundant optimism. Gone is the feeling of despair in the face of the malevolent works of 'Mother Nature', and in its place a new confidence in the technological abilities of man to subdue and to control for the common good. John Wilkins, a founder member of the Royal Society in Britain, wrote a book in 1638 on *The Discovery of a New World*, remarking that 'without any doubt some means of conveyance to the moon cannot seem more incredible to us than overseas navigation to the ancients, and that therefore there is no good reason to be discouraged in our hope of the like success'. Kepler was quite sure that as soon as man mastered the art of flying, then human colonies would be established on the moon.

Robert Boyle and Isaac Newton

Robert Boyle (1627–91), founder of modern chemistry, and an influential early member of the Royal Society, was at the forefront of the practical attempts to fulfil Bacon's vision and bring about the 'Great Instauration'. A fervent experimentalist, who published about 100 papers running to more than 2.5 million words, Boyle continued Bacon's attack on the deity of nature in his *Free Inquiry into the Vulgarly Received Notion of Nature* (1682). For Boyle, the 'vulgar notion' was the idea that 'Nature' had any kind of autonomous existence, or that it acted as a mediator between God and his works. He attacked the expression, popular at the time, that 'God and nature do nothing in vain', since this implied the old Greek idea of divine nature, rather than the relationship of 'creator and creature'. Since, said Boyle, God made the world by divine fiat, and sustained His creation at every moment in time, there was no need to invoke any necessity in nature, as if the created world had its own mind, or could operate as a separate agent. 'Nature', wrote Boyle, is not a 'separate agent' but a 'system of rules'. Any other view would hold back the investigation of the created order, since this would then depend not on the works of a rational Creator, but on the potentially capricious acts of the semi-divine 'forms' and 'intelligences' which were responsible for the 'Mother Nature' of Greek philosophy.

Boyle was not alone in making quite explicit his programme for the de-deification of nature. Writing some years before Boyle, the French physician Sebastian Basso in 1621 attacked the idea that the 'numinance' of Greek philosophy acted as God's lieutenants in the workings of nature, with the implication that there was a kind of cooperation between nature and God. Such ideas, said Basso, were completely superfluous since nature is but the observed consistencies in the actions of God.

The same point was repeatedly underlined by Sir Isaac Newton (1642–1727), for whom a correct understanding of God's creation was of fundamental importance to his science. Writing during the early years of the 18th century, Newton insisted that God

is not the soul of the world, but Lord over all... For God is a word
expressing a relation, and it refers to servants... a Being, however perfect,
without rule, cannot be called Lord God, for we say my God, your God,
the God of Israel... but not my Eternal, your Eternal, the Eternal of

Israel... or my Infinite, or my Perfect; these are titles that bear no relation to servants... for a God without rule, providence and design, is nothing but Necessity and Nature.

Ironically, the demythologizing of nature had developed to such an extent by Newton's time, that his very introduction of the idea of gravity to explain 'action at a distance' was criticized by some as smacking of powers that, because unseen and 'non-mechanical', must therefore be occult.

It should not be thought that the theological writings of natural philosophers such as Newton, Boyle, Bacon, Galileo and Kepler were simply rhetoric, or crop up so often in their scientific works because it happened to be a pious age and so was customary to make frequent religious allusions. Instead there seems little doubt that their theological worldview had profound effects upon their own scientific development and that their faith in God as Creator played a central role in their lives. Boyle, for example, was so convinced that his research was a kind of divine worship that he made a point of performing his experiments on Sundays. It is also intriguing to examine the topics of the books in Newton's library at the time of his death, as tabulated by R.J. Forbes (showing the major topical discussions only):

Topic	No. titles	Total (per cent)
Theology and philosophy	515	32
Mathematics, physics and astronomy	268	16
History and chronology	215	14
Classical authors	182	11
Chemistry and mineralogy	165	10

Robert Boyle learnt Hebrew, Greek, Chaldean and Syriac in order that he might understand the Bible more effectively, hardly the activities of a man for whom religion was merely peripheral to his daily concerns.

The belief in God as a creator, who acted by a 'system of rules', not only motivated the search for mathematical order in astronomy and physics, demythologizing nature so that it could be investigated without fear, but also focused attention on the *whole* of the natural world as reflecting God's works. It was in this spirit that John Ray (1627–1705), who was born in the same year as Boyle but whose background was as humble as Boyle's was privileged, published an immense array of works describing and classifying animals and plants in a series of observations which were to help to lay the foundations of modern biology. In his synopsis of British plants (1690) Ray writes in his preface of his gratitude to God that he had been born in an age when, within his own memory, scholasticism had been replaced by a new philosophy based on experiment.

Ray's highly popular book *The Wisdom of God Manifested in the Works of Creation* (1691) went through five large editions within twenty years of its publication. In it he tells us that

> the treasures of nature are inexhaustible... Some reproach methinks it is to learned men that there should be so many animals still in the world whose outward shape is not yet taken notice of or described... if man ought to reflect upon his Creator the glory of all his works, then ought he to take notice of them all.

And 'taking notice of them all' was precisely what John Ray did, publishing, for example, three great volumes containing 2,610 folios on the classification of 18,600 plants in the years 1686–1704, and cramming his cottage in the little hamlet of Black Notley in Essex with an immense collection of flora and fauna. At the age of seventy-seven Ray, now very close to the end of his long and productive life, struggled on with his descriptions of butterflies, moths, beetles, wasps and flies, and recording an astonishing 300 species of butterflies and moths within the grounds of his own very modest cottage.

Since the natural philosophers of the 16th and 17th centuries tell us so clearly and so repeatedly that the idea of God's creation was vital to *them* as they laid down the foundations for modern science, it might be good to pause for a moment and analyse a little more clearly the differences between their ideas of the creative actions of God and those which flowed from the Greek philosophers. Notice that what we are concerned with here is not 'creationism', a modern movement which began in the 20th century (as discussed in chapter 9), but rather the philosophical implications that flowed from a switch from Greek to Judeo-Christian views of nature.

The Judeo-Christian view of nature

In much Greek philosophy, the question of 'creation' does not arise, because such a concept only makes sense if one first presupposes a creator. Instead, there were Eternal Forms, of which matter was a pale and inadequate reflection. Yet, occasionally, one finds the concept of a 'god' or 'creator' whose role can be both compared and contrasted with the biblical idea of a creator-God. For Aristotle, 'Nature makes everything to a certain purpose', his Unmoved Mover being beyond the edge of the universe, and certainly not involved in anything so mundane as making chickens and octopuses. The rational forms of nature are perpetuated by self-reproduction. Perhaps the nearest we come to the concept of a creator is in Plato's *Timaeus*, in which a *demiourgos* ('demiurge') is involved in shaping the material of the world, already created, according to the Eternal Forms (or Ideas). The problem for Plato's demiurge is that the material of the world is in a chaotic state, without any order or reason, and resists the attempts of the demiurge to impose upon it the limitations imposed by the Eternal Forms. And so the demiurge is left in the unenviable position of making very imperfect imitations of the Eternal Forms out of recalcitrant matter, since matter itself offered him resistance that he was unable to overcome. Plato's 'story of creation' is therefore the pursuit of understanding the Eternal Forms which were thought to express, particularly in the language of mathematics, the pattern of the '*kosmos*'. However, there was little in this story to encourage the idea that the study of matter itself would yield a worthwhile dividend. Furthermore, it was beneath the dignity of Plato's demiurge to be involved in making living things, including man, since these were mortal beings. Instead, this role was delegated by the demiurge to the 'world soul', which was also responsible for sustaining the universe once it had been moulded by the demiurge into something resembling the Eternal Forms.

In contrast, the biblical theology of creation, which crops up so repeatedly in the writings of 17th-century scientists, had the following main strands.

First, there is one God who is the creator and sustainer of everything that exists. So the task of the natural philosopher is to analyse and describe the works of God or, as Kepler is reputed to have said, 'to think God's thoughts after him'. Since God is all-powerful, nothing can stand against his creative power and, in contrast to the limitations of Plato's demiurge, there is no hint in the biblical literature of matter itself having any autonomy over and against God's actions. Neither are there any fixed 'forms' that act as a kind of template according to which the world is then shaped. Quite the reverse; God speaks, and it happens, and the task of the natural philosopher is to describe what happens. It is God who is autonomous, not the created order, and scholastic rationalizing must therefore be replaced by the evidences of the senses.

Second, the universe is one of order and consistency. The Psalms are full of references to the repetition of the seasons, and the pattern of God's activity in the animal and plant world. So the biblical view of creation contributed to the idea of God as a lawgiver, and to the pursuit of finding the laws by which the universe is governed.

Third, nature itself was seen as being essentially good. The Hebrew creation account in Genesis chapter 1 reads as if it were a direct attack upon Platonic philosophy in its insistence, with regard to everything from the heavenly bodies to wild animals and plants, that 'God saw that it was good'. Far from being wild and terrifying, to be left strictly alone for fear of *hubris*, the created world is handed into the responsibility of people who should 'work it and take care of it' (Genesis 2:15). Rather than holding the heavenly bodies in fear because of their supposed malevolence, a reaction common to both Babylonian and Greek worldviews, they are seen as part of God's *good* creation (Genesis 1:16–18), and firmly under his control (Psalm 104:19–24). In the vivid poetry of Psalm 104, the whole of the created order is seen as reflecting the handiwork of God, including 'wine that gladdens the heart of man' (v. 15), the lions as they 'roar for their prey and seek their food from God' (v. 21), and 'the sea, vast and spacious, teeming with creatures beyond number' (v. 25). There is not much room in this earthy materialism for the neoplatonic shrinking from matter as if it were of no consequence.

The effects on the minds of 16th- and 17th-century scientists, as they were repeatedly exposed to this Judeo-Christian creation worldview, should not be underestimated. Unlike ourselves, they were living in an age in which religious sanction and theological validation were important factors in determining whether new streams of thought flourished or withered. As the Greek passion for logic and mathematics was baptized into a biblical framework of creation, there emerged a new synthesis that was to prove a powerful impetus for the emergence of modern science.

The role of the observer

One of the major implications of the Christian theology of creation was that the observer of the created world had immense value. For societies today in which the rights of the individual and the importance of personal views receive intense emphasis, the concept that anyone's accurate scientific observations should have no potential value appears bizarre. Yet in the medieval world of scholastic debate, there were still many forces, some psychological, some more external, which militated against the rights of the individual in investigating or expressing their views concerning the world about them.

Some of these forces were economic. Investigations of the natural world are clearly not a top priority when struggling to make a living or surviving the rigours of civil war. A turning point for Copernicus, for example, was when he took up his duties as a canon of Frauenberg Cathedral at the age of forty. His duties there were hardly exacting, and the Cathedral's sixteen canons led a relatively luxurious life and enjoyed substantial incomes. For the remaining thirty years of his life, Copernicus spent most of his time living in a tower behind the safe walls of Frauenberg, from where he could gaze at leisure at the heavens and compose his *De Revolutionibus* (Book of Revolutions) which was destined, after a long lapse of time, to turn upside down the view of the universe which had held sway for 2,000 years.

In England, the Elizabethan and then Stuart periods brought an expansion of trade, with the subsequent development of a wealthy leisured class who had not only the interest but also the time and money to make investigations of the natural world. Robert Boyle, for example, was the youngest and most favoured son of the Earl of Cork, who made an enormous fortune through his estates. Although Robert inherited only a small fraction of his father's fortune (having eleven siblings to compete with), his estates eventually brought him £3,000 a year which, in the second half of the 17th century, was not a bad income. Realizing the benefits of financial support for research, Boyle tried to persuade the ruling classes to support science, telling his nephew, heir to the Earldom of Cork, that the 'effectual pursuit' of science 'requires as well a purse as a brain' (a truism sadly overlooked by certain governments of our own day). As one wit remarked at the time in the light of his fund-raising efforts, Boyle was not only 'the father of chemistry' but also the 'uncle of the third Earl of Cork'.

Financial backing, however it came, was one of those crucial ingredients that contributed to the rapid growth of science during the 16th and 17th centuries by allowing the abilities and energies of natural philosophers to be focused on probing the world around them. Yet this point alone is insufficient to explain the growing stress placed on the role of the individual observer during this period. Through listening to what the natural philosophers of the period tell us, a further three factors can be discerned.

The growing respect for manual activity

First, there is a marked frustration with the contempt shown by classical antiquity for manual activity. Although manual work had been highly regarded in early Greek thought, it came to be despised by the later Athenian philosophers, who held that true philosophy operated in a different realm from lowly manual labour, which should be left to slaves. Plato scorned Pythagoras for his practical investigations of harmonics and, when his friends Eudoxus and Archytas tried to use mechanical instruments to demonstrate some points in geometry, Plato told them that such despicable manual work was no substitute for pure intellectual thought in such matters. A similarly jaundiced view was expressed by Archimedes, who made many mechanical instruments, but only for the defence of a city during a siege. As Plutarch said of him:

> Archimedes possessed such a lofty spirit, so profound a soul and such a wealth of scientific theory, but although his inventions had won for him a name and fame for superhuman sagacity, he would not consent to leave behind any treatise on this subject... *regarding the work of an engineer and every art that ministers to the needs of life as ignoble and vulgar...*[8] [my italics].

Later on, the Roman philosopher Cicero thought that a mechanical workshop 'contains nothing fit for a freeborn man', since manual labour was associated with slavery.

Several factors helped to provide social validation for the value of manual activity by educated people, so contributing to a more empirical approach in natural philosophy. The groundwork was laid by the monastic movement. Monastic orders such as the Benedictines established daily programmes of worship, contemplation and manual labour. The Renaissance period saw a growing cooperation between 'head and hand', and a greater willingness by natural philosophers to draw on the expertise of 'artificers' with their manual skills. The wide dissemination of the Bible which came about during the Reformation also encouraged the belief that any occupation was honourable, provided that it was carried out to the glory of God, so giving manual labour a religious sanction.[9] Gresham College, established in 1579 in London, was the first institute for teaching the new 'experimental philosophy' in Britain, and lectures were deliberately given in both Latin (the medium of philosophy) and in English (the language of daily life) to emphasize the fusion between the theoretical and the practical. Two of the college's seven professors were appointed for the sciences of geometry and astronomy, and were from the beginning urged to lecture on astronomical instruments that would be of benefit to seafarers. A few years later, Isaac Beeckman, who was trained both as a physician and as a minister of the Reformed Church, founded a Mechanical College in Rotterdam with the deliberate aim of bringing together lecturers of diverse backgrounds, including a silk-dyer, a merchant, a carpenter, a physician, a mathematician and a surgeon, who would teach through the practical example of their own hands.

Robert Boyle was also in the forefront of making philosophy acceptable by practising it himself. Coming from a noble background, Boyle, of all people, might have been expected to leave the 'dirty work' to others, but tells us that 'though my condition does... enable me to make experiments by others' hands; yet I have not been so nice, as to decline dissecting dogs, wolves, fishes, and even rats and mice, with my own hands. Nor, when I am in my laboratory, do I scruple with them naked to handle lute and charcoal.' As Boyle once remarked, a learned man who refused to learn from illiterate mechanics was 'indeed childish, and too unworthy of a philosopher to be worthy of a solemn answer'.[10] Francis Bacon, too, preached continuously against the prejudices that prevented people from investigating nature with the help of mechanical arts, such as agriculture, chemistry and glass-blowing.[11] Thomas Sprat, who wrote the first official *History of the Royal Society of London* in the 17th century, reported that in this society 'the tradesman, the merchant, the scholar' represented the 'union of Men's hands and Reasons' so that they preferred 'works before words'. It was Sprat's own opinion that 'philosophy will then attain to perfection, when either the mechanic labourers shall have philosophical heads, or the Philosophers shall have mechanical hands'.

This new respect for manual activity was coupled with a greater appreciation for the observations and ideas of uneducated people in general. Natural philosophy was no longer confined to the speculations of scholars, but became the domain of everyone who could touch, taste, see and work with their hands. The Huguenot potter Bernard Palissy told his visitors that they could learn more about fossils within two hours by touching and seeing them than they could by fifty years of studying the books of the philosophers. In astronomy, the observations of ordinary people flew in the face of centuries of scholastic teaching. For example, according to Aristotle the heavens were unchangeable. Yet, in 1572 a new star arose that was visible to everyone. Tycho Brahe, observing the new star for the first time on the way to his observatory, could not believe his own eyes, and asked his assistants whether they could see it as well. Even his assistants were not sure, and the whole group only believed the evidence of their own senses after the sighting of the new star had been confirmed by some sharp-eyed peasants. Tycho himself tells us that it was largely unlearned people who reported the new star, not the astronomers.[12] Robert Boyle pointed out that the ordinary seaman who travelled with Columbus, 'was able at his return to inform men of an hundred things that they could never have learned by Aristotle's philosophy'.[13]

There is a sense in which history has to repeat itself when science is established as an active enterprise in any country today. For example, the idea that manual labour is demeaning for an educated person is widely held in many cultures – and is often coupled with a respect for authority figures that is so deeply rooted that 'science' becomes the attempt to confirm what others have already found, rather than the pursuing of novel ideas. There is considerable evidence that such thinking retards the progress of science. When in an earlier phase of my career I was involved in setting up new laboratories in the Middle East, people were clearly puzzled by my insistence on donning a lab coat and doing experiments with my own hands. The expected role of the 'professor' was clearly to sit in an office and issue instructions to others, not to demean his status by getting his own hands dirty.

The clash with authority

The second factor in the scientific revolution of the 16th and 17th centuries which placed increasing stress on the role of the individual observer was the confrontation that occurred between the new natural philosophy and the authoritarianism of the old scholasticism.

Peter Harrison has convincingly argued that one important strand of this confrontation arose from changing views of how the biblical text should be interpreted.[14] Under the influence of Origen and Augustine, in turn influenced by neoplatonic thought, it had been customary for a thousand years of Church history to interpret the Bible in a largely allegorical sense. Within this framework of interpretation natural objects became important not in themselves but as signs to some deeper meaning. This neoplatonic style of interpretation was rather like unpeeling an onion with many layers. The simplest person could only aspire to the most basic meaning, the more advanced could also understand a moral sense of the passage, whereas the highest plane of interpretation belonged to the allegorical. This approach was also applied to the natural world as typified in the *Physiologus*, a small book of natural history, most likely written by a contemporary of Origen, which had enormous sales and influence right into the Middle Ages in Europe. But the *Physiologus* was unlike any natural history that you might read today. Every animal, every plant and every stone became endowed with layers of allegorical meaning. Similarly biblical references to natural objects were not intended to provide information about the world but about some deeper (and to our ears very speculative) meaning. Harrison argues that this way of thinking changed the way people thought about the natural world: 'It is difficult to overestimate the significance of this way of reading texts. Because the mentality which informs allegorical meanings of texts is so alien to the modern conception of the world, we have forgotten that for its medieval practitioners allegory had actually become a way of reading things, not words.'[15]

The medieval interpretation of nature, therefore, became like the interpretation of a text; the main aim was to relate the various parts to the larger scheme of things. The natural items were not looked on as being important in themselves. A speck of dust, said the 12th-century Robert Grosseteste, 'is an image of the whole universe' and 'a mirror of the creator'. The compilation of medieval natural histories were opportunities to display scholastic prowess. 'It was not the observation of animals and plants which counted, but whether all the relevant written sources had been consulted... Only gradually did it dawn on scholars that the empirical world might serve as a standard by which textual accounts of living things should be judged.'[16] A key step in this change of thinking was the Reformation emphasis on the literal interpretation of the Bible. All the major Reformers were deeply suspicious of allegory and Martin Luther argued that the Bible should be understood 'in its simplest meaning as far as possible'. Out went the onion layers of interpretation and in their place came the 'bare facts'.

This Protestant insistence on the literal sense of texts had profound and unintentioned consequences on the interpretation of the natural world. For if the text was 'demythologized' of its layers of allegory, then so too were the natural objects with which the allegorical meanings had previously been inextricably entangled. For example, the *Physiologus* had instigated a long medieval tradition of seeing the pelican as a symbol of Christ's suffering, a comparison odd to modern ears, which explains the presence of a pelican on the lectern of Norwich Cathedral and a pelican perched on the top of the 16th-century sundial in the front quadrangle of Corpus Christi College, Oxford. But from now on the pelican became just a pelican – just one more object to be studied in the natural world. 'Meaning and intelligibility were ascribed to words and texts, but denied to living things and inanimate objects... It was left to an emerging natural science to reinvest the created order with intelligibility. Thus was one of the hallmarks of modernity, the triumph of the written text and the identification of its meaning with authorial intention, to give rise to another – that systematic, materialistic understanding of the world embodied in the privileged discourses of natural science.'[17] Ironically a less allegorical and more literal understanding of the biblical text promoted the study of the natural world in a way which, in due course, led itself to a less literal interpretation of certain passages.

Forsaking the old authorities and ushering in the new ways of thinking did not happen without a great deal of resistance. We have already noted that Copernicus belonged in some ways more to the old era than to the new and his obsequious deference to the authority of the ancients serves to illustrate the point. When the Nuremburg mathematician Johannes Werner published a book in which he questioned the reliability of some of the observations passed down from the Greek astronomers ('the ancients'), Copernicus proceeded to lash out (in 1526) at his 'impiety':

> It is fitting for us to follow the methods of the ancients strictly and to hold fast to their observations which have been handed down to us like a Testament. And to him who thinks that they are not to be entirely trusted in this respect, the gates of our Science are certainly closed... he will get what he deserved for believing that he can lend support to his own hallucinations by slandering the ancients.[18]

When in 1559 the English physician John Geynes suggested that Galen might not be infallible, he was excluded from the Royal College until he acknowledged the error of his ways and signed a recantation.

Yet the 'slandering of the ancients' by the new natural philosophers gathered pace with increasing boldness. In 1654 John Webster lambasted the universities for their slavish adherence to Aristotle in his *Academiarum Examen*: 'Neither is it fit that *Authority* (whether of *Aristotle* or any other) should inchain us, but that there may be general freedom to try all things... so there may be a *Philosophical* liberty to be bound to the authority of none, but truth itself.' 'One insect is more in touch with Divine wisdom', wrote Malebranche, in a burst of excessive hyperbole, 'than the whole of Greek and Roman history.'

Kepler (who referred to himself as the 'Luther of astrology') describes in his

New Astronomy with undisguised glee the way in which a difference of only eight minutes between Tycho Brahe's observations and his own calculations of the orbit of Mars forced him to abandon the doctrine of circularity, an idea which had held sway for 2,000 years. As Kepler remarked 'If God has sent us an observer like Tycho, it is in order that we should make use of him', and it was by believing the accuracy of Tycho's observations rather than the authority of the ancients that Kepler was able justly to declare 'These eight minutes pave the way for the reformation of the whole of astronomy.' The difficulty of embracing the idea of an elliptical motion for the heavenly bodies, rather than a circular one, is illustrated by the fact that the very term 'ellipse' is derived from the Greek verb *elleipein*, meaning to 'fall short', 'to be imperfect'. For 2,000 years the authority of the ancients had rendered even the concept of such a motion for the planets as being imperfect, all the way from the Pythagoreans to Copernicus.

Whereas Kepler simply discarded those aspects of Greek philosophy that did not appear to fit with the 'harmony of the spheres', Galileo launched a frontal attack on the very idea that natural philosophy was to do with the rediscovery of the beliefs of ancient authorities, and that these beliefs were normative for succeeding generations. As Galileo wrote in his famous letter to the Grand Duchess Christina in 1615:

Who will assert that everything in the universe capable of being
perceived is already discovered?... Let us rather confess quite truly that
'Those truths which we know are very few in comparison with those
which we do not know'... No one should be scorned in physical disputes
for not holding to the opinions which happen to please other people best,
especially concerning problems which have been debated among the
greatest philosophers for thousands of years.

A few years later Galileo wrote his famous book called the *Dialogues on the Two Chief Systems of the World*, in which an imaginary character called Simplicio, supporting Aristotle, has his arguments overwhelmed by Salviati, the Platonist–Copernican presenting Galileo's own position, with a third character called Sagredo acting as a kind of referee, ostensibly to hold the combatants in balance, but in reality giving game, set and match to Salviati. Galileo's principal spokesman, Filippo Salviati, was an old friend of Galileo's, who had died in 1614. It was this book in particular that led to Galileo's clash with the church authorities, as we shall discuss further in the next chapter. Following his subsequent trial, Galileo wrote a bitter autobiographical note in the margin of his own copy of the *Dialogues*:

And who can doubt that it will lead to the worst disorders when minds created free by God are compelled to submit slavishly to an outside will? When we are told to deny our senses and subject them to the whim of others?

Meanwhile, in England the Lord High Chancellor, Francis Bacon, was launching his own attacks on Aristotle in his *Novum Organum* (1620). What Bacon was proposing was an entire sweeping bare of the old philosophical cupboard, with the construction of a New Learning which would have Bacon as its guide. 'It is idle to expect', wrote Bacon, 'any great advancement in science from the super-inducing and grafting of new things upon old.' Bacon observed that the study of nature had been obscured by four types of 'idol' which obstructed men's minds. For example, 'Idols of the Tribe' represented those tendencies in human nature to postulate more regularity in nature than it actually finds, to generalize hastily, and to overemphasize the value of confirming instances. 'Idols of the Theatre' were the received dogmas of the various philosophies and Bacon spent page after page in discrediting the philosophy of Aristotle. Aristotle and his followers made a haphazard and uncritical collection of data. Aristotelians generalized too easily. Aristotelians relied too much on induction. And so on. The problem with any clean sweep is that it leaves a heavy onus on those who have to restock the cupboard from scratch. Bacon himself was not really up to the task, and his own debt to Aristotle was much greater than he was prepared to admit, yet his campaign against scholasticism did much to set the tone of subsequent British science in a healthy anti-authoritarian direction.

The success of Bacon's campaign may be judged from the writings of early members of the Royal Society, such as John Wilkins,[19] who frequently started his discussions in science and mechanics with an examination of Aristotle's views on the subject but then proceeded to express his own very independent ideas. Wilkins wrote that we should not be

> so superstitiously devoted to Antiquity as for to take up everything as Canonical which drops from the pen of a Father, or was approved by the consent of the Ancients... It behoves everyone in the search of Truth, always to preserve a Philosophical liberty; not to be enslaved to the opinion of any man, as to think whatever he says to be infallible. We must labour to find out what things are in themselves by our own experience... not what another says of them. And if in such an impartial enquiry, we chance to light upon a new way, and that which is besides the common road, this is neither our fault, nor our unhappiness.

Occasionally the 16th- and 17th-century players in the scientific revolution sound so 'modern' in their observations and convictions that we are tempted to say 'so what' after reading them, simply because their remarks are so 'obvious' to our 21st-century ears. And yet it is precisely this 'so-whatness' which provides such dramatic evidence of the long-term effectiveness of their revolution. The success of any revolution may be judged by the extent to which the beliefs that it stands for become the norm for succeeding generations. The birth of modern science required a fresh discovery of the value of the individual and of his or her place both in society and in the universe. The medieval insistence on a monolithic structure for society validated by the pronouncements of authority figures supported by ancient texts crumbled in the face of pluralism.

Science as the servant of humanity

The third facet of the new natural philosophy to focus attention on the value of the individual was its utilitarianism, the idea that science should be harnessed for the control of the environment in the service of humanity. Francis Bacon was the champion of this view, maintaining that there were two motivations in the quest for knowledge, one religious, and the other humanitarian. The task of the new science was to instigate a 'great restoration' in which humanity would be restored to its rightful role in exerting its God-given dominion over the natural world.

Bacon's hostility to the philosophy of Aristotle was due as much to moral outrage, at its total irrelevance for the curing of the physical ills of humankind, as to its incompetence in extending an accurate knowledge of the natural world. It was Bacon's opinion that a natural philosophy that kept to words alone, and did not lead to practical works, was as dead as a faith without works. Bacon concluded the preface of his *Historia Naturalis* with a prayer:

> May God, the Founder, Preserver, and Renewer of the Universe, in His love
> and compassion to men, protect the work both in its ascent to His glory
> and its descent to the good of Man, through His only Son, God-with-us.

Yet Bacon never divorced the applications of science from the need to establish a solid foundation of pure science at the beginning. His 'New Atlantis' was a Utopian vision of life in which the benefits of science are used for the common good, established 'for finding out the true nature of all things, whereby God might have the more glory in the workmanship of them' while the practical application of knowledge was 'for the comfort of men'.

The novelty of Bacon's emphasis on the utility of science should not be underestimated. As G. Lloyd tells us 'the view that we find in Francis Bacon, that the goal of the acquisition of knowledge *is* its practical benefits, is quite foreign to the ancient world'[20] and Farrington sees the reason for the lack of progress of Greek and Roman science as its failure to become a transforming force in their conditions of life.[21] Bacon's 'was the philosophy that inspired science as an activity, a movement carried on in public and of concern to the public. This aspect of science scarcely existed before the 17th century.'[22]

However, from the 17th century onward it becomes commonplace to find natural philosophers writing on the utilitarian aspects of their work. The Royal Society encouraged the study of animals with a view to determining 'whether they may be of any advantage to mankind, as food or physic; and whether those or any other uses of them can be further improved'. "Tis no slight point of philosophy', said one of the first of the Royal Society's secretaries, Henry Oldenburg, 'to know... what animals may be tamed for human use and what commixtures with other animals may be advanced.' 'Man's dominion over nature', writes the social historian Keith Thomas, 'was the self-consciously proclaimed ideal of early modern scientists. Yet, despite the aggressively despotic imagery explicit in their talk of "mastery", "conquest" and "dominion", they saw their task, thanks to generations of Christian teaching, as morally innocent. "It never harmed any man", said Francis Bacon, "never burdened a conscience with remorse."'

It is hardly surprising that the responsibility for the worldwide rape of the environment currently in progress should frequently have been laid at Bacon's feet. Yet we should be careful to place Bacon's emphases within their correct historical context. At the time he was writing, natural philosophy had done virtually nothing to ameliorate poverty, disease and hunger. Most children did not survive into adulthood. Plagues decimated populations and nothing could be done to stop them. It was not unusual for university students to die before receiving their degrees. The Black Death (bubonic plague) killed one-quarter of Europe's population between 1346 and 1352, with death tolls ranging up to 70 per cent in some cities. Doctors were people to be avoided, for fear that their methods would kill rather than cure. All surgery, including amputations, was without anaesthetics. As always, Kepler writes vividly, describing in August 1599 the conditions in Gratz, where he had just lost his second child from cerebral meningitis:

> The ravages of dysentery kill people of all ages here, but particularly children. The trees stand with dry leaves on their crowns as if a scorching wind had passed over them. Yet it was not the heat that so disfigured them, but worms.

Given the preceding centuries of fatalistic acceptance of all that 'Mother Nature' brought one's way, Bacon's prophetic vision of an environment that could be controlled for the benefit of humanity stands as a radical change in emphasis. And although it took several more centuries for the benefits of science to make much practical impact on people's daily lives, Bacon at least pointed in the right direction.

How does science advance?

A central issue which marks yet another watershed between the world of Greek rationalism and the 17th-century scientific revolution is the question of how scientific knowledge is obtained. As with most other aspects of the scientific movement that we have looked at so far, theological considerations played an important part in the consensus that finally emerged.

Greek science was largely a rational and intellectual series of constructs. As Gillispie remarks 'it started inside the mind whence concepts like purpose, soul, life and organism were projected outward to explain phenomena in the familiar terms of self-knowledge. In these terms the success of an explanation depended only on its universality and capacity to satisfy the reason.' The arguments of Greek science started with axioms that were felt to be self-evident, and then proceeded to deduce a long series of supposed consequences. Observational data provided illustrations for the truth of those consequences but were rarely integral to the constructed knowledge itself.

Such processes of deduction dominated medieval scholastic thinking. 'Rational' philosophers were those who built great castles of deductions upon premises derived originally from Aristotle or Plato. While perfectly valid as a method in mathematics, this way of thinking proved immensely sterile for the advancement of science. Coupled with it came a passion for reasoning by analogy. The four supposed ages of man and his four supposed elements were constantly compared with the four seasons of the world, with its four compass points, and so on, and so forth. Analogy as a model or illustration to illuminate a concept has always been a helpful way of explaining a difficult point but arguing from analogy in the medieval sense proved as barren as chains of deductions as far as science was concerned.

One of the consequences of Greek rationalism was the belief that God was bound by the internal necessity inherent in the universe to act in certain ways, a view that came to be known as 'necessitarianism'. We have already noted an early example of this view, in that Plato's demiurge was restricted in his creative powers by recalcitrant matter that followed the precepts laid down by its own internal necessity. From time to time the medieval Church made vigorous attempts to combat such 'necessitarian' philosophy, recognizing that this Greek stream of thought was in direct contradiction to the biblical claim that God is entirely free and unfettered in his creative actions.[23] So the Bishop of Paris in 1277 condemned no less than 219 theses, many of which contained statements derived directly from Greek philosophy limiting God's creative powers. Among these theses were claims that God would not make an empty space, that he could not create a new species, that he could not make more than one planetary system, and that he could not make heavenly bodies to move in any way other than circular. The list of theses itself provides a dramatic demonstration, should it be needed, of the influence of Greek thought as it flowed into medieval Europe by translation and via the writings of Arab philosophers.

A hundred years later a fresh attack was made on necessitarianism by various theologians in a movement that came to be known as 'nominalism'. The Nominalists protested at the method of deducing systems from the final nature of things, as in Greek philosophy, which to them were mere *nomina* (Latin, 'names'). Thinkers such as Jean Buridan (c. 1300–c. 1358) and Nicole Oresme (c. 1320–82) attacked the idea that there is any necessity in the relation between God and natural phenomena. Oresme said that Aristotle's reasoning could not prove that the heavens move in circles and the earth is stationary, because God's will for the universe might be quite otherwise, and for the biblical creator there is no necessity whatsoever to cause these motions. Putting it crudely, God can do what he likes. The Nominalists therefore helped to pave the way for a more critical view of the ancients and their axioms, creating in the process a climate of opinion more open to empirical data, 'what really is the case', rather than simply clinging on to the rationalistic deductions of 'what ought to be the case'.

It is with this background that we can appreciate why the scientific revolution, at least in its early years, was largely seen as an *anti*-rationalistic movement. This is not some interpretation made by later historians, but rather what the 'old regime' protested at the time as the new natural philosophers around them dismantled the ancient ways of thinking.[24] New stars appearing in the supposedly unchanging heavens, planets that no longer moved in circles and an earth that moved – truly 'all coherence was gone', and these startling 'facts' flew directly in the face of the rationalistic deductions derived by centuries of medieval scholasticism. Apparent exceptions to this generalization came when the observations of the ancients, such as the apparently obvious fact (to the senses) that the earth does not move, had to be overcome by fresh reasoning based on new observations that started from different presuppositions. In Galileo's *Dialogue*, in which, as already mentioned, the viewpoint of Aristotle is represented by a fictional character called Simplicio, and Galileo's views are expounded by Salviati, it is *Simplicio* who defends the importance of observation, and Galileo has *Salviati* denying the claims of sense in favour of the power of reason:

> Nor can I ever sufficiently admire the outstanding acumen of those who have taken hold of this opinion [Copernicanism] and accepted it as true;

they have through sheer force of intellect done such violence to their own senses as to prefer what reason told them over that which sensible experience plainly showed them to the contrary.

However, it is clear from Galileo's other writings that he placed considerable value on empirical evidence, provided attempts were made to incorporate it into a mathematical framework – what is under attack here is not the value of data as such but the notion that our everyday 'common-sense' observations of the world are necessarily sufficient for an accurate natural philosophy. Galileo himself illustrated the difficulty of applying this principle consistently when he criticized Kepler for suggesting that the moon's gravitational pull affected tides on the earth. Galileo thought that this was absurd, commenting that Kepler had 'lent his ear and his assent to the moon's dominion over the waters, to occult properties and such puerilities'.

Francis Bacon was convinced that men ought to 'throw aside all thought of philosophy, or at least to expect but little and poor fruit from it, until an approved and careful natural and Experimental History be prepared and constructed'. 'Natural history' for Bacon was a collection of data, the fruits of enquiry. Followers of Aristotle, thought Bacon, had failed miserably in defining properly their starting predicates or axioms, such as 'attraction', 'generation', ' element' and so on, so making useless the long strings of deductions based upon them. Bacon lambasted the Aristotelians for reducing science to deductive logic, though this was not quite fair since Aristotle himself had always insisted that first principles be induced from observational evidence, a teaching frequently ignored by his disciples. Bacon was convinced that a new method for science was essential, based upon gradual, progressive induction. A proper inquiry would be like starting from the base of a pyramid and working up towards its apex. The new science was to start by building up a series of 'experimental histories' at the base of the pyramid that would describe natural phenomena. Once the facts had been established in a particular field, the natural philosophers would look for correlations within these facts, and would then start a gradual ascent up the pyramid, inducing broader and broader generalizations as they went. The more general the conclusions that could be described, the nearer to the apex of the pyramid one must be.

Though Bacon's method was not really as new as he claimed, it was argued forcibly with his usual vigour, and did much to focus on the need for data-gathering before any reliable generalizations could be made. 'The secrets of nature', he said, 'betray themselves more readily when tormented by art than when left to their own course.' Bacon was far from suggesting a dead kind of empiricism. As he said, the empirics were like ants merely heaping up a collection of earth. The natural philosophers of medieval scholasticism were like spiders spinning webs out of their own interiors. But the new natural philosophers, thought Bacon, should be more like bees, which extract matter from flowers and then re-fashion it by their own efforts. With a splendidly naive optimism, Bacon thought that his new method of scientific enquiry would require only a limited number of experiments, so that the scientific revolution would require only a decade or so.

The founders of the Royal Society certainly took the base of Bacon's pyramid seriously. The early proceedings of the Society contain an immense range of observations and experiments, including reports on various weird and wonderful phenomena that might have a problem scraping past the reviewers of today's scientific journals. In 1665 and 1666 alone Boyle made fifteen contributions to the society's *Philosophical Transactions*, which included titles such as 'Account of a monstrous calf', 'On a monstrous head of a colt', 'Of milk found in the veins instead of blood' and so forth. Boyle's enthusiasm for 'strange reports' was no isolated phenomena. Other articles of the period include a report by Nehemiah Grew of fowl whose feathers were produced by 'the urinous parts of their blood seeping through the skin' and there was some discussion about the observation of 'a production... from a male cat and a female rabbit'. Newton supported the Society's plans for an expedition to search for dragons in the Swiss Alps, a kind of 17th-century version of the hunt for the 'abominable snowman'. Many other reports were more prosaic, and included details on schemes for making seawater drinkable, Hooke's work on the design of carriages, and Wilkins' new designs of screws, wheels, pulleys, catapults and perpetual motion machines.[25] Many of the 'facts' gathered by the early members of the Royal Society were too isolated and disparate to form into any kind of coherent theory. Bacon's bees buzzed round the base of the pyramid, but many of them were unable, at least initially, to move very far up toward the apex.

In a radically different approach to scientific method, René Descartes (1596–1650) proposed that the apex of the pyramid was the right place to start rather than at its base. Descartes had attended the Jesuit College at La Fleche in France, and received a law degree from the University of Poitiers in 1616, but spent the remainder of his life based in Holland, where he did much of his productive thinking and writing. After experiencing a series of intense dreams in November 1619, Descartes began to believe that he had been called by the Spirit of Truth to make a complete reconstruction of human knowledge based on the certainties of mathematics. In his famous *Discourse on Method*, Descartes describes how he embarked on a course of systematic and methodological doubt, not in order to encourage scepticism, but with the ultimate aim of giving natural philosophy a more solid basis. Whereas Bacon had embarked on a progressive inductive ascent up the pyramid from 'facts' to 'generalizations',

Descartes started at the apex with his 'one great fact', and then tried to work downward by a deductive procedure. The 'one great fact' for Descartes was expressed in his celebrated phrase 'I think, therefore I am', by which Descartes meant that although one might doubt all else, there remains an intuitive perception of self as a cognitive agent, and it is from this primary certainty of one's own existence that other certainties should flow. Descartes' first rule in his new 'Method' was 'to include in my judgments nothing more than what presented itself so clearly and so distinctly to my mind that I might have no occasion to place it in doubt'. Since the idea of 'god' was one of those primary ideas that presented itself to Descartes, he placed 'god' in the cluster of certainties at the apex of the pyramid, and reasoned that a Perfect Being would not create man in such a way that his senses and reason should systematically deceive him. From such first principles Descartes then proceeded to deduce downward to the natural world, for as he said:

> These long chains of reasonings, quite simple and easy, which geometers are accustomed to using to teach their most difficult demonstrations, had given me cause to imagine that everything which can be encompassed by man's knowledge is linked in the same way.

Descartes was fully aware that one could not move very far down from the 'basic principles' at the apex of the pyramid without requiring empirical data in order to decide between competing theories of how such principles functioned in the real world. But his passion for generalizations frequently led him astray. For example, he deduced three laws of motion and, from these three laws, seven rules of impact for specific kinds of collisions, all of which proved to be incorrect. Descartes' tendency to suggest hypotheses based on analogies could also be misleading. For example, he built up his theory of blood circulation by suggesting that the heart spontaneously generated heat just as heat was generated in a mound of hay, and that this heat vaporized the venous blood as it entered, so expanding the heart and propelling the blood into the arterial system. This theory was opposite to the observations of William Harvey, who had already shown experimentally that the passage of the blood into the arteries is accompanied by a contraction of the heart. But although Descartes had read Harvey's famous book on the circulation of the blood, he still preferred to defend his own hypothesis. Experiments, for Descartes, were often no more than illustrations of general theories that had already been deduced from first principles, and it was this lack of attention to experimental data that has led to Descartes being remembered more for his contributions to maths and philosophy than for his science.

With the advantage of hindsight we can see that modern science has incorporated the general approaches of both Bacon and of Descartes, and the emphasis of either one or the other may be more important depending on the field of study involved, and also the stage of its development. For example, journals representing the biological sciences are often full of isolated facts in search of a theory, interesting observations which are left hanging for years without the benefit of a unifying hypothesis to give them a more general meaning. In contrast, it is the avowed aim of mathematical physics to propound unifying theories of the universe that will incorporate all known aspects of both matter and energy. Such theories tend to operate at the very tip of the pyramid, and are initially selected for their elegance or intrinsic coherence, with a wait of many years before they can be tested by crucial experiments. For example, the 'superstring theory' in physics claims to be a fundamental model for all the forces in the universe and is a theory held by many physicists, yet has also been vigorously criticized for its lack of empirical support. As Roland Dobbs has remarked, the superstring theorists 'start with their quantum gravity and attempt to come down to the 'massless' elementary particles, while the skeptics prefer to start with the known experimental facts and work up to a comprehensive theory'.[26] Bacon's pyramid analogy is by no means dead. Fortunately, the scientific community in any given discipline tends to be a heterogeneous mix of theorists and experimentalists, and as long as they keep talking to each other, then the pyramid will be built in the end.

As in most other aspects of 'early modern science', theological considerations were important in shaping the natural philosophers' understanding of how scientific knowledge should be extended. The belief that the whole universe was being actively created and sustained by God gave a strong incentive, as we have already seen, to the search for coherence and order, coupled with a conviction that physical phenomena were worth investigating since they reflected God's activity. The task of the natural philosopher was to study how the world *actually* worked, not to spin rationalistic theories about how it *ought* to work. Blaise Pascal was just one of a succession of scientists who took Descartes to task for his idea that because something comes clearly and rationally to our minds therefore it must be true. Pascal had a high view of human reason, claiming that 'our whole dignity consists in thinking', and yet pointed out that many physical phenomena take place which run counter to reason. It might seem irrational to philosophers, thought Pascal, that light goes through empty space and yet this is what light does – we must therefore accept the empirical data rather than submitting to the authority of the rationalists. In any case, to accept something as 'rational' often means no more than being accustomed to the idea. The theological reasons for making empirical data rather than man's reason the ultimate court of appeal in science were also clearly spelt out in Cote's preface to the second edition of Newton's *Principia Mathematica*:

Without all doubt this world... could arise from nothing but the perfectly free will of God... *These (laws of nature) therefore we must not seek from uncertain conjectures, but learn them from observations and experiments.* He who is presumptuous enough to think that he can find the true principles of physics and the laws of natural things by the force alone of his own mind, and the internal light of reason, must either suppose that the world exists by necessity, and by the same necessity follows the laws proposed; or, if the order of Nature was established by the will of God, that himself, a miserable reptile, can tell what was fittest to be done [my italics].

Bernard le Bouvier de Fontenelle, the secretary of the Paris Academy of Sciences, remarked that whereas Descartes started from what he clearly understood in order to find the cause of what he saw, Newton started from what he saw in order to find the causes, whether these turned out to be clear *or* obscure. According to Robert Hooke, 'science has to begin with the Hands and Eyes, to be continued by the Reason, and to come back to the Hands and Eyes again'.

It is hardly surprising, as Hooykaas remarks, that the defenders of the old scholastic philosophy accused the new natural philosophers of 'undermining religion, and of introducing materialistic principles instead of the approved, more spiritual, principles of Form, essence, Idea and purpose'. In contrast, the natural philosophers themselves 'considered their secularization of science to be its Christianization, because they had freed science from the human authority of theologians and philosophers and from the oppressive burden of its old idols, named Forms and Ideas'.

The new science was not anti-rational, but it was certainly anti-rationalistic.

Chapter 5

Aristotle's Ghost
The Roots of Modern Science (2) – Some Early Debates About Science and Faith

Men assert with assurance that God directs all things to a certain end… I shall enquire in the first place why so many fall into this error, and why all are by nature so prone to embrace it; then I shall show its falsity… Nature has no fixed aim in view, and all final causes are merely fabrications of men.

Spinoza

I have two sources of perpetual comfort – first, that in my writings there cannot be found the faintest shadow of irreverence towards the Holy Church; and second, the testimony of my own conscience, which only I and God in Heaven thoroughly know. And He knows that in this cause for which I suffer, though many might have spoken with more learning, none, not even the ancient Fathers, have spoken with more piety or with greater zeal for the church than I.

Galileo

Copernicus's work undermined the primacy of the biblical view of the universe and helped to weaken the religious establishment's power over scientific thought in medieval Europe.

***Nature*, 27 January 2000, p. 367**

Though God cannot alter the past, historians can.

Samuel Butler

We have noted in chapter 4 that modern science was born into a world in which new ideas failed to flourish unless theologically validated. Many of the natural philosophers of that world inform us that the biblical concepts of God and his relation to the world, concepts in which they firmly believed, played crucial roles in the development and practice of their 'new philosophy'. There is no reason why we should disbelieve them. Yet, as the new philosophy pulled away from the rigid moorings of medieval scholasticism, and as the world was exorcized of its old Greek empathies and sympathies, its Platonic Forms and Ideas, it was inevitable that the old order should feel threatened and that tensions should arise. In retrospect, considering the scale of the revolution in thought, what is truly surprising is not that tensions arose but that they should have remained so limited in their extent. The examples presented in this chapter suggest that these tensions had less to do with a 'conflict between science and faith', much more to do with conflicting theologies in which natural philosophers broke free from the constraints of the old scholasticism.

Galileo and the church

I was once invited to take part in a televised debate on the subject of 'miracles'. This entailed sitting under hot studio lights for some hours with an odd assortment of bishops, scientists, students and theologians, with a few token punks thrown in for colour, presumably to give the impression (quite false) that the programme might have some popular appeal. The debate was not a memorable one. However, I do remember the rhetorical question made by one of the main protagonists during one of those rare moments in the debate when only one person was speaking. 'And what', said he, 'about Galileo?' There was a pregnant pause. The very mention of the name was clearly supposed to spark off in our minds images of the gallant free-thinker confronting obscurantist religion in his quest for Scientific Truth. Galileo was the name to trigger all the reflex actions of the conflict thesis. What more needed to be said?

An enormous amount has been written about Galileo, and the brief comments that follow are only an introduction to the many published works available.[1]

Galileo Galilei was born at Pisa, in Italy, on 15 February 1564, the oldest of seven children, and died in 1642, the year that Newton was born. Pisa was then part of the Grand Duchy of Tuscany and it was a Tuscan tradition to name the firstborn of a family with a Christian name which repeated the surname. Galileo's father Vincenzio was an impoverished though accomplished musician, who also had some knowledge of mathematics. Galileo lived in Pisa until he was ten, when the family moved to Florence, from where he later joined a monastic order as a novice, being attracted by the quiet and studious life that he found there. However, Vincenzio had other plans, and took Galileo back to Florence to prepare him for a career in medicine, which Galileo began to study at the university of Pisa in 1581. Yet increasingly it was mathematics and philosophy that absorbed Galileo's attention, though in 1585 he was forced in any case to leave the university without a degree, having failed to obtain one of the forty scholarships currently available for students from poor families.

Galileo had a fascination with mechanical devices, and from 1585 onward he began a systematic investigation of the mechanical doctrines of Aristotle. His mathematical skills soon becoming recognized in the literary circles of Florence. In 1587 he discovered an ingenious way of determining the centre of gravity of certain solids, and it was this advance that opened up for Galileo that crucial ingredient for a successful career in late-16th-century Italy – patronage. It was through the patronage of influential friends that Galileo was appointed to the chair of mathematics at the University of Pisa in 1589, a rather poorly paid position since mathematics was not regarded as of great importance there. Yet it was this appointment that enabled Galileo, still supported by his patrons, to take up the far more prestigious chair of mathematics at the University of Padua three years later, a post that he held for the next eighteen years before moving to Florence.

Late-16th-century Europe remained dominated by Aristotle's universe. Unlike the present day, when universities are supposed to be pioneers of novelty in philosophy and scientific discovery, the universities of medieval Europe were, for the most part, bastions of conservative scholasticism. It was the entry of the major body of Aristotelian philosophy into Europe that had effectively created the universities as centres of learning during the 13th century. It was in the medieval universities that Aristotle was 'baptized and christianized' (to employ the phrase of Richard Westfall) and that Aristotle was known simply as 'the philosopher'. It is a striking fact that the new natural philosophy, which we now look upon as the direct forerunner of modern science, was promoted largely outside the universities during the 16th century and it was from the universities that the most vigorous rearguard action in defence of Aristotle frequently came. The University of Padua was no exception in this regard, being a hotbed of Aristotelianism, although the city of Padua itself was under the control of Venice, the most tolerant of all the Italian states, and so enjoyed a great measure of intellectual freedom. Apart from its relatively tolerant environment, Padua was renowned throughout Europe for its school of medicine, being the university where the great anatomist Vesalius had taught, and for its chair of philosophy, which had been occupied for many years by Giacomo Zabarella, the leading Renaissance exponent of Aristotelian method in natural philosophy. Copernicus had studied law and medicine there 100 years earlier.

In the early years of his academic life it seems clear that Galileo did little to question the prevailing Aristotelian orthodoxy, beyond some attempts to improve conventional treatments of motion. Some of his lecture manuscripts survive from 1606, and show that throughout this period Galileo was teaching the old astronomy of Ptolemy, and even specifically rejecting the heliocentric theory (the idea that the earth revolves around the sun) of Copernicus in public. Galileo published no scientific work until the age of forty-six, and his growing reputation, first at Pisa and then even more at Padua, rested on his mechanical inventions, the instruments that he had made in large numbers in his own workshop, and on the various ideas which he circulated in manuscript form. His ideas on cosmology, and on the laws of motion of falling bodies, were initially kept very private and Galileo discussed these with only a few personal correspondents, for reasons which he made clear in a letter written to Kepler on 4 August 1597. Kepler had sent Galileo a copy of his *Cosmic Mystery* and, in gratefully acknowledging the gift, Galileo wrote:

> I promise to read your book in tranquility, certain to find the most
> admirable things in it, and this I shall do the more gladly as I adopted the
> teaching of Copernicus many years ago, and his point of view enables me
> to explain many phenomena of nature which certainly remain inexplicable
> according to the more current hypotheses. I have written many arguments
> in support of him and in refutation of the opposite view – which, however,
> so far I have not dared to bring into the public light, frightened by the fate of
> Copernicus himself, our teacher, who, though he acquired immortal fame
> with some, is yet to an infinite multitude of others (for such is the number
> of fools) an object of ridicule* and derision. I would certainly dare to
> publish my reflections at once if more people like you existed; as they don't,
> I shall refrain from doing so (*literally *ridendus et explodendum*, which means
> 'laughed at and hissed off the stage').

I have quoted this section of Galileo's letter in full, because it shows unequivocally that it was fear of ridicule from his academic colleagues that kept Galileo from publicizing his Copernican beliefs during the early stages of his career. He was, after all, a relative newcomer to Padua and there were probably no more than a few professors in all of Europe's universities during the 16th century who paid any serious attention to the ideas of Copernicus.

Talk of the 'Copernican Revolution' can be misleading, since it conjures up a picture of a dramatic new heliocentric worldview sweeping Europe before it. Nothing can be further from the truth. Nicolas Copernicus completed his *On the Revolutions of the Heavenly Spheres* in 1530, but only published it right at the end of his life more than ten years later under strong pressure from others to do so. In the dedication of his book to Pope Paul III, Copernicus made the reasons for his hesitation to publish perfectly clear:

I may well presume, most Holy Father, that certain people, on learning that in this my book 'On the Revolutions of the Heavenly Spheres' I ascribe certain movements to the Earth, will cry out that, holding such views, I should at once be hissed off the stage... Therefore I have doubted for a long time whether I should publish these reflections written to prove the Earth's motion, or whether it would be better to follow the example of the Pythagoreans and others, who were wont to impart their philosophic mysteries only to intimates and friends, and then not in writing but by word of mouth... In considering this matter, fear of the scorn which my new and [apparently] absurd opinion would bring upon me, almost persuaded me to abandon my project.

It is intriguing that Galileo expresses the identical fear of being 'hissed off the stage' when explaining to Kepler sixty-seven years later why he was unwilling to publish his support for Copernicus, although Galileo certainly did not share Copernicus' infatuation with the Pythagorean cult of secrecy. There is no evidence in either case that fear of the church's reaction was a restraint upon publication. Copernicus' magnum opus was, after all, dedicated to the pope, and one of the people who persuaded him to publish was none other than the Cardinal Schoenberg, confidant of three successive popes, who wrote to Copernicus from Rome on 1 November 1536, that 'I beg you most emphatically to communicate your discovery to the learned world, and to send me as soon as possible your theories about the universe.' The man who finally persuaded Copernicus to publish was a protestant academic called Georg Rheticus (1514–74), Professor of Mathematics and Astronomy at the new University of Wittenberg. It was Rheticus who pored over the unwieldy manuscript, made many corrections, and finally arranged for its printing at Danzig.

Far from breaking upon the European scene like a thunderbolt, the ideas of Copernicus' *Revolutions* spread in very small and gradual ripples from the printing press at Danzig. There were a number of reasons for this lack of immediate impact. First, the book was very badly written and the first edition of 1,000 copies never sold out, there being only four reprints in the next four *centuries*. Second, the revolutionary aspect of the book's message, that the earth was *not* the centre of the universe, and that the sun did *not* encircle the earth, was lost in a plethora of detail about the number of epicycles required to make the heavenly bodies maintain their circular motion. Third, Copernicus never claimed that the earth rotates round the sun per se but rather round a point in space three times the sun's diameter away from the sun, the planets also revolving not around the sun but around the centre of the earth's orbit. Thus, both a point 'near' the sun and the theoretical point in space round which the earth orbits became the new 'centres of the universe'. This made the system geometrically simpler than Aristotle's universe as interpreted by Ptolemy, and it must have appeared to the casual reader that the book was a refinement of Aristotle's system, rather than the major departure from Aristotelian philosophy that, in retrospect, it was seen to be. This impression was reinforced by Copernicus himself, who maintained a slavish commitment to the concept of circularity and whose approach throughout the *Revolutions* was thoroughly committed to the classical authorities in almost every respect, as noted in the previous chapter. This was in spite of the fact that, in some academic circles at least, the onslaught on Aristotle had already begun. When Peter Ramus defended the proposition at the Sorbonne in 1536 that 'whatever is in Aristotle is false', he was applauded, but Copernicus would have none of this heresy.

As if all this was not enough to dull the impact of the *Revolutions*, Andreas Osiander (1498–1552), the leading Lutheran theologian of Nurenberg, added an anonymous preface to the first edition of the book in which he stated that the hypotheses presented 'need not be true or even probable', together with many other comments designed to give the impression that the work was presenting convenient mathematical fictions rather than absolute truth. Osiander's preface was written with the best of intentions, since he himself was a strong supporter of Copernicus, the aim being to placate the Aristotelians whose opposition Copernicus clearly feared. As Osiander himself explained to Rheticus, the best strategy was to defuse any opposition right at the beginning, so that eventually the readers would 'go over to the opinion of the author' (as is clear from a letter Osiander wrote to Copernicus on 20 April 1541). Overall, however, the net effect of the preface was rather unfortunate since it gave the impression that it was written by Copernicus himself, and so implied that he only half-believed what he was writing, which was untrue.

Given this background to the heliocentric theory of Copernicus, it is not surprising that Galileo hesitated to make his support public during the earlier years of his academic life. As already noted, his reasons were not fear of opposition from the church. After all, up to 1616 discussion of the Copernican system was actively encouraged by the leading astronomers among the Jesuits, provided that it was discussed as a possible theory, and not used to attack theology. As Cardinal Dini wrote to Galileo in 1615, 'One may write freely as long as one keeps out of the sacristy.' But as Galileo well knew, there were at the time no conclusive data which could force a decision between Aristotle's universe as codified by Ptolemy, the new heliocentric theory of Copernicus or, for that matter, the popular 'intermediate position' taught by Tycho Brahe who held that the earth was fixed but that the planets were in orbit round the sun. The chief redeeming feature of Copernicanism appeared to be its greater geometrical elegance compared with the older systems – but much more than that was needed to oust Aristotle's universe. The last thing Galileo wanted to do was to try and replace one great system of abstract philosophy based on shaky foundations with another great system, much preferring the approach of gradual accumulation of striking observations and experiments that would make piecemeal polemical points against the Aristotelian system.

Galileo's first public controversy was not with theologians but with philosophers. It arose out of a new supernova that appeared in the evening sky during October 1604. In Aristotle's universe the outer heavens were made of the 'quintessence' and were therefore fixed and unchangeable. Change could only occur in the basic elements of earth, water, air and fire. But both the new supernova, and the new star seen by Tycho Brahe back in 1572, were a direct challenge to this theory. Galileo gave three public lectures at Padua to press home the point. Aristotle must have been mistaken. Cesare Cremonini, professor of philosophy at Padua, sprang to Aristotle's defence and there followed a lengthy public feud, with an exchange of acrimonious booklets between the contestants using various noms de plume. What infuriated the philosophers of the day was not merely Galileo's attacks on Aristotle, which were bad enough, but that Galileo also refused to incorporate his own views into a 'grand system' that would, in their eyes, have qualified Galileo as a respectable natural philosopher. As Galileo succinctly expressed his position:

There is not a single effect in Nature, not even the least that exists,
such that the most ingenious theorists can ever arrive at a complete
understanding of it. This vain presumption of understanding everything
can have no other basis than never understanding anything.

Galileo's great fear of being 'laughed at and hissed off the stage' finally ended in 1609 with the invention of the telescope. Up until that time, with the exception of the supernova of 1604, the moon and stars had interested Galileo very little, his seminal work being carried out on the laws of motion. But now, quite suddenly, the new technology opened up a vista of new worlds. Basing his design on the initial telescopes made in Holland, Galileo soon had at his disposal instruments that could magnify objects nearly 1,000-fold and he made a present of one of the earlier models to the Venetian Senate, explaining that it would be a valuable tool to forewarn of armed invasion from the sea. The Senate immediately doubled Galileo's salary, and gave him security of tenure at Padua, so becoming part of a long tradition whereby scientists have often done rather well on those occasions when their work has found military application.

However, it would be quite unfair to suggest that Galileo developed the telescope for personal financial advantage, as his very first scientific publication, *The Messenger From the Stars* (1610), makes clear. In this booklet of only twenty-four pages, Galileo reported on the startling new observations that he had made.

The publication's terse and factual style was in total contrast to the diffuse mumblings that characterized some other scientific literature of the time. It was readable, an immediate bestseller and had an enormous impact. Galileo had seen the surface of the moon and reported that it was '*not* perfectly smooth, free from inequalities and exactly spherical, as a large school of philosophers considers with regard to the moon and the other heavenly bodies, but that, on the contrary, it is full of irregularities, uneven, full of hollows and protuberances, just like the surface of the earth itself'. Galileo went on to describe the existence of 'other stars, in myriads, which have never been seen before, and which surpass the old, previously known stars in number more than ten times'. Galileo considered that the most important of all his discoveries with the telescope was the novel observation of the four moons of Jupiter. If moons circulated round Jupiter, the whole system revolving round the sun, then was it not also just as likely that our single moon revolved round the earth, and that this system was also heliocentric, as in the Copernican system?

Whether Galileo was in fact the first to make some of these observations is debatable. The crucial point is that he was the first to publish his observations in a clear and readable form and, as many have learnt to their cost since Galileo, it is not necessarily the discoverer who wins the fame but the one who publishes first. *The Messenger From the Stars* aroused immediate controversy, but the discussion centred at first not on the significance of the findings but on whether the telescope was a reliable instrument. On the evenings of 24 and 25 April 1610, a party was held in Bologna at which Galileo was invited to demonstrate the existence of Jupiter's moons. However, none of the illustrious gathering of academic guests who looked through the telescope that evening admitted to seeing Jupiter's moons. The dots seen were, perhaps, optical illusions centred in the lens system of the telescope. In science it is always easier to see what you are expecting to see and it seems clear that the academics of Bologna were not suffering from over-expectation on those April evenings of 1610, though the telescope that Galileo brought with him to the party was crude compared with the instruments made only a short while later.

The best counter to the accusation of 'artefact' is to use better methods or better instruments. For Galileo it was better telescopes that saved the day, and the leading astronomer in Rome at the time, the Jesuit Father Clavius, together with other Jesuit scholars, not only saw Jupiter's moons but soon improved on Galileo's own observations. The controversy at this stage was largely scientific: did the extra planets and stars exist? But philosophical questions were coming to the fore, and the Aristotelian philosophers remained upset. How could there be mountains on the moon when Aristotle was so clear that the heavenly bodies were perfectly round and smooth? Lengthy debates took place in letters and pamphlets, but at this stage of Galileo's career there is little evidence of conflicts with theologians. Galileo was fêted by the Jesuit astronomers in Rome at a special conference. Pope Paul V granted him an audience. Cardinals and other churchmen attended Galileo's frequent exhibitions of his telescopic discoveries. Cardinal Francesco Maria del Monthe wrote to Grand Duke Cosimo II: 'Were we living in the ancient Roman Republic, I have no doubt that a statue would be erected in the Campidoglio in honour of his (Galileo's) outstanding merit.' When Galileo entered into further philosophical controversy in 1611 on the precise nature of ice, his side was taken in a public debate by no less a person than Cardinal Barberini, later to become Pope Urban Vlll.

So what was it that led to Galileo's clash with the Catholic Church? In summarizing the key events, it should be remembered that the Italy of Galileo's time was passing through a period marked by political and religious insecurity. Rome had been sacked in 1527 and Spain had increased its domination in the area. Ecclesiastical power was becoming more pronounced as the secular authorities appeared unable to prevent foreign domination. Europe was divided by the Reformation, and the Catholic Church was in a defensive phase, intent on preserving dogma and defending the faith. In 1559 Pope Paul IV had issued the first official Roman Index of Prohibited Books (which included all the works of the great humanist Erasmus and all translations of the Bible into local languages), and in 1571 Pope Pius had set up a 'Congregation of the Index' in order to supervise and enforce the banned list. Giordano Bruno was burned at the stake in 1600 for holding religious beliefs viewed to be heretical. Thomas Aquinas' baptism of Aristotelian beliefs into the church was vigorously defended by the Jesuit order and though a teacher in the Order could question details, anyone who departed from Aristotle's system as a whole faced dismissal. The Protestant insistence that anyone was free to read and interpret the Bible for themselves meant that any non-theologians who entered into public discussions about doctrinal matters were liable to be viewed with suspicion.

In 1613 Galileo published his *Letters on Sunspots*, his only work to clearly support the theory of Copernicus. Unfortunately the book contained a preface, inserted against Galileo's will, claiming his priority of discovery. A German Jesuit called Christopher Scheiner had already published a book about sunspots under a pseudonym, and the question of priority of discovery led to a long wrangle, during which Galileo, who was not always the most tactful of people, managed to anger not only Scheiner, but also a number of leading Jesuits who had formerly been his allies. The controversy with Scheiner broadened to include a whole range of issues which highlighted Galileo's insistence that natural philosophy was concerned only with observed events and the properties of things, whereas the Aristotelians saw the aim of science as determining the very essence of things.

In an appendix to his *Letters on Sunspots*, Galileo also presented what was, for him, evidence confirming beyond doubt that the Copernican theory was true. It was evidence derived from the discovery of the eclipses of Jupiter's satellites, which Galileo demonstrated could only be predicted correctly on the assumption that the earth moved. To an experienced astronomer the finding clinched the Copernican system. To the casual reader it remained rather an obscure point tucked away in the appendix. But the net effect was to confirm for Galileo that he was on the right track and his public pronouncements in favour of Copernicus and in opposition to Aristotle became more confident. Yet he was still not prepared for the Copernican theory to be taught to students. When Castelli was appointed in 1613 to Galileo's former Chair of Mathematics at the University of Pisa, Galileo warned him not to teach Copernicanism, saying that in twenty years of university teaching he had never done so.

Castelli was viewed from the beginning of his appointment as a follower of Galileo and soon became the focal point for attacks by the Pisan philosophers. Near the end of 1613 he was invited to a court breakfast of the ruling Medici family, Galileo's chief patrons in his career; Castelli's mother, Grand Duchess Christina of Lorraine, was also present. A professor of philosophy, who specialized in Plato, informed the grand duchess that Galileo, who was not present, was wrong in saying that the earth moved, since this contradicted the Bible. The outcome was a spirited defence of Galileo's position by Castelli, who maintained that scientific questions should be decided on the basis of scientific evidence alone. Castelli then sent an account of the incident to Galileo in Florence, who wrote a long reply in which he supported Castelli, and argued that theologians should allow freedom of thought in all matters that could be decided by 'sensate experiences and necessary demonstrations' alone. Nature was the 'executrix of God's will' and the Bible was the 'repository of God's word'. No contradictions could exist between them.

For the first time in his career Galileo found himself embroiled in a debate on theological matters and the trigger for the debate was the accusations made by a professor of philosophy directly to his own employer. True, there had been isolated incidents before, but none that either Galileo or the church authorities had taken seriously. Late in 1614 a young and ambitious Dominican named Thomas Caccini gave a sermon in the principal church of Florence attacking mathematicians in general and the followers of Galileo in particular, who had by this time started calling themselves 'Galileists'. It was clear that Caccini was aiming for a high appointment in Rome, and felt that public notoriety was the best route to the top. In the event a Dominican father at Rome wrote to Galileo and apologized for the uncouth behaviour of a member of his order; but by then the damage was done, and shock waves from this public controversy were felt far beyond Florence. The upshot was that Galileo's *Letter to Castelli* was sent to the Inquisition in Rome for their investigation. After receiving a report on its contents from a theologian, it was deemed theologically innocuous and no further action was taken – except by Galileo himself, who proceeded to expand the material into the much longer *Letter to the Duchess Christina* in 1615. This letter remains a classic in the early literature on the relationship between science and faith, and should be read by anyone who has an interest in the subject. What is clear from the events surrounding its composition is that the controversy was still largely between the mathematician Galileo and the philosophers, and that, apart from the intrigues of a few hotheads, the church had little interest in a confrontation at this stage.

Towards the end of 1615 Galileo made a crucial visit to Rome. His main reasons for the visit seem to have been a suspicion that the ambitious Caccini was plotting against him and Galileo was determined that his own views should be presented personally in the academic circles of Rome rather than by rumour. In some ways it was an unfortunate time to visit the city. The controversy between Catholics and Protestants was at its height and, since a major area of conflict was the Protestants' insistence that each individual was free to interpret the Bible for themselves, any apparent questioning of the Catholic interpretation of the Bible was likely to be viewed with suspicion. Galileo argued the Copernican position while in Rome with great passion and in 1616 presented his theory of tides, which depended on the motion of the earth, to Pope Paul V through the intermediary of Cardinal Orsini. But the pope was in no mood for further controversy and, on the recommendation of Cardinal Bellarmine, Galileo's Copernican theories were submitted to theological experts. These eventually came out with 'censures' of various propositions, including the claim 'that the earth is neither in the centre of the world nor immovable, but moves as a whole and in daily motion'. It is interesting to note that it was *philosophy* that was given the prime weight of authority in rejecting the theories of Copernicus. Aristotle had become so absorbed into the structure of the Catholic Church's dogma that an attack on Aristotle was tantamount to an attack on the church itself. As Galileo's contemporary Descartes observed at the time, 'theology has been so subjected to Aristotle that it is almost impossible to explain another philosophy without it seeming at first contrary to the Faith'. Stillman Drake comments that:

> It is a curious fact that historians have not blamed philosophers rather than theologians for the decision taken against freedom of scientific opinion in astronomy. Yet philosophers alone urged the intervention of theologians, confident that they would be on their side.[2]

Galileo himself was quite bemused that the theologians were making the philosophers the final arbiters of how to interpret scripture since the approach of the early Church authorities such as Augustine or Aquinas had been quite clear in such matters, maintaining that 'the mobility or stability of the earth or sun is neither a matter of faith nor one contrary to ethics'. It was quite inappropriate for the church of his day to defend as articles of faith views on astronomy that came from Aristotle, and which were nowhere found in the Bible. Galileo poured scorn on those who tried to prop up their scientific speculations by quoting from scripture:

If I may speak my opinion freely, I should say further that it would perhaps fit in better with the decorum and majesty of the sacred writings to take measures for preventing every shallow and vulgar writer from giving to his compositions (often grounded upon foolish fancies) an air of authority by inserting in them passages from the Bible, interpreted (or rather distorted) into senses as far from the right meaning of Scripture as those authors are near to absurdity who thus ostentatiously adorn their writings.[3]

The conclusions of the theological experts were read at a meeting of cardinals of the Inquisition on 24 February 1616. Two days later, by the express order of the pope, Cardinal Bellarmine summoned Galileo for an interview and an account of this encounter was later issued by Bellarmine at Galileo's request in order to dispel rumours that he had been punished by the Inquisition. The certificate issued, which Galileo carefully kept, stated clearly that he had been informed of the decisions of the 'Sacred Congregation of the Index', and that the 'doctrine attributed to Copernicus... cannot be defended or held', but also that Galileo had not been asked to recant. As it happened, an alternative version of this document later played a crucial part in Galileo's trial, stating that Galileo was also forbidden to *teach* Copernican views. Exactly how the alternative version came into being has remained a matter of debate until the present day. But the impression given to Galileo at the time was clearly that he was free to discuss and debate Copernican doctrines as astronomical theories, provided he did not defend or teach them as physical truths. Though to non-legal minds the distinction may appear academic, 17th-century Italy only operated socially as well as it did by the use of such face-saving devices.

On 5 March a decree was issued which placed on the Index of Prohibited Books any works in which the motion of the earth or the stability of the sun were held as real or were reconciled with the Bible. Copernicus' *De Revolutionibus* was suspended until corrections could be made, though in the event the corrections made were regarded by Galileo as being of little importance. In this modified form the work could again be read by 1620.

The main aim of the church authorities at this stage appears to have been to keep Galileo the mathematician 'out of the sacristy', away from affairs that would arouse philosophical and theological passions. Within a few days of receiving the warning, Galileo was granted a personal audience with the pope, during which he assured Galileo that he well knew of the intrigues against him, and that as long as he, Paul V, was alive, Galileo had nothing to fear. Armed with this assurance Galileo returned to Florence and busied himself with the question of how ships at sea could calculate their longitudes by using the positions of Jupiter's satellites. In the autumn of 1618 three comets appeared and, like all other changes which occurred in the heavens during this period, attracted much attention. A spate of books on comets appeared, one being written by a prominent Jesuit scholar called Grassi, defending the views of the mathematicians of the Jesuit College in Rome. In the controversy that followed, Galileo published a book called *The Assayer* in 1623, in which he not only commented on the nature of comets but also outlined in some detail his own views on the kind of knowledge that natural philosophy provided. Science was nothing to do with the 'sympathies', antipathies', 'occult properties' and 'influences' so beloved by the scholastics. Galileo ridiculed Grassi's views repeatedly and in so doing added yet another name to his list of Jesuit enemies. As Father Grienberger, a later head of the Jesuit College, remarked: 'If Galileo had not incurred the displeasure of the Company [i.e. of Jesuits], he could have gone on writing freely about the motion of the Earth to the end of his days.'

Just at the time that Galileo was completing *The Assayer*, Maffeo Barberini was elected to the papacy as Urban VIII. The Lincean Academy in Rome was about to publish the book and so Galileo quickly decided to dedicate it to the new pope. Barberini, an admirer of Galileo, was a Florentine, powerful, energetic, intellectual and immensely vain. In 1620 he had even written an ode in honour of Galileo and, after becoming Pope, a brother of a Roman cardinal wrote to Galileo a flowery invitation, which gives something of the flavour of court life at the time:

I swear to you that nothing pleased his Holiness so much as the mention of your name. After I had been speaking of you for some time, I told him that you, esteemed Sir, had an ardent desire to come and kiss his toes, if his Holiness would permit it, to which the Pope replied that it would give him, great pleasure, if it were not inconvenient to you... for great men like you must spare themselves, that they might live as long as possible.

As Koestler remarks, both Galileo and the new pope 'considered themselves supermen and started on a basis of mutual adulation – a type of relationship which, as a rule, comes to a bitter end'. It was not long before Galileo was back in Rome, being showered with gifts and favours during a series of six audiences with the new Pope. It was during this period that a friend of Galileo's in Rome, Cardinal Zollern, informed the pope that German Protestants were very much in favour of Copernicanism and that the Catholic Church must proceed very cautiously in its reactions to Copernican teachings. The pope replied that the church had never declared Copernican beliefs to be heretical and had no intention of doing so, but that final proof of the Copernican system might never in fact appear.

It was in this renewed glow of papal favour that Galileo felt at last able to embark on a major work of Copernican apologetics, which he intended to call *Dialogue on the Flux and Reflux of the Tides* and which he wrote during the period 1624–30. Just before publication he was instructed to change the title since it clearly implied physical arguments for the motions of the earth, whereas the censures of 1616 had allowed only public discussion of the hypothetical possibility of such a theory, the presentation of the movement of the earth as a physical reality being clearly banned. Nothing daunted, Galileo changed the title to *Dialogue Concerning the Two Chief Systems of the World – Ptolemaic and Copernican*, written in Italian rather than Latin with the aim of making a wide public impact. As one might expect, Galileo's spokesman Salviati dominates the proceedings, repeating the arguments against Copernicus made by the supporters of Aristotle and Ptolemy with great eloquence, and then proceeding to demolish them even more effectively, in the process winning Sagredo to his viewpoint, and making Simplicio, a pompous Aristotelian philosopher, look very foolish.

Galileo was only too aware that an entirely new system of physics was required to demolish the Aristotelian system, and much of the book is taken up with arguments about the motion of bodies on earth rather than with astronomy per se. In place of the Aristotelian idea that objects on earth are naturally at rest and motion requires the continual presence of a moving force, Galileo argued that bodies could continue in motion without the intervention of a force. This concept of inertia was crucial in clearing the way for the acceptance of a moving earth. The climax of the *Dialogue* came with Galileo's theory of the tides, in which Salviati argued that tides can occur only on the assumption that the earth is moving. As it happens, Galileo's theory of tides was wrong in almost all its aspects, and he scornfully rejected the theory held by Kepler, later shown to be correct, as already mentioned. Nevertheless, Galileo saw his theory of the tides as the *coup de grâce* for the opposition.

The *coup de grâce* for Galileo himself was, perhaps, Simplicio's closing speech, in which he expresses, almost verbatim, Pope Urban's argument that we should not have 'excessive boldness' in thinking that we could ever know for sure how God had chosen to arrange certain natural phenomena, such as the tides. Salviati replies with heavy irony, appearing to agree with Simplicio, but in the process hinting strongly that such a position reflects intellectual laziness.

Galileo's *Dialogue* was finally published at Florence in March 1632. The pope was furious. An order came from the Roman Inquisition to stop all sales but, unlike Copernicus' magnum opus, the edition of 1,000 copies had already sold out within months of publication. Galileo was ordered to Rome, a severe illness delaying his departure for a few months until the winter of 1632. On arrival in Rome it soon emerged that the problem was not simply the contents of the *Dialogue*, but the fact that Urban VIII had been shown an unsigned notary's memo from 1616 giving an alternative version of the certificate that had been handed to Galileo at the time by Cardinal Bellarmine. As noted above, in this version Galileo was expressly ordered not to *teach* Copernican propositions and it appeared to the pope that Galileo's *Dialogue* was therefore clearly illegal.

Galileo stayed in Rome in some comfort with the Tuscan ambassador and his trial began on Tuesday 12 April 1633. He was neither imprisoned nor tortured. The trial centred on the question of whether Galileo had presented the Copernican doctrine as a proved fact rather than a mere hypothesis and the 'alternative' ruling of 1616, which had been dug out of the church records, most probably by one of Galileo's Jesuit enemies, therefore played a crucial role in the proceedings. In his defence Galileo produced the authentic version of the certificate, written and signed by Cardinal Bellarmine. No signed document was ever produced to support the 'alternative' unsigned version which had been extracted from the archives and from a legal point of view Galileo's position therefore seemed secure. Yet it was clear that the Roman Inquisition were quite intent on maintaining the upper hand and, as the interrogations dragged on, Galileo, in contrast to his previous bombastic treatment of the authorities, gives the impression of being a tired and defeated man, ready to acquiesce for the sake of peace. During the final phase of the trial, Galileo was asked directly his opinion about which cosmological system was true, replying that before the decree of 1616 he had considered that either Ptolemy or Copernicus might be true, 'but after the said decision, assured of the wisdom of the authorities, I ceased to have any doubt; and I held, as I still hold, as most true and indisputable the opinion of Ptolemy, that is to say, the stability of the Earth'. The Inquisitors were unconvinced, and continued to press Galileo to express his true beliefs, receiving the same kind of reply each time. Galileo was also instructed to re-read his *Dialogue* and stated that there were several places in which he had gone too far. There seems little doubt that both Galileo and his Inquisitors knew that he was lying, at least in his insistence that he had never held Copernican beliefs since 1616, the *Dialogue* itself being perfectly clear in its defence of Copernicus.

No questions of science were raised at the trial, which was undertaken within a framework of legal technicalities. The charge against Galileo was 'vehement suspicion of heresy'. When the day came for the final verdict, Galileo was convinced that he would be let off lightly and so was shocked to hear that he was condemned to indefinite imprisonment. In the event the sentence was interpreted lightly. Archbishop Piccolomini of Siena managed to arrange for Galileo's 'imprisonment' to take place in his comfortable residence where, according to a visitor, Galileo worked 'in an apartment covered in silk and most richly furnished'. After this, Galileo returned to his farm at Arcetri and later to his house in Florence, where he remained for the rest of his life under surveillance of the officers of the Inquisition. The rest of the sentence prohibited the *Dialogue*, which remained on the Index of forbidden books until 1831, and insisted that Galileo was 'to abjure the Copernican opinion'. Galileo was also ordered for three years to repeat the seven penitential Psalms once a week, a duty which, with ecclesiastical approval, he delegated to his daughter Sister Marie Celeste, a Carmelite nun.

Galileo was downcast but, with Archbishop Piccolomini's encouragement, was soon engrossed in the preparation of another book which, by general consent, emerged as the most significant scientific work of his lifetime, the *Dialogues Concerning Two New Sciences*, in which Galileo expounded his science of dynamics. The book was completed in 1636 when Galileo was seventy-two and smuggled out to Holland where it was published by the Elseviers. A year later Galileo lost the sight of first one eye and then the other, but kept on dictating additional chapters for his new book. The death of his daughter Celeste dealt Galileo another blow and his health began to deteriorate, but Galileo continued to receive distinguished visitors until the end of his life, among them John Milton in 1638. A great encouragement was the spread of his books throughout Europe, particularly through the work of a French friar called Mersenne, who introduced Galileo's works to northern Europe. A Latin version of his *Letter to the Grand Duchess* was published by the Elseviers and helped to spread Galileo's views on the relation between scientific knowledge and scripture, but the Jesuits throughout Europe made strenuous efforts to prevent the publication of Galileo's writings.

What is perfectly clear is that Galileo remained firm in his own faith until the end of his days, despite the rough treatment that he had received from the church authorities. Galileo himself wrote to a sympathetic French correspondent who had heard of his condemnation and who was offering to campaign on his behalf in Rome:

> I have two sources of perpetual comfort – first, that in my writings there cannot be found the faintest shadow of irreverence towards the Holy Church; and second, the testimony of my own conscience, which only I and God in Heaven thoroughly know. And He knows that in this cause for which I suffer, though many might have spoken with more learning, none, not even the ancient Fathers, have spoken with more piety or with greater zeal for the church than I.

When Galileo died on 9 January 1642 it was in the sure knowledge that he had remained faithful both to the God whose glory and greatness 'are marvelously discerned in all his works', as well as to the 'sense-experiences and necessary demonstrations' which were so critical for the emerging scientific enterprise. 'Whatever the course of our lives,' Galileo wrote, 'we should receive them as the highest gift from the hand of God, in which equally reposed the power to do nothing whatever for us. Indeed, we should accept misfortune not only in thanks, but in infinite gratitude to Providence, which by such means detaches us from an excessive love for earthly things and elevates our minds to the celestial and divine.'

What can we say, therefore, about Galileo? His clash with the church authorities has been built over the years into the mythology of the science–faith 'conflict thesis'. Yet, as we have seen, the available evidence does not support such an interpretation. The conflict was no clash between 'science' and 'faith', but rather centred around competing theologies, with Galileo defending what he saw as the traditional Augustinian view of the relation between faith and natural philosophy against the rigid positions taken up by the Catholic authorities as they faced the twin threats of secular and religious pluralism. With the benefit of hindsight it is difficult to see how a clash could have been avoided between the new natural philosophy as it pulled away from the authority of the ancient philosophers and a church that had absorbed so much of the teaching of these philosophers into its dogmas. The clash, when it came, happened to centre on a man who was not afraid of public controversy, living in a society dominated by complex political cross-currents, in which power and prestige were won largely through patronage and intrigue. Galileo symbolizes not a conflict between science and faith but a conflict between the need for freedom in scientific enquiry and the restraints imposed by authoritarian regimes.

Did the early Protestants oppose Copernicanism?

Some of the early science–faith debates were generated not in the 16th and 17th centuries but in the fertile imaginations of 19th-century hagiographers who wrote imaginative accounts of how the scientific revolution should have happened according to their own particular agendas.

It is not easy to disbelieve statements which are repeated with great frequency and much assurance by a large number of experts writing in a wide range of scholarly publications. Consider, for example, the following string of quotations:

> There was an immediate and hostile reaction to Copernicanism from the leaders of the Protestant churches... in the 1530s Martin Luther made a contemptuous reference to Copernicus as the 'new astrologer who wants

to prove that the Earth moves and goes round'... Calvin also joined in the condemnation in his *Commentary on Genesis*, where he cited the opening verse of the 93rd Psalm, 'the world also is stablished that it cannot be moved', and asked 'who will venture to place the authority of Copernicus above that of the Holy Spirit?'[4]

Luther thought to refute Copernicus by quoting the Scriptures.[5]

The Lutherans, not the Catholics, had been the first to attack the Copernican system.[6]

The truth is that within the general range of religious opinion, Catholic, Lutheran and Calvinist alike, the Copernican view was dismissed as an absurdity. All the accepted authorities were against it.[7]

Thomas Kuhn similarly reports that:

Protestant leaders like Luther, Calvin, and Melanchthon led in citing Scripture against Copernicus and in urging repression of Copernicans.[8]

It would be possible to extend the list of such quotations across several more pages,[9] and I have to admit that I assumed for a long time that these statements accurately reflected the historical evidence available. However, there were several pieces of data that aroused my suspicions. The first was the fact that such statements were either backed by no references at all, or invariably channelled back to single historical sources of dubious authenticity. The second piece of data was the observation that early modern science flourished in a Protestant milieu and it was difficult to imagine that the new philosophy would have received such a welcome if the founders of the Protestant movement themselves had been as bitterly opposed as our commentators quoted above would suggest. Furthermore, following the Reformation, Catholics often appeared to identify Copernicanism with Protestantism. As already noted, in 1624 a cardinal warned the pope to be careful in deciding about Copernicus, since all heretics adhered to his opinion and held it for certain, and Galileo believed that 'all the most distinguished heretics' (meaning Protestants) accepted Copernican doctrines.[10] As Brooke and Cantor comment, at the time 'It would not have been difficult to perceive Galileo as a crypto-Protestant, tarred with the same brush as his friend Paolo Sarpi who had led a Venetian revolt against the papacy.'[11]

What did Martin Luther (1483–1546) himself believe about the matter? He was a theologian, not a natural philosopher, and there is no evidence that natural philosophy was at any time more than peripheral to his interests, nor is there any reason why it should have been. Luther was a man of his age and, though he viewed Aristotle with deep suspicion when it came to questions of theology, he most likely accepted the prevailing Aristotelian structure of the universe in the same way as his contemporaries. He was a great nature lover, a gardener by inclination, and repeatedly commented on the wonders of God in creation that he saw all around him. Luther had respect for astronomy, but ridiculed astrology, citing as evidence against it the example of twins such as Esau and Jacob who, though born under the same planets, were totally dissimilar in character (an argument originally put forward by Augustine back in the 4th century).

From about 1520 onward Luther used to assemble his disciples at a fixed time to discuss a wide range of topics. It seems to have been an early follower of Luther called Cordatus who, in 1531, first began to record Luther's comments during these discussion sessions. The practice was quickly taken up by others, who then proceeded to polish their texts, add to them from memory and improve their style. There was also some exchange of material between students and several distinct versions of the proceedings began to emerge. Luther himself appears to have condoned this note-taking which, at least at the beginning, must have seemed little different from students taking notes in lectures. Many of the discussions that they recorded were held over a meal in Luther's home, with the wine and his wife Kate's excellent home-brewed beer flowing freely, and no doubt comments were made in the heat of the moment or in jest which Luther never intended as serious academic material ready for publication. Despite this, twenty years after Luther's death, Johann Aurifaber, one of his disciples, published his notes in 1566 under the title of *Table Talk*, the only version available until about 1914. Unfortunately Aurifaber himself had only taken notes during the years 1545–46, and the rest of the text was taken from the notes of others, which themselves were largely second or third hand. However, there were other recorders who had been more careful, including Anton Lauterbach, whose version of the *Table Talk* was published in 1916, though some mistakes are also discernible in this version.[12]

On 4 June 1539, according to Lauterbach's diary, Luther held a 'table talk' during which he is alleged to have made the disparaging comments about Copernicus. The date is significant because it was in the spring of that year that the young Wittenberg mathematics lecturer Georg Rheticus had set out for Frauenberg in order to hear the news of the latest astronomical theories from the lips of Copernicus himself, then aged sixty-six. As we have already noted, the Protestant Rheticus soon became a passionate convert to Copernican theories and was instrumental in persuading Copernicus to publish his *De Revolutionibus*. It seems quite feasible that the departure of his colleague from the university would have been known to Luther, leading to discussion of the latest theories. Copernicus had produced a preliminary manuscript of some of his ideas around 1510–14, known as the *Commentariolus*, but the names of the scholars to whom he sent this unpublished work are unknown, its impact was slight, and it is unlikely that Luther had ever seen a copy. Thus, at the time of the table talk all was still rumour, no published work by Copernicus yet being available.

What did Luther actually say at the time? Unfortunately we do not know with any certainty, because the two versions of *Table Talk* disagree. Lauterbach's more reliable version reports that during dinner there was mention of a certain new astrologer (the terms astrologer and astronomer were not distinguished carefully at the time) who had new-fangled ideas and Luther is supposed to have commented:

Whoever wants to be clever must agree with nothing that others esteem.
He must do something of his own. This is what that fellow does who
wishes to turn the whole of astronomy upside down. Even in these things
that are thrown into disorder I believe the Holy Scriptures, for Joshua
commanded the sun to stand still and not the earth.[13]

Copernicus is nowhere mentioned by name, although it seems very likely that the astronomer being referred to is Copernicus, given the timing of the dinner-time conversation so soon after Rheticus had set out to make his visit. Aurifaber's less reliable version of the *Table Talk* uses the expression 'that fool' instead of 'that fellow' in the above text and it is this version of the conversation that has frequently been used to accuse Luther of anti-Copernicanism.

In the absence of any published evidence on the heliocentric theory, it is quite likely that Luther indeed reacted initially with scepticism to what, at the time, must have sounded a novel and preposterous rumour. In 1539 there was no direct evidence for the Copernican theory. But whichever version of the *Table Talk* might be true, or quite likely neither, makes little difference, since there is no evidence from Luther's own published works of any hostility to the new astronomy. As James Atkinson has remarked, 'No comment at table is accepted by a Luther scholar as authentic unless there is corroboration for its substance in Luther's writings.'[14] In fact Luther never referred to Copernicus even once in all his voluminous published works. Furthermore, publication of Copernicus' theories did not commence until 1540 (with a preliminary work produced by Rheticus), and Luther died only a few years later, making it even more unlikely that his views made any contribution to the reception of Copernican theories.

It is also interesting to note that Luther's own published views on astronomy and biblical interpretation are not at all in keeping with his *Table Talk* comments cited above. Luther was widely educated in the sciences, philosophy, mathematics and theology of his day and displayed a sophisticated view of the relation between natural philosophy and theology in which each discipline should be careful to adhere to its own particular language:

> [In biblical studies] one must accustom oneself to the Holy Spirit's way of expression. With the other sciences, too, no one is successful unless he has first duly learned their technical language. Thus lawyers have their terminology, which is unfamiliar to physicians and philosophers. On the other hand, these also have their own sort of language, which is unfamiliar to the other professions. Now no science should stand in the way of another science, but each should continue to have its own mode of procedure and its own terms.[15]

So Luther took the view that theology should tackle the overall question of the divine origin of the whole created order, whereas astronomers should get on with their task of describing God's universe:

> For the astronomers are the experts from whom it is most convenient to get what may be discussed about these subjects [sun, moon, stars, etc.]. For me it is enough that in those bodies [sun and moon], which are so elegant and necessary for life, we recognize both the goodness of God and His power.[16]

Far from being critical of astronomy, Luther here lavishes praise on the astronomers as 'the experts'!

Of perhaps greater interest are the views of those early Protestants who were themselves mathematicians or natural philosophers. Reactions among this group to Copernicus varied from enthusiastic endorsement (Rheticus, Kepler) to initial scepticism followed by grudging assent by Philip Melanchthon (1497–1560), who was not himself a natural philosopher but a gifted teacher and administrator who pioneered the educational arm of the Reformation in Germany. When Rheticus returned to Wittenberg in 1542 after a stay with Copernicus of two and a half years, he returned as a passionate convert, delighting like Kepler in the mathematical elegance of the 'remarkable symmetry and interconnection of the motions and spheres' exemplified by the Copernican system. Rheticus set about writing a *Treatise on Holy Scripture and the Motion of the Earth*, lost for many years but recently rediscovered, demonstrating the compatibility between the Bible and Copernican theories.[17]

Like Rheticus, the Lutheran Kepler, as we have already noted, embraced Copernicanism wholeheartedly. Kepler heard about Copernicus from his teacher in astronomy, Michael Mastlin, himself a convinced Copernican, while studying at the Protestant university of Tübingen, and records that while there, 'I often defended the opinions of Copernicus.' A year after taking up his teaching appointment in Gratz, Kepler became overwhelmed by the realization (as it happens, quite false) that the whole universe was constructed around geometrical figures, such as the triangle, square and so on, and proceeded to try and show that the orbits of the planets encompassed such mathematical forms, in a project which Kepler eventually published as his *Mysterium Cosmographicum* (1596). In the preface to this work, Kepler describes how

I lost almost the whole of the summer with this heavy work. Finally I came close to the true facts on a quite unimportant occasion. I believe Divine Providence arranged matters in such a way that what I could not obtain with all my efforts was given to me through chance. I believe all the more that this is so as I have always prayed to God that he should make my plan succeed, if what Copernicus had said was the truth.[18]

Later Kepler wrote about his hypothesis to a friend, remarking that 'I am satisfied to use my discovery to guard the gates of the temple in which Copernicus makes sacrifices at the high altar.'[19] Finding the mathematical principles that underlay the cosmos was, for Kepler, itself a religious calling. Meanwhile in England Copernicanism found a vigorous supporter in the Puritan Thomas Digges (1546–95?), whose *Perfit Description of the Caelestiall Orbes* contained a paraphrase of the first book of Copernicus' *De Revolutionibus*.

What about the alleged negative views of Calvin (1509–64) towards Copernicus alluded to above? The answer in this case is disarmingly simple. The supposed quote by Calvin in his Commentary on Genesis ('Who will venture to place the authority of Copernicus above that of the Holy Spirit?') is pure fabrication, and seems to have first appeared first in a work by F.W. Farrar in 1886[20] being repeated by other writers ad nauseam down the years since that time, too lazy to check their original source material.[21] In fact, there is not a single mention of Copernicus among *any* of Calvin's voluminous writings nor, for that matter, any firm evidence that Calvin had even heard of Copernicus. Calvin, a theologian like Luther, devoted his life to the progress of the Reformation and though he respected natural philosophy, it was peripheral to the major concerns of his life. As we have noted already, outside of a narrow circle of academics there were very few people in Europe at the time who took any notice of Copernican theories, either for or against, and Calvin himself appears to have accepted the prevailing scholastic consensus on astronomy. Yet, according to later natural philosophers who looked to Calvin for theological guidance, there was much in his writings to motivate their investigations of the natural world. Central to Calvin's theology was the biblical emphasis that *all* the faculties of people should be utilized to bring glory to God and that certainly included the intellect. Those who neglected the study of nature were as guilty as those who forgot the creator when investigating God's works. Opponents of science who thought that knowledge of the created world led only to pride were criticized for not recognizing that such knowledge led also to 'knowledge of God and the conduct of life'.[22]

> For astronomy is not only pleasant, but also very useful to be known:
> it cannot be denied that this art unfolds the admirable wisdom of God.
> Therefore, clever men who expend their labour upon it are to be praised and
> those who have ability and leisure ought not to neglect work of that kind.[23]

Calvin believed very firmly that truth should be appreciated wherever it might be found, for 'If we hold the Spirit of God to be the only source of Truth, we will neither reject, nor despise this Truth wherever it may reveal itself.' A similar point was made in rather more picturesque language by the Calvinist poet Johan de Brune: 'Wheresoever Truth may be, were it in a Turk or Tatar, it must be cherished... let us seek the honeycomb even within the lion's mouth.' Considering that these words were penned during a period when the Turks were at the gates of Vienna, threatening to conquer the whole of Europe, their publication must have taken some courage![24]

To summarize, then, the views of early Protestant thinkers towards Copernicanism were diverse, and there is little evidence to support the sweeping claims culled from the 'conflict thesis' literature and presented at the beginning of this section. Protestant thinkers included theologians such as Luther and Calvin who, to put it crudely, were too busy running the Reformation to pay more than passing attention to the new astronomy, as well as natural philosophers such as Rheticus and Kepler, whose commitment to Copernicus did much to ensure the eventual acceptance of the heliocentric worldview.

The Bible and Early Modern Science

We have already alluded in the previous chapter to the way in which both the Bible and the natural world began to be interpreted during the Reformation period less allegorically, thereby drawing attention to what things meant in themselves in place of their previous role as signifiers of some deeper symbolic moral or spiritual meaning. This led to a recurring discussion in both the scientific and theological literature of the 16th and 17th centuries as to whether the Bible is intended to teach natural philosophy, including astronomy, or whether its precepts cover only the areas of theology, history and ethics. No one at the time was in any doubt that the *theology* of creation was an inspiration to 'think God's thoughts after him', but the question still remained as to whether the Bible itself could be used to provide scientific information.

In our contemporary context the question might seem a curious one. Taken as a series of ancient texts, the Bible contains a great diversity of literary styles, including poetry, historical narratives, letters and theological essays. All of these texts predate the modern scientific movement by 1,400 years or more and the idea that their language can be press-ganged into contributing to the ever-changing kaleidoscope of constructed knowledge that we now call modern science appears bizarre. When Shakespeare's Macbeth, in the early part of the 17th century, pleads that 'Thou sure and firm-set earth, hear not my steps, which way they walk, for fear the very stones prate of my whereabouts,' (*Macbeth*, Act 2, Scene 1, in the court within Inverness castle), as far as we know Shakespeare was never accused by his contemporaries of being anti-Copernican as a result, nor of thinking that the earth had ears and could hear footsteps. Yet people of the same era had a habit of extracting quotations from equally poetical passages of the Bible and using them to support or attack current theories in natural philosophy. Why this crude literalism?

The answer lies partly in the deeply ingrained habits of medieval scholasticism. The lifeblood of that system, as already noted, was the recovery and translation of the texts of the ancients and the building of such 'discoveries' into great rationalistic schemes. The Bible was not generally available in the vernacular languages of medieval Europe and its translation was frequently opposed on the grounds that it was the task of professional theologians to interpret the Bible for the common people. There was a tendency, therefore, to view the Bible in the same kind of light as the ancient texts handed down from the Greek philosophers, with its contents only accessible to those of the right educational background. This pandered to the academic penchant for building up great schemes of interpretation in which layers of allegorical meanings were liberally applied to the text. Later the Reformation resulted in a dramatic increase in the general availability of the Bible, translated into vernacular languages, with a corresponding emphasis on the right of every individual to interpret it for themselves under the guidance of the Holy Spirit. The Reformation critique of allegorical interpretations of the biblical text also had the effect on some of swinging the pendulum in completely the opposite direction so that even passages that were clearly written as poetry were now trawled for truths about the natural world.

The main way in which the natural philosophers of the 16th and 17th centuries responded to these shifting trends in biblical interpretation was to relate their new philosophy to scriptural teaching by the theory of 'accommodation'. The idea is first found in Augustine in the 4th century, as

Rheticus explains in his *Treatise on Holy Scripture and the Motion of the Earth*: Augustine 'takes also into account how Scripture borrows a style of discourse, an idiom of speech or a method of teaching from popular usage, so that it may also fully accommodate itself to the people's understanding'. Therefore 'The obscurities of nature, which we sense as the work of God, the almighty Architect, should be dealt with, not by my making assertions, but by research.' Galileo continues the same theme in his *Letter to the Grand Duchess Christina*. According to Augustine, wrote Galileo, the writers of the Old and New Testaments had been well aware of the truths of astronomy:

> Hence let it be said briefly, touching the form of heaven, that our authors knew the truth but the Holy Spirit did not desire that men should learn things that are useful to no one for salvation.[25]

In Augustinian thought, the purpose of the Bible was not to propound astronomical theories, since in any case these would not have been understood by the great mass of people, but rather to explain to people the way of salvation. Galileo was particularly upset with some of his critics who tried to use poetic passages from the Psalms to oppose him (such as the passage in Psalm 93:1 which says 'The world is firmly established; it cannot be moved'). Today we would simply point out the rather obvious point that such passages are hymns of worship recorded in poetic stanzas that were never intended as a scientific text any more than Shakespeare's Macbeth. In the context of a long history of scholastic textual interpretation, Galileo's riposte was rather different, arguing that God could have revealed scientific truths in the Bible if he had so wished but that as a matter of fact he had chosen to adapt his revelation to the limited understanding of the general reader.

The widespread adoption of the principle of accommodation in this period was in part due to the influence of Calvin's writings on the Protestant natural philosophers. As Calvin put it, Moses 'adapted his writing to common usage'. The Bible was 'a book for laymen' and 'he who would learn astronomy and other recondite arts, let him go elsewhere'.[26]

> The Holy Spirit had no intention to teach astronomy; and, in proposing instruction meant to be common to the simplest and most uneducated persons, he made use by Moses and the other prophets of popular language... the Holy Spirit would rather speak childishly than unintelligibly to the humble and unlearned.[27]

Edward Wright echoes this theme when he wrote the preface to William Gilbert's *De Magnete* (1600), the first major original contribution to modern science published in England. In defending in his preface the idea of the motion of the earth that Gilbert was presenting, Wright explained that Moses had never intended to expound mathematical and physical theories, but rather 'accommodated himself to the understanding and the way of speech of the common people.' John Wilkins, an early member of the Royal Society in England who repeatedly referred to Calvin's commentaries in his writings, maintained that:

> It were happy for us, if we could exempt Scripture from Philosophical controversies: If we could be content to let it be perfect for that end unto which it was intended, for a Rule of our Faith and Obedience, and not to stretch it also to be a Judge of such Natural Truths as are to be found out by our own Industry and Experience.[28]

Wilkins was totally opposed to those who 'look for any Secrets of Nature from the Words of Scripture, or will examine all its Expressions by the exact Rules of Philosophy', telling us that he found neither Aristotelianism nor Copernicanism in the Bible, which does not express things as they 'are in themselves, but according to their appearances, and as they are conceived in common opinion'. When Kepler wrote his *New Astronomy* (1609) he argued that the biblical writers had accommodated their stories to the human sense of sight. So when Ecclesiastes (1:5) says that 'The sun rises, and the sun sets, and hurries back to where it rises', Kepler comments that 'The fable of life is ever the same; there is nothing new under the sun. You receive no instruction on physical matters [from the Bible]. The message is a moral one.'[29]

It has sometimes been thought that the theory of accommodation was a last-ditch stand by natural philosophers to defend the authority of the Bible in the face of the threat to religious belief posed by the newly emerging 'mechanical philosophy'. But this is not how the natural philosophers themselves viewed the situation. Instead it was generally held that Moses and the other biblical writers were perfectly well aware of the most modern scientific theories that were now being discovered, but had chosen to accommodate their language to the needs of ordinary people. Some thought that the new natural philosophy could shed light on the biblical text and that allegorical interpretations had blinded centuries of readers to the science that could be found within it. Isaac Newton maintained that the new discoveries in science involved the uncovering of truths that had been well known to the ancients, including atomic theory, the existence of the vacuum and universal gravitation. The Cambridge Platonist Henry More, whose writings had a great influence on Newton's thinking, believed that the corpuscular theory of Boyle and the Copernican view of the solar system, among other scientific theories, could be discerned in the writings of Moses. But most natural philosophers, as cited above, cautioned against the attempt to extract scientific truths from the Bible.

The accommodation theory appears to have been sufficiently powerful that it became virtually a consensus view among the natural philosophers of the period. Although the idea may now seem rather strange to us since, unlike the early natural philosophers, we are not emerging from centuries of medieval scholasticism, in retrospect we can see that it played an important role in clarifying the distinctive types of knowledge that either religion or science provided. The 'mainstream' opinion among the leading natural philosophers of the 17th century was that the Bible was *not* a kind of scientific textbook that could be looked to as an authority in matters of natural philosophy. The aims of the inspired text were rather theological and ethical, and the book could only be understood properly by those who took some effort to read it according to its historical context, and according to the particular literary style that was being used. It was not Moses' design, wrote George Hughes, 'to make men perfect in all natural and mathematical knowledge, but in that which might make them wise for salvation'. Or, in the pithy words of Galileo: 'The intention of the Holy Ghost is to teach us how one goes to heaven, not how heaven goes.'

Mechanism and meaning

A popular analogy used by the early natural philosophers was to liken the world, or the universe, to a giant machine which operated with clock-like precision. Today the idea of 'mechanism' is often brought into a conversation as if confronting the concept of 'meaning'. Intriguingly, this was not the dominant view of the early natural philosophers. It has also sometimes been suggested that the idea of the universe as a giant machine, and of natural philosophy as an enterprise to delineate the mechanisms of that machine, was inherited from the Greek Atomist philosophers, but was opposed by European theologians because they thought that such a view would be detrimental to a belief in God's creative activity. But neither does this view stand up to close scrutiny.

The new mechanical philosophy that began to prevail during the second half of the 17th century was espoused most vigorously by precisely those natural philosophers for whom belief in God was central to their science. There has been much discussion by historians as to the precise roots of this new vogue for mechanical analogies. Christian theism certainly appeared conducive to the new mechanical philosophy and may well have been one, among many, of the causal agents that led to its prominence in the early modern scientific movement. The debt to the Greek Atomists is not in question, Lucretius' poem *De Rerum Natura*, rediscovered in 1417, going through no less than thirty editions before 1600. But Greek atomism was put through a 'theistic filter' by the Catholic priest Pierre Gassendi (1592–1655), who saw that Christian doctrine was far more compatible with atomism than it was with Aristotelianism, atoms being the building blocks with which God chose to fashion the universe. In this form, far from being the tool of a materialistic philosophy as in the hands of Lucretius, atomism soon became absorbed into the wider stream of mechanical philosophy. Indeed, such was the driving force of 17th-century theism that atomism was soon being pressed as an argument supporting belief in God. As Bacon remarked:

> Nay, even that school which is most accused of atheism does most demonstrate religion; that is, the school of Leucippus, and Democritus, and Epicurus – for it is a thousand times more credible that four mutable elements and one immutable fifth essence, duly and eternally placed, need no God, than that an army of infinite small portions, or seeds unplaced, should have produced this order and beauty without a divine marshal... [30]

What were the essential elements of the 'mechanical philosophy', a term first coined by one of its most ardent proponents, Robert Boyle? Its emphases can best be discerned by comparing them with the Renaissance Naturalism which it rapidly replaced during the course of the 17th century. Renaissance thinking, inherited from the Greeks, had seen the world as ultimately mysterious and human reason quite inadequate to penetrate its depths. 'Ultimate Reality', having some of the characteristics of mind or spirit, was the active principle which permeated everything and everybody in the universe. There was no clear separation between mind and matter, spirit and body: the planets were deemed to be alive; the earth was full of magic signs, 'essences' and 'influences'; the blood contained vital spirits; the universe was constructed on the basis of mathematical harmonies; and 'sympathies' could relate objects separated by long distances in unexpected ways. Explanations of phenomena were dominated by teleology. Stones fell to earth in order to be reunited with their own kind of matter.

Such thinking is well illustrated by the belief, popularized by Paracelsus and Van Helmont, and widely held in the early 17th century, that the best way to heal a wound was not by rubbing ointment into the wound but rather by treating the weapon covered in blood that had caused the wound. William Foster explained the actions of such 'weapon salve' by claiming that the vital spirits in the blood on the weapon had 'sympathetical harmony' to the blood remaining in the body. The anointed weapon was therefore able to communicate 'in a direct invisible line' healing power from the weapon to the wounded person, just as the 'Sun-beames are a messenger betwixt heaven and Earth.'[31] Van Helmont was fond of explaining why the blood of a murdered man runs when the murderer comes near; the spirit in the blood boiled in rage at the presence of the mortal enemy, so causing the blood to flow.

Yet, by the end of the 17th century, mechanical explanations predominated over the 'organistic' as a method of explaining phenomena. When Robert Hooke wrote his *Micrographia* in 1665, the spontaneous growth of mushrooms was explained by use of the mechanical language of 'hammers', 'springs' and 'pins'. The fact that these mechanical analogies are not the most appropriate for describing mushroom growth is beside the point. Rather it was the mechanical analogies which link Hooke's biology of the mid-17th century with the genetic engineering and molecular detail of modern biology. A profound revolution in thought was taking place that eventually swept all before it. Mechanical chains of cause and effect were invoked in place of 'invisible lines' and 'sympathetical harmonies'.

In Descartes' radical dualism, reality became composed of two substances, the *res cogitans*, the 'thinking substance' – our minds – that had none of the properties characteristic of matter, and *res extensa*, material nature, which was completely inert and devoid of any source of activity on its own. Thus, in a single blow, did Descartes drive the spirits that so dominated Renaissance Naturalism out of matter, leaving it passive and waiting for its role in the machine of life. Descartes rejected the idea of atoms but instead promoted the idea of divisible corpuscles. All physical phenomena, such as heat, light and magnetism, could be explained by the behaviour of these invisible particles. When two competing theories were proposed that both explained phenomena equally well by the corpuscular theory, then this was, wrote Descartes, like two clocks that were identical on the outside but which differed in their internal mechanisms. The task of the new mechanical philosophy was to find out the internal mechanisms of the created world. What made the clock tick? The clock analogy was applied to the workings of the heart, Descartes seeing the arrangement of its various parts leading to its pumping action just as a clock worked by the arrangement of its cogs and wheels. Animals lacked rational souls, and so were nothing but complicated machines. If there were automata, said Descartes, 'possessing the organs and outward form of a monkey or some other animal without reason, we should not have had any means of ascertaining that they were not of the same nature as those animals'.

The corpuscular theory of Descartes was applied to the world of chemistry by Robert Boyle, who vigorously promoted the 'clearness of mechanical principles and explications' claiming that the theory was sufficient to explain 'all the phenomena of things corporeal'. In physics, Torricelli (1608–47) discovered the principle of the mercury barometer, finding mechanical explanations for the heights of columns of liquids in inverted tubes, Blaise Pascal (1623–62) confirming the power of mechanical explanations by a series of famous experiments. Harvey's analogy of the heart as a pump led to the first clear understanding of the circulation of the blood. It is generally recognized, said Dr Richard Mead, physician to Queen Anne and well imbued with the new mechanical philosophy, that the body of man is 'a hydraulic machine contrived with the most exquisite art, in which there are numberless tubes properly adjusted and disposed for the conveyance of fluids of different kinds'. The introduction of the microscope (1660–85) opened up a fascinating new world of detailed biological structure which readily lent itself to mechanical types of description, impressing even the cynicism of Jonathan Swift:

Fleas, so naturalists say,
  Have smaller fleas that on them prey.
These have smaller still to bite 'em,
  And so proceed ad infinitum.

The 17th-century scientists were unanimous in their belief that the machines that they described in the natural world around them were God's machines. As Descartes succinctly put the matter:

To those who know how many different *automata* or moving machines can be made by man's industry, with the use of very few pieces, compared to the great multitude of bones, muscles, nerves, arteries, veins and all other parts of an animal's body, it will not seem strange to consider the body as a machine, which being made by the hands of God, is incomparably better ordered, and has more admirable motions than anything which can be invented by man.[32]

Boyle was clearly fascinated by the clock analogy, writing that the world is

like a rare clock, such as may be that at Strasbourg, where all things are so skillfully contrived, that the engine being once set a-moving, all things proceed, according to the artificer's first design... by virtue of the general and primitive contrivance of the whole engine.[33]

Boyle was perfectly aware of the objection that the clock itself might be autonomous, with a God who 'wound up' the universe at the beginning, and then left it to its own mechanical devices, but went on to argue that the more a 'skilful artist' examined the mechanisms of the Strasbourg clock, discerning 'the aptness and sufficiency of the parts to produce the effects emergent from them', the more the artist would understand that the clock was made by 'the skill of an intelligent and ingenious contriver'.

With the exception of Leibniz, who continued to support Aristotle's belief that the laws of nature were internal to nature itself, the 17th-century mechanical natural philosophers saw law as being imposed on matter from outside. Just as well-run societies operated by the rule of law, so the matter of the universe operated according to God's laws, which could be expressed most elegantly in the language of mathematics. In promoting the idea of passive matter, organized by a system of laws, the mechanical philosophers were deliberately excluding the Aristotelian idea, prominent in the thinking of Thomas Aquinas, that God cooperated with the forces of nature in a way that respected their intrinsic properties while he accomplished his creative plan. Gary Deason has argued convincingly that Reformation theology encouraged the acceptance of the new mechanical philosophy precisely because of its insistence on the radical sovereignty of God in creation, leading to a denial of any autonomous role for matter in this process.[34] Calvin, for example, commented:

> Concerning inanimate objects, we ought to hold that, although each one has by nature been endowed with its own property, yet it does not exercise its own power except in so far as it is directed by God's ever-present hand. These are, thus, nothing but instruments to which God continually imparts as much effectiveness as he wills, and according to his own purpose bends and turns them to either one action or another.[35]

God's activity in nature, Calvin taught, was continuous and complete. There were no 'gaps' that could be attributed to forces or agents outside of God's immediate control. Nature was not autonomous. The Word or command of God was the only edict required to bring direction or purpose into inanimate matter. As Robert Boyle expressed it, seeing nature as a living being 'seems not to me very suitable to the profound reverence we owe the divine majesty, since it seems to make the Creator differ too little by far from a created (not to say imaginary) Being'. This same passivity of matter was central to Newton's thinking, clearly imbibed by his reading of Gassendi, Boyle and others during his early years at Cambridge. Material bodies, said Newton, 'cannot be truly understood independently of the Idea of God'. Gravity was not an innate property of matter, but stemmed directly from God's animating power. As Newton wrote to Bentley in 1693: 'That Gravity should be innate, inherent and essential to Matter... is to me so great an Absurdity, that I believe no Man who has in philosophical Matters a competent Faculty of thinking, can ever fall into it.'

There is little doubt that the introduction of mechanical ways of thinking into the minds of natural philosophers during the 17th century has had a most profound impact on the development of modern science. Although the earlier rather rigid mechanical clockwork analogies have long since given way, in physics at least, to the more fluid concepts of quantum mechanics and chaos theory, the idea that *mechanisms*, which can be analysed and understood, underlie complex and apparently mysterious natural phenomena, remains a vital ingredient of the scientific enterprise, not least in contemporary biology. But if something could be understood at a mechanistic level, was there still a role for God's creative activity? Or did God occasionally 'interfere' with machinery which otherwise operated independently, as Newton appears on occasion to have suggested? Or was it possible that the universe operated autonomously, with a role for a 'prime mover' back in the beginning who started the whole universe off, but who then left it to its own devices? It is by tracing some of the answers given to these questions during subsequent centuries that we will then be able to view current debates between the realms of science and faith within their proper historical context.

Chapter 6

Hubble's Warning
The Roots of Modern Science (3) — Science in Support of Conflicting Ideologies

When with bold telescopes I survey the old and newly discovered stars
and planets… when with excellent microscopes I discern… nature's
curious workmanship; when with the help of anatomical knives and the
light of chymical furnaces I study the book of nature… I find myself
exclaiming with the psalmist, How manifold are thy works, O God, in
wisdom hast thou made them all!

Robert Boyle

All errors in politics and morals are based on philosophical errors
and these in turn are connected with scientific errors. There is not
a religious system nor a supernatural extravagance that is not founded
on ignorance of the laws of nature. The inventors, the defenders of
these absurdities could not foresee the successive perfection of the
human mind.

Marquis de Condorcet

The book of nature, which we have to read, is written by the finger
of God.

Michael Faraday

Natural philosophy by the year 1700 was already emerging as an immensely
successful enterprise. Academies and journals had been founded. Scientific
discoveries had been so extensive that they affected the way most intelligent
people looked at the world around them. The earth was firmly in revolution
round the sun, and the sun itself had become merely one of thousands of stars
visible in the vast universe that the telescope had revealed. The new

understanding of matter and motion had been integrated with the new astronomy by the work of Newton. Mechanistic explanations had largely replaced the ancient Greek thinking of sympathies and empathies. The universe was no longer governed by 'souls', as William Gilbert had described it in 1600, but by laws. Mathematics had been successfully integrated into many spheres of natural philosophical enquiry. Natural historians had compiled great new classifications of the animal and plant world, and no country gentleman was complete without a collection of the flora and fauna of his locality. Microscopists had penetrated the fascinating world of the very small. Chemists had failed to transmute metals into gold but had gone some way towards elucidating the nature of elements and compounds.

In retrospect the advances made by the year 1700 may look more modest than they seemed at the time. But that is only because our view of the scientific enterprise itself has changed in the intervening years. At the time, the shores of scientific discovery were like the shores of new continents, there all the time, only waiting to be revealed by the efforts of the natural philosophers. As continent after continent was discovered, so it seemed to many that there would soon be little left for natural philosophers to do, apart from sitting back and contemplating the success of their labours.

The ideological context in which new scientific knowledge was propagated had long-lasting effects on the way the relationship between science and religion was perceived, effects that are still clearly discernible in the 21st century. In the year 1700 the emphasis that came to be known as 'natural theology' remained widely influential – 'the argument for a Designer from the design and purpose in the world especially disclosed by science'.[1] It was common for the new natural philosophy to be presented in such a way that it drew attention to God's creative handiwork. Such was Boyle's enthusiasm for natural theology that he left in his will the sum of £50 per annum 'for ever, or at least for a considerable number of years' in order to institute a series of sermons 'for proving the Christian Religion'. When Richard Bentley, Master of Trinity College, Cambridge, gave the first Boyle lecture in 1692, *A Confutation of Atheism*, he used arguments drawn 'from the structure of animate bodies and the origin and frame of the world'. Indeed, it is difficult to open any work of natural philosophy dating from the second half of the 17th century without persistent reference to the arguments of natural theology, through which certain assumptions run like persistent threads. For example, it was assumed that as science advanced, so the evidence of God's design in creation would become more and more compelling, and that as the works of nature were far above the wisdom of men, so the wisdom of their creator must be far beyond human wisdom.

Newton's natural philosophy was preached from prestigious pulpits to large and prosperous congregations, largely thanks to the Boyle Lectures. Numerous editions of these annual lectures became the means of disseminating Newtonian science to the educated laity both in England and on the Continent. This baptism of Newtonianism into Anglicanism was supported by Newton himself, and helped in creating a sober and rationalistic faith, strongly geared to the needs of a commercial class interested in capitalism, empire, scientific progress, and the applications of the new discoveries to navigation, industry and agriculture. 'Reasonable people must acknowledge a vast cosmic order, imposed by God, and attempt to imitate it in society and government.'[2] As the new philosophy was validated by the established church, so it continued to act as a bulwark against atheism, and in its turn validated the structures of the existing social order. It was rare to find an atheistic natural philosopher in 18th-century England but it also became increasingly rare to find natural philosophers with the kind of personal religious commitment demonstrated by those such as Kepler, Galileo, Boyle, Ray and many others, whose lives and work had so dominated the scientific revolution of the previous century.

The lens through which any form of knowledge is filtered has a profound influence on the associations which that knowledge then carries. The same news can be constructed in a myriad different ways depending on the varying editorial policies of different newspapers. Likewise scientific knowledge can accrue different associations depending on the ideological context in which it is popularized. The Hubble Space Telescope provides an unlikely metaphor. The two-billion-dollar telescope was found to be fatally flawed following its launch due to the inability of its giant polished lens to be focused correctly. This catastrophic error was finally traced to a tiny fleck of paint which had distorted the much smaller lens that had been used in the testing of the main lens. Only after immense further effort and expense was a space mission launched in 1993 to repair the telescope, enabling clearly focused images of deep space to then be successfully collected. One tiny aberration, in this case, was sufficient to completely change the final picture.

Considering the social prestige that the new natural philosophy had already accrued by 1700, it is not surprising to find that there were increasing attempts to utilize its growing influence to support competing worldviews. In some cases the use of natural philosophy to achieve distinctive political goals was overtly ideological. In other cases the 'lens effect' involved a more subtle influence in which science became associated with particular philosophical or religious contexts. In yet other cases the distorting lens involved not the realities of the original historical contexts at all, but the ability of later commentators to get their facts wrong.

The Philosophes in France were a group of scientific popularizers who did much to spread the new natural philosophy. Before considering the role of science in their philosophical and political campaigning, we shall briefly review a way of thinking which in England came to be known as Deism, since it serves as a useful bridge to the work of the Philosophes.

Deism

Deism represented an anticlerical rationalistic movement of the early 18th century. In his *Dictionary of the English Language* (1755) Samuel Johnson defined 'deist' as 'a man who follows no particular religion, but only acknowledges the existence of God, without any other article of faith'. Lord Edward Herbert of Cherbury (1583–1648) has been called 'the father of English deism'. Herbert maintained, rather like Descartes, that certain truths were 'self-evident', such as the existence of God and the need to worship God, and proceeded to berate the church for teaching 'mysteries, prophecies and miracles'. By this definition, 'deism' is probably the predominant worldview held by Europeans today, since belief in 'God' of some description is widespread but is frequently found in the absence of any considered doctrinal beliefs or institutional commitments. It has been remarked rather cynically, though perhaps with some measure of truth, that deism is the 'default button' of present secularized European culture, outright atheism requiring too much thought and commitment. This was not, however, the situation for the early exponents of deism, who wrote partly as a reaction to the Puritan emphasis on the Bible and Christian doctrine.

Later followers of Herbert were even more rigorous in criticizing the more 'supernatural' aspects of Christianity, miracles in particular coming in for special attack. These critics were philosophers or literary men, and were not themselves natural philosophers. Indeed, there is little tendency in the earlier deistic writings to use natural philosophy itself to attack religious precepts. The deists felt that they were defending 'true religion', derived from 'self-evident' or 'purely rational' assumptions, against the pagan and irrational accretions that had been brought into true religion by the machinations of uneducated priests combined with the force of tradition. The attack on miracles was made not in the name of natural philosophy but in the name of reason. As John Toland put it, 'Whatever is contrary to Reason can be no Miracle.'[3] Miracles were criticized not so much for their scientific impossibility as for their moral unreasonableness.

As the great laws of the Newtonian universe became more widely known, so the later deistic writings become more concerned with the impossibility of God 'interfering' with his laws in performing a miracle. Peter Annet (1693–1769), the last of the British deists, wrote that 'God has settled the laws of nature by His wisdom and power, and therefore cannot alter them consistently with His Perfections.'[4] Miracles were 'contrary to the course of nature'. It is this stream of thought that has left us the more modern meaning of the term 'deism', namely, the idea that a 'god' or 'intelligence' was responsible for making the universe 'at the beginning' according to certain fixed laws but that this universe ever since has operated autonomously according to these laws. In this view, the original 'god' or 'intelligence' is no longer involved with the ongoing properties or existence of the universe. In contrast, the relationship between God and his creation expressed in Christian theology is termed 'theism', the view held by the Keplers, Galileos and Boyles of the 17th century, that God not only created the universe in the beginning, but is in a moment by moment relationship with it, actively upholding and sustaining both its existence and its properties. In 'theism' the universe is viewed as contingent ('dependent') upon God's continuing creative actions, whereas in 'deism' the universe is non-contingent ('independent').

The early-18th-century discussion between the deists and those who espoused natural theology provides an interesting example of the way in which a heavy metaphysical burden can be placed on the sciences that they are quite unable to sustain. Toland emphasized gravity as an innate property of matter, existing independently of God's actions. Others, such as Newton himself, saw gravity (in the words of William Whiston, his successor as Lucasian Professor at Cambridge) as God's 'general, immechanical, immediate power'. Scientific theories became a focus for theological debate.

By the mid-18th century deism was already a spent force in England, but it was at just this time that it began to grow in influence in France and Germany, and many of the themes of deism were continued by the literary writers of the French Enlightenment.

The Philosophes

The Philosophes were a heterogeneous collection of French writers and philosophers who, during the 18th century, popularized the findings of the natural philosophers to the French public. Bernard le Bouvier de Fontenelle (whom we met in chapter 4) is generally held to represent the first of the Philosophes, his long life (1657–1757) encompassing the rise of the Newtonian worldview. For fifty of those years (1691–1741) De Fontenelle was secretary of the Paris Academy of Sciences and in this post transmitted natural philosophy to the French bourgeoisie with great success. As in England at the same period, natural philosophy met with great public interest among educated people. During the late 17th century we learn from De Fontenelle that Paris was full of foreigners who came to attend conferences or to observe demonstrations by various natural philosophers. Crowds of fashionable ladies were reported to be attending courses on chemistry given by Nicolas Lemery (1645–1715). De

Fontenelle was a writer and, though he later wrote some mathematical works, never himself made much contribution to natural philosophy. His gift was rather to publish the scientific discoveries of others in a clear, intelligible and witty prose. His famous dialogue *The Plurality of Worlds* (1686) went through many editions and became a model for future popularizers of science, although De Fontenelle's comment that the book was designed to bring the new astronomy 'within the grasp of the feminine intelligence' might not be received so warmly today. However, another comment of De Fontenelle could well act as a relevant motto for any modern laboratory: 'Make sure of the facts before you bother about their cause.'

De Fontenelle was a sceptic and, in contrast to the pulpits so often used to preach the Newtonian worldview in England, his reports of scientific discoveries were frequently cast in a distinctly anticlerical mould. This slant is also very noticeable in the funeral orations that De Fontenelle had to give as part of his job as secretary of the Academy of Sciences, which amounted to potted résumés of well-known members of the Academy. Again and again we are told that the *savant's* family had intended him to study theology prior to entering the church, but that the youth had found such an education restricting and, upon discovering the philosophy of Descartes, had 'seen the light' and taken up natural philosophy. The tone of these orations is distinctly triumphalist, the new philosophy being cast as the hero of a new age that would sweep away prejudice and traditional dogmas. Yet, as Butterfield remarks, De Fontenelle 'had held his sceptical views before coming into touch with the scientific movement at all... A scepticism which really had a literary genealogy combined to give to the results of the 17th-century scientific movement a bias which was rarely to be seen in the scientists themselves and which Descartes would have repudiated.'[5]

Another major figure of the Enlightenment was François Marie Arouet, better known under his pen name of Voltaire, whose long and turbulent life (1694–1778) was dedicated to fiery and satirical campaigns either for or against particular causes (Voltaire was not one to sit on the fence). Imprisoned in the Bastille during his early twenties for insulting the Regent, Voltaire was released after eleven months on condition that he went to England, where he spent the period 1726–29 in agreeable exile among the London intelligentsia. During this period Voltaire became deeply influenced by the empirical philosophy of John Locke and by the natural philosophy of Isaac Newton, whose funeral Voltaire attended in Westminster Abbey. Returning to France, Voltaire popularized Newtonianism in his *Elements de la Philosophie de Newton* (1738), and delivered the *coup de grâce* to Descartes in his *Lettres Philosophiques* (1734), Descartes' philosophy until then having dominated the educated French speaking world. Together with his mistress, Mme du Chatelet, Voltaire carried out some chemical research in a laboratory established in her chateau, at the same time continuing his study of Newton. However, Voltaire is remembered not for these modest incursions into science but for his substantial literary output, and for his bitter attacks upon the beliefs and practices of Catholics and Jews.

It should not be thought from Voltaire's anticlericalism that he was an atheist. Far from it. Voltaire campaigned vigorously against atheism, pointing out in the opening pages of his popularized version of Newton's views that 'the entire philosophy of Newton necessarily leads to the knowledge of a supreme Being, who has created everything and arranged everything freely'. Voltaire continued the theme with which Newton had finished his *Principia*, pointing out that God was at liberty to make the world as He, and not Descartes, had seen fit. In the same book Voltaire criticized Descartes for leading people away from God, pointing out that he had 'known many led by Cartesianism to admit no other God than the immensity of things; and I have on the contrary seen no Newtonian who was not a theist in the most rigorous sense'.

Voltaire's comments on philosophy and religion often made up for their lack of profundity by pithy sarcasm or mordant wit. In the article on 'atheism' in his *Dictionnaire Philosophique* Voltaire stated his position succinctly:

We are intelligent beings, and intelligent beings could not have been formed by a blind, brute, insensible thing; there is certainly some difference between the ideas of Newton and the droppings of a mule. Newton's intelligence, therefore, came from another intelligence.[6]

Voltaire's arguments for the existence of God were those of traditional natural theology, and in the same article in his *Dictionnaire* Voltaire carries on an imaginary debate with an atheist in which he maintains that God's intelligent design was demonstrated 'as much in the meanest insect as in the planets... The disposition of a fly's wings or of the feelers of a snail is sufficient to confound you.' Yet although Voltaire vigorously defended a deistic position, like the other Philosophes he was careful to emphasize current limitations of understanding about the natural world. It was precisely because Newton had refused to speculate on the mechanisms underlying gravitational attraction that Voltaire found his natural philosophy so appealing.

Not all the Philosophes were deists. Some were more rigorous materialists, a development hastened by startling scientific discoveries that appeared to undermine the arguments of natural theology. In 1740 it was observed that a hydra behaved like an animal, although it produced buds like a plant. When cut into pieces, new hydra could develop spontaneously out of the pieces. This discovery led to a flurry of speculation about the origins of life and the nature of animal souls. Was the soul of the hydra divisible? Was this an example of matter acting independently of God? The debate was intensified by the findings of John

Needham, an English Catholic priest, in 1745, when he thought that he had demonstrated conclusively the emergence of moving microscopic animals by spontaneous generation from a sample of heated gravy inside a sealed vessel. It took a further century before this observation was shown to be incorrect (clearly the air inside had not been as sterile as he thought). Such experiments were threatening to the tenets of natural theology since they appeared to show that matter could spontaneously organize itself into life, whereas the natural theologians thought that the creation of life could only occur by special divine action. Voltaire poured scorn on Needham, accusing him of atheism and saying that his observations must be mistaken.

A French doctor called Julien de la Mettrie (1709–51) was very impressed by the new data which appeared to support the idea that matter organized itself spontaneously, publishing his *L'Homme Machine* in 1747 anonymously in The Netherlands. La Mettrie concluded that if nature was spontaneously active, then living matter was 'nothing but' a machine and there was no need for a god. La Mettrie's book was soon banned in France for its rigorous materialism, and La Mettrie himself (who clearly did not manage to stay anonymous for long) was forced to seek refuge with Frederick the Great of Prussia. Descartes had warned long before that people might extend his theory of animal machines to man, and so promote atheism. La Mettrie fulfilled Descartes' worst forebodings, maintaining that man was just another piece of machinery like the animals, and that priests were motivated only by prejudice and fanaticism in thinking otherwise.

A thorough-going materialism was expounded most eloquently during this period by Baron d'Holbach (1723–89), a German who passed most of his life in Paris in the circle of the Philosophes. D'Holbach's *Système de la Nature* (1770) argued that matter was inherently moving and active, and that no outside force was needed to set it in motion. Just as microscopic animals could spontaneously arise from organic matter, so man also could appear by spontaneous generation. Far from nature being governed by chance, D'Holbach saw matter as being governed by a rigid determinism. The idea of creation was against reason, since the mind could not conceive of a time when nothing had existed, and neither could it conceive of a time when everything would have disappeared. As Goodman comments, 'D'Holbach's work is remarkable less for its originality than for its extreme opinions. Perhaps as clearly as any other work of the period, it developed that tendency of 18th-century French thought to exclude God from Nature. Nothing could be further removed from the type of natural philosophy which was determined to discover God everywhere in Nature (Boyle, Newton, Voltaire).'[7]

The most influential publication of the Philosophes was, without doubt, the *Encyclopedie*, which appeared in seventeen volumes between 1751 and 1765.

Inspired in part by the inductive philosophy of Francis Bacon, its subtitle was the *Analytical Dictionary of the Sciences, Arts and Trades*. Among the total of 160 contributors nearly all the Philosophes were represented, but there were also articles by working craftsmen who wrote technical articles describing their crafts. The editors Denis Diderot (1713–84) and D'Alembert (1717–83), set the optimistic and utilitarian tone of the volumes. The technology was presented in such a way that it carried the ideology with it. There were few if any direct attacks upon religion as such, but there was a strong underlying assumption that the cause of humanity would be promoted not by correct theological doctrines, but by right secular knowledge. Man was naturally good and was capable of perfection by the acquisition of knowledge. The *Encyclopedie* would ensure that 'our children, better instructed than we, may at the same time become more virtuous and happy'.

The various volumes of the *Encyclopedie* revealed the Newtonian world of harmony, order and cosmic law, which the Philosophes were quick to point out contrasted with the society of their day. In place of cosmic order they saw conflict and disorder, priests and noblemen who fostered ignorant superstitions and exploited them for power. The answer was to establish a new 'science of humanity' in which the rational laws of human nature would be applied to the organization of just and well-ordered societies. Obscurity and error would be purged by doubt and criticism. Reason would be the new tool to build a world devoid of superstition, supported by the prestige of natural philosophy. Natural science would become social science. As Gillispie points out, 'the noble 18th-century faith in natural law involved a fundamental confusion between the declarative and the normative senses of law, between 'is' and 'ought",[8] a point to which we shall return later.

Diderot's own progression from deism to a position closer to atheism during the course of his life appears, with the advantage of hindsight, as a logical progression. In his *Pensées Philosophiques* of 1746, Diderot was still using the classical arguments of deism: 'Is not the divinity as clearly imprinted on the eye of a mite as it is in the faculty to think in the works of the great Newton?' But three years later Diderot published his *Letter on the Blind for the Use of Those Who Can See*, in which he places sceptical comments in the mouth of a blind man for whom the beauties of the natural world had no meaning. The blind man complains to a minister of religion that 'god' is brought in to explain those aspects of the natural world which natural philosophy had not yet explained, a perfectly valid point that helps to explain why deistic arguments for the existence of God were doomed to failure. It was inevitable, as Diderot's blind man correctly realized, that a god who was simply a convenient 'explanation' to cope with gaps in our scientific knowledge would not last for very long. Diderot's blind man was in fact based on a contemporary character, the brilliant blind philosopher Nicholas Saunderson who, despite his disability, became Lucasian Professor of Mathematics at Cambridge University. In Diderot's hands the blind philosopher describes how his skills in geometry had attracted the curious 'from the ends of England', and how the ignorance of these people led them to introduce God into accounts of natural phenomena.

The spirit of the Enlightenment is perhaps best captured in the words of one of its most distinguished protagonists, the French mathematician the Marquis de Condorcet who, right at the end of the 18th century, looked back with obvious pleasure at the practical benefits that had been brought to society by natural philosophy, but with even greater enthusiasm at the radical changes in people's thinking that had occurred:

> All errors in politics and morals are based on philosophical errors and these in turn are connected with scientific errors. There is not a religious system nor a supernatural extravagance that is not founded on ignorance of the laws of nature. The inventors, the defenders of these absurdities could not foresee the successive perfection of the human mind.[9]

Condorcet's faith in the future of humankind was boundless. Science was going to remove the various sources of human misery and bring universal happiness. Science and 'reason' (which, in the usage of the day, often meant little more than what we would now call 'common sense') would sweep away prejudice, superstition, priests and despots, and would soon be replaced by enlightenment and liberty. Sadly Condorcet himself was pursued by the agents of the Jacobin Reign of Terror that followed the French Revolution, finally dying in prison in 1794. After the fall of Robespierre the rationalist tradition of the Enlightenment became institutionalized in the educational foundations of the new French Republic and, in this form, the ideas of the Philosophes, such as Condorcet, lived on.

It should not be thought that the emphases of the French Enlightenment were necessarily reflected in the beliefs of contemporary natural philosophers themselves. These spanned the range from devout Catholicism to atheism, with many shades in between. As the French scientist De Maupertuis observed in his *Essai de cosmologie* (1756):

> All the philosophers of our time belong to two sects. One group wishes to subjugate nature to a purely material order and to exclude all intelligent principles from it; or at least to banish final causes from the explanation of phenomena. The others, on the contrary, make constant use of these causes to discover through all of nature the views of the Creator, penetrating his intent in the smallest of phenomena. According to the first group, the

universe could do without God; or at the very least the marvels of nature do not prove Him to be a necessary agent. According to the latter, the tiniest parts of the universe constitute repeated demonstrations [of his being]: his power, wisdom and goodness are painted on the wings of butterflies and in every spider's web.[10]

One natural philosopher who belonged more to De Maupertuis' first group was Antoine Lavoisier (1743–94), one of the founders of the modern sciences of both chemistry and biochemistry.[11] Lavoisier's career flourished in the Paris Academy of Sciences, and his Parisian base brought him into close contact with leading members of the Enlightenment, with whose thinking Lavoisier appears to have been largely in sympathy. Nevertheless Lavoisier was no anticlericalist crusader, his own brilliant experimental investigations leaving little time for such pursuits. By the early 1790s Lavoisier was heavily involved in defending the Academy against increasingly bitter political attacks, falling victim to the guillotine in 1794, not because of his science but because he was a Farmer General, authorized to collect taxes for the pre-revolutionary government.

The mathematical astronomer Pierre Simon Laplace (1749–1827), whose quiet but persistent exclusion of God from his scientific writings was in marked contrast to many of his contemporaries, has often been cited as an example of a thoroughly atheistic and materialistic scientist of the period, embued with Enlightenment ideals. The historical data available suggests a more complex and in many ways more interesting picture. In a much quoted anecdote, when Napoleon Bonaparte asked Laplace what role God played in his natural philosophy, Laplace replied, 'Sir, I have no need of that hypothesis.' Although this incident is of doubtful historical accuracy, the tenor of Laplace's reply summarizes accurately his belief, apparent from his writings, that any concept of God as an 'explanation' for the gaps in our scientific knowledge is quite superfluous. The only room for 'god' in Laplace's scientific writings is as a Supreme Intelligence. Laplace suggested that this perfect philosophical mathematician could, in principle, determine everything that was going to happen to the objects in the universe 'for any instant of the past or future'. In practice humans could only estimate probabilities of events due to their 'ignorance of the diverse causes that produce the events and their complexity.'

In 1796 Laplace proposed the 'nebular hypothesis' in order to explain the physical origins of the solar system. Until that time the origins of the universe had been seen by the natural theologians as due to a first cause, God the Creator. But as Laplace is reported to have said to Bonaparte: 'a chain of natural causes would account for the construction and preservation of the wonderful system [of the world]'. By the turn of the century Laplace was widely perceived as being an atheistic scientist, and indeed is found listed in the *Dictionary of Atheists* that was published in 1800. Nevertheless in his personal life Laplace remained a practising Catholic and there is no foundation in the idea that he became an atheist.[12] It can be speculated that Laplace saw more clearly than many of his contemporaries that the 'god' of deistic philosophy, brought in as a 'hypothesis' to plug the gaps of scientific ignorance, was far from the theism of traditional Christian theology.

The French biologist Georges Cuvier was of Protestant background, being raised in the tiny principality of Montbeliard, now on the Swiss border of France.[13] Like Laplace, Cuvier was concerned to establish his science as a separate discipline, free from philosophical and theological controversies. Cuvier arrived in Paris in 1795 after the worst of the revolutionary excesses were over, there to show a particular ability in the art of social climbing, without which it was then impossible to obtain the necessary funding and influence to establish a career as a natural scientist, the role of patrons at the time being somewhat similar to that of grant-giving bodies today. Obtaining patronage from diverse directions enabled Cuvier to weather the rapid changes in fortune of his various patrons as the political intrigues of post-revolutionary Paris exerted their toll, much as a sensible laboratory now should be cautious about being over-dependent on a single source of income (for not dissimilar reasons...). As Cuvier progressed in his career, so he accumulated, as his contemporaries remarked, 'more posts than any single man had the right to'.

Cuvier joined the staff of the Museum of Natural History in Paris in 1795, and his subsequent career was largely based round the Museum. It was there that he began to unravel the earth's history by the study of fossils. His work had a strongly empirical emphasis, and Cuvier criticized those naturalists who 'seem to have scarcely any idea of the propriety of investigating facts before they construct their systems'. Nevertheless, Cuvier's own understanding of the natural world developed within a neoplatonic framework in which the natural world could be divided into a few basic plans of organization or 'types'. The animal kingdom was divided into four branches, and each branch consisted of innumerable species created according to their own fixed structural plans, each individual plan being a variation of the overall 'plan' of the particular branch. Each species was therefore fixed and could not change into another. Cuvier was the first to demonstrate from the fossil record that animal extinctions had occurred. Extinctions happened, said Cuvier, when an individual organism varied beyond the 'master plan' imposed upon it during its original creation. The geology of the planet could only be understood by supposing that 'this earth had often been troubled by terrible events... Living beings without number have been the victims of these upheavals... entire species have vanished for ever, leaving traces hardly recognizable even by the naturalist.'

Considering his support for the idea of 'fixed species', there is a certain irony in the fact that Cuvier's palaeontology later provided an important contribution to Darwin's theory of the origin of species. Cuvier also vigorously opposed the ideas of his older colleague at the Museum, Jean Baptiste Lamarck (1744–1829), who proposed a transformist theory of species in which nature produced an ordered Chain of Being, environmental forces then acting on this innate order to produce acquired characteristics. In Lamarck's view, the small changes in animals and plants so produced could then be passed on to offspring, the eventual accumulation of changes resulting in a new species.

In the more Whiggish literature on the history of science, the controversy between Cuvier and Lamarck has sometimes been pictured as the free-thinking Lamarck propounding a theory of evolution that was suppressed by the more religious and doctrinaire Cuvier. But both biologists were influenced by theological considerations. Lamarck's concept of God's activity in creation was immanent to the point of pantheism, holding that there was an innate power conferred on nature by God that impelled organisms to reach higher and higher levels of complexity until the pinnacle of creation was reached in the human species (ideas not dissimilar to those of Teilhard de Chardin in the 20th century). Cuvier's emphasis on a series of creative events, interspersed with a sequence of catastrophes, may have been more in keeping with the Protestant emphasis on the acts of God in creation, although his belief in the fixity of species seems to have depended much more on his neoplatonic philosophy than on his theology.

On another issue, theological considerations worked in a different way. Lamarck's deism led him to believe that God's creation was rationally ordered and intelligible, and so it was difficult for him to believe that species had become extinct since this seemed to indicate disorder. Cuvier, on the other hand, did believe that species had become extinct, because the fossil data pointed strongly in that direction, but seemed only mildly concerned that this posed questions for God's providence. Cuvier was certainly not a supporter of the 'Mosaic geology' that featured in geological controversies in England at the time, and apparently did not believe that scientific data on such matters could be derived from the Bible. In his *Preliminary Discourse*, perhaps his best-known popular work, Cuvier strongly supported the idea that the new field of geology should develop freely without becoming embroiled in theological and philosophical controversies. Cuvier was clearly concerned to accomplish for geology what his contemporary Laplace was achieving for mathematical astronomy – a new field of natural enquiry with well-defined borders that would deliberately exclude the wider questions of philosophy.

On a personal level Cuvier does not seem to have been particularly religious but was nevertheless a strong public supporter of the Protestant minority in France. However, as Outram reports, although Cuvier supported the Protestant communities at an administrative level 'he also manifested very little concern with the spirituality of Protestantism'.

The diverse religious opinions and practices of Lavoisier, Laplace and Cuvier illustrate how far were the lives of working natural philosophers of the period from the anticlerical crusades of the Philosophes. Yet it was the campaigns of the Philosophes that had the long-term effect of linking natural philosophy with materialism and anticlericalism in the French-speaking world.

The English Nonconformists

In contrast to the situation in France, in England the idea that there was a synergistic, or at least harmonious, relationship between science and religion was fostered not only by Anglican Newtonianism but also by various components of Nonconformism. The term 'Nonconformity' was used to describe any doctrine or practice that refused to conform to the established Church of England. Originally used of movements within the established church, the term took on a new meaning with the founding of several new denominations, such as the Presbyterians, Baptists and Quakers, during the 17th century. The movement to establish separate churches was accelerated by the Corporation Act of 1661, which barred Nonconformists from holding municipal office, and by the Act of Uniformity of 1662 which expelled all nonconforming clergy from positions within the established church. During the 18th century the term 'Nonconformist' was extended to include the newer denominations such as Methodists and Unitarians (Unitarians did not accept the deity of Christ).

A correlation between technical or scientific activity and Nonconformism during the 17th and 18th century has frequently been noted by historians. The precise reasons for historical correlations are notoriously difficult to delineate, this one being no exception.[14] Nevertheless, the fact that a correlation exists at all helps to explain why, in England at least, science generally continued to be viewed as being closely linked to theology. One reason for the association of science with Nonconformism was the influence of the 'Dissenting Academies', established as a result of Nonconformists being excluded by law from studying in the traditional educational institutions, then almost entirely under the control of the established Church of England. While the classics still dominated the curriculum in the universities, the Dissenting Academies placed much greater emphasis on scientific and technical subjects.

Three examples illustrate the diversity of Nonconformist contributions to science.

Joseph Priestley

Joseph Priestley (1733–1804), discoverer of oxygen and a co-founder with Lavoisier of modern chemistry, recalls in his autobiography that at the Dissenting Academy at Northampton that he attended:

We were permitted to ask whatever questions, and to make whatever remarks we pleased; and we did it with the greatest, but without any offensive, freedom. The general plan of our studies... was exceedingly favourable to free inquiry, as we were referred to authors on both sides of every question, and were even required to give an account of them... The public library contained all the books to which we were referred.[15]

There was a tendency at the academies to emphasize those aspects of science that had technical and commercial applications, and many of their graduates played prominent parts in the industrial revolution. Some were well equipped with scientific equipment and this, combined with the atmosphere of 'free inquiry' which Priestley describes, led others into careers in natural philosophy. John Dalton, Quaker and founder of the atomic theory, was a lecturer at the Manchester Academy, founded in 1786.

Dissenting religion also characterized the Lunar Society of Birmingham, so-called because their meetings were held on the nearest Monday to the new moon. This was an informal group of fourteen men linked by a common interest in science and its applications, many of whom were sympathetic to radical politics and favoured both the American Revolution and the French Revolution in its earlier stages. Its members included Erasmus Darwin, physician, botanist, poet and grandfather of Charles Darwin, James Watt the engineer and Joseph Priestley.

In many ways the life of Joseph Priestley typifies the linkage between science and Nonconformity in 18th-century England. Living before the age when specialization became the norm, Priestley is mainly remembered for his discoveries on the chemistry of gases. Yet he was made a Fellow of the Royal Society not for these discoveries, but for his *History of Electricity*, and the twenty or more books that he wrote during his lifetime ranged in topic from church history and politics to history and philosophy. Besides this, as Priestley himself records, he had 'a pretty good knowledge' of Greek, Latin, Hebrew, French, Italian, 'High Dutch', Chaldean and Syriac. After graduating from his Dissenting Academy, Priestley became a Nonconformist minister, running both a school and a chapel, and eventually earning enough to purchase his first 'philosophical instruments' (scientific equipment). During this period Priestley's theology gradually shifted to Unitarianism, and he became increasingly convinced that Christianity had been corrupted by various additions and distortions introduced since the days of the apostles. Coleridge considered that Priestley was the 'author of modern Unitarianism'. Highly independent in his attitudes and opinions, Priestley saw one of his life's tasks as demonstrating that his 'pure and original' form of Christianity was more amenable to 18th-century rationalism than the 'corrupted' versions then being practised.

In later life Priestley's scientific research was made much easier following his employment as librarian by the Earl of Shelburne, who later became Prime Minister in 1782, the post of librarian being designed by the Earl to leave plenty of time for experiments. Following this period (1773–80), Priestley became minister of a Unitarian Church in Birmingham, recording that this new job was 'highly favourable to every object I had in view, philosophical or theological'. It was during this period, for example, that Priestley was active in the Lunar Society. Josiah Wedgwood, Darwin's maternal grandfather, thought Priestley a genius, supporting his research with cash and laboratory equipment.

Priestley's visit to Paris in 1774 provides a good example of the immense gulf which then existed between the 'holy alliance' of science and religion in England, compared with the situation in France where science was so often used by the Philosophes as an ideological weapon for berating the church. As Priestley recounts in his usual robust style, the Philosophes were somewhat surprised to find that one of England's most famous natural philosophers of that era displayed a personal religious commitment:

I did not wonder... to find all the philosophical persons to whom I was introduced at Paris, unbelievers in Christianity, and even professed atheists. As I chose on all occasions to appear as a Christian, I was told by some of them that I was the only person they had ever met with, of whose understanding they had any opinion, who professed to believe Christianity. But on interrogating them on the subject, I soon found that they had given no proper attention to it, and did not really know what Christianity was.[16]

One of the fascinations with Priestley's writings is his serious attempt to relate the faith that so dominated his life with his thinking and experimentation in natural philosophy. The main aim of his *Disquisitions* was to demonstrate that a thoroughly materialistic view of man was perfectly compatible with Christian doctrine and that the Cartesian dualism between mind and body was quite unnecessary. There was no such thing as a separate immaterial 'soul', said Priestley, the idea of the soul as a substance distinct from the body being 'part of the system of heathenism, and was from thence introduced into Christianity which has derived the greatest part of its corruptions from this source'. The brain is the seat of thought, and thought does not survive the destruction of the brain. Thought was the property of a material brain and the brain did not require an immaterial 'extra' to provide this property. Priestley took the philosopher Locke to task for clinging to the idea of an immaterial soul. 'The common opinion of the soul of man surviving the body was... introduced in Christianity', wrote Priestley, 'from the Oriental and Greek philosophy, which in many respects exceedingly altered and debased the true Christian system.' The

Christian view of eternal life was dependent on the resurrection of the body, not on the immortality of the soul, Christians being convinced that matter itself was good because created by God, so rejecting the neoplatonic idea that matter itself was somehow evil. When someone dies, maintained Priestley, the body that decomposes may as well be recomposed by the being who first composed it, not by a miracle, but by some natural law unknown to us.

In his *Memoirs*, written in 1787, Priestley records his gratitude for having lived 'in an age and country in which I have been at full liberty both to investigate, and by preaching and writing to propagate, religious truth'. Unfortunately for Priestley, the Revolution in France was followed by hysterical reactions in England over the next few years in an attempt to defend both Church and King. As both a well-known Dissenter and virtually the only well-known natural philosopher of his day to hold radical political views, Priestley became a prime target for these reactions. While celebrating with some friends the anniversary of the French Revolution on 14 July 1791, a mob burnt down Priestley's church in Birmingham, and then proceeded to burn his house also, demolishing as Priestley records 'my library, apparatus, and, as far as they could, everything belonging to me'. Priestley was not attacked for his science, but for his politics. There is a certain irony in the fact that Lavoisier, whose scientific discoveries were so linked with those of Priestley, fell victim to the guillotine only three years later due to his political connections. However, fortunately for Priestley, killing the opposition was not an English tradition, at least not in the 18th century. Instead, Priestley set sail for America in the year that Lavoisier died, so inspiring the poet Coleridge to incorporate Priestley into a sonnet, surely one of the few natural philosophers to be featured in the poetry of the 18th century:

> *Though rous'd by that dark Vizir Riot rude*
> *Have driven our PRIESTLEY o'er the Ocean swell;*
> *Though Superstition and her wolfish brood*
> *Bay his mild radiance, impotent and fell;*
> *Calm in his halls of brightness he shall dwell!... (and so on)*

Priestley spent the last ten years of his life in America, where he was treated very well and showered with various honours (not the last example of an English person badly treated in his own country doing rather well on the other side of the Atlantic), eventually dying peacefully in his home in 1804 by the banks of the Susquehanna River.

John Wesley

A stream of Nonconformism very different from that espoused by Priestley was the Methodist movement started by John Wesley (1703–91). Wesley was an itinerant preacher and writer whose teaching had a widespread popular influence in England during the 18th century, his influence soon spreading via his followers to many other parts of the world. Wesley was no scientist, but popularized natural philosophy in the context of his particular religious commitment and work. He therefore provides a further interesting example of the way in which attitudes towards questions of science and faith can be moulded by the ideological context in which scientific information is communicated. In the world of 18th-century France, as we have seen, the communication of the latest discoveries in natural philosophy were carried out in the largely secular context of Enlightenment philosophy by popularizers of science who were, for the large part, not themselves scientists. Wesley's popularizing of science in England, in contrast, reinforced the notion that there was a 'holy alliance' between science and theology.[17]

It is not clear whether Wesley's interest in science was any less or greater than that of any other educated gentleman of an age in which it was fashionable to maintain a broad interest in the findings of natural philosophy. Wesley's influence lies simply in the fact that he was a great publicist of all his views, producing 230 original works during his lifetime, many of which were translated into other languages. Unlike the Nonconformist Priestley, the Anglican Wesley was educated at Oxford, the birth of Methodism as a separate denomination taking place late in his career. But, like Priestley, Wesley had an immensely broad education, mastering German, French, Spanish, Italian, Greek, Latin and Hebrew, and devouring an extraordinary number of books during his itinerant travels. As Wesley records in his journal, during one seven-year period he read 500 or 600 books on philosophy, history, theology and natural philosophy. Among the books on natural philosophy were Benjamin Franklin's *Experiments and Observations on Electricity*, Joseph Priestley's *History and Present State of Electricity* and a book by Gravesande on Newton's natural philosophy. Wesley was also in the habit of scanning the *Philosophical Transactions of the Royal Society*. Wesley's own books included a book on medicine called *Primitive Physic*, *The Desideratum: Or Electricity Made Plain and Useful* and a general treatise on natural philosophy, *A Survey of the Wisdom of God in the Creation: Or a Compendium of Natural Philosophy*. None of these books was particularly original, their aim being to communicate popular digests of natural philosophy, particularly information which would be of utilitarian benefit to the average reader. Despite Wesley's wide reading, the science was not always up-to-date, but the books had a wide distribution, his *Primitive Physic* alone going through at least thirty-two English editions from 1747 to 1828, and his book on electricity going through five editions between 1760 and 1781. Wesley not only wrote about science, but included it in his sermons, suggesting in one sermon that his hearers should amuse themselves by reading in several branches of natural philosophy and undertaking philosophical experiments.

Wesley seems to have had a particular fascination with electricity, a hot topic of research in the mid-18th century. In 1768 he recorded in his Journal:

> At my leisure hours this week, I read Dr Priestley's ingenious book on Electricity. He seems to have accurately collected and well digested all that is known on that curious subject. But how little is that all! Indeed the use of it we know; at least, in some good degree. We know it is a thousand medicines in one, in particular, that it is the most efficacious medicine, in nervous disorders of every kind, which has ever yet been discovered.

This passage illustrates well Wesley's penchant for practical science and medicine. He purchased four 'electrical machines' (examples of which have survived) for treating patients in the dispensaries that he established for the poor, and was not averse to trying out the machine on himself. In an age in which it was common for ministers to practice medicine, Wesley frequently commented on the medical condition of the thousands of people that he met during a normal week's travels, his observations on what we would now call psychosomatic medicine being particularly astute:

> The passions have a greater influence on health than most people are aware of... Till the passion, which caused the disease is calmed, medicine is applied in vain.
>
> Why do not all physicians consider how far bodily disorders are caused or influenced by the mind, and in those cases which are utterly out of their sphere call in the assistance of a minister...?

Wesley's popularizing of science was thoroughly within the Baconian tradition in being strong on experimentation and weak on theory and mathematics. His books on natural philosophy tend to be mere collections of observations, with little attempt at an overall synthesis of ideas, and it is clear that Wesley had a personal aversion to mathematics. The idea that Wesley was anti-Copernican in his views, a myth apparently created through the 'conflict' literature of Victorian England (on which more below), has no textual foundation, and indeed Wesley gave clear broad support to the Copernican system in his *Compendium*. However, he mistrusted contemporary astronomers, largely because of their disagreements and his own scepticism about the accuracy with which angles of parallax were then measured.

The holy alliance between science and religion in 18th-century England had less of the passion and conviction which had been its chief characteristic a century earlier. Yet the discourse of natural philosophy, varied as it was, still took place largely within a framework in which talk of God and his works was seen as normal, and it remained widely accepted that theology had a close bearing upon natural philosophy, convictions in natural philosophy having equally inevitable consequences for theology. This trend continued on into the first half of the 19th century, and within the Nonconformist tradition is symbolized by one of the most famous British scientists of all time, Michael Faraday.

Michael Faraday[18]

Faraday (1791–1867) managed to out-Nonconform all the Nonconformist scientists that have been mentioned so far by belonging to a tiny denomination called the Sandemanians, a splinter group from the Church of Scotland. Faraday was not, therefore, merely a dissenter, but a dissenter from other Protestant churches. His denomination was named after Robert Sandeman (1717–73), one of the church's early leaders. The aim of the Sandemanians was to return to a form of church organization based entirely on the Bible and to practise what they perceived as a pure form of New Testament Christianity. When Faraday made his own confession of faith in 1821 there were only about 600 members of the denomination, and the numbers were already in decline.

Victorian biographers have a tendency to iron all the wrinkles out of the lives of their heroes. Even taking this factor into consideration, there seems little doubt that Faraday was an exceptionally attractive character, whose humility in the midst of fame endeared him to a generation of scientific colleagues, as well as to a wider public to whom Faraday was so concerned to communicate the latest discoveries of science. Far from being the narrow-minded bigot that one might expect on learning that he was a member of such a tiny religious grouping, in reality Faraday had a generosity and calmness of spirit that inspired this poetic obituary in the magazine *Punch*:

A priest of Truth: his office to expound
 Earth's mysteries to all who willed to hear –
Who in the book of science sought and found,
 With love, that knew all reverence, but no fear.

The last few words reflect a trait recognized in Faraday by several observers – an empathy with the natural world that he was investigating, so that rather than 'wresting secrets from nature', Faraday gave the impression that 'nature's secrets' were readily available to someone who could think up the correct experiments. As Faraday told John Tyndall in 1851, 'Nature is our kindest friend'. Tyndall was Professor of Natural Philosophy at the Royal Institution and one of Faraday's collaborators over a period of many years. Although he had no sympathy for dogmatic religion, Tyndall was so impressed by Faraday that he wrote one of the many Victorian biographies of Faraday's life, asserting that his character 'approached what might, without extravagance, be called perfect'. Tyndall also recognized the tremendous drive that kept Faraday day after day at the laboratory bench:

> Underneath his sweetness and gentleness was the heat of a volcano. He was a man of excitable and fiery nature; but through his high self-discipline he converted the fire into a central glow and motive force of life, instead of permitting it to waste itself in useless passion.

Faraday's scientific career was quite different from those of the 18th-century Nonconformists like Priestley and Dalton, who had benefited from the scientific education provided by the Dissenting Academies. Coming from a poor background of non-Anglican stock, Faraday had no opportunity to go to university (Oxford was closed to dissenters; Cambridge accepted them, but they had to leave without a degree). Instead Faraday's scientific career was shaped by his apprenticeship to the chemist Humphry Davy, with whom he started working at the Royal Institution in London in 1813. By 1821 Faraday had already made his first major scientific breakthrough, the discovery of electromagnetic rotation, but this and other successes led to a strain in his relationship with Davy, by then President of the Royal Society, who appears to have become rather jealous of his assistant's dramatic advances. Davy tried to block Faraday's election to the Royal Society, but was overruled by a large group of members who ensured Faraday's eventual election. Only after Davy's death in 1829 did Faraday feel entirely free to pursue his own research programme. With the help of his faithful assistant Charles Anderson, Faraday then managed to publish many of the findings that form the basis of our modern understanding of electricity and electromagnetism. Today we might call Faraday a physicist, but the term did not come into usage until the late 1860s, and the description 'chemist, electrician and natural philosopher' more clearly describes the immense range of Faraday's investigations.

During the years 1831–55 Faraday read before the Royal Society a series of thirty papers that were published in his three-volume *Experimental Researches in Electricity*. His bibliography lists nearly 500 printed papers, of which only three were jointly written papers. In 1831 Faraday described electromagnetic induction, perhaps his most celebrated discovery, and in 1834 formulated his laws of electrochemical decomposition. By 1844 he had been elected to about seventy scientific societies. As Cantor remarks, 'as a Christian Faraday felt that no God-given moment should be wasted. His time had to be strictly controlled.

He pursued both his science and his religion with total dedication.' Faraday's advice to a younger scientist to 'work, finish, publish', is an aphorism that would serve as a useful reminder on the wall of any modern laboratory. Yet Faraday still found time to take a keen appreciation in the arts, read novels voraciously and spent many hours a week visiting the poor and sick in the context of his job as an elder of the Sandemanian church.

One of Faraday's jobs in the Royal Institute was to give regular public lectures that would bring the public up-to-date on the latest scientific discoveries. There was an immense public interest in science in early-Victorian England. Nervous at the start of his new responsibility, Faraday soon became a confident and gifted lecturer, incorporating experiments into his lectures and quickly establishing a rapport with his largely non-specialist audiences. His obvious enthusiasm for his subject was infectious. 'All is a sparking stream of eloquence and experimental illustration' enthused William Crookes after one of Faraday's lectures. Faraday rarely alluded to religion as such during his public lectures, but the religious message was implicit in the sense of wonder that he set out to evoke in the remarkable properties of God's world. In a private lecture given before Prince Albert in 1849 Faraday expounded the wonders of magnetism and the influence that it appeared to exert on every particle in the universe: 'What its great purpose is, seems to be looming in the distance before us... and I cannot doubt that a glorious discovery in natural knowledge, *and of the wisdom and power of God in the creation*, is awaiting our age.'

Another use Faraday made of his public lectures was to encourage a spirit of healthy scepticism concerning claims about spiritualism and the paranormal. The news that two sisters in New York state had received communications from beyond in the form of rappings during 1848 sent a wave of interest in spiritualism across America and Britain. During the 1850s a veritable stream of American mediums travelled across the Atlantic to fascinate respectable Victorian society with moving tables and voices from beyond. Alfred Russell Wallace, co-discoverer with Darwin of the theory of natural selection, was an enthusiastic convert to spiritualism, recording that his own table at home had tilted and, ever the accurate naturalist, that fresh flowers had appeared 'from the other side' to decorate it, including '15 chrysanthemums, 6 variegated anemones, 4 tulips'. Faraday would have none of this nonsense, writing critical letters to *The Times* (30 June 1853) and *The Athenaeum* (2 July 1853) to explain that, after some experiments on the matter, he had concluded that the movement of the table was due to 'a quasi involuntary muscular action (for the effect is with many subject to the wish or will)'. Spiritualism was no part of science, because it was unpredictable and therefore lacked one of the essential characteristics of scientific phenomena. Though in public Faraday's critique of spiritualism was based largely on purely scientific arguments, there seems little doubt that the motivation for such an energetic campaign was rooted in his religious beliefs. The Sandemanians were firmly in the biblical tradition in viewing all forms of spiritualism with suspicion. Randomly moving tables and voices from the 'other side' were no part of the consistency and law-like behaviour of God's world.

Faraday firmly believed in God as creator, but was critical of the natural theology that dominated much early-Victorian science, and neither did he look to the Bible as a source of scientific information. Like Bacon, Faraday was convinced that the book of God's world and the book of God's word had the same author, so that 'the natural works of God can never by any possibility come into contradiction with the higher things that belong to our future existence'. The source of knowledge about salvation was derived from the biblical revelation of God's working in history through the people of Israel in the Old Covenant, and then by God sending his Son to die on the cross and rise from the dead in order to secure the New Covenant. Such knowledge could not be derived by investigations of the natural world, which were sufficient only to indicate God's existence and power.

On at least two occasions before audiences at the Royal Institution, Faraday referred to Romans 1:20, which states that 'since the creation of the world God's invisible qualities – his eternal power and divine nature – have been clearly seen, being understood from what has been made'. For Faraday, investigation of God's world was therefore a holy enterprise, since science reveals 'the evidences in natural things of his eternal power and Godhead'. In his lecture on mental education Faraday declared that the 'book of nature, which we have to read, is written by the finger of God'. This vivid phrase was taken from Exodus 31:18 where Moses is receiving the ten commandments as 'inscribed by the finger of God'. For Faraday, God's 'book of nature' was written just as much by God as the Bible. But whereas God's handiwork reflected his wisdom, it was not there to teach us ethics or morality, neither could it lead a person to salvation, which was only possible through knowledge derived from the biblical revelation.

Faraday had a deep sense of the *order* of God's creation. The laws of nature 'were established from the beginning' and so were 'as old as creation'. The notes of one of his earliest lectures contain the pithy exhortation 'Search for laws'. Robert Sandeman himself had written a book called *The Law of Nature Defended by Scripture* (1760). The task of science was to discover those laws by a process of empirical investigation. As Faraday argued in a memorandum (1844) on the nature of matter: 'God has been pleased to work in his material creation by laws' and 'the Creator governs his material works by *definite laws* resulting from the forces impressed on matter'. The 'beauty of electricity...[is] that it is under *law*'. 'The *laws of nature*, as we understand them, are the foundations of our knowledge of natural things', he told the audience at his mental education lecture.

Several major themes constantly recur in Faraday's scientific writings which appear to have theological roots. One is Faraday's insistence that there is no waste in the natural order. 'Nothing is unproductive in nature,' Faraday told an audience in 1846, 'there is no residue of action that is useless. All the power that God has infused into matter, He uses for various effects in creation.' In a letter to Schoenbein, Faraday remarked that 'there is nothing superfluous, or deficient, or accidental, or indifferent, in nature'.

There is a certain irony in the fact that about the time that Faraday was extolling the frugality and balance of nature, his equally famous contemporary Charles Darwin was exploding in a letter to a friend 'What a book a Devil's Chaplain might write on the clumsy, wasteful, blundering low & horridly cruel works of nature!' The contrast perhaps stems from the very different theological backgrounds of Faraday and Darwin. Darwin had read theology at Cambridge, where he had been deeply influenced by Paley's classic work on natural theology, which espoused the traditional view that everything in the natural world reflected God's perfect character and workmanship. On uncovering biological mechanisms that offended his Victorian sensibilities, Darwin not unnaturally reacted against such a view. But Faraday, as we have seen, was no natural theologian, and his research field was in the physical forces that explain the universe, not the biological mechanisms that explain the diversity of biological organisms. The natural theologians tended to picture God as the skilled craftsman who fashioned the world, like the sculptor who makes a statue from a piece of formless stone. Faraday spoke more of God's action in the world as power that came into being as God spoke, power which 'God infused into matter' and which brought into existence all the various physical forces of electricity and magnetism that he so delighted in investigating. The Creator had 'gifted matter' with these powers.

The 'holy grail' of the relationship between the various powers of creation was a topic to which Faraday frequently referred, though it was a topic still so speculative that Faraday confided many of his most ambitious thoughts only to his diary. On 19 March 1849, his diary records: 'Gravity. Surely this force must be capable of an experimental relation to Electricity, Magnetism and the other forces, so as to bind it up with them in reciprocal action and equivalent effect. Consider for a moment how to set about touching this matter by facts and trial.' Many experiments followed, but Faraday was unable to detect any influence of falling objects on electric fields, reporting these negative results to the Royal Society in November 1850. Nevertheless, concluded Faraday, although the results were negative, they 'do not shake my strong feeling of the existence of a relation between gravity and electricity, though they give no proof that such a relation exists'. God's world was coherent, ruled by law. In such a world relationships between forces *had* to exist.

Faraday was a brilliant iconoclast. Einstein remarked of Faraday that he, of all people, 'had made the greatest change in our conception of reality'. Not by any stretch of the imagination was Faraday typical of the Nonconformists of his era. Nor, by his background, was he typical of other scientists of his day. Yet Faraday stands firmly in a tradition of natural philosophers like Kepler, Boyle, Ray, Newton, Pascal and many others, who took the biblical content of their faith seriously and who showed a particular delight in uncovering the regularities that characterized God's world.

Faraday was also living at a time when some distinct shifts in emphasis were becoming apparent in the relationships between science and theology in the English-speaking world, shifts which became both more acute and more visible during the second half of the 19th century. Two main factors, one scientific and the other sociological, led to this changing relationship. First, biological discoveries made it increasingly difficult to maintain some of the traditional forms of natural theology, undermining the very basis on which the 'holy alliance' had come to depend. Second, scientists finally emerged as a distinct professional class during this century, leading to a conflict of interests with other groups also committed to being the dominant intellectual voice in society. This shift to professionalism was particularly marked in the discipline that came to be known as geology.

Geology, Moses and the age of the earth

Speculations on the origin and age of the earth had been a common topic for books and pamphlets over a period of many centuries prior to the late 18th century, the time at which geology began to emerge as a distinct scientific discipline. Debate on the matter until that time had been largely carried out on religious and philosophical grounds, since no data were yet collected or recognized that would clarify the issue by scientific means. The debate had been used primarily to defend competing cosmologies, such as the Epicurean idea of eternally existing and eternally moving matter, or the opposing Christian idea that the universe had a specific beginning and was the work of a transcendent creator. The Epicurean philosophy had been popularized by Benoit de Maillet (1659–1738), one time French consul general in Egypt, who argued that the earth had developed by a cyclical process of generation and decay, passing through several distinct epochs in the process. De Maillet observed that sedimentary rock layers pointed to a long developmental process in the formation of the earth, rather than a sudden and instantaneous moment of creation, and suggested that the seas, which had once covered the dry land, would have required at least two million years to evaporate rather than the widely accepted timespan of thousands of years.

Following De Maillet, the Philosophe Baron d'Holbach (see above) also supported Epicureanism, maintaining that no external force had been required to set matter in motion, and therefore that there was no need to invoke the activities of a 'supernatural creator'. However, D'Holbach differed from classical Epicurean philosophy in believing that the universe was thoroughly deterministic rather than the outcome of purely 'chance' processes.

A rather different interpretation of time's cycle was given by Thomas Burnet, private chaplain to William III, who published the four books of his *Sacred History of the Earth* during the 1680s. In Stephen Jay Gould's elegant restoration of Burnet's reputation as a profound thinker of his era,[19] Gould shows how the frontispiece to Burnet's book summarizes his cosmology. Christ stands astride a circle of globes, with a quotation from the book of Revelation above his head: 'I am alpha and omega (the beginning and the end, the first and the last)'. History then proceeds clockwise from under Christ's left foot, which stands on a chaotic earth 'without form and void'. A succession of further stages of the world are then portrayed in circular form, the final stage being portrayed as being under Christ's right foot. Burnet's view of earth history is both cyclical and yet at the same time directional; there is a real beginning and a real ending. Such a view of 'time's arrow' is so much part of our culture that we take it for granted. The Judeo-Christian idea that history is unidirectional rather than cyclical or eternal, as in the Aristotelian universe, has had a profound effect on Western ideas of evolution and progress. Yet, as Gould points out, both cyclical and directional concepts of time played distinctive roles in shaping those views of earth history that eventually developed into the modern science of geology. The metaphor of time's cycle emphasized the regularity and law-keeping behaviour of earthly events, pointing to a narrative history of the earth that was progressive and even, to some extent, predictable.

Within the presuppositions of his interpretation of biblical history, Burnet was an arch rationalist. His task was to describe the natural causes that must explain the history specified by scripture. Observations of the natural world were to be used to interpret scripture for, as Burnet pointed out, echoing the writings of Augustine:

'Tis a dangerous thing to engage the authority of scripture in disputes about the natural world, in opposition to reason; lest time, which brings all things to light, should discover that to be evidently false which we had made scripture to assert... We are not to suppose that any truth concerning the natural world can be an enemy to religion; for truth cannot be an enemy to truth, God is not divided against himself.

Burnet refused to accept the lazy device of invoking a 'miracle' to try and explain those phenomena that could not yet be explained by natural philosophy, criticizing those who thought that God had simply made 'extra' water to bring about the deluge. No, the laws ordained by God for the universe were perfect, and therefore there *must* be natural laws underlying observed phenomena, however unusual those phenomena might be. Drawing on the 17th century's favourite analogy, Burnet commented that 'We think him a better artist that makes a clock that strikes regularly at every hour from the springs and wheels which he puts in the work, than he that hath so made his clock that he must put his finger to it every hour to make it strike.'

Burnet was no armchair speculator but made serious attempts to fill in the physics of his history. To find out if there was enough water for a universal deluge, he tried to calculate the amount of water in the oceans by using sample soundings of the depth of the water at various points. Burnet concluded that the Flood happened when the earth's crust cracked, allowing water to rise up from the abyss. In a long correspondence with Isaac Newton in 1681, Burnet remonstrated with Newton for maintaining that the earth's topography reflected its original form, rather than, as Burnet believed, having been sculpted into its present form by the waters of the Flood. He also disagreed with Newton on the interpretation of the 'days' in Genesis 1. Newton argued that the problem of creation in six days could be solved by postulating that the earth rotated much more slowly then, so producing a prolonged 'day'. Burnet, ever the rationalist, again followed Augustine in suggesting that the 'days' of Genesis 1 were allegorical.

One of the most famous of the Philosophes, the Comte de Buffon (1707–88), director of the Royal Botanical Collection in Paris, also interpreted the history of the earth as passing through a series of cycles or epochs, but his slant to history was considerably less theological than Burnet's account. Buffon maintained that the earth had been formed by the gradual action of natural causes rather than as the result of an instantaneous creation. In his forty-four-volume *Histoire Naturelle*, which remains as one of the most impressive monuments of the French Enlightenment, and in his *Epochs of Nature* (1778), Buffon argued that the earth was developing through a series of cycles but held that the dry land had been formed by the receding oceans, and would one day be covered with water again as the action of rain lowered the mountains and filled up the valleys. Buffon's historical account of the development of the earth's topography and of the distribution of living creatures over the globe was in sharp contrast to the static Epicurean views of De Maillet and Baron d'Holbach. On the basis of his own experiments on cooling, Buffon estimated that it had taken 72,000 years for the earth to cool sufficiently from its initially incandescent state in order for life to appear, though in private he considered periods as much as three million years, guesses in vast excess of the 6,000 years or so generally accepted as the age of the earth at that time. Buffon's ideas were criticized both by Voltaire (who disliked Buffon's theory that the earth had its origin as a result of a collision between a comet and the sun) and by the theologians of the Sorbonne, who were not unnaturally concerned about Buffon's apparent departure from the Genesis account. Buffon, as the more biblically minded Burnet before him, defended his theory by suggesting that the 'days' of the creation story could be interpreted as epochs.

By the late 18th century, therefore, there was an immense array of competing 'models' to try and explain the earth's origin and history. In 1764 the anthropologist De Pauw listed no less than forty-nine theories of the formation of the earth, and there were still thirty-five on the list of De la Metherie in 1797. The deist Voltaire lambasted all these system-builders in his inimitable style, reserving particular scorn for Buffon, 'an author who has made himself more famous than useful by his theory of the earth. It would take more time than the Deluge lasted to read all the authors who made beautiful systems about it; each of them destroys and renews the earth according to his own fancy.' It is perhaps not surprising to find that, after pulling down everyone else's system, Voltaire then proceeded to build one of his own. Curiously, though Voltaire had no love for the Bible, he preferred to keep the conception of a sudden creation as part of his model, which was then followed by a relatively stable state. A stable state implied the constancy of the species, a concept that Voltaire defended passionately in language as neoplatonic as anything written by Cuvier:

Do not lose sight of this great truth, that nature never gives the lie to herself. All species remain always the same. Animals, plants, minerals, metals, everything is invariable in that prodigious variety. Everything keeps its essence. The essence of the earth is to have mountains, without which it would be without rivers, consequently it is impossible that the mountains are not as ancient as the earth. One could as well say that our bodies have been a long time without heads...

By 1800, speculations that the earth was much older than a few thousand years were commonplace. However, belief in a relatively short history for the earth was still widely maintained. The claim that the creation of the world could be dated to the year 4004 BC had been popularized by the 17th-century archbishop James Ussher, a date that was even printed in the King James translation of the Bible into English. The Flood was widely held to be universal, and the growing awareness that fossils were the imprints of dead plants and animals was interpreted as evidence for the worldwide nature of the Flood. So accepted was the idea that the existence of fossils supported the historicity of the Flood that Voltaire, who wished to attack the historical accuracy of the Bible, denied their existence altogether! Those not in the Augustinian tradition, who thought that the language of the Genesis account of creation should be interpreted as if it were a scientific document, continued to defend the creation of the world in six literal days. J.E. Silberschlag expounded the Mosaic account in his *Geogenie* (1780) 'according to physical and mathematical principles', but remained a strict literalist. According to Silberschlag those who took the six 'days' of creation to refer to periods of time were but 'creators of amusing nonsense'.

It is a futile exercise to look back at a period in the history of science and judge one side as being 'right' or 'wrong' in the light of more recent knowledge and ideas. Aside from prior philosophical or religious commitments, very little data were available until the late 18th century that would make belief in a very short age for the earth untenable. In the absence of such data, it is hardly surprising that most people were content to envisage the history of the earth as having continued for thousands or, at the most, tens of thousands of years. Such a length of time had the advantage that it could be encompassed by the human imagination and fitted well with the deeply held belief that the world had been made for man, and it was therefore reasonable that the span of human history should be virtually the same in length as the earth's history.

Older histories describing the roots of modern geology have generally looked to the Scot James Hutton and his *Theory of the Earth* (1795) as a triumph of empirical data overcoming the prejudices of earlier generations of speculators and miracle-mongers. In Sir Archibald Geikie's account given in *The Founders of Geology* (1897) Hutton was the man who 'vigorously guarded himself against the admission of any principle which could not be founded on observation. He made no assumptions. Every step in his deductions was based upon actual fact, and the facts were so arranged as to yield naturally and inevitably the conclusions which he drew from them.' The mythological nature of this description has been clearly revealed by more recent historians. It is now realized that Hutton's theory of the earth was presented within a metaphysical system that was even more rigid than that of his various predecessors.

James Hutton was a brilliant polymath who wrote long and turgid prose. Nearly half the 1,000 pages of his *Theory of the Earth* comprises untranslated quotations from French sources. Fortunately, however, for posterity Hutton's ideas were popularized by his friend John Playfair, a mathematician and minister in the Church of Scotland, whose *Illustrations of the Huttonian Theory of the Earth* (1802) was far more widely read than Hutton himself. Hutton pictured the world as a great and perfect machine, drawing inspiration from Newton's reconstruction of space. Just as Newton's universe consisted of a complex network of planets moving round under the direction of divine law so, thought Hutton, must it be possible to describe our own world's 'constitution' as a cycle of orderly repeating events. Since the world was made by God as a work of infinite wisdom, there must be inbuilt mechanisms that maintained the earth in a state of cyclical renewal rather than continual decay. Hutton discovered this mechanism of renewal not by obtaining new empirical evidence, though he did himself engage in fieldwork on occasion, but by reinterpreting data already available. Previous histories of the planet had interpreted its topography as being due to a prolonged history of erosion, a gradual wearing down of the mountains that had continued unremittingly since the time of their creation. But Hutton realized that the geometry of geological strata could only be explained by assuming that layers once horizontal had been broken and forced vertically upward by immense heat (hence 'igneous' rocks) to recreate landscapes worn down by erosion. These 'unconformities' were illustrated by the 'fingers' of granite that penetrated up into a layer of limestone, showing that they had intruded in molten form from below, and were not the result of the erosion of a strata from above. So Hutton's earth was one of continual renewal, a giant benevolent machine ordered for the good of humankind in apparently endless cycles. Mountains were eroded into fertile valleys, useful for cultivation, which themselves eventually eroded, only to be replaced by new continents that rose up from the strata beneath by fiery forces.

Playfair understood Hutton's analogy with planetary motion very clearly:

> The geological system of Dr Hutton resembles, in many respects, that
> which appears to preside over the heavenly motions... In both, a provision is
> made for duration of unlimited extent, and the lapse of time has no effect to
> wear out or destroy a machine, constructed with so much wisdom. Where
> the movements are all so perfect, their beginning and end must be alike
> invisible.

It is only by using this analogy that we can understand Hutton's own ringing (and much-quoted) words with which he finished his *Theory of the Earth*: 'The result, therefore, of our present enquiry is, that we find no vestige of a beginning, – no prospect of an end.' Hutton was not suggesting that the world was eternal, only that it had been made as a work of such 'infinite power and wisdom' for the good of humankind that its powers of self-renewal kept it in constantly good condition. It was this that enabled Hutton to be so convinced about the immense age of the earth. The earth's cycles were as perfectly organized as the repetitive trajectories of Newton's planets. The last cycle of the earth was no different from the present for it saw 'an earth equally perfect with the present, and an earth equally productive of growing plants and living animals'.

Hutton himself was insistent that the intention of his theory was to simultaneously describe both the efficient causes (mechanisms) and final causes (why are things the way they are?) of the 'world machine'. 'We perceive a fabric erected in wisdom, to obtain a purpose worthy of the power that is apparent in the production of it.' The argument appears so circular, and is so foreign to our own separation of efficient from final cause, that we find it difficult to conceptualize. But Hutton presented his theory as a precise solution to solving an intellectual problem. The world 'was peculiarly adapted to the purposes of man', clearly demonstrating 'the presence and efficacy of design and intelligence in the power that conducts the world'. Man was 'happy from the appearance of wisdom and benevolence in the design, instead of being left to suspect in the Author of Nature any of that imperfection which he finds in himself'. How, then, in a world made in infinite wisdom, could there be constant renewal of the rich soil that was so necessary for agriculture, and therefore for the good of humankind? Observations about strata were presented by Hutton as illustrations of a theory that was already clearly true on the basis of a priori reasoning. As one of the chapter titles in the *Theory of the Earth* succinctly states the matter: 'The theory confirmed from observations made on purpose to elucidate the subject'. Hutton was an 18th-century James Lovelock (the originator of the Gaia theory in the 20th century) – the grand theory came first, to be followed in due course by some items of supporting data.

In stark contrast to the late-Victorian portrayal of Hutton as the founder of 'empirical geology', Hutton's own contemporaries viewed him as one of a long succession of armchair speculators. In 1817 *Blackwood's Magazine* commented that 'Had he studied nature, and then theorized, his genius would in all probability, have illustrated many difficult points; but it is obvious, from his own works, that he has frequently reversed this order of proceeding.' Cuvier was also quick to discard Hutton as a speculator rather than a serious fieldworker. But Hutton himself never pretended that he derived his theory from observations. The earth had a purpose, which clearly implied 'things which must necessarily be comprehended in the theory of the earth, if we are to give stability to it as a world sustaining plants and animals'.

As Gould remarks about Hutton's commitment to cycles, 'Hutton's rigidity' was 'both a boon and a trap. It gave us deep time, but we lost history in the process. Any adequate account of the earth requires both.' This sense of historical direction was partly supplied by those who continued to insist that the biblical Flood had played a key role in shaping the earth's topography. In contrast to endless cycles, the world according to this cosmology had been subjected to a series of dramatic upheavals, of which the Flood was the most prominent example. Already during the 18th century it had become commonplace to distinguish the most ancient rocks, which had no fossils, from the more recent fossil-bearing strata, which again were distinct from superficial deposits containing the bones of animals. The Flood became associated only with these most recent deposits, and were called 'diluvial' (dating from the Flood) to distinguish them from the 'antediluvial' or pre-Flood strata. In this way a longer pre-human history for the earth than previously expected gradually came to be accepted during the late 18th century based on reasoning quite different from that of Hutton's. It was even argued that fossils and strata were better guides to the history of the earth than written documents, since they were not subject to bias and forgery.

The so-called 'Neptunist geology' arose from the teachings of Abraham Werner, Professor of Mineralogy at Freiberg in Saxony, and was supported by Richard Kirwan, President of the Royal Irish Academy (1799–1819) and by Jean Deluc (1727–1817), a Swiss who lived in England after 1773. In contrast to the belief in the role of heat, as proposed by writers such as Hutton (sometimes called 'Vulcanism'), the Neptunists believed that water had played a major role in the formation of the earth's crust, an idea that they thought fitted well with the upheavals caused by the biblical Flood. Deluc built an immense geological system on Neptunist ideas, and then proceeded to demonstrate, at least to his own satisfaction, how remarkably well his system accorded with the Genesis account. Since Genesis gave such an accurate description of the physical origins of the earth, written by people who knew no science, thought Deluc, then clearly it must have come by divine revelation.

The debates between the Neptunists and the Vulcanists aroused much passion at the time, but at least had the useful net result that they brought the emerging science of geology to the public's attention and resulted in a large amount of new data accumulated by fieldworkers working within both schools of thought. The passions aroused were, no doubt, partly due to the different countries of origin and institutions represented by the competing theories. What is interesting to note in retrospect, however, is the way in which the cyclical history of the earth propounded by the 'Vulcanist' Hutton, *and* the more historical narrative propounded by the 'Neptunist' Werner, both contributed important elements to the concepts of time that underlay the science of geology that eventually emerged during the first part of the 19th century.

The foundation of the Geological Society of London in 1807 marks an important landmark in the emergence of geology as a distinct scientific discipline. For the first time natural philosophers investigating the earth's history started to call themselves 'geologists', and a professional class of geologists began to emerge. There was a conscious attempt by the new geologists to put aside the 'grand theories' of the earlier speculators and concentrate on fieldwork, although in practice there was initially some disagreement as to whether the geological record could, or could not, be utilized to support the arguments of natural theology. Nevertheless, the early history of geology is a very poor hunting ground for those who wish to sustain a 'conflict thesis' in relations between science and faith, for the simple reason that the early geologists operated almost entirely within their own religious frameworks, many of them, at least in private, though sometimes also in public, taking great pains to show that their discoveries were compatible with their Christian faith. The Reverend Adam Sedgwick (1785–1873), appointed as first Professor of Geology at Cambridge at the age of thirty-three, was pleased with the progressive character of the fossil record because it gave him a platform from which to attack deism. (The field of geology was so new that Sedgwick knew nothing about the subject when appointed, remarking that he 'had but one rival, Gorham of Queens, and he had not the slightest chance against me, for I knew absolutely nothing of geology, whereas he knew a great deal – but it was all wrong!') The deists held a static view of nature originally created by God but which was now held in a state of equilibrium by the actions of natural laws. Fossils for Sedgwick were the results of an orderly sequence of extinctions and creations of new species, and therefore evidence that God continued to be involved in the world that He created.

Sedgwick's geological counterpart at Oxford, the Reverend William Buckland (1784–1856), was no less concerned to demonstrate that the discoveries of geology were compatible with religious belief. In his *Reliquiae Diluvianae* (1823) Buckland argued for a recent, though non-miraculous, flood event, based on the discovery of a supposedly antediluvian hyena den containing the bones of mammals no longer seen in England. Geology, claimed Buckland, could prove the fact of a universal deluge 'had we never heard of such an event from Scripture, or any other authority'. A few years later Buckland quietly dropped his claim and instead became one of the first geologists to support the theory of Louis Agassiz (1807–73) that a recent Ice Age could better explain the animal remains in the hyena's den. Buckland's shift in interpretation did not mean that he had ceased to believe in the biblical Flood story, only that he was open to accepting better scientific explanations as they became available. By the mid-19th century it was, in any case, commonplace among geologists to view the Flood as a local inundation that had affected only the Fertile Crescent.

'Conflict', when it did occur, was often between the new professional class of geologists, which included a large number of clerics, and the 'amateurs', who were viewed as a threat to the hegemony of this new grouping. Charles Lyell, who did much to shape the development of the Geological Society, was particularly vigorous in denouncing any who challenged the authority of the new professionals, complaining:

> They do not scruple to promulgate theories concerning the creation and the deluge, derived from their own expositions of the sacred text, in which they endeavour to point out the accordance of the Mosaic history with

phenomena which they have never studied, and to judge of which every page of their writings proves their consummate incompetence.

Charles Lyell's outburst in the *Quarterly Review* seems to have been directed against those amateurs who wrote in popular magazines rather than against his fellow geologists, and Moore describes it as 'the challenge of an adolescent professionalism'. Indeed, by the early 19th century hardly any geologists continued to look to the Bible as a source of geological information. But the same was not true among the amateurs – a minority continued the attempt to extract a geological chronology from the first few pages of Genesis, a tradition that did not finally end until the 1850s. In part this so-called 'Mosaic geology' was itself a reaction against the increasing specialization in geology that tended to exclude the non-experts from an area of speculation previously open to all. From another perspective, 'Mosaic geology' represented a repeat of the debates of the 17th century as to whether cosmological theories could be derived from the Bible. Galileo, Wilkins, Kepler, Bacon and many others had argued in the Augustinian tradition that the Bible did not intend to teach such matters and it did not take very long for the professional geologists to follow in their footsteps in agreeing with this principle as far as their new scientific discipline was concerned.

The central point of discussion in early-19th-century geology has often been caricatured as a debate between the Catastrophists and the Uniformitarians. The Catastrophists believed that the geological record resulted from a series of cataclysms, each of which destroyed the animal world and each of which was followed by the introduction of new living things at a higher level of organization than before. The Uniformitarians, in contrast, argued that geological change had come about by gradual processes that were still operating to change the form of the world. According to this caricature, most of the leading British palaeontologists and geologists of the early 19th century could be classified as Catastrophists, including William Buckland at Oxford, and Adam Sedgwick at Cambridge, one of the founders of the British Association for the Advancement of Science. By the same account, the hero of the Uniformitarians was Charles Lyell, author of the *Principles of Geology* which was published in three volumes between 1830 and 1833. In an extension of this caricature the Catastrophists were viewed as prejudiced defenders of religion and the Bible, because they could more readily bring God into their account as the author of catastrophes, whereas the 'more empirically based' Uniformitarians were also more 'secular' because the gradual processes that they emphasized did not 'seem to leave so much room for God's actions'. This view is repeated ad nauseam in dozens of textbooks, of which one example reads:

Until Lyell published his book, most thinking people accepted the idea that the earth was young, and that even its most spectacular features such as mountains and valleys, islands and continents were the products of sudden, cataclysmic events, which included supernatural acts of God.[20]

Like many distortions of the 19th-century history of science, this account has suffered particularly badly at the hands of more recent historians. In this case the mythology was partly generated by Lyell himself, a barrister by training, who described his *Principles of Geology* as 'one long argument'. Early in his career Lyell had believed in a progressive view of the earth's history, but in 1827 he abandoned this view, apparently as a result of reading Lamarck. As we noted above, Lamarck had proposed a progressive evolutionary view of living organisms in which humble organisms started on the elevator of life by spontaneous generation and then gradually developed into higher organisms, a series of transformations that eventually led to humans. Such a view was anathema to Lyell, who had a very high view of humankind and apparently could not bear the thought that people might be descended from 'brute animals'. He countered this threat to human dignity, with all its overtones of radical and materialistic French politics, with a 'steady-state' view of history, in which species appeared and disappeared in an orderly fashion. There had been no progression, claimed Lyell, therefore no transformation of one species into another. The geology which underpinned such a scheme was that of Uniformitarianism.

In his attempt to emphasize the novelty of his ideas about the uniformity of the processes that had shaped the natural world, Lyell demonstrated the debater's natural inclination to create an 'opposition' and then to cast them in a rather poor light. Those who thought that there were events that had helped to shape the earth's topography that were no longer observably in action were lambasted by Lyell for their 'indolence'. Cuvier in particular was painted by Lyell as his 'Catastrophist' enemy. Cuvier, maintained Lyell, believed in a young earth; he thought that there was a miraculous recreation of life after each catastrophic extinction; he was working for the church against science, and so on. Yet in fact, as we have already noted above, Cuvier's work was carried out in the context of the French Enlightenment, he thought dogmatic theology was anathema to science, that the Bible should not be used as a source-book for scientific theories, and does not appear to have been particularly religious. Furthermore, Cuvier's earth was as old as Lyell's, and he was passionately committed to the empirical approach to science, believing in a rationalistic interpretation of geological phenomena. Cuvier's catastrophes were neither supernatural nor universal, being restricted to the inundation of land by water. Unfortunately lies become reinforced by endless repetition, and even in fairly recent textbooks of historical geology one finds legends like this one by Stokes (1973):

Cuvier believed that Noah's flood was universal and had prepared the earth for its present inhabitants. The Church was happy to have the support of such an eminent scientist, and there is no doubt that Cuvier's great reputation delayed the acceptance of the more accurate views that ultimately prevailed.[21]

There is not the slightest historical basis for these fantasies, which seem to have been passed down in a faithful but inaccurate pedigree from the time of Lyell. At least Lyell, unlike some more recent writers, did not accuse his geological colleagues of thinking that the world was only a few thousand years old, a belief that was already well on the way out by 1800, and was certainly not held by Cuvier.

The problem about historical legends is that they tend to mask the really substantive issues that underlie the development of a topic in a given era. The issue, in reality, was not whether past events could be explained by present events, but whether there were also geological phenomena that could only be explained by invoking explanations outside the range of observations normally made. The Catastrophists were convinced that the current topography of the earth could not be explained *only* by extrapolating from the present. Their conviction that occasional paroxysms had brought about geological change was rooted in a highly directional view of time in which a series of events had occurred as a direct result of the earth's cooling. In stark contrast, Lyell's view of time was much closer to Hutton's, maintaining that the earth was in a perfect dynamic equilibrium, always in motion, but never changing in general appearance.

Only late on in his life did Lyell finally abandon the 'steady-state' view of the earth's history that he had defended so vigorously and for so long, accepting in the end that life's history had indeed been progressive, and that there had been a development of life forms on the earth. But his caricature of his opponents' views remained in edition after edition of the *Principles*, to be copied and re-copied, finally being amplified into the legend of the 'secular empirical Uniformitarians' doing battle with the 'biblical anti-empirical Catastrophists'. As it happens, Lyell remained a chapel-going Unitarian until the end of his days, but the basis for his very high view of humankind appears to have been neither particularly biblical, nor theological, but rather, in Moore's words, 'was rather a complex religious longing – psychological, aesthetic, and social'.

In the end, therefore, all one can say about the geological debates of the early 19th century is that they had little to do with pitting 'religion' against 'science'. There was a conscious effort by the new professional geologists to address specifically geological questions and to leave the 'larger questions' on one side. In practice, however, as has happened so often in the history of science, geological theories were profoundly influenced by philosophical and religious considerations, particularly as these influenced concepts of time and the role of humankind in the earth's history.

The Philosophes, the Nonconformists and the early geologists all provide in their very distinctive ways examples of how science can be disseminated and debated through philosophical and theological lenses of widely varying focus. However, it was not until the professionalization of science occurred in the second half of the 19th century that the 'conflict thesis', at least in Britain, became an influential view of the relationship between science and religion.

Chapter 7

The Warfare Merchants
The Roots of Modern Science (4) – Darwin, Evolution and the Victorian Conflict Thesis

Extinguished theologians lie about the cradle of every science as the strangled snakes besides that of Hercules; and history records that wherever science and orthodoxy have been fairly opposed, the latter have been forced to retire from the lists, bleeding and crushed if not annihilated; scotched if not slain.

T.H. Huxley

I do not think that there is any general statement in the Bible or any part of the account of creation, either as given in Genesis 1 and 2 or elsewhere alluded to, that need be opposed to evolution.

B.B. Warfield

There are not, and cannot be, any Divine interpositions in nature, for God cannot interfere with Himself. His creative activity is present everywhere. There is no division of labour between God and nature, or God and law... For the Christian theologian the facts of nature are the acts of God.

Aubrey Moore

The growth of a large business is merely a survival of the fittest... The American Beauty rose can be produced in the splendor and fragrance which bring cheer to its beholder only by sacrificing the early buds which grow up around it. This is not an evil tendency in business. It is merely the working-out of a law of nature and a law of God.

J.D. Rockefeller

[All quotes are from 19th-century commentators]

The word 'evolution' in the late 18th and early 19th century had quite a different meaning from its more modern usage, being used in a scientific context within embryology to refer to the development ('evolution') of the fetus. Darwin used the term only rarely. By talking of an 'evolutionary' debate we are therefore already in danger of reading back into the thought of this era ideas derived from the contemporary theory of evolution. The term will be used here as a useful shorthand to refer to all those theories, many of which preceded Darwin, which claimed transformation of living things from one form into another over a period of time.

The evolutionary debate of the 19th century has often been presented as the ultimate example of the 'conflict' interpretation of the historical relation between science and faith. In Darwin's theory, it has been claimed, was the final nail in the coffin of the idea of God as creator. The theory of evolution was only accepted in the teeth of vigorous opposition from the clerical establishment, who thought that its acceptance would undermine morality in society and the influence of the church. The theory caused a deep division between scientists and religious believers that has remained to this very day. Such mythologies have been perpetuated and maintained in the media, in textbooks, and even by well-qualified popularizers of science. As with many aspects of the history of the interactions between science and faith, however, revisionist historians have been hard at work over the past few decades, and the picture of the evolutionary debate that has emerged is now considerably more nuanced. Many useful accounts are available, and we will focus here on one main question only: what were the religious and philosophical issues which surrounded the reception of Darwinism during the 19th century?

Charles Darwin

Charles Darwin[1] was born on 12 February 1809, the son of a wealthy Shrewsbury doctor and the grandson of the unorthodox Erasmus Darwin, who had published some rather speculative evolutionary ideas during the latter part of the 18th century. As a small boy Charles attended a Unitarian chapel but was later sent to an Anglican church by his free-thinking father, Anglican respectability no doubt being viewed with favour in light of business interests and the demands of a thriving medical practice. Charles' father was clearly not very impressed by his son's achievements at school, telling him that 'You care for nothing but shooting, dogs and rat-catching, and you will be a disgrace to yourself and all your family'. At the age of sixteen Darwin was packed off to Edinburgh to read medicine, but found the lectures dull and the witnessing of operations, carried out before the days of anaesthetics, disturbing. But it was in Edinburgh that Darwin developed an early interest in natural history, being strongly influenced by the sponge expert and radical Lamarckian evolutionist, Robert Grant, whose political views were far from those of Darwin's wealthy Whig background. Darwin became Grant's walking companion during excursions to collect specimens, in the process absorbing some of his enthusiasm for Lamarck. At the same time Darwin was exposed to Grant's conviction that the natural world was not caused by a series of divine creations, as taught by the clergy of Oxford and Cambridge, but instead had evolved due to purely natural causes.

Darwin left Edinburgh without a degree, having finally convinced his father of his utter loathing of medicine, who accordingly sent him off to Cambridge, to read divinity, the atmosphere there being more in accord with respectable Whig opinion. Darwin recounts in his autobiography that at the time he 'had scruples about declaring my belief in all the dogmas of the Church of England; though otherwise I liked the thought of being a country clergyman. Accordingly I read with care Pearson on the Creeds and a few other books on divinity; as I did not then in the least doubt the strict and literal truth of every word in the Bible, I soon persuaded myself that our Creed must be fully accepted.'

In the event Darwin's interest in his theological studies at Cambridge proved slight, though a final burst of cramming finally placed him tenth in a pass-list of 178 for a BA in divinity in 1831. One of the few theological books that captured Darwin's imagination was *The Evidences of Christianity* by the Reverend William Paley, a compulsory set-book for generations of Cambridge students that summarized the arguments of natural theology. Darwin revelled in Paley's cold, clear logic, effectively learning *The Evidences* by heart as he prepared for his exams. Paley's world was one of law and order, in which the tiniest details of the created world were not without meaning, illustrating the activities of a rational God who did nothing in vain. In later life Darwin recalled in his *Autobiography* the impact that Paley made on him during his time at Cambridge:

> I am convinced that I could have written out the whole of the *Evidences* with perfect correctness, but not of course in the clear language of Paley. The logic of this book, and, as I may add, of his *Natural Theology*, gave me as much delight as did Euclid. The careful study of these works... was the only part of the academical course which, as I then felt, and as I still believe, was of the least use to me in the education of my mind.

One of the passages that Darwin would have read in Paley's *Natural Theology* may, with the benefit of hindsight, be viewed as remarkably prescient of precisely the biological problem that Darwin was later to address so effectively. As Paley mulled over the way in which organisms are well adapted to their environments, he wrote:

There is another answer which has the same effect as the resolving of things into chance, which answer would persuade us to believe that the eye, the animal to which it belongs, every other animal, every plant, indeed every organized body which we see are only so many out of the possible varieties and combinations of being which the lapse of infinite ages has brought into existence; that the present world is the relic of that variety; millions of other bodily forms and other species having perished, being, by the defect of their constitution, incapable of preservation, or of continuance by generation.

Paley rejected such a possibility, partly because he could not conceive of such countless numbers of species disappearing when extant animals in general seemed so adaptable to their environments. Much later Darwin was to revive a very similar idea, an idea which he called 'natural selection'.

Though Darwin's commitment to divinity while at Cambridge was never excessive, other interests were pursued with considerably more passion, including his old pastimes of shooting and hunting. Darwin was also a founder member of the Glutton Club, a society devoted to the consumption of unusual meat. His fascination with natural history was stimulated by his friendships with John Henslow, the Professor of Botany, and with Adam Sedgwick, Professor of Geology. Henslow recommended that Darwin serve as naturalist on board the *Beagle* during a hydrographic survey of South America. Darwin's father thought the idea quite wild and opposed it on the grounds that Charles would be distracted from his calling as a clergyman. Fortunately Darwin's uncle Josiah Wedgwood came to his aid, writing to Charles' father that 'the pursuit of Natural History, though certainly not professional, is very suitable to a clergyman', and on 27 December 1831, Darwin finally set sail on what was to become a five-year voyage.

Darwin's voyage on the *Beagle* had a profound effect on his thinking about the natural world and it was out of the immense body of data collected during this period that the twin concepts of biological variation and natural selection eventually crystallized. His later description published as *The Voyage of the Beagle* still remains one of the classic accounts of scientific exploration. Among the many scenes that deeply impressed Darwin,

none exceed in sublimity the primeval forests undefaced by the hand of man; whether those of Brazil, where the powers of life are predominant, or those of Tierra del Fuego, where Death and Decay prevail. Both are temples filled with the varied productions of the God of Nature: no one can stand in these solitudes unmoved, and not feel that there is more in man than the mere breath of his body.

Volume 1 of Lyell's *Principles of Geology* went with Darwin on his voyage, Volume 2 catching up with him later. Lyell's emphasis on very gradual geological changes began to lay the groundwork in Darwin's thinking for the possibility of a long series of small biological changes eventually producing new life forms. Yet Lyell's proposition that species were created at the time and place when the conditions seemed right was not so satisfactory. The immense scale of animal extinction was overwhelming, and the extraordinary number of species and the remarkable variation in the flora and fauna from country to country made Darwin ponder whether each species could really have been created separately. The vivid images of untamed nature, in which animals struggled for survival and earthquakes devastated the environment, also did much to shake Darwin's faith in natural theology, the comforting scheme of an ordered world in which everything had a fixed purpose. In Chile Darwin himself witnessed a major earthquake. Could one still believe in divinely ordained nature when only the rubble remained from the cathedral at Concepción? Nature in the raw, where giant condors devoured sheep and cattle, was very different from the tidy world of English gardens and the manicured lawns of Cambridge colleges...

Returning to England in 1836, Darwin joined his opium-smoking literary brother Erasmus in London, later marrying his religious first cousin Emma, daughter of Josiah Wedgwood, who had become famous through his development of the porcelain industry. The wedding dinner consisted of sandwiches eaten on the train from Staffordshire back to London, and on his wedding night Darwin, never one to waste any time when it came to natural history, managed to record some notes on the properties of turnips. Settling down in Gower Street in London, Darwin was soon immersed in London's scientific circles, joining the prestigious London Geological Society, and becoming its secretary shortly afterwards. Emma's firstborn was called Willy, and Darwin studiously compared Willy's behaviour with that of Jenny the orang-utan recently obtained by London Zoo.

Darwin's new circle of London friends exposed him to a wide range of political and social views, some of which were to prove crucial in the development of his theory of 'transmutation'. The theories of the Reverend Malthus were a frequent topic of conversation at select dinner parties. Malthus had pointed out that populations grow geometrically, whereas food supplies grew arithmetically, particularly easy to believe during early-19th-century Britain when from 1801 to 1831 the population doubled from 12 to 24 million. The inevitable consequence was that population size would tend to outstrip the food supply, leading to famine and the reduction in size of the population. The Whigs supported Malthus, maintaining that the social world was part of nature, and should therefore be allowed to struggle and progress in accordance with God's laws. In contrast, conservative Anglican Tories thought that the Almighty had laid down fixed laws at the beginning for man, for animals and indeed for the whole universe. If the church were overthrown, everything would collapse.

Darwin was surrounded by these debates as he mulled over the enormous body of data culled from the *Beagle* voyage. He became convinced that indeed 'the Creator creates... by laws'. The problem with traditional views of the natural world were that they tended to invoke God to 'explain' phenomena that had not yet been brought under the sway of natural law. Darwin complained that 'we can allow satellites, planets, suns, universe, nay whole systems of universe[s], to be governed by laws, but the smallest insect, we wish to be created at once by special act'. His task was to uncover the laws whereby living organisms had arrived on the planet in such bewildering diversity, that 'origin of species' that had so often been referred to by his fellow naturalists as 'the mystery of mysteries'.

It was a further ten years before all the data obtained on the *Beagle* were classified, and Darwin then spent a further eight years in a detailed study of barnacles. Yet throughout this period he continued to work on 'my theory', as he came to call it. Darwin realized that the Malthusian struggle for survival in the animal world between competing individuals for a limited food supply would mean that only the fittest would survive. Beneficial variations would be passed on to progeny and the gradual accumulation of small variations would eventually lead to the origin of a new species. By early 1844 Darwin could write to his mentor Joseph Hooker that 'gleams of light have come, and I am almost convinced (quite contrary to the opinion I started with) that species are not (it is like confessing a murder) immutable... I think I have found out (here's presumption!) the simple way by which species become exquisitely adapted to various ends.' As Darwin later recounted:

> Here then I had at last got a theory by which to work; but I was so anxious to avoid prejudice, that I determined not for some time to write even the briefest sketch of it. In June 1842 I first allowed myself the satisfaction of writing a very brief abstract of my theory in pencil in 35 pages; and this was enlarged during the summer of 1844 into one of 230 pages, which I had fairly copied out and still possess.

What was the 'prejudice' that Darwin was so anxious to avoid? And why was it not until 1859, a full seventeen years after Darwin wrote the first brief description of his theory, that *The Origin of Species* finally appeared?

A crucial factor that explains Darwin's reticence in publishing his views was the political climate of England during the 1830s and 1840s, an era of poverty and social upheaval. In July 1830, when Darwin was still at Cambridge, the reactionary French king Charles X had abolished the government and Paris had tottered once more towards revolution. The exiled king fled to England, there to be sheltered by a Tory government, the Tories being the traditional defenders of Church and Crown. The parallel English movement for reform was accompanied by massive campaigns of civic disobedience, landowners and the fat and self-satisfied Anglican church alike becoming the focus for bitter attacks by starving agricultural labourers. As Darwin returned to England from the *Beagle*, the Duke of Wellington was complaining that the power of decent Tory Anglicans was being lost into the hands of Whig manufacturers, shopkeepers and atheists. The introduction of the New Poor Law, which abolished charity and forced the poor to compete for jobs or face the workhouse, was perceived by many as the direct outcome of Malthusian principles.

The late 1830s, that critical period when Darwin was forming his views on transmutation, were marked by a deep depression. There was widespread suffering among the poor as factories closed and workers were laid off, with 400,000 annually leaving the shores of Britain to look for a new life in the colonies. Dissident groups joined together to form the reformist Chartist movement, strongly tainted with the materialistic ideas of the French Revolution, which campaigned for a People's Charter demanding universal suffrage, annual elections and salaried MPs. The words 'atheism' and 'materialism' were used as derogatory terms by the government to attack the Chartist movement, raising the spectre that the terrors of the French Revolution might be repeated in England. This was no idle threat. A general strike was called by the Chartists in 1842 and half a million workers came out. Troops opened fire, killing demonstrators in several towns. Darwin's anatomist collaborator, Richard Owen, marched with the Honourable Artillery Company as they supported the police in their attempts to quell the mobs. The summer of 1842 was probably the closest that England came to revolution during the course of the 19th century, the very year in which Darwin first composed his theory in a written form. To have published evolutionary views at that time would have been to play straight into the hands of the radicals. Darwin, whose close scientific friends were largely from the Anglican elite, had no intention of his views on transmutation being turned into Lamarckian revolutionary rhetoric on the streets. As a respectable Whig gentleman, a member of the Athenaeum Club, the haunt of lords, bishops and cabinet ministers, Darwin had a profound belief in the rule of law. Nothing would have been more disturbing than for 'his theory' to be used as a slogan for revolution.

In 1842 Darwin finally left the noise and radical rhetoric of London to settle in the peace of the Kent countryside at Down, there to occupy a one-time vicarage and pursue a lifestyle reminiscent of a typical clerical–naturalist. While Emma fulfilled the Victorian goal of bearing a long succession of offspring, Darwin continued to polish his private written views on the origin of species. In 1844 an event took place that must have made Darwin even more reticent at the thought of making his views public. This was the anonymous publication of the *Vestiges of Creation* by Robert Chambers, a self-taught Scottish natural historian and publisher. The *Vestiges* was Chamber's response to the challenge which the Catastrophists had presented to Lyell: how could one unvarying natural law produce a steady progression of distinct organic forms? Chamber's answer was along the lines of German Nature Philosophy, proposing that there was a law of development, 'gradual evolution of higher from lower, of complicated from simple, of special from general, all in unvarying order, and therefore all natural, although all of divine ordination'. Chamber's analogy was the stages that a mammalian fetus appeared to go through prior to birth. The fetus of fish, reptile, bird and mammal all passed through the same initial stages of development. Any factor which prolonged gestation might then result in the emergence of a new type. Not content with applying his evolutionary ideas to the natural world, Chambers extended his ideas to build up a giant cosmic scheme, which extended to the formation of the solar system, in which all events reflected the unfolding of invariable laws.

The publication of the *Vestiges* aroused immediate controversy, and the book faced vigorous denunciations from both geologists and theologians. Its anonymity helped its publicity, the sale of its twelve editions boosted by a rumour that the author was none other than Prince Albert. There seemed to be something in the book calculated to annoy almost everybody. The natural philosophers did not like it, because it contained little in the way of science. Darwin commented that the book's 'writing and arrangement are certainly admirable, but the geology strikes me as bad and his zoology far worse'. If Chambers was right, declared Lyell, then 'all our morality is in vain'. Thomas Huxley moaned about the 'prodigious ignorance and thoroughly unscientific habit of mind manifested by the writer'. Adam Sedgwick, Darwin's geological mentor at Cambridge, made an emotional attack on *Vestiges* on the grounds that it propounded a materialistic philosophy and blurred all distinctions between the physical and the moral. Later on, when his identity became known, Chambers responded to such accusations by protesting that his work was a treatise on natural theology, arguing that 'I believe in a personal and intelligent God, and cannot conceive of dead matter receiving life otherwise than from Him, though of course in the manner of order or law.'

The passions aroused by the *Vestiges*, as well as the radical political climate, must surely have made Darwin wonder whether the 1840s was an appropriate time in which to publish 'his theory'. The way in which the book was torn to shreds by its scientific critics was also a warning to those who published controversial theories without the backing of solid evidence. As Darwin later recounted in his autobiography:

It has sometimes been said that the success of the *Origin* proved 'that the subject was in the air' or 'that men's minds were prepared for it'. I do not think this is strictly true, for I occasionally sounded not a few naturalists, and never happened to come across a single one who seemed to doubt the permanence of species...

Only in 1854 did Darwin finally write to his mentor Hooker: 'I have been frittering away my time... sending 10,000 barnacles out of the house all over the world. But I shall now in a day or two begin to look over my old notes on species.' The climate of the 1850s was very different from the 1840s. A new and more confident England was emerging, one of imperial supremacy driven by the machines of the industrial revolution. The ideas of progress and technological achievement were in the air, culminating in the Great Exhibition held in the giant iron-and-glass Crystal Palace at Hyde Park in 1851, a triumphant display of the mechanical fruits of the Industrial Revolution, ushering in a new age committed to progress and technology. The glistening Palace symbolized the aspirations of an emerging class of scientists and technocrats, who were gradually realizing that they had as much right as the old Anglican establishment of 'gentlemen natural philosophers' to receive the status and rewards of their profession.

The Origin of Species

In May 1856, Darwin embarked on what he intended to be a massive book, one that would encompass all his previous twenty years of painstaking observations and thinking about the natural world. But in 1858 Darwin received a letter from another naturalist, Alfred Russell Wallace, with an enclosed twenty-page manuscript that neatly encapsulated 'his' theory of the origin of species. Wallace, who had originally been attracted to the idea of evolution by reading Chambers' *Vestiges*, had even come to the idea of natural selection by a similar route to that of Darwin. While lying sick of malaria on the island of Ternate, near New Guinea, pondering on the reasons why some animals lived and others died, Wallace had realized that the inexorable law of population growth proposed by Malthus would ensure that only the fittest survived. Darwin was dumbfounded. At a stroke it seemed as if priority of publication would be taken from him, for Wallace's paper clearly seemed ready for publication. To his credit, Darwin behaved like a true Victorian gentleman, commenting to Lyell:

As I had not intended to publish any sketch, can I do so honourably because Wallace has sent me an outline of his doctrine? I would far rather burn my whole book, than that he or any other man should think that I had behaved in a paltry spirit.

But at the same time Darwin confessed that he would certainly 'be vexed if any one were to publish my doctrines before me'. Finally a group of friends arranged that both Wallace's paper and an extract from Darwin's 1844 manuscript should be read together at a meeting of the Linnean Society, together with a letter that Darwin had written to the American botanist Asa Gray in order to bring the material up to date. The papers were duly read on 1 July 1858, to about thirty Fellows of the society, but Darwin himself was unable to be present. Stricken with grief, he was attending the funeral of his retarded son, Charles Waring, who had died of scarlet fever. As it happened, the presentation of Darwin's and Wallace's papers made little impact at the time and when the President of the Linnean Society reviewed the year 1858 in his annual report, he recorded laconically:

The year which has passed... has not, indeed, been marked by any of those striking discoveries which at once revolutionize, so to speak, the department of science on which they bear.

Far more immediate impact was made by the publication of *The Origin of Species* in 1859, fourteen chapters and 155,000 words of detailed observation and argument, written for the new class of specialists in natural history. Wallace received a complimentary copy, with a covering letter from Darwin explaining that 'the book is only an abstract, and very much condensed. God knows what the public will think. No one has read it, except Lyell.' To allay any public concerns, Darwin placed a quotation at the front of his book taken from the Cambridge philosopher and clergyman William Whewell's *Bridgewater Treatise*, one of a series of volumes on natural theology:

With regard to the material world, we can at least go so far as this – we can perceive that events are brought about not by insulated interpositions of Divine power, exerted in each particular case, but by the establishment of general laws.

Clearly Darwin wanted to explain the origin of species without the need to refer to divine intervention. The quotation was certainly suitable for this purpose. But Darwin no doubt was also concerned that a stamp of respectability be given to a theory that, up until that time, was associated with political radicals and critics of natural theology. Darwin may also have been expressing his own genuine feeling of debt to the natural theologians. In his *Autobiography* he later mentions that when he was at work on the *Origin* (presumably in the 1840s) he still believed that this 'immense and wonderful' universe must have a First Cause, the source of the law-like behaviour in the natural world that Darwin was so committed to elucidating.

How did the public react to the publication of *The Origin of Species*? The mythology of the 'conflict thesis' has it that there was an immediate public outcry, with a sharp division soon developing between the church, with its doctrine of creation, and the scientists (as they were now beginning to be called) with their new 'law of evolution' that made any notion of creation unnecessary. In fact the response was extremely diverse. The introduction of any radically new theory invariably encounters a wide range of reactions. Darwin's revolutionary theory was no exception. There were scientists who opposed the theory on purely scientific grounds. There were scientists, both religious and secular, who rapidly incorporated the theory into their scientific worldview with the minimum of fuss. There were other scientists who opposed the theory on religious grounds. There were scientific popularizers and clerics who readily accepted Darwin's theory and quickly adapted it into the traditional framework of natural theology. And so the list could go on. The reception of Darwinism depended also on geography. As David Livingstone points out, three academic centres of the time shared in common a similar theological tradition, but the reception was warm in Edinburgh, negative in Belfast, and ambivalent in Princeton. To do proper justice to such heterogeneity would take a complete book, and all we can do here is to draw on a few examples to illustrate the diversity.

Scientific reactions to The Origin of Species

The major opposition to Darwin's theory came firstly from fellow scientists. As Huxley recalled when looking back in later years at the way in which *The Origin of Species* had been received: 'There is not the slightest doubt that, if a general council of the church scientific had been held at that time, we should have been condemned by an overwhelming majority.' Most of the scientific objections were ones that Darwin had himself anticipated, and which were discussed within successive editions of *The Origin of Species*. St George Mivart (1827–1900), a Catholic who in later life became Professor of the Philosophy of Natural History at Louvain University, was initially a strong supporter of Darwin's theory and never forsook his commitment to a theory of organic evolution. However, ten years after the publication of the *Origin*, Mivart shifted his position, holding that natural selection was only one of the mechanisms involved in evolution and that 'special powers and tendencies existing in each organism' were even more important. Mivart criticized natural selection for its inability to explain the persistence of apparently useless structures and for the difficulty, as he saw it, of explaining the evolution of structures that were only of use in their fully developed form, popularizing his views in a bestselling book called the *Genesis of Species*. Darwin commented on Mivart's book that it was 'producing a great effect against Natural Selection, and more especially against me'.

There were many converts to the theory of evolution, but few to the idea of natural selection, even strong supporters of Darwin, like Thomas Huxley, finding it difficult to accept that such an apparently random mechanism could generate such complexity of biological form and function. In response, Darwin modified the role played by natural selection in later editions of the *Origin*, giving greater emphasis to Lamarck's view that acquired characteristics could be inherited. By the time Darwin published his *The Descent of Man* in 1871, he was admitting

that in the earlier editions of *The Origin of Species* I probably attributed too much to the action of natural selection or the survival of the fittest... I had not formerly sufficiently considered the existence of many structures which appear to be, as far as we can judge, neither beneficial or injurious; and this I believe to be one of the greatest oversights as yet detected in my work.

To the end of his life Darwin defended the Lamarckian (and now discredited) idea that acquired characteristics could be inherited.

The rarity of transitional forms in the fossil record and the lack of a satisfactory mechanism to explain variation were other favourite objections raised by scientific critics of Darwin, who again had anticipated these points in extensive discussions within the *Origin*. The causes of variation, thought Darwin (wrongly as it turned out), lay within the environment, arising from 'new conditions of life'. By changing their habits in response to a changing environment, and by so doing using or disusing certain organs, animals could bring about variation in their offspring. Darwin's views on variation became the target for the physicist Henry Jenkins, who argued mathematically that useful variations would be swamped by subsequent breeding.

The lack of a satisfactory mechanism of inheritance was another gap in Darwin's theory that he freely admitted remained 'quite unknown'. Ironically, Johann Gregor Mendel (1822–84), a monk from Austrian Silesia (in what is now Czechoslovakia), published his particulate theory of inheritance in the *Proceedings of the Bonn Natural History Society* in 1866, but there is no evidence that Darwin ever read this paper. Given the mathematical content of Mendel's paper, it is doubtful that Darwin would have appreciated it. But it was the rediscovery of Mendel's pioneering work at the turn of the century that eventually led to the fusion of Darwinian evolution with modern genetic theory, the 'new synthesis' that developed into the current understanding of evolution. We now know that genes are the basis of both inheritance and variation between organisms, but Darwin had the arduous task of defending his theory without the advantages of such insights.

The scientific criticism that Darwin himself found most difficult to handle was the problem of time. The evolution of species through a myriad intermediate forms differing only in tiny details demanded an immense length of time. When the *Origin* was first published, Darwin was free to postulate from geological data 'incomprehensibly vast' aeons of time in which evolution had occurred. But Lord Kelvin (1824–1907), arguably the most important British physicist during the 19th century, gradually whittled away the age of the earth by basing his calculations on the rate of its cooling. In 1862 Kelvin thought that the maximum age of the earth was 400 million years, a time re-estimated to 100 million years by 1868 and to a mere 50 million years by 1876. Although the assumptions upon which Kelvin's calculations were based are now known to be incorrect, at the time they caused Darwin great concern, and he remarked that of all the problems that had been raised against his theory, the difficulty with time was 'probably one of the gravest as yet advanced'. The mathematical physicists like Kelvin remained largely sceptical about Darwinism during the latter half of the century. George Stokes, a physicist President of the Royal Society, remarked that 'Darwin's theory has been accepted by many eminent biologists with a readiness which is puzzling to an outsider, especially one accustomed to the severe demands for evidence that are required in the physical sciences.'

The geologist Lyell's very distinct concept of time, outlined in chapter 6, proved an obstacle to his acceptance of Darwinism for many years for reasons very different from those of Kelvin. Lyell believed that species appeared (by unknown means) already perfectly adapted to their environment in a steady and orderly manner, and that their extinction was equally orderly. The appearance of 'abruptness' in the geological record was an illusion created by its imperfections. Only when Lyell finally accepted that there had been true progression in the development of life forms of increasing complexity was he prepared to admit that evolution might be true. But his *Antiquity of Man* (1863) said little about the evidence for transmutation. Lyell never accepted natural selection and still baulked at the idea that man had descended from the apes. Lyell's hesitations were particularly hard for Darwin to accept, for it was Lyell's own gradualist emphasis that had helped to shape Darwin's own ideas about the pace of biological change. But, ironically, Darwin's theory of progressive transmutation turned out to be much closer in the end, at least in its concept of time, to the more historical accounts of the earth's history provided by the Catastrophists than to the steady-state ideas of the Uniformitarians. The earth *did* have a history, and the end-point of that history was the emergence of observers intelligent enough to have debates about it.

Certainly it would be quite mistaken to suggest that anyone who opposed Darwin's theory during the 19th century was obscurantist. Natural philosophers like Lyell and Kelvin were among the most famous of their time. Scientists have sometimes been guilty of triumphalist views of scientific theories, using the benefit of hindsight to extrapolate their modern understanding back into history in order to berate those who should have 'accepted the correct theory earlier'. Darwin's theory of evolution was a risky enterprise, a theory open to refutation, as Darwin himself was keenly aware. Given the complete lack of understanding of the mechanistic basis for key elements in the theory, such as inheritance, variance and natural selection, it is indeed remarkable that the vast majority of scientists had accepted Darwin's theory within a few decades of its publication. But for many the acceptance came slowly and only after a considerable period of initial hesitation and criticism.

Philosophical responses to The Origin of Species

The hesitations or outright opposition of some were rooted deeply in a neoplatonic stream of philosophy represented by an influential group of contemporary biologists. We have already noted that the anatomical ideas of Cuvier were based on the concept of a limited number of ideal fixed 'plans' of biological organization. Cuvier's main disciple in England was the distinguished anatomist Richard Owen (1804–92), whose declared aim in his anatomy textbooks was to reveal 'the unity which underlies the diversity of animal structures; to show in these structures the evidence of a predetermining will, producing them in reference to a final purpose'. Owen did not believe that there was any outside creative force animating inert matter. Instead, matter became living by an 'internal energy'. This life-force was limited, and could not stretch beyond the organizational plan that had already been marked out for its species. Any idea of conversion of one species into another was therefore impossible.

Not many went as far as Owen in their commitment to platonic idealism. But the platonic conviction that the various entities of the physical world were but imperfect reflections of underlying 'forms' or 'essences' had deep roots. As far as the heavens were concerned, the ideal world of platonic essences had crumbled with the revolution in astronomy, but in biology the old platonic ideas lived on, enshrined in the great systems of taxonomic classification introduced by John Ray in the 17th century and Carolus Linnaeus in the 18th century. As already noted in the previous chapter, deists like Voltaire believed even more firmly in the static nature of species than did theists like Ray. The impact of many centuries of platonic thinking helps to explain why it was so difficult for biologists steeped in this tradition to cope with Darwin's new concept of variable populations composed of unique individuals. In place of the 'fixed essence' of unchanging species was a dynamic system of evolving species, demonstrating an apparently endless array of variation.

Darwin's main scientific opposition in North America came from Louis Agassiz (1807–73), Professor of Geology and Zoology at Harvard, another biologist strongly influenced by Cuvier's platonic essentialism. Agassiz's distinctive approach was to baptize the ideas of Cuvier into the *Naturphilosophie* that he had imbibed during his education in his native Switzerland, that pantheistic idealism that identifies the activity of God as being one with nature. Agassiz has sometimes been presented as a precursor of the modern 'creationist' movement due to his anti-evolutionary views. However, it was Agassiz's conviction that the creative power of God could be discovered by the study of nature itself, quite apart from the Bible. As Numbers comments 'his creationism owed more to philosophy than to revelation'. Furthermore, Agassiz himself appears to have made little effort to practise the faith of his father, a Swiss Protestant pastor, making him an unlikely candidate as a 'creationist precursor'. Shortly before his death in 1873 Agassiz conceded that the idea of organic development had won 'universal acceptance'. Indeed, there were few scientists in North America who continued Agassiz's antagonism to evolution. Numbers reports that 'Beyond Dawson, and to a lesser extent Guyot, one searches in vain for a prominent late-19th-century North American scientist who actively opposed organic evolution.'

Darwin's willingness to incorporate new features into his theory in response to his critics as time went on is to his credit. It was his passionate commitment to detail that led Darwin into five painstaking revisions of the *Origin*. But it was this very flexibility to shape his theory according to the prevailing winds of criticism that helped convince others of Darwin's critics that his theory was not really 'scientific' anyway. The background to such philosophical attacks came from the continued dominance of Bacon's ideas about inductive science. Bacon's proposition that the scientific method involved the dispassionate collection of a large number of facts, followed by the induction of generalized laws derived from such facts, had been modified by earlier Victorian philosophers, such as William Whewell and John Stuart Mill, into a system in which deduction played a greater role. Nevertheless, even such a modified Baconian system was still expected to lead to 'scientific proof', a position of full and final certainty with regard to statements about the physical world. Darwin's theory of evolution was clearly far from such certainty, since the theory of natural selection depended on the interpretation of a large number of disparate observations, and no one had actually observed one species changing into another, for obvious reasons. Today Darwin's theory would be called a 'model', believable because of the elegant way in which it incorporates consistently such a wide variety of observations. But in Darwin's day his theory smacked of 'speculation', 'conjecture' and 'clever invention', being far from the public image of the 'assured results of science'. As usual, Darwin had anticipated such objections, writing at the end of the *Origin* that 'Any one whose disposition leads him to attach more weight to unexplained difficulties than to the explanation of a certain number of facts, will certainly reject my theory.' But this did not prevent popular magazines like *Punch* (in 1871) lampooning Darwin's failure to achieve the level of certainty that had supposedly been reached by scientific 'giants' such as Newton:

> *'Hypotheses non fingo',*
>   *Sir Isaac Newton said*
> *And that was true, by Jingo!*
>   *As proof demonstrated*
> *But Darwin's speculation*
>   *Is of another sort*
> *'Tis one which demonstration*
>   *In no wise doth support.*

The twin philosophical themes of platonic essentialism and Baconian inductivism recur repeatedly in the literature critical of Darwin during the three decades after 1859. Frequently, either or both of these philosophical strands are found thoroughly intertwined with specifically theological considerations, illustrating the ease with which secular philosophies have frequently been absorbed into the mainstream of the church's teaching, and then defended vigorously as if they were part and parcel of revealed dogma.

Christian responses to The Origin of Species

There were many scientists, both secular and religious, who accepted Darwinian evolution into their scientific worldview with very little fuss, although confusion over the precise understanding of 'natural selection' continued for many years. There was also a variety of opinions concerning the possible evolutionary origins of man, an issue that Darwin did not address directly until publication of his *Descent of Man* in 1871. Asa Gray, Professor of Natural History at Harvard, an orthodox Presbyterian in belief, had long been Darwin's confidante, and was one of the privileged few to receive advance complimentary copies of the *Origin*. It was Gray, whom Darwin described as a 'cautious... reasoner' but a 'loveable man', who had supplied much of the botanical data that contributed to Darwin's chapter on 'Variation' in the *Origin*. It was to Gray that Darwin sent a long letter describing his theory several years before publication of the *Origin*, a letter that was to prove crucial when read before the Linnean Society in establishing his priority. Gray responded by cautioning Darwin not to personify 'natural selection' as if it was itself a causal agent of change, instead of simply a way of winning life's race. Later Gray reviewed the *Origin* very favourably in the *American Journal of Science and Arts*, arranged for its publication in America and personally confronted neoplatonists such as Louis Agassiz over the question of transmutation at meetings of the American Academy of Arts and Sciences.

Since Darwin had no clear idea as to the source of variation in animals and plants, Gray proposed that 'variation had been led along certain beneficial lines' like a stream 'along definite and useful lines of irrigation', and that 'in each variation lies hidden *the mystery of a beginning*'. Not surprisingly, such a 'God-of-the-gaps' theology did not withstand the ravages of further scientific advances. But Gray did much to make evolution respectable in America, arguing that Darwinism liberated natural theology from common objections:

Darwinian teleology has the special advantage of accounting for the imperfections and failures as well as the successes. It not only accounts for them, but turns them to practical account. It explains the seeming waste as being part and parcel of a great economical process. Without the competing multitude, no struggle for life; and, without this, no natural selection and the survival of the fittest, no continuous adaptation to changing surroundings, no diversifications, and improvement, leading from lower up to higher and nobler forms. So the most puzzling things of all to the old-school teleologists are the *principia* of the Darwinian.

Though Darwin himself did not agree with Gray's idea of a 'divinely directed' evolutionary process, he was nevertheless happy to have Gray on his side to soothe theological concerns. When Gray printed some articles under the title *Natural Selection Not Inconsistent with Natural Theology*, Darwin was delighted, paying half the cost and posting 100 copies to both scientists and theologians in England. When Darwin in later life was replying to a letter asking whether theism and evolution were compatible, he replied saying that indeed it was possible to be 'an ardent Theist and an Evolutionist' – look at the example of Asa Gray. Gray was initially cautious in extending the theory of evolution to human origins, but became gradually convinced after reading Darwin's *Descent of Man*. In 1880, near the end of a distinguished scientific career, Gray was invited to give two lectures to the Theological School of Yale, declaring that:

Man, while on the one side a wholly exceptional being, is on the other an object of natural history – a part of the animal kingdom... He is as certainly and completely an animal as he is certainly something more.

We are sharers not only of animal but of vegetable life, sharers with the higher brute animals in common instincts and feelings and affections. It seems to me that there is a sort of meanness in the wish to ignore the tie.

Gray also reminded his audience that 'the high Calvinist and the Darwinian have a goodly number of points in common', referring to his Calvinist belief that God could use a long series of apparently random and even painful events to bring some beneficial outcome.

Gray is just one example of a considerable number of American scientists of Christian persuasion who rapidly absorbed Darwinian evolution into their view of natural history during the latter half of the 19th century. Joseph Henry, like his friend Asa Gray, was a churchgoing Presbyterian physicist who served as head of the Smithsonian Institute. 'I have given the subject of evolution much thought', wrote Henry to Gray, 'and have come to the conclusion that it is the best working hypothesis which you naturalists ever had.' The theologian and geologist George Wright (1838–1921), whose books on glacial geology were for years the standard texts on the subject, was not only a vigorous proponent of Darwinism, but held, as Moore points out, 'that Darwin's work actually allies itself with the Reformed faith in discouraging romantic, sentimental, and optimistic interpretations of nature'. Wright even wrote 'that Darwinism has not improperly been styled "the Calvinistic interpretation of nature"', agreeing with Gray's point that the purposes of God might well be achieved through events that appear entirely random to the observer.

As a leading spokesman among the Methodists, Alexander Winchell, Professor of Geology and Palaeontology at the University of Michigan, was clearly not in the Calvinist tradition but during the course of his career came progressively closer to a Darwinian understanding of evolution. Winchell played a major role in organizing geology as a science in the USA and was a founding member of the American Geological Society. By 1877 Winchell was assuring the readers of the *Methodist Quarterly Review*, in an article entitled *Huxley and Evolution*, that it was now preferable to accept the 'doctrine of derivative descent of animal and vegetal forms' than to reject it. James Dana, Professor of Natural History at Yale, and editor of *The American Journal of Science*, was another American geologist of orthodox Christian conviction who accepted Darwinian evolution after some initial doubts, initiating an influential series of lectures on evolution at Yale in 1883. Dana's concluding remarks of his opening lecture are informative, because they summarize what was clearly an influential emphasis in American academic circles of the late 19th century:

1. That it is not atheism to believe in a development theory, if it be admitted at the same time that Nature exists by the will and continued act of God.

2. That we cannot tell when we have ascertained the last limit of discovery with regard to secondary causes.

3. That God is ever near us, ever working in and through Nature...

In 1872, fewer than thirteen years after the *Origin*, the palaeontologist Edward Cope (1840–97) noted that 'the modern theory of evolution has been spread everywhere with unexampled rapidity, thanks to our means of printing and transportation. It has met with remarkably rapid acceptance by those best qualified to judge of its merits, viz., the zoologists and botanists.' By 1880 nearly all American naturalists were evolutionists and it is clear that a substantial number among them, of whom perhaps Gray, Wright and Dana are the most prominent examples, were insistent that Darwinism both could and should be baptized into a modified form of natural theology. The term 'Christian Darwinism' was being used as early as 1867. On details they certainly did not agree. Dana emphasized a much larger role for Lamarckian evolution (the inheritance of acquired characteristics) than either Darwin or Gray was willing to accept, although as noted above Darwin wavered considerably on this point in successive editions of the *Origin*. Many held that natural selection applied to the whole natural world, with the exception of a 'special creative act' that had been responsible for the origin of the first humans. In this respect they were far from the thoroughly non-providential tone of Darwin's *Ascent of Man*. But the overall impact of those American scientists who tried to relate the theory of Darwinian evolution to their religious beliefs was to validate the theory to segments of the church who might otherwise have viewed it with suspicion.

Although the *Origin of Species* was non-providential in tone, in the sense that it did not look to concepts such as 'design' or 'creative acts' as explanations for biological phenomena, it is not without good reason that the book has also been called 'the last great work of Victorian natural theology'. It was precisely Darwin's concern to demonstrate that the natural world was ruled by rational laws that attracted the sympathies of scientists such as Gray, Dana and Wright, who wished to maintain natural selection within the overall boundaries of God's providence. Darwin had, after all, been raised on Paley's natural theology, had received his scientific education almost entirely from clerics, and apparently believed for much of his life that the biological laws that he was discovering were but 'direct consequences of still higher laws'. Manier has observed that Darwin 'often employed the patterns of speech, the argumentative structures, and the basic concepts of Paley as if they were his own'. In his final chapter of the *Origin* Darwin underlined this point by stating that 'to my mind it accords better with what we know of the laws impressed on matter by the Creator, that the production and extinction of the past and present inhabitants of the world should have been due to secondary causes, like those determining the birth and death of the individual'.

As Darwin's son William later wrote of his father (1887): 'As regards his respect for the laws of Nature, it might be called reverence if not a religious feeling. No man could feel more intensely the vastness and the inviolability of the laws of nature, and especially the helplessness of mankind except so far as the laws were obeyed.'

For much of his life Darwin preferred to call himself an 'agnostic', the new term invented by Thomas Huxley, but he could still write to Asa Gray, 'I can see no reason why a man, or other animal, may not have been expressly designed by an omniscient Creator, who foresaw every future event and consequence.' Yet as far as Paley's argument from design was concerned, Darwin would have none of it, once confiding to Hooker (in a sentence already quoted in the last chapter): 'What a book a Devil's Chaplain might write on the clumsy, wasteful, blundering low & horridly cruel works of nature!' These two contrasting remarks illustrate Darwin's own ambivalent feelings toward religious belief, feelings which oscillated quite markedly during the latter half of his life. In 1879, during the time that he was writing his *Autobiography*, Darwin wrote: 'My judgment *often fluctuates*... In my most extreme fluctuations I have never been an Atheist in the sense of denying the existence of God. I think that generally (and more and more as I grow older), *but not always*, that an Agnostic would be the more correct description of my state of mind.' 'I am in an utterly hopeless muddle,' wrote Darwin on one occasion to Asa Gray, 'I cannot think that the world, as we see it, is the result of chance; and yet I cannot look at each separate thing as the result of Design.' Darwin continued the same theme in a letter to William Graham after reading Graham's book *The Creed of Science*: 'You have expressed *my inward conviction*, though far more vividly and clearly than I could have done, that *the universe is not the result of chance*. But then with me the *horrid doubt* always arises whether the convictions of man's mind, which has been developed from the mind of the lower animals, are of any value or at all trustworthy.'

Just as the responses of scientists to the *Origin* were immensely varied, so were the reactions of church leaders on both sides of the Atlantic, a point well illustrated by the very different approaches taken by two leading Anglican churchmen at the 1860 meeting of the British Association for the Advancement of Science in Oxford. The official sermon at the meeting was preached by Frederick Temple, the future archbishop of Canterbury, who argued that the activity of God was to be discerned throughout the laws governing the natural world, not in the gaps in current scientific knowledge. Although Temple did not mention Darwin by name, one member of his congregation recounted afterwards that 'he espoused Darwin's ideas fully!' Later Temple was to develop this theme in his Bampton lectures of 1884, in which he presented a specifically Darwinian view of evolution.

On the last day of the 1860 meeting (June 30) William Draper, first President of the American Chemical Society, was scheduled to read a paper on the

Intellectual Development of Europe considered with reference to the views of Mr Darwin. Huxley had not intended to attend this last session, but was persuaded to stay by Chambers, the anonymous author of the *Vestiges*, who was eager to see opponents of evolution publicly defeated. The only item in the session that everyone who was there appears to agree about was the interminably long and boring address by Draper, whose brand of social Darwinism was never very popular among British scientists. What happened in the rest of the session has become part of the heroic mythology of the 'conflict thesis'. 'Soapy Sam' Wilberforce, Bishop of Oxford and a Vice-President of the British Association, well known for his eloquence, spoke for about half-an-hour in response to Draper, taking the opportunity to attack Darwin's *Origin*, summarizing many of the points soon to be published in his critical review of the *Origin* which appeared in the July issue of the Tory *Quarterly Review*. Owen had lodged with Wilberforce the previous night and had apparently primed him well from his anti-evolutionary repertoire, although Wilberforce probably needed little assistance, having just written his own critical review for the *Quarterly Review*. According to Huxley's account, written down thirty-one years after the event, Wilberforce then tried to lighten the proceedings by turning to Huxley and asking whether it was on his grandfather's or grandmother's side that he was descended from an ape, thereby casting aspersions on that peculiarly sensitive Victorian nerve of female ancestry. Huxley's account then goes on to describe how he muttered in an undertone 'The Lord hath delivered him into mine hands', and so proceeded to 'let him have it', referring to the combative reply with which he demolished 'Soapy Sam's' arguments.

Although the Huxley–Wilberforce debate of 1860 was for a long time one of the star events in the 'warfare' interpretation of the relation between science and religion, even providing material for TV reconstructions, more recent scholarship has thrown doubt on Huxley's version of the events. For example, Wilberforce's comments on apes have been called into question by alternative versions of his words given by others present at the meeting. Furthermore, Darwin's botanizing confidante, Joseph Hooker, also present, recounted later in a letter to Darwin that Huxley indeed made some comments in reply to Wilberforce, but Huxley 'could not throw his voice over so large an assembly, nor command the audience; & he did not allude to *Sam's* weak points nor put the matter in a form or way that carried the audience'. Instead Hooker recounts how *he* eventually asked permission to speak '& then proceeded to demonstrate... 1 that he could never have read your book & 2 that he was absolutely ignorant of the rudiments of Bot[anical] Science'. Both Hooker and Huxley left Oxford clearly convinced that they had been the hero of the hour, though Hooker's version of his role in the final session is supported by a contemporary report in *The Athenaeum*. In contrast, an account of the debate in Wilberforce's biography does not present it as a defeat for the bishop. At least one early convert to Darwinian evolution, the naturalist Henry Baker Tristram, actually stopped believing in evolution as a result of the debate, so convinced was he by Wilberforce's criticisms. *The Athenaeum* was correct in stating that 'the most eminent naturalists assembled at Oxford' were on Wilberforce's side. Wilberforce was paid £60 to review the *Origin* in the *Quarterly Review*, so it seems very unlikely that he had not read the book as Hooker claimed. As it happens, many of the critical points that Wilberforce raised were the very ones that had caused Darwin so much anguish as he wrote the *Origin*. After reading Wilberforce's review, Darwin commented that 'it picks out with skill all the most conjectural parts, and brings forward well all the difficulties'. A passage from the concluding section of Wilberforce's review certainly does not give the impression that he was quite the obscurantist cleric that Huxley tried to make out:

> Our readers will not have failed to notice that we have objected to the views with which we are dealing solely on scientific grounds. We have done so from our fixed conviction that it is thus that the truth or falsehood of such arguments should be tried. We have no sympathy with those who object to any facts or alleged facts in nature, or to any inference logically deduced from them, because they believe them to contradict what it appears to them is taught by Revelation. We think that all such objections savour of a timidity which is really inconsistent with a firm and well-intrusted faith.

Wilberforce was convinced that the weight of scientific evidence was against the theory of natural selection. Considering the lack in 1860 of evidence for intermediate forms, of any known mechanism of inheritance, and the fact that the breeding of hybrids was invariably sterile, the grounds for believing Darwinian evolution in 1860 were certainly much weaker than they were to become 100 years later.

What really happened in the legendary debate of 1860? Certainly there was an exchange of scientific views, probably debated with some passion and perhaps rudeness. But the sociological roots of the debate, so thoroughly reviewed over the past few decades, ran far deeper. Science in Britain had been dominated by gentlemen-clerics for so long, imbued with the traditions of natural theology, frequently from secure and privileged backgrounds that allowed them the finance and the freedom to pursue their research. Darwin himself was a typical example of this older type of natural historian. But by 1860 the pattern was changing. A new professional class of scientists was emerging who had risen to prominence from a variety of backgrounds, and who were now eager to use the growing status of science in society to win the kind of privileges previously given only to the gentlemen-clerics. This new professional class became increasingly hostile towards the non-specialist 'amateurs'. When the British Association for the Advancement of Science had been founded in the early 1830s, clerics had formed about 30 per cent of its membership. From 1831 to 1865, forty-one Anglican clergy had presided over its various sections but from 1866 to 1900 this number was only three. Much of this shift towards professionalism was due to a younger breed of scientists, like Huxley, a schoolmaster's son who had experienced the greatest difficulty in seeing his career as a naturalist established. So the legendary encounter at Oxford in 1860 must be viewed against this background. What right had these meddling clerics to comment on a subject that was now firmly in the hands of the specialists?

As far as the debate within the Anglican Church was concerned, Temple was by no means the only prominent clerical voice to advocate the acceptance of Darwinian evolution soon after the *Origin* appeared. The novelist and socialist Charles Kingsley, who later became Professor of Modern History at Cambridge, was delighted with the *Origin*, writing to Darwin that the book '*awes* me... if you be right I must give up much that I have believed'. Kingsley proceeded to do just that, remarking that the theory of natural selection provided 'just as noble a conception of Deity, to believe that He created primal forms capable of self-development... as to believe that He required a fresh act of intervention to supply the *lacunas* which He Himself had made'. Darwin was so impressed with this response that he quoted these lines in the second edition of the *Origin* hoping, no doubt, to sway the clerical doubters.

Kingsley's emphasis on the continued creative activity of God in generating biological diversity is also found in the writings of the Oxford Anglo-Catholic Aubrey Moore (1843–90), theologian, Fellow of St John's College, Oxford, and curator of the Oxford Botanical Gardens. Moore maintained that evolution should be 'specially attractive to those whose first thought is to hold and to guard every jot and tittle of the Catholic faith'. The reason for this attraction, claimed Moore, was based on the intimate involvement of God in His creation, for:

There are not, and cannot be, any Divine interpositions in nature, for God cannot interfere with Himself. His creative activity is present everywhere. There is no division of labour between God and nature, or God and law... *For the Christian theologian the facts of nature are the acts of God.*

Moore did much to attack the earlier ideas, which tended to crop up in the concepts of natural theology, that God's activity was to be looked for in those aspects of the natural world that science could not yet explain. Darwin's close friend, the botanist Hooker, was also well aware of the dangers of natural theology to Christian faith. Natural theology was, said Hooker, 'the most dangerous of all two-edged weapons... it seeks to weigh the infinite in the balance of the finite, and shifts the ground to meet the requirements of every new fact that science establishes, and every old error that science exposes. Thus pursued, Natural Theology is to the scientific man a delusion, and to the religious man a snare.'

Historians have sometimes suggested that Darwin *stole* his universe from the natural theologians, in the sense that he replaced God by natural selection. There is certainly truth in this claim, in that the acceptance of Darwin's theory marked a decline in the popularity of the old arguments from design. Nevertheless, at the same time, one could also say that Darwinian evolution *disinfected* Christian theology of some of the accretions that had grown up round it over the centuries, in particular the idea that knowledge of the character and being of God could be derived from a detailed study of the natural world. One result of this disinfecting process was that theologians were forced back to what, as it happens, was a more biblical concept of the relationship between God and the world, which we shall review further in chapter 10.

Some of Darwin's supporters among the theologians were almost embarrassing in their excesses. Henry Drummond, Scottish naturalist and Professor in the Free Church College in Glasgow, believed with Herbert Spencer that evolution could be applied to every aspect of life. Drummond thought that natural selection was 'a real and beautiful acquisition to natural theology' and that the *Origin* was 'perhaps the most important contribution to the literature of apologetics' to have appeared during the 19th century. In his *Ascent of Man* Drummond argued that the 'Struggle for Life' had resulted in the evolution of man, but that the process had gradually developed into the 'Struggle for the Life of Others', the physical forces that produced evolution having spiritual and moral aspects. These wild extrapolations from biological evolution to society as a whole were rather typical of the social Darwinists of the period, but Darwin had little time for them, preferring evolution as a biological theory, not as a theory 'for the explanation of everything'.

Other supporters of Darwin among the theologians either tended to be in the same Calvinist tradition as Gray and Wright in the United States, or in the Anglo-Catholic tradition of Aubrey Moore. Although in many respects these traditions were very different, the readiness with which they absorbed Darwinian evolution was rooted in the same conviction that God was actively sustaining His world in every aspect and that biological explanations were simply descriptions using a different language of how God had chosen to order things. James McCosh, for example, who was firmly in the Calvinist tradition, held the Chair in Metaphysics in Queen's College, Belfast, before crossing the Atlantic to become President of the College of New Jersey (later to become Princeton University). McCosh held strongly to the concept of natural selection, but believed equally firmly that 'the natural origin of species is not inconsistent with intelligent design in nature or with the existence of a personal

Creator of the world'. Upon looking back over twenty years as President of the College of New Jersey, McCosh remarked that 'I have been defending Evolution but, in so doing, have given the proper account of it as the method of God's procedure, and find that when so understood it is in no way inconsistent with Scripture.' The Princeton theologian B.B. Warfield supported McCosh in his providentialist interpretation of God's activity in the world, remarking in later life that he had been a 'Darwinian of the purest water' even before McCosh became president of Princeton. In his series of lectures on anthropology, Warfield persistently emphasized that theists could hold to a completely mechanistic theory of life and origins, provided they also believed that natural laws were the expression of divine supervision. In light of the contemporary 'creationist' belief that the Bible is in some sense opposed to the theory of evolution, it is of interest to note Warfield's remark of a century ago that 'I do not think that there is any general statement in the Bible or any part of the account of creation, either as given in Genesis 1 and 2 or elsewhere alluded to, that need be opposed to evolution.'

By mentioning certain church traditions as having prominent adherents who were vocal in their support of Darwinian evolution, it would be a distortion to imply that any one tradition was entirely consistent in this respect. For example, William Whewell, the polymath cleric and Master of Trinity College, Cambridge, represented the older tradition of natural theology and resisted the *Origin*. The reasons for his resistance remain as a classic statement of the 'God-of-the-gaps' position:

It still appears to me that in tracing the history of the world backwards,
so far as the palaeontological sciences enable us to do so, all the lines of
connection stop short of a beginning explicable by natural causes; and the
absence of any conceivable natural beginning leaves room for, and requires,
a supernatural beginning. Nor do Mr Darwin's speculations alter this result.
For when he has accumulated a vast array of hypotheses, still there is an
inexplicable gap at the beginning of the series.

Charles Hodge (1797–1878), Professor of Theology at Princeton, who had been raised in the same school of Calvinism that characterized Gray, Wright and Warfield, was even more opposed to Darwinism than Whewell, writing in 1874: 'We have thus arrived at the answer to our question, What is Darwinism? It is atheism.' The reasons for Hodge's opposition to Darwinism are intriguing. He was a great admirer of the Baconian ideal in science, thinking that an industrious collection of 'facts' would eventually give rise to generalized scientific laws. Hodge followed Agassiz in maintaining that 'facts' were sacred, whereas theories were mere speculations that should therefore be discounted.

So in his book *What is Darwinism?*, Hodge explains that the greatest weakness in Darwinism is that it was a 'mere hypothesis... incapable of proof'. A similar misunderstanding of the status of scientific knowledge in general, and of evolutionary theory in particular, can still be found in contemporary 'creationist' literature. It is also clear that Hodge had his own particular definition of Darwinian evolution, writing that 'the most important and only distinctive element' of the theory was the idea that 'natural selection is without design, being conducted by unintelligent causes':

> It is... neither evolution nor natural selection, which gives Darwinism its peculiar character and importance. It is that Darwin rejects all teleology, or the doctrine of final causes. He denies design in any of the organisms in the vegetable or animal world... As it is this feature of his system which brings it into conflict not only with Christianity, but with the fundamental principles of natural religion, it should be clearly established.

Darwin himself remained agnostic as to whether there was some ultimate 'intelligent cause' that supervised the natural world, while accepting that his theory of natural selection was not inimical to belief in God. Hodge thought otherwise, maintaining that one could be a theist and an evolutionist, but not a theist and a Darwinian evolutionist, since this would involve acceptance of natural selection which, for Hodge, meant giving up the traditional claims of natural theology. Hodge even accused Gray, Darwin's main defender in America, of not being a real Darwinian at all because he still held on to the idea of God's design in creation! It is clear that the central problem with Darwinism for Hodge was not particular scientific or biblical objections, but rather the apparent threat to the accumulated traditions of centuries of natural theology. For Darwin himself, Hodge maintained a correct gentlemanly respect, remarking that Darwin was 'on all sides respected not only for his knowledge and his skill in observation and description, but for his frankness and fairness'.

Such politeness was not always shown by others of Darwin's less academic clerical opponents. The ornithologist rector of Nunburnholme in Yorkshire, Francis Morris (1810–93), spent more than twenty years in crusading against Darwinism, writing:

> Ineffable contempt and indignation is the only feeling which any person of common sense and of a right mind must feel at the astounding puerilities of Darwinism.

The Reverend Morris was not the only one to be long on robust prose, but short on argument. Some sections of the popular press, from which the less well-read clerics derived their information about evolution, had a field day with Darwinism. The Victorian era was the age of periodicals. The satirical magazine *Punch* published a series of articles and cartoons, playing on the theme of man's monkey origin, a theme which the average Victorian appears to have found either threatening or hilarious, depending on taste. The *Family Herald* claimed, on 20 May 1871, 'Society must fall to pieces if Darwinism be true.' Nevertheless, such comments were not necessarily typical of the periodicals of the time. In an exhaustive study of the treatment of Darwinism in 115 British periodicals, including forty-five religious serials, published over the period 1859–72, Ellegard reports that the reviews of the *Origin* ranged from fair to favourable.

No doubt the fears of many members of the general public were allayed when Darwin himself was buried in Westminster Abbey in 1882, Huxley, Hooker and Wallace being among the pallbearers. It was, above all, a patriotic occasion. As Darwin was laid to rest alongside Isaac Newton, David Livingstone and the other 'greats' of English history, it was as if Darwinian evolution itself was baptized into respectable Victorian society. How could such a theory be threatening when its author was accorded such respect by the full weight of the secular and religious organs of the state? Francis Galton, who had campaigned for Darwin's burial in the Abbey, captured the feeling when he spoke of the thrill of 'national honour and glory' at the ceremony, which illustrated the moral duty that scientists had in fusing the ideas of human evolution with the ideals of religion 'upon which the social fabric depends'. Following the funeral the secular and religious press alike vied with each other in their praise of Darwin. *The Times* thought that Darwin gave the Abbey 'an increased sanctity, a new cause for reverence' by being buried there. Darwin was described as a 'true Christian gentleman'. *The Church Times* adulated Darwin for his patience, calmness, industry and moderation. In New York a Unitarian preacher, John Chadwick, declared that 'The nation's grandest temple of religion opened its gates and lifted up its everlasting doors and bade the king of science come in.' Evolution, finally, had been 'respectified'.

Towards the end of the 19th century, Asa Gray commented to the Bishop of Rochester that 'he could not say that there had been any undue or improper delay on the part of the Christian mind and conscience in accepting, in such a sense as he deemed they ought to be accepted, Mr Darwin's doctrines'. In retrospect, considering the enormous paradigm shift in biological thinking that arose from the theory of natural selection, and bearing in mind the threat that evolutionary theory presented to traditional natural theology, it is remarkable that Darwinian theory was accepted so widely and so rapidly. By 1885, according to Owen Chadwick, acceptance of the view that evolution and Christian doctrine were compatible was more or less complete among more educated Christians, although there were some who continued to believe in a special act of creation for humans, while holding to a theory of natural selection for the evolution of plants and animals. 'If you are *in even so slight a degree* staggered,' Darwin had written to his old friend Henslow, referring to the implications of 'his theory', 'then I am convinced with further reflection you will become more and more staggered, for this has been the process through which my mind has gone.' Along with Darwin, the Victorian world staggered, but then, as the older revolutionary associations of the word 'evolution' receded into history, happily absorbed the new 'law of natural selection' into the established social order.

Ironically, Darwinian evolution as a scientific theory went into decline at the turn of the century, then to be revived in the 1920s by the fusion of Mendelian genetics with natural selection, to generate the 'synthesis' that forms the basis of contemporary theory. The 1920s also saw the beginnings of the 'creationist' movement in America, the roots of the so-called 'scientific creationists' of today, whose claims will be further examined in chapters 9 and 10. But it is important to emphasize that 'scientific creationism' began as a 20th-century phenomenon quite alien to the dominant views of the late-Victorian churches.

Beyond biological evolution

We have surveyed some of the varied responses to Darwin's *scientific* theory of 'natural selection', particularly with reference to religious responses. But in practice, as John Brooke remarks with reference to the debate on evolution, 'scientific and religious beliefs were so enmeshed in broader social and political debates that attempts to extricate them and relate them one to the other can be extremely artificial'. This was particularly so because 'evolution' itself was used with so many shades of meaning, often as a weapon to support nearly every major ideology of the 19th century, many of them mutually incompatible. Not surprisingly, when presented in such ideological packages, 'evolution' tended to be embraced or rejected for reasons that had little to do with science.

One complicating factor was that the churches during this period were passing through a period of debate and inner turmoil, and occasionally these debates became obfuscated with scientific issues. *The Spectator* reported in 1861 that 'of all tastes common among the middle class, the taste for discussing half-understood theology is perhaps the most pronounced'. For example, only three months after Darwin's *Origin* appeared, seven Anglican clerics produced a book called *Essays and Reviews* in which they attempted to publicize some of the more moderate theories of German biblical criticism. The book sold 22,000 copies in two years, more than the *Origin* sold in the next two decades, and was met by public and ecclesiastical uproar. More than 400 books, pamphlets and articles were written in reply. There was little about evolution in the *Essays*, though one of the authors, the Reverend Baden Powell, Professor of Geometry at Oxford, who was already strongly supportive of evolution, predicted that the *Origin* 'must soon bring about an entire revolution in opinion in favour of the grand principle of the self-evolving powers of nature'. Another contributor, C.W. Goodwin, attacked the habit of reading scientific meanings into the biblical text, giving as an example the various mutually contradictory ways in which attempts had been made to reconcile the Genesis account of creation with geology during the earlier part of the century. The opening essay was by Frederick Temple, who argued that to fear the result of scientific investigation was nothing short of 'high treason against the faith'. But the *Essays* only mentioned science in passing. Their main thrust was a plea to understand the Bible in its historical context. Clearly some felt that this was an attack on the faith itself. But the *Essays* appear to have contributed little, if any, fuel to the idea of 'conflict' between science and faith. The debate that they aroused was one carried on in a religious context, the 'conflict' largely being one between the liberal and conservative wings of the Anglican church.

It should be said that Darwin, country gentleman that he was, experienced frequent horror at many of the ways in which his theory was used, preferring to avoid all controversies of religion and politics. The *Origin* was translated into French by Clemence Royer, complete with an anticlerical harangue as a preface, which presented the reader with a stark choice between the 'rational revelation' of scientific progress and the 'obsolete revelation' of Christianity. Meanwhile Vladimir Kovalevsky was translating the same book into Russian as part of his evolutionary crusade against Russia's Orthodox autocracy. In Germany, Darwin's main defender was the zoologist Ernst Haeckel. But, unlike the pragmatic Darwin, Haeckel had imbibed Goethe's mystical philosophy of Nature-worship while at the University of Wurzburg, and tried to apply the principle of natural selection to the evolution of the whole of society, arguing that it drove 'the peoples irresistibly onward... to higher cultural stages'. Haeckel wanted to take the churches over and redecorate them with symbols of nature and science, and hoped that eventually he would be elected the 'anti-pope' by apostles of free thought. His view of nature has been described as resembling 'a giant work of art, almost yearning for the creator he kept begrudging it'. When Haeckel met Darwin for the first time, he described the encounter in quasi-religious terms. Darwin was

> tall and venerable... with the broad shoulders of an Atlas that bore a world of thought: a Jove-like forehead, as we see in Goethe, with a lofty and broad vault, deeply furrowed by the plough of intellectual work. The tender and friendly eyes were overshadowed by the great roof of the

prominent brows. The gentle mouth was framed in a long, silvery white beard.

But when Haeckel's two 500-page volumes of his *Generelle Morphologie* reached Down House soon afterwards, Darwin was less than happy. Haeckel had managed to incorporate natural selection into a 'universal Theory of Development, which embraces in its vast range the whole domain of human knowledge'. To make matters worse, Haeckel envisaged that the laws of biological and national evolution would lead to a new Teutonic superiority in a unified Germany, and that a new *phylum* of superior people would emerge as a result of evolutionary struggle. When Haeckel welcomed Bismarck to Jena he declared that 'While the booming of guns at the Battle of Koniggratz in 1866 announced the demise of the old Federal German Diet and the beginning of a splendid period in the history of the German Reich, here in Jena the history of the *phylum* was born.' In retrospect the sentiments seem sinister; for Darwin at the time they were simply frustrating – the obfuscation of a strictly biological theory by layer upon layer of philosophizing. Furthermore, Haeckel's evolution came packaged in a vindictively anticlerical package that Darwin found distasteful. It was small wonder that 'evolution' in Germany became associated in the public mind with assaults on religion and theories about society rather than with biology alone.

The British equivalent to Haeckel was the philosopher Herbert Spencer. 'Petty, monotonous, self-pitying, cantankerous – Spencer was the Eeyore of Victorian science', Jim Moore records, clearly reflecting Darwin and Huxley's opinions about the matter, at least in later life. From the 1840s onward Spencer had begun to develop a grandiose sociological system, expanded in a verbose series of ten volumes published from the 1860s onward entitled *System of Synthetic Philosophy*. Spencer believed that there was an 'Unknowable Power that makes for righteousness' that was gradually but inevitably manifesting itself through an evolutionary process not unlike that proposed by Lamarck. Whereas Darwin had imbibed the optimistic mid-Victorian view that humanity had evolved so far that it was likely that it would continue to progress from barbarity to civility, he would never make any promises that evolution *would* continue in that direction. As he once remarked, 'There is nothing in my theory necessitating in each case progression of organization, though Natural Selection tends in this line, and has generally thus acted.' In contrast, Spencer was convinced that progress was 'not an accident, not a thing within human control, but a beneficent necessity'. Spencer maintained that the entire universe was ascending towards ultimate perfection through the operation of inexorable physical laws – a true forerunner of Teilhard de Chardin. It was he, not Darwin, who coined the phrase 'survival of the fittest' (in 1852), using the word 'fittest' with distinct moral overtones.

It is not surprising that Spencer's optimistic progress-oriented philosophy proved so popular, because it fitted well with the spirit of the age – particularly in the USA, where evolution was seen by the general reading public largely through Spencerian spectacles. John Fiske toured around giving lectures on Spencer's views, extending them to include an evolutionary version of American history. America had a 'manifest destiny' whereby the 'Anglo-Saxon' race would eventually bring peace and prosperity to the entire human race by means of an evolutionary process. In Scotland Henry Drummond, as we have noted, reinterpreted Spencer's philosophy in optimistic theological terms. But Spencer's grandiose 'theories of everything' proved too much for his fellow countrymen, and Darwin summarized his own views on Spencer in a passage carefully edited out of his published autobiography by his son Francis:

> I am not conscious of having profited in my own work by Spencer's writings. His deductive manner of treating every subject is wholly opposed to my frame of mind. His conclusions never convince me... His fundamental generalizations (which have been compared in importance by some persons with Newton's laws!)... are of such a nature that they do not seem to me to be of any strictly scientific use. They partake more of the nature of definitions than of laws of nature... they have not been of any use to me.

Spencer was a member of the 'X club', a dining club for the scientific elite, so-called because the intention was to have ten members, though a tenth was never in fact included. The other X club members seem to have shared Darwin's sentiments, partly because Spencer tended to philosophize at their dinners at great length, and was generally so boring and unable to listen to anyone else that they closed the proceedings early when he attended meetings.

'Evolution' in the most general sense was a wonderful argument for almost anything. As G.B. Shaw once remarked: Darwin 'had the luck to please everybody who had an axe to grind'. The Tories liked natural selection because it seemed to underpin ideas of capitalist laissez-faire economics in which only the 'economically fit' survived. When Spencer visited America in 1882, the businessman Andrew Carnegie was there to hear him. Later Carnegie wrote *The Gospel of Wealth* (1890) in which he argued that the wealth and improvements of modern civilization had only happened because of the law of competition. We must 'accept and welcome... great inequality' wrote Carnegie, 'the concentration of business, industrial and commercial, in the hands of a few; and the law of competition between these, as being not only beneficial, but essential to the future progress of the race'. Why? Because capitalism alone 'ensures the survival of the fittest'. The American W.G. Sumner, who preached a social Darwinism, maintained that 'If we do not like the survival of the fittest, we have only one possible alternative, and that is the survival of the unfittest. The former is the law of civilization; the latter is the law of anti-civilization'. J.D. Rockefeller (1839–1937) later maintained:

> The growth of a large business is merely a survival of the fittest... The American Beauty rose can be produced in the splendor and fragrance which bring cheer to its beholder only by sacrificing the early buds which grow up around it. This is not an evil tendency in business. It is merely the working-out of a law of nature and a law of God.

Meanwhile socialists were trying to use evolution to prop up theories of class conflict in which progress occurred in society as one class overthrew another. Karl Marx (or possibly his de facto son-in-law Aveling[2]) wanted to dedicate *Das Kapital* to Darwin, who politely declined. Marx wrote to Lassalle (16 January 1861) that 'Darwin's book is very important and it suits me well that it supports the class struggle in history from the point of view of natural science. One has, of course, to put up with the crude English method of discourse.' When Engels was giving Marx's graveside eulogy at Highgate cemetery in 1883, he declared, 'Just as Darwin discovered the law of development of organic nature, so Marx discovered the law of development of human history.' Socialists in Britain clearly agreed. The *Bradford Labour Echo* asked rhetorically in 1871, 'What is Socialism but the development of a new social organism, where each part works for all, and all for each? It is in the direct line of evolution.' The Fabian Annie Besant declared in a pamphlet of this era, 'I am a Socialist *because* I believe in evolution.'

Darwin himself was a shrewd capitalist, investing very successfully in the stocks of railway companies, noting that England would only stay a vital and progressive country if there was unimpeded competition with minimal state interference. In 1875 the expenditure on meat in the Darwin household hit a five-year low, only £221, and total expenditure was £900, only 10 per cent of Darwin's earnings, which included substantial interest from investments. The total wages for the Darwins' seven servants in the same year came to just £86. Such ratios were not abnormal for a large Victorian household, but they illustrate how the Malthusian struggle for existence certainly validated the status quo. Nevertheless, as Darwin cheerfully explained, the forces of natural selection were somewhat suppressed among the civilized nations: 'With highly civilized nations continued progress depends in a subordinate degree on natural selection, for such nations do not supplant and exterminate one another as do savage tribes.' Despite this 'subordinate role' for natural selection, Darwin clearly thought that the struggle between nations was similar to the struggle going on in the natural world, asking a correspondent to 'Remember what risk the nations of Europe ran, not so many centuries ago of being overwhelmed by the Turks, and how ridiculous such an idea now is! The more civilized so-called Caucasian races have beaten the Turkish hollow in the struggle for existence.' Furthermore, Darwin was in no doubt that the European aristocracy were more handsome than the middle classes; evolution had ensured that the most powerful members of society really did deserve their status. There was no doubt, also, that women were 'inferior intellectually' to men, as Darwin wrote enthusiastically to an American feminist.

As we noted in chapter 2, Darwin himself never consciously used his theory to support racist theories, but simply absorbed the racist stereotypes typically held by a Victorian gentleman. Others were not so restrained. If the 'struggle for existence' had brought the 'civilized nations' to the pinnacle of power, then surely it was only logical and 'natural' that they should continue to suppress the 'lower races'? In his book *Sunshine and Storm in Rhodesia* (1896), F.C. Selous tried to defend the brutalities of colonial rule, arguing that the black should either accept the white man's rule, or die in trying to resist it, since this was

a destiny which the broadest philanthropy cannot avert, while the British colonist is but the irresponsible atom employed in carrying out a preordained law – the law which has ruled upon this planet ever since... organic life was first evolved upon the earth – the inexorable law which Darwin has aptly termed the 'Survival of the Fittest'.

Clearly, being an 'irresponsible atom' in a 'preordained law' was a very convenient role for someone engaged in suppressing another nation.

Given the immense range of understandings during the 19th century of the terms 'natural selection', 'evolution', 'survival of the fittest', and so on, the difficulty of making broad generalizations about the factors that affected the reception of Darwinism is hardly surprising. What is clear, however, is that Darwinism was not itself so much the source of new religious, political or sociological theories but rather a convenient prop that could be used to support ideas that in most cases had already been around for a very long time. Indeed, it seems to be the mark of all highly successful scientific theories that attempts are usually made by society, sooner or later, to utilize their intellectual prestige for non-scientific ends.

Where, then, are the real roots of the 'conflict thesis' theory of the relationship between science and faith in the English-speaking world? Certainly not in the debate about evolution. For those roots we must look elsewhere: to the growing professionalization of science that was taking place during the latter half of the 19th century.

The Victorian 'conflict thesis'

In 1800 science in Britain was largely an activity run by amateurs. Financial support for science was mainly by patronage, the level of government funding being trivial in comparison. There were few opportunities for scientific employment. Most scientific research was carried out by gentlemen of leisure with private funding, typically clerics or those with lands, and the Royal Society provided a fashionable forum in which such gentlemen could meet in a convivial atmosphere to present their findings. Specialization was rare, dabbling in a broad range of scientific interests still common. Natural philosophers frequently expressed the hope that their findings would support the tenets of natural theology. Patronage and employment in the sciences was much easier to find for clergy, or for laymen known for their religious commitment. There were few scientific journals. The universities and secondary schools were dominated by clerics and the teaching of science was marginalized by the major emphasis placed on the arts, particularly the classics. Only in the Dissenting Academies, as mentioned above, was there a systematic attempt at a scientific education.

By 1900 all this had changed. The scientific enterprise by then was not dissimilar to the one that we know today. 'Scientists' had both a name that everyone agreed upon, a new status as a group of professionals, and numerically were far greater than in 1800. Public spending on science had increased dramatically, though of course never to the extent that the scientists wanted. Science had become more specialized, reflected in a plethora of specialist societies and journals. Clerics were less represented in the scientific world, their own calling having become increasingly professionalized during the century in response to the needs of rapidly expanding urbanized populations. Scientists were motivated less by the tenets of natural theology to pursue their professions, being more likely to practise their religious beliefs as an activity separate from their professional lives as scientists. Scientific education was now a major emphasis in both the universities and secondary schools.

It has been convincingly argued that the social changes required for such a dramatic transition of the scientific enterprise from its 1800 form to its 1900 form lie at the heart of the Victorian 'conflict thesis'.[3] In 1851 Charles Babbage complained that 'Science in England is not a profession: its cultivators are scarcely recognized even as a class. Our language itself contains no *single* term by which their occupation can be expressed.' But from the 1850s onward a new group of scientists emerged, a group that Leonard Huxley later called 'the young guard of science', who began to campaign for greater recognition of the professional rights and status of scientists. Among these early campaigners in the X Club were: Thomas Huxley, a biology lecturer at the School of Mines (which later became Imperial College); Joseph Hooker, Director of the Royal

Botanic Gardens at Kew; and a pugnacious Irish physicist called John Tyndall. In 1864 the X Club comprised these three, together with George Busk (surgeon), John Lubbock (astronomy and mathematics, and a neighbour of Darwin's at Down), T.A. Hirst (mathematician), Edward Frankland (chemist), William Spottiswoode (publisher and mathematician) and Herbert Spencer (author). All except Spencer were Fellows of the Royal Society and three held office as its President at various times.

Although the extent to which the X Club members acted as an organized body in campaigning for their goals remains unclear, it is apparent that individual members of the group were highly effective campaigners for the rights of scientists, drawing moral support from the other members. The X Club members comprised scientists who had grown up on the peripheries of the Victorian establishment, well outside the privileged circle who had easy access to financial support for their science. They had mostly been educated in London medical schools, the civil service, Scottish universities or in Dissenters' colleges. Huxley, for example, had worked as a medical student among the poor of the East London slums, then spent four years working as a biologist on a surveying ship, making his name for his studies on sea squirts. He was then duly elected as a Fellow of the Royal Society, but was unable to obtain a job, being turned down by a succession of universities. There were simply too few jobs available that depended on merit rather than patronage. Indeed, Huxley was in such dire financial straits for a while that he was unable even to afford decent lodgings or to bring his fiancée to England from Australia – they were forced to spend six years apart before finally marrying in 1855. Although Huxley eventually obtained his lecturing job at the School of Mines, he never forgot the humiliation of being excluded from the financial benefits enjoyed by the English scientific elite, even though his scientific research was clearly worthy of recognition. One of the earliest campaigns of the 'young guard' was to fight for more pay for London's science lecturers, much inferior at the time to that enjoyed by the clerical naturalists up at Cambridge.

The X Club members were, to a man, 'scientific naturalists', that is they saw their science as providing a particular worldview that encompassed 'rational facts' in contrast to the world of religion that dealt with metaphysical theories and opinions. It was therefore of vital importance that scientists as a profession exerted their own domination over their science, not allowing it to be controlled, as in the past, by the 'amateurish' clerics. This professional domination was particularly important in those cases in which clerical opinion appeared to threaten the freedom of scientific enquiry by propounding 'dogma' in the place of 'scientific facts'. Edward Frankland reported of his X Club colleagues that they were all 'of one mind on theological topics', and even suggested that Darwin, Huxley and Spencer were 'the three great modern evangelists whose literary work will guide the thoughts and actions of men long after the teachings of the four older evangelists have become obsolete'.

Of all the X Club members, Huxley was the one who campaigned against clerical prestige and 'interference' in scientific affairs with the greatest vigour and bombast. As a propagandist for the cause he was brilliant. Huxley used the classic strategy of portraying his 'minority group' as being unjustly treated by the majority, then proceeding to attack the majority with venom so that the views of the minority could be made crystal clear in the resulting conflict. 'If I have a wish to live thirty years' wrote Huxley in 1859, 'it is that I may see the foot of Science on the necks of her enemies.' A year later we find him exploding:

> Extinguished theologians lie about the cradle of every science as the
> strangled snakes besides that of Hercules; and history records that
> wherever science and orthodoxy have been fairly opposed, the latter have
> been forced to retire from the lists, bleeding and crushed if not annihilated;
> scotched if not slain.

Huxley's campaign required Enemies, and fortunately Enemies in abundance were available. Enemy Number One was clearly the Catholic Church, which Huxley described as 'our great antagonist' and 'that damnable perverter of mankind', apparently playing on the public anti-papal sentiments then prevalent. After the hapless Mivart had defected from the Darwin camp by ceasing to accept natural selection as a satisfactory mechanism to explain evolution, Huxley pursued him relentlessly, accusing him of being 'poisoned with... accursed Popery and fear for his soul'. Mivart had added insult to injury by claiming in print that evolution was fully compatible with the Catholic fathers such as Augustine and Aquinas, and with the last great scholastic, Suarez. For Huxley, this was too much. To have a clearly defined Enemy was one thing, but the idea that a divinely directed form of evolution had always been part of the Catholic faith (apart from being historically fanciful) ran the risk of making the Enemy look more respectable. In a review Huxley snarled:

> If Suarez has rightly stated Catholic doctrine, then is evolution utter
> heresy. And such I believe it to be... Indeed, one of its greatest merits in my
> eyes, is the fact that it occupies a position of complete and irreconcilable
> antagonism to that vigorous and consistent enemy of the highest
> intellectual, moral, and social life of mankind – the Catholic Church.

Mivart was understandably puzzled that Huxley should be so upset by his 'attempt to show that there is no real antagonism between the Christian religion and evolution', not realizing what is easy to see in retrospect – that the antagonism that Huxley was trying to engender between science and religion had little to do with ideas, but much to do with the institutional control of society.

Huxley's rhetoric was also closely linked with nationalism. It was Science that was going to keep England great. It was Science that was going to keep British industry ahead of her German competitors. When Huxley lectured at the Royal Institution on Darwinism in 1860, he questioned whether England would play a noble role in this 'revolution' of thought, answering his own question with this ringing challenge:

> That depends upon how you, the public, deal with science. Cherish her, venerate her, follow her methods faithfully and implicitly in their application to all branches of human thought, and the future of this people will be greater than the past. Listen to those who would silence and crush her, and I fear our children will see the glory of England vanishing like Arthur in the mist.

Huxley, nicknamed the 'General' by his followers, was an immensely popular public speaker and drew large crowds. In 1866, 2,000 people had to be turned away at St Martins Hall in London when Huxley was inaugurating his 'Sunday evenings for the People'. These were designed to provide scientific lectures at a time when the Victorian faithful were supposed to be in church. Huxley cultivated the style and the dress of a cleric, canvassing for 'scientific Sunday Schools', speaking of 'the church scientific' and referring to himself as its 'Bishop' (though probably not taking kindly to those who lampooned him as being its 'Pope'). In some ways Huxley was not so far from the world of the French Philosophe De Fontenelle, who once remarked of physics that it 'becomes a kind of theology when it is pursued correctly'. Those in the X Club's sphere, like Darwin's cousin Francis Galton, tended to slip into the same language, Galton referring to the new class of professional scientists as the 'church scientific'. The rule of Natural Law was the new religion to replace the old and scientists were to be the new guardians of public morals. When Huxley lectured to the working classes he taught them that 'physical virtue is the base of all other, and that they are to be clean and temperate and all the rest – not because fellows in black with white ties tell them so, but because these are plain and patent laws of nature which they must obey "under penalties"'. In an echo of the Athanasian creed, Huxley called his trust in scientific method the 'agnostic faith, which if a man keep whole and undefiled, he shall not be ashamed to look the universe in the face, whatever the future may have in store for him'.

Huxley was much more sympathetic to Anglican clerics than he was to his pet hate, the Catholic Church. This was particularly true when they came out publicly in support of Darwin, or when disrespect to Anglicanism might be interpreted as anti-English sentiment, something that Huxley abhorred. In his personal life, Huxley maintained a strongly Puritan streak, admiring the Old Testament prophets for their denouncements of injustice and oppression and, in his work for the London Education Board, fighting for the inclusion of Bible-reading in the school curriculum. Huxley's eulogies of science and scientists were highly moralistic, again echoing the world of De Fontenelle who had assigned to the scientific prophet the virtues of 'dedication, unswerving allegiance to truth, fortitude, tranquillity, and even righteousness'.

Only when it seemed that clerics of any hue were claiming territory that rightfully belonged to Science did Huxley move into full combat in order to 'smite the Amalekites' (clerical opposition). He wrote of his 'untiring opposition to that ecclesiastical spirit, that clericalism, which in England, as everywhere else, and to whatever denomination it may belong, is the deadly enemy of science'. John Tyndall put the point equally succinctly in his address to the British Association in Belfast in 1874, when he declared that men of science 'claim, and... shall wrest from theology, the entire domain of cosmological theory. All schemes and systems which infringe upon the domain of science must, in so far as they do this, submit to its control, and relinquish all thought of controlling it.' It is precisely this point which helps to explain why Huxley wanted to build up the story of his encounter with Wilberforce 1859 to such legendary proportions. Wilberforce stood for all that Huxley abhorred, a clerical 'amateur' meddling in the 'domain of science'. Wilberforce had a first in maths from Cambridge, was a keen geologist and ornithologist, and was a vice-president of the British Association, originally founded for scientifically minded clerics just like himself. No wonder he symbolized for Huxley a threat to the dominance of the newly emerging class of professional scientists.

Ironically Darwin persisted in calling himself a 'naturalist', and was firmly in the tradition of the gentlemen amateur naturalists who, supported by their own finances, had no particular professional position or duties. But Huxley, Darwin's 'bulldog', called himself a biologist and struggled for more science teaching posts in schools and universities. The words used to describe the new breed of 'scientists' were sensitive issues and Huxley fought over them long and hard. Darwin himself hated public conflict and debate, and was far happier at home with his barnacles and his worms. He was grateful for Huxley's support, but baulked at his abrasive style, seeing little point in being so confrontational. It was probably just as well, then, that Darwin did not read the letter sent by Huxley to Hooker in 1859 concerning a proposed research fund:

> If there is to be any fund raised at all, I am quite of your mind that it should be a scientific fund and not a mere naturalists' fund... For the word

'Naturalist' unfortunately includes a far lower order of men than chemist, physicist, or mathematician. You don't call a man a mathematician because he has spent his life in getting as far as quadratics; but every fool who can make bad species and worse genera is a 'Naturalist'.

By 1880 Huxley and his 'professionals' had largely attained their goals. Members of the X Club and their circle had achieved editorships, professorships and offices in all the major scientific societies. It is surely no coincidence that of all the eligible chemists who might have been chosen in 1877 to preside over the first professional association for scientists, the one chosen was Edward Frankland, the only chemical member of the X Club. Three members of the X Club, Huxley, Hooker and Spottiswoode, occupied the presidency of the Royal Society during the period from 1873 to 1885. At the same time there was a spectacular growth in the number of scientists in Britain, and the membership and prestige of the scientific societies likewise grew. In 1847 the membership rules of the Royal Society were changed in favour of those with scientific rather than social qualifications, and in the same year the Philosophical Club of the Royal Society was founded, limited to forty-seven members who had to be scientists engaged in research. With the increasing professionalization of the scientific community, the percentage of clerics in the scientific societies steadily fell (10 per cent of the Royal Society's membership was Anglican clergymen in 1849, 3 per cent in 1899). During the first thirty-five years of the British Association's history (1831–65) nine clergymen held the office of president; during the following thirty-five years there were none. Though these figures reflect a clear shift to scientific professionalism, they do not necessarily imply that the membership of these societies were becoming more secular in their personal beliefs. According to an analysis by Harrison of the officers of the Royal Society from 1850 to 1900, 170 'man-years' of office-holding were accounted for by men committed to Christianity, whereas 108 'man-years' were by men committed to 'scientific naturalism', the brand of anticlerical religious agnosticism espoused by Huxley.

Huxley and his fellow campaigners also saw education as a key area that had to be 'wrested' from clerical control. Education in Britain remained largely in the hands of the Anglican and Catholic Churches until the Education Act of 1870, which destroyed their monopoly. The new professional scientists wanted full control of scientific teaching positions and school curricula, goals that brought them into direct opposition with these churches, though not with the Nonconformists, who were also campaigning for non-sectarian education. In 1874 the Orangeman John Tyndall directed a particularly bitter attack on the Catholic Church and its grip on education in Ireland during a meeting of the British Association in Belfast. At the time his speech caused a far greater stir than the legendary encounter between Huxley and Wilberforce at Oxford fourteen years earlier, apparently because those who read the speech later in England interpreted it as a general attack on religion. However, a few months before the Belfast meeting the Irish Catholic authorities had refused a request to incorporate physical science in the curriculum of the Catholic University, so there seem to have been good local reasons for Tyndall's attack. The competition for institutional control of education clearly contributed to the idea that there was 'conflict' between the competing agendas of scientists and clerics.

Despite the minority status of scientists committed to 'scientific naturalism', therefore, there seems little doubt that hostility towards religion became associated in many people's minds with the emergence of science as a separate and prestigious professional community during the latter half of the 19th century. This association was reinforced by a series of popular books, all published in London, that hammered home the metaphor of 'warfare' between science and religion. The titles speak for themselves: *History of the Conflict between Religion and Science* by J.W. Draper (1875); *A History of the Warfare of Science with Theology in Christendom* by A.D. White (1896); and *Landmarks in the Struggle Between Science and Religion* by J.Y. Simpson (1925). These books achieved immense sales and helped in shaping the views of several generations concerning the relationship between science and religion. They stand as classic examples of the Whiggish interpretation of history: tales of triumphant Scientists winning great victories over the Enemies of Science – the retrograde clerics who were keeping the people in ignorance and darkness. No modern historian of science now accepts the 'warfare' metaphor proposed by these titles as an adequate description of the historical relationship between science and faith. Furthermore, the many historical inaccuracies and distortions in these volumes have been thoroughly catalogued in earlier generations, and need not detain us. Of greater interest is the way that the 'warfare' metaphor was so readily absorbed by generations of readers, and the particular historical reasons why each of these books was written.

The Victorians were familiar with war at a distance: the horrors of the Crimea and the heroic Florence Nightingale; the siege of Khartoum and Gordon's tragic sacrifice; the Indian mutiny; the Boer war; endless 'skirmishes with the natives' in remote corners of the Empire. But few outside the armed forces had any personal experience of war. Far from war's brutal realities, it was relatively easy to take the military metaphor and use it for a multitude of ends. This was the era of 'Onward Christian Soldiers, Marching as to War' and, in America, the 'Battle Hymn of the Republic', the era which saw the founding of the 'Church Army' and the 'Salvation Army'. The churches in general do not appear to have felt uncomfortable in using military imagery on a massive scale. When Huxley and his followers took up military metaphors they were only echoing phrases and terminology which were already part of religious discourse. 'Under the circumstances of the time' explained Huxley, 'warfare has been my business and duty', reminding the mild-mannered Darwin as he read a pre-publication copy of the *Origin* that 'some of your friends... are endowed with an amount of combativeness which... may stand you in good stead. I am sharpening up my claws and beak in readiness.' In a lecture at the Royal Institution in 1860 Huxley painted a graphic portrait of Science as being 'Crushed and maimed in every battle, it yet seems never to be slain; and after 100 defeats it is at this day as rampant, though happily not so mischievous, as in the time of Galileo'.

Those who described the 'conflicts' in their bestselling books had particular reasons of their own to further the 'warfare' metaphor. John Draper was a Professor of Chemistry and Physics in New York. The son of a Methodist minister, Draper's later religious development is difficult to assess, since he ordered his correspondence to be destroyed at the time of his death. Nevertheless, it is clear that his own religious beliefs were deistic rather than theistic, God being the great cosmic architect who had set the whole universe in motion, a universe now developing inexorably by the laws of evolution. It was Draper who had droned on so interminably about Darwinism and the 'intellectual development of Europe' before Huxley's legendary encounter with Wilberforce at Oxford. But one does not need to read many pages of Draper's *History* to realize that the prime target for Draper's *Conflict* story was not 'Religion', but in fact the Roman Catholic Church. Like Huxley, Draper had been dismayed by the various papal edicts pronounced during the decade after 1860, culminating in the declaration of papal infallibility in 1870. 'Roman Christianity and Science', wrote Draper, 'are recognized by their respective adherents as being absolutely incompatible; they cannot exist together; one must yield to the other; mankind must make its choice – it cannot have both.' In order to bolster his case, Draper painted a graphic and greatly exaggerated picture of the power of the Catholic Church – 'the most widely diffused and the most powerfully organized of all modern societies'. There is, therefore, a certain irony in the observation that it was precisely the crumbling of Catholic temporal power in Italy during this era that led to such vigorous attempts to maintain centralized control of the Catholic Church at large. A crystallizing of papal authority had nothing to do with science, but much to do with the army of Victor Emmanuel II, King of Piedmont and Sardinia, who was at that very time decimating the papal lands, until they were finally restricted to their present tiny dimensions. To have a roaring lion in distant lands was a useful fiction for Draper's conflict thesis, but in reality there is no evidence that any papal pronouncements had the slightest effect in impeding the progress of science during the time when the fifty printings of Draper's book were appearing in the United States during the second half of the 19th century. The many Catholic scientists making active advances in research during this period, including such household names as Pasteur, Ampère and Volta, do not appear to have felt unduly restricted in their work by their Catholicism, despite Draper's 'narrative of... two contending powers'.

Unlike Draper, Andrew White was a historian, who became in 1868 President of Cornell University, one of the first non-sectarian universities in the USA. The founding of Cornell was clearly a threat to those denominations that, until then, had exerted complete domination over college education in America. White's *History of the Warfare of Science with Theology in Christendom* was an attack not on religion, but on dogmatic theology. As a professional historian White was a little more accurate than Draper in his pronouncements but still highly selective in his choice of material. Many of his claims have been shown to be misleading by more recent historians.[4] White's main concern was to defend the ideals of non-sectarian education in the USA from the opposition of religious and educational traditionalists. As the Cornell historian Carl Becker later commented, White was 'essentially a crusader... His crusading spirit extended to every aspect of life on campus.' White's 'warfare of science with theology' was a convenient platform from which to campaign for secular education, much as the circle round the X Club somewhat earlier had used warfare terminology in their fight against ecclesiastical control over education in Britain. In his personal beliefs Draper remained a respectable 'churchman' (his own term), commenting in his magnum opus that the 'most mistaken of all mistaken ideas' was 'the conviction that religion and science are enemies'. Unfortunately his book had the long-term effect of reinforcing precisely this mythology. The realization that science, like theology, could to some extent be culturally determined did not fit easily with White's triumphalist view of science, nor with the spirit of his age. As Colin Russell remarks, the ideas of Draper, White and many of their contemporaries, that there existed 'an endemic hostility between science and religion could well be a cultural artefact, reflecting social tensions, aspirations and fears in the 19th century... one is not too far from the mark to assert that the conflict thesis... is an artefact of Victorian social ambition'.

The 19th-century legacy

The 19th-century 'conflict thesis' set the agenda for the interpretation of the relation between science and faith for at least the first half of the 20th century. The conflict was real enough within its own historical context. The century did see the professionalization of science, with all the social tensions that this entailed. There was competition between religious and secular institutions in the areas of education and public funding, and over the question of who was to be the dominant intellectual voice in society. The century did see a decline in the popularity of natural theology as a motivation for carrying out scientific research and as a way of viewing the natural world.

But during the second half of the 20th century the roots of the conflict thesis withered. While public attitudes towards scientists are ambivalent, scientific communities no longer find themselves competing with ecclesiastical institutions for intellectual or educational dominance in society. Professionalization of science and privatization of religion in modern Western society normally ensures that everyone goes about their own business with little interference from competing claims. At the same time, triumphalist accounts of scientific progress have become less common. A vast wealth of modern research has revealed historical interactions between science and faith far more subtle and complicated than the black-and-white battle-lines drawn by the protagonists of the Victorian era. The 'conflict' metaphor has been found inappropriate by modern historians in writing the history of science. Cultural influences in the building of science as a body of constructed knowledge are now more frequently recognized. A static view of theology as a fixed body of beliefs held in sterilized isolation from surrounding culture, is no longer popular.

To pretend that the 'conflict thesis' had died, however, would be an exaggeration. Though it has largely died in academic research, it remains alive and well in the public consciousness. As we considered in chapter 1, the idea that 'science' and 'faith' are mutually incompatible is a presupposition that tends to be absorbed unconsciously as a 'fact', usually during schooling and via the impact of mass media. In sociological and psychological terms, the 19th-century legacy is an enduring one.

The question of course still remains as to whether scientific knowledge does, as a matter of fact, make religious knowledge irrelevant or untenable. We may accept that the Christian religion, in particular, has had a significant effect on the development of modern science, and that many leading scientists down the centuries have not only been committed to a personal faith in God, but have also seen their faith as being profoundly relevant to their research. Nevertheless, we might still maintain that scientific knowledge has now developed to the point at which genuine conflict with religious ideas becomes inevitable, and that the 'conflict thesis', though bankrupt as an accurate metaphor for the historical relationship between science and faith, now *ought* to be the way in which that relationship should be described. The remainder of this book addresses this contemporary question.

Chapter 8

Reweaving the Rainbow
Scientific Knowledge and Religious Knowledge

When we run over libraries, persuaded of these principles, what
havoc must we make? If we take in our hand any volume — of divinity
or school metaphysics, for instance — let us ask, Does it contain
any abstract reasoning concerning quantity or number? No. Does it
contain any experimental reasoning concerning matter of fact and
existence? No. Commit it then to the flames, for it can contain
nothing but sophistry and illusion.

David Hume, *An Enquiry Concerning Human Understanding*

Religious believers, unlike scientists, typically and characteristically seek to preserve their favoured models from criticism at
all costs and in the face of whatever difficulties they encounter —
something that would certainly be seen as irrational in a scientist.

A. O'Hear, *Experience, Explanation and Faith*

You clearly can be a scientist and have religious beliefs. But I don't
think you can be a real scientist in the deepest sense of the word
because they are such alien categories of knowledge.

Peter Atkins

When we first begin to believe anything, what we believe is not a
single proposition, it is a whole system of propositions. (Light
dawns gradually over the whole.)

Ludwig Wittgenstein, *On Certainty*

At the heart of discussions about science and faith lies the question of *knowledge*.
What *is* scientific knowledge? And what *is* religious knowledge? And what is the
relationship between the two?

Studying scientists themselves is of little help in arriving at an understanding of the content of scientific knowledge. Scientists are a nondescript and often rather scruffy-looking bunch of people, and an investigation of their immensely varied backgrounds, personalities, research interests, artistic tastes and political views would be unlikely to generate any useful information about the kind of constructed knowledge that they spend their lives in generating. As the Nobel prize-winning immunologist Peter Medawar once wrote: 'Scientists are people of very dissimilar temperaments doing different things in very different ways. Among scientists are collectors, classifiers and compulsive tidiers-up; many are detectives by temperament and many are explorers; some are artists and others artisans. There are poet-scientists and philosopher-scientists and even a few mystics.'[1]

The best way of elucidating the distinctive characteristics of scientific knowledge is not to look at scientists themselves, but at that voluminous weekly outpouring of results and discussion that fills up the many thousands of scientific journals currently being published. What constitutes scientific knowledge is not some abstract definition in a textbook of philosophy but the articles written and published by the international scientific community following a process of peer review and editorial selection. Read your daily paper, and then dip into a selection of journals picked at random off the shelves of the science section of a university library. What are the crucial differences between these two forms of communication?

A restriction on the questions being addressed

It does not take much reading to conclude that the contents of scientific journals, while vast in scope with reference to their coverage of the natural world, are deliberately restricted to lists of topics that are considered appropriate for scientific analysis. No one doubts that the working of lasers, the influence of drugs on the brain, the sequencing of genes, the evolution of humans, the birth of stars or the search for the ultimate physical particles, are entirely suitable topics for submission to scientific journals. But a vast amount of human activity and discourse, the very material that makes your daily paper so saleable, is carefully weeded out of scientific discourse.

Aesthetics
One whole area of human experience that is excluded from scientific journals is *aesthetics*, for the simple reason that the appreciation of art, music, theatre and cinema is a matter of subjective judgment made by individuals acting as human agents who describe their impressions of a particular art-form within the

context of their own personal histories and experiences. The art critic who writes in your newspaper uses the same grammar, syntax and rational modes of persuasion and argument that are used by the scientist in the laboratory, but what counts as 'relevant data' for the art critic is obviously very different from the kind of data acceptable for a scientific publication. Someone who compares the opinions of five different art critics writing about the same art exhibition in five different newspapers will not be in the least surprised to read five quite different opinions. Which opinion they tend to accept will depend on their faith in a particular critic as an expert guide in the world of art. Nevertheless, when they go personally to view the art exhibition they may disagree with all five opinions and come away with some very different impressions of their own. People are not expected to appreciate a work of art in exactly the same way. A scientist may come along and record the opinions of thousands of people about the same work of art, even attempting to tabulate their opinions in some numerical form and giving the numbers statistical validation, but such information is quite different from the individual's personal experience of the painting, and no amount of tabulation can tell anyone whether or not their experience of a particular work of art is 'correct'.

One poet who writes about a sunset may write full of foreboding for what the next day may bring, because this was the sunset that marked the last day of peace before an expected outbreak of war. Another poet may watch an identical sunset and write only of the changing kaleidoscope of colours lighting the sky over the misty blue mountains. For a third poet the same sunset may act as a trigger to write about the day that her father died, when she held his lifeless hand as the weak rays from the setting sun lit up the hospital ward with their ghostly glow. All three poetic reactions to the same event are entirely appropriate, thoroughly rational and dictated uniquely by the circumstances of the individual's recent history. If the three poems were published in the same volume, no one would be likely to complain that the descriptions of the sunset were contradictory. In contrast, if three physicists analysed the wavelengths of the various colours emanating from the same sunset at the same moment, we would worry about their skill or the accuracy of their instruments if the results reported were not in close agreement. Reproducible observations are boring in poetry, valued in science. Aesthetic judgment is personal and idiosyncratic. Scientific knowledge comprises generalizations that are potentially valid and reproducible for any observer in any country under a given set of carefully defined circumstances.

The strongly personal element of aesthetic appreciation is not the only reason why it is excluded from the scientific reporting process. Data-gathering by scientists is in no sense an impersonal exercise – far from it; the primary reality that we all experience as conscious, sentient beings is that which comes via our senses, and scientific data are gathered via the same senses that provide the raw data which we interpret as an aesthetic experience. But the collecting of scientific data is generally directed towards solving a problem or elucidating some aspect of the physical world with the ultimate aim of constructing generalized statements that make phenomena both understandable and predictable. In contrast, Bach, disco music, Rembrandt or Picasso are not exercises in problem solving (at least, not for the listener/viewer) but personal experiences to enjoy and savour (or dislike). An audience will not be censured for their inability to construct generalized statements about their combined experiences at the end of an enjoyable concert. They may all have enjoyed the music for very different reasons. And why not.

The view expressed here is somewhat different from that put forward by Edward Wilson in his book *Consilience* (1998) in which Wilson argues that there is an essential unity of knowledge that transcends the boundaries between the arts and the sciences. Wilson attempts to break down the boundaries between the two disciplinary areas by recourse to evolutionary naturalism, the view, expanded on more fully in chapter 11, that all forms of human experience and behaviour find their ultimate explanation in evolutionary biology. Wilson sees the essential unifying factor in the arts as being 'human nature' and because the natural sciences are beginning to form a picture of the mind, he thinks this will eventually lead to insights into the creative process itself. While agreeing that evolutionary biology and brain science may eventually provide clues as to how art emerged as a product of human culture, it is not immediately apparent why more and more detailed descriptions of our brain states while artistically engaged will contribute to an understanding of artistic appreciation per se. Such a view is far from pitching the arts against the sciences, but simply admits that they are different and both valid within their own distinctive frameworks of reference. Real unity often comes not by the attempt to press-gang all forms of knowledge into one paradigm (evolutionary biology in this case), but by affirming the validity of diverse perspectives. The refusal to publish critical comparisons of Bach and Beethoven in the scientific literature implies no slur on these forms of music, only that science has nothing to say on the matter.

Personal knowledge

Aesthetic appreciation is just one subgroup of a large class of personal experiences which can be collected loosely under the heading of 'personal knowledge'. 'Personal knowledge' comprises all of those aspects of our experiences throughout life that can only be communicated by description to a very inadequate extent, since the communication, however effective and by whatever medium, is never equivalent to the experience itself. The panic at being totally lost as a small child, the exhilaration of reaching a mountain peak, the coziness of chatting with a group of close friends over a pint, the surge of fear as the surgeon announces the results of exploratory surgery, the first gasping wail of the newborn, the bitterness of breaking up an intimate relationship – such experiences and thousands more make up that complex web of daily personal experience that we label 'normal human existence'. Even imagining a super-scientist who could provide a complete description of our behaviour and experiences at each moment in life, such that our psychology, physiology, biochemistry, and so on, were recorded in total detail, it is apparent that the final scientific description, while complete in itself, would not be equivalent to our life history of personal experiences. In the final analysis you can only *have* experiences. There is nothing mystical or irrational about this very mundane observation, which reflects our status as *agents*, conscious beings who constantly express their belief in their own human agency by their use of the little word 'I'. It is no accident that it is precisely this same word 'I' that is carefully weeded out of scientific papers ('we' being allowed if used sparingly), not because anyone is in any doubt that the experiments were performed by flesh-and-blood individuals like themselves, but as a reminder that the results are being reported by someone who is making an effort to be as objective as possible (however difficult objectivity may be in reality).

The ultimate form of personal knowledge is 'knowing a person', such a matter-of-fact part of our everyday experience that we rarely bother to think about it. Clearly 'knowing a person' is very different from 'knowing about a person'. We can know a lot *about* a person without having met them. Knowing about people and their behaviour forms a common basis for the submission of data to various kinds of scientific journal, particularly in the field of psychology. The description of human behaviour is a fascinating, though difficult, branch of science. Along with other impecunious PhD students from my department of biochemistry at the Institute of Psychiatry, I used to volunteer as a subject for the research laboratory of Hans Eysenck, at one time Professor of Psychology in the University of London. Studying the biochemistry of the brain gave us the convincing illusion that we were somehow superior to mere psychologists who never got their hands dirty by analysing the molecular machinery inside the brain. The game was therefore to try and outwit Eysenck's researchers so that we would discern the real purpose behind their questionnaires, psychological games and one-way viewing mirrors, and convince them experimentally that we were other than what we knew we were. I am ashamed to admit that we were frequently successful in this enterprise, and shudder to think of the models of introversion–extroversion that may have been based on such perverse human material.

Data based on 'knowing about a person' may be gathered satisfactorily whether you know the person or not. Interview records from many countries may be pooled to provide statistical data. The psychologist may interview a person in their office to obtain data, and might well be justified in claiming at the end of the interview that they did not really *know* the interviewee – they had only *met* them, or 'knew them only a little'. Yet there remains a widely accepted 'all-or-nothingness' about 'knowing a person'. In answer to the question 'Do you know so-and-so?' we would be misleading if we answered 'no' when in fact we had met them, however fleetingly, although we might well proceed with a qualification concerning the extent of our personal knowledge.

It is clear that 'knowing a person' does not provide subject material for submission to scientific journals. A particular encounter, perhaps even with a famous scientist, may change the course of your career, but your report of that encounter submitted to a scientific journal is unlikely to proceed very far (as far as the bin, most likely).

Ethics

A further notable absentee from the list of topics included in scientific journals is the subject of *ethics*. Ethical statements are those that address the question of what *ought* to be the case or what *ought* to be done. Journals of anthropology may describe human behaviour in all its varied and bizarre manifestations, but do not lead to conclusions concerning whether one type of behaviour is more appropriate than another. Such conclusions rest on philosophical or religious presuppositions, but are not generated via scientific data. Scientists may analyse the anatomy of a famine in a given country in immense and convincing detail, so that if you read their analysis you may achieve a very full understanding of the various aspects of climate and geography that led to the famine in the first place, but their analysis will not tell you whether you should cancel your expensive holiday and give the proceeds to relieve the famine, nor whether you ought to risk damaging your career by going out to that country to help in relieving the suffering. Such decisions will be educated by the scientific analysis provided but will not be dictated by it. Indeed, someone may conclude after reading the analysis that the people of the country concerned had misused the resources of their environment to such an extent that they deserved to pay the full penalty of their misuse. Equally, another person might read the same report, feel very sorry about the situation for a few minutes, and then carry on planning their expensive holiday anyway. Scientific descriptions per se do not provide answers to the question of what *ought* to be done.

Despite this conclusion it should not be thought that ethical concerns are of little interest to the scientific community as a whole. Far from it. For many different reasons ethical questions regularly receive intensive coverage and scrutiny in the news and views sections of popular scientific journals like *Nature* and *Science*. Cases of scientific fraud are greeted with alarm and despondency, because if the procedures of data generation and presentation are not carried out with rigorous honesty, then research programmes can be led off into false lines of enquiry with consequent loss of time and energy. Of greater public concern are the ethical questions raised by advances in the biomedical sciences which place increasingly sophisticated powers of manipulation into human hands. How far should scientists go in the use of fetal tissue for research? Are there limits to the extent to which human cells should be altered by the techniques of genetic engineering? Should reproductive cloning be carried out? There is widespread acceptance within the scientific community that such issues cannot be addressed solely by the application of scientific methods. Whereas scientists may often be in the best position to assess the possible risks and ethical implications of their technologies, in the final analysis the value-judgments that are inevitable in all applications of scientific knowledge are neither derived from science itself nor are they the prerogative of any special grouping within society. That the scientific community is very aware of this fact is illustrated by the grants awarded by the National Institutes of Health to bodies such as the Center for Theology and the Natural Sciences (USA) to carry out research and consultation on the theological and ethical issues raised by the programme to sequence the complete human genome. Science is generating enough new ethical questions to keep theologians, philosophers and government committees discussing, philosophizing and legislating for many years to come, but no scientist is naive enough to imagine that the answers to these complex questions will be generated by simple perusal of more and more scientific data.

A restriction on the language being used

A very obvious difference between the discourse of scientific journals and the discourse of everyday life is the highly specialized use of language found in the journals. It is not uncommon for scientists to sit in blank incomprehension through seminars presented by other scientists on topics somewhat distant from their own research fields, not because the ideas involved are necessarily difficult but because the jargon has become so specialized. Switching research fields involves a process not unlike learning a foreign language. At first the everyday chatter of the new laboratory is as confusing as being plunged into a foreign culture. Yet, despite the inconvenience, the specialized language is crucial, because along with it comes the assumptions and theories that permeate a particular research field and which provide the signposts for future research initiatives.

For years philosophers have tried to generate an observational language which is free of theoretical assumptions, but in practice this has proved impossible. Words used are frequently 'theory-laden' in the sense that their meanings may only be understood within the context of a particular theory. Antoni van Leeuwenhoek, the 17th-century Dutch microscopist, was proud of his ability to describe what he saw down his microscope without making any theoretical assumptions, but when he examined some stale water and observed some tiny creatures (probably *Euglena*), he gave them the name 'animalcules' because they moved, even though we now know that these single-celled organisms contain chlorophyll and are more closely related to plants than to animals. The term 'planticules' might have been more appropriate. Today thousands of other specialized scientific terms may be found in the literature, and while some may be purely descriptive, most carry with them various theoretical assumptions. Words such as 'gene', black hole', 'intelligence quotient', 'charm', 'particle' and so on, are all derived from particular theories and may only be properly understood within the context of those theories. Even an apparently straightforward observational statement such as 'the temperature in this room is 20 degrees centigrade' contains a large number of theoretical considerations.

Science is of course not the only body of constructed knowledge which utilizes a specialized language; almost every field of human endeavour generates its own jargon, from cooking to hang-gliding. Theological discourse equally contains specialized terms, and miscommunication in the area of science and faith has frequently occurred due to theological terms being misunderstood by scientists as if they were scientific terms, or scientific terms being misunderstood by theologians as if they were theological terms. For example, Stephen Hawking in his book *A Brief History of Time* refers to the goal of constructing 'a complete unified theory of everything in the universe', but by this term he does not really mean a 'theory of everything' that we would like to know, but instead the 'golden grail' of modern physics, the attempt to unite the general theory of relativity and quantum mechanics in a new 'quantum theory of gravity'.[2] Therefore Hawking's term 'a theory of everything' has a specialized meaning derived from contemporary theories of physics and the term does not necessarily carry any theological implications.

Further scope for confusion has come with words such as 'creation'. The term can be used to refer to artistic forms of creativity or to new styles in clothes displayed at fashion shows. It is also used by theists to refer to their belief that the universe is contingent upon the creative activity of God, that nothing occurs without his continued say-so, irrespective of the precise mechanisms that scientists may describe. The term is further used by some to refer to the belief that God made the world in a period of six days. As we shall consider further in the next chapter, it is the precise meaning attached to the term which determines views about the relationship between creation and evolution.

Science, therefore, is certainly not unique in its use of a specialized language to express its theories and concepts, but the degree of specialization is so extensive as to make many types of scientific literature largely inaccessible to those without the relevant education, underlining the potential for miscommunication when science is related to other domains of constructed knowledge.

A restriction on the methods being used

It does not take much browsing in the scientific literature to perceive that the gathering of scientific data is heavily dependent on specialized methods and techniques. The physical world can be 'interrogated' in a myriad different ways and the methods used vary enormously depending on the question being addressed. There is no such thing as *the* scientific method. Nevertheless, there are certain common features to be found in many of the methods and approaches utilized in science. For example, methods in science are particularly valued if they provide *quantitative* data. Key experiments may need to be repeated over and over again before statistically significant results emerge. Invalid conclusions in science often emerge because the experiment has not been repeated enough times. The expectation is that valid results will be *reproducible*, not only in the laboratory in which the results were originally obtained, but also in other laboratories in which the experiments are repeated under identical conditions. This is why methods should be carefully described in scientific papers so that others may repeat the experiments if they wish to do so. An inability to reproduce the findings of others is not unusual and may produce a considerable level of hand-wringing, though contradictory findings between laboratories are usually reconciled in the end by using exactly the same reagents or by the discovery of an unexpected variable in the experimental protocol.

Another characteristic of scientific methods is the conscious attempt to reduce the chances of *self-deception*. In drug trials, 'double-blind' procedures are followed whereby neither the patients nor those administering the trial know whether the drug being tested or a placebo is being ingested. It is also common procedure for samples being sent for testing to a laboratory to be identified only by numbers so that there will be no expectations on the part of the receiving laboratory about the outcome of their tests. All of these tricks of the trade and many more aim to minimize the prejudices of the investigator.

The risks of self-deception are as high in science as they are in any other human endeavour, and there are plenty of examples from the history of science. For example, in the early part of the 20th century there was a vigorous debate in astronomy about the nature of what were then called 'spiral nebulae', diffuse spirals of light that powerful telescopes had revealed and which were surprisingly common in the night sky. Some astronomers, such as Adriaan van Maanen of the Mount Wilson Observatory, were convinced that these were clouds of gas within our own galaxy, whereas other astronomers thought that these nebulae were other galaxies so far away from our own that individual stars could not be distinguished. Van Maanen addressed the question by comparing photographs of the nebulae taken several years apart and reported that during this time the nebulae were 'unwinding', and therefore must be within our galaxy since motion would be impossible to detect in distant objects. However, shortly after this announcement, Edwin Hubble, a colleague of Van Maanen who was using the new and more powerful 100 inch telescope at Mount Wilson, showed conclusively that the nebulae were in fact distant galaxies. There is no evidence of any particular errors in Van Maanen's observations, and in retrospect it is easy to see how he may have interpreted his photographs within the framework of his theory. Probably every scientist who has spent much time in research has experienced at some stage the same strong desire to cling on to a theory or preliminary finding that later turns out to be false. But an interesting point about this story is the way in which a more powerful instrument settled the question clearly.

Science can advance no further and no faster than its reagents, instruments and techniques allow. This is particularly true when investigating very small or very large objects. The light microscope opened up a whole new world for biologists which was then magnified still further by the electron microscope. Study of the collisions of particles accelerated towards each other at great speeds has enabled the more fundamental components of matter to be elucidated. The light telescope opened up a vista of new stars and planets but this was very limited compared to the vastness of the universe later revealed through the radio-telescope. Each method may be looked on as a 'net' designed to catch fish of a certain size, the 'fish' in this case being particular types of data which are being collected in order to test a theory. By making the mesh in the net of a particular size the precise size of the fish can be specified. No one method provides a complete 'slice' of reality. The data obtained from many different techniques have to be combined to provide a comprehensive understanding of a given aspect of the physical world.

Scientific data are not isolated pieces of information that exist independently from the theories, methods and instruments whereby they were generated. Most scientific facts are method-dependent and/or instrument-dependent facts, being difficult to assess or appreciate unless something is known about the procedures used to obtain them. Even heads (cynics might add 'especially heads') of research laboratories can be deceived by data gathered in their own laboratory if it has been some time since they did any experiments themselves. There is nothing like hands-on experience of the techniques being used when it comes to assessing whether a result is significant or not. This is why the methods of science together comprise the *craft* of science, a word which covers that ability of a good scientist to design good experiments, use appropriate techniques to obtain accurate data and then assess the data judiciously so that what is significant may be discerned out of a background of mere 'noise'. What counts as 'noise' will be interpreted according to the previous experience of the investigator and also according to the current assumptions of the research field. Not infrequently pieces of data are excluded initially because they do not appear relevant to the theory being tested, but later – sometimes many years later – the same data are seen as highly significant due to new findings which shed fresh light on them.

Furthermore, the use of different methods in a research programme is a social enterprise, pursued within (hopefully) interactive communities of scientists who help, criticize, get in the way, provide useful suggestions and generally act as a support group for the work of their colleagues. Entry into the research world by the process of obtaining a doctorate is based on the idea that the experience of spending three years (or more) carrying out experiments with a scientific 'craftsman' (otherwise known as a supervisor) is of greater value than any amount of pure academic study. Although science has always been a communal endeavour, increasing specialization has made it even more necessary for research groups to be interactive as each individual contributes their particular skills and knowledge for the good of the whole team. Today's biomedical research laboratories are large open-plan areas with researchers crammed into every available nook and cranny, the philosophy being that the negative effects of overcrowding are more than outweighed by the enforced communication that results.

Science is successful because it has learnt to construct a body of knowledge which is restricted to addressing one particular slice of reality. By focusing on potentially soluble questions, by using a precise and specialized language, and by creating methods which enable investigation of the chosen questions by communities of specialists, the scientific community continues to fill thousands of scientific journals every week with a mass of scientific knowledge. But is this great body of scientific knowledge locked away in a watertight compartment, isolated from the kinds of ultimate questions that religion seeks to address? Or are there some similarities in the ways in which scientific and religious types of questions are investigated?

Scientific knowledge and religious knowledge

The standard view of science and its critics

The 'standard view' of science is that which developed with the growth of modern science itself. This is that common-sense inductivist picture of scientific progress, that started with Bacon, was continued by the empirical approach of the mechanical philosophers of the next few centuries, and was finally completed by the Logical Positivists. According to this view, the natural world is regarded as real and objective, and the preferences or intentions of its observers make no difference to its characteristics. As Galileo once said, 'The conclusions of natural science are true and necessary, and the judgment of man has nothing to do with them.' In Newtonian physics theories were equally thought to represent the world as it really is, quite independently of the observer. Since space and time were viewed as absolute frameworks in which every event is located, those qualities of the world that can be expressed mathematically, such as mass and velocity, were perceived as objective characteristics of the real world. According to the 'standard view', therefore, the task of the scientist is to make a large number of accurate observations, and then induce from such facts a general theory which, provided it is supported by a large body of consistent data, is viewed as an 'immutable law of nature'. Discovering a law then becomes like discovering a new continent – it was there all the time, only waiting to be revealed. As Lord Kelvin concluded in a speech to the British Association for the Advancement of Science around 1900: 'There is nothing new to be discovered in physics now. All that remains is more and more precise measurement.'[3] In Medawar's parody of this view, the creation of scientific knowledge 'begins with the plain and unembroidered evidence of the senses, with innocent, unprejudiced observation... and builds upon it a great mansion of natural law'.[4] Scientific knowledge is seen as being immune from subjective factors such as prejudice and self interest, since it depends upon facts that are obtained according to the stringent criteria of the experimental method.

It should be noted that this 'naive realist' view, as it has been dubbed, places the authority of science firmly in the techniques involved in the method of enquiry itself. This authority comes by exorcizing extraneous values to a realm outside of science, so that Bacon saw the fruit of science as being its social application and benefit, whereas science itself was the realm of *facts*. The Positivists of the 19th and early 20th century took this whole approach a step further by defining meaning and rationality itself according to whether it was empirically verifiable. According to Logical Positivism – an anti-metaphysical movement influential in the earlier half of the 20th century, promoted in Britain by A.J. Ayer in his *Language, Truth and Logic* (1936) – a sentence can only be true or false either if it can be justified as being true on the basis of sensory experience, i.e. it is empirically verifiable, or if it can be shown to be true or false on the basis of meaning alone, i.e. it is logically consistent. The 'scientific method' came to be the arbiter of what was designed as rational. The Positivists had a field day in declaring to be nonsense (in the strict sense of that term) all kinds of claims and statements that did not seem to be meaningful according to these stringent criteria, not least in the arts and in religion. However, they finally found themselves hoist by their own petard with the realization that their own stringent criteria for meaning rendered the criteria themselves meaningless as they could not be empirically supported. As it happens, the more extreme tenets of Positivism proved very stale for science, as men like Mach tried to eliminate reference to all unobservable entities from scientific discourse, a process that would rapidly reduce most laboratories to a state of complete silence![5] It is certainly a useful exercise to identify criteria with which to define the boundaries of scientific discourse, but it is a different matter altogether to claim that scientific discourse provides the *only* valid kind of knowledge that exists. Although Positivism as an organized philosophy is no longer with us, its ghost still lives on in popular culture under the label of 'scientism', which we will discuss further below.

The 20th century witnessed a gradual loss of confidence in the naive realist view of science. In 1934 the philosopher Sir Karl Popper made a central attack on one of the tenets of Logical Positivism in his *Logic of Scientific Discovery* by claiming that, far from scientific theories gaining more and more credibility as they are buttressed by increasing quantities of empirical evidence, theories are really only useful to science insofar as they can be *dis*proved. Later Popper popularized his views further during his tenure as professor of logic and scientific method at the London School of Economics from 1949 to 1969. The crucial line for Popper which separated physics and metaphysics was not, therefore, whether statements are empirically verifiable, but rather the extent to which statements can be falsified by the methods of science. However long a theory might survive, a single crucial experiment or observation might yet turn up to overthrow it, as with the replacement of Newton's mechanical theory by Einstein's relativity, an event which itself had a great influence on the development of Popper's philosophy of science. The idea, once popular, that certain markings visible by telescope on the surface of Mars represented giant canals, and therefore provided evidence for sentient life, was a scientific theory in the sense that one day it would be possible to travel to Mars and find out if the markings were canals. As it happens, later space probes showed that they were not; the theory was disproved. So all we can learn from science is that some tests survive better than others, but this is no guarantee of their truth because their turn for overthrow may come soon, rather as in evolution 'fitness' for an environment is a temporary rather than an absolute concept. Once a theory has been refuted, then it is time to think up a new one that can be tested and refuted in turn. 'Acceptance of a theory' for a scientist is therefore supposed to be a very tentative and temporary affair. As Lakatos has remarked: '*Belief* in Popper's view 'may be a regrettably unavoidable biological weakness to be kept under the control of criticism: but *commitment* is for Popper an outright crime'.[6]

Clearly there was little room in Popper's philosophy for the old inductionist view of 'standard science' in that the past successes of a theory are no guarantee that it will continue to be successful in the future. According to this view the 'immutable laws of nature' have disappeared, to be replaced by an infinite regress of increasingly sophisticated theories. But note that at least one feature of 'standard science' has been retained – the view that scientific theories are to be treated as descriptions of the real world. Popper was therefore a 'realist' rather than an 'instrumentalist', the latter being one who believes that the theories of science are merely instruments for prediction or approximate models for technological application. But it is not difficult to see how Popper's influential view of science shifted the focus of attention, away from the 'facts in the external world' that force the theory upon us (as in the inductionist view), onto the scientific community whose logic and expertise generate better theories, and whose important task it is to decide the criteria for adequate testing of theories in order to attempt their falsification. It is by this process that data become 'theory-laden', so that observations are only meaningful within the context of a specific theory and outside of that theory could mean something quite different.

There is little doubt that Popper's philosophy of science has been immensely influential both inside and outside the scientific community. Many scientists are practising Popperians, at least in principle, even though they may have never read any Popper. The idea of potential falsifiability by the methods of science provides a tidy and convenient borderline for differentiating science from non-science, and underlies the choice of material for publication in scientific journals, as discussed above. This is not to say that the demarcation line between science and non-science is invariably a sharp one – and it is certainly not static since the concept of what is 'potentially falsifiable' changes according to the development of new techniques. What counts as a scientific theory worthy of serious testing may also be controversial. For example, tests of homeopathic claims that extremely dilute compounds have beneficial medical affects have occasionally been published in scientific journals like *Nature* on the grounds that homeopathic theories are in principle refutable and therefore potentially scientific. Nevertheless, the degree of dilution is sometimes so great that one homeopathic dose may contain only a few molecules of the relevant compound. Since the idea that the ingestion of a few molecules of a compound can have any significant biochemical effect whatsoever on bodily functions is contrary to the findings of many decades of biomedical research, one can certainly sympathize with the argument that further tests of homeopathic claims is a waste of time and resources. For Popperian views to make sense the scientific community must act as policeman to control what counts as a significant theory to be tested. Someone may claim that rings that appear on their lawn are due to the activities of fairies. This claim passes Popper's test of potential falsifiability, but clearly more than this is required to establish that a theory is potentially scientific. For example, the theory will have a greater chance of being taken seriously if it demonstrates at least some continuity with the notions already current in the research field. In practice, therefore, it is very difficult to avoid inductive inferences in science, because the judgment by the scientific community that a theory is worth testing is based on the inductive inference that the type of theory which withstood tests well in the past is also likely to do so in the future.

In attempting to provide demarcation lines to distinguish between science and non-science, Popper is clearly not suggesting that scientific knowledge is the *only* significant form of knowledge, which is the fallacy underlying Logical Positivism. Sir Karl recounts how he was discussing the validity of moral rules in a seminar when the linguistic philosopher, Wittgenstein, who was sitting near the fire, jumped up, brandishing a poker, shouting, 'Give me an example of a moral rule!', to which Popper replied: 'Not to threaten visiting lecturers with pokers'. Rather more formally, Popper has written:

> It is important to realize that science does not make assertions about
> ultimate questions – about the riddles of existence, or about man's task in
> this world. This has often been well understood. But some great scientists,
> and many lesser ones, have misunderstood the situation. The fact that
> science cannot make any pronouncement about ethical principles has
> been misinterpreted as indicating that there are no such principles whilst
> in fact the search for truth presupposes ethics.[7]

By far the most weighty critiques of Popper's views on the nature of scientific knowledge have come from those who have pointed out that they do not accurately reflect the actual historical development of the sciences. First, far from merely *proposing* theories as Popper suggests, in practice scientists usually *believe* their theories and defend them with passion and vigour. Observe the discussions that occur at any major scientific conference and you will soon find untenable the idea that scientists are emotionally detached with regard to their theories. Sometimes scientists will doggedly continue to defend their theories long after the rest of the research field has moved on to new convictions, and the death of outworn theories often only occurs with the retirement or death of the scientists who first proposed them. When during the last year of his life Henri Poincaré (1854–1912) returned from the 1911 Solvay Conference at which many physicists heard the first exposition of quantum theory by Max Planck, Poincaré expressed the majority view of those present when he recorded:

> The old theories, which seemed until recently able to account for all
> known phenomena, have recently met with an unexpected check... A
> hypothesis has been suggested by M. Planck, but so strange a hypothesis

that every possible means must be sought for escaping it. The search has revealed no escape so far... Is discontinuity destined to reign over the physical universe, and will its triumph be final?[8]

Second, as Thomas Kuhn has pointed out, 'No process yet disclosed by the historical study of scientific development at all resembles the methodological stereotype of falsification by direct comparison with nature.'[9] In other words, it is simply not true that scientists give up their theories that easily after they have set up tests for the theory which have turned out not to support it. In practice the anomalous data are explained away, or reinterpreted or, more often, seen in retrospect not to provide a very good test of the theory. A classical example of this claim may be seen in the way in which the early Newtonians treated 'facts' that appeared to threaten Newton's theory of universal gravitation. This theory was only moderately successful in predicting the positions of the planets. For example, its prediction about the moon's perigee, the time at which the moon makes its closest approach to the earth during its orbit, was found to be significantly wrong. Despite this anomaly, the Newtonian scientists did not behave in a correct Popperian manner. Far from abandoning their theory because its predictions had been clearly falsified, they went on to demonstrate that the mathematics used for the application of their theory to planetary locations had been wrong; and once this was rectified (by Clairaut) the moon's perigee could indeed be correctly predicted. Another strategy used by the Newtonians when faced with unfavourable findings was to inform the natural philosophers involved that their observations were inaccurate. Indeed, on several occasions the observers were forced to admit that their data were wrong and the theory was correct. When irregularities were observed in the orbit of the planet Uranus, Newton's theory predicted the existence of another planet, as yet undetected, which was causing these irregularities. Scientists predicted the exact location where this planet had to be if Newton's gravitational theory was correct and, sure enough, when the great telescope at Berlin was pointed at the prescribed spot, the planet Neptune was discovered. As Laplace once commented, the Newtonians 'turned each new difficulty into a victory of their programme'. But one anomaly that the Newtonians were unable to explain by their gravitational theory was a similar irregularity in the behaviour of the planet Mercury, and in this case there was no gravitational disturbance caused by a neighbouring planet to explain it. For decades this anomaly remained and yet, despite Popper, the Newtonians did not forsake their theory. Only with Einstein's relativity theory was the anomaly in Mercury's orbit satisfactorily explained. And suddenly the explanation became a striking 'refutation' of Newtonian physics, although it had certainly not been so prior to the advent of this new theory.

A somewhat analogous process may be seen in Darwin's defence of his theory of natural selection. As we noted in chapter 7, Darwin was only too aware of the evidence that was amassed against his theory, which, if anything, tended to become greater during his lifetime rather than less. But as Lord Kelvin's estimates for the age of the earth became shorter and shorter, far from abandoning his theory because there no longer appeared to have been sufficient time for the development of all life forms to have occurred by a process of random natural selection, Darwin proceeded to incorporate more of the Lamarckian idea of the inheritance of acquired characteristics into later editions of *The Origin of Species*, a stratagem that would shorten the time required for evolutionary processes. As it happens, Kelvin was wrong and Darwin's emphasis on evolution by natural selection, as expounded in the very first edition of his *Origin*, was right, further illustrating the difficulties involved in successfully refuting theories.

Tenacity in holding to theories is not therefore necessarily counter-productive in the advance of science, though the decision to commend someone for their tenacity rather than to criticize them for their obstinacy is more easily made with the advantage of hindsight. What does appear clear is that a theory, particularly one which incorporates a large mass of disparate data, should be allowed time to develop and to be tested adequately. If it makes coherent a wide range of data it should certainly not be dropped merely because of a few anomalous findings. This leads directly to the third main critique of Popper's philosophy of science, namely, that in practice scientists do believe theories more firmly as their predictions are confirmed by experiments carried out in a wide range of reputable laboratories. Far from a desire to refute a theory in order to establish a better one, in real life scientists demonstrate a distinctly non-Popperian habit of becoming more and more convinced of the truth of a theory as its predictive powers are vindicated by tests of increasing sophistication.

All three of these critiques of Popper's philosophy have been expounded with great vigour in the writings of Thomas Kuhn. We have already referred in chapter 1 to Kuhn's understanding of a 'scientific paradigm' as introduced in his seminal work *The Structure of Scientific Revolutions* (1962). In Kuhn's own words, a paradigm consists of a 'strong network of commitments – conceptual, theoretical, instrumental, and methodological', the framework of beliefs that are accepted in common by a community of research scientists and which form the basis for their daily activities. Therefore, for Kuhn, 'normal science' is that period of scientific research which concentrates on puzzle-solving within the framework of the paradigm. The aim of 'normal science' is to fit the pieces of nature into the patterns designed by the paradigm. 'Testing' within normal science is not seen so much as a test of the paradigm itself as of a particular research worker's skill in providing a good fit between the data and the paradigm. Anomalies are treated not as refutations of the paradigm but as problems for which solutions which will eventually be forthcoming. However, as soon as enough anomalies accumulate – data that do not readily fit the paradigm – science gradually enters into a process of crisis that continues until the revolutionary creation of a new paradigm, which not only includes all that the old theory explained but the anomalous data as well.

According to the standard view, science develops gradually as facts pile up in favour of one theory but against another. There is a steady progression of theories determined by the rules of science which show that a new theory is better than the old. In contrast, Kuhn has proposed that the 'shift' from one scientific paradigm to another occurs not so much as a result of reasoned argument, more by a process akin to revolutionary change that occurs as a result of ideological and political persuasion. Paradigms are not 'out-argued' but overthrown. This is because the argument in favour of a new paradigm

> cannot be made logically or even probabilistically compelling for those who refuse to step into the circle. The premises and values shared by the two parties to a debate over paradigms are not sufficiently extensive for that. As in political revolutions, so in paradigm choice – there is no higher standard than the assent of the relevant community.[10]

It is this last phrase perhaps more than any other that sets Kuhn's philosophy of science aside from its predecessors. No longer is there a particular set of methods that gives to scientific knowledge its special status. Instead the final scientific authority now lies in the hands of the scientific community itself, which decides between competing paradigms on grounds that go well beyond the mere application of rules. Little wonder that the philosopher of science Imre Lakatos has accused Kuhn of making science 'a matter for mob psychology'.

A famous debate between Popper and Kuhn helped to clarify their views, though certainly not to the satisfaction of all. It is good to remember that Popper played the role of the philosophical prophet, trying to pave the way for a science with more clearly defined boundaries that would free humankind from dogmatism and from the 'neurotic and hopeless search for certainty and justification'. On the other hand, Kuhn is a social historian, looking back at how science has actually worked in practice and finding a very different picture from the idealist claims that scientists often make for themselves. Popper's way as a philosopher was more proscriptive, Kuhn's way as a historian more descriptive; provided that we bear this in mind, it is perfectly possible to benefit from the very different insights utilized in these two approaches.[11] In reacting against certain aspects of Kuhn's theory, philosophers such as Lakatos have also generated new models to describe how scientific knowledge is generated. In place of Kuhn's 'paradigm', Lakatos refers to a 'research programme' which possesses a hard core of unquestioned assumptions that are used as the starting point for tackling new questions. As long as the programme keeps predicting novel facts with some degree of success, then the programme will thrive, but once the programme becomes static or merely provides *post hoc* explanations for discoveries made by others, then the programme is set to decline.[12] When the programme becomes fully defunct (astrology, phrenology) then it can no longer be considered a science.

Kuhn's ideas have been taken in relativizing directions further than he himself would allow, by placing an even more extreme emphasis on the workings of the scientific community itself rather than on the workings of the world that science is supposed to be describing. Paul Feyarabend has argued that no one approach to the pursuit of knowledge should be allowed to dominate all others.[13] For this reason, rival and totally different theories should be thrown into the arena of ideas – 'anything goes' at the level of methodology – and there are no fixed criteria for deciding what is within or without the boundaries of science. A less anarchic but no less contentious school of thought has emerged from the Science Studies Unit set up at the University of Edinburgh in the 1960s in an attempt to bridge the gap between the arts and the sciences – the famous 'two cultures' described by C.P. Snow. Barry Barnes, a sociologist, David Bloor, a philosopher of science, and Steven Shapin, a historian, have developed the so-called 'strong programme' to emphasize the ways in which the social circumstances and social goals of scientists affect the content of their claimed knowledge. The key question then becomes the way in which a particular piece of knowledge has been constructed and used in order to serve whose cultural interests in what particular social context. Ironically, considering the earlier aspirations of the Edinburgh school to bridge the divide between the arts and the sciences, their school of thought culminated in a bad-tempered debate in the 1990s between sociologists and scientists dubbed the 'Science Wars' in journalistic parlance,[14] a debate which now appears to be in decline. Sometimes the scientists have been too defensive in such debates. It can readily be admitted that all kinds of social and political considerations have impinged on the practice of science over the centuries without giving up the core assumption that, through all its vicissitudes, as a matter of fact science does generate maps of increasing accuracy in its descriptions of physical reality.

It is perhaps not surprising that scientists themselves are often rather bemused when (and if) they read philosophical and sociological accounts of how science is supposed to work (I have heard the remark that the philosophy of science is about as useful to scientists as ornithology is to birds). One reason for this bemusement is that the various accounts given seem to differ so wildly from what scientists know they do in their laboratories every day. This is a useful reminder that no one approach in the philosophy of science can possibly do justice to the immense variety of experimental strategies used in different scientific disciplines, nor to the complex histories displayed by the various branches of science. There is a danger in building a philosophy or sociology of science based on the experiences of scientists in one particular discipline. For example, the role of experiments varies considerably from one field to another. In some branches of science it is possible to have an idea over breakfast, test it during the day in the lab and have an answer before arriving back home. By contrast it took the best part of half a century before Einstein's theory of relativity was adequately tested and confirmed. Einstein himself was not at all impressed by the experimental confirmations of his theory, once remarking that 'I do not by any means find the chief significance of the general theory of relativity in the fact that it has predicted a few minute observable facts, but rather in the simplicity of its foundation and in its logical consistency.'[15] As with the situation when the theory of general relativity was first put forward, so today much contemporary theorizing about cosmology depends on mathematical elegance as a criterion for acceptance rather than on its ability to generate obvious tests, although empirical testing may eventually become feasible. There is therefore a danger in constructing comprehensive 'theories of scientific method' which make grandiose claims about their applicability to all branches of science.

Scientists who have read some history of science will be ready to admit that social, religious and political factors have at various times contributed to the emergence and acceptance (or non-acceptance) of scientific theories. Such has particularly been the case for the 'grand theories of science', such as evolution and theories relating to the origins of the universe, which have commonly been thought to carry wider implications for society. Such a view can readily be held alongside the conviction that the theories in question are valid and well supported by the data. The social and personal factors involved in the lives of the scientists who proposed that DNA is a double-helix make for fascinating reading, but do not alter the fact that as a matter of fact DNA does have a double-helical structure.

Postmodernism

This perspective is very different from that espoused by postmodernism, a philosophical movement that goes much further in denying any privileged position to scientific knowledge. If modernism is characterized by the 'standard' view of science outlined above, enthroning the scientific method as an arbiter of what is rational, then postmodernism proclaims that science provides only one (among many) culture-bound ways of looking at the world. Science may thus be treated as one option on the worldview shelf displayed by multicultural societies in which occult or mystical worldviews may be looked on as equally valid. One strand of postmodernism that has proved highly influential argues that language is purely conventional and specific to a particular community. More radically, there is no way of knowing whether a language mirrors reality, since the criteria for its correct use are internal to a particular linguistic community. The suspicion is that all language, and thus all articulations of 'knowledge', are masks for power relationships. The result is a profound scepticism about all claims to objectivity.

Postmodernism, as Professor Roger Trigg comments, 'dethrones science by attacking the very human rationality which has produced science'.[16] An expounder of one particular stream of postmodernist thought, Jean-François Lyotard, echoes Kuhn when he writes:

It is recognized that the conditions of truth, in other words the rules of the game of science, are immanent in that game, that they can only be established within the bounds of a debate that is already scientific in nature, and that there is no other proof that the rules are good than the consensus extended to them by the experts.[17]

According to this view, there is no 'grand narrative' that could validate one set of rules or the beliefs of one linguistic community above another. Postmodernism is therefore defined by Lyotard as 'incredulity toward metanarratives', disbelief in the idea that knowledge can be anything but rooted in a particular historical context and culture. The possibility of universally shared human experiences is excluded. Even were such shared experiences possible, we could not discover them since we have no universal means of communication.

At first sight it might appear that the ideas of postmodernism could provide a fruitful way of reinterpreting the relationship between science and religion. After all, if all forms of constructed knowledge are 'language games', why should it not be possible for science and religion to busy themselves in isolation with their own 'set of rules'? The drawback to such a view is that if the postmodernist worldview is valid, then both science and theism must abandon their claims to map objective reality. This probably explains why postmodernism has had some influence in the arts, and is popular among enthusiasts for pantheistic mysticism, but has made little impression on scientists – for the very good reason that their profession would cease to exist were the beliefs of postmodernism accurate! For example, science operates on the assumption that the world is consistent in its properties and therefore that experiments will work in the same way irrespective of the cultural, linguistic or social context in which they are carried out. The reality of gravity means that people fall out of trees with the same acceleration irrespective of their language, although they may interpret their experiences differently. The properties of DNA are not time-bound geography-bound cultural artefacts. And so the 'game of science' is worth playing for the very good reason that its models and maps claim to say something that is true about the physical structure of the universe, something which anyone in the world would be right to believe and wrong to disbelieve. Science *does* have a 'grand narrative' that validates its knowledge, an elegant 'mathematical narrative' written into the structure of the universe, which expresses those physical realities that ultimately dictate what will be believed by scientists following a process of investigation and rational argument. Language for the scientist, therefore, is not what the 'game' is all about but rather an essential tool through which the character of the world is encountered. Language may be a human construction, but what we talk about is certainly not.[18]

If postmodernism were true, then much of religion would be as futile as science, in particular those religions which make specific claims about the way the world is and about the role and meaning of humanity within it. For example, it is part of the Christian worldview that there is a God who is distinct from the universe that he has created and that humankind is responsible to God for the care of this planet and its resources. This worldview certainly qualifies for the description 'grand narrative', particularly since it is seen as being globally true and to be the case in a way that is not ultimately determined by geography or by a particular culture. The responsibility of humankind for the environment is absolutely binding irrespective of such localizing factors. Clearly, were the assumptions of postmodernism valid, the claimed universality of such a view would be as impossible as the universal claims of science, for both make 'an explicit appeal to some grand narrative', neither being willing for banishment to the realm of culture-bound language games.

It should be noted that the assumptions of postmodernism comprise a system of thought as metaphysical as anything that underlies 'modernism'. The claim that there is no 'grand narrative' that can validate particular forms of human knowledge is of course itself a 'grand narrative' on a majestic scale which itself lacks validation, and indeed there seems to be no particularly good reason for believing it. The beliefs of postmodernism therefore find themselves hoist by their own petard in rather the same way that Logical Positivism came aground on the realization that its own claims could not be validated by empirical data. In some ways postmodernism is in a worse position than this, because its new 'grand-narrative' – that no branch of human knowledge can be legitimated – must, if believed, lead to the conclusion that the claims of 'postmodernism' themselves comprise a language-game that need not detain us for very long. Indeed, it is difficult to avoid the slide from such conclusions into futility and cynicism. If various branches of human knowledge are ultimately mere sets of language games, why bother to play them? We may as well stick to trivial pursuits.

In a few pages we have now spanned the complete spectrum of philosophies of science, from the complete objectivity of the earlier standard view of science, all the way to the relativistic notion of science as the product of one particular culture-bound community. Against this backcloth we will now examine six distinct themes which can be discerned in the various attempts by the scientific community to construct a body of reliable scientific knowledge. Each one of these themes has parallels in religious knowledge, and we will consider each theme in the context of both science and religion.

1. Critical realism

The description 'critical realism' refers to the belief held by the vast majority of scientists, implicitly if not explicitly, that the data they collect in their experiments tells them something about the real world 'out there' of which they are the observers. Pattern, order and reproducibility are not qualities created out of their own heads but reflect properties inherent in the physical world under investigation. No scientist in his or her right mind would sweat long hours in the laboratory for low pay, write endless grant applications and papers, struggle with obstinate instruments and techniques, wrestle over conflicting data and experience the disappointment of someone else publishing their key findings before them, unless they actually believed that their theories were providing coherent information about the real world. To that extent effectively all scientists are realists. But the word 'critical' separates off this view from the type of realism found in the 'standard view' of science that was so prevalent a century ago. Scientists are not (for the most part) 'naive realists'. They do not believe that their theories provide exhaustive knowledge of the world around them. Neither do they believe in the earlier view that laws were like lost continents, there already but just waiting to be found. Instead they recognize the 'theory-laden' status of scientific data and acknowledge the fact that all data reach their senses through the filters provided not only by prior theoretical assumptions, but also via the processing effects of their techniques and instruments. They are therefore far more open than a century ago to accept the inevitable human component of the scientific enterprise. Realists tended to separate scientific knowledge into a separate compartment as if the keeping of certain rules alone would guarantee this pool of sure and certain knowledge about the physical world. Critical realists still believe in the objectivity of science, but have realized that complete objectivity is an impossibility in practice. Far from being immutable laws, good scientific theories provide a series of maps that help to make the workings of the physical world coherent and which act as useful starting points for the next series of exploratory investigations.

Nevertheless, the maps are congruent with the data derived from the physical world as presently understood; they are not mere social constructs.

It is this last point which provides the strongest argument in support of the critical realist position. In the final analysis, science *works*. For example, over the past two centuries there have been enormous advances in our understanding of the biochemistry and cell biology of the living world. These advances have proved highly successful in leading to the development of better drugs and vaccines, and in improving general health care. The sequencing of the human genome has provided a further useful databank that can be utilized in understanding and preventing genetic diseases. It is highly unlikely that such success in utilizing the natural world for human welfare would ever have been achieved had the theories and models underpinning modern biological research not been at least to some extent congruent with the reality of the natural world. A major weakness of the more extreme sociological interpretations of the advance of science is that they are unable to explain why science has been so successful. If it is the case that all forms of constructed human knowledge are equally valid, why is modern medicine more successful than the theories of witch-doctors in curing the sick?

Some close parallels have been noted between the 'critical realism' that characterizes a large segment of contemporary scientific communities and the 'critical realism' espoused by certain religious traditions. In a classic paper,[19] M.B. Foster argued that the Christian doctrine of creation provided a key element in the development of modern science in that it emphasizes the *contingent* status of the created order in relation to the creator. In other words, matter is dependent for its properties upon the continued say-so of the creator who voluntarily wills it into being and wills that it has such properties. As we noted in chapters 4 and 5, this is a very different idea from that prevalent in much Greek philosophy in which the properties of matter were defined by their inherent essences which were seen as being largely autonomous with respect to divine activity. According to Christian theism there is a real world, which is not an illusion, having physical properties that are consistent and reproducible because contingent on God's continued activity – a world that can therefore be investigated by the methods of science. Such a worldview is highly consistent with the position of the scientific realist.

At the same time there are 'data' about the world and one's experience of it that require a canvas much broader than scientific knowledge alone can provide. These data are derived from a diverse array of observations, including information obtained from the study of history; facts about human behaviour and the operations of human social structures, political systems and religious communities; experiences in the realm of aesthetics, religion and personal relationships; experiences of moral imperatives and obligations; and information obtained by the study of particular religions. This heterogeneous collection of observations and experiences comprises a body of data that has to be reckoned with, which is just as much part of the real world as that tiny segment of the physical world investigated by the scientist in the laboratory. But the Christian theist is a *critical* realist in insisting that such observations and experiences will, at the best of times, provide only a very partial view of the total picture, and that our understanding of the world around us is invariably filtered through all kinds of cultural and philosophical assumptions. Nevertheless, despite such caveats, our observations and experiences of the world, according to this view, are not merely human constructs but provide data that can be cited during the rational process of deciding between conflicting worldviews.

'Truth-telling' plays a foundational role for the 'critical realist' in science as in religion. As Harry Collins, Professor of Sociology at the University of Bath, has remarked:

> Science, like any other social institution, relies on trust because not every scientist can check every fact. With trust comes an obligation to truthfulness, for if we were all to lie as readily as we speak the truth then trust would cease to exist and information would no longer be a property of discourse...[20] all societies rest on truth-telling and its correlate, trust. If people will as easily tell a lie as a truth, then nothing they say or do has meaning or consistency and there can be no social order.[21]

Striking illustrations of this point come from the history of science in which, for example, the early Royal Society, with its motto *Nullius in verba* (take no one's word for it), came to equate trustworthiness with gentlemanly origins. As Shapin has pointed out, early scientists like Robert Boyle were listened to precisely because of their social status. A gentleman was held to be competent in describing sensory experiences; had to tell the truth in order to preserve his social reputation; was a Christian, and was deemed to be a disinterested and financially independent observer who had no interest in personal gain from his observations. In contrast, those of lowly birth, who were likely employed as research assistants, were not deemed to be accurate conveyors of truth or knowledge (even though they may have done all the experiments!).[22] Although the contemporary situation is radically different in that now it is the scientific credentials and publication records of scientists that act as criteria for their belief-worthiness, truth-telling per se continues to retain its fundamental importance as a foundation for the scientific enterprise.

It is therefore no accident, as already pointed out in chapters 4–7, that modern science flourished within a theistic worldview in which curiosity-driven research was driven by a desire to find out how God's universe actually worked.

Since God was deemed to be the source of all truth, and everything that existed was created and sustained by his ongoing activity, a central goal of the scientific enterprise was to engage in truth-telling about God's creative actions. The motivation for truth-telling was underpinned by a particular theological worldview. In religion, as in science, 'truth-telling' plays a critical role because the task is no less than trying to describe accurately, although incompletely, what God has done in the created order. As we will note in the next chapter, the question of truth-telling is also one of the critical issues in the debate about creation and evolution.

'Critical realism' therefore takes a position intermediate between the older standard view of science at one extreme and the radical relativism of postmodernism at the other. As it happens, postmodernism has done much to draw attention to the shared assumptions between science and theism. These are based on centuries of shared history. The worldviews of science and Christian theism are highly congruent.

2. Coherence

An important shared goal of both science and theology is to render coherent observations about the world around us that remain incoherent in the absence of the proffered scientific or theological frameworks of understanding. In the realm of science, Darwin's theory of evolution has often been taken as an example of the way in which a novel theory can bring coherence to a wide range of facts that otherwise remain incoherent.[23] As Ernst Mayr has written: 'The theory of evolution is quite rightly called the greatest unifying theory in biology. The diversity of organisms, similarities and differences between kinds of organisms, patterns of distribution and behaviour, adaptation and interaction, all this was merely a bewildering chaos of facts until given meaning by the evolutionary theory.'

Similarly Darwin wrote, in his *Origin of Species*, that 'Light has been thrown on several facts, which on the theory of independent creation are utterly obscure.' The task of his book, which, echoing Lyell's words, he referred to as 'one long argument', was to marshal an enormous array of varied evidence that only made sense if the theory of natural selection was correct. Many of the pieces of data that Darwin gathered together had been known for a very long time; other observations were his own, particularly those made during his voyage on the *Beagle*. One point to which Darwin returns again and again in the *Origin* is why similar flora and fauna had not developed in countries and islands sharing similar climates and terrains. This was difficult to explain if each species had been created separately to fit a particular climate, but much easier to explain if it were assumed that the species had a history of transitions that was unique to their part of the world. Darwin also noted that species could be classified according to family resemblances, and that subgroups within a particular class of animals shared a cluster of similarities pointing to a linkage between them by gradual steps. 'Why should not Nature have taken a leap from structure to structure? On the theory of natural selection we can clearly understand why she should not; for natural selection can act only by taking advantage of slight successive variations; she can never take a leap but must advance by the shortest route and slowest steps.'[24] Again, similar morphologies reflecting similar bone structures and functions were found throughout the animal kingdom:

> What can be more curious than that the hand of man, formed for grasping, that of a mole for digging, the leg of the horse, the paddle of the porpoise, and the wing of the bat, should all be constructed on the same pattern, and should include the same bones, in the same relative positions?[25]

Natural selection was proposed, therefore, not so much because of striking new discoveries, but rather as an overarching theory that would draw together many different threads and weave them into a coherent whole. It is the challenge of all great scientific theories to perform a similar function. Theories make coherent what was incoherent before, not necessarily on such a grand scale as Darwin's theory, but with the same goal of linking together observations to provide an inference to the best explanation for particular phenomena. Einstein's theory, as noted above, provided a more coherent theory than Newtonian science because it was able to explain the anomaly in Mercury's orbit satisfactorily. Many scientific papers finish with a model as their last figure that forms the basis for the discussion section. The critical question in every case is the same – how coherent is the model in its ability to explain the data presented?

The challenge of coherence is equally pertinent when it comes to assessing competing metaphysical worldviews. For example, it has frequently been suggested that atheism, a metaphysical worldview that denies the existence of God, lacks coherence in its inability to explain the universe that we inhabit and our experience of it as observers. The conviction that there is no God is, for many people, difficult to sustain in light of the fine tuning of the physical constants of the universe which have enabled carbon-based life forms to emerge on this planet. The extent to which such an argument can be used to support belief in God will be considered further in chapter 12. Irrespective of the validity or otherwise of such 'anthropic arguments', it is a fact that we as conscious beings have arisen after a process of evolution stretching back millions of years to become observers, possibly the only conscious observers, of a universe characterized by mathematical elegance that with rational brains we can analyse and begin to comprehend, a universe of such immense size as to fill us with awe, in which our own tiny planet is crammed with a startling array of biological diversity. Yet, if atheism is correct, our own existence in this amazing universe must be a bizarre accident, with no more ultimate meaning than the blowing of the wind in the trees. The metaphysics of atheism insists that there can be no meanings in the universe beyond those that people construct themselves in order to give their lives a sense of significance. On the timescale of the universe, or of this planet's geology – it makes little difference – each human lifespan is little more than the time taken by one blink of the eyes, and within the worldview of atheism it is difficult to see how any particular blink could be of any possible ultimate significance. The most brilliant Nobel prize-winner, the greatest works of art, the best music, the noblest acts of sacrifice, the pinnacles of political success, the deepest human relationships – all these will soon be lost in the unthinking void, events destroyed for ever by the inevitable march of the second law of thermodynamics. Either the universe will continue to expand or will eventually contract back on itself in the 'big crunch', but in either case the whole span of human history will appear as a tiny flicker in comparison with the vast scale of the history of the universe. Struggles for justice in human societies may assume epic proportions on the localized timescale of a country's short history, but if atheism is correct the struggle must be futile in any ultimate sense because the oppressors and the oppressed will likewise be swallowed up and forgotten by the inevitable passage of time; and when the sun's energy reserves are finally exhausted and human societies on this planet come to a final end, there will be no conscious beings left to remember struggles for justice, least of all to reflect on how meaningless they were in light of the ultimate demise of the human race. Within the worldview of atheism, the bodies of rapists and of saints, of mass murderers and of hospice workers, of mad dictators who burn millions of people in gas ovens and of great social reformers who transform societies – all will return to the same chemical elements from which they were formed and their deeds, noble or evil, will be irrelevant because all memory of them will ultimately be ablated.

This is a bleak view of the universe and, outside of various works of art, music and literature, is not a view that most atheists allow to impinge too deeply upon their daily lives – life is far too interesting and enjoyable for that. But the dichotomy between a philosophical position that denies any ultimate meaning to the universe, or to individual lives, and the reality of a world that bursts with apparent meaning and purpose, at least at the level of human relationships and personal biography, certainly provides food for thought. It is for this very reason, I would suggest, that atheism fails to convince: as a metaphysical system it involves a profound mismatch between commitment to a life in which goals and

247

achievements are deemed to carry some significance, and a worldview in which the existence of life itself must, by definition, be ultimately futile.

A contemporary response to such comments echoes the parable composed by G.E. Lessing more than two centuries ago. A father has a magic ring and the time comes to leave it to one of his three sons. Since he loves them all equally and does not wish to show favouritism he has two imitation rings made so that each of his sons can have one. This leads to a dispute in which each son claims that he has the only magic ring. The dispute is resolved by Nathan the Wise who offers the following judgment: 'Let each think his own ring true and in the meantime show forth gentleness and heartfelt tolerance.' In other words, in the context of the present discussion, it does not really matter what worldview people hold, as long as it keeps them happy, and as long as their beliefs do not interfere with those of anyone else.

The value of 'heartfelt tolerance' should certainly not be downplayed, but the idea that all worldviews are equally coherent is less than satisfactory for a scientist committed to the critical realist view that models should 'fit' with observational data. If atheism points to a profound mismatch between belief in ultimate philosophical futility and a world that provides strong hints of purpose and transcendence, does theism provide a more coherent account? The comments that follow are not intended as an attempt to answer such a question comprehensively but rather as a brief sketch of the kind of observations that theists might put forward in support of the coherence of their worldview, remembering that the aim of our present exercise is to explore the extent to which the concept of model-testing, familiar in scientific investigation, can be extended to the rational assessment of metaphysical systems.

Theism is the belief that there is a God who is actively involved in creating and sustaining the universe; God is not part of the universe, but the universe and its properties are contingent upon God's will. We have already presented evidence in chapters 4–7 suggesting that this belief contributed to the emergence of modern science. In its Christian version, theism also maintains that God has qualities that can only be described, albeit very inadequately, by analogy with persons, and that these qualities include love and forgiveness. Christian theism perceives God not as a philosophical construct required to solve a knotty metaphysical problem, but as a personal God, the God and Father of Jesus Christ of Nazareth, without whom nothing would exist, and by whose continued say-so the universe has the properties that the scientific community struggles to describe adequately.

Theism is as much a metaphysical belief system as atheism. The possession of a metaphysical worldview is an inevitable consequence of being human. As considered in chapter 1, we all carry around in our heads philosophical systems with long pedigrees in the history of philosophy that impinge upon our daily actions. Clearly there are no knock-down arguments establishing that theism is the most coherent worldview, any more than there are for atheism – otherwise the world would be much more neatly divided into adherents of one worldview or the other than it is at present. Nevertheless, on balance theism as a model appears to 'fit' better with the properties of the world that we observe. For example, as Einstein was fond of remarking, the truly incomprehensible fact about the universe is that it is comprehensible, and moreover it contains conscious rational beings who can appreciate its comprehensibility. The theistic worldview predicates precisely such a universe. In the 20th century, Dirac and Schrödinger, two of the founders of quantum theory, remarked that:

It was a sort of act of faith with us that any equations which describe fundamental laws of Nature must have great mathematical beauty in them. It was a very profitable religion to hold and can be considered as the basis of much of our success.[26]

In a similar vein the physicist Steven Weinberg has commented:

There is reason to believe that in elementary particle physics we are learning something about the logical structure of the universe... the rules that we have discovered become increasingly coherent and universal... there is simplicity, a beauty, that we are finding in the rules that govern matter that mirrors something that is built into the logical structure of the universe at a very deep level.[27]

Another physicist, Paul Davies, formerly Professor of Theoretical Physics at Newcastle, has written of the profound effect that the comprehensibility of the universe has had on his own thinking:

Through science we human beings are able to grasp at least some of nature's secrets... Why should this be, just why *Homo sapiens* should carry the spark of rationality that provides the key to the universe is a deep enigma. We who are children of the universe – animated stardust – can nevertheless reflect on the nature of the same universe, even to the extent of glimpsing the rules on which it runs... I cannot believe that our existence in this universe is a mere quirk of fate, an accident of fate, an incidental blip in the great cosmic drama. Our involvement is just too intimate. The physical species *Homo* may count for nothing, but the existence of mind in some organism on some planet in the universe is surely a fact of fundamental significance... This can be no trivial detail, no minor by-product of mindless purposeless forces. We are truly meant to be here.[28]

It was in light of such reflections that Davies has also commented that 'It may be bizarre but in my opinion science offers a surer road to God than religion.'[29] Davies makes no claim to traditional theistic belief as a result of travelling such a road and it would be a mistake to suggest that Christian theism could be derived merely from the physical properties of the natural order. The claim here is very different – the remarkably fine tuning of the physical constants that have resulted in the properties of the universe and, consequently, our own existence as conscious agents, are more consistent with theism than with atheism. As Peacocke has remarked, 'Only the dullest could fail to react with awe at the immense inbuilt and inventive creativity of the world in which we have evolved,'[30] and Wolpert has commented: 'Why the world should conform to mathematical descriptions is a deep question. Whatever the answer, it is astonishing.'[31]

Note that no attempt is being made here to derive metaphysics from science, only to ask the question as to whether metaphysical model A fits the data better than model B or vice versa. A theistic universe is one in which the comprehensibility and mathematical elegance of the physical world and the existence of conscious persons is both coherent and expected; an atheistic universe is one in which such findings remain bizarre anomalies.

A similar line of reasoning may be applied to the existence of persons and of personal relationships. The theistic concept of a personal God who is far more then abstract intelligence is consistent with a world of personal beings who are called into relationships both with God and with one another. Indeed, it is the depth, joy and intensity of human relationships (of course experienced by any person, irrespective of their worldview), that has often led to a recoil against the absurdity of the assumption that such experiences have only temporal significance. At the level of relationships between humankind and God, there is also the universal experience of religious awe, the sense of the numinous, that has been documented in widely differing cultures. Human beings have every appearance of being incurably religious animals and if their sense of transcendence is suppressed it is likely to reappear in other guises. It is precisely the universality of religious belief and its power to shape culture and political structures that has led to its incredible abuse over the centuries. One has the greatest sympathy for those who find religious belief difficult due to the widespread use of religion to support or even motivate human conflict (the Crusades, the religious wars of Europe during the Middle Ages, the conflict in Northern Ireland, the Shiite–Sunni conflicts within Islam, and so forth), although it has to be said that in many cases it is precisely the great power of religion that makes governments or the leaders of political parties so eager to utilize it for their own unscrupulous goals. Furthermore, other basic human drives have equally been the source of human tragedy on a vast scale. Human economic greed has been the driving force for as many wars as religion but we do not give up the use of money. Human gluttony, particularly in the Western world, causes the ill health and premature death of millions, yet we do not give up eating. Neither do we give up sex because of the existence of rape. The answer to the abuse of basic human drives is not confrontation but the attempt to prevent misuse. Ironically, therefore, it is the widespread abuse of religion as a tool to achieve political goals that illustrates so vividly both its power and its universality, and it is precisely such universality that would be expected within a theistic worldview.

What about the old Freudian argument that belief in God represents wish-fulfilment, the projection of a father figure into the sky? Curiously this is one of the few Freudian beliefs that can be assessed by the gathering of scientific data. Should Freud's theory be true, then one might expect that the type of matriarchal or patriarchal social structures of differing cultures might influence the concept of god prevalent in that particular culture, since it would presumably be the qualities of the dominant social figures in the family structures of that society that would be reflected in the characteristics of the god-figure(s). To the best of my knowledge no such data have been published and the theory therefore lacks empirical support. If some correlation could indeed be demonstrated between the character of authority figures in a society and the characteristics of the god(s) worshipped in that society, there would still remain the knotty question of whether the god was a projection of the human authority figure or whether (equally likely) the particular social role and character of the human authority figure had been moulded by that society's belief in a god deemed to possess those same qualities.

A rather vague derivative of Freud's argument is sometimes expressed in the idea that belief in God is some kind of 'wish-fulfilment' or, in Richard Dawkins's even vaguer phrase, the 'argument from personal comfort'.[32] The idea being proposed is that it is more comfortable to accept a theistic worldview since this guarantees immediate purpose and meaning in the universe in contrast to the rather bleak outlook implied by atheism as outlined above. But it should be noted that the fact that a belief does or does not bring comfort has no necessary bearing on its truth content. A general might spread a false rumour to his hard-pressed troops in battle that reinforcements were on the way in an effort to revive their flagging spirits. But, however successful he might be in achieving this goal, it would not alter the fact that no reinforcements were forthcoming. Conversely a mother might comfort a child who failed to get to sleep because of a fear that there were hobgoblins in the garden with the words that 'there was nothing to be afraid of because there are no such things as hobgoblins', and her statement would in fact be both true and comforting. It is also worth noting that the type of psychological prop implied by the 'argument from personal comfort' is certainly not provided by the God of Christian theism, worship of whom can be highly demanding. Belief in such a God is a dangerous business, because worship could involve, for example, giving up a lucrative job in order to serve people in a socially deprived area. Indeed, one might even imagine that there could be some wishful thinking in *not* believing in such a God, given the risky nature of such an enterprise. At the end of the day, however, assertions that a particular individual believes something because of a certain psychological explanation invariably results in intellectual sterility. Such arguments can be used about any belief – theism, atheism, agnosticism or whatever, with equal futility, since the claims simply cancel out. Psychological explanations can readily be generated for any set of beliefs. So what? They do nothing to elucidate the truth or falsity of the beliefs, which have to be assessed on other grounds.

Equally unhelpful in this respect is another analogy introduced by Dawkins to try to 'explain' religious belief, namely his concept of 'memes'. Memes, Dawkins has suggested, are ideas or beliefs which are analogous to genes in that they replicate rapidly and 'infect' people's minds:

> Examples of memes are tunes, ideas, catch-phrases, clothes fashions, ways of making pots or of building arches. Just as genes propagate themselves in the gene pool by leaping from body to body via sperm or eggs, so memes propagate themselves in the meme pool by leaping from brain to brain...[33]

Dawkins further suggests:

> The survival value of the god meme in the meme pool results from its great psychological appeal. It provides a superficially plausible answer to deep and troubling questions about existence. It suggests that injustices in this world may be rectified in the next. The 'everlasting arms' hold out a cushion against our own inadequacies which, like a doctor's placebo, is none the less effective for being imaginary.[34]

Now there is little doubt that analogies have often played a fruitful role in the development of scientific theories, not least in biology, but the fruitfulness of a good analogy can be tested by the way it provides new insight into a particular problem, or suggests novel ways of testing a particular theory. In this context there are two problems with 'meme' as an analogy: the first is that it is inaccurate, and the second is that it is fruitless.

With regard to the first problem, it is simply not the case that ideas or beliefs are transmitted in a way similar to genes. Genes are transmitted as DNA sequences incorporated into chromosomes. The communication of ideas and beliefs is made by verbal, pictorial or written communication and is nothing like DNA replication. As pointed out in chapter 1, many of our beliefs are absorbed with little thought through our early upbringing, but equally we can assess our beliefs in later life, think rationally about them and change them if we wish to do so. This is quite dissimilar from our genetic inheritance, about which we can do relatively little. Of course there is the trivial point that there is a struggle for ideas in human societies, and there is also competition between genes in the gene pool, but the processes that lead to competition between genes and competition between ideas are so different that any analogy between them is far-fetched.

The fruitlessness of Dawkins's meme analogy stems from the same critique used above to address the 'argument from personal comfort'. If a 'god meme' is transmitted like a virus, for example from parents to children, then presumably an 'atheist meme' can be transmitted equally effectively, if the analogy is to hold true. It is even possible that 'believing in a meme as a valid analogy for the transmission of beliefs meme' could be transmitted equally effectively. If such automatic modes of thought transmission were the case, then there is clearly no basis for the rational justification of *any* belief. The analogy therefore suffers the same futility by infinite regress as the 'personal comfort' argument. It leads nowhere and is therefore best ignored.

So far we have suggested that the fine tuning of the physical constants of the universe, the existence of persons who have conscious awareness of such a universe and the global phenomenon of religious belief, are all coherent facts within a theistic worldview. The existence and enjoyment of music and the arts are also frequently cited as being coherent within such a framework. Their existence in our evolutionary history is far too recent to have had any impact on our biological evolution and, besides, even the most ardent sociobiologist might baulk at attributing greater reproductive success to the effects of listening to Brahms rather than to Beethoven. If the universe has no ultimate purpose, as atheism suggests, then the universal experience of being moved by works of great music or by other great acts of human creativity is difficult to explain. Most people at some points in their lives, and some people quite frequently, experience strong feelings of transcendence, often triggered by their exposure to the arts, although similar feelings may be evoked also by experiences of the natural world. I remember a friend at university, who happened to be an atheist and who went climbing at weekends. One Friday he went off to climb in the mountains of Skye in Scotland. By the time he returned on Monday he was a theist. This was not the result of having heard some new knock-down argument for belief in God over the weekend, but rather, as he explained, that he had found it impossible to continue believing that such overpowering natural beauty did not point to some reality beyond the natural order. Such experiences of nature and of the arts sit more comfortably within a theistic worldview, with its insistence on human creativity as a pale reflection of God's creativity, rather than an atheistic worldview, in which such experiences stand out as rather odd and fragmented episodes.

Each one of these points could of course be developed, discussed and criticized at great length. They are mentioned here only to illustrate the point that metaphysical 'models' or 'worldviews' can be tested by rational argument in a way not dissimilar from the arguments and counter-arguments used to discuss scientific data. In each case the goal of the discussion is the same: what observations or pieces of data are most coherent with the proffered model? Similarly, even though many observations may cohere with the model under discussion, is there one particular observation that does not fit with the model to such an extent that the coherence of the whole model is called into question? This point will be pursued further under the section below on 'refutation'.

3. Common sense

It is sometimes thought that the scientific enterprise is largely a common-sense exercise in which scientists describe in somewhat esoteric language what anyone could conclude using more normal terminology by the application of a little common sense. As the philosopher and mathematician Alfred North Whitehead once claimed, 'Science is rooted in the whole apparatus of common-sense thought.' Lewis Wolpert has convincingly argued that this 'common-sense' view of science is quite mistaken and that frequently scientists are forced by the data to believe theories that are counter-intuitive and quite alien to common sense.[35] It is often such 'lateral thinking' that plays a key role in novel scientific breakthroughs – the ability to think things and to believe things that no one has believed or thought before. The molecular biologist Sydney Brenner describes how he shared an office for twenty years with another Nobel prize-winning scientist, Francis Crick, and how

> we had a rule that you could say anything that came into your head. Now most of those conversations were just complete nonsense. But every now and then a half-formed idea could be taken up by the other one and really refined. I think a lot of the good things we produced came from those completely mad sessions. But at one stage or another we have convinced each other of theories which have never seen the light of day... I mean completely crazy things.[36]

Now it may appear perverse to cite such an approach to science immediately after a section entitled 'coherence'. But note that the apparent 'anarchy' in such comments is at the level of openness to new ideas and to novelty, openness to believing something that has never been believed before, perhaps to see old data but this time from a completely new angle. Such an openness does not remove the hard experimental slog of trying to refute or confirm the novel ideas, but without such a stream of novel ideas the scientific enterprise dries up and becomes sterile.

Very often the novel theory which best fits the data is quite foreign to common sense. As Newton wrote when commenting on the nature of gravity:

It is inconceivable that inanimate brute matter, would without the modification of something else which is not material, operate on, and affect other matter without material contact... That gravity should be innate, inherent and essential to matter, so that one body may act upon another at a distance through a vacuum without the mediation of something else... is to me so great an absurdity that I believe no man who has in philosophical matter a competent faculty of thinking can ever fall into it.[37]

Yet despite this apparent reluctance to believe the impossible, Newton goes on to comment that 'Gravity must be caused by an agent acting constantly according to certain law but whether this agent be material or immaterial is a question I have left to the consideration of my readers.' Since a universe in which bodies exerted forces at a distance upon each other was the only universe that made sense, the forces had to be believed even though the precise nature of those forces was undefined. This is an interesting example in which the very drive towards constructing a coherent theory generates an essential belief in something that in itself is quite alien to common sense.

Similarly today it is the cosmologists' quest for coherence in describing the state of the universe during the first second after the Big Bang that generates a theory in which all the mass of the universe would fit comfortably through the eye of a needle! It would be something of an understatement to suggest that such an idea could be generated by common-sense criteria. As Wolpert remarks:

Both the ideas that science generates and the way in which science is carried out are entirely counter-intuitive and against common sense – by which I mean that scientific ideas cannot be acquired by simple inspection of phenomena and that they are very often outside everyday experience.[38]

It is important that this insight neither be exaggerated nor taken out of context. Wolpert is not making a plea to believe nonsense, but rather to emphasize that the scientific way of thinking is in many cases quite different from the everyday common-sense way of thinking that we normally use for conducting our daily lives. There is nothing wrong with common sense per se, but as a tool for the scientific enterprise it is severely limited.

Is it possible to make the same point within the context of religion? I believe it is, although it is important to hedge this parallel around carefully with certain qualifications. As in science, so in religion, disbelief in common-sense ways of thinking as a means to arriving at truth should never be a justification for belief in nonsense. Nevertheless, if it is indeed the case that there is an all-powerful God who exists and who is the ultimate and continuing source of the universe and its properties, then it would be surprising indeed if our knowledge of this being and his ways was not accompanied by a considerable element of surprise and novelty. A God whose ways fitted too comfortably with our common-sense preconceived notions is the one that we should be suspicious of trying to worship, since it is precisely such a God that is likely to represent a merely human construct.

Similar considerations apply to the more earthy everyday world of ethical choices. It is not a common-sense view that people should risk their own careers and lives in order to go to far-off countries to help people whom they do not know and to whom they are not related. Nevertheless many people out of religious motivation do take such a step. As in science, so in religion, such actions, in themselves so alien to everyday common sense, should be assessed within the criteria of their own worldview. Just as in science it is quite a common event that data can only become coherent by believing something that is quite foreign to our everyday common-sense ways of thinking, so within a theistic framework the 'absurd' action of sacrificially helping genetically unrelated individuals can become perfectly coherent.

Scientists, of all people, are those who have to live with novel beliefs that, until they become more familiar, appear quite absurd. Who could ever believe that the whole universe could pass through the eye of a needle – tell me another old wives' tale!

4. Objectivity

We have already ruled out of court the possibility of total objectivity in science; the history of science makes it clear that theories have often been pursued for quite unscientific reasons, and in chapters 4–7 examples have been given of research goals that were pursued for particular cultural or religious reasons. Nevertheless, at the end of the day, the body of knowledge known as science is constructed by practitioners from widely different cultures and languages, any one of whom can, in principle, reproduce the experimental results obtained by others in the scientific community. It has been argued that this strongly suggests that science is not an artefact of a particular culture, but represents a reliable body of knowledge that reflects the reality and reproducibility of the properties of the physical world, gathered by a community who at least make objectivity their goal.

Could there be an analogous situation with religion? At first sight this might appear a forlorn hope. It is clear that if I had been brought up in Saudi Arabia, then I would most likely now be a Muslim rather than a Christian. But, by the same token, it would probably be considerably less likely that I would be a biochemist. Nevertheless, despite this truism, I do not discount my biochemistry or reject its validity because I was led into it for particular historical and cultural reasons. Neither do I discount democracy because the country in which I was born happens to practise a democratic system of government. Culture and upbringing do not necessarily dictate what people end up believing, particularly if they travel or deliberately expose themselves to alternative ways of thinking or believing. I know of British people who, despite the Christian roots of their families, have become Hindus, Buddhists or Muslims. Likewise I have met people brought up as Muslims in Muslim countries who have decided to become Christians. I have also met Christians from families that have been atheist over several generations and atheists from families that have been Christian over several generations. These observations per se do not demonstrate that these choices have been made objectively but they certainly suggest that it is possible for people to 'stand back' from their own beliefs, assess them somewhat dispassionately, and choose to believe something different if they so wish. Such choices may be far from trivial in their implications in those parts of the world that disapprove of people choosing differently from the dominant beliefs of the majority community.

A further observation that supports the possibility of a degree of objectivity in making religious choices is that *none* of our choices in life are made as if we were a *tabula rasa*, a blank sheet waiting for choices to be written on it. In practice we make decisions with our prejudices and beliefs already in place. In science it is essential to accept the beliefs and assumptions of a particular research community in order to function at all within that community. Once we have taken that essential step, it is then possible to begin introducing novelty as we then (hopefully) begin to push back the boundaries of scientific knowledge by new observations and discoveries. But without the prior commitment to the norms of the scientific community we cannot even begin. Similarly, in daily life the least committed person is not necessarily the most objective. Objectivity is the ability to assess other views or beliefs dispassionately from a particular framework or point of view.

A development in Western societies that has encouraged the possibility of objectivity in religious belief is the emergence of highly pluralistic societies in which many different religious beliefs (or none) are afforded a place in school timetables and a role to play in society in general. A course in comparative religion can be chosen as an academic subject. There is a vast literature available describing various belief systems, many of them producing their own journals and magazines. For the secular humanist there is the *Freethinker*, for the skeptic the *Skeptical Inquirer*, for the Anglican the *Church Times*, and so forth. Furthermore, in a secular society it is possible to meet people in the course of daily life who hold very different beliefs from your own. If you are so inclined you can listen to other people's reasons for believing things (or not). Even better, you can go and live in another country with a religious and/or political emphasis very different from your own. Very often you will find that a religion practised in a country where it is the dominant belief system has very different characteristics from the rather arid summaries of its beliefs that you might study in an academic course on comparative religions.

In summary, therefore, it is fallacious to assume that true objectivity is a characteristic of science, whereas all other forms of knowledge are consigned to purely subjective opinion. Objectivity is a goal in science, but in practice is a goal only partially attained since there is no such animal as an unprejudiced scientist.[39] Likewise, dispassionate and rational thinking about competing metaphysical worldviews can be carried out with a fair degree of objectivity, always remembering that in this case, as with science, unprejudiced observers do not exist.

5. Refutation

O'Hear's quote at the beginning of this chapter claimed that 'Religious believers, unlike scientists, typically and characteristically seek to preserve their favoured models from criticism *at all costs* and *in the face of whatever difficulties they* encounter – something that would certainly be seen as irrational in a scientist.' There are several problems with such a claim. The first, as we have already noted in discussing Popper and Kuhn, is that in practice scientists do not easily give up theories to which they are committed, particularly if the theory makes coherent a large body of data relative to the anomalies that yet remain to be explained. Newtonians did not give up their research programme when the first counter-evidence was obtained any more than Darwin forsook his theory of evolution as Kelvin's estimate for the age of the earth became shorter and shorter, so apparently making the timescale for evolution impossibly short. But neither was Kelvin any quicker to shed old theories as new data came along. Throughout his long and illustrious career in science Kelvin never discarded the concept that an atom is an indivisible unit, remaining resistant to Rutherford's theory of the electronic composition of the atom, one of the fundamental discoveries of modern physics.[40] General agreement by the scientific community of what might count as refutation for one of the 'grand theories' of science is frequently not obtained and refutation, when it finally comes, is more likely to comprise a whole series of anomalous findings rather than one single observation that suddenly collapses the whole theory. It is quite common, indeed even respectable, to continue commitment to a grand theory of science despite its inability to explain everything satisfactorily. Anomalies, as we have already noted, are often seen as challenges to further research rather than as fatal flaws in the whole theory. As Kuhn has pointed out:

> Scientists may conclude that no solution will be forthcoming in the present state of their field. The problem is labelled and set aside for a future generation with more developed tools.[41]

In contrast to the situation with the 'grand theories' of science, refutations in the course of everyday 'mundane science' are generally quite clear and uncontroversial. If you measure a specific parameter or characteristic using a specialized instrument or technique to gather the data and the result obtained does not confirm your idea, then your idea has been refuted. If the same idea can be reproducibly refuted in other laboratories by people using the same instruments and techniques, then it is relatively easy to arrive at a general conclusion that your idea was false.

Can religious claims, or other types of metaphysical belief such as atheism, be refuted? It must be stated at once that there are no universally accepted criteria for refutation in religion or in philosophy analogous to the refutations of daily 'mundane science' that we have just described. It is precisely the possession of such criteria that gives power to scientific methods as tools for constructing a body of reliable knowledge about the physical world. The price paid for such reliability is, of course, the restriction of science to questions about the properties of the physical world. The topics mentioned earlier that are not found within the pages of scientific journals are precisely those to which the idea of refutability as practised in daily 'mundane science' cannot be applied. There are no universally accepted criteria for refuting the claim that a certain piece of music is beautiful, or a particular painting is inspired. It would be equally difficult to draw up a list of universally accepted observations that would allow you to refute the claim that two people were in a meaningful relationship, because ideas about what that means varies enormously between cultures. 'Straightforward refutation' in this sense is the province of science.

However, a strong case can be made for an analogy between the function of refutation in the 'grand theories' of science and the refutation of metaphysical belief systems. In both cases the aim is to make coherent a very broad array of observations. So broad can a theory be in science, such as Darwinian evolution, that it encompasses the whole of biology, and is therefore a true paradigm in the Kuhnian sense. The purpose of biology is not to gather evidence to support evolutionary theory, but rather the whole biological research enterprise – encompassing ecology, molecular biology, biochemistry, animal behaviour and everything else – is pursued within the evolutionary framework. Problems with the theory are typically seen as challenges to further research rather than as fatal flaws. A biologist cannot function properly without breathing the 'evolutionary air' that permeates his or her discipline. Could the theory of evolution in principle be refuted? Certainly. If the footprints of dinosaurs and those of *Homo sapiens* were without question found in material of the same geological age then this would be a challenge to current theory, to say the least. (There have been some claims for the coexistence of dinosaur footprints with human footprints on the Paluxy river bed in the USA, but these have been discredited.) Likewise, if each animal phylum was found to have a quite different genetic code then this would also be difficult to fit into current evolutionary theory (in fact the code for nuclear DNA is universal, bar a few trivial variations). So the theory is not immune to counter-evidence, any more than any other of the 'grand theories' of science. Nevertheless, the anomalies in the theory are currently so weak, in comparison with the vast amount of data that the theory explains, that refutation, although possible in principle, is not something that biologists expect to happen in practice.

Could similar considerations apply to religious models? We have argued above that the 'grand theory' of Christian theism provides coherence to a very wide diversity of different observations about the universe and our existence as conscious agents within it. Can it be refuted? First, it is worth noting that individuals who have given up the theism they once held to be true clearly believe that this is the case. For them it is certainly refutable, and they can give their reasons, otherwise they would not have stopped believing it. Precisely the same comment can be made about the reverse traffic from atheism to theism. If atheism was not refutable then rational people would not forsake it for theism. It should be noted, however, that the reasons given by individuals for forsaking either theism or atheism show considerable heterogeneity. Such reasons do not comprise a body of criteria that would be accepted by everyone as refuting belief or disbelief, even though recurring themes may be detected among the various reasons given, as we shall discuss further below.

Are there common criteria that could universally be accepted by anyone as a refutation of theism? The early Christians clearly thought so in their defence of the historical claims of Christian theism. For example, the apostle Paul wrote to the early church in Corinth that 'if Christ has not been raised, our preaching is useless and so is your faith'.[42] In other words he perceived both his faith and that of the early church as resting on a historical claim which, if untrue, would clearly refute his belief system. Since Paul was writing his letter to Corinth within a few decades of the purported event, he was clearly putting his message at risk by raising the possibility of refutation, since it might still have been possible for someone to produce the dead body of Jesus, recognizable due to embalmment, and so demonstrate that the resurrection had never happened. Equally, had the body of Jesus been stolen, so beginning the mythology of his resurrection,[43] the thieves might have produced the body at a later date, so discrediting the early Christian movement. Clearly we are not in the same position as the apostle Paul, now being separated from the purported event by nearly 2,000 years. Nevertheless, in principle there could be new historical discoveries that could cast severe doubt on the historical claims of 1st-century Christianity. Let us imagine, for example, that a tomb was discovered and that evidence was uncovered that it had acted as a pilgrimage site for early Christians – such a finding would not fit easily with the idea that Jesus had risen. Or let us imagine that a manuscript was discovered written by one of the disciples confessing that he had stolen the body and, furthermore, that there were good literary and historical grounds for thinking that such a manuscript might be genuine – then again the historical foundations of Christian theism would clearly be called into question. Such counter-evidence would be closely analogous to the possibility, mentioned above, that current evolutionary theory could be refuted by the finding of human and dinosaur tracks in material from the same geological era. Most believers in Darwinian evolution would find such a possibility extremely remote but, if pressed, would admit that new data might always be discovered that could refute current dogma, since this is the characteristic of scientific theories. Likewise, Christian theists who believe that the historical aspects of their religion are important would find the possibility that further discoveries might be made casting doubt on the resurrection of Jesus equally implausible. Nevertheless, if pressed, they would find it difficult to rule out of court. Therefore, when it comes to the historical claims of religious beliefs, the possibility of universally accepted criteria of refutation becomes more closely analogous to the type of refutation practised in science, at least in its 'grand theories'. Both the apostle Paul and Charles Darwin took great risks in making their respective claims, because their claims in both cases were wide open to the possibility of refutation, as they were only too well aware.

When considering the possibility of refutation in either scientific theories or religious belief systems, it is important to distinguish between genuine anomalies, which do not fit easily with the theory, and gaps in the evidence for the theory that would be expected if it is the case that the theory is indeed true. For example, if speciation within biological evolution has occurred relatively rapidly within the timescale of geological time, then fossil evidence for transitions would be expected to be rare, since the number of animals that are fossilized is tiny in comparison with the whole. This is indeed the case and is therefore an example of a gap in the theory, not of an anomaly. It could be argued that there is circularity in this argument, but an acceptable amount of circular reasoning is characteristic of most scientific theories. Trying to fit a model to the data is like trying to fit the right connecting plug to the back of a computer. If one of the holes in the socket is missing at the precise place at which the plug is also missing a pin, then one might safely assume that the plug is the correct one. Gaps in theories are acceptable if predicated by the theory itself.

It has been suggested above that although individuals provide different reasons for their belief that theism has been refuted, recurring themes may nevertheless be detected among the various reasons given. Without doubt the major reason cited as refuting belief in a loving God is the existence of suffering in the world. As Michael Ruse, Professor of Philosophy and Zoology at the University of Guelph, Canada, has commented when writing on his struggles to come to theism out of agnosticism:

> The problem of evil is most troubling of all. Frankly the free-will defense seems to me just not to wash, logically. If God be all-powerful, why did He not simply make us to do good freely? Far worse than the logic, however, is the dreadful implication of the free-will defense. God, this all-loving father, is prepared to let small children suffer in agony to satisfy the freedom of monsters like Hitler. As one of the Brothers Karamazov says, I simply do not want salvation at that price. How can one enjoy eternity, if it be bought by the blood of innocents?[44]

Is this a knock-down argument which refutes theism, as Ruse appears to be suggesting? It is certainly a weighty argument and one frequently put forward as a reason for disbelief. The argument per se is a good illustration of the possibility of religious beliefs being refuted, at least at the level of an individual's belief system. But does it belong to the category of criteria, like human and dinosaur footprints being found in the same material, or stolen bodies being produced when they were supposed to have been resurrected, that would be universally accepted as challenging scientific or religious claims? To provide a complete answer to that question would go well beyond the scope of this book,[45] and we will here only sketch a brief outline to suggest that aspects of Ruse's arguments are in fact more characteristic of an expected gap in a theory than they are of an anomaly that brings refutation in its wake.

First, a few empirical observations are in order. It should be emphasized at once that the problem of suffering is a problem for the whole of humankind, irrespective of their belief systems. Only people who never suffer could enjoy the luxury of discussing suffering as if it were a purely intellectual exercise. Even if we had a completely satisfactory answer to the problem of suffering, which of course we do not, our insights would not necessarily help us through our suffering. My dentist may inform me in great detail about the medical causes of my agonizing toothache but his objective analysis will not necessarily be of help in enduring the pain. Suffering raises intensely practical as well as profound intellectual questions that no one can escape.

Second, it is perversely the case, at least from the point of view of the non-theist, that many people become Christians either through their own experience of personal suffering or by observing the presence of evil in the world. While working at the American University Hospital in Beirut, which took in most of the casualties from the Muslim west side of the city during the Lebanese civil war, I had ample opportunity to observe the effects of suffering on people. My observation was that suffering could produce acts of enormous compassion, heroism and sacrificial care, or it could bring in its wake bitterness, despair and revenge. It was like living with a giant amplifying system in which the qualities of people were pushed to their extremities in both good and bad directions. During that time I met a woman while attending a church who had become a Christian since the outbreak of the civil war. Upon asking her why she had taken this step, she explained that she had observed so much evil in people during the conflicts of the civil war that she had become disillusioned with her previously held optimistic humanism and had been drawn to a religion which both recognized the reality of evil in people and held out the promise of doing something practical about it.

One alternative to believing that there is a loving God who allows suffering in the world is the belief, inherent in atheism, that all forms of suffering are meaningless in any ultimate sense. If there is no God, or no ultimate reason for human existence or human experiences, then by definition human suffering must be seen as a perverse by-product of the way the world is and of the way people are, afflicting individuals on a random basis with no rhyme or reason. Life is then a giant lottery wheel and suffering can never be more than a stoic acceptance of what the wheel of fortune has served up for us. This is surely one of the reasons why experiences of personal suffering are frequently cited by people when giving the reasons why they came to faith in God. Believing in the possibility that suffering may have some ultimate meaning, even though it may not be apparent in the present, is infinitely preferable to believing that it cannot possibly have any meaning at all. This rather obvious point immediately takes some of the sting out of Ruse's comments quoted above, since such comments would have much greater force were they being made by the holder of some other theory of the universe in which the problem of suffering had found a substantial intellectual and practical solution. However, atheism provides neither. Intellectually, it is difficult to believe that all of the vast arena of human suffering down the ages, including our own personal suffering at this present time, has absolutely no meaning in any ultimate sense. Practically, it is difficult to hold the hand of a dying person who has suffered all their life and inform them that it was all a total waste of time and effort because within a century or less it is very likely that their heroic fight against illness will be largely if not totally forgotten. Critiques of the idea of a God of love in a world of suffering do not start from positions of great intellectual or pastoral strength.

If Christian theism provides at least the possibility of finding some meaning for human suffering, either at a personal level and/or as a rationalization of the way the world is, then what type of meaning might this be? It should be noted that the 'free-will defence' argument is considerably more potent than Ruse suggests. It is incontrovertibly the case that the vast majority of human suffering is the result of the actions or lack of actions by other humans. Most famines now arise as a result of war. There is sufficient wealth, food and medical knowledge in the world so that no one need go to bed hungry or with their basic medical needs unmet. In practice this is far from being the case because of human mismanagement of resources, the gap between rich and poor, human conflict, the greed of multinational companies for profit and many other reasons. Famine and war are clearly human responsibilities and only the fatalist will try and palm such things off as God's fault. But why then could not God have created us so that we always choose the good? Why could God not have made creatures who always lived in harmony with their environment and with each other? Or who stopped wars once they broke out so that the innocent would not suffer unduly? The classic 'free-will defence' argument maintains that since the purpose of our existence is to respond to the love of God by entering of our own free choice into a relationship with him and into relationships of genuine love with other people, in harmony with our environment, such an outcome would have been impossible had we been programmed only to choose the good. Genuine love only becomes possible as a result of genuine choice. Love implies the possibility of the existence of hate. Every time I switch on my Macintosh computer to write this book it announces 'Welcome to Macintosh' because it has been programmed that way, but I feel considerably less welcomed than I do when greeted in the street by a total stranger who need not have made the effort. Of course God could have programmed us so that we always did the good, but then real love for God and for other human beings would have been impossible because it is of the essence of real love that it involves choice. Programmed love is not real love. Therefore the existence of love implies the possibility of the existence of evil as a result of human choice.

At this point it may be objected, as Ruse does, that the scale of suffering generated by the free but evil choices of human beings is so vast that it would have been preferable not to have had freedom rather than to run the risk of monsters like Hitler causing the suffering of millions of innocent people. If that is the risk of having free choice, let's do without. Clearly this objection has a certain appeal. But there is a problem in dreaming up the way that we think the world should have been. First, we are in a very poor position to judge whether such a world would have been either possible or meaningful. On the face of it, a world of robot-like do-gooders is not very attractive. One is reminded of Virginia Woolf's comment about characters in a novel: 'I like people to be unhappy because I like them to have souls.'[46] A world lacking in genuine choices would also be a grey world lacking in compassion, heroism and true altruism. Would that be a preferable world to the one we live in? We really have no way of telling. We are not in a position of a supercomputer programmer ready to run n possible world scenarios through y vast computers to see what the possible outcomes might be. While such material is fun as science fiction it is difficult to see how such speculations could possibly find adequate answers. This brings us to the second problem with the objection under consideration: if we are in the slightest bit interested in scientific ways of thinking, then we will be more concerned with how the world actually is than with alternative possible worlds. Aside from the esoteric shores of cosmological theory, most scientists are firmly rooted to a research programme that grapples with the way the world is and speculating about how it might have been is not a very meaningful exercise in such an endeavour. Similarly, when comparing metaphysical worldviews, we are more likely to arrive at sensible answers by examining the world we in fact live in, with its properties and qualities that are at least partially accessible to us, rather than speculating about imaginary worlds, about which we have no information at all. In the real world human beings make good or evil choices that have profound consequences for themselves and for others. In the context of the human suffering that arises from evil choices, the 'free-will defence' simply points to the obvious: human existence as we know it, with its love and hate, generosity and greed, heroism and cowardice, altruism and selfishness, acts of justice and acts of injustice, is indissolubly linked to the concept of the freedom of the will, and these pairs of opposites are bound up with the exercise of that will.

Not all human suffering arises from evil choices. There are earthquakes, fires, viruses, bacteria, genetic diseases, storms at sea, bolts of lightning and a host of other threats to our peace and well-being. The question under discussion is whether the existence of such varied sources of human suffering can be cited as counter-evidence to refute the worldview of Christian theism. Clearly there are people who do indeed cite such sources of human suffering as a reason for their atheism, thereby underlining the status of metaphysical belief systems as being open to counter-evidence and to rational debate. However, as already noted above, there is a perverse tendency for theists to cite suffering in their own lives as being signposts on their own personal pilgrimage to faith. Clearly this should not be the case if suffering per se provided the kind of refutation of theism that anyone would be irrational to disbelieve. But in fact theists will often recount how a particular illness or tragic accident played a critical role in leading them to faith in God or in deepening their relationship with God. Therefore in these particular cases it can be demonstrated that a particular good came out of a particular experience of suffering. Such examples of suffering then become coherent to at least some extent through their beneficial outcomes, outcomes that could only occur in an environment in which suffering was a possibility.

It would be convenient for the theist's position if it could be shown that some good came out of *every* experience of human suffering. This is impossible to demonstrate for there are many examples of human suffering that apparently have no such outcome. Of course it might be argued that there is always *some* good that comes out of human suffering, but we are not God and therefore not in a position to know what that good might be in every case. This certainly may be true, but goes well beyond the data available to us, which is that only *some* examples of suffering have an obviously visible and beneficial outcome. A more defensible argument is therefore the one that suggests that it is only the kind of world that we do in fact inhabit that displays possibilities for moral and spiritual growth for people in general.

To elucidate this point we may imagine, for example, a world in which rock-climbers would be kept happy and fulfilled and be able to advance their experience and abilities in their chosen sport. It goes without saying that an ideal world for such people would be full of abundant rock faces of all shapes and sizes to cater for every taste in climbing. Since the thrill and the risks of the sport appear to be part of its allure, the laws of this world would have to include gravity, since it would be difficult to imagine any thrill in attempting a difficult climb if you knew that if you fell off you would simply float. Furthermore, such a gravity-less world would not provide the challenge required to stimulate people to become better and better climbers, since the whole point of the sport seems to be to defy gravity in climbs requiring increasing levels of strength, skill and technical prowess. However, once the value of gravity as a way of promoting climbing has been admitted, the possibility then arises that a climber may fall off a cliff, so opening an avenue for human suffering. It is the very existence of a world in which rock-climbing is possible that *ipso facto* allows the possibility of suffering, not in the sense that every item of suffering has its own particular individual explanation, but rather that *no one* would enjoy the joys of rock-climbing without simultaneously admitting the possibility that someone might suffer as a result of the existence of such a world (as a matter of fact up to forty people each year die climbing Mont Blanc and 160 are seriously injured – and that is only one mountain out of thousands, albeit a very popular one for climbers).

In a parallel way the theist can argue that in the world we in fact live in, it is the existence of possible sources of human suffering that challenge our own self-dependence and which stimulate us to reach out in compassion to help others in need. Hick addresses this point as follows:

> In order to be an environment in which they can grow as moral and spiritual persons the world need not of course contain the particular pattern of hazards and challenges which it does contain. But it would need to contain either this or some other set; and whatever set this might be would inevitably seem both arbitrary and excessive to those who have to live in that world.[47]

The force of this argument is therefore not that every individual sample of human suffering has a transparent meaning, although some do, but rather that the kind of world that we live in, with its challenges to human complacency and to human compassion, is the kind of world in which moral and spiritual growth is possible. The level of suffering which in fact prevails might indeed seem 'arbitrary and excessive' to us, to quote Hick's words, but we really have no way of telling whether this is indeed the case. This is the point at which we expect gaps in the theory just as gaping as the absence of transitional forms in the fossil record in the context of the theory of evolution. The gap in this case is our total inability to guess whether a world with less sources of suffering than our world contains would be a world in which moral and spiritual growth would still have been possible. However, what we do know is that precisely this type of growth is indeed possible in the world in which we in fact live.

It is also worth emphasizing that all the examples of sources of human suffering listed above are in principle amenable to human control by scientific and technological advances. Happily even previously intractable medical problems such as inherited genetic diseases are beginning to yield to the applications of genetic engineering. As pointed out in chapter 4, the utilitarian application of science stemmed from a specifically Christian impetus in the 17th century starting a tradition that has continued to the present day. Theists have no time for stoicism nor for masochism. One of the practical challenges of living in a world of suffering is to invest one's life in tackling the sources of that suffering.

The Christian theist would also want to point out that a symbol of suffering, indeed of capital punishment, lies at the heart of his or her faith. The cross for the Christian speaks of a time when God became involved in the suffering of the world in such a deep way that he himself experienced its anguish and pain, including the full consequences of the evil choices of humankind. This is why the God of Christian faith can never be the distant god of deism, remote from the needs of the world and indifferent to its suffering. It is precisely this personal involvement of God alongside suffering humanity that speaks so powerfully at a pastoral level to those who are going through the deep waters of suffering themselves. And beyond the cross is resurrection and the resurrection for the Christian is the basis for their belief that our human experience is not limited to this world, but has a dimension that reaches beyond it for which the present is a preparation. It is not necessary to accept this belief in order to appreciate that it provides within the theistic worldview a further rationalization for the beneficial outcomes that can ensue from particular experiences of suffering.

It would be foolish to suggest that we have done more than scratch the surface of a vast subject and I am not so naive as to think that the pointers sketched so briefly in this section provide some global 'answer' to the weighty problem of human suffering. Nevertheless I think it is possible to make a more modest claim based on such arguments, namely, that human suffering per se does not provide a refutation of theism.

To summarize this section, therefore, we have considered whether religious worldviews can be refuted and have concluded that no universally accepted criteria of refutation are available that parallel those which pertain to the everyday practices of laboratory science. However, it has been suggested that the refutation of the 'grand theories' of science is more complex and that both anomalies and acceptable gaps can continue in such theories for considerable periods of time. Nobody expects comprehensive theories of this kind to be perfect, otherwise further research would be unnecessary and scientists would be out of business. Nevertheless, even 'grand theories' in science can, in principle, be refuted, and this usually occurs by the weight of anomalies building up to an intolerable limit, the demise of the old 'grand theory' being hastened by the proposal of a rival and more comprehensive theory. It was then argued that a 'grand religious theory', like theism, could in a parallel way face refutation by an accumulation of weighty anomalies, of which novel historical data might count as the most weighty counter-evidence in those cases where religious beliefs are based on historical claims. The specific problem of suffering was then considered on the basis that it is often cited as if it were a refutation of theism and it was concluded: first, that this cannot be the case because many people come to faith through suffering; second, that the 'free-will defence' provides a valid explanation for the existence of evil brought about by evil human choices; and, third, that the existence of other types of suffering are part and parcel of a world in which moral and spiritual growth are possible. Furthermore, it is an expected and acceptable 'gap' in the theory that we have no way of ascertaining whether the level of suffering that we observe is more than is necessary for achieving such goals. After surveying such arguments the theist may feel a little like Darwin as he made his first lengthy defence of his theory:

> A crowd of difficulties will have occurred to the reader. Some of them are so grave that to this day I can never reflect on them without being staggered; but, to the best of my judgment, the greater number are only apparent, and those that are real are not, I think, fatal to my theory.[48]

6. Commitment

A further theme that raises interesting parallels between religious worldviews and the work of the scientific community in constructing a body of reliable scientific knowledge, relates to *commitment*. Within the scientific community the word 'commitment' is characteristic of two quite distinct phenomena.

The first is that scientists frequently have a very high level of commitment to their research effort, particularly if they are working in a highly competitive field and/or environment. Scientists will work for long hours, frequently for pay far lower than their contemporaries who have parallel or lesser academic qualifications, driven on by a complicated mixture of motives which will surely vary from person to person, but which will almost certainly include a fundamental curiosity to find the answers, the desire to find these answers before other people, so enabling prior publication, peer recognition for discoveries so made and the basic satisfaction that comes from the design and execution of a successful experiment. The level of competitiveness varies in intensity from country to country and from laboratory to laboratory within countries, but it is notorious that in some laboratories, particularly in the USA, the pressure to get results and publish them is extremely intense. It is amusing on occasion to hear scientists criticizing religious fanaticism, for although religious fanaticism certainly exists and is clearly dangerous, alarmingly high levels of fanaticism also characterize some sections of the scientific community, particularly when it comes to the struggle to establish priority in discoveries. The need to prevent commitment, in this first sense, from sliding into fanaticism is therefore important in both scientific and religious communities.

The second type of commitment that characterizes the scientific enterprise is of greater interest when making parallels with religious belief, since this is that commitment to theories without which grants would never be written, laboratories would never be established, novel instruments would never be built and scientific conferences would not be the argumentative types of forums for human debate that they in fact so often prove to be. Scientists do not come to the laboratory with open minds, but with ideas, hunches, intuitions, insights and prejudices, subsumed under the more respectable title of 'hypotheses' or 'theories', which they then set about testing. Their degree of commitment to theories will vary considerably depending on factors like how successful the theory has already proven to be in the past, the implications for the rest of their work if the theory proves to be false, the question of whether the theory originated in their laboratory or someone else's, and the degree to which they personally have previously published papers defending the theory. It would also be absurd to suggest that commitment to the theory of evolution or quantum theory could or should be on the same level as commitment to a theory which, if refuted, would have far less profound implications for a given research field if proved false. The 'grander' the scientific theory in question, the higher the level of commitment is likely to be, since the stakes get higher and higher as theories get bigger and bigger in terms of their explanatory power, and the consequences of their possible falsification therefore increase in like horrendous manner. This is why, to the outsider at least, scientists appear remarkably sanguine about novel data that appear to challenge a 'big theory'. If the theory is long-established and forms the basis for a whole research field, then the chances are that the commitment level to the theory will be very high and the anomalous data will be explained away or left on one side in the expectation that it will be accommodated comfortably into the theory in due course.

Commitment to a theory will also tend to increase as other possible explanations of data, such as artefacts due to the technique(s) being used, are excluded in favour of the theory being proposed. For example, palaeontologist Alan Cheetham started out his career in evolutionary biology with the conviction that speciation was a slow process that took millions of years. However, after undertaking a very detailed study of speciation occurring in coral-like animals known as bryozoa, Cheetham finally concluded that for these animals, at least, the theory of punctuated equilibrium (the idea originally proposed by Niles Eldredge and Stephen Jay Gould that speciation occurred relatively rapidly interspersed by long periods of stasis) was correct. What Cheetham observed was that individual species persisted unchanged for millions of years and then, in a short period of geological time lasting a mere 100,000 years, gave rise to a new species. However, there were several possible alternative explanations for Cheetham's data. One was that the morphological differences in use to define the various species were not detailed enough and that several different species were being grouped as one. To exclude such a possibility, Cheetham therefore made a detailed study of the genetics of living specimens of bryozoa from each species and clearly established that the morphological distinctions he was using had a solid foundation. It was at this point that Cheetham's collaborator Jeremy Jackson was finally persuaded by the data and, as he expressed it in his own words, 'became a believer' in the theory of punctuated equilibrium with reference to the evolution of bryozoa. So belief in and commitment to a particular theory is not an all-or-nothing state of mind, but a growing conviction of the essential correctness of a certain model once evidence begins to pile up in its favour and rival explanations are gradually excluded.[49]

The high commitment levels of scientists to the 'grand theories', as well as to some of the 'lesser theories' of science, has a certain parallel with the commitments of atheists or theists to their respective metaphysical worldviews. The commitment of the theist to belief in God appears as annoyingly impervious to anomalies as the complacency of the scientist who continues in their commitment to a 'grand theory' of science in the face of apparent difficulties. In both cases the 'anomaly level' is clearly not yet high enough to be perceived by the believer as sufficiently substantial to challenge the theory. Certainly the high levels of commitment observed in both cases makes it difficult to believe that scientists go around believing in tentative hypotheses that may be disproved at any moment, whereas religious believers are so committed to their worldview that they will refuse to listen to counter-evidence. As we have already noted, the existence of an active two-way flow between atheism and theism does not support such a mythology.

Nevertheless the theist will want to point out that their religious commitment goes well beyond mere commitment to a theory. As the mathematical physicist John Polkinghorne has remarked: 'I believe in quarks, but the acknowledgment of their existence does not touch or threaten me in my own being. It is very different with belief in God, which has consequences for all that I do and hope for.'[50] Faith in God for the Christian involves confidence, loyalty and personal trust. Similar qualities are apparent when someone puts their life into the hands of a surgeon during a particularly delicate operation. Their commitment may be based on perfectly rational considerations, such as the long history of the successes of the surgeon in carrying out just this type of operation, but at the end of the day there is always an element of risk involved in such a step. Faith is no blind leap into the dark, but personal trust based on rational arguments and a careful weighing up of the available evidence. It has been suggested above that the types of argumentation employed prior to taking such a step of religious commitment are not dissimilar to those used when assessing the 'grand theories' of science, even though the data that are accepted as allowable are distinctive in each case. But, however convincing may be the arguments, there is an element of risk in taking a step of faith just as real as the risk involved in placing yourself under the surgeon's scalpel. There are no cast-iron guarantees.

At this point the atheist may object that once someone has taken this step of personal faith in God they then become 'blind' to any counter-evidence and totally set in their beliefs. There is a sense in which this is clearly the case, because trust, confidence and loyalty are inescapable elements of personal faith in God, as they are of enduring relationships between two people. The idea of commitment between two people in an exclusive human relationship, involving loyalty and trust, is not very coherent if either partner or both are constantly casting around for alternative relationships. But even a bride or groom on their wedding day making vows of personal allegiance 'until death doth us part' would, if pressed, have to admit that the divorce statistics are very high and that no one could guarantee that eventually their marriage might not break up, however deeply they might be in love at that moment with divorce the furthest intention from their minds. It is not therefore unreasonable to suggest that a high level of personal faith and commitment, to God for example, can coexist with the realistic assessment that unbelief can never be totally ruled out as a possibility for the future, however far that may be removed from a person's present thoughts and intentions. As already emphasized, this is in fact what happens to a subset of people. Even the most lifelong committed atheists can backslide and the same can happen to theists. I remember a friend who studied biochemistry with me at university who boasted that he came from a long line of atheists, which included his parents and his grandparents, before he then decided to become a Christian several months later. Another friend who was an atheist became a Christian through reading Bertrand Russell's book *Why I Am Not a Christian* on the grounds, as he explained later, that if such a brilliant man could present such weak arguments for disbelieving in Christianity then there must be a lot going for it. However, I remember a further friend who was a theist and who lost his faith about the same time (perhaps he should have read Russell...). Such events are going on continuously in these and many other directions in the pluralistic societies in which we live. Therefore it is simply not the case that religious commitment, involving personal trust in God within the Christian context, is incompatible with the possibility of a future loss of faith, suggesting that religious commitment is not the continuing blind trust in the face of any counter-evidence that is sometimes suggested.

Furthermore it is perfectly possible to have faith in God involving trust, confidence and loyalty, but at the same time to read widely and think dispassionately on worldviews quite different from one's own. Just as it is very noticeable that those most secure in their own culture are best able to adapt to the culture of others, for example when they move to another country, so it is not at all impossible for the person with atheistic or theistic beliefs to consider alternative worldviews sympathetically and with a degree of objectivity. For example, to the best of my knowledge Geoffrey Cantor claims no particular personal faith but has written a highly acclaimed biography of Michael Faraday, including a sympathetic portrait of his Christian worldview that so influenced

Faraday's professional and personal life as a scientist.[51] In the same way theists, despite (because of?) their religious commitment are perfectly able to enter sympathetically into the thinking of those who hold quite different worldviews from their own.[52]

Scientism

It has been suggested above that the price to be paid for the construction of a body of universally reliable scientific knowledge, fit to be published in reputable scientific journals, is the imposing of certain restrictions – restrictions on the type of questions addressed, restrictions on the language employed and restrictions on the methods used. Despite these restrictions it has also been pointed out that there are many interesting parallels between the way in which we make rational assessments of scientific and religious knowledge, although there are some important differences as well.

We now turn to consider a view of scientific knowledge which lingers on in popular culture and which is also actively promoted by some scientists and philosophers of science. This comprises a rather amorphous mixture of beliefs, the mixture varying somewhat in emphasis depending on who is propounding it, but the beliefs are linked sufficiently to subsume them under the general title of 'scientific naturalism' or, less formally, 'scientism'. In a way this latter term is an unfortunate title, since it implies that this is a philosophy which is inherent in the scientific enterprise itself, whereas it would be far closer to the truth to say that 'scientism' is parasitic upon science but certainly not part of it. Scientific naturalism, or scientism, refers to the view that only scientific knowledge is reliable and that science can, in principle, explain everything.

It will be clear from this definition that scientism remains in the tradition of Logical Positivism which, as we have already noted, ultimately foundered due to the undermining of its major claim by its own assumptions: no empirical data exist to support the claim that scientific explanations are the only ones that provide real knowledge. It is likewise fair to ask whether science itself can be used to justify scientism. It cannot. The data which science generates can provide no support for or against such a philosophy. Since the truth of scientific naturalism cannot be scientifically demonstrated, it cannot be a valid form of knowledge, and so is hoist by its own petard.

Furthermore, it is not clear why precedence should invariably be given to scientific explanations, as if the particular form of constructed knowledge that they represent were the form against which all other forms of knowledge should be measured. This smacks of 'scientific imperialism'. As already indicated above, there is a wealth of human knowledge, including all of the arts, that is not amenable to scientific investigation, and to write it all off as less than real knowledge smacks of a remarkable arrogance, not to say misunderstanding of the nature of scientific knowledge. As Stephen Jay Gould has commented, 'We live with poets and politicians, preachers and philosophers. All have their ways of knowing, and all are valid in their proper domains. The world is too complex and interesting for one way to hold all the answers.'[53]

One of the many flaws of scientism is the fallacy that once all the possible scientific descriptions of something have been made, then this body of knowledge provides the *only* possible significant description of the object or phenomenon. For example Dawkins has claimed:

> We are machines built by DNA whose purpose is to make more copies of the same DNA... Flowers are for the same thing as everything else in the living kingdoms, for spreading 'copy-me' programmes about, written in DNA language.
>
> That is EXACTLY what we are for. We are machines for propagating DNA, and the propagation of DNA is a self sustaining process. It is every living objects' sole reason for living.[54]

These words faithfully echo those of the sociobiologist E.O. Wilson:

> The individual organism is only the vehicle (of genes), part of an elaborate device to preserve and spread them with the least possible biochemical perturbation... The organism is only DNA's way of making more DNA.[55]

Now no self-respecting biologist would wish to deny that a property of all biological organisms is the passing on of DNA to their progeny, but it is puzzling why Dawkins wishes to claim that this is our *sole* reason for living. You do not need to have religious beliefs in order to think that there may be more to life than simply propagating your DNA to the next generation. People have all kinds of reasons for living – the ambition to be a great writer, a desire to travel the world, sporting success, financial achievements or even the goal of being a successful scientist. There seems no particular reason why any or all of these reasons for living should be incompatible with also believing in the importance of passing on one's DNA.

So concerned was Dawkins about the reactions of his readers to the 'cold, bleak message' of his earlier writings, that he wrote a book extolling the 'deep aesthetic passion' of science which ranks 'with the finest that music and poetry can deliver'.[56] The aesthetic experiences of scientists are not in question, but Dawkins should admit that the existence of 'aesthetic passions' cannot be adequately accounted for by the creed of scientific naturalism. Francis Crick was more faithful to the creed when he wrote that science has shown that '"you", your joys and your sorrows, your memories and your ambitions, your sense of identity and free will, are in fact no more than the behaviour of a vast assembly of nerve cells and their associated molecules'.[57] Scientific naturalism *is* a bleak creed which excludes precisely those experiences in life that, for most people, make it worth living. In practice no one lives as if science were enough.

The fallacy of scientism may be illustrated by the following scenario. A team of scientists from various branches of science carry out a study on the musical instruments of the London Philharmonic Orchestra. They analyse the woods and the metals and determine their origins: the physicists measure all the wavelengths of the noises that can be extracted from each instrument; the biochemist triumphantly concludes that certain components of the older violins are biological in origin, and so forth. But at the end of the day the team's written analysis of their data would be necessarily devoid of concepts like 'orchestra', 'concert' or 'Brahms concerto'. Their scientific explanations of each musical instrument would not be *rival* descriptions for these 'upper level' explanations of these physical phenomena, but *complementary* explanations. It is both true that a violin string gives out notes of a certain wavelength that can be recorded *and* that the string may be made from catgut *and* that the real meaning of the violin's existence is that it can be played with feeling and sensitivity in the context of a Brahms concerto. When listening to the concerto it is doubtful that one will be overly worried about the wavelengths given out by the catgut. Someone who claimed that the *only* meaning of the violin's existence was to emit sounds of a certain wavelength would be deemed eccentric.

The particular claim, therefore, that makes Dawkins's comments quoted above eccentric is that the *sole* reason for the existence of all living organisms is to propagate DNA. This type of statement has frequently been criticized under the general title of 'nothing buttery', because the ideas of scientism are so frequently expressed by the formula 'such-and-such a phenomenon is *nothing but* a collection of atoms, or DNA, or whatever the particular claim might be'.[58] The phrase is found in Hume's *Dialogues Concerning Natural Religion* in a passage remarkably similar in language to that used by Dawkins:

> Look round the world: Contemplate the whole and every part of it: You will find it to be nothing but one great machine, subdivided into an infinite number of lesser machines...[59]

As it happens Hume puts these words into the mouth of the theist, Cleanthes, who adopts the Newtonian design argument in Hume's treatise. Physicists would be unlikely now to view the world as a giant Newtonian machine, although the machine analogy has some remaining value in biology. But irrespective of the value of 'machine' analogies in modern science, it is the 'nothing but' phrase or its various equivalents (such as 'merely') that so frequently acts as a signpost for the presence of scientistic claims. In the immortal words of James Watson, 'there are only atoms. Everything else is merely social work.'[60]

Underlying the 'nothing buttery' critique is a particular form of 'reductionism'. Reductionism comes in two flavours. The first is 'methodological reductionism', a research strategy which is absolutely essential in the scientific enterprise. This is the process of taking a system apart and analysing the properties of the components one by one so that they can be understood in isolation. The number of components in any system, physical, chemical, biological or whatever, are so vast that the scientist tries to keep as many parts of the system as possible constant while investigating one particular aspect of the system. Having analysed each aspect separately there is then the challenging task of trying to see how all the various components interact to make the system what it is. This approach has been enormously successful and reductionism in this sense is therefore integral to science.

It is perhaps the very success of methodological reductionism which has led to the growth of 'ontological reductionism' (*ontology* is the study of existence, of being), the type of reductionism being attacked here by the term 'nothing buttery'. It is that form which wishes to claim that humans are *only* machines for propagating DNA, or that sounds given out by violins are *only* vibrations in the air of a certain wavelength. The greater the success in understanding a complex phenomenon by methodological reductionism, the greater will be the tendency to think that there is nothing more to say than the level of explanation generated by the particular method of scientific investigation being used. But this involves equating the method of investigation with the nature of the reality itself that is being investigated. The two should not be confused. When they are confused the results can be disastrous both for a given research field and also for the wider task of relating scientific knowledge to other forms of knowledge. In a previous era the psychologist B.F. Skinner argued that all behaviour could be explained by genetic factors and the history of reinforcement to which an organism had been exposed, explicitly denying the existence of mind or the validity of conscious reasons as a basis for behaviour. This externalist account of behaviour (descriptions of an observer) became in Skinner's account the *only* account that mattered – all 'internalist' accounts (what I think, feel, choose, and so on) were simply classified as irrelevant. As the psychologist Stuart Sutherland has commented, 'By his over-simplification, Skinner held back the progress of animal – and to a lesser extent human – psychology for a generation.'[61]

How can such confusions be avoided? A commonly used approach to relate the various levels of explanation generated by the use of methodological reductionism has been to utilize a concept already introduced above in the context of our orchestral analogy, that of *complementarity*. The term has had a chequered past and therefore needs some explanation. It was originally introduced by the physicist Niels Bohr in response to the introduction of quantum field theory by Paul Dirac in 1927 and was later expanded by Bohr to encompass many other types of human knowledge.[62] By the time of Dirac it was already clear that light behaved either like a series of waves spreading through space or like a stream of particles, and that the type of behaviour displayed by light depended on the experimental context. Light could therefore be understood in terms of the positions of individual particles ('configuration space') or in terms of momentum ('momentum space'), and the relationship between the two could be satisfactorily described by quantum theory. Bohr suggested that the relationship between these two ways of perceiving the properties of light was one of complementarity. The view that light behaved in some respects like waves was not a *rival* view to the concept that light behaved like particles, but a belief forced upon the observer by experimental observations that could only be interpreted by holding both views simultaneously. And while the belief that something could behave both like a wave and a particle was counter-intuitive in terms of models, at the level of transformation theory in quantum mechanics the two could be related in a satisfactory way.

Not all physical phenomena can be related so satisfactorily, and in extending the idea of complementarity to the relationship between scientific and religious explanations, later writers such as Donald MacKay have cautioned against using the concept to relate two phenomena that are in fact contradictory. 'When *are* we justified in insisting that two pictures must be complementary?' The answer that MacKay suggested to his own question was: 'Only when we find both are necessary to do justice to experience.'[63] The principle must never therefore be invoked as a cloak for intellectual laziness or to retard the pursuit of better ways of explaining the relationships between different types of experience. In this sense it is perhaps unfortunate that the concept arose out of Bohr's attempt to describe the relationship between two models for the behaviour of light that appear at first sight counter-intuitive or even flatly contradictory. The usage of the term complementarity to describe the relationship between scientific and religious explanations can therefore carry with it, for historical reasons, the notion that there is an apparent contradiction which is waiting to be reconciled.

A more mundane and, I would suggest, more fruitful use of the term 'complementarity' in the context of scientific and religious explanations emanates not from physics but from biology. Arthur Peacocke has emphasized the hierarchical nature of scientific explanations in biology.[64] Every plant and animal, humans included, could in principle be described using the language and techniques of physics, a description that would be unbelievably complex since it would be a description at the atomic level of the swirl of elementary particles and their energy relationships which comprise the ultimate building blocks of all living matter. Whether it was the human body that was being described, or some other biological organism, it would be perfectly correct to say that there was nothing else in the body but that which the physicist described. Yet from the biologist's point of view the description would be quite inadequate by itself to explain how the organism functioned. To become useful a number of other levels in the hierarchy of description would need to come into play. At the next level 'up' from physics would come biochemical descriptions, explanations concerning molecules that would include the functions of DNA and the way in which its genetic code is translated into protein sequences, and then the ways in which those proteins are involved in converting the energy derived from food into sustaining the life of the organism. A level 'up' from biochemistry comes cell biology. At this level the organism is seen no longer in terms of the interactions between molecules but in terms of cells and the organelles within cells, each one containing billions of molecules. This level of explanation is required in order to investigate questions such as the development of the organism. Since all the information that encodes our bodies is present in the DNA of every cell, how does the cell know how to develop into a kidney cell rather than a brain cell? And how do tissues (collections of cells) become the shape that they do become? One level 'up' from cell biology comes physiology, the study of the dynamic interactions between the various organs of the body in order to understand homeostasis, the various regulatory devices whereby the internal environment of the body is kept stable in the face of a changing environment. For brainy primates like humans there is then the need for yet a further level of explanation that requires the language and techniques of psychology. As goal-oriented human agents, what are the various factors that explain the different goals chosen by the agent? What can we say about human behaviour when the agent fails to achieve those goals? After this level of explanation we would then wish to study the organism in the context of its interaction with the environment using the language and concepts of environmental biology and, in the particular context of human societies, social anthropology. At a still higher level, and still in the human context, many people would then want a level of explanation relating to the ultimate purpose and goal of human agents together with a study of the basis for their ethical concerns, the domain of religious and philosophical discourse.

The term 'complementarity' seems a very appropriate way of relating these various levels of description. No biochemist (in their right mind) thinks that their biochemical explanations comprise the *only* relevant body of knowledge in the study of an organism, least of all that their explanations are in any sense *rival* to those supplied by the physicist, cell biologist, psychologist, or whoever. It is tacitly recognized that many layers of explanatory understanding are not only preferable but essential if a reasonable and complete description of a phenomenon so complex as a biological organism is to be achieved. The distinctive nature of the language, concepts and techniques necessary for explanations at each level are critical for this enterprise. Terms such as gene, metabolism, hormone or enzyme are not simply reducible into the language of physics but only make sense within the context of their own particular explanatory level (biochemical in this case). This does not mean that there is anything beyond physics that is required for their existence, only that the language and techniques of physics are as insufficient for their elucidation as would be the language and techniques of psychology. The biological properties of an organism 'emerge from' the matter that comprises that organism and which can be properly described by physics, but these emergent properties require more than the language and techniques of physics if they are to be understood correctly. 'As one goes to the higher and higher levels of organization, new concepts emerge that are needed to understand the behaviour at that level.'[65]

It should also be noted that I have used the word 'up' firmly straddled by inverted commas while describing this hierarchical series of explanatory levels, for although it is impossible to use the word hierarchy without some concept of 'up' and 'down', the idea of complementarity implies no value judgment about whether one level of explanation per se is necessarily any more important than another. What *is* really crucial, however, is to ensure that the questions and language appropriate to one level are not confused with those of another level. Such 'category mistakes' occur frequently during discussions of science and faith and can lead to endless and unnecessary confusion. It is as absurd to address theological questions as if they were referring to biological explanations as it is to attempt biochemical explanations using the techniques and language of psychology. 'Category mixing' also underlies many of the statements made by scientistic writers. For example, Peter Atkins expresses the scientistic creed clearly when he comments that 'Humanity should accept that science has eliminated the justification for believing in cosmic purpose, and that any survival of purpose is inspired solely by sentiment.'[66] But it is not at all clear why scientific explanations should be expected to eliminate questions of 'cosmic purpose'. The language of science and the language of ultimate purpose are complementary domains of human discourse with their own distinctive categories.

The idea of complementarity that emerges from its use here in considering the hierarchical nature of biological descriptions carries no suggestion that the types of knowledge being related are in any sense contradictory or counter-intuitive. On the contrary, the complementary nature of the levels of description are an inevitable consequence of the use of methodological reductionism as a research strategy. The scientist investigating the biological organism is very well aware that it is one single organism that is being studied but is equally aware that s/he will never really understand it without investigating one or a few bits of the organism at a time. Part of the fascination of biology is to determine how the various bits of an organism function to make an integrated whole and, equally, how the single organism survives and reproduces while living within complex populations of other organisms. Another fascination is to find out how the different levels at which a single organism is studied relate to each other. For example, certain human mutations which involve only tiny changes in the structure of DNA are sufficient to cause profound changes in development or intelligence, and the challenge is therefore to track the consequences of those changes all the way from the DNA molecule through to the major bodily changes which ensue. Tracking these consequences will probably involve virtually every level of biological explanation mentioned above, a reminder that the various complementary levels of explanation in the hierarchy are certainly not in watertight compartments but together form one integrated whole. To return to the orchestra analogy used above, the mutation would be equivalent to the breaking of a single piece of catgut in a single violin within the orchestra – the consequent jarring note in the overall symphony would be readily discernible to the musical ear, a further reminder that complementarity refers to the many connected aspects of a single reality, not to the relations between disconnected realities.

As mentioned already, in his book *Consilience – the Unity of Knowledge*, E.O Wilson proposes the unification of all human knowledge by pressing it into the framework of his own particular brand of scientific naturalism. Whether the underpinning of evolutionary biology is robust enough to derive human value and a valid ethical system will be considered further in chapter 11. For the moment it is worth noting the irony that in his section on 'Ethics and Religion', Wilson, far from deriving the unity of knowledge from his philosophical position, ends by pitting 'transcendentalism' (by which Wilson means all ethical views that derive from religious beliefs) against 'empiricism' (by which Wilson means the view that ethics can be derived by better biological research on human nature): 'Which worldview prevails, religious transcendentalism or scientific empiricism, will make a great difference in the way humanity claims the future.'[67] But this is a false dichotomy. It is entirely possible that there is a God who has intentions and purposes for his creation which are worked out by biological processes and that theological descriptions of his intentions and biological descriptions of the processes provide complementary insights into the same reality from different perspectives. Wilson provides no evidence why this should not be the case, and the fact that his scientistic presuppositions fail to achieve his quest for 'consilience' (unity of human knowledge) may suggest that his starting assumptions need re-examining.

There are many different ways in which religious explanations may be viewed as complementary to those of science. For example, if someone makes the theological claim that 'God healed Susan in answer to prayer' in the full knowledge that Susan had just undergone an extensive series of tests and operations in a leading hospital, they need not by this statement imply any deficiencies in the hospital or in the doctors involved in the case. Far from it, they might instead be recognizing the providential actions of God over the whole created order, including the biochemistry and physiology of Susan and over the skilled hands of the doctors, in seeing a particular result come to pass. The sceptic would naturally want to say that the outcome would have been the same without the prayer, a point which is clearly not amenable to testing in this instance. But, irrespective of whether someone believes in prayer or not, the point at this stage is to see that the claims of religious discourse are frequently about the overall interpretation or ultimate purpose of a particular series of events and are therefore complementary to other levels of explanation that might be provided. Some further striking examples of this point will emerge during the discussion of creation and evolution in the next chapter, and again in our consideration of miracles in chapter 13.

At this point it might be objected in defence of scientism that scientific explanations of a given phenomenon are in fact the *only* ones that are required – religious discourse is redundant because it adds nothing to the explanation. Religious explanations, the objector would point out, may indeed be logically allowable in the complementary sense of explanation that has been suggested, but on the principle that excess explanations should be dropped if they add nothing further, religious explanations are deemed unnecessary.

If such a comment is made solely in the context of explanations of physical phenomena, then it is certainly true, but in this case it becomes not an objection in defence of scientism but a valid defence of the way that the scientific enterprise itself should be carried out. Questions about physical phenomena require physical answers. However, if the defence of scientism is made by suggesting that religious explanations are redundant because they add nothing to scientific explanations in the context of *all* classes of human knowledge, then this objection is an example of the 'category error' type to which we have already referred. It has been argued in this chapter that the scientific enterprise has advanced so successfully by deliberately restricting its scope to investigations of the physical world. By definition, therefore, a vast swathe of human knowledge and experience, encompassing the arts, ethics, personal relationships, philosophy and religion, lies outside the scope of science. Within this sphere of non-science, religion in particular addresses questions of ultimate meaning and purpose and the closely related question of how we ought to live our lives. No one can escape such questions in practice because everyone has a life to be lived and, it has been argued, a metaphysical set of beliefs which are used in decision-making with regard to that life. Scientific information tells us nothing about ultimate meaning and purpose nor gives any indication as to how we should live our lives. Such things have to be sorted out using other types of criteria that science does not provide. As Steve Jones comments in *The Language of the Genes*:

> Science cannot answer the question that philosophers – or children – ask; why are we here, what is the point of being alive, how ought we to behave? Genetics has almost nothing to say about what makes us more than just machines driven by biology, about what makes us human. These questions may be interesting, but scientists are no more qualified to comment on them than is anyone else.[68]

Therefore within this particular context it is quite correct and proper to see religious and scientific explanations as being complementary to each other.

It is once again the human species that provides the most striking examples of such types of complementary levels of explanation. A person may believe that her ultimate aim in life is to worship god *and* make it a personal goal to become a successful scientist *and* to become a mother and raise children *and* to believe that her body can be described very successfully within the framework provided by modern biochemistry, molecular biology and physiology. Each one of these levels at which the individual operates, either with the internalist perspective of human agency or with the externalist perspective of a human observer, may be seen as complementary to each of the others. But to suggest that in this hierarchy the religious 'meaning level' is necessarily redundant is simply to ignore the actual experience of the great majority of the world's population. Many people would wish to say that it is this level which places all the others in their correct perspective. The relationship between these levels also meets the criterion espoused by MacKay for the correct use of the complementarity concept in that the individual clearly *does* find that all levels are 'necessary to do justice to experience'. One level is not reducible to another.

The notion of complementarity implies no incompleteness in any particular level of description. Naturally when a scientist tries to describe a biological organism there are gaping holes in the descriptions at whichever level we try and make them. But it is not this incompleteness that generates the need for complementarity. The need for a complementary understanding of the relationship between the various descriptive levels would be equally pressing even if our knowledge at all the levels was total. If 'all' we had in our hands was the complete biochemical description of an organism at the molecular level provided by a super-biochemist, we would nevertheless remain in great ignorance about that organism. Of necessity concepts such as 'shape of nose', 'how many legs' and 'reproductive habits' would be missing from our description. The complementary descriptions provided by cell biologists, physiologists, anatomists and evolutionary biologists, would all be essential to an understanding of the organism. This would imply no slur on the work of the super-biochemist, but merely reflect the need to tackle our analysis of complex objects like organisms at several different levels.

It should by now be apparent that someone making religious claims, for example, about the ultimate aims and purposes of our lives, will be unsympathetic to the idea that such claims imply the need for some incompleteness in the biological or psychological 'stories' that scientists may provide in describing the human species. This point is often misunderstood by people critical of religion who think that religious claims necessarily imply deficits in the scientific explanations provided by human biology. Not so. No 'ghost-in-the-machine' or special mystical little hidden corners of the human psyche are necessary to justify religious claims about human aims and purposes. Far from it, religious claims are introduced at a very mundane non-mystical level of human experience in questions such as 'how should I live my life', 'does my life have any ultimate meaning/purpose', and so forth. The concepts of ultimate meaning and purpose are no more reducible to physiology, genetics or physics than the concept of 'liver' or 'gene' are reducible to physics. Again, let it be underlined, this is not to imply that anything other than what can also be described by physics is present in the human body, only that different complementary levels of language and description are essential if we are to do justice to the complexities of our experience in both being a human and studying other humans in our capacity as scientists.

Equally it should also be apparent, at least within a theistic understanding of the world, that it would be quite mistaken to take the level of human existence at which religious language is appropriate – the language of 'god', 'purpose', 'goals' and 'ethical decisions' – and mix this with any of the various levels of scientific description. The concepts of 'god' or 'ultimate purpose' have no more place at the descriptive levels of genetics or molecular biology than the concepts of 'genes' and 'enzymes' have relevance to discourse about 'ultimate purpose'. Least of all can 'god' be reduced to a kind of causal agent acting at one or more levels of scientific description as if god was acting in the present gaps in our scientific knowledge, for example by making up sequences for the genetic code (an area of science in which our present ignorance provides a rich hunting ground for 'god-of-the-gaps' type arguments by creationists).

Map-making

A useful analogy that has often been used to illustrate the appropriate relationship between complementary levels of knowledge relating to the same reality is that of map-making. As with all analogies, it is important that it is not pressed too far, but the map analogy provides certain insights both into the type of knowledge that science provides and also the way in which it may relate to other types of knowledge.

First, maps are representations of reality but they are not the reality itself. In this way they are similar to scientific data, which represent a slice of reality delivered to our sense organs following extensive filtration through a selection of instruments by means of specialized techniques. The theories that make sense of the data are like the contour lines on the map that join the various objects on the scientific landscape and link them together into a coherent whole. When the contour lines are packed tightly together on a geographical map we know that our planned climb will be a steep one, but the actual climb is a very different matter from running our finger with great ease over tightly packed contour lines on a map. The map is an accurate representation of reality that has to be taken seriously, and which we ignore at our peril, but it is certainly not synonymous with that reality.

Second, the best way to provide useful information about a country in map form is to provide a whole series of specialized maps. It would be confusing to try and pack all the information on to a single map. Instead we make separate maps for geology, communications, urbanization, rainfall, population, topography, crops grown, church attendance, voting preferences, economic parameters, length of queues for hospital treatment and so forth, an almost endless potential for representing the same geographical area from some new and specialized angle. The various maps are not rivals but provide complementary information. They are all about the same reality but viewed from different angles, just as the various levels of description of a human being are all necessary to give a complete picture of what that organism is really like. If each level of biological description was converted into a 'map format', then a special list of symbols, terms and definitions would be required to find our way successfully round any particular map. The biochemical map of the human would be full of metabolic and signalling pathways all interconnected in highly complex ways. The genetic map of the human would incorporate the locations of genes on chromosomes, genetic sequences and an idea of how these are translated into the proteins that then 'run' the body. The psychological map of the human would have a completely different set of symbols, including terms like motivation, drive, complex and phobia. The religious map of the human would be different again, characterized by further specialized language like ultimate goal, ethical decision, feeling of transcendence and commitment to God. None of these maps need be rival to any of the others, but mixing of symbols and language between maps will lead to muddles and category mistakes. Trying to find 'motivations' and 'drives' on the genetic map will be an experience as fruitless as the search for transcendence on the chromosomes. This is not at all to deny that the person who experiences 'drives' does so using a brain having an anatomy encoded by genes, just as transcendence is experienced by the same person using the same brain encoded by genes located on chromosomes, but the internalist and externalist accounts of these various facets of human experience require two quite distinctive accounts to do them justice.

The third useful aspect of the map-making analogy is that while maps are intended to provide reliable knowledge, they are never final nor complete. The development of scientific theories of increasing sophistication may be viewed as akin to the development of a series of maps, each related to and dependent upon the edition that came just before, but no one would be so naive as to think that the contemporary 'map' of their particular research field was in any sense exhaustive in its explanations. Likewise, the person who defends their religious beliefs on the basis that they form a body of reliable knowledge does not need to imply that the particular map of reality that they are espousing is a static one which is not equally open to new understanding as time goes on. Nevertheless, as with the scientific maps that are never redrawn from scratch but which always rely on the previous ones, the religious maps will also want to include the important and valid points of the previous edition while at the same time incorporating new insights.

It should be noted that the map-making analogy is hostile to scientism in all its aspects. First, by reminding us that a scientific theory is only a representation of reality, not the reality itself, the analogy helps to deflate the exaggerated claims for scientific descriptions that often characterize scientism. Second, the fact that many different complementary maps are essential to build up an accurate picture of reality is anathema to scientistic philosophies, which maintain that scientific knowledge is the only reliable body of knowledge that exists. Third, the idea that any given map is never the final and complete answer sits uneasily with the Baconian assumption, often implicit rather than explicit in scientistic writings, that science is there to give us the 'bare unchangeable facts', as if facts could be divorced from the theories into which they are currently incorporated and which will develop further and become increasingly sophisticated with time. This does not mean that the 'facts' will change, but they will certainly be cast in a different light as theories which incorporate them become more sophisticated.

Models

Both scientific and religious understandings of the world are deeply wedded to the use of models and the way in which such models are utilized in these respective spheres has proved a useful point of contact. John Polkinghorne has proposed the word 'model' to be:

> a frankly heuristic device by which one attempts to gain some purchase on reality or some insight into complexity, without believing that one is giving a totally accurate account of that reality or a fully adequate characterization of that complexity. A model is potentially illuminating but not exhaustively descriptive.[69]

Unlike the analogy of map-making which, useful though it may be, remains an analogy, the process of model building plays a much deeper role in both science and theology than that of mere analogy. Although it is clear that the model is not the reality itself, nevertheless the model can often assume such importance in scientific enquiry that it becomes a major driving force within a particular research field. The race to elucidate the structure of the DNA molecule within a model that satisfied its physical properties, as well as providing for its replication and role as the carrier of the genetic code, provided an important focus for biochemical research during the early 1950s. The triumphant double-helical model for DNA has dominated the biological sciences ever since. The double-helix provides a model of great power and elegance. Yet no biochemist thinks that if only you had the right type of powerful microscope you could look into the cell and see double-helical molecules of DNA neatly stacked up in the nucleus which would look anything like the neat and static model of DNA which dominates the front of the MRC Laboratory of Molecular Biology in Cambridge a few hundred metres from where I type these words. The model is not the reality itself. For a start, DNA is not only a double-helix but has a further level of structure whereby, along with attendant proteins, it is packed into structures called chromosomes. Furthermore, each DNA molecule *in situ* is a hive of activity, not unlike a busy dock-side with ships loading and unloading, in which regulatory proteins shuttle to and fro to switch genes (stretches of DNA) on and off, and in which the helix is busy winding or unwinding, depending on the need of the moment.

Even though the double-helical model is not the reality itself, it nevertheless incorporates an enormous amount of vital information about DNA and continues to form a focus for research in molecular biology. The double-helical model also excludes other rival accounts of DNA. For example, DNA is not a triple-helix. Neither is biology going to 'advance' to the point at which a new model is proposed suggesting that DNA is a triple-helix – the possibility of a triple-helix was excluded back in the 1950s. In this sense the double-helical model of DNA is a 'fact' just as the encoding of genes within stretches of DNA is a 'fact'. It is this point which helps to distinguish the term 'model' in science from a scientific theory. A model is an attempt to bring something which is right outside our everyday experience into a realm of discourse that depends on the language and concepts of that experience. It may well be that the first model proposed is shown to be inappropriate as more data become available, in which case the need to make up a better model will be apparent.

In contrast the term 'scientific theory' is generally used to describe the attempt to make sense of a wide assortment of data, which may involve several different models, by assembling them into a coherent whole. For example, a comprehensive theory of protein biosynthesis requires not only the correct model for DNA but also the correct models for RNA and protein structure to boot. Or, to switch to the world of physics, the wave and particle models of light were introduced to do justice to the results of two distinct types of experiment, and both models remain necessary so that we can translate the properties of light into language more amenable to our daily perceptions. But it was quantum field theory that showed how both these models could be incorporated consistently into a single scientific theory.

Inevitably associated with the process of making up scientific models is the use of metaphor. Metaphor has been described as 'a strategy of desperation, not decoration; it is an attempt to say something about the unfamiliar in terms of the familiar, an attempt to speak about what we do not know in terms of what we do know'.[70] Scientific discourse is loaded with metaphors, some helpful, some unhelpful, but they are an attempt, sometimes a desperate attempt, to enable us to grapple with some slice of physical reality. Occasionally the metaphors chosen are unfortunate in that their scientific usage becomes confused with their ordinary daily usage, thereby leading to miscommunication. For example, metaphors such as 'selfish genes' and 'altruistic behaviour' have precise biological meanings which are distinct from the everyday usage of these terms. Occasionally the choice of metaphor is downright quirky, like the choice to call one of the quantum numbers 'charm' in the sense of 'amulet' since this provided a way of warding off the evil of an unobserved experimental consequence which would otherwise be present in the theory![71]

The use of models and metaphors in science is so deeply embedded and so taken for granted that scientists are often surprised when informed that a very analogous process goes on in religious discourse. As in science, so in religion, there is the challenge to bring a slice of reality well beyond our daily experience into a realm of discourse to which we can relate. Talk about God is full of such challenges. Christian theism, for example, speaks of a personal God. Biblical descriptions of the character of God are full of words that are used to describe humans, such as loving, displeased, caring, willing and so forth. In applying these words to humans such terms have clear meanings that can be defined. But the application of such terms to God is strictly metaphorical. They can never give a *complete* description of what it means for God to be loving, or displeased, or caring. This does not mean that such statements are untrue, any more than it is untrue to say that a gene is 'selfish' (given the technical biological definition of that term). A 'model' of God as being personal is only coherent because of our human experience of interrelating as persons. Without that experience such a metaphor would be vacuous. A very similar point could be made about many of the metaphors used in science. Talk of DNA as a double-helix would make no sense unless we had received some personal experience of helical structures from our everyday world of mathematics and twisted columbine creepers. Talk of 'black holes' in cosmology would be of little value unless we had experienced a hole for ourselves. Even though we realize that 'black holes' in cosmology are nothing like the ones that we have experienced, nevertheless the metaphor is not devoid of value.

When people talk of God using personal language they are sometimes accused of being anthropomorphic. But the fact is that there is no other language to use than that which is derived from our daily personal experiences, no more in religion than there is in science. Both spheres of investigation demand metaphor for understanding. Just how important it is not to interpret metaphors too literally, either in science or in religion, will be illustrated by the topic of the next chapter.

Chapter 9

Headquarters Nights
Creation and Evolution

You poor fools, God can make a cow out of a tree, but has he ever done so? Therefore show some reason why a thing is so, or cease to hold that it is so.
William of Conches, 12th century

The antagonism of science is not to religion, but to the heathen survivals and the bad philosophy under which religion herself is often well-nigh crusted. And, for my part, I trust that this antagonism will never cease; but that, to the end of time, true science will continue to fulfil one of her most beneficent functions, that of relieving men from the burden of false science which is imposed upon them in the name of religion.
T.H. Huxley, *Lectures on Evolution*, 1876

But can't we be Christian evolutionists, they say. Yes, no doubt it is possible to be a Christian and an evolutionist. Likewise, one can be a Christian thief, or a Christian adulterer, or a Christian liar! Christians can be inconsistent and illogical about many things but that doesn't make them right.
Henry Morris, *King of Creation*, 1980

To hear Ayala talking lovingly of his fruit flies and Gould of his fossils was to realize so vividly that it is those who deny evolution who are anti-God, not those who affirm it.
Michael Ruse, *A Philosopher's Day in Court*, 1988

The Darwinian theory of evolution provides a paradigm within which all contemporary biological research is carried out. The theory gives coherence to an immense and varied array of research fields, including molecular biology, biochemistry, immunology, developmental biology, zoology, botany, anatomy, anthropology, geology, ecology and behavioural psychology, to name but a few. Despite occasional journalistic claims to the contrary, there is currently no rival scientific theory to explain the origins of biological diversity. This certainly does not imply that Darwinian theory is a perfect theory; many aspects of the theory remain active areas of investigation, not least the mechanisms involved in speciation and the particular lineages involved in human origins. Nevertheless, within the biological research community no other theory has been seriously considered as an alternative explanation for biological diversity since Darwin's theory became established during the latter half of the 19th century.

Darwin's theory claims that the form and diversity of the living world is due to a theory of variation *and* to a theory of selection. *Variation* is generated by genetic mutations that occasionally affect the survival and reproductive fitness of individuals. *Natural selection* is the process whereby genes which promote the greatest reproductive success of individuals in a given environment are more likely to be passed on to the next generation. It is not the purpose of this chapter either to explain or to defend Darwin's theory further than providing this bare definition, although some aspects of the theory will be discussed in more detail insofar as it is claimed that they have ethical or religious implications. As far as the biological theory itself is concerned, the best way to appreciate it is to attend a relevant course in biology and many excellent textbooks of evolution are also available.[1]

'With but few exceptions the leading Christian thinkers in Great Britain and America came to terms quite readily with Darwinism and evolution'[2] and, 'with the exception of Harvard's Louis Agassiz, virtually every American Protestant zoologist and botanist accepted some form of evolution by the early 1870s'.[3] Yet despite this wide acceptance of Darwinian evolution, which included its adoption by virtually all the mainstream Christian denominations by the 1880s to 1890s, it is a surprising fact that for a period during the 1920s, and then for the last few decades of the 20th century, a vigorous campaign has been carried out against the theory by so-called 'creationists', mainly based in the USA. The USA is arguably one of the most technologically advanced nations in the world and certainly the world leader in terms of its output of biological research, yet nearly half the population do not believe in evolution.[4] A 1985 survey at Ohio State University revealed that 62 per cent of the student body accepted evolution but a sizeable minority (25 per cent) believed that scientists doubted evolution, even though publicly supporting it. According to a 1991 Gallup poll, 47 per cent, including one-fourth of the college graduates polled, continued to believe that 'God created man pretty much in his present form at one time within the last 10,000 years.' On a much smaller scale this opposition to evolution has been exported to other countries, such as Holland, Australia and Britain.

The existence of this anti-evolutionary campaign in precisely those countries in which Darwinian evolution was most rapidly accepted in the last century is in itself a phenomenon of great interest and has received widespread analysis. The roots of the campaign are complex and will be analysed further below, but clearly stem to at least some extent from the belief that evolutionary theory has certain moral implications which comprise a threat to religious belief. As a direct result of such anti-evolutionary crusading, scientists have frequently reacted, not surprisingly, in vigorous defence, but in the process a minority of scientists have also made exaggerated claims concerning both the status of scientific theories as well as the supposed theological and moral implications of Darwinian theory. The extreme poles of opposing positions normally rely on each other for their very existence and the often murky debates between 'creationists' and their opponents have been no exception in this respect. Extreme poles are frequently characterized by greater similarities of thought than is first imagined, and there is a certain irony in the reflection that both 'creationists' and those who believe that science is hostile to religious belief often share the same basic misconceptions both about theology and about the nature and scope of scientific enquiry.

I shall argue in this and the following two chapters that the Darwinian theory of evolution, whatever may have been the various ideological uses to which it has been put since 1859, is essentially devoid of either religious or moral significance, and that those who try to derive such significance from it are mistaken. We shall first consider the roots and claims of the creationist movement and then outline and defend a more traditional religious view that expresses a very different concept of the relationship between God and the universe than that espoused by the creationists. Finally the various points of supposed conflict between religious beliefs and evolutionary theory will be discussed and the views of those 'evolutionary naturalists' who believe that ethical beliefs can be extracted from evolutionary theory will be analysed.

The roots of the creationist movement

The terms 'creator', 'create' or 'creation' as used in the English language within a theological context were generally used well into the 19th century as referring to the activity of God in bringing the physical universe into being, including the world with its biological diversity, irrespective of the mechanisms that may have been used. For example, the astronomer Sir John Herschel, whose scientific writings were later to inspire Darwin as an undergraduate at Cambridge, spent some time during the 1830s mapping the southern skies from his vantage point on the Cape of Good Hope (astronomers have always found good excuses to travel). In 1836 Herschel wrote to Lyell to comment on the immense biological diversity that he was observing in the region and on 'that mystery of mysteries the replacement of extinct species by others'. It was his opinion, stated Herschel, that both the origin and the extinction of species were due to natural causes and that to think otherwise was to hold 'an inadequate conception of the Creator' since 'in this, as in all his other works we are led by all analogy to suppose that he operates through a series of intermediate causes'. Consequently, if we could ever observe the origin of new species, it 'would be found to be a natural in contradistinction to a miraculous process'.[5]

As we have already noted in chapter 7, it was a quote from Whewell, expressing a very similar view, that Darwin later placed at the front of the *Origin*, stating that events were not brought about by 'insulated interpositions of Divine power, exerted in each particular case, but by the establishment of general laws'. As Darwin well realized, Whewell did not apply his own theology rigorously enough, but this provides a further illustration of the way in which God's creative activity was perceived by one of the leading thinkers of that era. The same underlying concept of 'creation' is to be found in the writings of Wallace, Darwin's co-discoverer of evolution, during the period in which he was beginning to publish his findings. In his paper of 1855 Wallace made quite clear that 'every species has come into existence coincident both in space and time with a pre-existing closely allied species'. As Young points out 'Wallace employed the language of creation but left no doubt that he envisaged a natural mechanism for the origin of species.' The present living world, wrote Wallace, 'is clearly derived by a natural process of gradual extinction and creation of species from that of the latest geological periods', making plain in his later writings that he intended by the term 'natural process' the process of evolution.[6]

During this same period the Reverend Henry Baker Tristram was both a canon of Durham and a distinguished naturalist specializing in the fauna of Palestine and North Africa, continuing that long tradition of involvement in natural history that was so characteristic of the Victorian clergy. When the theory of evolution was first published by Darwin and Wallace in the *Proceedings* of the Linnean Society in 1858, Tristram not only took note of the theory but was the first to publicly accept it prior to the publication of the *Origin*. 'Writing with a series of about 100 Larks of various species from the Sahara before me', Tristram wrote in a paper published in 1859, 'I cannot help feeling convinced of the views set forth by Messrs Darwin and Wallace in their communication to the Linnean Society.' There were, continued Tristram, 'perfectly natural causes' that 'serve to *create* as it were a new species from an old one', adding that such causes 'must have occurred, and are possibly occurring still'.[7] However, as we noted in chapter 7, Tristram actually stopped believing in evolution as a result of the Huxley–Wilberforce debate.

It was only during the latter half of the 19th century, following the publication of the *Origin*, that the term 'creation' began to be used by some writers, critical of Darwin's theory, as if it referred to an explanation of events that supposedly remained unexplained by evolutionary theory or could not be described in purely physical terms. As already noted in chapter 7, the Swiss naturalist Agassiz as well as Darwin's old teacher, the geologist Sedgwick, continued to believe that each species had been created separately in its own particular habitat. But even those scientists who were initially most critical of evolution were still very far in their beliefs from the 20th-century 'creationists' who first started their vocal campaign in the USA during the 1920s. It was only then that creationists began to proclaim their belief in a 'young earth', created only some 10,000 years ago, belief in a creation period of six literal days of twenty-four hours, creation *ex nihilo* ('out of nothing') of each separate species and a universal flood which contributed to the geological record. As a leading contemporary creationist writer, Duane Gish, has stated:

> By creation we mean the bringing into being by a supernatural Creator of the basic kinds of plants and animals by the process of sudden, or fiat, creation. We do not know how the Creator created, what processes He used, *for He used processes which are not now operating anywhere in the natural universe* [Gish's italics]. This is why we refer to creation as special creation. We cannot discover by scientific investigations anything about the creative processes used by the Creator.[8]

Not since the late 17th century have such 'creationist' beliefs in a young earth, flood geology and six literal days of creation been widely propounded, and then of course because there was little reason to believe otherwise. The last mainstream natural philosopher to advocate the 20th-century creationists' form of flood geology is generally held to be John Woodward in 1695. Even Darwin's most bitter scientific critics in the 19th century were certainly not 'creationists' by this 20th-century definition of the term. Sedgwick, for example, referred in his critical review of the *Origin* published in *The Spectator* in 1860 to the 'millions of years' involved in laying down the various geological strata and it was in any case he more than anyone else, together with Murchison, who established the geological column. It is therefore misleading, contra the claims of both creationists and their opponents, to suggest a continuity of belief between the 20th-century creationists and those who were most vocal in their opposition to Darwin in the 1860s. Critics like Sedgwick were not people who doubted the geological record, nor the extreme age of the earth, nor indeed who held to six literal days of creation, but scientists who were genuinely puzzled by the apparently sudden appearance of new species in the geological column and who found it difficult to believe that the slow processes underlying natural selection could possibly explain them. Despite their belief that God had 'intervened' at particular points to bring about the formation of new species, they would nevertheless have been shocked by Gish's comment that God's creative activity involved 'processes which are not now operating anywhere in the natural universe', since it was precisely the drive to uncover the mechanisms that God had chosen to use in his creation that had provided such a powerful motivation for natural philosophers in their work over a period of so many centuries. The novelty of the 20th-century package of creationist beliefs should not be underestimated, nor the discontinuity of these beliefs with those held by Darwin's critics during the 19th century.

Creationism and fundamentalism

Given the marked discontinuity of belief between 20th-century creationists and the concepts of creation commonly espoused in the previous century, how can we explain this sudden exotic flowering of 18th-century beliefs in the midst of the 20th and on into the 21st centuries? The term 'fundamentalist', which has often been used to describe such beliefs both in the press and in the scientific literature, has done little to enlighten the roots of this phenomenon. The term stems from a mass-produced series of twelve booklets entitled *The Fundamentals* published in the period 1910–15, which were intended to reform and strengthen the basic beliefs of Christianity around the world. But the tone of the booklets towards evolution was ambivalent and generally lacked the strident anti-evolutionary rhetoric that characterized the creationist movement of the 1920s. Furthermore, several writers were asked to contribute to *The Fundamentals* who were well known for their acceptance of evolutionary theory. For example, the Christian Darwinian George Wright's contribution to volume 7 of *The Fundamentals* commented that the word evolution 'has come into much deserved disrepute by the injection into it of erroneous and harmful theological and philosophical implications'. Wright's critique centred not on evolutionary theory per se but on the various attempts that had been made to extract out of it a materialistic philosophy. R.A. Torrey, who edited the last two volumes in the series, once referred to Darwin as 'the greatest scientific thinker of the 19th century' and with reference to the interpretation of the creation story in Genesis, Torrey wrote that 'Anyone who is at all familiar with the Bible and the Bible usage of words knows that the use of the word "day" is not limited to periods of twenty-four hours. It is frequently used of a period of time of an entirely undefined length.' In the same vein another frequent contributor to *The Fundamentals*, James Orr, reminded his readers that the 'Bible was never given us in order to anticipate or forestall the discoveries of modern 20th-century science'.[9] It is difficult to believe that such sentiments provided much help to the later 'fundamentalists' who began to proclaim that the Bible was a scientific textbook teaching that the world was made in six days. Clearly the word 'fundamentalist' underwent its own rapid evolution during the course of the 20th century.

The crusade against evolution, which began in the USA during the 1920s, developed against a background of rapid social change in which scapegoats were actively sought for the loss of faith and breakdown in morality which, it was widely held, was 'sapping the strength of America as a great nation'. Furthermore, there were very real fears that although Germany was now defeated, the philosophy that 'might is right', which underlay German militarism, might be imported into American life and culture. The channel, so it was thought, by which such a doctrine could spread through the nation was Darwinian evolution. The man who campaigned for this view and popularized it with great vigour was William Jennings Bryan and it is highly unlikely that the anti-evolutionary campaign of the 1920s would have gained such strength or notoriety without Bryan's leadership.

William Bryan and 1920s' creationism

Bryan was a three-time defeated Democratic candidate for the presidency of the United States, a Presbyterian layman and one of America's greatest populist reformers of that era. Bryan had been at the forefront of campaigns for women's suffrage and the direct election of senators, and against American imperialism and involvement in the First World War. Indeed, as a pacifist, Bryan had resigned as USA President Woodrow Wilson's secretary of state over the issue of maintaining America's neutrality during the war. Until the war Bryan had apparently maintained an ambivalent attitude towards evolution and had certainly not singled it out as a target for his campaigning zeal. However, in 1904 he wrote in a book entitled the *Prince of Peace*:

> The Darwinian theory represents man as reaching his present perfection by
> the operation of the law of hate – the merciless law by which the strong
> crowd out and kill off the weak. If this is the law of our development then,
> if there is any logic that can bind the human mind, we shall turn backward
> toward the beast in proportion as we substitute the law of love. I prefer to
> believe that love rather than hatred is the law of development.[10]

This passage reveals deep misunderstandings about the meaning and scope of Darwinian evolution to which we shall return below. Given such misunderstandings it is perhaps not surprising that the Great War, with all its demonstrations of 'merciless law' and turning 'backward toward the beast' should have directed Bryan's campaigning temperament against evolution.

According to Bryan's own account, there were two books in particular that sparked his campaign, and both are worth considering in some detail since they illustrate very vividly the reasons that underlie much of the anti-evolutionary fervour that continues up to the present day. These two books were *Headquarters Nights* by Vernon Kellogg (1917) and *The Science of Power*, by Benjamin Kidd (1918).[11] Vernon Kellogg, a professor at Stanford, was an entomologist and a leading evolutionary biologist of his time. During the earlier period of the First World War when America remained officially neutral, Kellogg was posted to the headquarters of the German General Staff in his capacity as a high official in the international effort for Belgian relief. *Headquarters Nights* is the account of Kellogg's conversations with the Kaiser's military officers during which, night after night at the dinner table, they extolled the virtues of German militarism according to the philosophy of 'might is right'. Many of the officers had been university professors before the war and were therefore of a similar background to Kellogg, who recounts:

> Professor von Flussen is Neo-Darwinian, as are most German biologists and natural philosophers. The creed of the *Allmacht* ['all might' or omnipotence] of a natural selection based on violent and competitive struggle is the gospel of the German intellectuals; all else is illusion and anathema... This struggle not only must go on, for that is the natural law, but it should go on so that this natural law may work out in its cruel, inevitable way the salvation of the human species... That human group which is in the most advanced evolutionary stage... should win in the struggle for existence, and this struggle should occur precisely that the various types may be tested, and the best not only preserved, but put in position to impose its kind of social organization – its *Kultur* – on the others, or, alternatively, to destroy and replace them. This is the disheartening kind of argument that I faced at Headquarters...

Kellogg was well aware of the spurious nature of such extrapolations from biology into philosophy, but the experience of being repeatedly exposed to such arguments shook his pacifism to such an extent that he later returned to America determined to see German militarism destroyed by force. It is perhaps not surprising that when Bryan read *Headquarters Nights* it spurred his anti-evolutionary campaign. Ignoring Kellogg's own protestations to the contrary, Bryan misunderstood the implications of evolutionary theory just as profoundly as the Kaiser's officers and reacted with horror to the idea that 'this natural law may work out in its cruel, inevitable way the salvation of the human species'.

The Science of Power, by Benjamin Kidd, was a very different kind of book. Kidd was a philosophical idealist, believing that the true goal of life could only be achieved by a rejection of struggle and individual benefit, a view diametrically opposed to the philosophy of 'might is right'. Kidd maintained that society could only advance by integration, whereas Darwinism depended on the struggle of the individual. This was the pathway that led to war: 'Darwin's theories', wrote Kidd, 'came to be openly set out in political and military textbooks as the full justification for war and highly organized schemes of national policy in which the doctrine of force became the doctrine of Right.'

It is in such mistaken extrapolations from evolutionary theory that the roots of much of Bryan's anti-evolutionary campaigning are to be found. But it would be wrong to think that such a campaign was merely an aberration that occurred towards the end of a life otherwise dedicated to the support of liberal causes. Bryan clearly saw his anti-evolutionary rhetoric as being one of a piece with his previous populist campaigns on behalf of women's rights and for greater justice in the tax system. Evolution became the target because it was perceived to support a morality in which the powerful triumphed over the weak and helpless in society, and which provided a justification for aggressive nations to go to war with their neighbours. Furthermore, then as now, there were strong supporters of biological evolution who, like the Kaiser's officers, provided plenty of ammunition to fuel the anti-evolutionary lobby. Evolution was still frequently taught as if it represented a grand Spencerian philosophy for the whole of life, history and human progress, rather than in its straightforward Darwinian form of a biological theory to explain the origins of biological diversity. Not infrequently it was used to support rabid racist views which, as we reviewed in chapter 2, had dominated so much scientific thinking and enquiry during the 19th century. For example, when John Scopes taught his schoolchildren evolution at Dayton, Tennessee, he used a textbook called *A Civic Biology* by George Hunter (1914); under the heading 'Parasitism and Its Cost to Society – the Remedy', Hunter wrote:

> Hundreds of families such as those described above exist today, spreading
> disease, immorality and crime to all parts of this country. The cost to
> society of such families is very severe. Just as certain animals or plants
> become parasitic on other plants or animals, these families have become
> parasitic on society. They not only do harm to others by corrupting,
> stealing or spreading disease, but they are actually protected and cared
> for by the state out of public money. Largely for them the poorhouse and
> the asylum exist. They take from society, but they give nothing in return.
> They are true parasites.
>
> If such people were lower animals we would probably kill them off
> to prevent them from spreading. Humanity will not allow this, but we do
> have the remedy of separating the sexes in asylums or other places and in

various ways preventing intermarriage and the possibilities of perpetuating such a low and degenerate race.

Biologists of Bryan's era promoted eugenics as a natural and logical outcome of their science in a brazen manner that makes the post-holocaust reader cringe. In the 1920s and 1930s, nearly all geneticists took it for granted that 'mental defectives' should be prevented from breeding.[12] The geneticist Charles Davenport suggested that American society should

> prevent the feebleminded, drunkards, paupers, sex offenders, and criminalistic from marrying their like or cousins or any person belonging to a neuropathic strain. Practically it might be well to segregate such persons for one generation. Then the crop of defectives will be reduced to practically nothing.[13]

S.J. Holmes, Professor of Zoology in the University of California, worried in his textbook on evolution that 'If most of humanity comes to consist of what is called the dull normal class with an increased percentage of high grade morons the stability of civilization will be in peril' and suggested that 'Society may accomplish much by checking the multiplication of the feeble-minded, the criminals, and the insane; but how to keep from being swallowed up in the fecundity of mediocrity is a much more difficult problem.'[14] The possible implications of natural selection for the black population was also an active topic for discussion in American scientific journals. In an article in the *American Journal of Hygiene*, R. Pearl expressed the following opinion:

> The Negro is biologically a less fit animal, in the American environment, physical, social, and general, than the white... Under conditions as they are, Nature, by the slow but dreadfully sure processes of biological evolution is apparently solving the Negro problem in the United States, in a manner which, when finished, will be like all Nature's solutions, final, complete, and absolutely definite.[15]

Lest it be thought that American biologists were unusual in their commitment to 'might is right' in the context of eugenic theories, it is worth remembering that:

> In Germany, not one geneticist criticized the inter-war eugenics movements. After the Nazis came to power, genetics was invoked on behalf of ever more extreme measures of racial purification. Nevertheless, most of Germany's leading geneticists, including those who

before 1933 had criticized anti-Semitism, actively helped to build the racial state. They served on important commissions, provided opinions on racial ancestry and participated in the drafting of racial laws. More than half of all academic biologists joined the Nazi Party, the highest membership rate of any professional group.[16]

Thus when campaigners such as Bryan vented their anti-evolutionary rhetoric, whereas their arguments may have been ill-founded, their rhetoric was not without good reason. As long as evolution was perceived to be a 'pernicious theory' undermining traditional morality and providing a basis for aggressive, racist and eugenic views, then so long would populist opposition continue to flourish.

By the end of the 1920s more than twenty state legislatures had debated anti-evolution laws and four of them proceeded to ban the teaching of evolution in state-funded schools. One of these states was Tennessee and in 1925, John Scopes, the teacher mentioned above, 'confessed' to violating the recently passed law banning the teaching of human evolution in his state. The subsequent trial focused international attention on the anti-evolutionary campaign and Bryan came to assist the prosecution. Not a single scientist was found to support the prosecution and it emerged that Bryan himself was not the strict creationist that many had believed, confiding to a Dr Kelly shortly before the trial that he had no objection to 'evolution before man'. In the event the trial was somewhat of a farce and, although the court found Scopes guilty as charged, the creationists emerged from this episode publicly ridiculed and Bryan himself died several days after the trial, its pressure no doubt contributing to his death. The creationist campaign continued on vigorously for a while without its main leader, but eventually ran out of steam in the late 1920s, particularly with the advent of the depression. Nevertheless there is good evidence that the campaign had a long-lasting impact on the contents of the nation's textbooks of biology. In 1942, a nationwide survey of secondary school teachers indicated that fewer than 50 per cent of high-school biology teachers were teaching anything about organic evolution in their science courses[17] and it has been reported that 25–30 per cent of USA high-school biology teachers believe in 'special creation'.[18] Anti-evolution laws were not in fact enforced in the states where they existed for the simple reason that publishers, with an eye on sales, eliminated all references to evolution in their textbooks.

Late-20th-century creationism

It was not until the early 1960s that the creationist campaign was revived in America in a form recognizably similar to the 1920s anti-evolution movement, but this time on a much grander scale. As Marsden comments: 'Before 1960, what is today known as "creation science" had only the most meagre support even among the conservative evangelical or fundamentalist communities in the United States.'[19] This more recent campaign was triggered not by a populist politician but by a lecturer in civil engineering from the Rice Institute called Henry Morris.[20] Together with a young theologian called John Whitcomb, Morris published a book in 1961 called *The Genesis Flood*, which basically repeated much of the material published by the Seventh Day Adventist self-styled geologist George McReady Price back in 1923 in his book *New Geology*. In the 1920s, as Numbers reports, Price had 'won few true converts to flood geology outside his own small... Adventist sect'.[21] But now Whitcomb and Morris argued once again for a recent creation of the entire universe, a 'fall' that brought about the second law of thermodynamics and a worldwide flood that in a single year laid down most of the geological strata. To their great surprise, and the surprise of the public at large, Price's once marginalized beliefs now began to enjoy a wide readership and notoriety. Within a quarter of a century *The Genesis Flood* went through twenty-nine printings and sold over 200,000 copies. The interest stimulated by this book led to the formation of the Creation Research Society (CRS) in 1963, which required its members to sign a statement of belief accepting the inerrancy of the Bible, the special creation of 'all basic types of living things' and a worldwide deluge. Unlike the 1920s creationist movement, which was largely devoid of any support from scientists, the CRS made a particular point of recruiting scientists onto its committee and into its membership. CRS founders referred to themselves as 'scientific creationists'. A second lay organization called the Bible-Science Association was founded to popularize creationism to the public at large. As the movement grew it spawned further organizations such as the Creation-Science Research Center and the Institute for Creation Research. By including the word 'research' in the title of such organizations the impression has been fostered that, unlike their more flamboyant forebears of the 1920s, the new creationist movement is concerned with serious scientific research. In practice, however, creationists have published very little in the scientific literature.

Many of the creationists are from the applied physical sciences and engineering with, perhaps not surprisingly, relatively few people from the biological sciences. They claim that biologists have been 'brainwashed' with evolutionary theory whereas applied scientists are more practical people who 'have their feet on the ground and are heavily committed to test out theories'. Creationists also argue 'that people in technical professions, working in highly structured and ordered contexts, are inclined to think in terms of order and design'.[22]

The creationist activity that has most aroused the ire of the scientific community has been their campaign to include 'scientific creationism' together with evolutionary theory in biology textbooks and in school teaching. As

Dorothy Nelkin has commented 'The history of American educational reform has reflected an abiding faith that schools are a means to remedy social problems and to bring about social reform. Education is often viewed as an ideological instrument, a means of changing social perceptions, such as racial or sexual prejudices.'[23] The creationists campaigned according to this tradition, viewing the teaching of evolution as carrying with it an ideological materialistic worldview which would undermine morality and promote atheism. But, as good campaigners, the focus of their arguments in court was not about morality but about questions of 'rights' and 'equal time'. By claiming that 'scientific creationism' was a valid alternative hypothesis to Darwinian evolution, it was then possible to argue that equal time should be given in the classroom to both theories. Success in any political struggle depends on taking the moral high-ground and in capturing the definition of the relevant terminology in the debate for your own use. The creationist lobby has been particularly adept in such strategies. 'Let us present as many theories as possible', commented Henry Morris, 'and give the child the right to choose the one that seems most logical to him. We are working to have students receive a fair shake.'[24] Eventually creationists were successful in introducing, although not enacting, legislation in at least thirty-five states seeking to legalize the teaching of creationism alongside evolution in the classroom. In Arkansas and Louisiana such laws were actually passed but the Arkansas law was declared unconstitutional by Judge Overton in 1982 and the Louisiana law was overthrown in the landmark supreme court decision of 1987 in which the court found by a seven to two majority that the law violated the first amendment and served to advance a particular religious belief. The creationists did not give up: in several states, particularly Texas and California, both centres for textbook publishing, the creationist lobby was still able to influence heavily the contents of textbooks through state education committees,[25] and the Kansas Board of Education managed to halt the study of evolutionary biology in public schools, at least for a couple of years.[26] Overall the creationist campaign has left a legacy of unnecessary bitterness and confusion that has done little to improve the understanding of either science or religion.

What reasons might there be for the extraordinary virility of the creationist movement during the latter half of the 20th century? Giving pejorative labels of 'anti-science' and 'irrationality' to the movement has done little to elucidate its underlying vigour. Three major themes may be detected in the creationist campaign and its literature, which provide more relevant insights.

1. Evolution as an attack on religion and morality

A dominant theme in creationist writings is that belief in evolution undermines morality and represents an attack upon religious accounts of biological origins.

'The evolutionary hypothesis', claimed Bryan, in a moment of excessive hyperbole, 'is the only thing that has seriously menaced religion since the birth of Christ; and it menaces... civilization as well as religion'.[27] Or, as Henry Morris robustly stated the case nearly sixty years later:

> But can't we be Christian evolutionists, they say. Yes, no doubt it is possible to be a Christian and an evolutionist. Likewise, one can be a Christian thief, or a Christian adulterer, or a Christian liar! Christians can be inconsistent and illogical about many things but that doesn't make them right.[28]

One can, at least, not fault creationist writers for lack of clarity in their claims. And such claims are by no means rare in the creationist literature. 'It may astonish you', wrote another creationist writer, in a book significantly entitled *The Evolution Conspiracy*, 'but belief in the evolution of life is the source of much of our present society's confusion and waning morality. Evolutionism in all its forms has become so firmly entrenched that it now tears at the very fabric of our moral structure.'[29]

How can a biological theory possibly have become so encrusted with moral and metaphysical meaning? Is this merely a perverse misunderstanding of a reasonably straightforward biological theory which, I will argue below, has neither moral nor religious implications? It is perhaps no coincidence that the creationist movement has flourished in American soil in which, as we noted in chapter 7, the writings of Spencer sold in their hundreds of thousands in the late 19th century. Whereas scientists like Asa Gray popularized Darwinian evolution as a biological theory, Spencer, it will be recalled, insisted on generating a 'cosmic evolutionary' scheme in which humanity was advancing up the escalator of life towards ever higher planes:

> The advance from the simple to the complex, through a process of successive differentiations, is seen alike in the earlier changes of the universe to which we can reason our way back... it is seen in the unfolding of every single organism... it is seen in the evolution of Humanity, whether contemplated in the civilized individual, or in the aggregate of races; it is seen in the evolution of Society in respects alike of its political, its religious, and its economic organization.[30]

Clearly the meaning of 'evolution' here has moved far from its Darwinian roots and has taken on all the trappings of a 'grand metaphysical theory' with strong religious overtones. It is surely no accident that Spencer's voluminous works remained popular at the time that Kellogg was listening to the no less grandiose claims from the Kaiser's officers which were to galvanize Bryan into his creationist campaign. Those scientists who have continued to promote the Spencerian understanding of the word 'evolution' have much to answer for in terms of explaining the popularity of creationism. And in case this seems unfair, just read the extraordinary claims made by the highly respected geneticist H.J. Muller back in the 1930s, in which he suggests that biological evolution is but the first phase in an escalator leading ever upward to the deification of man:

> And so we foresee the history of life divided into three main phases. In the long preparatory phase it was the helpless creature of its environment, and natural selection gradually ground it into a human shape. In the second – our own short transitional phase – it reaches out at the immediate environment, shaking, shaping and grinding to suit the form, the requirements, the wishes, and the whims of man. And in the long third phase, it will reach down into the secret places of its own nature, and by aid of its ever-growing intelligence and co-operation, shape itself into an increasingly sublime creation – a being beside which the mythical divinities of the past will seem more and more ridiculous, and which setting its own marvellous inner powers against the brute Goliath of the suns and planets, challenges them to contest.[31]

The language clearly seems closer to Greek mythology than to genetics. In the same era the Marxist physicist J.D. Bernal was envisaging that Evolution with a capital 'E' would eventually lead to a world that would be run by 'the aristocracy of scientific intelligence'. Scientific institutions would eventually become the government itself and so achieve 'a further stage of the Marxian hierarchy of domination'. The end result would be that scientists 'would emerge as a new species and leave humanity behind'.[32] There is a terrifying irony in the observation that only a decade after Bernal described his Marxist utopia, Hitler was extrapolating evolutionary theory to justify his philosophy of 'might is right' just as the Kaiser had before him, reminding his dinner-guests:

> If we did not respect the law of nature, imposing our will by the right of the stronger, a day would come when the wild animals would again devour us – then the insects would eat the wild animals, and finally nothing would exist except the microbes... By means of the struggle the elites are continually renewed. The law of selection justifies this incessant struggle by allowing the survival of the fittest. Christianity is a rebellion against natural law, a protest against nature.[33]

Given the wild extrapolations of evolutionary theory, from the epic heights of Muller's god-like humans 'challenging the suns to contest' and Bernal's ruling 'scientific aristocracy', down to the vicious depths of Hitler's 'survival of the fittest' in the Nazi extermination camps, one can perhaps feel sympathy for creationists who misunderstand the scope of Darwinian evolution. The continued exaggerated claims made by a small subset of scientists are partly to blame. Dawkins is firmly in this tradition in his claim that 'The more you understand the significance of evolution, the more you are pushed away from the agnostic position and towards atheism.'[34] As long as scientists continue their attempts to construct metaphysical worldviews out of biological theories, so long will creationism continue to thrive.

It is precisely the suspicion of evolution as a 'threat to morality' and as 'promoting atheism' that has made it so easy to package along with all the other 'isms' that the Moral Majority are supposed to be against in American society. Evolution has not infrequently been cited as a common enemy along with communism. In January 1961, a bill to repeal Tennessee's 'monkey laws', still in force thirty years after the Scope trial, was passionately opposed by people who argued that evolution 'drives God out of the universe' and 'leads to communism'.[35] The growth of the 1960s creationist movement was associated with a time of rapid social change and social disintegration partly associated with American involvement in the Vietnam War. The Creation-Science Research Center announced that its research proved that evolution fostered 'the moral decay of spiritual values which contribute to the destruction of mental health and... [the prevalence of] divorce, abortion, and rampant venereal disease'.[36] At the same time areas of the USA such as Texas and southern California, where creationist support was most vocal, saw high population growth and economic fluctuations associated largely with science-based industry. These social undercurrents created an atmosphere in which traditional values were seen to be under threat, and provided a spur for the scientists and engineers active in these industries to become involved in the creationist cause. The growth of the creationist movement also coincided with the 1963 Supreme Court decision which forbade public prayers in American schools, a decision which triggered general alarm about the force of secularizing influences in the nation's schools. Effective campaigns require clear targets. Evolutionism, atheism and communism together comprised a neat package of 'isms' against which it was not difficult to mobilize millions of Americans using funds, somewhat ironically, generated largely from the nation's high tech science-based industries.

2. Evolution as a conspiracy

A second common theme that runs through the creationist literature is that evolution is propagated as a conspiracy by the scientific community, or by government, or by school boards, or by other sinister forces, to corrupt the nation's youth and promote atheism. Such feelings are frequently allied with populist resentment against the perceived dominance of centralized political power and were dominant, for example, in Bryan's 1920s campaign. Bryan resented the attempt of a few thousand scientists 'to establish an oligarchy over the forty million American Christians' to dictate what should be taught in the schools. 'Forget, if need be,' said Bryan, 'the high-brows both in the political and college world, and carry this cause to the people. They are the final and efficiently corrective power.'[37] Such considerations were particularly powerful when it came to the campaign to control what should be taught in schools. As Nelkin remarks, 'The public education system is one of the last grass-roots institutions in America. School systems have traditionally been decentralized, run by local boards composed of elected citizens (non-professionals).'[38] Therefore federally funded attempts to usurp this local autonomy have been viewed with suspicion. Congressional indignation has been expressed about

> the insidious attempt to impose particular school courses... on local school districts, using the power and financial resources of the Federal government to set up a network of educator lobbyists to control education throughout America... We Americans place a high value on local autonomy. Local school boards, reflecting the prevailing social norms of the community, should be the final arbiter of curriculum development.[39]

Such indignation fuelled the campaign by parents to retain parental control over the contents of the biology textbooks that their offspring would be taught at school, fearing that a grand federal conspiracy was under way to finance a system of education that would corrupt the nation's youth by its teaching of evolution.

How deep is the creationist fear of evolution as a conspiracy may be gleaned by casting an eye down the chapter titles and subheadings of creationist writings such as *The Evolution Conspiracy* (1991) by Matrisciana and Oakland. Part one is 'The Hidden Agenda', in which we find 'Seducing the Masses', 'Silent Brainwashing', 'Evolutionary Sabotage', and so forth. Evolution is being portrayed here not as a scientific theory to explain biological diversity, but as a grand metaphysical worldview being foisted on an unsuspecting public.

3. 'Evolution is just a theory'

Another idea that crops up very often in creationist literature is that science is about 'facts' not 'theories'. There is a strong Baconian undercurrent in many creationist writings. The task of science is seen as the gathering of facts by careful observation and experimentation, followed by a process of induction in which the facts are classified and generalizations are drawn. Speculative hypotheses incapable of verification by observation are beyond the scope of true science. So Henry Morris writes:

> Science is *knowledge* and the essence of the scientific method is experimentation and observation. Since it is impossible to make observations or experiments on the origin of the universe... the very definition of science ought to preclude the use of the term when talking about evolution.[40]

Duane Gish picks up the same theme when he writes that 'For a theory to qualify as a scientific theory, it must be supported by events, processes or properties which can be observed, and the theory must be useful in predicting the outcome of future natural phenomena or laboratory experiments'.[41] Such statements have great appeal to a public, strongly influenced by pragmatism, which perceives science as a tool 'to make things work' – whereas academic theorizing is viewed with suspicion.

As it happens Darwinian theory *has* generated an enormous amount of research in which the theory of evolution is being tested in animal, plant and microbial populations under carefully controlled laboratory conditions. By choosing living organisms with rapid replication rates it becomes much easier to investigate the effects of environmental changes, crowded ecosystems and reproductive strategies on changes in genotype and phenotype. Although Darwin thought that evolution works 'silently and insensibly', and was therefore not amenable to normal methods of scientific investigation, it is now possible to test his theory in ways that he never dreamt, not least in computer modelling in which Darwinian predictions can be tested over thousands of generations.[42]

But, irrespective of these more recent developments, which tend to undermine the comments of Morris and Gish quoted above, there is a more fundamental problem with the Baconian claims of the creationists. As discussed in the previous chapter, they do not accurately reflect the way in which the scientific community carries out its work in practice. All scientific investigations are theory-laden and all scientific observations require interpretation, often long after the purported events occurred. 'Bare facts' divorced from theories do not occur in science. Therefore to talk about a passionate commitment to 'evolutionary *theory*' is certainly not a contradiction in terms. Calling a scientific model of explanation a 'theory' is not to demean it, least of all an indication of disbelief, but a reminder that the purpose of science is to provide frameworks of increasing coherence within which 'facts' and 'observations' can connect and make sense.

Unfortunately the response of some scientists to creationist Baconianism has not always been very clear. Stephen Jay Gould, normally so judicious in his comments on such matters, did not help at this point by writing a critique of creationism entitled *Evolution as Fact and Theory*. Gould wrote that 'evolution is a theory. It is also a fact,' and 'Evolutionists have been clear about this distinction of fact and theory from the very beginning, if only because we have always acknowledged how far we are from completely understanding the mechanisms (theory) by which evolution (fact) occurred.'[43] But this is to confuse the issue. 'Facts' are normally taken to refer to the data that scientists collect in the course of their investigations. These data may be as diverse as mutation rates, fossils, bird beak length, animal courting behaviour and population genetics. Theories, such as evolutionary theory, are the theoretical constructs within which the data are connected and made coherent. The observation of a certain animal courting ritual cannot be refuted. Assuming that the naturalist was not hallucinating, this is indeed the behaviour that characterizes this particular species of animal prior to mating. Similarly a mutation in a particular piece of DNA is a fact that any scientist can measure anywhere in the world if they possess the right equipment and are working on an identical piece of DNA. In this sense, however, evolution is not a fact, but a theory that gives sense to such facts. Furthermore, whereas the facts cited above as illustrations cannot be refuted, the theory of evolution could, in principle, be refuted, for the reasons outlined in the previous chapter. It is precisely this possibility of refutation that supports the status of Darwinian evolution as a scientific theory.

It is for the same reason that the term 'scientific creationism', used so frequently within the creationist movement, *must* be an oxymoron. 'Science' is a term referring to the attempt to generate testable theories about the workings of the physical world. 'Creation' is a theological term referring to a purported relationship between God as creator and the universe that he has created. 'Science' refers to a research programme, an attempt to construct a body of reliable knowledge about the physical world; 'creation' is a claim about the source and ultimate meaning of this physical world, a claim about why anything should exist rather than nothing. If there was no creation there would be no science – no physical world to investigate and no scientists to carry out the investigations. To conflate the term 'science' with 'creation' is therefore a category error, the mixing of two terms which refer to two very different kinds of concept and which therefore should not be mixed. Conflating the two categories would be rather like the characters within a novel trying to confirm the existence of the author from clues provided by a few detailed descriptions of the natural world provided in one of the chapters. Authorship is either a property of the whole novel or not at all; it is not something that can be derived from a particular little piece of the novel.

Besides the fundamental error of mixing categories, at a practical level the difference between science and creationism is illustrated most strikingly by the manifesto that has to be signed on becoming a member of the Creation Research Society. This includes the statement: 'All basic types of living thing, including man, were made by direct creative acts of God during Creation Week as described in Genesis. Whatever biological changes have occurred since Creation have accomplished only changes within the original created kinds.'[44] The manifesto also affirms belief in a worldwide flood. Now if the aim of an organization is to carry out a programme of scientific research, it is clearly incompatible with this aim if you have to sign a statement at the beginning agreeing to the conclusions of the programme before it has even started. A characteristic of science is a willingness to change your beliefs about the natural world as new data become available. But if you sign a statement to the effect that you will never change your mind no matter what, then it is difficult to see how this fits with the idea of a 'Research Society'. Not surprisingly, bearing this point in mind, 'scientific creationism' has made few contributions to the scientific literature and has scarcely generated a serious research programme, apart from a few forays by creationists into the natural world to seek evidence which might support their manifesto.[45]

As it happens, the beliefs held by creationists about the natural world are perfectly amenable to testing, as may be seen by a perusal of the CRS manifesto, quoted above, or of the 1981 Arkansas law, which provided a useful summary of the beliefs of 'creation science':

> Creation-science includes the scientific evidences and related inferences that indicate: 1. Sudden creation of the universe, energy, and life from nothing; 2. The insufficiency of mutation and natural selection in bringing about development of all living kinds from a single organism; 3. Changes only within fixed limits of originally created kinds of plants and animals; 4. Separate ancestry for man and apes; 5. Explanation of the earth's geology by catastrophism, including the occurrence of a worldwide flood; and 6. A relatively recent inception of the earth and living kinds.[46]

If, for example, point 3 is correct, and all 'kinds' (or species) of plants and animals are dependent upon God's instantaneous 'creative interventions', then the fossil record should show signs of such 'instant' speciation. If, for example, point 6 is correct, which in fact means for many creationists that the world was created about 10,000 years ago, then this is clearly amenable to refutation. Yet, despite the overwhelming evidence that the earth is extremely old, the subset of creationists who maintain that the world is only 10,000 years old usually show little sign of giving up their particular understanding of creationism. To append the term 'scientific' to the theological term 'creationism' is therefore oxymoronic in practice, and not just in principle, since it is an ideal of science (not always put into practice, as noted in the last chapter) that beliefs are changed if the accumulation of conflicting data becomes overwhelming.

If the beliefs of creationists are, in principle, refutable, then is it not correct to assign the term 'scientific' to such a set of beliefs? The possibility of refutation was cited in the last chapter as one of several criteria for distinguishing scientific knowledge from other forms of knowledge. If creationism is a valid 'alternative' model to the theory of evolution, then why not give both 'models' equal time in the classroom? The problem with such a view is that refutation is not the *only* criterion for demarcating the boundaries of scientific knowledge. A further criterion is that if a theory has been deemed to have been tested adequately by the scientific community and found to be totally lacking in support, then it is judged to be a waste of time and money to go on testing it. It is also deemed to be bad scientific educational policy if a theory that has been discarded by the scientific community as lacking any support continues to be taught in schools as if it were a genuine alternative to the normally accepted theory. There is no justification for giving equal educational time to theories that are not true.

More recently in the creationist movement there has been an attempt to utilize Kuhnian concepts of paradigms within science to promote the idea of creationism as being simply an 'alternative paradigm' to the evolutionary paradigm. But this attempt suffers from the same fatal flaw. The creationist beliefs about the origins of biological diversity within the natural world are not accepted within the scientific community as a serious alternative paradigm to evolutionary theory precisely because the paradigm rests on assumptions, such as a young earth and instantaneous speciation, that are unsupported by scientific data. Paradigm switches occur in science not merely because one group of people shout louder about their theory than anyone else, but because, at the end of the day, the rival paradigm makes the data more coherent. Creationist beliefs about the natural world do not make the data more coherent.

To be fair to the creationist movement, it should be noted that some leading creationists have left the movement after careful consideration of the scientific data and not all creationists believe in a young earth. For example, Larry Butler was appointed President of the Creation Research Society while teaching in the department of biochemistry at Purdue University, but later resigned from the CRS after becoming disillusioned with its negative approach to evolution. Butler commented how his own research on enzymes had revealed 'amazing similarities... which suggest strong inherited relationships between organisms as different and distinct as bacteria and snakes and higher animals'.[47] Even more striking is the example of the chemist P. Edgar Hare who was selected as one of the founding members of the Geoscience Research Institute, an organization started in 1957 and funded by the Seventh Day Adventist denomination with the specific aim of promoting creationism. Hare, who studied at the California Institute of Technology before joining the Institute, set out to see whether he could use his research on the amino-acid content of marine animals to 'show that fossils found in the different strata are essentially the same age'. But Hare's research did not support such an assumption, rather suggesting that life on this earth was immensely old, and he later resigned.[48] Hare's experience illustrates well the refutability of creationist beliefs by scientific data, insofar as these beliefs relate to the natural world, as well as the vital role that truth-telling plays within the scientific community.

Ironically, it is the creationist conflation of science and theology that unites them with some of their bitterest enemies. Richard Dawkins, for example, in contrast to most recent work by philosophers of science, maintains that theological statements are identical in kind to scientific statements:

> Until recently one of religion's main functions was scientific; the
> explanation of existence, of the universe, of life... So the most basic
> claims of religion are scientific. Religion is a scientific theory.[49]

In agreement with the creationist view, Dawkins specifically sees the 'hypothesis of God' as being a rival explanation in competition with the theory of evolution by natural selection. 'God and natural selection are, after all, the only two workable theories we have of why we exist.'[50] As an example of category confusion this statement rivals anything that may be found in the creationist literature, and perhaps helps to explain why the extremist poles in the science–religion debate promote each other's continuing campaigns so successfully. The possibility that reasons for existence may be considered at several different levels at once seems to occur neither to the creationists nor to Professor Dawkins.

Having considered three of the themes which occur most frequently in the creationist literature – evolution as an attack on religion and morality, evolution as a conspiracy and evolution as 'just a theory' – we will now consider a more mainstream Christian view of evolutionary theory and discuss the various ways in which this view addresses both the points raised by the creationists as well as the ideological campaigns of those who wish to use evolution as a prop for atheism.

A mainstream theistic view of creation

Since creationists make much of biblical authority in support of their views, it seems appropriate to begin this section by carrying out a brief survey of the central themes in the biblical doctrine of creation, not least because all Christian denominations take the Bible as a basis for their beliefs. In the process we will find that biblical teaching parts company from the 'creationist' position at a number of important points and at the same time undermines attempts to invest scientific theories with religious content. Most of the themes outlined below have already been touched on briefly during chapters 4–7 in describing the role of the biblical view of creation in the historical development of modern science. Even for those today who, in contrast to the early scientists who established the foundations of modern science, no longer hold to such a theistic worldview, it should nevertheless be possible to understand from what follows why traditional theism and contemporary biology remain such mutually supportive partners.

The word 'partnership' should not, however, be taken as a claim that belief in God can somehow be derived from a study of biology. The scientific approach to problem-solving, as discussed in the last chapter, usually involves the adoption of a model followed by a process of testing in which the degree to which the data fit the model is empirically investigated. In contrast the approach of the classical philosopher is to start from postulate A and then derive a series of supposed logical consequences until one arrives at conclusion P by a process of deductive reasoning. Although such philosophical reasoning is perfectly valid in its context, it has to be said that such an approach is quite alien to the way that scientists approach their science in daily practice. The scientist starts out in an investigation with a model, frequently not their own. Most often it has been learnt from the scientific literature or from the head of their laboratory. The model may include all kinds of assumptions, hunches and speculations, but the scientist is committed enough to the model to make a start on the long process of empirical investigation in order to test its credence. In this respect the biblical approach to belief in God is much closer to the approach of the scientist than to that of the philosopher. The traditional philosophical 'proofs' for the existence of God were never very satisfactory because the most they could end up with was an abstract philosophical concept of God that was so distant from the personal God of biblical theism as to be unrecognizable. Instead the Bible starts with a 'grand theory'. This is summarized very briefly by the first four words of the Bible: 'In the beginning God...' (Genesis 1:1). The rest of the biblical record then provides historically based claims about the implications of this starting presupposition, through the events that took place in the nation of Israel, and then on to the life, death and resurrection of Jesus of Nazareth. And it is the central thrust of this biblical account that the events recorded are coherent within a theistic framework. The 'data' fit the starting model. Had the Bible been a work of philosophy it would have ended up with the 'QED' that God exists as its conclusion on the *final* page. But as an account of 'salvation history' it sets to work on the very *first* page to tell us what God is doing in his world.

The brief survey provided below of the biblical understanding of God's relationship to the created order is not therefore intended to provide a rationale for *why* theists believe in God, but rather to explain the model to which Christian theists are committed as they think about God's relationship with the world. As with the models that scientists inherit from the scientific literature, so Christians have inherited their 'model' of how God interacts with the world from the biblical literature – they did not make it up themselves. In what follows we will focus on the major themes that comprise this model and which occur repeatedly throughout the biblical text, before briefly considering the Genesis account.

God's transcendence in creation

One of the most striking features of the biblical text for those who are coming to it for the first time is its convinced monotheism. This is all the more remarkable when one considers the extensive polytheism that characterized the other dominant religious systems of that era in the Middle East. God's *transcendence* is a term describing the particular character of this monotheism, that God is separate from his creation, totally 'other' in comparison with it, not localized within it, nor needing it in any way to be fully God. It is on the basis of the transcendence of God that it is possible to speak about the 'creator' and the 'created'. Pantheism disallows such a vocabulary since in pantheism god *is* everything and everything *is* god. The transcendence of God is made explicit throughout the biblical text of both the Old and New Testaments and hundreds of examples could be provided. For example in Psalm 90 the psalmist prays:

> *Before the mountains were born*
> *or you brought forth the earth and the world,*
> *from everlasting to everlasting you are God.*
> *You turn men back to dust,*
> *saying, 'Return to dust, O sons of men.'*
> *For a thousand years in your sight*
> *are like a day that has just gone by,*
> *or like a watch in the night.*
> **Psalm 90:2–4**

The phrase 'from everlasting to everlasting you are God' provides a very useful definition of transcendence. God's time and his being are not like our time nor like our being. The same theme is picked up in the majestic poetry of Isaiah 40:

> *Do you not know?*
> *Have you not heard?*
> *The Lord is the everlasting God,*

312

the Creator of the ends of the earth.
He will not grow tired or weary,
* and his understanding no one can fathom.*
Isaiah 40:28

God, in this understanding, is not a local or tribal god who can be pinned down to some neat time-bound or culture-bound formula. He is either the God of the whole universe or not really God at all. In the story of Jonah when Jonah was out in a storm at sea running away from what God wanted him to do, the non-Jewish captain and crew questioned him closely about his faith. Jonah's confession of faith in one creator-God is illuminating since it was clearly so distinctive from anything believed by the people around:

So they asked him [Jonah], 'Tell us, who is responsible for making all this trouble for us? What do you do? Where do you come from? What is your country? From what people are you?'
    He answered, 'I am a Hebrew and I worship the Lord, the God of heaven, who made the sea and the land.'
Jonah 1:8–9

The understanding of God as transcendent is as foundational to New Testament teaching as it is to the Old. Jonah's credal statement, repeated so often throughout the Old Testament to emphasize the otherness of God, that the real God could not possibly be a local tribal deity, was frequently used in the New Testament to provide the same reminder. When Jesus prayed it was to his 'Father, Lord of heaven and earth' (Matthew 11:25). When the early church prayed they said:

Sovereign Lord... you made the heaven and the earth and the sea, and everything in them.
Acts 4:24

And when Paul and Barnabas were mistaken for the local versions of the Greek gods Zeus and Hermes as they travelled round 1st-century Asia Minor (today's Turkey), they rushed into the crowd shouting:

'Men, why are you doing this? We too are only men, human like you. We are bringing you good news, telling you to turn from these worthless things to the living God, who made heaven and earth and sea and everything in them.'
Acts 14:15

Dozens of other examples of variations on this basic phrase 'the God of heaven and earth and sea' are scattered throughout the Bible, a credal formula that constantly reiterated the conviction that God was the source of everything that existed, a transcendent God so totally beyond and unlike the gods which human beings insisted on continually making in their own image.

The immanence of God in creation

A concept of God which depended only on the notion of transcendence could easily degenerate into the deistic idea of a distant and remote God who winds up the universe at the beginning and then occasionally returns to 'intervene' or meddle around with it. Such a scenario is disallowed by the biblical insistence that God is not only *transcendent* but that he is also *immanent* in his creation, meaning that God is intimately involved in continued creative activity in relation to his universe. All that exists only continues to do so because of his continued say-so. The properties of matter continue to be what they are because God wills that they should continue to have such properties. This provides the foundation for the *contingent* universe which, it has been noted in previous chapters, stimulated the growth of the scientific movement. It is the belief in the immanence of God that encourages the idea that the properties of matter are consistent and therefore worth investigating, and also at the same time the value of empiricism, since we cannot rationalize from first principles what properties of matter God may have willed – we can only discover them by a rigorous process of investigation.

As with the transcendence of God, so with his immanence, many biblical passages could be cited to illustrate God's continuing activity and sustaining work in his creation.[51] When the early Jews prayed they did so remembering both the transcendence of God and his immanence in the same breath:

> You alone are the Lord. You made the heavens, even the highest heavens, and all their starry host, the earth and all that is on it, the seas and all that is in them. You give life to everything, and the multitudes of heaven worship you.
> **Nehemiah 9:6**

Both the past tense and the present tense are equally appropriate in referring to God's creative activity. His activity in giving life now 'to everything' is perceived as being no more and no less relevant than his activity in making the 'earth and the heavens' in the past. All are of one piece in the ongoing creative drama. Such a theme is brought out very forcibly in the theology of the Psalms with their evocative poetic descriptions of God's continuous activity in the natural world. Psalm 104, for example, speaks of God bringing the present natural order into being in the past (vv. 1–9), but also speaks of God making rivers flow to supply the needs of animals (v. 11), making grass grow for cattle (v. 14), supplying 'wine that gladdens the heart of man' (v. 15), bringing darkness (v. 20) and supplying food for lions and other wild animals (v. 21). God is even seen as the one who makes animals die (by taking away their 'breath', v. 29) and then creating them with his Spirit when they are born (v. 30). The Hebrew word *bara* used here for 'create' is the same word frequently used in Genesis and elsewhere in the Old Testament to refer to God's creative activity in bringing the earth and heavens into being. Obviously this Psalm is providing us with a theological and not a biological interpretation of the natural world as perceived by the Jews of that time. As a rural and agricultural people they were perfectly aware of the natural processes of animal birth and death. The poetic description that is being provided is not, therefore, some *rival* theological description to what everyone knew by simple observation took place in the natural world, but a theological interpretation of a deeper reality that underlay all events without exception, of which the natural world provided many interesting and prominent examples.

A striking aspect of the biblical descriptions of God's immanence in creation is the way that they often focus on the most mundane and least dramatic aspects of the natural world. These are seen as being as much reflections of God's creativity as the creation of the earth or the stars. The modern tendency to look for God at the boundaries of our present knowledge is quite alien to biblical thought. When God is pictured as answering Job out of the storm while Job was struggling with the problem of evil (Job 38), it is to the whole gamut of his creative activity that he draws attention, not merely to big things like the 'laying of earth's foundations' (v. 4) and organizing the stars (vv. 31–33), but also to its more mundane aspects like watering deserts (vv. 25–26), frost-formation (v. 29) and providing food for lions (v. 39) and for the raven 'when its young cry out to God and wander about for lack of food' (v. 41). The God who sorts out stars and constellations is also the one who is immanent in sustaining the ongoing natural order with its cycles of food-chains and birth and death. Creation, in this view, is a seamless cloth, all of a piece.

The same emphasis is found in the New Testament. Jesus said that his Father (in the present tense) 'causes his sun to rise on the evil and the good, and sends rain on the righteous and the unrighteous' (Matthew 5:45), and this same God also feeds the 'birds of the air' (Matthew 6:26) and 'clothes the grass of the field' (Matthew 6:30). When Paul spoke in Athens, a melting-pot of 1st-century religious pluralism, he was careful to emphasize both the transcendence of God and his immanence:

> The God who made the world and everything in it is the Lord of heaven and earth and does not live in temples built by hands. And he is not

served by human hands, as if he needed anything, because he himself
gives all men life and breath and everything else.

Acts 17:24–25

There is a finely tuned balance here. The real God, claims Paul, is not restrained
within the confines of human buildings, however much we might capture him
in our grasp and try to make him in our own image. He is far beyond us, but at
the same time we cannot breathe without him. Paul picks up this theme of the
immanence of God later on when writing to the new church at Colossae:

He [Jesus] is the image of the invisible God, the firstborn over all creation.
For by him all things were created: things in heaven and on earth, visible
and invisible, whether thrones or powers or rulers or authorities; all
things were created by him and for him. He is before all things, *and in him
all things hold together.*

Colossians 1:15–17 [my italics]

Paul makes here some very remarkable claims about the divinity of Jesus, not
only that 'he is the image of the invisible God', but also that Jesus was intimately
involved in the bringing into being of the whole created order and that creation
only continues to exist because of this continuing involvement. This
extraordinary claim is repeated by the writer to the Hebrews:

But in these last days he [God] has spoken to us by his Son, whom he
appointed heir of all things, and through whom he made the universe.
The Son is the radiance of God's glory and the exact representation of his
being, *sustaining all things by his powerful word.*

Hebrews 1:2–3 [my italics]

Whatever may be your own personal beliefs about the claimed divinity of Christ,
you cannot take the biblical text seriously and at the same time be a deist. God's
activity in creation is no more or less now than it was when the universe came
into being. Stars, animals, the weather, plants, human life, the sun, all equally
go on existing because God continues to will that it is so – that is the claim.

It should be noted, however, that the Bible makes no attempt to construct a
theory of *how* precisely God's creative activity is mediated to the universe. The
difficulties of such an enterprise must immediately be apparent. If it were
possible that God's relation to the physical universe could be understood
scientifically, then this might imply that God was *part* of the physical universe.
Such a relationship would be like studying the possible effects of one physical
entity within the universe upon another. But if God is the transcendent creator

of the universe, then such a scenario is impossible: God is the author of the universe, not an entity within it. The question of God's relationship to the universe is therefore an ontological question, not a scientific question, involving no claims about religiously inspired natural science. Ontology is about how one sort of being relates to another and belongs to the realm of metaphysics, not the realm of science.

Suggesting analogies that shed light on what it means for God to be immanent in creation is difficult, since analogies can give the false impression that God is part of the universe. Nevertheless, as long as a 'disclaimer' to the contrary is provided, they may then have some value. For example, the immanence of God in relation to the universe has been likened to the sun in relation to biological life on the earth. Both the origin and continued existence of living organisms depend on the sun's energy, although that energy is harvested and distributed by a network of complex secondary causes. But remove the primary cause, the sun's energy source, and biological life will soon cease to exist. There is therefore a sense in which the sun is both transcendent in relation to the earth (totally distinct and different from anything on it), but also immanent in the ongoing existence and richness of its biological diversity.

The apostle Peter used a rather different analogy when he told the startled crowds at the birth of the church that they had killed 'the author of life, but God raised him from the dead' (Acts 3:15). The idea of authorship has already been used as another way of expressing the immanence of God in relation to the universe. The author is separate from the play or novel that is created, but at the same time is intimately involved in upholding it in all its aspects. In a variant on this analogy, which places greater emphasis on human freedom, Donald MacKay has likened God's creative activity to the continual flow of electrons being diverted by a changing magnetic field, without which there would be no picture on our TV screen. Your favourite TV soap is a self-contained drama, and talk of electrons and magnetic fields will add nothing to it, yet without the continued flow of electrons the drama would cease to be conveyed to your living-room.

Arthur Peacocke has also suggested the analogy of God as musical composer in relation to a symphony or a fugue.[52] This is a particularly rich analogy because it draws attention to the gradual unfolding of the creator's intentions as the music is played. Music has subtle twists and turns, often unexpected, the nuances of which may keep the listener guessing right up to the end of the piece. The same composition may contain majestic cadences, cheerful interludes and passages of quiet despair, but all flow from the creativity of the one composer who is distinct from the music as it is played, yet thoroughly immanent in all the sounds that eventually emerge.

A right understanding of the immanence of God in creation has profound implications for the biblical assessment of 'creationism', implications that were already very clear to Aubrey Moore more than a century ago when he wrote (in 1889) that:

> The scientific evidence in favour of evolution, *as a theory* is infinitely more Christian than the theory of 'special creation'. For it implies the immanence of God in nature, and the omnipresence of His creative power. Those who oppose the doctrine of evolution in defence of a 'continued intervention' of God, seem to have failed to notice that *a theory of occasional intervention implies as its correlative a theory of ordinary absence*[53] [author's italics].

Moore even suggested that it was Darwinism that had given a helping hand in restoring the doctrine of the immanence of God to its rightful place in Christian theology:

> The one absolutely impossible conception of God, in the present day, is that which represents him as an occasional visitor. Science has pushed the deist's God further and further away, and at the moment when it seemed as if He would be thrust out all together, Darwinism appeared, and, under the guise of a foe, did the work of a friend... Either God is everywhere present in nature, or He is nowhere.[54]

The personal nature of God in creation

The transcendent-immanent character of God's creative relationship to the universe could, in principle, be claimed as referring to a God who was essentially an ultimate form of abstract intelligence, or some kind of heavenly supercomputer. The biblical claim, however, about the God who is both transcendent and immanent in his creation, is quite distinctive in its insistence that this creator–God is a *personal* God and that the emergence of personality is therefore what one expects in a universe that exists because of his creative activity.

In talking about claims of a 'personal God' we are forced inescapably into the use of human analogies (anthropomorphic language). As pointed out in the previous chapter, this is not surprising since anthropomorphic language is the only one we have. All our linguistic attempts to describe realities that are beyond our direct everyday sensory experience are full of metaphors, analogies and poetic licence as we attempt to communicate *something* about such realities, the only alternative being complete silence. In talking about 'black holes' or 'selfish genes' or 'protein denaturation' everyday speech is being pressed into metaphors in attempts to describe what are in fact highly complex physical phenomena. As we have already noted, scientific laboratories would become very quiet places if metaphors were banned from science. But no one actually believes that 'black holes' are like holes you find in the road outside your front door, or that the metaphor 'selfish gene' implies that genes lead independent and self-centred lives, or that 'protein denaturation' means that when a protein is warmed slightly it completely loses its original nature (in fact its primary structure does not change). So all of these metaphors are inadequate in their attempts to translate phenomena into the world of our everyday sense experience. Nevertheless, none of these metaphors is totally vacuous; they all communicate *something* that is true about the phenomena to which they refer. Frequently a whole package of metaphors may be necessary to do justice to a phenomenon that is well beyond our language of daily discourse.

Very similar considerations apply in talk about a 'personal' God. Biblical language uses a rich panoply of words and metaphors to paint a picture of the creator-God as a personal being. Early on in Jewish history Moses reminds the people of Israel:

Is he [the Lord] not your Father, your Creator, who made you and formed you?
Deuteronomy 32:6

and Abraham is called the 'friend' of God (Isaiah 41:8). These twin themes of the fatherhood and friendship of God continue throughout the Old and New Testaments and are particularly characteristic of the biblical concept of God. In the Old Testament the prophet Malachi specifically linked the idea of the fatherhood of God with his creative activity:

Have we not all one Father? Did not one God create us?
Malachi 2:10

This link between creation and the fatherhood of God is reiterated in the New Testament:

There is but one God, the Father, from whom all things came and for whom we live; and there is but one Lord, Jesus Christ, through whom all things came and through whom we live.
I Corinthians 8:6

When Jesus wished to underscore the value and worth of animals in general, and of human beings in particular, his teaching was carried out based on a personal not an impersonal God:

319

> Are not two sparrows sold for a penny? Yet not one of them will fall to the
> ground apart from the will of your Father... don't be afraid; you are
> worth more than many sparrows.
>
> **Matthew 10:29–31**

The biblical language makes it clear that the creator-God is not a demiurge,
nor a vague force underlying the mathematical elegance of the structure of the
universe, but a personal God who is distinct from the world and yet intimately
involved in it.

The Genesis creation account

The biblical story of the world and the creation of its biological diversity in six
days is a familiar one. However, it is surprising how many people who refer
(disparagingly or otherwise) to this section of the Bible have never read the
chapters in question, nor considered what kind of literature they represent, nor
tried to place them in the context of other Near Eastern creation stories that date
from the same era. Although it is not the intention here to provide a full
discussion of such points, even a cursory reading of the chapters in question,
and of the relevant literature required to put them in their cultural and
theological context, make two points abundantly clear: first, this creation
literature has certain fascinating parallels with other Near Eastern creation
stories, but at heart is profoundly different; second, the creationist reading of
these passages ignores a large amount of research that has shed light on the
meaning of the text.

Long before the fruits of such research became available, it had been recognized
by Jewish and Christian commentators that the early chapters of Genesis contain
much figurative language that can only be understood in their original context.
Origen, an important scholar of the early Greek church, commenting in AD 231 on
certain expressions used in the early chapters of Genesis, wrote that 'I do not think
anyone will doubt that these are figurative expressions which indicate mysteries
through a semblance of history.'[55] In the next century we find Augustine in his
monumental *Commentary on Genesis* (c. AD 391) writing: 'In the case of a narrative
of events, the question arises as to whether everything must be taken according to
the figurative sense only, or whether it must be expounded and defended also as a
faithful record of what happened. No Christian would dare say that the narrative
must not be taken in a figurative sense.'[56] Augustine therefore suggested that the
days of creation were not periods of time but rather categories in which creatures
were arranged by the author for didactic reasons to describe all the works of
creation. Intriguingly, Augustine's commentary was entitled 'The Literal Meaning
of Genesis' but in it he makes clear that the 'literal meaning' was for him the
original meaning intended by the author. Although Augustine was the first to

admit that the extraction of this meaning from the text was not a trivial exercise, the main themes were as clear for him as they are for us, and these themes have been brought into sharper focus for us by the Near Eastern cuneiform discoveries of the last century.

The first few chapters of Genesis comprise a profound theological essay which forms an important introduction to the early history of the Jewish people, including the patriarchs, the exodus of Israel from Egypt and the subsequent lawgiving at Sinai. Genesis is divided into ten sections, each one introduced by the phrase, 'this is the account of'. The first section, which starts at chapter 2 verse 4, is distinctive in that it provides 'an account of the heavens and earth when they were created', whereas the subsequent nine sections all relate to family histories. Genesis 1:1 – 2:3 acts as the overture to these ten accounts by placing the creation of humankind in the context of the creation of the rest of the physical order.

The idea that such passages may be read as if proffering a scientific text is, I would suggest, bizarre. As we saw in the last chapter, contemporary science refers to a programme of generating testable theories to provide maps of increasing sophistication with reference to their ability to explain the physical world. Genesis offers us no such programme, but is concerned rather with the very different goal of providing a theological explanation for the order which characterizes the world together with a basis for the meaning and purpose of humankind within that order. So deeply and successfully over the centuries has the theology of Genesis penetrated into Western thought that it is now virtually impossible for us to appreciate how starkly its message contrasted with the worldviews expressed in other contemporary literature of its era. Fortunately extensive Mesopotamian creation accounts have come down to us, including the *Enuma Elish* ('The Epic of Creation'), the Epic of Gilgamesh, the Atrahasis Epic, the Sumerian flood story, as well as many other more fragmentary accounts.[57]

Coming from King Ashurbanipal's great library at Nineveh and dating from the 7th century BC, the *Enuma Elish* was the first Mesopotamian creation account to be discovered and was named *Enuma Elish* after its opening words ('When above'), but is relatively late in composition compared with other cuneiform texts that subsequently came to light. Most of these were written in Akkadian, the international language of the ancient Near East for two millennia, Babylonian and Assyrian being dialects of Akkadian. Other important texts have been discovered in Ugaritic, discovered at the site of Ugarit, now on the Mediterranean coast of modern Syria. A third language used in texts from the Near East was Aramaic, which became popular in the 1st millennium BC and was used by city-states lying to the north of Israel. Like Hebrew, all of these languages are Semitic and therefore provide valuable material that casts light on the text and thought-forms of Genesis.

At one level Genesis 1:1 – 2:3 may be read as a polemical and sometimes sarcastic attack on the Babylonian and Sumerian creation stories that were widespread in the Near East during the period from 500 to 2000 BC. From this perspective the material reads more like *Private Eye* than traditional theology. The passage lampooned the pathetic gods and superstitions of the time, undermining faith in the power of the heavenly bodies as effectively then as it does today in its critique of the type of fatalism which continues to make the astrological predictions in today's newspapers so profitable to their purveyors.

From a literary point of view the passage is tightly structured. The earth is described 'in the beginning' by the vivid onomatopoetic Hebrew term *tohu bohu*, meaning 'formless and empty'. There was emptiness and disorder waiting to be filled up by the creative activity of God. The rest of the chapter then uses a series of literary devices to show how God introduced structure and order into this emptiness. There is a fascination with the number seven, the number frequently used to express order, perfection and completeness in biblical texts, and here also used to present teaching about the Jewish Sabbath. Even the Hebrew verses of Genesis chapter 1 comprise multiples of seven words, with the first verse containing seven words, the second verse fourteen words, and the summary in 2:1–3 at the end of the passage containing thirty-five words. The word 'God' is mentioned thirty-five (5×7) times in the passage, whereas 'earth' and 'heaven/firmament' occur twenty-one (3×7) times each.[58] The order which God introduced into *tohu bohu* is further emphasized by the six days of creative activity culminating in the seventh day of Sabbath rest.

The six days of creation are also arranged according to a carefully organized literary structure in which the creative activities on days 1–3 are symmetrically balanced by those on days 4–6. In days 1–3 the outline of the created order is established with light on day 1, sky on day 2 and land with its vegetation on day 3. Days 4–6 then fill in the details of this sketched outline as the luminaries are established to regulate light and darkness on day 4, the sky is filled up with creatures on day 5 and the land is filled with animals on day 6. The climax of the account comes on day 6 with the creation of *Adam*, humankind, whose task it is to care for the created order (1:26–28). In this context in its very first usage in the book of Genesis, the word *Adam* is clearly used to refer to humanity in general, both male and female (1:27).

As the Genesis account progresses, it becomes clear that *Adam* can either mean humanity, 'man' as distinct from 'woman', or be used as a personal name for a particular person. In Genesis 2 and 3 the word generally has the meaning of man as distinct from woman, since the definite article appears before the word in these chapters and in Hebrew personal names do not occur with the definite article.[59] Not until Genesis 4:25 is there an unambiguous use of *Adam* without the definite article as a reference to a particular individual. But throughout these chapters it is made clear that this particular word for 'man' was deliberately chosen in place of the more common Hebrew word for man, *iš*, to make a theological point. *Adam* sounds very similar to the Hebrew word *adamah*, meaning ground, and the word-play involved in this similarity is made explicit in 2:7 and 3:19. Man is from the ground and to the ground he will return. Furthermore, the common Hebrew word for man, *iš*, is also commonly used throughout the Old Testament in the context of titles of occupations such as 'priest' (Leviticus 21:9), 'ruler' (Exodus 2:14) and 'warrior' (Joel 2:7). The use of a word for 'man' followed by a place name, as Hess reports, 'is also common in the Near East of the 2nd millennium BC as a means to describe the rulership of a town or other place. Thus the leader of the town of Kumidi is called "man of Kumidi" in the 14th century BC Amarna correspondence.'[60] The term *Adam* therefore seems to have been chosen deliberately to emphasize not only that humankind is *from* the ground, but also that *Adam* has God-given responsibilities *towards* the *adamah*, 'to work it and take care of it' (2:15) and to name all the animals and birds that likewise came out of the *adamah* (2:19–20). *Adam* is the 'man-in-charge-of-the-ground', God's earth-keeper.

There has been much discussion as to the possible links between the early chapters of Genesis and other contemporary Mesopotamian and Egyptian creation accounts. By about 1800 BC Babylonian writing had been disseminated as far west as Cappadocia (now in modern Turkey). A number of documents composed in Babylonian have been discovered in the ancient Hittite capital Hattusas, also now in Turkey.[61] There was a widespread dissemination of cuneiform literary texts throughout the Near East, particularly in the Amarna period (late 15th century BC). However, whereas there is clear evidence of common source material with respect to the story of Noah and the flood, in particular the Epic of Gilgamesh and the Atrahasis Epic, the creation material found in the first few chapters of Genesis displays no unambiguous literary dependence on other source material that has come to light so far. Rather the writer appears to be familiar with the general themes of the creation stories current at the time and deliberately picks on these themes to provide a very different theological interpretation from that which has come down to us in the Mesopotamian and Egyptian cuneiform creation epics. Indeed, as already mentioned, the writer of Genesis appears to take polemical delight in demythologizing the other creation stories that were widespread in the Near East at the time, and the differences between the Genesis record and other contemporary accounts in circulation are far more striking than the similarities. At least seven distinct differences may be discerned.

First, the Genesis account is striking in its monotheism. In contrast, the other creation epics are uniform in their polytheism, and in them the gods struggle and squabble as they carry out their creative activities. In Genesis God is perceived to be all powerful and when he speaks things happen. In the epics, as has often been remarked, the gods are made in the image of man, whereas in Genesis 1 man is made in the image of God. *Enuma Elish* therefore pictures successive generations of gods and goddesses as proceeding from the ancestors of all the gods, Apsu and Tiamat, gods who have human form and are clothed in garments similar to human dress. They also have human needs such as food, drink and sleep. When in the Epic of Gilgamesh those saved from the flood gave a thank-offering:

The gods smelt the fragrance,
The gods smelt the pleasant fragrance
The gods like flies gathered over the sacrifice.
Tablet XI

According to the Atrahasis epic, it was because the gods were losing their sleep, due to the noise made by the people they had created, that they became irritable and sent all kinds of illnesses and judgments upon humankind, including the flood.[62] The narratives also describe wars breaking out among the gods. For example, the god Ea kills another god, Apsu, and with his dead body forms the subterranean sea upon which the earth rests. Such accounts are quite alien to the book of Genesis.

Second, in the Genesis account God does all the work of creation and provides for the physical and spiritual needs of humankind, whereas in the epics man is created to be a slave of the gods. According to the *Enuma Elish* one group of gods rebelled against another and was defeated. As a punishment they were imprisoned and forced to act as servants of the victors. But Marduk, one of the victorious gods, decided to relieve the vanquished gods of these duties and create man instead to be the servant of the victors. The ring-leader of the rebels, Kingu, was therefore killed, his arteries were severed and humankind was created with his blood. A similar reason for the creation of man is found in the Atrahasis epic:

Belet-li the womb-goddess is present –
Let her create a mortal man
So that he may bear the yoke...
Let man bear the load of the gods![63]

In contrast men and women are created in Genesis not as slaves, but with major responsibilities over the created order which has been given to them for their well-being (1:29–30). The psalmist expressed the situation like this:

May you be blessed by the Lord,
the Maker of heaven and earth.

The highest heavens belong to the Lord,
   but the earth he has given to man.
   Psalm 115:15–16

Third, there is a strong ethical and moral element in the early chapters of Genesis that is lacking from the Mesopotamian creation stories. Seven times after each creative activity it is reported that 'God saw that it was good' (vv. 4, 10, 12, 18, 21, 25, 31). Matter is not evil but has divine approval. There is no hint here of the platonic concept that the spiritual is on a higher plane than the material. The creation of humankind is marked by a strikingly earthy materialism. You cannot get more earthy than by being called *Adam*! Already by Genesis 2 *Adam* is being faced with choices of obedience or disobedience, good and evil. The way of evil lies totally opposed to God's clear command. But in the Babylonian epics the gods are as corrupt as humankind.

Marduk, the top god in the *Enuma Elish*, defeated the rebel goddess Tiamat, split her skull with his club, cut her arteries, and finally divided her enormous body into two parts to create the universe. With one half of her corpse he formed the sky and with the other he made the earth.[64] This creation of the world out of a murder does not bode too well for what is to follow and, all-in-all, the gods continue to act like a murderous bunch of thugs, sending vicious plagues onto humankind for trivial offences like making too much noise and forcing them to be their slaves. As another Babylonian source remarks:

Narru, king from of old, the creator of mankind; gigantic Zulummar,
who pinched off their clay; and lady Mama, the queen, who fashioned
them, have presented to mankind perverse speech, lies and untruth they
presented to them forever.[65]

Since humans were made from the blood of the gods in Babylonian mythology, how could they possibly shake off the nature of the gods? In Genesis humankind was created in communion with God but then fell by moral choice. In the Babylonian accounts there was no possibility of a fall, for humankind was made morally flawed.

Fourth, in the Mesopotamian creation accounts matter is viewed as being eternal, whereas in the Genesis narrative God is seen as the ultimate source of the whole created order. In the *Enuma Elish* Apsu and Tiamat are not perceived merely as the ancestors of the gods, but as living, uncreated matter out of which all else was formed. Apsu is pictured as being the 'primeval sweet-water ocean, and Tiamat the primeval salt-water ocean', so that in them matter and divine spirit were coexistent and eternal. This Babylonian view was clearly expressed by Diodorus Siculus, a historian of the last century BC, when he reported that

'The Chaldeans say that the substance of the world is eternal and that it neither had a first beginning nor that it will at a later time suffer destruction.'[66] In contrast the opening words of the Genesis account – 'In the beginning God created' – imply that it was God, not matter, that was at the very beginning of all things. The Hebrew word *bara* used in this opening sentence and elsewhere in the Genesis account, while not necessarily carrying the meaning of 'created out of nothing', does carry a stress in Hebrew on the creator's freedom and authority.[67] The rest of the Bible interprets such passages as referring to God as the creative source of everything that exists. The all-inclusive language is striking. For example, in the prologue to John's Gospel we read:

> In the beginning was the Word, and the Word was with God, and the Word was God. He was with God in the beginning. Through him all things were made; without him nothing was made that has been made.
> John 1:1–3

The writer to the Hebrews has a similar emphasis:

> By faith we understand that the universe was formed at God's command, so that what is seen was not made out of what was visible.
> Hebrews 11:3

There is no hint in any biblical passage about a God-of-the-gaps or a God who is an absentee landlord from his creation, or who is baffled by the resistance of matter to his creative will. God commands and the universe is made. God speaks and the created order is continued, diversified and sustained.

Fifth, the Genesis account attacks the idea, commonly held throughout the Near East, that the sun, moon and stars are divine in nature and exert a baleful influence over human affairs. It is presumably with reference to such a worldview that the psalmist promises that:

> *The Lord watches over you –*
> *the Lord is your shade at your right hand;*
> *The sun will not harm you by day,*
> *nor the moon by night.*
> Psalm 121:5–6

What God promises to protect us from here is not sunburn, but rather the fear of the malevolent intentions of the heavenly bodies. When Marduk, the top god of the *Enuma Elish* account, was born, he was hailed as 'Son of the sun-god, the sun-god of the gods' (Tablet I). Later on in the account in Tablet V Marduk 'created stations for the great gods; the stars their likeness(es), the signs of the zodiac he set up'. The stars were therefore perceived to be stamped with the divine image of the Babylonian pantheon of gods and goddesses, and in Near Eastern thought were credited with controlling human destiny.[68] In contrast Genesis 1 takes great pains to demythologize the divine powers of the heavenly bodies. On day 1, 'God said "Let there be light", and there was light,' without even a *mention* at this stage of the sun. Talk about marginalization! Not until day 4 is there a detailed and carefully worded exposition of the creation of the heavenly bodies, clearly relegated here to the second division. Like the rest of creation, the heavenly bodies are created in response to the divine word; they are objects with no powers of their own outside of God's say-so. Instead of giving them their usual Hebrew names, which might suggest an identification with Shamash the sun god or Yarih the moon god, the writer calls the sun and moon 'the larger' and 'the smaller light' (v. 16).[69] The sun and moon are to 'serve as signs to mark seasons and days and years' (v. 14), quite lowly functions in comparison with their elevated status in most Mesopotamian literature of that era. The Hebrew word 'light, lamp' used to refer to the sun and moon in this passage is also used to refer to the sanctuary lamp in the Jewish tabernacle – and it is possible that the writer is pointing out by this usage that the order introduced by God into the days and seasons by such heavenly 'lamps' is parallel to the God-given order that characterized the running of the tabernacle. Far from having any control over human affairs, the stars are created almost as an afterthought: 'He also made the stars' (v. 16). Not much encouragement here is given to astrologers, who are also seen later on as fair game for mockery by the Old Testament prophets (e.g. Isaiah 47:12–14). Even today such demythologizing of the baleful powers of the heavenly bodies has only partially been successful. As I write this a total eclipse of the sun has just taken place across a large swathe of Asia. Today's newspaper report said that:

Astrologers were in despair at the ominous portents. They said India faced a period of dire events and declared that anybody touched by the moon's shadow would suffer ill-fortune. Hundreds of thousands plunged into holy rivers to be cleansed of malevolent influences. Pregnant women were careful to avoid the shadow, fearing it would cause the birth of a deformed child, and millions heeded astrologers' advice not to eat during the eclipse... In Bombay, thousands of vendors of milk, bread and eggs did their rounds early to avoid being touched by the shadow.[70]

Sixth, those facets of the created order that were deemed most terrifying and threatening to human existence in the ancient Mesopotamian and Egyptian worldviews are picked on in Genesis as being opportunities for God to demonstrate his complete control over every aspect of his creation. For example, in some Near Eastern accounts the gods struggle to separate the 'upper waters from the lower waters', whereas in Genesis 1:6–10 this is accomplished by simple divine fiat. In myths from both Ugarit and Babylon the chief deity did battle with the sea and conquered it. In Genesis the sea was under God's control from the beginning.[71] Dragons or sea-monsters in such accounts are pictured as threatening rivals of the gods who therefore have to be conquered. In Genesis 1:21 these 'great creatures of the sea' are seen as totally under God's control and, far from having any threatening mythological powers, are viewed as being merely one of the many creatures 'with which the water teems'. The word *bara* is used to describe the creation of the 'great creatures', and they are declared 'good' along with the rest of the sea-creatures and birds (v. 21).

Seventh, according to one Babylonian tradition, the 7th, 14th, 19th, 21st and 28th days of each month were regarded as unlucky,[72] whereas in Genesis the 7th day is set aside as being a special day characterized by God's blessing, a day of rest consecrated to him (2:2–3). It seems likely that the Israelite Sabbath was introduced as a deliberate replacement for this lunar-related cycle. Far from being a day of ill omen, the Sabbath was to be a day blessed and made especially holy by the creator. Furthermore, in contrast to the account provided in the Atrahasis Epic, God rested not because there were now humans that he could use as slaves but because the work of creation was complete.

This brief survey of the way in which the Genesis creation account attacks the worldviews that dominated contemporary Near Eastern thought is necessarily incomplete – the references provided should be pursued for those who require a fuller discussion. But sufficient material has been provided to emphasize that the creationist reading of Genesis, as well its critique by scientists who demonstrate little understanding of the nuances of ancient Near East literature, lead to understandings of the text that are distant from the author's intentions. Removing ancient texts from their linguistic and cultural contexts not only distorts their meaning but, more importantly, often results in the modern reader missing the punchlines altogether. The sad consequence, in this case, is both bad theology and bad science.

Yet, despite such modern misunderstandings, with a more historical perspective it has to be said that the creation account provided by Genesis has been enormously successful. Had the ancient Mesopotamian creation accounts come to dominate European thought, rather than the Genesis account which in fact triumphed, the emergence of modern science may have proved a much slower process. Capricious argumentative gods with very limited powers over the natural world would be unlikely to provide hope that the properties of the physical world would be consistent or reproducible enough to be worth investigating. Neither is it likely that natural laws describing the properties of such a world would have been generated from such a worldview. The frightening opposition of certain forms of eternal matter to the will of gods and humans alike might also not prove conducive to its investigation, a situation not helped by the malevolent intentions of the sun, moon and stars casting their baleful influences over any attempts by the slaves of the gods to investigate the properties of the natural order. The Genesis creation account does not contain science, but without the widespread dominance of its worldview at a critical period during European history, it is unlikely that the scientific enterprise would have developed as rapidly and as effectively as it did.

Chapter 10

The Fox and the Hedgehog
Does Evolution Have Any Religious Implications?

The fox knows many things, but the hedgehog knows one big thing.
Fragment of Greek poetry

Science has demythologized most of human experience by disproving traditional religious accounts of the origin of the world and substituting in their place a network of precise and experimentally testable, materialistic explanations.
Edward O. Wilson

Unless at least half my colleagues are dunces, there can be – on the most raw and empirical grounds – no conflict between science and religion. I know hundreds of scientists who share a conviction about the fact of evolution, and teach it in the same way. Among these people I note an entire spectrum of religious attitudes – from devout daily prayer and worship to resolute atheism. Either there's no correlation between religious belief and confidence in evolution – or else half of these people are fools.
Stephen Jay Gould

It is beyond the scope of this book to discuss all the commonly quoted objections to the theory of evolution, a task which has in any case been performed adequately by many previous publications.[1] Our focus here will be to address the question of whether the theory of evolution has any religious implications. Three issues have often been raised in this context: the issue of chance and design; the related issue of whether the mechanisms utilized in the evolutionary process are compatible with a personal God of love as portrayed in Christian theology; and the issue of the morality of the evolutionary process.

The blind watchmaker?

Richard Dawkins's book *The Blind Watchmaker* remains one of the best popular expositions of evolutionary theory.[2] It is therefore a pity that the book is cast as a critique of Paley's natural theology, a way of thinking that was already losing its popularity prior to the publication of the *Origin of Species* and which was decisively undermined in the decades that followed. Quite why Dawkins chose as his target a type of thinking that was abandoned by mainstream theology more than a century ago is unclear, but such tilting at windmills tends to detract from the book's otherwise excellent qualities.

The particular windmill in question is Paley's contention that the natural world, and in particular biological organisms, provide many examples of design – and that from these examples we may infer the existence of the great Designer. Paley likened the natural world to a finely tuned watch which, if we stumbled across it for the first time, would immediately suggest to us the existence of a watchmaker. The argument had some force in a culture that had been dominated for two centuries by natural theology, although it is interesting to note in passing that the biblical account of God's activity in creation is quite devoid of such arguments. In Dawkins's account natural selection becomes the 'blind watchmaker'.

Three fatal flaws in Paley's argument should be noted. First, he was by no means the first to make the mistake of bringing God into his account of the natural order as if he were a physical entity within the universe interacting with other physical entities. As already pointed out, if the theistic account of God's relationship to the universe has any validity, then God is the author of the universe, not an entity within it. We cannot therefore reduce God to being a 'scientific explanation' for anything, for in that case God would become part of our causal explanatory net and, at the same moment, would cease to be the God portrayed in traditional theism. That this is indeed the implication of Paley's argument is made clear by the ready substitution by Dawkins of 'natural selection' in place of Paley's watchmaker, since Dawkins correctly surmised that evolution provided a better and more scientific explanation for the existence of 'design' in biological organisms than the concept of a 'watchmaker'. Indeed, it is most likely this flaw in Paley's argument that has led Dawkins to conflate *all* theological claims with scientific claims as if they were rival explanations, a confusion that has already been criticized in the last chapter. In contrast to Paley's view, however, the theist may perfectly well point to the existence of the complete universe, with ourselves as conscious observers within it, and argue that theism provides the best explanation both for its existence and for our own significance as observers. This is at least consistent with the idea of God as the author and sustainer of all that exists.

The second flaw in Paley's 'design' argument, which flows directly from the first, is that it lends itself to a God-of-the-gaps argument in which the 'watchmaker' is conveniently provided as an explanation for those biological adaptations which appear particularly remarkable. Not surprisingly, however, the need for the 'god' fades as scientific explanations for the phenomena become available.

The third flaw is this: even were such a 'design' argument valid, the most that one might infer would be the existence of a designer. This would appear to be a disadvantage from the point of view of someone arguing the case for traditional Christian theology. The biblical descriptions of God contain many rich metaphors but 'designer' is not one of them. Of course the immanence of God in the created order implies that nothing exists without his continued sustaining. But this is very far from the claim that a particular animal x was designed by God to have characteristics y, or that God is like some heavenly engineer tinkering with the DNA code or with the designs of his creatures. This point raises the whole question of whether natural theology can be looked to as a source of information about God's interaction with the world. The existence of God may provide an inference to the best explanation for the existence and properties of the universe, but how much of God's character and purposes can we 'read off' from a scientific study of the created order? My own view, for reasons that I hope will become clearer as we proceed, is 'not a lot'.

Chance and necessity

In his *Autobiography* Darwin discusses his religious beliefs, making the very reasonable point that religion is not necessarily true because many people believe it to be so, and then comments that:

> Another source of conviction in the existence of God, connected with the reason and not with the feelings, impresses me as having much more weight. This follows from the extreme difficulty or rather impossibility of conceiving this immense and wonderful universe, including man with his capacity of looking far backwards and far into the future, as the result of blind chance or necessity. When thus reflecting I feel compelled to look to a First Cause having an intelligent mind in some degree analogous to that of man, and I deserve to be called a Theist.[3]

Darwin then goes on to provide a marginal note explaining that 'This conclusion was strong in my mind about the time... when I wrote the *Origin of Species*, and it is since that time that it has very gradually, and with many fluctuations, become weaker. But then arises the doubt – can the mind of man, which has, I fully believe, been developed from a mind as low as that possessed by the lowest animal, be trusted when it draws such grand conclusions?' It is on such a basis, Darwin goes on to inform us, that his agnosticism is based. Curiously Darwin's doubts about the inability of human reason to grapple with such matters are not consistently applied to all his other beliefs, for example his belief in the theory of natural selection. Since all our faculties, both for believing and disbelieving, have been passed down to us as a result of evolutionary processes, it is not clear why this insight should cause us to be selective in distrusting one of our beliefs more or less than any other. But the important point to note for our present context is that in his earlier life Darwin clearly perceived the impossibility of conceiving that 'this immense and wonderful universe' could be the product of 'blind chance'. Chance was therefore a reality for Darwin that had clear theological implications.

This was certainly not the case for Darwin's 'bulldog' T.H. Huxley who denied the existence of chance altogether, confidently asserting in 1876 during a lecture on evolution given in New York that:

> It has ceased to be conceivable that chance should have any place in the universe, or that events should depend upon any but the natural sequence of cause and effect... And as we have excluded chance from a place in the universe, so we ignore, even as a possibility, the notion of any interference with the order of Nature.[4]

All kinds of assumptions are built into these brief sentences which are easier to unpack with the benefit of hindsight. Clearly Huxley was expressing the opinion, non-controversial in the late 19th century, that the universe was built as a tightly structured causal network in which long deterministic chains of 'cause and effect' proceeded according to 'nature's laws'. Any 'interference' in such a causal network by chance events was therefore viewed by a secular thinker such as Huxley with suspicion as smacking of 'miraculous intervention'. Long sequences of causes and effects appeared to leave no room for God's actions or interventions.

Such a view has long since been left behind by the advent of Heisenberg's uncertainty principle, chaos theory and the contemporary understanding of the important role of chance in biological events. Ironically, considering the context of Huxley's lecture, it is Darwinian evolution that illustrates chance events so strikingly and Darwin appears to have been more prescient than Huxley in understanding this point. There is also a certain irony in the observation that whereas Huxley clearly perceived chance as possessing theological overtones that threatened his agnosticism, once chance became scientifically respectable in the 20th century, secular thinkers were then quick to take up the opposite position and suggest that it was hostile to theism.

The meanings of chance

Chance is a slippery word and in any discussion of chance events it is always worth checking on the particular way in which the word is being used before jumping to conclusions. The word chance may be used in three quite distinct ways, which I will label A, B and C. First, it can refer to events that are unpredictable because we cannot, for practical reasons, possess the necessary information that would enable us to predict the future outcome: this is Chance A. Coin tossing exemplifies such an event. No one imagines that when we toss a coin the movement of the coin moves outside the realm of normal physical behaviour. Indeed we could, in principle, design a sophisticated machine that would analyse the flick of the finger with which we toss the coin, and the consequent forces influencing the flight of the coin, in such detail that the machine would be able to predict a heads or tails outcome before the coin had reached the ground. The existence of such a machine would not contradict the claim that the outcome of coin tossing represented a chance event. This sense of chance can also be used for events that arise from the interaction between two causal chains. Out in the forest a deer is frightened by the sound of a hunter's gun and runs into the path of an express train that happens to be passing at that moment. Both sets of events have separate causal antecedents and it is their intersection by chance that results in the death of the deer.

The second major meaning of chance, Chance B, refers to events that are physically indeterminate, as in the conventional interpretation of quantum mechanics. According to Heisenberg's uncertainty principle both the position and the momentum of an electron, a constituent part of all atoms, cannot be defined simultaneously with any certainty. In quantum mechanics the electron behaves like a wave and a wave equation is therefore used to describe it. If a wave of electrons hits a barrier, such as a metal surface, some of the electrons will pass through and others will be reflected. The wave equation will enable the probability of a given electron being reflected or passing through the barrier to be predicted, but the outcome for any one electron cannot be predicted. The event is indeterminate. Equally when radioactive atoms decay it is possible to observe the emission of particles over a period of time and to find that the frequency distribution of the numbers in successive intervals of time conforms to a simple pattern (Poisson's law), but it is impossible to predict when a single particle will be emitted. The term 'pure chance' is sometimes applied to these types of quantum events because they are indeterminate in principle and not just in practice.

There has been some discussion as to whether chaos theory should rightly be classified as belonging to Chance A or Chance B. Chaos theory deals with situations in which outcomes are highly dependent on small variations in the starting conditions. 'Chaos' is therefore somewhat of a misnomer, since chaos theory demonstrates how different *ordered* systems can arise from such different starting conditions. The importance of tiny variations in initial conditions was discovered by a Professor of Meteorology at the Massachusetts Institute of Technology, Edward Lorenz, who came across chaos theory 'by chance' while using an early computer (this was 1961) to calculate how convection currents might vary in the atmosphere with time. Lorenz had three variable quantities in his equations and these had to be retyped into his old-fashioned computer by hand once a certain stage had been reached in the calculations. One day Lorenz was surprised to find that his computer had generated a very different meteorological outcome even though the variables typed in were identical. However, on closer inspection it turned out that whereas the number 0.506127 had been entered as the variable on one occasion, in another run this had been rounded off to 0.506. This apparently trivial difference in one of the starting variables resulted in a striking difference in the modelled changes in convection currents by the time the computer had finished its calculations.

Since this initial insight there has been an enormous amount of research into the way that very small differences in starting conditions can have major implications for eventual outcome. Chaos theory has been found to be applicable to fields as diverse as variations in animal populations, the spread of disease, the swing of a pendulum and certain chemical reactions. The impossibility of making accurate long-term weather predictions has also been underlined by further study of chaos theory in meteorological research. In 1979 Lorenz gave a lecture with the whimsical title 'Predictability; does the flap of a butterfly's wings in Brazil set off a tornado in Texas?', thereby generating the 'butterfly effect' as a shorthand and widely used term to refer to the implications of chaos theory. To bring chaos theory into a more prosaic context, consider the gas particles that comprise the air that you breathe in a room. In one ten thousand millionth of a second each molecule has about fifty collisions with its neighbours. How accurately do we need to know the starting conditions in order to predict how any one of these molecules will be moving after its first fifty collisions? The answer turns out to be quite surprising. If in our calculations we ignore the effect of an electron on the other side of the observable universe interacting with the molecule by the force of gravity, then a major error in our prediction is likely to emerge.

Yet, as John Houghton has emphasized, 'Considered from the point of view of classical physics, events in... chaotic systems... are as predictable in theory as they are in any Newtonian system. What we have been at pains to point out is the extreme difficulty of any attempt at such a calculation.'[5] If a complete account of the movement of the fundamental particles in the whole universe is necessary to make an accurate prediction, then it might seem reasonable to suggest that the predicted event is indeterminate. Nevertheless, for the sake of tidiness, chaos theory will be classified here with Chance A, in recognition of the fact that it refers to classes of events that are unpredictable in practice, not unpredictable in principle. As it happens, for the purposes of the discussion below its classification makes no difference.

The third major definition of chance is what I will call 'metaphysical chance', Chance C, a term which embraces several shades of meaning. 'Metaphysical chance' is the idea that chance is the ultimate principle or power which rules the universe, often with the implication that there can be no rival because 'ultimately all is by accident'. One version of metaphysical chance was expressed in the qualities of *Tyche*, the Greek goddess of chance, together with *Fortuna* her Roman counterpart. This tradition of 'Lady Luck' was kept alive by the TV advertisements for the British national lottery when it was first introduced, in which a deep voice called from heaven 'It could be you!' as a star-spangled finger pointed to the lucky winner. The personification of chance in this sense is quite incompatible with the two more technical meanings of Chance A and Chance B that we have introduced so far, since it is clear from their definitions that chance is not a causal agency that makes things happen but rather a description of the way in which we as observers understand the workings of certain events within the world around us. Chance itself *does* nothing. Despite this rather obvious point, it is remarkable how often heroic attempts have been made to extrapolate Chance C out of Chance A and/or Chance B, as will be considered below.

Chance and DNA

The generation of genetic variation in DNA (mutations) may be described within the context of either chance A or B. 'Point mutations' involve the change of a single 'base' (the letter in the 'genetic alphabet'), whereas other mutations may be caused by loss of a whole sequence of bases, or a gain of sequences of DNA that have been added inappropriately from some other chromosome in the same cell. Such events occur fairly frequently during the process of cell division in which the DNA makes copies of itself for the daughter cells. The copying process is extremely accurate, but the enormous rate at which cell division occurs in some tissues leads to errors in replication. Many of these are rectified by the actions of DNA repair enzymes, which are constantly on the look out for infidelity. But even with the actions of such enzymes, some mutations may be passed on to the daughter cells. Other mutations may be caused by chemical compounds in the environment that cause mutations (mutagens) or by exposure to radiation. As noted above, the emission of a given radioactive particle is, in principle, indeterminate, since its emission is described by quantum theory. Yet it is the single radioactive particle that can cause a mutation in the DNA. So mutations may arise in DNA either due to processes describable as chance A (mistakes in DNA copying, exposure to chemical mutagens) or chance B (damage due to radiation). In either case it is only if mutations take place in eggs or sperm (collectively called 'germ-line' cells) that they will be passed on to the next generation. If they occur in the other cells of the body they may have implications for that individual's own health, but such mutations will not be inherited.

Some mutations have no effect because of what is called the 'redundancy' of the genetic code. Proteins are composed of amino acids and each amino acid is encoded by more than one triplet of the bases that make up the DNA sequence. A mutation may therefore cause a change in the triplet of bases, but the alternative version will still encode for the same amino acid. The protein encoded by the gene will therefore be identical to what it was before the mutation occurred. In other cases, however, the mutation will generate a triplet of bases that encode for quite a different amino acid. This may cause subtle changes in the properties of the protein that the gene encodes. In most cases the protein will do its job less well than before but occasionally a mutation will enable it to do its job better. An even more dramatic result will ensue if the mutation causes generation of a triplet of bases which encodes a 'stop codon'. This is the equivalent of a red light for protein synthesis and a truncated protein will be synthesized in the cell, which may be much shorter than the original protein. Again, such truncations are normally deleterious for the protein's function. Occasionally, however, a protein may be produced which can carry out quite a different task, or can do the same task more efficiently.

Natural selection is the process whereby the effects of mutations on the 'phenotype' are tested. The 'phenotype' refers to the net result in the body of the possession of the total sequences of one individual's genes (called the 'genotype'). The testing of the phenotype is with reference to reproductive success, defined as the relative ability of an organism to survive and to leave offspring that themselves can survive and leave offspring. Note that simply leaving many offspring is, by itself, insufficient to define such 'reproductive success' since the offspring could be numerous but not very reproductive, or even sterile. A full definition of 'reproductive success' must therefore include the transmission of the genes down the generations, although for many species (including our own) such a full definition is difficult to apply to practical measurements. The winnowing process of natural selection sorts out the genes containing mutations, which encode proteins that promote reproductive success, from those that do not. In practice, for most proteins the net result is immensely conservative, which means that the sequence of the protein remains remarkably conserved through evolution. For example, the amino acid sequence of one particular enzyme (protein) on which I have carried out some research is identical between human and rabbit – it differs not once in its approximately 370 amino acids. Such high conservation is not unusual. This explains why every year millions of pounds of cancer research money are spent on yeast, even though humans separated from yeast in evolution more than a billion years ago. The rationale for this research strategy is based on the fact that many of the proteins that regulate cell division in yeast have been conserved through all these millions of years of evolution so that they carry out similar or even identical tasks in the organization of our own cells as they do in yeast. If a protein is doing a good job, why change it? When a protein is highly conserved it implies that it is carrying out such an essential task inside the cell that even a minor change in its sequence may be lethal. Natural selection has the effect of conserving the 'best' proteins – those that contribute to the well-being of the individual as measured by their reproductive success.

Taken as a whole, therefore, the evolutionary process is very far from being a 'chance' process. Variation in the DNA is indeed generated by chance, but the consequences of variation are then tested over millions of years of evolutionary time in which only those mutations that confer advantages in terms of reproductive success are passed on to succeeding generations. This explains why Dawkins states that one of his tasks in *The Blind Watchmaker* is 'to destroy this eagerly believed myth that Darwinism is a theory of "chance"... This belief, that Darwinian evolution is "random", is not merely false. It is the exact opposite of the truth. Chance is a minor ingredient in the Darwinian recipe, but the most important ingredient is cumulative selection which is quintessentially *non-random*.'[6] My only quibble with Dawkins at this point would be over his use of the word 'minor'. Chance occurrences play a *major* role in that without them there would be no variation in DNA and so no basis for natural selection to even get started.

It should also be noted that the generation of mutations in DNA is not the only chance process in operation in evolution. Chance events may operate at the level of the phenotype as well. For example, as noted above, meteorological conditions are fickle and best described within the boundaries of chaos theory, a special case of Chance A. Yet it is changes in such conditions that have caused the extinctions of many millions of the world's species. It has been estimated (by reference to the fossil record) that more than 99 per cent of the species that have ever lived on this planet are now extinct, and most of these went extinct long before we came on the scene. There may be as many as 30 million species alive today, but these represent only a tiny proportion of the thousands of millions of species that have probably existed since life began. Although our detailed knowledge of how the great majority of these extinctions occurred is very limited, it is clear that extremes of weather may have 'tipped the balance' in many cases, so that a struggling population finally succumbed to drought – or to a new ice-age. Chaos theory is certainly not irrelevant to the processes of evolutionary change.

Chance events apart from changes in the weather can also have dramatic effects on biological populations. The drifting apart of whole continents has separated populations, which have then proceeded to evolve in very distinctive directions. The massive explosions of volcanoes through geological time is likely to have rendered extinct certain populations local to that region. If, as has been suggested, a meteorite hitting the earth was responsible for the extinction of the dinosaurs, then this was a 'chance event' par excellence that had a major impact (literally) on biological diversity. Gould has suggested that in the major catastrophe at the end of the Permian period, about 225 million years ago, up to 96 per cent of all species existing at that time may have become extinct.

Metaphysical chance

Given this major role of chance events in the generation of biological diversity, and therefore of ourselves as a species, are we justified in extrapolating Chance C from such observations? Chance C, it will be recalled, is that version of chance whereby it is reified to become the principle or power that reigns supreme in the universe and against which all else must be measured. A vivid description of Chance C was provided by the molecular biologist Jacques Monod in his book *Chance and Necessity*. With respect to mutations Monod wrote:

> We say that these events are accidental, due to chance. And since they constitute the *only* possible source of modifications in the genetic text, itself the *sole* repository of the organism's hereditary structures, it necessarily follows that chance *alone* is at the source of every innovation, of all creation in the biosphere. Pure chance, absolutely free but blind, at the very root of the stupendous edifice of evolution: this central concept of modern biology is no longer one among other possible or even conceivable hypotheses. It is today the *sole* conceivable hypothesis, the only one compatible with observed and tested fact. And nothing warrants the supposition (or the hope) that conceptions about this should, or ever could, be revised[7] [Monod's italics].

Based on these observations of mechanisms operating in molecular biology, Monod then goes on to conclude, in a much quoted passage, that 'Man knows now that he is like a gypsy camping on the edge of the universe where he must live. The universe is deaf to his music, indifferent to his hopes, as to his suffering or his crimes.' Monod has further claimed that we now have 'biological proof of the absence of a master-plan' and 'belief in a universe in which man was destined to appear is contrary to modern biology'.[8]

There are several points to make about Monod's claims. First, as noted above, within the evolutionary context it is not true that 'chance *alone* is at the source of every innovation'; without the sieving effect of natural selection occurring at the level of the phenotype the innovations to which Monod refers would never see the light of day, or certainly not for very long. Second, if evolution has any 'message' at all, it surely indicates the precise reverse of our proposed status as 'alienation from the universe'. Far from being gypsies on the move the evolutionary 'message' is that we are superbly adapted for our particular ecological niche in the universe and are biologically linked with all other life forms on this planet. Third, and most importantly, it is impossible to make metaphysical extrapolations from molecular biology all the way to the supposed lack of meaning in the universe. Why should the mechanisms described by molecular biology tell us anything about ultimate questions of meaning? One cannot help thinking that Monod is the mirror image of the natural theologians, like Paley, who tried to extract far too much metaphysics by his observations of the natural world about him. Just as evidence for engineering design in the biological world provides an insufficient basis per se from which to extrapolate the existence of a heavenly Engineer–Designer, so the existence of chance mechanisms in generating such design tells us equally little about questions of ultimate purpose and meaning in the universe. Either way biology is being pressed into service to generate metaphysical schemes that it is ill-equipped to provide.

Chance and the notion of God as creator

Does the existence of chance mechanisms in generating biological diversity have any implications for the theology of creation as expressed in traditional Christian theism? It is difficult to see why there should be any implications at all, either positive or negative. The theistic claim is that the created order, complete with its biological diversity, has been brought into being and continues to exist by God's will. The claim says nothing about the mechanisms by which this has occurred in the past or continues to occur in the present. It is the task of biologists (and others) to elucidate such mechanisms. It so happens that processes best described from our perspective as 'chance processes' have made a central and substantial contribution to the generation of biological diversity, of which the human race comprises a particular example. So what?

At this juncture it might be good to head off a complaint that could, with some justification, be made by the atheist. Surely, they might object, the theist's belief in God is vacuous because whatever physicists or biologists uncover about the origins of the structure of the universe or of biological diversity, then the theist will simply say that this is the way that God has chosen to bring about what we in fact observe. There is therefore nothing that scientists could, in principle, describe within the confines of their discipline that would have any bearing on the validity or otherwise of theistic belief. Precisely so. The traditional Christian theist has a 'voluntaristic' doctrine of God, meaning that, unlike Plato's demiurge, God is free to act in any way he chooses, unrestricted and unfettered. As we noted in surveying the history of science, this doctrine provided a powerful impetus for science in stimulating the early natural philosophers to investigate what God had actually done in the created order in contradistinction to the rationalistic scholastic philosophers who thought they could derive what God *ought* to have done from first principles. Therefore when it comes to scientific explanations and models of how things work, the theist need have no hidden theological investment in supporting one model over another. Theistic belief in God is 'vacuous' only to those who believe in a 'God-of-the-gaps' God who is supposed to act as a plug for our scientific ignorance until such time as a satisfactory scientific explanation becomes available. But Christian theists neither believe in such an entity nor in such intellectual laziness. And, as pointed out in chapter 8, neither do they believe that scientific knowledge per se is relevant to a whole range of important human questions and beliefs, of which theism is but one example of many. The study of evolutionary mechanisms is a fascinating area of research which deserves all the funding that it can get, but it has no bearing on the question of whether or not God exists.

James Rachels raises precisely the objection cited above in his book *Created from Animals: the Moral Implications of Darwinism*. In considering the theistic interpretation of evolution, Rachels writes:

> It is possible to construe the theistic interpretation in such a way as to *guarantee* that there could never be any evidence against it. This could be done by refusing to specify any details at all, leaving it a perfectly open question how God works through the evolutionary process. Given no specific content, the theistic interpretation would imply nothing at all about what nature is like. Then, no matter what discoveries are made, the theist could always say: 'Yes, that is the way things are, and that is the way God planned it.' If one takes this approach, then the challenge to provide evidence against the theistic interpretation can never be met[9] [Rachels' italics].

Rachels then goes on to suggest that this 'is an unsatisfactory way of defending the theistic interpretation'. But I think Rachels misses the point here. The position is not a way of *defending* the theistic interpretation at all, but a *statement* of what this doctrine of creation *means* – this is what is entailed if a robustly theistic view of the created order is to be maintained. The theistic argument is that we have no way of knowing ahead of time what a 'theistic' biological mechanism would look like as opposed to an 'atheistic' biological mechanism, and therefore an examination of such mechanisms is neutral in the context of a comparison between theism and atheism. In the theistic interpretation the relationship between the created order and God may be likened to the relationship between a natural history programme on TV and the TV station transmitting the programme. It would make no sense to argue that one aspect of the natural history being portrayed on the screen was an argument for the existence of the transmitting station, whereas another aspect of the natural history being shown was not. Either the existence of the whole natural history programme is contingent on the transmitting station or it is not. Examining bits of the programme is irrelevant in such a context, a point which must surely be as disappointing for creationists as it is for their atheistic 'mirror-image' critics.

To take this analogy one step further, it might be interesting to take people straight out of a culture that knew nothing of physics nor of TVs and show them a TV natural history programme. What would be their interpretation of where the programme was coming from? Whatever their explanations might be, it is unlikely that they would depend on any particular aspect of the programme more than another, but would rather be directed at deriving the best explanation for the existence of the programme *as a whole*. Human beings are innately curious and it is unlikely that they would be fobbed off from asking such ultimate types of questions as they sat enjoying the programme.

Strangely Rachels maintains that the understanding of theistic evolution outlined above represents some kind of 'retreat' to deism. But I would suggest the reverse is in fact the case. Deism represents God to a greater or lesser extent as being only partially involved in the created order. In its most extreme form deism envisages a God who starts the universe off 'at the beginning' and then (perhaps) occasionally interferes at a later date. Creationism represents a less extreme form of Deism in its insistence that God has 'intervened' numerous times to start up life at the beginning (e.g. by generating the genetic code) and then to generate biological diversity by creating separate species. But as Aubrey Moore put the point so succinctly more than a century ago in a passage already quoted above: 'a theory of occasional intervention implies as its correlative a theory of ordinary absence'. The argument that a particular biological event (rather than all biological events) provides an argument for God's activity in nature (or his absence) certainly has deistic overtones. But classical theism will have none of this and sees the whole created order as a seamless cloth.

Chance and order

If God has purposes for his creation and particular plans for humankind, as the biblical record insists, how can such purposes and plans be consistent with such a long drawn-out and *messy* evolutionary process in which vast numbers of biological lineages have become extinct and in which chance processes have played such a key role? After all, if we stretch out one arm and picture the age of the earth as the length from our head to the tip of our index finger, one passage of a nail-file across the nail of that finger will remove the whole timespan of *Homo sapiens* upon this planet. Is not our existence, therefore, just an unlikely evolutionary accident, of little significance when compared to the vast aeons of time that comprise the geological history of our planet? If our number just happened to come up in the roulette game of life, then why should this be of any significance?

In response it is worth noting that the biblical claim is that God has brought not engineering perfection, but order, out of *tohu bohu* (disorder). Random events may play a key role in the creative process, but the consequences are decidedly non-random. If the universe was random in the sense that deliberately scrambled series of numbers are random, then the universe would have as much order as the 'noise' on our TV screens when something has gone wrong with the signal, and clearly as a consequence we ourselves would not be around to wonder whether the universe has any meaning.

How has this order come into being? Time plus chance are clearly two key components of its coming into being, but we need to look at these components with a somewhat more critical eye. From our human perspective within time, Chance A and Chance B are only too real. But in the theistic model God is outside time in his transcendence, albeit interacting with the universe in his immanence. Modern physics has made it easier to picture such a model with its proposal that time may be considered as a dimension with similar characteristics to a dimension of space. So God may be viewed as existing outside of our space–time dimension but simultaneously acting into our space–time in its entirety in his creative activity. Now let us do a thought experiment. What might a God's-eye view of Chance A look like? Surely little different from any other aspect of the created order. Chance A arises from our inability to predict the consequences of complicated physical events, but we realize that there are causes for these events and that if we had sufficient knowledge of these causes then prediction would, in principle, be possible. Clearly no such limitation is of relevance to the God of the whole universe, outside space–time, whose knowledge and upholding of every elementary particle at every moment (in our space–time dimension) is complete and absolute.

If we accept that chaos theory is a special example of Chance A, then how would those events, described best by chaos theory from our human perspective, look from a God's-eye perspective? Again, it is difficult to see why they should look any different from any other events. Quantifying very small differences in starting conditions is certainly a problem for us but it is hard to imagine that it would be a problem for the all-powerful God who is the source and sustainer of all that exists.

What about quantum theory and Chance B? In Einstein's oft-quoted phrase 'God does not play dice', he expressed his conviction that the unpredictability of energy states within the atom were merely expressions of ignorance by the quantum physicists and that one day discoveries about the finer structure of matter would make everything determinate once again. As it happens, the further investigation of matter since Einstein's day has provided no basis for such an expectation. But in the context of biological diversity, quantum theory is likely to be of limited significance. Mutations may be generated by radiation which requires quantum theory for its fuller understanding, but the sieving effects of natural selection operate irrespective of the precise way in which changes in DNA have been generated. Mutations are random irrespective of whether they have been generated by processes best described by Chance A or Chance B. Quantum theory is highly relevant for understanding things on a very small scale, such as the behaviour of the elementary particles that comprise atoms. But biology operates at higher levels of organization in terms of molecules, multi-molecular complexes, cellular organelles, cells, tissues, organs, bodies and environments. The behaviour of molecules is described perfectly well by the laws of chemistry. From a God's-eye perspective there appears to be no particular reason, therefore, why Chance B should be of any particular relevance in the context of the generation of biological diversity.

The emergence of order out of disorder is often more apparent when the scale is changed or the process is speeded up. Study the early development of any organism at a molecular level on a slow timescale and all you see is a seething and apparently random array of molecules. But speed up the film and look at the organism as a whole and the various stages of development can then be viewed as an orderly unfolding of carefully orchestrated events. From our human perspective the process of evolution might seem unimaginably slow, meandering and inefficient. But imagine now a super-observer looking at a speeded-up version using lapsed-time photography. What would we see of biological interest should the history of this planet be compressed into a single day of twenty-four hours? Lest such a thought-experiment appear too mind-stretching, it is worth remembering that whereas the light from the sun takes 8.5 minutes to reach us, when we stare at the most distant galaxies through our most powerful telescopes, we are seeing them as they were ten billion years ago because it has taken that amount of time for their light to reach us. Note that this is a period more than twice as old as the lifespan of our own planet. So the observation of events that took place ten billion years ago is not that bizarre – indeed, it occurs every time someone looks down a powerful telescope.

So what happens if we start our twenty-four-hour clock at zero around 4.6 billion years ago, the estimated age of our planet, and imagine that midnight is the present moment in time? What would we observe? Simple forms of life would already be appearing by 2.40 a.m. with single-celled organisms (prokaryotes) flourishing by around 5.20 a.m. The great oceans of the world start to change colour as cyanobacteria (blue-green algae) spread across the planet. At the same time the genetic code becomes established that will dominate the generation of biological diversity for the remainder of the day. After this early morning start, there would then be quite a long wait until single-celled organisms containing nuclei (eukaryotes) become visible around lunchtime. A further seven hours pass before multicellular organisms start appearing in the sea by 8.15 p.m. About half-an-hour later the planet changes colour as cyanobacteria and green algae invade the land. From then on the biological pace hots up and there is a busy evening of observation ahead. The Cambrian explosion starts at 9.10 p.m. and in an amazing three minutes an immense diversity of phyla appear, each with a distinctive body-plan, with many of the anatomical features introduced continuing in many of the phyla right up to midnight. Twenty minutes later plants start appearing on land for the first time, followed very soon afterwards by the earliest land animals. At 9.58 p.m. this is followed by the mass extinctions of the Devonian period. At 10.11 p.m. reptiles start roaming the land, followed half-an-hour later by the mass extinctions which mark the end of the Palaeozoic period. By 10.50 p.m. the earliest mammals and dinosaurs are appearing, but five minutes later there is further mass extinction at the start of the Jurassic period. By 11.15 p.m. Archaeopteryx, the reptile/bird, are flapping around and within minutes the sky begins to fill with birds. Another mass extinction occurs at 11.39 p.m. in which the dinosaurs are wiped out. Just two minutes before midnight hominids start to appear and a mere three seconds before midnight anatomically modern humans make their entry onto the scene, the whole of recorded human history until now being compressed into less than one-fifth of the second before midnight, the mere blink of a human eyelid.

Such a graphic presentation of the planet's history acts as a vivid reminder of the immensely fruitful role that chance events (chance, that is, from our perspective) have played in generating the order in the biological world that in fact we observe. Random events may have played key roles in the processes involved, but the products of those processes are far from random. With the benefit of hindsight, the reasons are rather obvious. There are potent morphological constraints in living in a world of gravity, of light and darkness, of heat and cold, where the atmosphere has a certain percentage of oxygen, nitrogen and carbon dioxide, and so forth. Some fairly hefty flying organisms have been observed in the fossil record, but elephants are not among them. Flying may be very advantageous if you want to escape predators and search for new sources of food, but when you become the size of an elephant such considerations become less pressing, especially when considering the energy required for lift-off.

The consequences of living in a world with certain physical constraints are illustrated most strikingly by convergent evolution in which similar design solutions to particular problems have arisen many times, even though the convergence may not be total. For example it is likely that eyes have evolved not once but dozens of times during evolutionary history, since in a world of light the contribution of such an organ to the reproductive fitness of an organism is enormous. A more mundane example is the hypocone, a small modification of the molar tooth that allows mammals to feed on a more diverse range of vegetation. It has been estimated that the hypocone has evolved convergently more than twenty times among mammals during the Cenozoic period alone.[10] Such 'design tricks' can render great advantages to the organisms that possess them, whether it be major innovations, like eyes, or relatively trivial modifications, like the hypocone. Mutations can be seen as a way of scanning 'design space', the sifting process of natural selection allowing species to flourish in a certain ecological niche if they possess the right 'design tricks' for reproducing successfully in that particular environment. Because of the constraints of living on planet earth, the same designs have emerged repeatedly.

Cosmology, biology and the origin of life

Further constraints on the kinds of biological diversity that have emerged are provided by the chemical starting materials from which all living organisms have evolved. If we accept a 'big bang' model for the origin of the universe some fifteen billion years ago, then one hundredth of a second after the big bang occurred there were still no atoms because the universe was still too hot for atoms to survive (more than 100 billion degrees Kelvin). Only after three minutes had elapsed did the universe cool down sufficiently – to less than a billion degrees – for the nuclei of hydrogen and helium to form, leaving the universe with 76 per cent hydrogen and 24 per cent helium. Aside from a little lithium and deuterium, there were no other elements around at this stage. Only after a further million years did the universe cool down sufficiently so that electrons were then added to these nuclei to form atoms. Over the next few billion years stars and galaxies formed out of hydrogen clouds, but it was only as these stars began to die that the elements were generated, which would eventually lead to life on our planet.

The life of stars is determined by the length of time that thermonuclear reactions continue in their cores, reactions very similar to those that occur during the explosion of a hydrogen bomb. The nuclei of hydrogen atoms are combined to form helium with a massive release of energy. As this reaction progresses, so the helium nuclei combine to form heavier nuclei, which recombine to form even heavier nuclei until finally iron is formed. Elements heavier than iron are rarely formed because of the large amounts of energy required. This process of nucleosynthesis continues until the hydrogen fuel runs out. Our own sun, for example, is a typical star and is likely to run out of hydrogen fuel in around five billion years, so on our twenty-four-hour 'thought experiment' timescale for the history of our planet to date, our planet has another twenty-four hours to run (unless we manage to destroy it ourselves first). When the sun dies it will expand to become a red giant before shrinking down to a white dwarf, less than 1 per cent of its present size.

The key to life on our planet lies not with stars like our sun, which become white dwarfs when they die, but with stars that are more than 1.4 times the mass of the sun. In these stars the gravitational attraction within the star is so great that when it dies it collapses to form a 'neutron star' of extremely high density and with a diameter of only about ten miles. This contraction is accompanied by a massive explosion and the ejection of the outer regions of the star into space, a phenomenon known as a supernova in which the brightness of the star increases about a billion-fold for a short period of a few weeks. So much energy is released during this explosion that elements even heavier than iron are produced and these are flung into space during the explosion to mix with the hydrogen and helium that is already there. This enriched hydrogen and helium now collapses under the force of gravity to form a second-generation star. If there are planets associated with this star, as is the case with our own star, then they will also contain the same mix of atoms. Most of the hydrogen and helium has dispersed in the case of our own planet because they are very light elements and the force of gravity is insufficient to hold them (although some helium remains trapped in the earth's mantle). The heavier elements remain, and it is these elements that comprise our own bodies and those of all other biological organisms. We are indeed 'animated star dust', with our origins in the fiery furnaces of supernovae.

Life appeared on this planet remarkably quickly following its origin – probably as early as 2.40 a.m. on our thought-experiment timescale (half-a-billion years after the earth began). The precise chemical events that led to the emergence of life remain an active research area and there are many aspects of the sequence of events that remain speculative. But it is both bad theology and intellectually lazy to invoke the activity of God to 'explain' any one particular part of this process. Theism, as we have been taking pains to insist, implies that God is either the author of all or else not at all. It is the task of the biochemist helped by the geophysicist and the astronomer to try and sort through the various clues and experimental data and put together likely scenarios of how the origin of life may have occurred. With the benefit of hindsight we can see that the chemical and environmental constraints were enormous.

The versatile combining powers of carbon, one of the elements flung into space during the explosion of dying stars, have played an absolutely central role in the origin of life. Carbon-based compounds are abundant in interstellar space and range in complexity from having only two or three atoms (e.g. CO and HCN) to having as many as thirteen atoms (e.g. cyano-penta-acetylene [$H(C_2)_5CN$]). Organic compounds are also common within our own solar system. For example, one of Saturn's moons, Titan, contains methane and it has a reddish-brown colour due to the presence of organic matter. Therefore carbon-based compounds are common in the universe and there is good evidence that this carbon-based material was contributing to the surface of the early earth in the form of tiny particles with a size of only a few tens of microns. The possibility that actual life forms existed on nearby planets such as Mars and were then carried to the earth on meteorites remains a subject of active debate.

The composition of the earth's early atmosphere is also not yet clearly established. The early earth may have had a mildly reducing oxygen-free atmosphere comprising mainly carbon dioxide and nitrogen, somewhat more reducing than are present-day volcanic gases and containing greater amounts of hydrogen, ammonia and methane. The oceans would have been anoxic (oxygen-free) like the atmosphere and the iron extracted from the igneous rocks by weathering would therefore have been in its reduced (ferrous) form. Because the ferrous form of iron is much more soluble in water than the oxidized ferric form which is more common today, the early oceans likely contained far more dissolved iron than today, perhaps 1,000-fold more. Interestingly, carbon-dioxide can be reduced to formaldehyde (HCHO) by irradiation with ultraviolet light if it is in solution containing ferrous iron, so iron may have played a critical role in the production of organic compounds in the pre-biotic earth. Ultraviolet radiation, particularly powerful in the early earth due to the lack of a protecting ozone layer, can also cause the production of methanol (CH_3OH) and other simple organic compounds in water containing suspended clay particles and dissolved carbon dioxide.

With mildly reducing conditions, electrical discharges through solutions of HCN can generate low yields of amino acids, the building blocks of proteins. Heating mixtures of amino acids results in polymerization. Upon cooling, protein-like polymers called proteinoids can be formed with many of the properties of polypeptides. When mixtures of amino acids are heated together, they do not combine with each other randomly but preferentially form peptides (strings of amino acids joined together) containing some combinations of amino acids but not others. Further specificity may have been introduced into chemical reactions by the adsorption of chemicals onto clay surfaces.

The further fascinating details of how the early genetic code may have become established, first by the use of RNA, then of DNA, and of how the first cells could have come into being, may be found in most textbooks of evolution.[11] The main point in our present context is that the role of chance was constrained and channelled by the laws of chemistry. Carbon-based life can have only so many properties in a given environmental context, and the evolutionary history of our planet has been one in which the potentialities of those properties have been very fully explored. Would those same potentialities be explored if we could rewind the tape of life and play it all over again under the same environmental conditions? Of course we do not really know, but given the constraints imposed by chemistry, gravity, the composition of the atmosphere, together with mechanical considerations, it is difficult to imagine that the life forms that would emerge would be so dissimilar in their diversity from those that now exist. Would creatures like us re-emerge as we rerun the tape of life? Again, we really have no idea, but as we look back at recent mammalian evolutionary history, it is a striking fact that brain power has markedly increased in relation to body weight during a relatively short geological period. The greater the competition for scarce resources, the more sophisticated becomes the organizational and predictive powers of the competing organisms. Although the word 'inevitable' is treated with great suspicion by evolutionary biologists, surely for the best of reasons, it is nevertheless tempting to speculate that if we could rerun the tape of life, the eventual outcomes in terms of biological diversity might not look so very different from the outcomes that we in fact observe. Of course the timescale might be very different. For example the rerun might not reach the present level of organizational complexity as illustrated, for example, by the human brain, for ten billion years (which would be unfortunate, given the future prospects for our sun), rather than the mere 4.6 billion years which it has in fact taken. But given time plus chance plus natural selection plus the occasional catastrophe, together with the severe biochemical and morphological constraints already outlined, it is not impossible that the rerun might not turn out so very different.

We have now clearly moved into the realm of speculation. But such speculations at least serve to highlight the fact that we live in a highly ordered world, a world so constrained by its physical properties that we can reasonably suppose that life forms are almost bound to appear eventually. If this is not the case, then it seems to make little sense to attempt calculations of how many other planets there might be in the universe upon which life might exist. Estimates of such possibilities vary wildly, but even if only one other planet exists with conditions similar to those found on planet earth, then it is likely that life forms would eventually emerge on such a planet. If we also take into account the fact that dying stars distribute the same mix of elements all over the universe, plus the observed richness of carbon compounds in interstellar space, it is reasonable to suppose that other life forms evolving in some other corner of the universe could well be carbon-based. As far as our own planet is concerned, the conservation of protein sequences throughout 3.5 billion years of evolutionary history does not appear to provide much support for the notion of metaphysical chance, Chance C. The universe in general, and our planet in particular, are ordered entities, as far from the meaningless fuzz on the screen of a faulty TV screen as one could imagine.

It should not be imagined that this description of chance and its constraints in the ordering of the universe provides any kind of knock-down argument for theism. Unlike enthusiasts for natural theology, and their 'mirror image' atheistic detractors, I do not believe it possible to argue for either theism or atheism simply by an analysis of the particular physical properties that our universe possesses. Nevertheless, the highly ordered universe that we observe certainly seems very consistent with the basic presuppositions of theism, and is certainly not inconsistent with the Christian idea that the universe has an overall meaning and plan that is ultimately under God's providential control. There seems little to support Monod's espousal of chance as if it were some overarching metaphysical principle which ruled the universe, Chance C. The universe that we in fact observe just does not seem to have the type of properties that one might expect should such an assumption be true.

Evolution, materialism and theism

It should be noted that the Darwinian view espoused so far is a thoroughly materialistic one in the sense that it requires no empathies, sympathies, vital spirits, ghosts-in-the-machine, special biological drives, hidden religious tricks, miracles or other special effects, in order to occur. Quite the contrary – the Christian view now, just as it was in the 17th century, is that the natural order has been demythologized of such entities by the realization that all that exists is contingent upon God's continuing creative activity. The universe that science struggles to describe accurately consists of material that God, in the theological language of Genesis 1, has proclaimed to be good. The materialistic universe is a good universe. The evolution of biological diversity on this planet, in this view, is no more and no less part of God's creative activity than the birth and death of distant stars. As we have noted, these events are indeed indissolubly linked. The material stuff of our bodies has its origins in the dying moments of long-forgotten stars. The reason that we have the properties of human beings and not of very small pieces of stars is because of the particular arrangement of atoms and molecules in our bodies. It is the precise organization of matter in this particular way that comprises a thinking, feeling human being with the capacity for love, hatred, poetry, war, peace and worshipping (or not worshipping) God. Darwinian evolution provides a very good (albeit as yet incomplete) biological account of the way in which the matter in our bodies has come to be organized in this particular way and not another. Where Darwinian theory does not help us very much is in deciding whether or not the universe, and our own lives within it, has any kind of ultimate meaning.

Intriguingly this materialistic view of the created order is very close to that espoused by the philosopher Daniel Dennett (among others). Yet, in *Darwin's Dangerous Idea*, Dennett presents such a worldview as if it were a convincing argument for atheism, maintaining that Darwinism is 'dangerous' because it shows how 'Design can emerge from mere Order via an algorithmic process that makes no use of pre-existing Mind'.[12] Whether describing natural selection as an 'algorithmic process' really adds anything to our understanding of how it works is open to question, but the important point to note here is that Dennett is trying to exclude the notion that anything else other than the evolutionary mechanism itself is required to explain the mechanism. To emphasize the same point, Dennett repeatedly criticizes the notion of 'skyhooks', meaning any kind of 'miracle', 'intervention', 'special pleading' or 'saltations' that people might wish to use to explain difficult feats of design engineering in biology. As an attack on some of the more deistic ideas implicit in the creationist literature, then this critique has some potency. But it is difficult to follow the logic of the argument in the context of theism. Dennett is clearly under the impression that the concept of 'pre-existing Mind' is contiguous with the Christian concept of God. But, for reasons already outlined above, it makes no sense to invoke God as the 'scientific explanation' of a particular biological mechanism, since by such a manoeuvre we are implicitly denying at least two basic tenets of theism, first that God is continually sustaining the *complete* created order and, second, that God is not part of his creation and therefore cannot be invoked as if he were just one further mechanism within the created order to explain how things work. In fact, if we substitute the term 'God-of-the-gaps' for Dennett's term 'skyhook' every time that it appears in *Darwin's Dangerous Idea*, then it reads much more like a work defending traditional theism.

A rhetorical device much loved by writers such as Dennett and Dawkins is to repeatedly describe the processes involved in evolution as being 'mindless', 'blind' or even 'pointless'. For example Dawkins comments that the 'watchmaker that is cumulative natural selection is blind to the future and has no long-term goal',[13] and Dennett writes that 'We are not just designed, we are designers, and all our talents as designers, and our products, must emerge non-miraculously from the blind, mechanical processes of Darwinian mechanisms.'[14] The trick, it will be noted, is to attach as often as possible the words that describe your personal ideology to a prestigious scientific theory, in this case evolution. It will then prove much easier to use the same words to describe your personal metaphysical view of the world that can be produced like a rabbit out of the hat with a great flourish at some later stage of the argument. But the use of such words to describe natural selection really adds nothing to the biological understanding of such processes. Is there anyone who really believes that natural selection is 'visual' or 'mindful' and, if not, then what can it possibly mean to call evolution 'blind' and 'mindless'? The terms are redundant. People can see or have minds but mechanisms, by definition, cannot. However, the fact that any mechanism per se is by definition 'mindless' does not exclude the possibility that it has a meaning and purpose defined by its incorporation into the larger scheme of things. The fact that the operations of pistons, spark plugs and carburettors in a car engine are 'mindless' does not imply that the car-driver has no chosen destination. The fact that the various mechanisms that comprise the operating parts of jet engines are 'mindless' has no implications for the existence of Frank Whittle who originally designed the jet engine. The existence of God is not an engineering question, a point which both Dawkins and Dennett seem to have missed.

Nature red in tooth and claw?

There are two distinct although ultimately related moral questions that are often raised in the context of evolution. The first concerns the apparent cruelty involved in the evolutionary process and the question as to whether such a process is compatible with the idea of a God of love as portrayed in biblical theism. The second concerns the degree to which morality itself may be a product of evolutionary processes and, if so, in what ways this understanding may impinge on more traditional understandings of morality.

The first question was encapsulated in Tennyson's much quoted reference to 'nature red in tooth and claw' and was an issue that clearly troubled Darwin on more than one occasion. Darwin could not persuade himself, for example, that 'a beneficent and omnipotent God would have designedly created the Ichneumonidae [parasitic wasps] with the express intention of their feeding within the living bodies of caterpillars'.[15] Some far more stomach-churning examples of nature's delights have come to light since Darwin's day of the type that are best not described just before having lunch. Clearly evolution has involved the killing of animals and plants on a mind-boggling scale. Cats continue to play with mice. Killer whales continue to throw seals around in the air before devouring them. Does it matter?

The properties of carbon-based life forms
First it should be noted that once multicellular carbon-based life forms began to exist, then a dynamic natural order in which life and death are integral parts became an inevitable consequence. No change or development into new life

forms would be possible without the death of the old. Carbon-based organisms (which are the only types that exist on planet earth) can only live by feeding on carbon-based molecules derived from other plants and animals. No multicellular animal can live by deriving all its energy needs from chemical elements – all are completely dependent on the food-chain whereby organic molecules synthesized in other organisms are passed on to them. A world like our own without biological death of any kind would be a magical world, a nonsensical world by any understanding of the properties of matter. Even if an organism as relatively simple as a bacterium continued to divide in an unrestricted manner without death, its mass would soon fill the whole earth, its nutrients would become depleted and death would be inevitable. Carbon-based life and death are biologically so integrated that life is impossible without death.

As the complexity of living forms has increased during evolution, and no one can deny that a kangaroo is a more complex organism than an earthworm (for example), so there has been an increase in the sophistication of the sensory organs required to inform the kangaroo's brain about its environment. With this growing sophistication has come increased brain size and complexity and a concomitant increase (presumably) in awareness of the environment and, in particular, awareness to pain. Such assumptions underlie the very strict UK Home Office regulations which control the distribution of animal licences to those using animals for experiments. It is animals that, to the best of our knowledge, experience pain, or that demonstrate complex behaviours consistent with a complex nervous system, which are quite correctly protected under such regulations. The octopus was included in the list of animals requiring a licence for experimentation precisely because of its complex behavioural patterns.

Humans have the most complex brains of any known animals, are the only organisms, as far as we know, that possess consciousness, and have an exquisite awareness of pain. Therefore brain complexity, awareness of the environment and experience of pain appear to increase in parallel. Possessors of consciousness are uniquely aware of the joys of sex, good food, a beautiful sunset and an enjoyable evening at the theatre, but by the same token can be acutely aware of pain when it happens. Clearly pain for us, as for all living organisms, is essential for survival. But do we really need so *much* pain to ensure our survival? The biological answer is almost certainly 'yes'. Our nervous system has been honed by millions of years of evolution to generate precisely the types of pain that will be most likely to ensure our survival. The mammals whose nervous systems worked inefficiently and failed to pass urgent 'action' messages back to the brain are presumably among the species that became extinct and failed to pass their genes on to us. The pain levels that we experience, however much we might dislike the idea, have played a critical role in our evolutionary past and continue to be essential for ensuring our survival in the present.

Without pain we would be walking around on broken legs, happily going to school with meningitis, merrily ignoring fatal tumours and munching on broken glass with rotting teeth. In short, our lives would be considerably briefer than they are at present.

Food-chains, life and death, pain – all are part and parcel of living as carbon-based life forms. We might wish it otherwise but, in so wishing, at least let us be clear that we are dreaming of a universe with properties unimaginably different from our own. Could God have created a universe with different properties altogether, with no carbon-based life forms and so perhaps no pain and no death? Surely if God is all-powerful the answer must be 'yes', and for all we know perhaps he has, but the fact remains that we ourselves happen to have carbon-based bodies and are living in a world of carbon-based biological diversity which reflects that brute fact. Those who have been influenced by the scientific way of thinking, with its emphasis on investigating the properties of the real world, will be more interested in grappling with our role as conscious agents in the world we do know rather than making up imaginary worlds about which we can know nothing.

Sentimentality, competition and cooperation

The phrase 'nature red in tooth and claw' epitomizes a certain attitude towards nature which, if not uniquely British, has most certainly flourished particularly well in British soil. For various complex religious, social and economic reasons, attitudes towards the natural world had been changing dramatically in Britain during the centuries before Tennyson penned his immortal words in the 19th century. 'In early modern England' writes the social historian Keith Thomas, 'the official concept of the animal was a negative one, helping to define, by contrast, what was supposedly distinctive and admirable about the human species'.[16] This official attitude towards animals was accompanied by a considerable level of cruelty towards animals in society. But largely as a result of opposition from the churches, cruelty against animals was far less widespread by the time of Tennyson.[17] Indeed, there had been an enormous growth in the keeping of animals as pets and, during the 18th century, a marked tendency to bestow human names upon pets and generally treat animals more anthropomorphically. There was an unspoken rule that pets were never eaten, and birds such as larks, linnets and robins, which were most familiar around English gardens and woodlands, and which had once been such a popular feature of the English diet, began to disappear from the menu. When Mountstuart Elphinstone, the ex-Governor of Bombay, was travelling in Italy in the 1840s, 'he reacted with horror to the local habit of cooking nightingales, goldfinches and, worst of all, robins: "What! Robins! Our household birds! I would as soon as eat a child."'[18] Anthropomorphic sentiments towards animals have received a further enormous stimulus with the proliferation of children's books centred around animal characters, which in turn has stimulated a toy industry devoted to the seemingly insatiable demand for more cuddly animals to take to bed. The sentimentality of the British towards animals is frequently remarked on by people from other nations who do not share our religious and social history. During fifteen years of teaching biological subjects in Middle Eastern universities I was often asked by puzzled students the reasons for such sentimentality. The British often assume that the rest of the world shares their attitudes towards animals, but this is not the case.

How, then, could God make such a cruel world in which cuddly animals engage in titanic struggles to kill each other for food? The anthropomorphic presuppositions of the question immediately begin to provide an answer. The notion of cruelty implies forethought and the conscious decision to act in a cruel way, qualities of thought that are usually uniquely assigned to humans. While cruel rats and malevolent weasels might exercise such wicked designs in the pages of children's books, to the best of our knowledge the real animal world is amoral and has no ethics. Whether there is genuine animal intentionality rather than 'merely' animal behaviour remains a hotly debated issue, but irrespective of the answer to this question there is general agreement that animals are not responsible for their actions in any way resembling human responsibilities. A lion may be shot for mauling someone who enters its enclosure, but this is to prevent further mauling, not because the lion needs punishment. Or, as a recent news item reported, Lucy the bull terrier was not culpable in killing fourteen-year-old Fluffy the cat, despite her owner being taken to court on the basis of section 2 of the 1871 Dogs Act; for as the court wisely concluded: 'It is a matter of common knowledge that dogs chase cats. You can't find a dog dangerous for doing what dogs naturally do.'[19] The accusation of cruelty is therefore fallacious; animals follow their instincts in order to survive and reproduce. Of course most of us do not like looking at animal blood and gore, and surely for the best of reasons. But the antipathy towards seeing animals being killed (or killing each other) varies drastically between cultures depending on the degree of exposure to such things that has occurred in childhood. I have often watched sheep having their throats cut in the streets around our home in Turkey during the time of the 'Sacrifice Holiday', and small children barely able to walk would frequently be among the circle of onlookers watching the blood pumping into the gutter from the dying sheep. But I have never detected any negative reactions from the children upon watching what, to many people in Britain, would be a gruesome episode. If seeing animals being killed is a normal part of your life from an early age then it is unlikely to be viewed with sentimentality, any more than it is in Western abattoirs in which the killing of millions of animals each year is clinically compartmentalized away from societies no longer accustomed to the sight of real blood.

None of these considerations should remotely be thought of as justifying human cruelty to animals. Clearly we do have ethical duties towards animals, and if we behaved towards animals in the ways in which they behaved towards each other, we could rightly be accused of acting cruelly since we do have conscious choice and the possibility of acting otherwise.

If human sentimentality frequently leads to anthropomorphic attitudes towards nature that are not justified by the amoral nature of animal behaviour, then is it not still the case that the titanic struggles in which animals engage for the 'survival of the fittest' provide an unsavoury spectacle? The background for such comments often lies in a misunderstanding of the way that the biological world operates. Darwinian evolution depends on a competition for resources that may often be scarce or limiting, but equally it depends on cooperation between individuals, provided only that it is individual organisms that receive the eventual genetic benefits in terms of reproductive fitness. 'Survival of the fittest' rarely involves battles to the death between individual animals; much more commonly animals have evolved patterns of behaviour that avoid conflict. In many cases the 'struggle for survival' refers to the survival of a species in a harsh environment rather than struggle against a competing species. The idea that nature is one long litany of bloody battles is therefore as false as the idea that at heart animals are really quite cooperative and that any blood spilt is an unfortunate accident. Certainly there are no rational grounds for 'reading into nature' our own particular value-system – the diversity of animal behaviours provide no secure grounds for such an exercise. As Stephen Jay Gould comments:

> I like to apply a somewhat cynical rule of thumb in judging arguments about nature that also have overt social implications: When such claims imbue nature with just those properties that make us feel good or fuel our prejudices, be doubly suspicious. I am especially wary of arguments that find kindness, mutuality, synergism, harmony – the very elements that we strive mightily, and so often unsuccessfully, to put into our own lives – intrinsically in nature. I see no evidence for Teilhard's noosphere, for Capra's California style of holism, for Sheldrake's morphic resonance.[20]

The natural world provides a constant source of wonder and fascination, but it is an amoral world, devoid of those qualities of foresight, conscious deliberation and ethical choice that would justify assessing it as either cruel or cooperative. It just is and that's the way it is.

Creation's functional integrity

A concern of Darwin's that we have not yet addressed is whether, for the theist, God is perceived as being concerned for any one *particular* aspect of the natural world. In other words, does God's sustaining of the created order imply that he has a specific will for its every detail, or only a general will that defines its general properties? 'Do you believe', wrote Darwin to the theist Asa Gray, 'that when a swallow snaps up a gnat that God designed that that particular swallow should snap up that particular gnat at that particular instant?'[21] The answer is surely 'no', not because God's sustaining power is in any way distant from his created order, but because of what Van Till has termed 'creation's functional integrity'. By this term Van Till wishes to remind us that the historic biblical picture of creation is not of an interfering God who continually (or occasionally) has to tinker with the natural world as if its original specification was in some sense incomplete but rather of a God who bestows the natural order with consistent and coherent properties that are autonomous, in the sense that they require no further specification. Drawing primarily from the 4th- and 5th-century works of Basil and Augustine, Van Till comments:

> I find a substantial basis for articulating a 'doctrine of Creation's functional integrity' that envisions a world that was brought into being (and is continuously sustained in being) only by the effective will of God, a world radically dependent upon God for every one of its capacities for creaturely action, a world gifted by God from the outset with all of the form-producing capacities necessary for the actualization of the multitude of physical structures and life forms that have appeared in the course of Creation's formative history.[22]

Van Till goes on to speak 'of a universe, brought into being from nothing, pregnant with potentialities conceived in the mind of the Creator', so that 'In a manner rich with both pattern and novelty, both continuity and contingency, both coherence and freedom, some of these latent potentialities would be actualized in the course of time – galaxies and galagos, stars and starfish, hulking quasars and human questioners.'

Although all our human analogies are severely limited in their ability to elucidate the relationship between God and the created order, and certainly we 'see through a glass darkly', the analogy used above of the sun's power and immanence in sustaining the natural world perhaps sheds some light on 'creation's functional integrity'. Biological life and diversity are contingent upon the sun's heat and light. Remove the sun and all would quickly die. But such utter dependence does not imply that the details or direction of that biological diversity are guided by the sun. Radical contingency is coupled to a quasi-autonomy.

A rather different perspective derives from another analogy, also previously used, involving the relationship between the novelist and his/her novel. In a big novel there may be many pages of details which are not essential for the development of the characters, nor for the plot, but which provide the texture and backcloth for the events as they unfold. The details could be different in countless ways without significantly altering the actions of the characters in the story. In a way the details are autonomous, not in the sense that they do not originate in the novelist's creativity but in the sense that they could well have been otherwise and it would not make a scrap of difference. It really does not matter to the overall plot whether a particular swallow eats a particular gnat. As in novels, perhaps so in real life, something may be both contingent and trivial at the same time, and I would suggest that gnats provide a good example of such a category.

The moral scale of the universe

Someone supporting a non-theistic account of evolution might at this point object that there has been so *much* biological diversity that has taken *so* many millions of years to evolve. So how on earth can we think of ourselves as being in any way special, especially when we consider that our own species has been present on the planet for such a tiny amount of time compared with many other species before us. The thought experiment in which we compressed the history of our planet into a single day might appear to support the case for own insignificance – a mere blink of the eye just before midnight. The argument becomes even more impressive when we compare our own puny existence with the vast spaces of the universe with its unimaginably huge numbers of stars and galaxies.

If size and time are the main criteria for assessing value and importance, then clearly this objection has some basis. But now let us carry out a further thought experiment. Suppose that the history of our planet was again compressed into twenty-four hours, but this time instead of a linear timescale the scale was set according to the appearance of morality and ethics on the planet. Clearly the picture would look diametrically opposite to the one we had before. This time the complete evolution of life with all its biological diversity would be crammed into the first few seconds, and then human beings would completely dominate for almost the entire twenty-four hours for, to the best of our knowledge, no other animals with the capacity for moral choice have ever roamed this planet. And if our planet appears ridiculously small from a physical perspective in comparison with the vastness of the universe, then for all we know if we apply the scale of morality to the universe then our planet might look ridiculously large. Of course we have no idea whether there might be other moral beings in the universe, but even if there were nine other planets in the universe with moral beings living on them (many people would be surprised by even one), then our planet would take up around 10 per cent of this unusual 'map' of the universe, should the scale be one of morality rather than sheer size.

As with geographical maps that describe countries, everything depends on which items you choose to highlight on your map, and very different perspectives will emerge depending on whether you choose terrain, languages, economics, biological diversity, religious belief or the frequency with which people play the national lottery. A theistic understanding of the natural order certainly gives a different shading to the map compared with an atheistic perspective.

In his famous account of Leo Tolstoy entitled *The Hedgehog and the Fox*, Isaiah Berlin took a fragment of Greek poetry and used it to express a typology of human thought: 'The fox knows many things, but the hedgehog knows one big thing'.[23] According to Berlin, there are those who pursue many ideas and those who like to subsume everything under one overarching principle; the latter are hedgehogs and the former are foxes. In the present context the theist would wish to stick up for the hedgehog but emphasize in the same breath that foxes are crucial as well. The scientific details of the evolutionary account are truly important but such mechanistic descriptions are by no means incompatible with an overarching account that bestows ultimate meaning on the system taken as a whole.

Chapter 11

Determined to Love?
A Critique of Evolutionary Naturalism

A devil, a born devil, on whose nature nurture can never stick, on whom my pains, humanely taken, all, all lost, quite lost.

Prospero about Caliban in Shakespeare's *The Tempest*

Christianity is a rebellion against natural law, a protest against nature.

Adolf Hitler

The naturalistic approach, locating morality in the dispositions produced by the epigenetic rules, makes our sense of obligation a direct function of human nature. We feel that we ought to help others and to cooperate with them, because of the way that we are. That is the complete answer to the origins and status of morality. There is no need to invoke... some Platonic world of values. Morality has neither meaning nor justification, outside the human context. Morality is subjective.

Michael Ruse, *Taking Darwin Seriously*

The abandonment of lofty conceptions of human nature, and grandiose ideas about the place of humans in the scheme of things, inevitably diminishes our moral status. God and nature are powerful allies; losing them does mean losing something.

James Rachels, *Created from Animals – the Moral Implications of Darwinism*

To us in Asia, an individual is an ant. To you, he's a child of God. It is an amazing concept.

Lee Khan Yew, Senior Minister of Singapore (in response to the outcry in the West over the sentence of flogging of a certain Michael Fay for vandalism in 1994)

Does evolution have any moral significance? So far we have suggested that the natural world is essentially amoral and that our anthropomorphic sensibilities about the reality of biological food-chains provide little support for the notion that 'nature red in tooth and claw' is in any sense immoral. But a far weightier claim for the moral significance of Darwinian evolution has been made by those biologists and philosophers who have insisted that the roots of morality itself are to be found in our evolutionary heritage and that the moral content of our beliefs continues to be shaped by our biology. Such a view is most frequently put forward within the context of evolutionary naturalism.

Scientific naturalism has already been defined (in chapter 8) as the view that only scientific knowledge is reliable and that science can, in principle, explain everything.[1] Evolutionary naturalism then becomes the attempt to construct a coherent worldview that depends on the explanatory powers of evolutionary theory. Moral beliefs, it is generally accepted, are a distinctive feature of humanity, but in an evolutionary naturalistic worldview they are a feature that must have arisen, and which must now be justified, by appeals to the theory of evolution.

Taking Darwin seriously

How can such beliefs about morality be justified? A number of recent attempts have been made to provide an evolutionary justification, mostly variants of similar themes. We will therefore summarize here the particular justification presented by the philosopher Michael Ruse as a fairly typical example of this genre. In his *Taking Darwin Seriously* (1986)[2] Ruse presents the following line of reasoning, and I supply quotes and relevant page numbers to help in tracking his argument.

Ruse maintains that moral beliefs are no mere cultural constructs representing rules for living in a particular local society, but rather 'morality... crosses national boundaries' and 'what distinguishes a moral claim is that it is set against some universal standard of required thought or behaviour' (p. 69). 'Morality is about what we *ought or should* or *may* do, and about what we ought or should or may not do.' Morality is therefore prescriptive and not merely descriptive – substantive ethics rather than an expression of our likes and dislikes. Initially, therefore, evolution does not appear to provide promising material for generating true morality because of its descriptive nature (p. 71). However, 'It is our moral task to see that evolution does indeed continue' (p. 72). Such a task could be fulfilled either by not standing in the way of the evolutionary process or by actively trying to promote the ends towards which a given evolutionary process appears to be leading. 'Therefore it can be seen that in our aiding evolution we are contributing to the morally worthwhile, which is the accomplished evolution itself. The rules of conduct do not exist in splendid isolation, but are rooted in the very essence of living beings, just as the dictates of the Sermon on the Mount are rooted in the very essence of the living God. As you must therefore now recognize, evolutionary ethics is thus a naturalistic philosophy par excellence' (p. 72).

Cultural factors alone are insufficient to explain human nature. 'I shall show that the humans-are-purely-cultural argument has simply been overtaken by the march of science' (p. 124). The aspect of the 'march of science' which is most pertinent to Ruse's argument are the epigenetic rules expounded by Wilson and Lumsden in their book *Genes, Mind and Culture*.[3] An epigenetic rule 'is a constraint which obtains on some facet of human development, having its origin in evolutionary needs, and channeling the way in which the growing or grown human thinks and acts' (p. 143). Epigenetic rules may be divided into primary or secondary. An example of a primary epigenetic rule is the way the physiology of colour vision, rooted in the various colour cones of the retina, causes humans to classify colours in ways that are common to all languages and cultures. An example of a secondary epigenetic rule is provided by incest taboos in which humans appear to pass through a negative imprinting stage during early childhood, so that those in sibling relationships (biological or social) will be unlikely to have sex together when they reach adulthood. The suggestion is not that the incest taboo is directly encoded in the genes, but rather that there are genes which ensure that when children are exposed to a particular environment – that in which they find themselves in daily contact with other children – mechanisms are then set in motion to ensure that they are 'turned off' from them sexually as they grow older. Thus 'Human culture, meaning human thought and action, is informed and structured by biological factors. Natural selection and adaptive advantage reach through to the very core of our being. And the link between our genes and our culture is the epigenetic rule' (p. 147).

Ruse then goes on to argue for a theory of knowledge (epistemology) based on Hume in which our grasp of notions such as causality is very much dependent on our own human nature, rather than on some ideal to which we can appeal that is removed from our own biologically based awareness of it. Ruse is well aware that such a position can easily lead to a position of total scepticism since if all our beliefs are ultimately subjective, even to the extent that natural selection can 'deceive' organisms for their own biological good, how do we know that our belief in Darwinian evolution is not a similar type of deception? Ruse maintains that 'There is no guarantee that a philosophically satisfying answer will emerge. Fortunately, in real life this does not matter, for we have the world of common-sense reality. Moreover, natural selection has seen to it that we are psychologically inured against the torments of metaphysical doubt' (p. 206).

What about Darwinian ethics? Ruse outlines the role of the philosopher – it is to understand the nature of morality and the grounds that support it. The first of these tasks is 'substantive' or 'normative ethics', in which the basic premises of moral thought and action are investigated. The second task is 'metaethics', which refers to the meaning and support that render morality plausible or reasonable (p. 207). Ruse hopes to press a Darwinian investigation into both of these traditional tasks of moral philosophy. Certainly values can not simply be 'read off' from evolutionary facts about the world (p. 213). This is at the heart of the difference between 'is' and 'ought'. Therefore what is the ultimate metaethical justification of morality? Broadly speaking there are two options. Either morality is objective, rooted, for example, in belief in God or a platonic ultimate Good, or morality is subjective, a function perhaps of likes and dislikes backed up by gut emotions. At first look Darwinian evolution might appear an unlikely source to back up either position. How can the struggles involved in natural selection, 'nature red in tooth and claw' contribute anything to morality? As Huxley wrote: 'Let us understand, once for all, that the ethical progress of society depends not on imitating the cosmic process, still less in running away from it, but in combating it' (p. 218). To counter such a position Ruse expounds two concepts: 'reciprocal altruism' and 'kin selection', which are familiar to anyone who has browsed through the literature on sociobiology.

'Reciprocal altruism' refers to the mechanism whereby the reproductive success of an individual is promoted by helping others. If we all stand in risk of drowning and I save you from drowning because I have a 'biological urge' to do so, this may put me at a one in twenty risk of drowning myself, but I in turn avoid a one in two risk of drowning myself were you never to respond to my cry for help. 'One throws one's help into the general pool, as it were, and expects to be able to draw on the pool as needed' (p. 219). For such a mechanism genetic relatedness is unnecessary.

In contrast 'kin selection' refers to that particular form of altruism in which our relatives are the selected beneficiaries of our behaviour. As our relatives reproduce so our own genes are being passed on, although the number of our genes passed on grows progressively less the more distant the degree of relatedness becomes. Thus help given to relatives rebounds to the favour of one's own reproductive interests even though the relatives themselves may reciprocate with little help. Wilson has termed reciprocal altruism 'soft core' altruism because it occurs between non-relatives and there is some expectation of return, whereas kin selection is 'hard core' altruism since it occurs uniquely between relatives and there is no expectation of direct return (p. 221).

All that remains, suggests Ruse, is to see how 'biological altruism', which depends upon mechanisms for biologically working together harmoniously to achieve reproductive ends, can be converted into 'real altruism', which demands 'genuine sentiments about right and wrong' (p. 221). Morality is the option that natural selection has generated in order to set within us epigenetic rules that will incline us towards actions that are, unknown to us, 'altruistic' in the biological sense (p. 221). Moral feelings therefore become evolution's way of backing up the dictates of the epigenetic rules. 'The Darwinian's point is that our moral sense is a biological adaptation, just like hands and feet. We think in terms of right and wrong. It so happens that the overall effects are biological' (p. 222). Epigenetic rules giving us a sense of obligation have adaptive value. 'Biology demands that we be "altruistic" in its (metaphorical) sense. For ants, that is it. They are programmed to do what they do. In the case of humans, biology achieves its ends by making us altruistic in the literal sense. We are aware of dictates of morality – given through the epigenetic rules – which we should obey' (p. 237). However, 'I doubt', writes Ruse, 'that natural selection would set up any strong sense of obligation towards people from whom there is absolutely no possibility of return, or who never were, are, or could reasonably be expected to be in my community' (p. 239). Such a 'Darwinian view' may therefore 'mesh happily with utilitarianism' in broad outlines, but would 'part company with the view that every individual counts as an equal moral being, deserving of as much attention as any other'. Nevertheless, the epigenetic rules generating the moral 'whisperings within' have real bite – 'The sense of obligation could well be and often is working against our basic selfish desires' (p. 240).

Can there be a 'Darwinian metaethics', that is, a framework which can ground all that Ruse has been claiming on a solid basis? Can the Humean prohibition against confusing 'is' and 'ought' be overcome? Ruse thinks that it can, because there is an important difference between 'statements about matters of fact, like normal feelings, and statements about matters of obligation, as occur in morality' (p. 250). Ruse therefore presents a subjectivist view in which 'ought' is equated not with a mere description of what is the case but with a strong conviction, stemming from the epigenetic rules, that something should be the case. 'The naturalistic approach, locating morality in the dispositions produced by the epigenetic rules, makes our sense of obligation a direct function of human nature. We feel that we ought to help others and to cooperate with them, because of the way that we are. That is the complete answer to the origins and status of morality. There is no need to invoke... some Platonic world of values. Morality has neither meaning nor justification, outside the human context. Morality is subjective' (p. 252). 'Ought' thus *really* means having a strong feeling about something. It is precisely the air of objectivity which morality has about it that gets us moving into action so that we faithfully act out the epigenetic rules. 'In a sense, therefore, morality is a collective illusion foisted upon us by our genes. Note, however, that the illusion lies not in the morality itself, but in its sense of objectivity' (p. 253). Our moral code, claims Ruse, is as innate as our chromosome number. 'For the Darwinian, the very essence of morality is that it is shared and not relative. It does not work as a biological adaptation, unless we all join in... It is only in my biological interests to have moral sentiments if you likewise have such sentiments. Otherwise, I will be moral; you will cheat; and I shall be left a loser' (pp. 255–56). Ruse's approach to the Humean is/ought distinction is therefore not to address the problem directly, but rather to sidestep it (Ruse's own expression, p. 256). 'Ought' is subsumed into psychology.

Despite strong overtones of genetic determinism, Ruse ends his argument with a resounding defence of free will, emphasizing that 'we are conscious beings, aware of the dictates imposed by our epigenetic rules – aware of the prescriptions of morality. Far from Darwinism denying freedom, it demands it!' Indeed, 'we do break sometimes (often) with our sense of morality' (p. 259). But we should not drift too far from our Darwinian sense of morality. 'My only hope' says Ruse in closing his final chapter, sounding a little like the Queen's speech on Christmas Day, 'is to have shown that a Darwinian approach to morality does not call for a repudiation of standards and values cherished by decent people of all nations' (p. 272).

Clearly this brief summary of Ruse's position cannot do justice to its various nuances and finer points – only a reading of the original volume can do that. Nevertheless, I hope that enough of Ruse's thesis has been provided so that we can see how it may be broken down into five basic steps that attempt to create a path leading from biology to morality. These steps may be summarized as follows:

Step 1: Complex human behaviours, such as moral decision-making processes, can be inherited.
Step 2: These innate dispositions have, or once had, adaptive value: they increased the chance of parents passing on their genes to their descendants.
Step 3: The force of the 'ought' which is implicit in all genuine ethical discourse is based on such innate biological drives derived from our genetic inheritance. There is no objective morality, only subjective awareness of our own biology.
Step 4: Such biological drives result in ethical impulses which, as a matter of fact, are broadly in line with traditional morality, promoting the 'values cherished by decent people of all nations'.
Step 5: We have a moral duty to aid the process of evolution.

Two types of critique may be levelled at Ruse's position, empirical and philosophical. The empirical critique relates to steps 1, 2 and 4 and the philosophical to steps 3 and 5. I will now present evidence and arguments, both biological and philosophical, that suggest that all five steps involve either faulty reasoning or are incompletely supported by empirical data. As a consequence Ruse's pathway from biology to morality fails to reach its goal.

Step 1 – Are complex human behaviours inherited?

Can complex and varied forms of human behaviour be inherited? No one is in any doubt that the overall parameters for our behaviour as humans are defined by our biology. For example, we do not fly, neither can we breathe under water without mechanical aids, we walk upright on land and we talk a lot. Presumably early hominid socialization was shaped by evolutionary pressures. Our brains are the products of millions of years of primate evolution. The human brain is built by perhaps as many as half of all the gene products (proteins) present in the body and is by far the most complex entity that we know about. It is much more complex, for example, than stars, which have turned out to be relatively simple to understand. Today we know of hundreds of genetic diseases in which chromosomal abnormalities or specific mutations in known proteins or metabolic pathways have effects on how the brain functions, sometimes mild, sometimes devastating. When the hardware goes wrong, the software does not run properly. When we think, look at things, make decisions, then biochemical events occur in our brains ('physical correlates') that can be measured. The biology of the brain does not provide support for a 'platonic mind' that exists as an entity independent from the brain which embodies mind.

The notion that complex human behaviours might be inherited is therefore by no means implausible. This clearly happens in animals and since our brains are derived by an evolutionary process from our primate forebears, it is not unreasonable to suppose that inherited complex behaviours have 'carried over' into the human brain. Studies on twins might, at first glance, support such a notion. Identical twins, sharing identical genes, are separated at birth and raised in different environments. When studied in later life they are found to share a wide range of characteristics in common, including personality variables and similarities in social and even religious attitudes.[4] The interpretations appear straightforward: compare the similarities in such parameters between identical twins reared either apart or together, along with studies on non-identical twins and sibs, and this provides an indication of the degree of genetic heritability of the parameter under study. Unfortunately, however, studies on humans are never quite that easy. It turns out that twins reared apart are in fact together for variable times (ranging from 0 to 49 months in the study cited) before being separated. Furthermore, some are not completely apart but have significant contact time prior to investigation (ranging from 0 to 1,233 weeks in the cited study). Nevertheless it is suggested that similarities in the measured parameters do not arise from such contact. But other difficult questions arise. Adoption agencies for the best of reasons have often tended to choose home environments for adoptees that are similar to those of the biological parents. And to what extent does the physical similarity between identical twins reared apart cause people in their differing environments to behave similarly toward them, thereby shaping their upbringing in similar ways? Behavioural geneticists have made vigorous attempts to address such sources of bias in their estimates of heritability, but the list of assumptions grows larger as more and more variables have to be taken into account. The effects of sharing the same maternal womb also appear to explain a significant proportion of the similarities between identical twins reared apart.[5] This is particularly remarkable because identical twins can experience very different environments in the uterus due to competition for limited resources. In the shared uterine space twins will also be exposed to the same infectious agents that may contribute to common medical conditions in later life, medical histories which will in any case be likely to be similar due to known genetic components in many diseases.

For the sake of argument, let us say that we accept the estimated high levels of heritability for various psychological parameters and social attitudes that are reported in studies of identical twins reared apart (typically in the range 30–50 per cent). Does this mean that complex human behaviours are inherited? Not necessarily. At present such findings remain interesting phenomena in search of a satisfactory explanatory model. It is quite plausible that variable genes have effects on early childhood responses (excitability, passivity or whatever) which in turn impinge on the way in which parents respond to the needs of the child. Parents react very differently to their children depending on their level of aggression. Rather than 'nature versus nurture', Professor Robert Plomin prefers to rename the debate as the 'nature of nurture'. Genes and environment are in practice so intricately entangled that attempts to split human behaviours artificially into 'inherited' and 'learnt' components fail to do justice to the way in which human development involves a continual two-way traffic between bodies built by genes and the environment. This two-way traffic begins at the moment of fertilization and continues until death.

As it happens the debate about twins is not helpful to Ruse's thesis, and the reason why twins studies do not feature much in the literature on sociobiology are not difficult to ascertain. What behavioural geneticists wish to study is the putative effects of genetic variation on behaviours. But this fails to deliver what Ruse wishes to maintain, which is a genetically derived and universal morality that is as innate as our chromosome number. If twins studies provide clues about heritability then the clues are about the normal range of genetic variation in human populations. But Ruse's biological source for morality requires the commonality of a species' behaviour rather than the diversity of behaviours which are supposedly generated by diverse genes. This point alone is, I think, fatal to his cause, and it will be considered further below.

We will now return to the kind of arguments which have been used by sociobiologists to argue for the inheritance of complex human behaviours. Since Ruse wrote *Taking Darwin Seriously* the term 'sociobiology' has tended to go out of fashion in favour of the less ideologically tainted 'evolutionary psychology'. *Plus ça change, plus c'est la meme chose.* E.O. Wilson, who may justly be cited as the founder of sociobiology, defined the discipline as 'the systematic study of the biological basis of all social behaviour'[6] – which is what evolutionary psychology appears to be as well. The terms will therefore be used here as having the same meaning, a stance promoted by Wilson himself.[7]

Three faces of human sociobiology

Three types of human sociobiology may be distinguished, which correlate approximately with historical developments within the field itself. The distinctions between these three types can be made by considering the various ways in which genotypes and phenotypes may be related. The genotype refers to the total set of genetic instructions encoded in the DNA of an individual. The phenotype refers to the description of the organism as a whole, including its anatomy, biochemistry, physiology, behaviour and so forth. Genotypes are inherited from parents, phenotypes are not, since they depend upon the development of an organism carrying a particular genotype within a particular environment.

Sociobiology Mark 1

The first model, which we will label Sociobiology Mark 1, is roughly contiguous with the earlier sociobiological literature as represented by books such as *Sociobiology: the New Synthesis* (1975) and *On Human Nature* (1978) by E.O. Wilson,[8] and *Sociobiology and Behavior* by David Barash (1977).[9] The assumption in these earlier writings was that there was a fairly direct link between the genotype and the phenotype as far as human behaviour was concerned. Despite the accusations made by their opponents, these writers were not so naive as to downplay the role of culture and the environment altogether. Nevertheless, in discussing the development of moral systems in *On Human Nature*, Wilson asks:

> Can the cultural evolution of higher ethical values gain a direction and momentum of its own and completely replace genetic evolution? I think not. The genes hold culture on a leash. The leash is very long, but inevitably values will be constrained in accordance with their effects on the human gene pool.[10]

The type of relationship envisaged between genotype and phenotype is well illustrated by the title of another book by Barash, *The Whisperings Within* (1979)[11] in which Barash pictured genetically encoded programmes nudging us towards choosing behaviour A rather than behaviour B because behaviour A was adaptively advantageous in our hominid past. As the earlier E.O. Wilson assured his readers, in a passage that he may later have regretted: 'In hunter-gatherer societies, men hunt and women stay at home. This strong bias persists in most agricultural and industrial societies and, on that ground alone, appears to have a genetic origin... My own guess is that the genetic bias is intense enough to cause a substantial division of labour.'[12]

That Sociobiology Mark 1 is not completely dead was well illustrated by the more recent publication of *A Natural History of Rape: Biological Bases of Sexual Coercion* (2000),[13] which maintains that human males are by nature rapists, murderers, warriors and perpetrators of genocide, and *The Dark Side of Man: Tracing the Origins of Male Violence* (1999),[14] in which the authors argue that rape is an adaptation to increase the reproductive success of men who would otherwise have little sexual access to women. Neither volume seems to cohere very well with Ruse's hope that our biology generates a morality which 'does not call for a repudiation of standards and values cherished by decent people of all nations'. In neither book is there any coherent argument for how genetic variation is supposed to account for the fact that some males commit rape whereas others do not, or that some are murderers whereas others are not.

Sociobiology Mark 2

Sociobiology Mark 2 is closest to the position that Ruse espouses and arose out of the intensive critique to which earlier sociobiological speculations were subjected, not least by feminists concerned about the deterministic stereotypes of female roles that were rife in such literature; by Marxists concerned that the forces of economic change were being drowned in a wave of genetic determinism; by anthropologists who thought sociobiologists were being naive about the power of culture; and by biologists who could anyway find little hard genetic data suggesting that human behaviours were inherited. Sociobiology Mark 2 was expressed most typically by C.J. Lumsden and E.O. Wilson in their book *Genes, Mind, and Culture* (1981)[15] and allows for a much larger role for cultural inheritance than is found in the earlier sociobiological writings. If culture was normally held on a rather tight genetic leash in Sociobiology Mark 1, in the Mark 2 version the leash was intended to become much more flexible. So Lumsden and Wilson introduce their work by asking the question:

> Why has gene-culture coevolution been so poorly explored? The principal reason is the remarkable fact that sociobiology has not taken into proper

account either the human mind or the diversity of cultures. Thus in the great circuit that runs from the DNA blueprint through all the steps of epigenesis to culture and back again, the central piece – the development of the individual mind – has been largely ignored. This omission, and not intrinsic epistemological difficulties or imagined political dangers, is the root cause of the confusion and controversy that have swirled around sociobiology.[16]

So 'in order to have a real evolutionary theory of mind and culture, one must begin with genes and the mechanisms that the genes actually prescribe. In human beings the genes do not specify social behavior. They generate organic processes, which we have called epigenetic rules, that feed on culture to assemble the mind and channel its operation.'[17] As C.J. Lumsden has claimed for this view: 'The existence of epigenetic rules for gene–culture transmission in no way implies that cognition and behaviour are genetically "hardwired" or that they are in any meaningful sense "genetically determined" (i.e. that knowledge of an individual's genome allows us to predict the behavioural or cognitive phenotype)... Rather, the epigenetic rules express the logic of the phenotype's developmental response to experience... Evolved constraints therefore help to match the developmental needs of the individual to the contents of the social system, assembling knowledge, attitudes, and beliefs into an evolutionarily competitive phenotype.'[18]

On the face of it this Mark 2 version of sociobiology, espoused also by Ruse, appears to be a welcome shift away from the more crudely deterministic claims of the earlier literature. The obvious and potent power of human culture to transmit ideas and influence human decisions is now freely admitted. Nevertheless in reading *Genes, Mind, and Culture* the genetic leash never seems too far away. As Lumsden and Wilson comment 'The central tenet of human sociobiology is that social behaviors are shaped by natural selection' (p. 99). The claim is not merely that our basic biological needs and cognitive capacities to make decisions are derived from our evolutionary past, which is non-controversial, but rather that the propensities for individuals to choose certain paths are channelled in certain directions by epigenetic rules that are themselves genetically determined. Genes and culture co-evolve, but in the final analysis it is the genes which have the upper hand.

If genes are transmitted via DNA, then how might culture be transmitted? Genes are transmitted by individuals, and so Lumsden and Wilson atomize units of culture into 'culturgens' which are likewise transmitted via individuals, proposing that cultures are then composed of the various 'culturgens' that are found within them. Culturgens (the forerunners of Dawkins's memes that we have already discussed earlier) may refer to virtually any *individual* human belief, prejudice, cultural practice or behaviour provided they are 'relatively homogeneous' and can be defined by at least one set of attributes. So culturgens might be 'an assortment of food items, an array of carpenter's tools, a variety of alternative marriage customs to be adopted or discarded, or any comparable array of choices'. The culturgens are processed by the epigenetic rules which regulate the probability of using one culturgen as opposed to another' (p. 7). The focus of Lumsden and Wilson's model is therefore on the social transmission of cultural variants within human populations and on the genetic constraints that lead to the choice of one culturgen in preference to another.

The problem, however, with the definition of culturgen that Lumsden and Wilson provide is that it is so vague that virtually any human behaviours can be grouped together by choosing a selection of attributes. Furthermore, it is difficult in practice to disentangle individual culturgens from the rules of the society that relate to those culturgens. Philip Kitcher, for example, imagines three different hypothetical societies in which there are taboos against incest,[19] a favourite topic of the sociobiological literature. Among the Shunsib there is almost universal avoidance of brother–sister incest. However, the Shunsib people do not express any distaste for the actions of others. So there is no public criticism of incest. It is simply avoided. In contrast, in the Moralmaj there is exactly the same pattern of incest avoidance but this time accompanied by personal sanctions against brothers and sisters who break the taboo. Moralmaj adults teach their children not to engage in incest, but no public punishments are involved. The Tabuit, likewise, have the same pattern of incest avoidance, but in their culture it is forbidden by an explicit taboo, written in the Tabuit book of laws. Anyone caught breaking the taboo will be punished in public. The important question that Kitcher raises is how will the culturgen be defined in these three societies? The behaviour of incest avoidance is the same in each case, but there are three different cultural states involved in these societies. The state of 'criticizing those who engage in incest' can be distinguished from the state of 'not criticizing those who engage in incest' and also from the state of 'punishing those who engage in incest'. Therefore it is not a trivial matter to atomize items of culture and pretend that they are inherited in a manner analogous to genes. In the present example the propensity for the culturgen of punishing incest is a *group property*, since it involves punishment by society, whereas the propensity for incest avoidance is present in *individuals*. So a wedge has already been driven between the inheritance of 'culturgens' by the individual, upon which Lumsden and Wilson's definition of a culturgen depends, and the reality that actually exists in human cultures, which is that the behaviours of individuals are frequently regulated by social institutions. Yet their mathematical treatments of the inheritance of culturgens, which fill the pages of *Genes, Mind, and Culture* so profusely, are lethally undermined if culturgens are no longer things that individuals can adopt or refrain from adopting.[20]

Sociobiology Mark 3

A discussion of culturgens leads readily into a definition of Sociobiology Mark 3, which claims that 'culturgens', or 'memes' in the language of Dawkins, are essentially divorced from the life of the genes altogether and have their own 'fast track' of inheritance by processes which are closely analogous to the transmission of genes. Therefore the question of the genetic inheritance of complex forms of human behaviour does not arise in this version of sociobiological theory since such inheritance is deemed not to occur, at least not to any significant degree. Some writers would not include this Mark 3 version as part of sociobiology at all, since it requires reference to evolutionary biology only by analogy. For our present purpose the precise classification is immaterial, since Ruse's theory under consideration clearly requires some kind of genetic input into human behaviour, and we will therefore focus on the claims of Sociobiology Mark 2.

Sociobiology Mark 2 in the spotlight

There are two key issues: first, are there convincing empirical data to support the notion that genes encode not only the 'hardware' required for cultural transmission but also contribute to the 'software' that influences human cultural choices, either directly or indirectly, by the so-called 'epigenetic rules'? Second, is the co-evolution of genes and culture the only model which will satisfactorily explain the examples cited in support of sociobiological claims? Consideration of a few concrete examples frequently discussed in the sociobiological literature will serve to illustrate these issues.

The language of colour

Prior to 1969 it was generally thought that the words used for colours in different cultures were arbitrary, that each language performed the coding of experience into sound in a unique manner. However, in that year a study by the anthropologists Brent Berlin and Paul Kay was published showing precisely the opposite.[21] Based on their investigation of twenty different languages, Berlin and Kay found that a basic set of eleven categories were determined as being common to all the languages studied – white, black, red, green, yellow, blue, brown, purple, pink, orange and grey. Surprisingly Berlin and Kay also found that if a language encoded fewer than eleven basic colour categories, then there were strict limitations on which categories it could encode, so that '(1) all languages contain terms for white and black; (2) if a language contains three terms, then it contains a term for red; (3) if a language contains four terms, then it contains a term for either green or yellow (but not both); (4) if a language contains five terms, then it contains terms for both green and yellow; (5) if a language contains six terms, then it contains a term for blue; (6) if a language contains seven terms, then it contains a term for brown; (7) if a language contains eight or more terms, then it contains a term for purple, pink, orange, grey, or some combination of these.'[22]

Much further research has been carried out on this topic since Berlin and Kay's pioneering work, and their findings have now been confirmed and extended by the study of a much wider range of languages. A clinching experiment came from the psychologist Eleanor Rosch who studied colour-term learning among the Dani people of highland New Guinea. The Dani people had only two terms for colour 'light/white' and 'dark/black'. Rosch therefore set out to teach three groups of Dani schoolchildren eight completely new colour words using sets of coloured chips as aids. Group 1 were shown chips corresponding to the 'natural' clusters of colours worked out by Berlin and Kay, whereas the other two groups were taught from deliberately 'non-natural' clusters of coloured chips. All three groups were taught to associate familiar non-colour Dani words with each of these colour categories. The results were unambiguous. The Group 1 schoolchildren learnt the terms with much greater ease than the children who had been taught from the 'unnatural' colour categories. The clear conclusion from all these studies is that the linguistic designation of colour categories in all cultures of the world studied so far is not arbitrary but is determined by something innate within the human brain.

In parallel with these anthropological findings has come a great increase in our knowledge of the neurophysiology that underlies colour vision.[23] There are three main stages in the neural coding of colour. At the first stage light energy is received by 125 million specialized photoreceptor cells, known as rods and cones, that convert light impulses into neuronal impulses. In primates the number of dimensions of colour vision as determined by perceptual colour matching tests is usually the same as the number of types of visual pigments found in the cones. Along with Old World monkeys and apes, humans are trichromatic, since they possess three types of cone, containing three different pigments, which are stimulated optimally by light in different parts of the visible spectrum of wavelengths. The pigments absorb light at short, middle or long wavelengths, and the cone photoreceptors containing them are therefore commonly termed the blue, green and red cones.

The decoding of signals takes place in a part of the brain called the lateral geniculate nucleus. There a special group of nerve cells receive nerve impulses transmitted from mixtures of the various types of cone. The cells are able to respond positively to light of one wavelength and negatively to light of another, so that one cell type responds positively to red light and negatively to green, whereas for another cell type the situation is reversed. Interestingly, each type of nerve cell responds positively to only one colour in each of the pairs, implying that the nervous system grades these as distinct categories of colour. In contrast the intermediate categories of reddish green and bluish yellow are not so generated, in keeping with the absence of words for such categories in different languages. Further decoding of visual information then takes place in the visual cortex of the brain.

The study of colour word vocabulary in various cultures, therefore, together with a parallel increase in our understanding of the physiology and genetics of colour vision, have together provided a convincing story linking genes with a particular aspect of linguistics. Words for colours 'map' onto the biochemical and neuronal mechanisms that identify light wavelengths at discrete and universally recognized boundaries. What does this show? Lumsden and Wilson have dubbed such phenomena 'primary epigenetic rules' in that there appears to be a direct linkage between genes and a particular human behaviour in such instances. People who develop with genes encoding a particular configuration of rods, cones and neuronal computing apparatus will tend to develop colour words which describe similar categories of colour perception. It is possible that the language of colour vision will eventually prove to be paralleled in other modes of sensory perception, such as smell, touch and hearing.

There are also strong grounds for believing that language acquisition itself is a property of being human that is as biologically rooted as walking on two legs.[24] The language acquiring apparatus that our brains possess is common to all humankind.

If the human brain, coupled to the various mechanisms of sensory perception, were not extremely similar in all of humankind, then there would be no possibility of genuine cross-cultural communication concerning the nature of physical phenomena in the world, and science as an international enterprise would be impossible. If a shape viewed as a triangle in one culture was viewed as a square by another, then scientific communication would certainly be a problem. As it happens, this is not the case and all the evidence suggests that what people see, touch and smell in their various environments around the world are closely similar for the simple reason that they all share a common genetic heritage that ensures that their brains and apparatus for gathering and interpreting sensory data are highly similar. The symbolism and meanings that people attach to their sensory data may vary considerably according to their culture, but the perceptions themselves appear to be strikingly similar. In traditional Chinese society, for example, white symbolizes the colour of mourning whereas in Western societies mourning is conveyed by wearing black. In the West red often stands for danger, whereas in China the colour red is associated with joy and happiness (remember Chairman Mao's little red book?). But what is firmly agreed upon by people, whether in China or the West, is what counts as red, black or white objects.

'Primary epigenetic rules' are not particularly controversial. They certainly contribute to the unity of the human species and undermine the more extreme claims of postmodernism that all human knowledge is relative and culture-bound. But they are still far from the kind of 'secondary epigenetic rules', Ruse would have us believe, that lie at the root of our deepest moral convictions. Are there any convincing examples of these?

Incest taboos and inbreeding avoidance

It has been widely suggested that the existence of incest taboos in all cultures of the world provides an example of such a 'secondary epigenetic rule'. Since the sociobiological literature frequently confuses incest taboos with the avoidance of inbreeding, some definitions will be necessary at the outset. The incest taboo can be taken to be any rule or set of rules that prohibits sexual activity among kin.[25] It is therefore not necessarily the same as inbreeding avoidance. For example, there can be non-incestuous inbreeding, as when sexual intercourse among certain categories of kin is not prohibited, and there can also be incest taboos which do not involve inbreeding, as in the prohibitions which apply between parents and their adopted or step children. Incest taboos are normally taken to describe *all* forms of sexual activity that are prohibited between kin in a population, not necessarily only sexual intercourse itself. Furthermore, as we have already noted in the example borrowed from Kitcher, incest taboos and their institutional reinforcement vary widely from culture to culture, particularly with regard to the range of relatives who are forbidden from sexual activity and the severity of punishments that are given to those who break the taboo. Taboos often extend to those who share 25 per cent of their genes in common, such as first cousins, but invariably include members of the nuclear family who share 50 per cent of their genes.

The way that incest taboos are transmitted from generation to generation is very similar to the transmission of any other cultural rule within society. Taboos represent a cognitive understanding of what ought or ought not to be the case in society and this information is clearly intended to have a guiding influence upon human behaviour; but equally clearly it is not the behaviour itself. The preservation of taboos depends on social transmission backed up by various levels of institutional reinforcement. Incest taboos are not reinvented in every generation but have long histories. Nevertheless the formulation of the taboo can undergo rapid change, for example when ethnic groups migrate to settle in a different geographical area. Incest taboos also have powerful symbolic overtones, and in many cultures incest is associated with cannibalism, witchcraft and the desecration of major cultural values.

Incest taboos are nearly but not completely universal. For example, convincing historical evidence has been presented showing that brother–sister marriages were relatively frequent among commoners during the Roman period (about 30 BC to AD 324).[26] But brother–sister incest has been cited more frequently within royal families, as in the royal lines of Hawaii, the Incas and Egypt. In only eight societies is there evidence of incest being tolerated among commoners.[27] But even in the vast majority of societies in which taboos exist, incest remains surprisingly common. Exactly how common is difficult to gauge as the topic is understandably surrounded by a fog of anecdotal evidence, and the frequency is heavily dependent on how the incest taboo is understood. If the taboo refers to all forms of sexual activity, then its reported incidence will clearly be much higher than if it refers specifically to sexual intercourse.

In contrast to incest taboos, inbreeding avoidance refers to the actual set of behaviours that such taboos are intended to deter. The Finnish sociologist Edward Westermarck proposed in 1891 that a psychological aversion to sexual intercourse develops between human beings who have been reared together in childhood. Westermarck himself presented little hard data for his assertion, but his proposal has been supported by a series of modern studies, in particular those carried out on the children of the Israeli kibbutzim in which children are reared together.[28] A further example of such aversion which is often cited in the sociobiological literature is that of 'minor marriage' in Taiwan in which the bride entered her future husband's home as a child, generally between the age of one and three, and was raised as if she were a sibling of her future husband.[29]

Are incest taboos inherited?
Is it likely that the development of aversion between non-related children who are raised together has a genetic basis? Is this a case where a mechanism to prevent genetic abnormalities is being switched on simply by the continued close proximity of non-related infants? The devastating genetic effects arising from the marriage of close relatives have been well documented.

It is quite reasonable to suppose, therefore, that strong selection pressure has induced the evolution of a set of genes influencing behaviour that ensure sexual avoidance behaviour between children raised together. This selection pressure would have been directed towards the prevention of genetically unfit offspring during the course of evolution, but the mechanism in place (as yet unspecified) is so strong that it operates among any children raised as if they were siblings, even though they are in fact unrelated. This evolutionary interpretation is supported by many observations of inbreeding avoidance in other species such as Japanese quail, olive baboons and chimpanzees,[30] although there are other species, such as the wolves of Isle Royale, in which there are high degrees of inbreeding.[31]

Nevertheless, attractive as the idea of a genetically encoded incest avoidance mechanism might seem, the evidence for such a 'secondary epigenetic rule' remains ambiguous. First, if inbreeding avoidance is so powerful, then why do we need a taboo anyway? An incest taboo is a rule or set of rules that prohibits sexual activity among kin, and is therefore reinforced by institutions within society. Unfortunately Lumsden and Wilson conflate incest avoidance, disapproval of incest and the presence of an incest taboo as if they could all be covered by a single 'anti-incest' culturgen, when in reality these three facets of human behaviour are distinct. Lumsden and Wilson inform us quite clearly that culturgens are things that individuals are free to adopt or not to adopt:

> [The mind] searches for new solutions and occasionally invents additional culturgens to be added to the repertory. Out of a vast number of such decisions across many categories of thought and behavior, culture grows and alters its form through time. The flux of culture comprises an unceasing torrent of changes in individual decision making.[32]

According to Lumsden and Wilson, the reason that people adopt one culturgen over another is because they are 'biased' in their decisions by epigenetic rules. But the claim fails to explain the presence of social institutions in society that support incest taboos. For if people are already genetically biased in their decisions such that inbreeding avoidance is the norm, then the social reinforcement appears unnecessary.

Second, there is no evidence that inbreeding avoidance is genetically inherited in humans. Behavioural geneticists like studying genetic variation. Do people who commit incest have certain genes which differ from those who do not? We have no idea. In a decade or so it might take only a week to obtain the complete genomic sequence of a given individual. Then we can do the experiment. Until then we will have to wait. In the absence of relevant data, for the moment any firm claims about epigenetic rules, even in forms which avoid crude genetic determinism, should be treated with caution. Although *Genes, Mind and Culture* presents many pages of impressive equations that may give the impression of a high level of objectivity on the matter, the maths is only of use if it expresses assumptions that are in fact true. As Philip Kitcher has so elegantly shown,[33] it is quite possible to arrive at the same mathematical conclusions as Lumsden and Wilson without invoking the influence of genes at all. Straightforward calculations based on probability theory will do the job just as well as assumptions based on genetic inheritance. The same problem besets a wide range of examples which are frequently cited in the sociobiological literature. In every single case the data provided are just as readily explained by cultural transmission as by genetic transmission, and mathematical models will comfortably fit either type of assumption.

Third, in the particular case of incest there are convincing alternative explanations for taboos that do not require genetic explanations. For example, the psychologist Roger Burton has suggested a 'recognition and attribution theory' based on his observations that 'the most common reason given in both primitive and modern societies for the incest taboo is that it [inbreeding] produces bad stock'.[34] The first element of this theory is that native populations recognize the catastrophic consequences of inbreeding and the second element is that these consequences are interpreted as a form of supernatural punishment. As Burton comments, with an average 50 per cent of abnormal offspring arising from incestual relationships within the nuclear family 'even non-scientific, non-record-keeping people would perceive the bad results of such close inbreeding and would want to control it'. Understanding physical paternity is unnecessary for such a theory as long as close inbreeding stands out as the particular act that displeases deities. The theory also predicts the variation in intensity of opposition with the degree of relatedness of the relatives involved in incest, since the greater the degree of relatedness the more the number of abnormal offspring and therefore the greater the intensity of the taboo. Contemporary anthropological data support the contention that many societies do note the deleterious effects of inbreeding and act accordingly.[35] Sociological theories have also been advanced for the aversion to inbreeding in kibbutzim and in Taiwanese minor marriages that are just as convincing as genetic explanations.[36]

Fourth, genetic explanations face other types of conceptual difficulty. For example, fathers and daughters, like brothers and sisters, share 50 per cent of their genes, but sociobiological ideas about the presumed epigenetic basis for incest taboos do not address the question of father–daughter incest. Little evidence is available to suggest that aversion to inbreeding develops between the generations in a manner analogous to its development between individuals of the same generation. Yet if evolution has endowed brothers and sisters who share 50 per cent of their genes in common with an aversion to sex, then the evolution of a similar mechanism to prevent sex between fathers and daughters might have been expected. This point has been highlighted by data gathered following Britain's Access to Birth Records Act of 1975 which enabled anyone over eighteen who had been adopted to trace their parents. In expectation that reunions with unknown family members in later life would lead to difficulties, a counselling clause was included in the Act. Surprisingly, a survey of reports from counsellors in London, who had been involved in giving advice to pairs of long lost relatives following their reunions, found that more than 50 per cent of their clients experienced strong sexual feelings in reunions, a phenomenon dubbed 'genetic sexual attraction'.[37] These feelings led to sexual intercourse in a significant number of cases, both between generations (mother–son, father–daughter) as well as between siblings. These results were obtained in people who had been adopted prior to the age of six months, and the average age on contacting their biological family was thirty-seven, so one could argue that as far as siblings were concerned there had been insufficient time to establish inbreeding avoidance by co-socialization. But this only serves to highlight the powerful intergenerational feelings that were reported, sufficient in some cases to lead to the divorce of the older partner from their current husband or wife. Whatever may be the explanation for such phenomena, such findings do little to support the idea of an epigenetic rule channelling human behaviour into a powerful instinctive antipathy to incest, particularly considering the continued illegality of incest according to British Law (passed in 1908).

In summary, therefore, there is insufficient empirical evidence at present to support the claim that inbreeding avoidance or incest taboos represent a 'secondary epigenetic rule' as frequently claimed in the sociobiological literature. The claim cannot be excluded, but the genetic arguments remain weak and cultural factors are at least as adequate in explaining the available data. This conclusion is important because, as Lumsden and Wilson state: 'The best research strategy for gene–culture coevolutionary theory... would seem to be the same as that employed in biology and ethnography: start with examples in which the units are most sharply and readily definable, establish them as paradigms, and then proceed into more complex phenomena entailing less easily defined units.'[38] Inbreeding avoidance or incest taboos are usually presented by sociobiologists as being the 'sharply and readily definable' paradigm for other epigenetic rules, but if the support even for this example remains weak, then this does not generate confidence that other more complex 'culturgens', such as universal moral ideals, will find a convincing genetic basis.

'What is the direct evidence for genetic control of human social behaviour? At the moment, the answer is none whatever', writes Stephen Jay Gould. Unless this situation changes, Step 1 looks decidedly insecure.

Step 2 – Innate dispositions with adaptive value?

Step 2 of Ruse's argument, it will be recalled, proposes that complex forms of human behaviour, in particular those which we now categorize as universally valid moral beliefs, do have adaptive value either in our past evolutionary history and/or in the present. Therefore moral behaviour is behaviour that promotes the reproductive success of individuals. To spend time in assessing this step might seem redundant if Step 1 is as weak as has been suggested. For if genetic variation makes no difference to any complex human behaviour, let alone our deepest moral convictions, then there is clearly no Darwinian sense in which we can speak of behaviours as having adaptive value, since there is no relevant genetic variation upon which natural selection can act. This is not to say that certain moral behaviours might not be adaptive in the analogous sense that they increase the reproductive success of the individuals who practise them, at least as far as their own immediate offspring are concerned. But the analogy is rather weak because without a genetic contribution to the practice of the moral behaviour the reproductive success of the individual would have no particular benefits to the progeny, and is therefore not Darwinian.

Such considerations set the scene for what has been a long and often acrimonious debate in the evolutionary and sociobiological literature. The debate has centred on the precise meanings of the term 'adaptation' and on the question of whether contemporary human behaviours can be said to be adaptive when the environmental conditions in which they supposedly evolved were clearly different from those pertaining to the present time. It is useful to make a distinction between 'organic adaptations' and 'cultural adaptations'. 'Organic adaptations' refer to those features that promote fitness measured in terms of reproductive success which have been built by genetic selection for the functions that they now perform. Gould has suggested the further term 'exaptation' for those 'useful structures... that are fit for their current role [but] were not designed by natural selection'. For example, the human nose plays a useful function for holding spectacles in the correct position, but most people would accept this benefit as an exaptation rather than as adaptive in the strict sense. 'Cultural adaptations' refer to features that also contribute to fitness and reproductive success but which have been shaped by sociocultural processes. These two categories of adaptive behaviour are not mutually exclusive, but to distinguish between them is important when considering the mechanisms that may underlie adaptive behaviour. It is also important to notice that human behaviours that contribute to fitness and reproductive success can fit comfortably into either category. The observation that a particular behaviour contributes to reproductive success is in itself insufficient to demonstrate a genetic contribution to such a behaviour.

Real-life adaptations

Ruse is quite specific in claiming that the evolution of morality represents an organic adaptation. It is therefore instructive to compare such a speculation with human organic adaptations that are already well established and for which detailed genetic data are already available. Such examples are provided by the prevalence of certain genetically inherited blood diseases in parts of the world where malaria is prevalent. People heterozygous for genes that encode variant forms of the red blood cell protein haemoglobin are more resistant to infection by virulent malarial protozoans such as *Plasmodium falciparum*. Being heterozygous means that only one copy of the two copies of the gene for haemoglobin is defective. If two people both heterozygous for the defective gene marry, there is a 25 per cent chance that any one of their children will carry two copies of the defective gene and the child will therefore suffer from the disease sickle cell anaemia. The parents who are heterozygous do not have the disease, but the single copy of the defective gene that they carry does give them greater resistance to malaria and is therefore adaptive in terms of their fitness and reproductive success. The children who have the disease are clearly less fit and are therefore less likely to pass on their genes to the next generation. However, the number of heterozygotes in the population is maintained at a relatively high level due to the prevalence of malaria in the area and the resistance to malarial infection that a single copy of the 'bad' gene bestows. In a given environment a genetic equilibrium is therefore reached in an inbreeding population with reference to the genes for haemoglobin due to the decrease in fitness of homozygotes (diseased) who carry two copies of the defective gene, balanced against the increase in fitness of the heterozygotes (healthy carriers).

Such examples of organic adaptations are convincing because a genetic evolutionary explanation of human diversity has been provided by causally linking the genotypic differences with the phenotypic consequences. The relevant genes have been identified and are well characterized. These are adaptations that both promote reproductive fitness in the present and were historically favoured by genetic selection in the past. It should be noted, however, that the carriers of the defective genes comprise only a small fraction of the populations who are exposed to malarial infection, and so the benefits of the adaptation are experienced by only a small proportion of the people in such geographical areas. Furthermore, such adaptive solutions to the problem of malarial infection are far from being Panglossian. Dr Pangloss, it will be remembered, maintained that we lived in the 'best of all possible worlds' and Gould has claimed that 'Dr Pangloss is reborn in human sociobiology. The adaptationist paradigm is his agent.'[39] Gould's point is well illustrated by the genetic 'solution' to the problem of malarial infection in humans, which is certainly far from Panglossian, for it is precisely the maintenance of a high level of defective haemoglobin genes in the population bestowing resistance to malaria that also guarantees that more children will be born with debilitating blood diseases. There is a paradox in that the conditions that create an adaptation to malarial resistance also increases the frequency of maladaptive phenotypes. The phrase 'survival of the fittest' should therefore be interpreted judiciously. The term certainly does not mean 'as fit as the organism possibly can be in a given environment'. There is a constant flow of genetic information through populations as the generations pass by, and the fitness of each individual in the population is a function of a combination of interacting gene products (the proteins). This means that the contribution of any given gene to overall fitness will be defined by the genetic company that it keeps. It has long been recognized by population geneticists that under certain conditions the fittest combinations of two genes may even be driven out of a population altogether.[40]

Such considerations raise particular problems for human sociobiologists who wish to persuade us that a particular aspect of human behaviour has an adaptive history by maintaining that the optimizing power of natural selection has fixed the best available genotype (namely this very behaviour!) in the population. The sociobiological literature is rife with examples of all kinds of human behaviours that are presented as adaptations, but the stories of how they supposedly became adaptive in the first place frequently sound too good to be true. A set of constraints are presented for the population under study, then it is shown that with such and such constraints a particular trait would maximize something that is taken to contribute to the fitness of the population in a given environment, and then, amazingly, precisely such a trait is identified in the population. In practice, however, the way evolution works is more like the belt and braces principle in which the set of genes that happen to be available are cobbled together to generate a surviving phenotype, but there is no guarantee that this phenotype is optimal for a given environment. This is one of the reasons why reliable adaptationist histories are so difficult to construct. Without an intimate knowledge of all the factors involved, both genetic and environmental, it is very easy to get the story completely wrong. For example, in the absence of a detailed knowledge of how resistance to malaria is generated, the idea that a defective gene which leads to a debilitating blood disease can in some way be adaptive would be completely counter-intuitive.

A related problem in constructing adaptationist histories is to know whether a particular contemporary human behavioural trait that appears to increase fitness would also have had the same contribution to fitness in the very different environments in which traits were supposed to have evolved. If complex behavioural traits evolved during the Pleistocene era, the period when most of human evolution took place, then it can be argued that the fact that a given trait is adaptive in a Western industrialized society today makes it very unlikely that it would have had adaptive value in the hunter–gatherer societies of the Pleistocene era, since the selection pressures on such a trait would have been very different. But equally the fact that a behavioural trait appears to be maladaptive in contemporary populations is no guarantee that the trait was not once adaptive in an earlier phase of human development. In perusing the literature of sociobiology it is difficult to avoid the impression that the interpretations of human behaviour are so versatile that with sufficient imagination, adaptive or maladaptive explanations can be found for virtually any eventuality. The fact of the matter is that we know very little about hominid behaviour during the Pleistocene and so the ideas continue to float without any anchoring in empirical data.

The 'hawks' and the 'doves'

Such considerations become particularly acute when considering Ruse's claims about the evolution of morality. It will be remembered that, in Ruse's account, our deepest moral convictions were supposedly shaped by natural selection during the Pleistocene era into the universally shared intuitions that now characterize the human race. These moral convictions were selected for their adaptive value arising from the processes of both 'reciprocal altruism' and 'kin selection'. Biological altruism, as defined by E.O. Wilson, occurs 'when a person or animal increases the fitness of another at the expense of his own fitness'. Fitness in the evolutionary context refers to the number of adult offspring in succeeding generations attributable to an individual's reproductive behaviour. Ruse's argument is based on the concept of 'inclusive fitness', which was introduced by the biologist W.D. Hamilton (1964). Inclusive fitness explains genetically costly actions in terms of their joint effects on both the fitness of the individuals that perform them as well as their genetically related social partners. In kin selection, the closer the degree of genetic relatedness between the altruistic individual and the benefited social partners, the greater the probability that altruistic behaviour results in the preservation of the altruistic individual's genotype. In 'reciprocal altruism' no genetic relatedness is involved, but the reproductive success of an individual is promoted by the net effects of helping others in a way which has the immediate effect of decreasing their fitness, but which in the long run increases their fitness due to the cumulative effects of the reciprocated help received from other members of the same species.[41]

The concept of inclusive fitness has been a successful tool for analysing the social structures of animal societies, particularly in the study of social insects such as ants, explaining self-sacrificing behaviour in a way that does justice to Darwinian natural selection. The theory has also been successfully applied to the evolution of the sterile 'worker' caste in naked mole rats, a species of mammal, and to the behaviour of other animal species. However, some of the original predictions made by 'Hamilton's rule' have not been supported by more recent evidence.[41] But, in any case, can the concept bear the weight that Ruse places upon it, so that universally valid moral instincts in humans are derived as biological adaptations from a long evolutionary process in the Pleistocene era? Game theory, first introduced into the evolutionary literature by Richard Lewontin (1961), has helped in visualizing the application of inclusive fitness to animal populations, but game theory also raises some problems for Ruse's claims. Thus, a population may be regarded as a collection of players in a game, each one pursuing various strategies in order to gain advantage in winning the game. We can then try to analyse the expected payoffs, in terms of future genetic representation, for each strategy. The concept of game theory has been developed by John Maynard Smith with a series of examples of varying degrees of complexity, of which the match between 'hawks' and 'doves' is perhaps the best known. Two 'hawks' meet and there is a fight. The winner takes all and the loser limps away in a bad condition, reproductively less fit. The game is set up so that all 'hawks' are equal and so will win half their encounters with other 'hawks'. When 'dove' meets 'dove' there are no fights. When 'hawk' meets 'dove' the 'hawk' runs away with everything (a key food resource, for example) and the 'dove' is left with nothing. The expected average payoffs to each 'hawk' and 'dove' can now be calculated. The strategies of each player in the game describe their characteristic ways of behaving. More subtle strategies can of course be introduced than the black-and-white ones provided here. For example, 'indecisives' can play being 'hawks' half the time and being 'doves' the other half, whereas 'deceivers' could pretend to behave like a 'dove' at first encounter but then proceed with a 'hawk'-like strategy.

Maynard Smith has shown that evolutionary stable strategies (ESSs) can emerge in such contests in which the competing demands of differing strategies by individuals are maintained in equilibrium. An ESS is a strategy such that, if almost all individuals in a group use it, no alternative strategy can invade the population. In theory ESSs can be accomplished in a population in several different ways. For example, each individual could demonstrate genetically based, individual differences in the use of single strategies, so that each individual consistently uses the same strategy in every situation, as with the hawks and doves example above. Alternatively all individuals within a population could use a genetically fixed optimal mix of strategies, whereby every individual uses the same statistical mix of strategies but does so randomly and unpredictably in relation to the situation. A further type of ESS could emerge in which every individual has an initial potential to use every type of strategy but, after exposure to particular environmental events in the course of development, is channelled into using only a small fraction of possible strategies. Other scenarios are also possible,[42] but the important point to note is that ESSs develop by selection pressures acting on variations in behaviour until these differing strategies stabilize in a given population in a particular environment.

The way in which reciprocal altruism works to develop an ESS is illustrated by the 'tit-for-tat' rule, which imagines a genetically endowed response rule that says that an individual should do favours for others with the exception of those individuals who have previously refused to do favours for that individual.[43] To make the idea work, there has to be a bias towards generosity in those cases where there has been no previous experience of the other individual. The system is set up so that the cost of helping someone is not that risky, e.g. I throw you a rope when you are drowning, which does not cost me much but which saves your life. If everyone in a population of interacting individuals adheres to this response rule, and if every individual is as likely to require as many favours as are requested from him, then an ESS will emerge. The individuals who refuse to join in by refusing to provide favours to others may later be unable to obtain the help they need. Stingy individuals will lose out, and so the genes encoding stingy behaviour will eventually be weeded out of the population.

If only life were that easy! There is a big difference between the world of genetic games played out on computer screens and the real world of human behaviour. Certainly game theory has been quite successful in explaining the strategies used by individuals within various animal populations, but if inclusive fitness is to generate a universally valid morality in human populations, there is a problem. The problem is that there is no guarantee that a universally shared set of moral behaviours will emerge from such a theoretical scheme. An ESS, as already noted, develops out of *variations* in behaviour in populations, and the commonality of 'tit-for-tat' is only one of a myriad possible scenarios that could emerge. Indeed, for someone who believed that the concept of an ESS was a valid way of interpreting human behaviour, the immense variation in moral behaviours and convictions between individuals throughout the world might strongly suggest that it is variety that has been selected for, not commonality as suggested by the 'tit-for-tat' example.

As it happens, in contrast to Ruse, the way that sociobiologists commonly apply ESSs to human populations is precisely with this understanding in mind. So Linda Mealey, writing on the 'sociobiology of sociopathy', is explicit in her premise 'that sociopaths are designed for the successful execution of social deception and that they are the product of evolutionary pressures which, through a complex interaction of environmental and genetic factors, lead some individuals to pursue a life strategy of manipulative and predatory social interactions'.[44] Sociopaths are also sometimes known as psychopaths or antisocial personalities. Mealey argues that there is a genetic predisposition underlying sociopathy which is normally distributed in the population and that sociopaths represent the people who in game theory are referred to as 'cheater–defectors' in terms of their behavioural strategy. Clearly there are a large number of assumptions here (which receive a detailed critique at the end of Mealey's paper), but Mealey cannot be faulted for her application of the ESS model to human populations. What the ESS model generates is not, as Ruse suggests, universally moral instincts that all right-thinking people should share, but a variety of moral behaviours that are in conflict with respect to those resources which contribute to human fitness or, more strictly, contributed to fitness in the environments in which humans evolved.

Ruse suggests:

The Darwinian's claim is that we have genetically based dispositions to approve of certain courses of action and to disapprove of other courses of action. But they are more than mere likes and dislikes. Here we start to move towards genuine morality and its evolution – from 'altruism' (in the biological sense of working harmoniously together, thus promoting reproductive ends), to altruism (in the literal sense, demanding genuine sentiments about right and wrong).[45]

But inclusive fitness does not necessarily involve this rather bland picture of 'working harmoniously together' but rather the competition by different individuals for scarce resources using different behavioural strategies to achieve their ends. If one of these strategies involves cheating or, as Mealey points out, being a sociopath, so be it. Ruse seems in other places to accept this for he also remarks that 'I, like you, have forty-six chromosomes. I, like you, have a shared moral sense. People who do not have forty-six chromosomes are considered abnormal, and (probably) sick. People who do not have our moral sense are considered abnormal, and (probably) sick.'[46]

It seems rather difficult to make any coherent sense of Ruse's position at this point. For if ideas of biological altruism and inclusive fitness are applicable to the evolution of human moral behaviours, then all we know about the genetic operations of such processes in animal populations suggests that what will evolve will be a diverse array of genetically influenced behaviours directed towards increasing individual fitness by competition for scarce resources. Some will be 'hawks', some 'doves', some 'deceivers', some 'cheats', and so forth. E.O. Wilson appears to accept this point when he writes that 'While individuals *within* a particular society vary greatly in behavioural genes, the differences mostly wash out statistically *between* societies.'[47] But Ruse wants to derive from Darwinian theory a universally shared moral understanding with common 'standards and values cherished by decent people of all nations'. Yet in the same breath he appears to admit that what has in fact evolved is not universal, so that those who do not share 'our moral sense' (who are these mysterious 'our'?) 'are sick'. So in reality two quite separate theories are being presented and the conclusions from both are being confusingly conflated. In his first theory Ruse would have us believe that a universally valid moral understanding has evolved that is common to all humans, based on the concept of biological altruism. But the problem with this theory is that commonality is not what biological altruistic theories deliver, but competition for scarce resources by a variety of behaviours, some of which may not seem very moral to us at all. In his second theory, Ruse would have us believe that those not characterized by his idealized universally valid moral understanding must be 'sick', but if the biological basis for his first theory were taken seriously, then these are precisely the individuals within a population that one expects to find flourishing. Whoever said that a minority of cheats do badly? The problem is that Ruse wants to have his cake and eat it and his biological theorizing (let alone any biological data) fails to generate the idealized universal moral understanding that he has in mind.

Genes for self-deception?

If universal morality as a Darwinian adaptation does not really work when looked at from the perspective of the commonality of moral instinct that Ruse wishes to derive, then a further 'adaptation' that he proposes fares even worse. This relates to his suggestion that our feeling that morality is objective has evolved adaptively, since it is only then that we will obey the moral dictates of our consciences satisfactorily. Ruse claims:

> The point about morality... is that it is an adaptation to get us to go
> beyond regular wishes, desires and fears, and to interact socially with
> people... In a sense, therefore, morality is a collective illusion foisted upon
> us by our genes. Note, however, that the illusion lies not in the morality
> itself, but in its sense of objectivity.[48]

Here Ruse succeeds in smuggling a Trojan horse into the human psyche. For if our genes can deceive us into thinking that our deepest moral convictions are objective, when *really* we know that they are not, then the moral force behind such convictions is clearly lessened. For if we know that we are being deceived by something, then it is a normal human response to take compensatory action for the deception. For example, it is common after suffering from a bad bout of flu to feel depressed for a while and see the events of life through rather dark glasses, even though the events of life may have changed not one whit. But once you become aware of this commonplace of human physiology, then you can allow for the deception involved and decide not to take the vagaries of your body's biochemistry quite so seriously.

And if Ruse is correct, how do we know that our genes have not foisted upon us a sense of objectivity about our *scientific beliefs* which are in fact quite illusory? Perhaps the reasoning necessary for science to emerge had some adaptive value for our hominid forebears during the Pleistocene era, but the sense of objective knowledge so engendered is actually quite mistaken. In which case perhaps our conviction that evolution is a satisfactory theory to explain the origins of biological diversity is an illusion foisted upon us by our genes since it contributes to our reproductive success. But if this is true, then Ruse's objective belief, presented by rational arguments in many books, that true Darwinians can only believe in a subjective basis for morality, is also based on an illusion foisted upon him by his genetic inheritance, and so we would be correct to ignore what he claims.

Once 'genes for self-deception' are allowed into the philosopher's repertoire for explaining how things happen then, like those computer viruses which cause all the words written on your computer screen to disintegrate and crash to the bottom of the screen, further rational discourse becomes effectively impossible. The form of the argument is very similar to the attempt to assign all unwanted beliefs to the category of memes which 'infest' brains. Once 'brain infestation' is allowed as a valid argument to undermine one belief, then of course it can be allowed as an argument to undermine any belief, as we have already noted, and the real consequence is intellectual sterility.

Big brains and the fast track to cultural change

When arguments end with sterility then it is generally time to take a different tack. The problem with many sociobiological arguments about the inheritance of complex human behaviours and the origins of our moral convictions is that they are using the wrong tools to tackle the question. In addressing a novel problem in science, there is little point in dreaming up a highly esoteric theory, difficult to test and hard to refute, when a perfectly obvious and testable theory is ready to hand. Every biologist agrees that we humans have evolved with big brains that have enabled us to be extraordinarily adept at learning, incredibly flexible at adapting to different environments, gifted with the benefit of language and diligent at socializing and passing on our cultural and religious beliefs to the next generation. Presumably our sophisticated on-board computers evolved under selection pressures for survival and reproductive success in an environment in which those who could run faster, calculate distances quicker, communicate more effectively and have a greater capacity for learning, would have a greater chance of passing their genes on to succeeding generations. No biologist doubts that the essential characteristics which give us an identity as a species are defined by the information content contained in our genes, perhaps supremely in the genes responsible for encoding brains that generate phenotypes characterized by consciousness and language. There also seems no reason to disbelieve the idea that the basic human instincts relating to survival and reproductive success, namely, those instincts relating to food, sex and nurturing of the young, are directly dependent upon our genetic endowment, although establishing rigorous genetically encoded mechanisms for even this modest repertoire of behaviours is not a trivial exercise. But when it comes to human behaviours of increasing complexity and diversity, then any changes generated by genetic diversity are likely to be too slow and unwieldy in comparison with the 'fast track' of learning and the cultural transmission of new ideas. Hundreds of human generations might be necessary for any phenotypically significant genetic change to occur, and even then some useful adaptation, like resistance to malaria, might be possessed only by a small minority in a population. But once you learn that malaria is spread by mosquitoes biting people, you can take steps to avoid mosquito bites, or kill all the mosquitoes in the region – and, if you are so inclined, you can spread this immensely adaptive piece of information round a whole community in a single generation.

The process of transition from genetically encoded behaviour patterns in animals to human behaviour based on learning, may be likened to what has happened with the introduction of the Internet as a system of communication. Originally introduced as a way in which a few academics could communicate their scientific results, the Internet or World Wide Web (WWW) now encircles the planet linking millions of people in a global village with, like any new communication system, enormous potential for both good and ill. The WWW now has applications that could hardly have been dreamt of when it was first introduced, including electronic shopping, scanning airlines for travel bargains, linking members of clubs and societies, propagating pornography, passing on cooking recipes, explaining how to make bombs, and linking up lonely hearts, some of whom end up getting married. The concept of e-mail never 'evolved' with any of these present 'adaptations' in mind but, once it arrived on the scene, its potential for such adaptations became apparent. So with our sophisticated on-board computers. The fact that they evolved to improve our abilities at hunting and gathering makes our enjoyment of choral music, playing football or driving fast cars no less special. It is perfectly possible to remain a good Darwinian and yet not believe that any of these human activities emerged as adaptations contributing to reproductive success during the Pleistocene era. Humans have big brains with big learning capacities for new tricks. Why not just accept this biological reality?

Curiously, sociobiologists occasionally give the game away by providing examples of how new ideas or new motivations can come into societies and transform them in a single generation. E.O. Wilson provides such an example in his book *On Human Nature*. In a chapter headed 'Aggression' Wilson informs us that 'there is an innate predisposition to manufacture the cultural apparatus of aggression, in a way that separates the conscious mind from the raw biological processes that the genes encode. Culture gives a particular form to the aggression and sanctifies the uniformity of its practice by all members of the tribe.'[49] But Wilson also informs us about the Maori tribes of New Zealand who for centuries massacred each other in tribal warfare. This appears to provide ample support for his claims about human aggression, but Wilson then reports that 'In the late 1830s and early 1840s the Maoris as a whole converted rapidly and massively to Christianity, and warfare among the tribes ceased entirely.'[50] If there is in humankind any innate predisposition to aggression, as Wilson suggests (a point that of course remains highly controversial), then it is not so rooted that it cannot be overcome, sometimes quite dramatically, by a change in the value system and motivations of the people involved.

The power of religious beliefs and social structures rather than epigenetic rules is also well illustrated by communities such as the Hutterites. The Hutterites are a religious sect which originated in Europe in the 16th century and migrated to North America to escape conscription. They have no private ownership, sharing all goods in common. They also cultivate an attitude of selflessness, despising nepotism and reciprocal altruism, the two principles that sociobiologists often use to explain human behaviour. Giving must be without regard to relatedness and without any expectation of return.[51] Yet despite these counter-Darwinian behaviours the Hutterites are reported to have the highest birth rate of any known human society. 'In present-day Canada, Hutterites thrive in marginal farming habitat without the benefit of modern technology and almost certainly would displace the non-Hutterite population in the absence of laws that restrict their expansion.'[52] The Hutterites have only been in existence for four centuries, which in terms of genetic change is a trivial amount of time. There is no doubt, therefore, that Hutterite religious beliefs and social structures have nothing to do with Hutterite genes. The beliefs and social practices of the Hutterites, like that of any other human community, have long ago become detached from any direct genetic contribution to their content, and are on the 'fast track' of learning and social transmission.

Philip Hallie recounts a further example from the Second World War of a community whose altruistic behaviour hardly fits with sociobiological assumptions. The residents of the French Huguenot village of Le Chambon risked their lives to save over 6,000 Jews, mostly children, from the Nazi holocaust. Their actions, reports Hallie,[53] depended on their faith that God was embodied in sacrificial love, that we should be our brother's keeper, we should defend the fatherless, and we should not murder or betray one another. The people of Le Chambon put their own children, families and property at risk in order to save complete strangers. How can their behaviour, motivated by faith in God, be accounted for in sociobiological terms? Ruse would have us believe that they were acting upon a necessary illusion. But had they been told that their beliefs were illusory, and had they accepted such an explanation, would they have pursued their altruistic course of behaviour? It is very unlikely. As Richard Busse remarks: 'Would they help the Jews if their faith was founded on a "noble lie"? Can altruistic actions such as taking in the Jewish refugees and helping them to escape to Switzerland, actions exemplifying unselfishness, heroism, unbounded love for humanity, and devotion based on the love of God and all of humanity as the children of God, be explained by the aims of survival and adaptation? The goodness of the people from Le Chambon cannot be accounted for by ethics based on sociobiology.'[54]

Step 3 – The naturalistic fallacy

The third step in Ruse's argument leading from biology to morality proposes that epigenetic rules have generated a *genuine* morality, morality that invokes the force of an 'ought', an understanding of morality that does not involve us breaking the dictates of what Ruse terms the 'naturalistic fallacy'. The spectre of the 'fallacy' hangs so heavily over his writings that it requires some careful consideration. The traditional place to start with such discussions is with Hume, and he is worth quoting in full at this point:

> In every system of morality, which I have hitherto met with, I have always remark'd, that the author proceeds for some time in the ordinary way of reasoning, and establishes the being of a God, or makes observations concerning human affairs; when of a sudden I am surpriz'd to find, that instead of the usual copulations of propositions, *is*, and *is not*, I meet with no proposition that is not connected with an *ought*, or an *ought not*. This change is imperceptible; but is, however, of the last consequence. For as this *ought*, or *ought not*, expresses some new relation or affirmation, 'tis necessary that it shou'd be observ'd and explain'd; and at the same time that a reason should be given, for what seems altogether inconceivable, how this new relation can be a deduction from others, which are entirely different from it.[55]

Hume's statement has generally been taken to imply that you cannot logically make the shift from 'is' statements to 'ought' statements; however much you may describe that something *is* the case, such statements provide no justification for the claim that such *ought* to be the case. The argument was taken further by the Cambridge philosopher G.E. Moore in his *Principia Ethica* (1903) who maintained that all attempts to justify moral claims by reference to descriptions of the physical world were doomed to failure.[56] Moore used examples from the voluminous writings of Herbert Spencer to illustrate his point. Spencer's *Data of Ethics* published in 1879 had argued the pressing need for 'the establishment of rules of conduct on a scientific basis', claiming that 'good conduct' really meant 'more evolved conduct'. Moore pointed out, surely correctly, that 'good' and 'relatively more evolved' are quite different types of concept and that it was impossible to move logically from the latter to the former.

How then can the sociobiologist extract a truly prescriptive morality out of descriptions of the natural world? Ruse tries to bypass the fallacy by redefining 'ought' so that the word no longer has its traditional sense of an implicit appeal to an objective yardstick of morality, but instead refers merely to innate dispositions deriving from our evolutionary past. Our strong sense of obligation is therefore 'a direct function of human nature'; it is rooted in our biology. The naturalistic fallacy is supposedly sidestepped by the claim that 'ought' sentences are justified not by logical deductions from descriptions of what is the case but as empirical descriptions of the way that humans actually feel about their obligations. There is therefore no truly objective morality in such a view and, in the final analysis, morality is a collective illusion foisted upon us by our genes, not because the morality is fallacious, but because the sense of objectivity that we have about it is illusory. 'The feeling of objectivity is the price we pay for reproductive success.'

It should be noted in assessing such claims that it is entirely possible that we have innate genetically influenced dispositions that direct our care and attention towards close relatives. No data that we have considered so far have excluded such a possibility. On the other hand neither have any data convincingly shown that this is the case. It remains equally possible that all the undoubted extra care and attention, which, on average, humans bestow on close relatives compared with non-relatives, is due to powerful cultural and social factors. Irrespective of the eventual resolution of this issue, it is quite clear that our moral obligations extend much further than our own backyards, and include questions of our responsibility to starving non-relatives in other countries, to homeless people in our big cities whom we have never met and to paying our taxes honestly so that non-relatives to whom we are strangers might benefit from the fruit of our labours. Ruse envisages a 'moral gradient' of ethical responsibilities that fall away steeply as our degree of relatedness with individuals declines. But in admitting our undoubted responsibilities to close relatives, it is also apparent that in the global village in which we now live we are faced daily with ethical issues that involve people remote from us genetically and geographically. Whether it be words or images down the Internet, or our investments in multinational companies that are over-utilizing natural resources thousands of miles away, we cannot readily escape the issue of our human responsibilities to non-relatives.

Given the global nature of our moral choices, and the diversity of moral opinion across different cultures, it is perhaps not surprising that Ruse never attempts listing those 'core moral beliefs' that our common evolutionary heritage has supposedly succeeded in generating within us as innate dispositions. No doubt 'killing is wrong' is fairly universally accepted, but it is doubtful that complex epigenetic theories are necessary to explain this essential criterion for a moderate level of human (or animal) social cohesion. And even this apparently straightforward moral dictate becomes the subject of endless discussion when it comes to the ethics of killing as part of war, capital punishment, euthanasia, abortion and so forth. Therefore in practice it turns out that the great majority of moral decisions are subjects for discussion and debate, leaving us with the question in each case as to what *ought* we to do on this particular issue? Far from the answers being 'obvious' due to our innate biological dispositions, the solutions are frequently very far from being obvious, particularly when the discussion spans many cultures and social structures in different geographical locations. If Ruse's model were correct, such moral diversity would be surprising, given that we all share the same human genes. In fact Ruse appears to admit this, since he states that 'Certainly at times our thoughts and behaviours put us in active opposition to our moral sentiments. And it is selfishness which often wins. It is open to the Darwinian to argue that morality is but one of the urges promoted by reciprocal altruism. Non-moral, restricting feelings are also produced by the same mechanism.'[57] But if this is true, then how can one set of feelings ('altruistic') be described as 'moral', when another set of feelings ('restricting') are described as 'non-moral'? The biological perspective is simply that people have different urges to do different things, and it is not clear from this perspective why one set of urges should be labelled more 'moral' than another. Moral obligations founded on a disposition to do something are not really obligations at all.

What ought we to do?

At the end of the day, then, we are still left discussing what is it that we *ought* to do? To what actions is this *ought* directed? It is formally possible, although I think unlikely, that the feelings of moral and social obligation which may be engendered when we use the word *ought* could indeed derive from biologically based dispositions with an evolutionary history. Whether this is the case requires much more data to resolve. However, even if it were the case, it would still be a matter of human choice as to what we attach these feelings of *ought*. We could then be compared to a machine which turns a spinning wheel. The energy from the spinning wheel could be harnessed for all kinds of purposes, from driving a dynamo to generate electricity, to pumping water on to dry fields for irrigation. If the spinning wheel represents the innate feelings to which the term *ought* relates, then the various uses to which its energy may be coupled represent our moral decisions. If 'ought' were really equivalent to 'having an extra strong feeling about doing something', then there seems no reason why this 'spinning wheel' could not be engaged with all kinds of practices that most people would accept as evil. A strong obligation to carry out one's duty and to obey orders was used with chilling efficiency by the Nazi regime to organize the

Jewish holocaust. Ordinary people felt that they *ought* to use their organizational abilities to please their paymasters; it would be wrong to protest. Collusion with the Nazi regime was widespread, particularly among academics.[58]

But if morality is a description of the biologically innate dispositions of a majority, as Ruse's theory implies, then on what basis can it be rationally criticized? If, as Ruse suggests, there is no objective morality, then all the onlooker can do is to provide an empirical account of what he sees. 'I look upon the philosopher' writes Ruse, 'as being, in a sense, an applied scientist.'[59] Then all the scientist–philosopher can do with Ruse's set of presuppositions is to describe the set of human instincts and dispositions manifest by the Nazi regime and say 'so this is where biological instincts lead under these circumstances'. There is really nothing else to say. Criticize and you have already begun to smuggle in value-judgments that are quite unjustified by the concept of human dispositions based on epigenetic rules. Far from sidestepping the 'naturalistic fallacy', Ruse's strategy of pretending that 'ought' refers to psychological feelings merely draws renewed attention to the central question as to whether there can be a solid basis for a metaethics that might justify such deep feelings. The moral decisions still remain to be made.

The ambiguities in Ruse's position on metaethics are also well illustrated by his treatment of altruism. 'Biology achieves its ends', says Ruse, 'by making us altruistic in the literal sense.' But what does this really mean? The definition of biological altruism, already provided above, is unambiguous in meaning, although not always easy to measure in practice. The problem comes when, sometimes by sleight of hand, this clear biological definition is conflated with the ordinary dictionary definition of the term as 'regard for others as a principle of action'. The implications of this muddle are brought out well in Ruse's discussion of people like Mother Theresa who, well past child-bearing age, set up a programme of caring for the dying in the slums of Calcutta. 'As far as the saint is concerned', writes Ruse, 'given the variation which exists in all populations... one fully expects some people to be more sensitive to their moral urges than others. Even if sainthood takes you into the biologically maladaptive, the Darwinian would think this no more than the occasional price you pay for a first-class social-facilitating mechanism like morality.'[60] And as if to underline the assumption that true altruists are some kind of genetic freak, Ruse states that 'I doubt that natural selection would set up any strong sense of obligation towards people from whom there is absolutely no possibility of return, or who never were, are, or could reasonably be expected to be in my community, as it were.'[61] But there are of course thousands of people all round the world who are engaged in selflessly helping non-relatives, often in cultures different from their own, in a myriad different ways. Very often the work they carry out to help others is voluntary or lowly paid, and there is no doubt that it involves a 'strong sense of obligation'. In many cases they give up opportunities to raise a family by performing this work and it therefore lowers their reproductive success. Indeed, it is precisely such work that the dictionary labels as being 'altruistic'. Ruse is correct, therefore, in suggesting that such behaviour is 'biologically maladaptive', at least as far as the transmission of the individual's genes is concerned, which is all that matters in the Darwinian context. But in that case it cannot *also* refer to 'people who are more sensitive to their moral urges than others' since his argument depends on morality being *adaptive*, otherwise the presumed epigenetic rules, which supposedly gave rise to morality, would never have evolved. Logically Ruse should therefore label truly altruistic behaviour as immoral because maladaptive, yet in the same breath he labels such truly altruistic behaviour as being due to heightened moral awareness. This seems to be yet another case of trying to have one's cake and eat it. An alternative Darwinian strategy in this context would be for Ruse to argue that true altruists were rare specimens whose behaviour was maintained in a population as an ESS, whereas the majority practised biological altruism with its spinoffs in self-interest measured as reproductive success. The problem with this approach, of course, and perhaps the reason that Ruse ignores it, although it fits well enough with his presuppositions, is that the true altruists then become equivalent to the psychopaths and the misfits. An argument which starts out trying to provide a solid basis for metaethics and ends up labelling saints as psychopaths should be viewed with suspicion.

Ruse's discussion of altruism highlights a problem frequently encountered in the sociobiological literature which leads to the justified criticism that no evidence could be produced which could possibly falsify the model being presented. Notice, for example, the strategy used in this context. Biological altruism is used to explain the evolution of morality. Morality is held to be all those socially facilitating mechanisms which we have innate dispositions to believe, generating a strong feeling that we 'ought' to do them. But in practice we frequently do the opposite. Well, never mind, this just shows that 'non-moral, restricting feelings are also produced by the same mechanism'. So how do we know which list of innate dispositions to label as moral and which to label as non-moral? It turns out that the list we label as moral looks remarkably similar to the traditional Judeo-Christian morality which North American humanists like Ruse espouse. So what about real altruism, which is often maladaptive from a Darwinian perspective? Ah well, these are the variants in society – there will always be the variants... And so the argument weaves and turns, moving now more in the direction of genetic determinism, now more in the direction of human free will, depending on the need of the moment. Despite Ruse's promotion of the idea of the 'scientist–philosopher', it is often not clear what new data would count against such poorly defined concepts.

Human intentions

It will also be clear by now that a vital ingredient has been left out of Ruse's biological definition of altruism that is at the heart of real altruism, and that is human intention. In biological altruism the question of intentionality is irrelevant, since the only criterion of any significance is that of reproductive success. In real altruism, by contrast, it is accepted that a person acts with the intention of advancing the welfare of another person in conscious recognition of some disadvantage to themselves. It is not even the final ends of an action that determines whether it was altruistic, but the intentions of the doer. Consider, for example, a family who forsakes their own summer holiday so that they can fund a holiday for a group of children from an orphanage. Most people would accept such an action as altruistic. Unfortunately, however, on the way to the seaside the coach carrying the orphans has a bad accident and they are all killed or badly injured. The unforeseen outcome of altruism was, in this case, disastrous, yet we still have no hesitation in labelling the family's generosity as altruistic.

Conversely, there are plenty of situations in which selfish and decidedly non-altruistic acts work out for the benefits of others in sometimes quite unexpected ways. Imagine, for example, a person driving back into Cambridge after a morning's pigeon shooting out in the countryside. Forced to stop suddenly at traffic lights, another car collides with his and in the ensuing argument he loses his temper, pulls out his shotgun and shoots the offending driver dead. When the police come to arrest him and to inspect the body and the damaged cars, it emerges that the man shot dead was coincidentally a terrorist whose car was packed with explosives and who was on the way to set off his car bomb by remote control in the middle of Cambridge as the streets were packed with shoppers. His fortuitous death prevented the almost certain death and wounding of hundreds of people. A murderous act has been rewarded with unexpected benefits.

Hanging over such discussions is the shadow of Thomas Hobbes. Hobbes claimed that although people are capable of good actions, when their motives are fully revealed they are found to be full of calculating self-interest. The consistent follower of Hobbes would therefore say that although it *appears* that a person's intentions may be altruistic, in *reality* this is only a cover for a hidden agenda in which the individual's self-interests are at heart. As one sociobiologist has succinctly stated the case: 'Evolutionary biology is quite clear that "What's in it for me?" is an ancient refrain for all life, and there is no reason to exclude *Homo sapiens*.'[62] But in recognizing that human motives may be sometimes mixed and are rarely totally transparent, there is no need to lurch to the opposite and cynical view that all acts that appear altruistic are in reality self-serving. As already noted, there are simply too many cases around where human beings serve the needs of others and, as a matter of empirical fact, their service works to the detriment of their own interests. Anyone who does not believe this probably has not travelled enough and met enough people in different societies or, if they do not like travelling, they could always take a few biographies out of the local library.

A true Hobbesian with sociobiological leanings could claim at this point that although the intention of the person to help someone else at cost to themselves appears like true altruism, what people are really doing in such circumstances is to calculate the consequences of their actions in terms of their inclusive fitness, either consciously or (in Ruse's argument) unconsciously. We need not be so impressed by their altruism once we understand the subconscious well from which it springs. One problem with this position is that there is no evidence that people have little computers in their heads with which they go around making conscious or unconscious calculations concerning the implications of their actions for inclusive fitness. This is a sociobiological construct that is often assumed for the sake of the argument, but there are no data pressing us to believe in such cerebral calculators. It is more convincing to suggest that evolutionary mechanisms have endowed us with cognitive abilities that enable us to make decisions, on occasion, which detract from our inclusive fitness. There is nothing un-Darwinian about such a statement. Darwin was as aware as contemporary biologists that the capacities of the human brain are profoundly different from those of the nervous systems of ants and bees. It should not therefore be surprising if concepts of altruism prove to be rather different in these two contrasting biological contexts.

Neither should it be thought that, because kin-selection may have been involved as an evolutionary mechanism in the development of the caring acts of parents towards their children, this thereby implies that the actions of those parents cease to be truly altruistic. Take, for example, some acquaintances of mine, both highly qualified academically, whose firstborn suffered from meningitis as a baby, thereby suffering a complete loss of hearing. The result was that the mother gave up her own academic career to devote herself to the welfare of her deaf child, in particular teaching her to speak and providing extra education for her at home. The mother's investment in time and energy has paid off more than she dared to hope, as her deaf daughter is now in the process of qualifying to be a doctor. Do we judge the altruism of the parents to be any less remarkable because, as a coincidental consequence of their caring, it may eventually make it more likely that their daughter will marry and have offspring? Surely not. Nobody in their right mind thinks that parents make conscious decisions about the investment of their genes in future generations. As has often been remarked, using this as a basis for parental actions would strike us as crazy, not as selfish.

In the case of the caring mother with the sick child, what we are impressed by is not some remote evolutionary consequences of parental actions, but the altruism which they in fact demonstrate in their present circumstances. That the biological disposition to practice such altruism (if it exists) is remarkably weak is suggested by the unfortunate observation that our daily newspapers are full of examples where in the parental context it has been so little practised. The evolutionary consequences of having a large brain is that we enjoy a unique cognitive capacity for making conscious and considered decisions in which the potential outcomes of our decision-making can be weighed. It is such human decision-making that can lead to altruistic intentions, even when the outcome of those intentions are not invariably beneficial for the good of others. Sometimes our altruistic actions will lead incidentally to the greater welfare and reproductive success of relatives or non-relatives. Sometimes they will not. Either way there appears to be no more necessary connection between our altruistic actions and distal evolutionary mechanisms than there is between those evolutionary mechanisms and playing the trombone. Real altruism, as opposed to biological altruism is, like trombone playing, a uniquely human capability that can only be understood within its own social context, and the social context has been made possible by millions of years of evolution that have provided us with big brains and impressive cognitive capacities.

Step 4 – Evolutionary origins of decent values?

Step 4 of Ruse's argument, it will be remembered, suggests that our biological drives result in ethical impulses which, as a matter of fact, are broadly in line with traditional morality, promoting the 'values cherished by decent people of all nations'. The problem with this argument is that it is empirically false. In reality there is a great variety of different 'traditional moralities' around the world in various cultures and in practice many people much of the time do not behave according to the minimalist dictates of 'biological altruism' let alone the greater demands of real altruism. The liberal humanism which Ruse espouses may play well in the elite enclaves of Western academia where Ruse finds his intellectual home (although surely even here one smells the occasional whiff of cordite?), but is miles from other traditional moralities. Millions of women worldwide still undergo forcible circumcision when they reach their teen years. It is looked on as a necessary part of local culture. In Zimbabwe, where the AIDS epidemic (as in other countries) has reached epidemic proportions, witch-doctors teach that HIV-positive men will lose their HIV infection if they have sex with a virgin girl. In India the practice of suttee – burning alive the widow of her dead husband on his funeral pyre – was still actively practised in India until banned in the 19th century. A few weeks before writing this I visited Uzbekistan in Central Asia, a trip which included a tour round a small museum in the city of Khiva depicting some of the punishments meted out by the 19th century Khans of the area. Women (but not men) caught in acts of immorality were buried up to their necks and then stoned to death. Another favourite was to tie hapless victims in sacks shared by wild and hungry cats. What is striking in the prints from that time displayed in the museum was the large and curious crowds who would be drawn by such spectacles. All of these contemporary and historical gems are items of traditional morality, all practised by people having, on average, no more genetic variation between them as ethnic communities than do individuals within any given population. The question still remains: which traditional morality are we going to choose? No biological urges appear to be welling up within human communities to bring about the kind of moral consensus which Ruse's theory demands.

Biologists are often the first to face up to the realities of human nature. Richard Dawkins is blunt: 'Let us try to teach generosity and altruism because we are born selfish.'[63] George Williams comments that 'An unremitting effort is required to expand the circle of sympathy for others. This effort is in opposition to much of human nature.'[64] The empirical reality is that people taken worldwide do not practise a communal traditional morality, which is what one might expect in the event that Ruse's proposed biological drives generated common ethical impulses. If this is the case in contemporary societies, the claim becomes even less believable when we take into consideration millennia of recorded history during which traditional moralities have been marked by enormous diversity, a period yet too short to involve significant genetic change.

Step 5 – Our moral duty to support evolution?

The final step of the argument proposes that we have a moral duty to aid the process of evolution. But Ruse never makes clear *why* it is 'our moral task to see that evolution does indeed continue'. As Ruse admits, on the basis of rational thought we can choose to behave differently from the direction that our innate biological desires (if they exist) might direct us. Since, in that respect at least, we are not like ants, why should we choose to conform to these supposedly innate evolutionary impulses? Indeed, it is difficult not to conclude that the argument smacks of fatalism. Many people take the view that the world is in a very sorry state and that the reason for this is largely due to human folly. Yet if human folly is based on epigenetic rules, as it presumably must be if Ruse's thesis is correct, then perhaps our moral duty should be to oppose the processes of evolution at every opportunity. If we have free will, as Ruse claims, then let's use it to stop the rot. And if the feeling of objectivity that we have about moral beliefs is a collective illusion foisted on us by our genes, then let's rid ourselves of it as soon as possible. Who wants to believe an illusion?

Another problem with the argument is that it is also not clear why we should have a moral duty to support the process of evolution when Ruse then spends the rest of his thesis arguing that moral values are subjective and innate and are therefore as natural to us as our number of chromosomes or having two legs. If this were really the case, then people would promote the processes of evolution naturally by the normal actions of epigenetic rules and would require no exhortations to do so, but these epigenetic rules then certainly seem to be lacking in at least 50 per cent of the population of the USA who apparently do not believe in evolution...

Building a thesis by promoting belief in evolution as a 'moral duty', when the ultimate intention of the thesis is to demonstrate that evolution itself generates innate moral beliefs, sounds incoherent.

Naturalism and metaethics

If the attempt to extract moral foundations from biology fails, then where does morality come from? A thorough answer to that question lies well beyond the scope of this book, but it is worth noting that as far as metaethics is concerned there are really only two broad positions. The first believes that objectivity in morality has a basis in religious belief or in, for example, some Platonic concept of the ultimate Good. In this view morality really is objective because it is rooted in a source outside of ourselves, such as in God or in gods, and our strong feelings of its objectivity therefore reflect a state of affairs that is in fact the case. The second is the naturalistic position which maintains that morality is a purely human construct and that if there is objectivity in morality it must be rooted in some way in the natural order. Ruse of course defends this second position, with the particular nuance that objectivity derives from our evolutionary history. However, there are numerous alternative versions of this second position which would deny that evolution tells us much if anything about morality. Arguably the aspect of Ruse's position that has the greatest implications for the actual practice of morality is not its evolutionary claims but its naturalistic assumptions. Whether you believe that evolution has any relevance to morality or not, at the end of the day inescapable moral decisions have to be made.

Moral individualism

I have, therefore, much greater sympathy for other writers in the naturalistic tradition who have grappled with precisely the same questions as Ruse, but who have come to rather different conclusions. For example, James Rachels in *Created from Animals – the Moral Implications of Darwinism* (1990), argues that Darwinian evolution does undermine traditional values and in particular 'it undermines the traditional idea that human life has a special, unique worth'.[65] Rachels suggests that the high value placed on the individual in the Western world derives from what he calls the 'image of God thesis', namely, the Christian teaching that humankind has an absolute value that is rooted in the description found in Genesis 1:27: 'So God created man in his own image, in the image of God he created him; male and female he created them.' This theme continues through the rest of the biblical account and is re-emphasized in the teaching of Jesus. Rachels argues that the teaching of an absolute basis for human value permeated the Western world over many centuries so that even the later more secularized accounts of the absolute value of humankind, as provided by philosophers such as Kant, were cast in the same mould. As Rachels remarks: 'A religious tradition can influence the whole shape of a culture, and even determine the form that secular thought takes within it. Only a little reflection is needed to see that secular moral thought within the Western tradition follows the pattern set by these religious teachings.'[66] As Lee Khan Yew, Senior Minister of Singapore, commented in response to the outcry in the West over the sentence of flogging of a certain Michael Fay for vandalism: 'To us in Asia, an individual is an ant. To you, he's a child of God. It is an amazing concept.'[67]

Rachels' own view is that this religious framework for justifying the absolute value of human individuals is no longer tenable (although he provides few reasons for this position). But he is certainly acutely aware that if the 'image of God thesis' is no longer accepted, then there are profound consequences:

> The big issue in all this is the value of human life. Darwin's early readers – his friends as well as his enemies – worried that, if they were to abandon the traditional conception of humans as exalted beings, they could no longer justify the traditional belief in the value of human life. They were right to see this as a serious problem. The difficulty is that Darwinism leaves us with fewer resources from which to construct an account of the value of life. Traditional theorists could invoke mankind's divine origins and special place in God's plan, as well as the idea that human nature is radically different from animal nature. Using these notions, they could derive a robust account of the sanctity of human life and its consequent inviolability. A Darwinian must make do with skimpier materials. With the old resources no longer available, one might well wonder whether we are left with enough to construct a viable theory.[68]

Substitute the phrase 'evolutionary naturalism' for 'a Darwinian' in the above passage and then, I think, Rachels is essentially correct. As argued above, Darwinism can be expressed equally well within a theistic or an atheistic worldview, so Rachels' focus on the 'Darwinian' view as being necessarily expressed within a naturalistic framework is mistaken. However, the critical point for the present context is that if naturalistic presuppositions are correct, and the scientific account of the world is the *only* expression of valid knowledge, then finding a firm basis for the continued belief in human value is not a trivial exercise.

Rachels' own replacement for the 'doctrine of human dignity' is 'moral individualism' by which he means that the way an individual, be it human or animal, is treated should be determined not by considerations of group membership but by considering the individual's own characteristics. Therefore we cannot speak of the 'value of humankind' as a generalization but only of the 'value of particular humans', which in turn will depend upon their circumstances. 'If A is to be treated differently from B, the justification must be in terms of A's individual characteristics and B's individual characteristics.'[69] Rachels explicitly states that the 'individuals' in this comparison may be human or animal. For example, moral individualism sees no reason to prefer the value of a human baby with severe brain damage over the life of a healthy monkey. Suicide and euthanasia may be justified in cases where life has become intolerable. Moral individualism dictates that the value of an infant with Tay–Sachs disease, who will inevitably die within a few months, is inevitably less than that of a healthy baby who has a long life ahead of it.[70] As Rachels remarks: 'The abandonment of lofty conceptions of human nature, and grandiose ideas about the place of humans in the scheme of things, inevitably diminishes our moral status. God and nature are powerful allies; losing them does mean losing something.'[71] Rachels goes on to suggest that this 'does not mean losing everything', but his point is well made. At the end of the day, what determines the rational foundations of moral beliefs and practices is not people's belief (or otherwise) in evolution, but on whether they justify their moral system within a theistic or naturalistic account of the world. Evolution per se may be comfortably accommodated within either framework. What makes the two worldviews different is whether human value has to be generated from a descriptive account of the world, as in naturalism, or whether human value is grounded in a reality beyond such descriptions, as in theism.

Rachels' helpful insights are highly relevant also to Ruse's discussion of the putative biological base for morality and the foundation of 'ought'. In the final analysis evolution is not very relevant for the discussion. If one starts with naturalistic assumptions, as Ruse does, then inevitably there will be naturalistic conclusions and 'ought' *must* dissolve into some form of psychological explanation since no firm underpinning for the concept remains. Evolution may be invoked to try to explain the source of these feelings, but adds nothing to the conclusions that are implicit in the starting assumptions. Likewise, the theistic framework, with its idea of a God who acts as the final arbiter of what is right or wrong, good or evil, generates a strong concept of 'ought' that is implicit in such a framework. The truth or otherwise of evolution is irrelevant to such a framework. The choice is not between evolution and non-evolution but between God as the ultimate source of all there is and the belief that there is no God. That such choices are no mere intellectual exercises is well illustrated by Rachels' insights. If God is dead, then sustaining a rational basis for a strong view of human value and of moral obligations is not easy. It may therefore be predicted that secularization of a culture with its accompanying absorption of a naturalistic worldview will be accompanied by an acceptance of moral choices precisely along the lines that Rachels indicates. For example, it is more likely that in such a society laws on suicide and euthanasia will be liberalized, and that human members of that society least likely to have a 'future biography', such as the handicapped newborn and the infirm elderly, will be accorded less care.

The reconstruction of morality

It should certainly not be assumed that the Judeo-Christian view of the value of the individual will remain a focus of moral attention as the logic of the naturalistic worldview is pressed in directions very different from those espoused by traditional secular humanists like Ruse and Dennett. The shadow of Friedrich Nietzsche, for example, still hangs heavily over contemporary thought. Nietzsche insisted that God was dead and that with him had died all notions of a universal human nature or of absolute moral laws. 'There are no moral facts whatever', Nietzsche declared. Far from being 'given' by religion or by biology, Nietzsche saw our nature and our values as being self-invented. We should be involved, said Nietzsche, in 'the creation of our own new tables of values... we want to be those who give themselves their own law, those who create themselves!'[72] The creative path lay in unlocking the wild, untamed, animal energy within, one's own personal *daimon*. 'Man needs what is most evil in him for what is best in him.' Only by exercising the 'will to power' could one discover transcendence.

In many ways Nietzsche was the grandfather of postmodernism. The entire life of the postmodernist thinker Michel Foucault (1926–84), for example, has been called a 'a great Nietzschean quest'.[73] Foucault pointed out that if one does not believe in a creator-God, then it is hard to see how people could be endowed with the 'natural rights' which were proclaimed by the thinkers of the Enlightenment. Foucault echoes Nietzsche in his claim that there is no fixed human nature – all is waiting to be created. And so, as James Miller's biography

The Passion of Michel Foucault (1993) demonstrates, Foucault saw himself as the active agent who was deeply involved in turning his life into a personal work of art. There was no authentic self waiting to be revealed as the earlier existentialist thinkers like Sartre had claimed – quite the opposite, all was yet waiting to be created. With Nietzsche, Foucault thought that the tools for self-creation were to be found in 'limit experiences', those extreme experiences in one's life that release powerful creative forces. It was this philosophy that fuelled his reckless fascination with madness, violence, perversion and suicide. As Miller recounts, as a student Foucault decorated his room with Goya's etchings illustrating the grotesque violence of war, and revered the actor Antonin Artaud, whose 'theatre of cruelty' was marked by obscenity, glossolalia, rage, and incoherent incantations. Foucault also immersed himself in the pornographic writings of the Marquis de Sade, who claimed that through sexual torture one could experience transfiguration.[74] 'To die for the love of boys', said Foucault, who eventually himself died from AIDS, 'What could be more beautiful?'

Foucault's life and writings seem very far from the measured tones of Ruse's moral philosophy with its insistence that biology underpins the moral code to which all decent people adhere. Ruse thinks that 'molesting children is just plain wrong' and that our biology tells us so. Foucault starts with the same naturalistic assumptions but finishes with rather different conclusions. If paedophilia is the price of 'limit experiences' through which, according to Foucault, the self will be created, well so be it. Biology therefore provides no guarantee of moral uniformity or continuity. Morality is not something held by the genes on a leash, but can be reshaped and reconstructed in all kinds of different directions within a naturalistic framework that lacks an objective basis for human value or for the underpinning of the 'oughtness' of 'ought'. At the end of the day, Ruse's moral system is derived not from epigenetic rules but from his own personal choices shaped, no doubt, by an early Quaker upbringing and by a father who was a conscientious objector 'in a household for which religion was an all-important factor'.[75] But based on a naturalistic framework there seems no grounds for Ruse to suppose that people may not choose a very different moral path compared with his own, as of course they do, biology notwithstanding.

Perhaps the creationists of the 1920s had a point after all, but for the wrong reasons. Their concerns, that the teaching of evolution in American schools could be used to spread the 'might is right' philosophy of First World War German militarism, proved groundless. But their conviction that evolutionary ideas could be abused in order to achieve political and racial goals was frighteningly confirmed in the rise of Hitler to power during the 1930s. It was surely no coincidence that Hitler's biography *Mein Kampf* ('My Struggle') contained as its title part of the phrase associated with the Darwinian struggle for survival. *Mein Kampf* preached a blatant racist message on the supremacy of the Aryan race. 'Whoever is not bodily and spiritually healthy and worthy', Hitler wrote, 'shall not have the right to pass on his suffering in the body of his children.' Hitler's eugenic programme based at Hamburg resulted in 400,000 sterilizations of those who were deemed unworthy of passing on their genes. The German psychiatric geneticist, Professor Ernst Rudin, was appointed Director of the Kaiser Wilhelm Institute of Psychiatry in Munich in 1928. Rudin was one of the principal advocates of the Nazi programme of enforced sterilization. Criteria for sterilization in Rudin's institute included being a conscientious objector, a frame of mind that was considered to be a form of schizophrenia and consequently classified as hereditary.

The Wannsee Conference, which decided on the final solution of the Jewish problem, was attended by many scientists, half of whom had doctorates, mainly in anthropology. About 45 per cent of German medical doctors ultimately joined the Nazi Party, a step which was certainly not necessary for their career to proceed normally. The extermination of Jews was largely carried out by medically trained doctors. Scientists played a leading part in the initiation, administration and execution of Nazi racial policy.[76] The 'Euthanasia' programme was intended to eradicate all mental illness by extermination of the patients. One of the doctors at Auschwitz, called Munch, describes how the doctors' talk at the camp centred round the technical problems associated with killing such large numbers of people, the most important of which was not the killing itself but the disposal of corpses. Robert Lifton's research revealed that the typical Nazi doctor appeared as a normal, warm-hearted person with his family, children and friends, but that he had numbed all feelings towards Jews in Auschwitz, and had a valueless, scientific and technological view of the realities of the death camps.[77] Just as the creationists had feared, the doctrine of 'might is right', coupled to a passion for racial purity and supremacy, so deadened the minds of thousands of highly educated people that their minds and consciences became numb to the human suffering of the racially excluded group.

The abuse of scientific theories no more invalidates the theories than the abuses of religion invalidate religion as a whole. As one of the 'grand theories' of science, evolutionary theory has been most terribly abused in the decades since Darwin, that most gentlemanly of the old breed of Victorian natural philosophers, and pressed into service in attempts to support diametrically opposed philosophies. As a theory to explain the origins of biological diversity, evolution has, I would suggest, no philosophical, theological, racist, economic or political implications whatsoever. Such a position will be equally disappointing to that subset of atheists who look to the theory as an ultimate prop for their atheism, as it will be to creationists who, ironically, agree with the atheists in their convictions and therefore feel duty bound to be hostile towards the theory.

Evolutionary theory is like a ship that has been so long voyaging at sea that its hull has become encrusted with some rather strange barnacles which are hitching a ride. But the barnacles themselves do not belong to the hull and need to be stripped off. That process needs to continue so that the good ship evolution can steam ahead more forcefully, unencumbered by such a weight of unnecessary philosophical and religious baggage.

Chapter 12

King of Infinite Space?
God and the New Cosmology

I could be bounded in a nutshell, and count myself as king of infinite space.
Hamlet

The unrest which keeps the never stopping clock of metaphysics going is the thought that the non-existence of the world is just as possible as its existence.
W. James

[Consider] the view now held by most physicists, namely that the sun with all the planets will in time grow too cold for life... believing as I do that man in the distant future will be a far more perfect creature than he now is, it is an intolerable thought that he and all other sentient beings are doomed to complete annihilation after such long-continued slow progress.
Charles Darwin, *Autobiography*

'Any coincidence', said Miss Marple to herself, 'is always worth noticing. You can throw it away later if it is only a coincidence.'
Agatha Christie

Scientists like explanations for things. It is supposed to be one of their jobs that they tackle difficult questions and come up with good explanations to answer them. Scientists who fail to ask questions about the ultimate purpose and meaning of the universe therefore display an odd lack of curiosity which contrasts strikingly with the explanatory quest so characteristic of the scientific enterprise as a whole.

The question this chapter addresses is the extent to which it is possible, or impossible, to derive conclusions about the existence and characteristics of God from the properties of the universe, a question often described by the term 'natural theology'. Until well into the 19th century the answer to the question seemed fairly obvious to most scientists. As surveyed in chapters 4–7, the existence of scientific laws, the richness of biological diversity and the predictable properties of the solar system were all routinely cited as convincing evidence that there was a divine lawgiver.

The 20th century saw both a marked decline and a remarkable revival of natural theology. On one hand Darwinian theory made the traditional biological 'argument from design' less plausible – although we have argued in chapters 9 to 11 that this did not make the theory any less compatible with theism – whereas on the other hand the discoveries of physics and cosmology concerning the fine tuning of the universe put natural theology back on the agenda. One form of natural theology was ushered in the front door even as the other form was bundled unceremoniously out the back.

Before considering whether this new form of natural theology will fare any better than its predecessor, it is worth tackling a prior objection that is sometimes made when this topic is broached. This objection is sometimes based on 'Ockham's razor', referring to the principle that explanations should be of the simplest form possible and should not be multiplied when a single explanation will suffice. For example, if the properties of the universe could, in principle, be explicable by a 'Grand Unified Theory' that integrates all the forces governing the macrophysical world then, it is maintained, there would be no need to look for any other type of explanation for its properties. It is curious that the name of Ockham is invoked to make this particular point, for William of Ockham was a 14th-century theologian with a refined and well thought out view of the relationship between the actions of God and the properties of his creation. But in any case, as with any razor, 'Ockham's razor' needs to be applied with some care. First, it is not true that the simplest explanation is invariably the correct one. Many phenomena in my own field of immunology have complex explanations and earlier much simpler explanations have been shown to be quite false. Second, multiple explanations for things are commonplace and acceptable, provided they operate at different levels. Ockham's razor is only relevant in those cases where an unnecessarily complex explanation is put forward when a much simpler explanation *operating at the same level* does the job better. If one day you look out of your kitchen window and see armed men wearing camouflage storming across your vegetable patch, you could conclude that, unknown to you, your country had gone to war, that an invasion had already occurred, and that troops had already entered your village. However, the simpler explanation, that your neighbours' sons are practising for a forthcoming village theatre production involving a war scene, quickly wins the day. Both explanations could, in principle, be correct, and both are operating at the teleological level of 'what plans and purposes are being accomplished by people with guns storming across my vegetable patch?' but in this case Ockham's razor points to a local rather than an international explanation.

So commonplace is our tendency to look for multiple explanations that we hardly notice it. Think, for example, about 'explanations' for the fact that your car is parked in the front drive. It is there because you drove it out of the garage this morning. It is there because you plan to drive to the airport this afternoon. It is there because dutiful mechanics in the past have carried out its 6,000-mile services on time and thereby maintained it in a functional state. It is there because a friend of yours was leaving the country to take up a position overseas and sold it to you in a hurry. It is there because you are a successful accountant with a good salary which allows you to indulge in buying such classy looking cars. It is there because you live in a culture in which car possession is an assumed cultural norm. On and on the explanations can proceed, each tackling a different kind of explanation from a distinctive angle. All the explanations in this case may be complementary. There is no reason to believe that the various explanations are in any sense rivals. However, if someone else claimed that the real reason that the car was in the front drive was not because you intended to drive to the airport but because you planned to run off with your secretary to a quiet hotel in Scotland, then a rival explanation would indeed appear, because in this case the alternative explanation is operating at the same level as its competitor, at the level of human intentions.

It is very likely that there are a number of explanations for why the universe exists and for why it exists in a way that allows the presence of conscious observers within it, but there is no reason why those explanations should be viewed as rivals unless more than one explanation is proffered at precisely the same level of explanation, in which case the criteria for choice will, as always, be based on coherence, elegance and the evidence presented for the rival explanation.

The anthropic principle

In the latter part of the 20th century, explanations for the existence of conscious observers in a finely tuned universe were dominated by the 'anthropic principle', which is really a set of ideas which differ quite widely in their claims and implications. Although the seeds of anthropic ideas may be found scattered widely round the earlier scientific literature, the anthropic principles were first formulated in 1970 in an unpublished Cambridge University pre-print by Brandon Carter entitled 'The significance of large numbers in cosmology'. More recently these ideas have been expounded at length by John Barrow and Frank Tipler in their book *The Anthropic Cosmological Principle* (1988)[1] and by others in numerous books and papers.[2] Brandon Carter introduced the idea of a '*weak anthropic principle'* (WAP) which suggests that 'Observed values of all physical and cosmological quantities are not equally probable because we must take into account the fact that our location is necessarily privileged to the extent of being compatible with observers.' As Barrow & Tipler comment: 'Features of the universe which appear to us astonishingly improbable, a priori, can only be judged in their correct perspective when due allowance has been made for the fact that certain properties of the universe are necessary if it is to contain carbonaceous astronomers like ourselves.'[3] The WAP therefore focuses on those particular properties of the universe which have enabled life to evolve on our planet and so to be pondered on by conscious carbonaceous observers. For all we know there may be other conscious observers, not necessarily carbonaceous, also pondering on the significance of the universe on some other planet, but we do not know for sure.[4] What we do know for sure is that we exist and the WAP is therefore definitely anthropic.

The *'strong anthropic principle'* states that 'The universe must be such as to admit the creation of observers within it at some stage.' In its most exotic form, given the title the *'participatory anthropic principle'* by Wheeler, the claim is made that 'Observers are necessary to bring the universe into being.'[5] Here the role of the observer in quantum theory is invoked to suggest that only universes with observers are actualized. The participation of the observer actualizes a universe in a manner analogous to the role of the observer in causing the collapse of a quantum mechanical wave function. But most commentators have found the notion highly implausible that an observer who appeared billions of years after the start of the universe could in some way have brought it into being. The strong anthropic principle will not therefore be considered further here.

What of the WAP? The fine tuning of the cosmological constants has been thoroughly surveyed by others – all we need to do is provide a brief overview of some of the most striking features of our universe that have enabled conscious life to emerge. These concrete examples will illustrate the WAP, and enable us then to address the important 'So what?' response, particularly the objection that the argument implied in the WAP is circular, since the universe has to be the way it is otherwise we would be unable to exist to observe it.

In the standard 'big bang' cosmology the universe started about fifteen billion years ago in a fireball of unimaginable energetic intensity in which the temperature, after about one-tenth of a second, was ten billion degrees Kelvin (nearly two million times hotter than the surface of the sun). In the first moments of the big bang the physical laws themselves were laid down which have defined the properties of matter and the characteristics of the universe ever since. So great was the energy of the early universe that it was at first a soup of boiling quarks, gluons and leptons. But already by the time it was one ten-thousandth of a second old the matter of the universe began to take on its more familiar form of protons, neutrons and electrons. Not until the first three minutes were completed did the universe cool sufficiently for nuclear reactions to slow to completion, setting the gross nuclear structure of the universe just as it remains today with its one-quarter helium and three-quarters hydrogen. Yet it was still far too hot for atoms to form round these nuclei – this did not take place until a million years had elapsed. At about 3,000 degrees, cooler than the surface of the sun, the universe became cool enough for matter and radiation to become distinct until today the background radiation of the universe has a temperature of only three degrees Kelvin, the lingering remnant of the dense fireball from which our universe emerged.

The Cosmic Microwave Background Explorer (COBE) satellite established that there were fluctuations in the microwave background that acted as a signature of the density fluctuations in the early universe that made the formation of galactic structures possible. When this astonishing discovery was announced at the American Astronomical Society in 1990, the 1,500-strong audience greeted the announcement with prolonged applause. The finding was a key observation in supporting a big bang cosmology.

Although the early universe is thought to have been almost completely uniform, the tiny fluctuations detected by COBE are thought to have been present in its constitution from the beginning. As these were acted on by gravity, so regions were produced at which there was an excess of matter. Gravity further acted on these regions until stars and galaxies began to 'crystallize out' after the universe was a billion or so years old. Had the early universe expanded in a completely uniform way, gravitational effects would have been exerted equally throughout all matter and the universe would have finished up featureless and boring. Once the forces of gravity had caused stars to contract to a critical density, nuclear reactions began which turned them into giant balls of incandescent gas, generating not only light but also the energy required to synthesize heavier elements. Stars are fuelled by the same process that makes hydrogen bombs explode. Hydrogen fusion in our sun requires fifteen million degrees. A series of reactions fuse four nuclei of hydrogen (protons) into one helium nucleus, which weighs 0.7 per cent less than the four protons from which it was made, thereby releasing enough energy to keep a star shining for several billions of years. So, as already noted, even though our own sun has been shining for about 4.6 billion years, it still has enough hydrogen fuel in its core to keep shining for a further 5 billion years. From the perspective of our sun, it is only about half-time.

About 10 billion years after the big bang the first stars began to die. Stars which are heavier than our sun have a spectacular way of dying. All their central hydrogen is consumed and is turned into helium, and then gravity squeezes these stars so that the temperature rises even higher than before, so providing the energy to synthesize the nuclei of heavier atoms such as carbon (six protons), oxygen (eight protons) and iron (26 protons). Finally the core of the star is turned into iron and the pressure of gravity then becomes so vast that its central core is compressed to the density of an atomic nucleus, leading to an enormous explosion known as a supernova. This causes the outer layers of the star to blast off into space, including the elements such as carbon, oxygen and iron which are essential to life as we know it. At the same time the immense energy generated in the dying moments of the star before it explodes drives the synthesis of even heavier elements, such as gold and uranium, which are likewise scattered into interstellar space. A supernova is so bright that for a few weeks it will visibly outshine the galaxy in which it is located. Eventually the scattered elements from the supernova find themselves in a new star, where once again the process of nuclear synthesis is continued. So stars may be viewed as a series of stellar factories which take in elements and process them further up the periodic table until they are once again scattered into space, then to continue the process in another star, perhaps hundreds of millions of years later.

Our own galaxy, the Milky Way, is about 100,000 light years across and contains 100 billion stars. Its oldest stars were formed more than ten billion years ago, in contrast to our own sun which was formed, together with its planetary system, about 4.6 billion years ago. The sun was born in an interstellar cloud. The cloud started to rotate, building up an increasing centrifugal force, rather as you would when swinging around on one heel with your arms spread out. Contraction of the stellar cloud continued until its centre became hot enough to trigger hydrogen fusion, turning the compressed cloud of matter into a star, burning in its interior at about fifteen million degrees. Meanwhile the surrounding disc cooled and some of the gas condensed into dust and rock that peeled off the surface as planets. By the time our sun was formed, heavy stars within our galaxy could have been through several generations of birth and death, generating the heavier elements that eventually became the building blocks of life on planet earth. Our own solar system condensed from the matter left over from a vast array of earlier stars. Our sun contains about 2 per cent of the heavier elements because it is a second or third generation star, a composition reflected in our own planet, thereby rendering biological life possible. The atoms that today comprise a single DNA molecule in our bodies were once spread out throughout our galaxy. Chemically we are all the products of the ashes of burnt-out stars.

Fine tuning of physical constants

Modern cosmology has revealed a remarkable set of finely tuned constants without which our universe would not have had the properties that it in fact displays, and without which our own presence in the universe would have been impossible. As Carr and Rees pointed out in a seminal paper: 'The possibility of life as we know it evolving in the universe depends on the values of a few physical constants – and is in some respects remarkably sensitive to their numerical values.'[6] The significance, or otherwise, of such findings for anthropic arguments will be considered further below. Here we will select a few striking examples out of the many that could be cited.

The properties of matter are governed by four fundamental physical forces or interactions: gravity, electromagnetism, and the weak and strong nuclear forces. These define, for example, the properties of hydrogen that are crucial to the way in which it is burnt as fuel inside stars, during which process the hydrogen is converted to helium. The production of deuterium is the first step in this nuclear reaction and involves the fusion of two protons. Proton–proton fusion is controlled by the weak force and is a reaction 10^{18} times slower than one based on the strong nuclear force that controls the further conversion of deuterium to helium nuclei. The weak and strong forces are finely tuned in such a way that the conversion of hydrogen to helium continues by this tightly regulated reaction pathway. Without such fine tuning all the matter in the universe would have burnt to helium before the first galaxies started to condense, and we would certainly not exist. At the same time, if these values were a few per cent different, a catastrophic consumption of hydrogen and enormous release of energy would occur. In short, the stars would not burn by steadily consuming their hydrogen fuel, as they in fact do, and would certainly not shine long enough for life to evolve anywhere in their vicinity. Tiny changes in the strong and weak forces could even have meant that no hydrogen at all would have emerged from the big bang, so no stars would have emerged, and the universe would be a dark and gloomy void.

Another remarkable example of the way in which the strong force is tuned to make life possible was discovered by Fred Hoyle. This example has been described as the 'only genuine prediction'[7] of an anthropic principle because the finding was predicted based on anthropic reasoning, and only later then shown to be true experimentally. This prediction arose because of Hoyle's efforts to explain how carbon could have been formed inside stars. As already noted, once hydrogen has been converted to helium in stars, the heavier elements are then generally made by fusing together helium nuclei, which consist of two protons and two neutrons. However, the element beryllium, which consists of two helium atoms fused together, is very unstable. Astrophysicists knew that it was necessary to make beryllium first before obtaining carbon, which consists of three helium nuclei fused together, and which is of course quite stable, being the basic building block of life. So how could carbon be synthesized when beryllium was so unstable? The beryllium would simply decay immediately it was formed.

There was no way out of this conundrum unless beryllium and helium could stick together particularly easily. Hoyle realized that this could only happen if there happened to be a 'resonance' in the carbon nucleus which matched that of the fusing beryllium and helium nuclei.

In the 1950s carbon nuclei had not yet been investigated very thoroughly, so Hoyle managed to persuade one of his collaborators in California to determine whether carbon had the properties he predicted, namely, that the carbon nucleus should have a resonance of 7.7 million electronvolts, a measure of the energy involved in nuclear reactions. The Californian collaborator experimentally measured a resonance value of carbon of 7.65 million electronvolts, an incredibly close fit. Without this particular resonance no carbon would have been made in the stars and we would not be here. 'Nothing', remarked Hoyle later, 'has shaken my atheism as much as this discovery.' In fact for carbon to survive there has to be a further requirement – that it does not capture a fourth helium nucleus too quickly and be turned into oxygen. This particular step is not that efficient, but if the oxygen nucleus was only 1 per cent different, all the carbon would disappear rapidly into oxygen, and then on into other elements as soon as it was made. So it is the very finely tuned properties of atomic nuclei that have led to the ratios between carbon and oxygen which we observe and that have rendered life possible.

The exact strength of the weak nuclear force is important for the emergence of life in a number of other ways. For example, the weak force regulates the hydrogen/helium ratio known as η (the Greek letter *eta* – scientists love calling things by Greek letters). Eta is the ratio of baryons to photons in the universe. Baryons are a class of fundamental particles that include the proton and the neutron. Photons are quanta ('small packets') of radiation. The value of η, the baryon-to-proton ratio, turns out to be extremely small. There is only one baryon for every billion photons (viz $\eta = 10^{-9}$). This tiny value for η is also required for the smooth development of galaxy formation and if its value was greater than 10^{-7} or less than 10^{-12}, then galaxy formation would not occur.

The weak force is also important in the way that the heavier elements are distributed around the universe. If the elements synthesized in stars simply remained there, then they would not have the opportunity to become synthesized to even heavier elements in other stars, nor to end up in planets like our own. Supernovae only occur, as outlined above, because of the precise strength of the weak force. When a star explodes, the neutrinos provide a critical burst of energy that causes the matter in the star to be distributed around the galaxy. The weak force determines how the neutrinos interact with other forms of matter. So if the weak force was weaker than it is, then neutrinos would not interact significantly with other forms of matter at all, and the heavy elements in the exploding star would not be distributed. However, if the weak force was stronger, then neutrinos would become trapped in the core of the star, since their interaction with other matter would be so tenacious, and the heavier elements such as carbon would then not be dispersed around the galaxy.

The presence on our planet of elements, such as carbon and oxygen, which are essential to life as we know it, is therefore due to multiple coincidences in the fundamental forces which define the properties of matter, and all of these forces have to be *exactly* right in order for these elements not only to exist, but to end up in the right place to make life possible.

A cosmological question which has received considerable attention, but which awaits clear resolution, is whether the universe is destined to expand 'for ever', until it finally runs out of energy in a final 'heat death' in which all stars are extinguished as they run out of fuel, or whether the force of gravity will eventually cause all the matter of the universe to stop expanding and then to implode in a 'big crunch' scenario. The basic concept is a familiar one: if we throw a javelin up into the air, it will continue to rise until the force of gravity finally brings it back to earth. But if we threw the javelin extremely hard with a sufficient 'escape velocity', it would then break free of the earth's gravity and take off into space. The big bang generated such an enormous 'escape velocity' that all the matter in the universe has been moving apart ever since. But is the total gravity exerted within the universe sufficient to bring it all back together again?

At present we do not know if we are living in an 'open universe', in which matter will continue expanding, or whether it is a 'closed universe', destined to end up in a 'big crunch'. The constant which determines the outcome is known as the relative density parameter Ω (the Greek symbol for the letter *Omega*). The value of Ω is the present matter density of the universe divided by the critical matter density of an 'escape velocity'. If omega is less than one then the universe will expand for ever; if it's greater than one then the universe will eventually collapse. Calculations show that if the density of the universe was more than about five atoms per cubic metre, then this would be sufficient density to eventually bring the expansion of the universe to a halt. This is an extremely low density, much lower than can be achieved in any vacuum that we can generate on earth. But in fact if all the matter in all the stars in all the galaxies were dismantled and then spread evenly throughout space, all this matter would provide only about one-tenth of an atom per cubic metre, fifty times lower than the critical number of five atoms. This is a density so low that we can barely conceive it. It is equivalent to taking the atoms in a single snowflake and spreading them around in a volume the size of the earth.

So at first glance, the chances of there being sufficient matter in the universe to cause it to cease expanding appear rather slim. But there are good reasons for thinking that Ω is not as small as one-fiftieth, as suggested by working it out from the density of the known matter in the universe. It is thought that only about 10 per cent of every galaxy is visible. The remaining 90 per cent is made up by so-called 'dark matter'. The presence of the dark matter can be inferred from the gravitational effects that it exerts on the movement of galaxies, and even of clusters of galaxies. Without the presence of such dark matter clusters of galaxies would fly apart. Dark matter may consist of small faint stars ('brown dwarfs'), so small that their density is insufficient to ignite their nuclear fuel; dark matter could be the remnants of massive stars hidden away in black holes; or dark matter could be made up of exotic particles such as neutrinos.

But it has been calculated that even if we take on board all this inferred dark matter, it will still bring Ω only up to a value of 0.2, just one-fifth of the critical density needed to stop the universe expanding. Whether there is enough matter out there to 'bridge the gap' between 0.2 and 1.0 remains to be seen. But what is already known is that the value of Ω is critical for the emergence of the universe. It is possible to calculate the value of Ω at a time of 10^{-2} seconds after the big bang. At that moment 1 minus Ω was less than or equal to 10^{-15}. This is an incredibly finely tuned value. If we had picked a value of Ω of 2.0 at a time when the universe was only one-hundredth of a second old, then the universe would have continued to expand for a further 0.02 seconds before collapsing into a hot fireball just 0.06 seconds after the start of the big bang.[8] During the history of this briefest of universes the temperature would never have dropped below ten billion degrees. At the same one-hundredth of a second after the big bang, had the value of Ω been 0.1 instead of 2.0, then the present universe would have had such a low density that there would be only about one proton in every million cubic kilometres, so there would be no stars or planets. In either scenario the universe would be dead and lifeless.

It has sometimes been suggested that the creator is wasteful since he has made a universe that is so vast and so old. But the fact is that the universe needs to be this vast and this old in order for elements such as carbon and oxygen to be synthesized, and so for life to be able to emerge. The present size of the universe is related to its present age multiplied by the speed of light. If the universe were the size of our solar system, then it would last for only about one hour. Even if the universe contained as much as a single galaxy, such as our own Milky Way, containing 'only' 10^{11} stars, instead of the 10^{12} galaxies that it in fact contains, it would have expanded only for about a month. 'No observers could have evolved to witness such an economy-sized universe.'[9] Our universe needs its 10^{22} stars in order for us to exist. As we look up into the night sky, the vastness of its myriad stars and galaxies should remind us of how small we are, but the fact remains that without those stars we would not exist. The only universe that we can exist in is one that is 'big and old, dark and cold'.

The cosmological constant is perhaps the most finely tuned constant of all those which define the properties of our universe. Known by the Greek capital letter lambda (Λ), the meaning of the cosmological constant itself has changed somewhat since Einstein first introduced it into his equations as a long-range repulsive force in order to 'balance the books' so that the universe would end up a static universe. A decade later Einstein realized that by doing this he had completely missed the key point that we are living in an expanding universe – the fact was masked by the introduction of the constant – later describing the introduction of Λ as 'the biggest blunder of my life'. Today the cosmological constant Λ is viewed more as a fixed background vacuum energy density in the universe. This means that as the expansion of the universe tends to slow down, due to the decreasing gravity interactions between the matter of the universe as it becomes more disperse, so this is compensated for by the opposite 'vacuum force' tending to speed the expansion up again. Contrary to all expectation, it seems that the universe is currently expanding at about twice the speed of its escape velocity, the speed required to overcome the gravitational pull of all the matter in the universe.[10] The implication is that we are living at rather a special time. In the past the universe was more dense and its expansion rate was slowing down. In the future the expansion rate may well speed up yet more as it comes under the influence of a new sort of matter that has been called 'quintessence'. Quintessence is related to the cosmological constant Λ and has negative gravitational mass. This means that its 'gravity' pushes things apart rather than draws them together.

Measurements of Λ are possible because distant galaxies are viewed by cosmologists as they were in the distant past, due to the immense time that it takes light to reach our radio telescopes. The formation of distant stars and galaxies can be observed even though these events took place before the emergence of our own solar system. It seems that the expansion rate of the universe started increasing when the universe was 60 per cent of its present size. Curiously this release of the gravitational brake on the expansion of the universe coincided with the time when life emerged on earth. But in our present context the greatest fascination is with the extreme fine tuning of Λ, which Hawking describes as the most accurately determined constant in nature because it is observed to be 10^{121} times smaller than would be predicted by quantum gravity theory alone. There are strong anthropic reasons why the value of Λ should be so small, since if it were a fraction larger the formation of galaxies would have been prevented. Like Ω, the cosmological constant is a key determinant of the present size and age of the universe.

So what?

A common response to the finely tuned physical and cosmological constants that make life feasible is to point out that our observation of them is not surprising since, had they not been as they are, life would not have evolved and so we would not be here to observe them. This 'so what?' response is closely linked to the suggestion that multiple universes may exist and we happen to be in the universe in which life is feasible. The multiple universe assumption underlies the treatment given to the anthropic principle by writers such as Barrow and Tipler[11] and Martin Rees.[12]

As early as 1951, well before the finely tuned physical constants essential for the properties of the universe had been thoroughly described, a British zoologist called Charles Pantin suggested the idea of a multiple universes scenario:

> The properties of the material universe are uniquely suitable for the evolution of living creatures. To be of scientific value any explanation must have predictable consequences. These do not seem to be attainable. If we could know that our own universe was only one of an indefinite number with varying properties we could perhaps invoke a solution analogous to the principle of Natural Selection, that only in certain universes, which happen to include ours, are the conditions suitable for the existence of life, and unless that condition is fulfilled there will be no observers to note the fact. But even if there were any conceivable way of testing such a hypothesis we should only have put off the problem of why, in all those universes, our own should be possible?![13]

The sting in Pantin's comment lies in the tail. But for the moment let us consider the first part of his argument, which has received considerable attention during the past few decades.

Several different mechanisms have been proposed for the way in which multiple universes may have been generated. For example, Hawking has proposed that quantum fluctuations within a mother universe could give rise to baby universes that are connected by a worm-hole to a black hole in the mother universe. As the black hole evaporates the worm-hole is severed, creating an independent and separate universe.[14] An idea popular in the 1970s was that our own universe could pass through many cycles of expansion and contraction, generating multiple universes in the process. However, the proposal lost its appeal with the realization that the mass in the universe may prove insufficient for even one 'big crunch' to occur.

It should be noted that these and other suggested mechanisms (which are many) can only be tested for their mathematical consistency. The presence or absence of other universes cannot, by definition, be detected, since if empirical data were cited that had a bearing on their existence, the availability of such data would itself prove that the proposed alternate universe was not really distinct from ours at all, and so not alternate. For example, there is a barrier imposed by the speed of light which means that there is a natural horizon from beyond which signals could not yet have reached us. Speculations about multiple universes belong strictly to the realm of metaphysical speculation. Though such speculations are entertaining, it is important to keep in mind that scientific data for their existence do not exist, and quite probably cannot exist for the reason noted above.

The idea of multiple universes also provides a 'catch-all' kind of explanation which usually proves rather unproductive for science. Rodney Holder comments that the 'Many worlds theories remind me of the argument put forward by Christian fundamentalist Philip Henry Gosse in the 19th century to reconcile a literal reading of Genesis with geology. Nature is really cyclical and God created it instantaneously in mid-cycle – Adam with a navel, trees in Eden appearing to be 50 years old, fossil birds with half-digested food in their mouths! Anything can be explained on this basis and no observation can possibly contradict the theory. Many worlds theories are equally sterile.'[15]

But let us accept for the sake of argument that multiple universes do exist. It is often maintained that if a very large series of multiple universes is generated, then sooner or later one will occur in which the cosmological constants are finely tuned in such a way as to render the evolution of life possible. Surprise, surprise, we then evolve to observe it. However, such an argument depends on universes being generated by the random selection of cosmological constants akin to the throwing of dice. It is such a scenario that gives rise to Pantin's picture of a 'natural selection' of universes for those in which life is possible, an argument pursued in more graphic detail by Daniel Dennett.[16] Nevertheless there can be no assurance that the generation of such putative universes is random. It might be that there are certain deep physical principles, of which we are entirely ignorant, which determine that multiple universes will only have properties within a certain range of parameters. There is no guarantee, then, that even an infinite number of such universes would ever generate conditions conducive for life. If you roll two dice the range of numbers you can obtain on a single throw is between 2 and 12. Placing this analogy in the context of cosmological constants, if 50 per cent of all cosmological constants need to be in the range 2–12, but the remaining 50 per cent in the range 13–17, in order to generate a viable universe in which life is possible, then it does not matter how many times you roll the dice, the values are loaded against you ever achieving such a goal.

Even if we accept the wildly speculative premise that there are multiple universes, and then the even more wildly speculative suggestion that the properties of such universes are generated randomly until such time as one is achieved in which life is possible, such speculations barely count as an argument against purposeful explanations for the existence of conscious life. The reasons for this are twofold. First, the fact remains that if there is an ensemble of universes in which conscious life is feasible, rather than a single universe, then there is still the task of inferring to the best explanation the reason(s) for the existence of such an ensemble. Why should such an ensemble of universes exist in one or more of which conscious life is feasible? Scientists still like asking questions, even when they have moved into the realm of the strictly metaphysical. Hawking's questions about the present universe might equally well be directed to an ensemble of universes: 'What is it that breathes fire into the equations and makes a universe for them to describe? The usual approach of science of constructing a mathematical model cannot answer the questions of why there should be a universe for the models to describe. Why does the universe go to all the bother of existing?'[17] Change the word 'universe' to the plural in this quote and the questions still remain essentially the same. For the believer in God as creator of the universe, the concept of God as creator of an ensemble of universes instead is no big deal, though from a scientific perspective the believer might wish to be cautious before giving thanks to God for something that might in any case not exist. Our present universe has the great advantage that at least we know it exists. Judging by the enthusiasm of some for multiple universes you might even imagine from their writings that other universes have a greater reality than the one we in fact know about. Plenty of scope for wishful thinking here.

A second type of argument has also done much to undermine the potency of the multiple universe scenario as an argument for critiquing anthropic principles. Although at first sight the core of the anthropic principle appears to be based on circular reasoning – 'isn't it remarkable that we exist in a universe which is finely tuned for own existence' – closer analysis reveals that there is a genuine mystery in our existence which requires explanation. This point has been drawn out by William Craig,[18] who emphasizes that in fact 'we should be surprised that we do observe basic features of the universe which individually or collectively are excessively improbable and are necessary conditions of our own existence'. In practice we do not know what the odds are that the cosmological and physical constants that define the properties of the universe are what they are. But we do know that their numerical values, at least in theory, might have been vastly different from what they are.

To illustrate Craig's argument, imagine an intelligent but malevolent team of research scientists who visit earth from outer space. To carry out their research they kidnap an accountant and inform him that he must enter the national lottery using a single ticket each time over the coming ten consecutive weeks and that unless he wins the national lottery for every one of these ten weeks he will be struck by a mysterious disease that will kill him within a day. The visitors from space then leave, promising to return when the experiment is completed. The accountant is much depressed by the unbelievably high odds stacked against his survival. For the sake of argument we will say that the chances of winning the national lottery in each round are one in ten million. But, amazingly, he wins the national lottery the first week and so survives to buy his ticket again the second week, and his extraordinary run of luck then continues so that he wins the national lottery in each of the ten consecutive weeks. The chances of this happening are one in ten million multiplied by itself ten times (i.e. one in 10^{60}), a very small chance indeed. But it happened and the accountant survives in an amazed and shocked state to tell the tale. The visitors from outer space then return to interview the accountant, informing him that he should not be surprised that such an unlikely event happened for, had it not, he would not have been alive to observe it. But the accountant protests that his amazed and shocked state is perfectly justified, for it is unheard of for one person to win the national lottery in two consecutive weeks, let alone ten. And the accountant is surely correct in his protest. Something very remarkable and unexpected has happened which demands an explanation.

A further illustration may help to clarify this point. Let us suppose, for example, that a gambler in London needs to achieve a series of ten heads in a row by coin tossing to win a million pounds, a series that he then immediately achieves. The gambler is initially very surprised (and pleased) at this run of heads, but then remembers that there are probably hundreds of gamblers around London tossing coins, so someone has to be the one that has a run of ten heads. But although the gambler is correct in thinking it likely that some gambler in London that night will have a run of ten heads, he is wrong in his common-sense view that he personally should not be surprised in obtaining a run of ten heads, since the presence of other gamblers tossing coins in London makes the probability that he will get ten heads in a row no different. The chances remain at one in 1024. This fallacy has been called by Ian Hacking the 'inverse gambler's fallacy'. The fact that other coin tossing sessions may be going on in parallel, at other times, or that they occur in the same place spread out in a long temporal sequence, makes no difference to the odds of one person getting ten heads in a row, which remain stubbornly at one in 1024. If we further imagine that the gambler is killed unless the result is ten heads, the fact of the gambler still being alive does not explain why he got ten heads in a row – the probability of this unlikely event remains at one in 1024.[19] What requires explanation is not that the gambler is alive and therefore observing something but rather that he is not dead.

How strong are anthropic arguments?

We have argued so far that the universe has some very unusual properties that render conscious life possible – and that those properties are not unusual because we observe them but because the physical constants that make them unusual could, presumably, have been otherwise. Postulating a multiplicity of universes, even if accepted as a possibility, fails to address the central mystery of our existence as conscious observers within an ensemble of universes in which ours is both understandable and mathematically elegant. 'The enormous usefulness of mathematics in the natural sciences', the physicist Eugene Wigner comments, 'is something bordering on the mysterious and there is no rational explanation for it. It is not at all natural that "laws of nature" exist, much less that man is able to discover them. The miracle of the appropriateness of the language of mathematics for the formulation of the laws of physics is a wonderful gift which we neither understand nor deserve.'[20]

At the least such anthropic arguments are an embarrassment to atheism. Atheism provides no explanation for why the universe, as Hawking puts it 'should bother to exist'. As Sartre was fond of pointing out, the fundamental philosophical question is why something exists rather than nothing. And our finely tuned universe is not just any old 'something', but contains within it a planet full of people who postulate theories about cosmology and the meaning of the universe, who write poetry, fall in love, build socially complex societies, and who believe in justice, freedom, ethics and the reality of good and evil. Atheism provides no insights into why such an odd entity should exist, nor for why the physical parameters of the universe should be so precisely correct as to make the existence of such an entity possible. If atheism is true, then it can be argued that the emergence of conscious life and personhood within this vast and largely, if not completely, impersonal universe remains a total enigma. For scientists who look for explanations for things, this is not a very satisfactory position to adopt. One is reminded of Steven Weinberg's much quoted comment from his best selling book on cosmology, *The First Three Minutes*:

> It is almost irresistible for humans to believe that we have some special relation to the universe, that human life is not just a more-or-less farcical outcome of a chain of accidents reaching back to the first three minutes [of the Universe's existence], but that we were somehow built in from the beginning... It is very hard to realize that [the entire earth] is just a tiny part of an overwhelmingly hostile universe. It is even harder to realize that this present universe has evolved from an unspeakably unfamiliar early condition, and faces a future extinction of endless cold or intolerable heat. The more the universe seems comprehensible, the more it also seems pointless.[21]

The problem with this credo is that it is stating as if certain what remains the central point of the discussion – whether there is some kind of overall purpose to the universe, the existence of which is consistent with its finely tuned structure. The first sentence is clearly false – if the belief was irresistible there would be less atheists. Furthermore, because a belief is attractive does not imply that it is mistaken. But the main problem comes in the final sentence of the quotation from Weinberg. In science if some useful data are collected that fail to fit within the current theory, it is time to throw out the theory and try another one. If atheistic presuppositions are unable to render data coherent, which on other grounds appear comprehensible, this may be a hint that the starting presuppositions are incorrect.

It has to be admitted, however, that whereas anthropic arguments are clearly an embarrassment to atheism, the degree to which religious inferences can be drawn directly from the physical properties of the universe is quite limited. And to be fair to Weinberg, his hostility to anthropic arguments appears to stem partly from the exaggerated claims that are occasionally made for them. 'When physicists use the word "God" mostly they are just using it in a metaphorical sense', Weinberg suggests. The bulk of God-talk in physics is little more than a metaphor for 'the laws of nature, the principles that govern everything'. 'I rather grieve when physicists use the word, because I do think one should have some loyalty to the way words are used historically, and that's not what people have historically meant by "God".' 'What the word has meant historically', Weinberg says, 'is an interested personality. But that's not something we are finding scientifically.'[22]

It may well be, as Weinberg proposes, that some physicists in their bestselling books have tended to use the word 'God' as little more than a useful way of describing the mathematical principles that underlie the laws of nature. However, there are certainly other physicists who use the word in its historical sense (at least historical in the sense that their cultures have been historically influenced by the Christian notion of a personal God). Irrespective of these quibbles, the main problem with Weinberg's line of argument, insofar as it attempts to draw prestige from science, is that it does not proceed in the way that scientific argumentation normally proceeds. As we noted in chapter 8, it is particularly the case with the 'big theories' of science, such as evolutionary theory in biology or big bang cosmology, that their appeal lies in the fact that they are inferences to the best explanation of large bodies of very different kinds of data. The theory of evolution was proposed because it provided a good explanation for the biological diversity that we presently observe. The theory itself evolved over many years and through many intellectual struggles, as Darwin's notebooks make clear. Evolution could not simply be 'read off' from the natural world in some obvious or common sense way, as if it were an obvious inference to the best explanation that was immediately apparent to any unprejudiced observer.

Clearly the idea of an all-powerful God, who chose to create a universe with particular properties such that conscious life would be possible, was not a theory postulated in quite the same way as a scientific theory. On the other hand, the style of reasoning which suggests that the properties of the universe are indeed consistent with such an idea is quite similar to the form of reasoning with which scientists are rather familiar. The data pointing to a series of remarkably finely tuned constants which have promoted the emergence of conscious life sit more comfortably with the idea of a God with plans and purposes for the universe than they do with the atheistic presupposition that 'it just happened'. It is intriguing to follow the writings of Paul Davies in this context. As noted in chapter 8, Davies is a physicist who has written widely on cosmology in general and on the anthropic principle in particular, commenting that 'I cannot believe that our existence in this universe is a mere quirk of fate... an incidental blip in the great cosmic drama. Our involvement is just too intimate.' In considering the coherence of the properties of matter that has made this possible, Davies reflects:

> The very fact that the universe is creative, and that the laws have
> permitted complex structures to emerge and develop to the point of
> consciousness – in other words that the universe has organised its own
> self-awareness – is for me powerful evidence that there is 'something
> going on' behind it all. The impression of design is overwhelming.[23]

The comments of Davies are particularly interesting because they probably reflect the furthest extent to which strictly anthropic reasoning can go, namely, that the odd physical properties of the universe at least point to 'something going on' behind it all. The astronomer Fred Hoyle's pathway out of atheism provides a similar example of the limits of anthropic reasoning. Hoyle's concept of a deity is of an impersonal intelligence: 'I believe', says Hoyle, 'that we are the emergence of software that has basically been designed by another intelligence, probably to represent itself. In a way, software is the soul.'[24] For scientists such as Davies and Hoyle, the impression of anthropic design in the universe is a clue to keep thinking and to keep searching for satisfying explanations.

But there is still a further point to make. If we leave now the arena of scientific data, and ask the wider question of whether the notion of a personal God – Weinberg's 'interested personality' – is consistent with a universe in which persons have evolved, and in which persons form relationships and communities, then the answer has to be in the affirmative. Whereas strictly anthropic reasoning may not move us beyond the position that Davies appears to advocate – 'there is something going on' – once we adopt a standard method of scientific reasoning, postulate a Big Theory, and then accept as data the whole gamut of human knowledge and experience to test it, including science but by no means restricted to science, then one can accept that the Christian notion of a personal God is highly consistent with what we observe. The personal God has plans and intentions for his universe and has ensured that the properties of the universe should be such as to bring about conscious observers who are able to come into relationship with him, thereby actualizing his intentions.

Using the broader question, 'What grand theories are the data consistent with?', we can in this way begin to sort through some of the 'grand theories' towards which anthropic arguments point us. For example, let us say that on anthropic grounds we become persuaded that 'something is going on' in the universe that cannot be encompassed satisfactorily by the idea that 'it just happened'. We could then further postulate that there is a powerful but abstract intelligence in the universe, the 'Force', which mediates coherence to the physical properties of matter. However, if we now start with this 'grand theory' and start asking 'consistent with' type questions, we soon encounter a problem. If the 'Force' is impersonal, why do we find persons within the universe? An abstract, impersonal universe might be more consistent with its source in an abstract, impersonal intelligence.

What is being argued in this chapter, therefore, is barely a WAP, more like a V-WAP – a 'very weak anthropic principle'. The V-WAP is an embarrassment to atheism, so that, in that sense, maybe it's not so weak – but it is certainly weak compared with the old natural theology. A V-WAP makes no attempt to derive the Christian doctrine of a personal God from the properties of matter, but it does act as a pointer to something going on in the universe. Things are arranged too amazingly just right for conscious life to emerge to believe that it was merely a giant fluke. Multiple universe scenarios just push the questions back one step – they do not remove the questions.

But if all a V-WAP can do is exclude atheism and generate curiosity about the universe, acting as a generator of speculations about its ultimate origins, a more traditional style of scientific argumentation can then be used to sort through the speculations to see which one fits the available data most coherently, provided no attempt is made to restrict the evidence allowed to scientific data alone. The speculations, or 'grand theories', about ultimate origins can be tested by the notion of 'consistent with'. Overall, the historical idea of God as an 'interested personality', as Weinberg puts it, comes out rather well from this reasoning process. The finely tuned physical and cosmological constants of the universe, together with the presence in the universe of conscious beings, are together clearly consistent with the notion of a personal God who has intentions for the universe that he has brought into being and continues to sustain.

Chapter 13

Impossible Events
A Critical Look at Miracles, Ancient and Modern

A miracle is a violation of the laws of nature; and as a firm and
unalterable experience has established these laws, the proof against
a miracle, from the very nature of the fact, is as entire as any
argument from experience can possibly be imagined.
David Hume, *Enquiry Concerning Human Understanding*, 1748

Miracles are things which never happen; only credulous people
believe they have seen them.
J.E. Renan, *Life of Jesus*, 1863

When such a thing happens, it appears to us as an event contrary to
nature. But with God it is not so; for him 'nature' is what he does.
Augustine (on miracles), *Literal Commentary on Genesis*, c. AD 391

There is nothing that God hath established in a constant course of
nature, and which is therefore done every day, but would seeme a
Miracle and exercise our admiration, if it were done but once; Nay,
the ordinary things in Nature, would be greater miracles than the
extraordinary, which we admire most, if they were done but once... and
onely the daily doing takes off the admiration.
John Donne, Dean of St Paul's Cathedral, London,
in a sermon given on 25 March 1627

I have witnessed many miracles during my career.
James Watson, 1990

In the spirit of David Hume, miracles are viewed by many scientists as things that simply do not happen. The topic is tainted with fake faith healers, weird claims that are never substantiated, bleeding statues of the Virgin, Hindu gods drinking milk and perpetual images of the incredulous crowd swayed by the religious sentiment of the moment. Altogether it is not a pretty sight. Since modernism dictates that science provides the ultimate criteria of what counts as knowledge and, since miracles cannot lie within the remit of scientific knowledge, therefore miracles do not happen.

In contrast, the postmodernist perspective accommodates miracles comfortably as valid expressions of groups or individuals within certain cultures undergoing particular experiences in particular historical contexts. The interpretation of their experience as a miracle may be entirely appropriate for their context, and the question that the scientist insists on asking – whether the purported event actually occurred – is deemed, if not irrelevant, at least impossible to ever know.

When some years ago the Anglican Church appointed a bishop of Durham who, according to newspaper reports, described the story of Christ's bodily resurrection as 'a conjuring trick with bones', the appointment naturally led to some debate in both the national and scientific press. Since many of the issues aired in that debate will be revisited in this chapter, it is of interest to quote a letter published in *The Times* newspaper, written at the time by six Fellows of the Royal Society and eight university professors of science, and then to read the vigorous rebuttal written by the then editor of *Nature* shortly afterwards. The letter to *The Times* read as follows:

> In view of the recent discussions about the views of Bishops on miracles we wish to make the following comments. It is not logically valid to use science as an argument against miracles. To believe that miracles cannot happen is as much an act of faith as to believe that they can happen. We gladly accept the Virgin Birth, the Gospel miracles, and the Resurrection of Christ as historical events. We know that we are representative of many other scientists who are also Christians standing in the historical tradition of the churches.
>
> Miracles are unprecedented events. Whatever the current fashions in philosophy or the revelations of opinion polls may suggest it is important to affirm that science (based as it is upon the observation of precedents) can have nothing to say on the subject. Its 'laws' are only generalisations of our experience. Faith rests on other grounds.[1]

Six days letter this letter was confronted by a *Nature* editorial, written under the nearest that this leading scientific journal ever comes to a banner headline, which contained a stinging refutation, of which the second section is reproduced below:

MIRACLES DO NOT HAPPEN
A group has invited trouble by claiming that science has nothing to say about miracles...

Nobody can sensibly complain that scientists of various kinds are often religious people of one persuasion or another, or quarrel with the conclusion of Berry *et al.* that the 'laws' of science are 'only generalisations of our experience' and that 'faith rests on other grounds'. But it is a travesty of something to assert that science has 'nothing to say' about miracles.

Take an uncontentious miracle, such as the turning of water into wine. This is said to have happened at a wedding feast, when the supply of wine was unexpectedly exhausted. The only published account has it that jars of drinking water were found to have been transformed into wine in the socially embarrassing circumstances that had arisen. The account is now firmly a part of the Christian legend, but that is not the same as saying it is the account of a phenomenon. Obvious alternative explanations abound. As scientists, the signatories would not have given a favourable referee's opinion of such an account for a scientific journal. And far from science having 'nothing to say' about miracles, the truth is quite the opposite. Miracles, which are inexplicable and irreproducible phenomena, do not occur – a definition by exclusion of the concept.

Ordinarily, the point would not be worth making. The trouble with the publication from Berry *et al.* is that it provides a licence not merely for religious belief (which, on other grounds, is unexceptionable) but for mischievous reports of all things paranormal, from ghosts to flying saucers.[2]

This editorial set in motion a debate on miracles that meandered on in the correspondence columns of *Nature* for several months afterwards, so providing a rich vein of argument and counter-argument on the subject.

What this exchange between an assortment of science professors and the then Editor of *Nature* at least minimally establishes is that there is certainly no monolithic view on miracles expressed by the scientific community as a whole, although it would probably be fair to say that the opening paragraph of this chapter, together with the *Nature* editorial, express something not far from the views of the majority. This chapter will, first, assess the arguments of Hume on miracles and then propose an understanding of miracles that is different from both Hume and *Nature*'s editorial but compatible with both science and a theistic understanding of the natural order. Whether and under what circumstances a miracle can ever be belief-worthy will then be assessed, and then finally the question of contemporary claims for the miraculous will be considered. The conclusion of this chapter is that there are indeed concepts of the miraculous that are hostile to science, but also that there is a view on miracles which can sit comfortably with science and that can even be nurtured by science.

Hume's arguments on miracles

Discussions of miracles have often been labelled 'footnotes on Hume', and no consideration of the topic would be complete without an assessment of his influential arguments. The aim of this section is not to provide an exhaustive treatment of Hume, an exercise carried out many times by others,[3] but rather to summarize the pith of Hume's arguments so that they can be assessed in light of contemporary views of scientific and religious knowledge.

David Hume (1711–76) was a Scottish philosopher and historian who became best known for his 'attempts to introduce the experimental method of reasoning into moral subjects', the subtitle of one of his best-known works. Hume was a dominant influence on empiricist philosophers of the 20th century. Hume's influential essay 'Of Miracles' is a mere twenty pages tucked away in his *Enquiries Concerning Human Understanding* (1748).[4] It is written against a background of deistic arguments that had been thoroughly aired in the decades before 1748, and in fact there is little that is completely novel in Hume's essay.[5] Its long-term impact seems to stem more from the fame that Hume eventually achieved, the brevity of the essay, and the way in which it summarized so succinctly arguments that had been circulating more loquaciously in the writings of others.

To understand the backlash expressed in some of the deistic writings against miracles, it should be remembered that many of the Christian natural philosophers who were active in the emergence of modern science in the 17th century also promoted a strongly evidentialist role for the biblical miracles. Just as scientific theories should be supported by empirical data, it was maintained, so the veracity of the biblical accounts were supported by appeals to their descriptions of miracles. Thomas Sprat, secretary of the Royal Society, and its first historian, even referred in 1667 to miracles as God's 'Divine Experiments' which he used to assert the biblical truths without which 'no age nor place had been obliged to believe his message'.[6] This notion, that miracles provided powerful evidence in support of the truth of Christianity, was commonplace in the late 17th century and it was against such ideas that the deists reacted. Many of them, including to some extent Hume in his essay 'On Miracles', were not so much concerned to attack miracles per se as they were to demonstrate that miracles could not be used as arguments for the historical claims of Christianity.

Hume's essay is separated into two parts. The first part summarizes his a priori arguments for the impossibility of miracles, referring to those arguments which, Hume thought, ruled miracles out of court as a matter of principle. Hume's opening gambit is to underline the point that experience 'is our only guide in reasoning concerning matters of fact'. However, experience is not an infallible guide as nature is not always predictable and neither do we know all the possible range of natural causes. Therefore 'A wise man... proportions his belief to the evidence.' The observer should balance up the type of evidence that is available to him and establish a kind of certainty–uncertainty scale in which beliefs will vary in their position on the scale depending on the available data. In presenting this argument, Hume also reiterated his notorious critique of cause–effect relationships, maintaining that the connection between causes and effects is not something that is strictly observable, but rather causal connection is something that 'we feel in the mind' as the product of the 'imagination' due to the 'constant and regular conjunction' of causes and effects. Fortunately scientists have always cheerfully ignored this particular Humean argument since cause–effect relationships are precisely what they spend their time investigating.

Nevertheless the fact of our *experience* of the 'constant and regular conjunction' between events (even though, according to Hume, we cannot actually see causes in themselves but only the succession of events) plays a key role in Hume's argument as to how testimony should be evaluated. All evidence based on testimony is founded on past experience and we will tend to believe that testimony to the degree that it accords with our own previous experience of events, or the extent to which we can make an analogy between the alleged event and our own experience:

> The reason why we place any credit in witnesses and historians, is not
> derived from any connexion, which we perceive a priori, between
> testimony and reality, but because we are accustomed to find a
> conformity between them.[7]

Things are therefore much more probable when we have observed them to happen frequently in conjunction. Hume therefore goes on to propose that:

> A miracle is a violation of the laws of nature; and as a firm and
> unalterable experience has established these laws, the proof against a
> miracle, from the very nature of the fact, is as entire as any argument
> from experience can possibly be imagined.[8]

A 'law of nature' for Hume was something in which our own experience had established a regularity of concurrence between events to such a high degree that not a single occasion had ever been observed when this concurrence was lacking, so giving rise to this high level of certainty based on 'firm and unalterable experience'. Given such a high level of certainty, Hume then argues that no level of testimony would in practice be sufficient to persuade him that a miracle could in fact happen, since the probability that the testimony of the event is mistaken will always be so much higher than the probability that a 'law of nature' has been violated.

So part 1 of Hume's essay intends to establish that in principle no testimony under any circumstances would be sufficient to establish the veracity of any miraculous event. Natural laws are built on uniformity of experience which, for Hume, is what makes something into a 'proof'. Miracles are alleged violations of natural laws. Therefore the 'proof' of natural laws always outweighs the 'proof' of the testimony relating to any particular alleged miracle. The wise person should always choose to believe what has the greater weight of evidence. Therefore miracles can never be believed by a wise person.

Part 2 of Hume's essay is dedicated to a posteriori arguments, those that depend on assessment of evidence after it has already been presented. The arguments that Hume collects in part 2 would have been familiar to anyone of that era who had followed the deistic debate and there is no hint of novelty in this section of Hume's essay. Hume presents four arguments:

First, witnesses to alleged miracles are all incompetent, or suffering from delusions, or are not beyond suspicion in some other way, so we cannot really trust them.

Second, people love gossip and so there is an innate human tendency to pass on stories that become exaggerated in the telling.

Third, miracles 'are observed chiefly to abound among ignorant and barbarous nations' and were not often observed among educated people, so rendering them intrinsically unlikely.

Fourth, rival religions claim miracles which oppose each other and so they in effect cancel each other out.

Hume then provides a number of historical or contemporary examples of miracles, including the stories, well known at the time, of the alleged miracles of healing connected with the tomb of the François de Paris in France. As Hume freely admits, the evidence for such healings having occurred was really rather strong, so his conclusions on the matter are therefore quite informative:

Where shall we find such a number of circumstances, agreeing to the corroboration of one fact? And what have we to oppose to such a cloud of witnesses, but the absolute impossibility or miraculous nature of the events, which they relate? And this surely, in the eyes of all reasonable people, will alone be regarded as a sufficient refutation.[9]

In other words, since miracles cannot happen, even though the witnesses are both vocal and numerous, nevertheless their combined testimony cannot possibly accumulate to provide sufficient weight to believe that miracles have occurred.[10]

A critique of Hume

It should be at once admitted that Hume made some very reasonable points, particularly in his discussion of miracles in part 2 of his essay. The deistic critique of contemporary accounts of miracles was in many cases as valid in the early 18th century as it is centuries later. Alleged contemporary miracles do often seem to be surrounded by an atmosphere of hysteria in which witnesses appear gullible or unduly influenced by the psychological influences of a crowd. There is also no doubt that stories can easily become exaggerated upon being re-told, not least via a media machine which knows that the unusual or the quirky sells well in mass markets. The value of a scientific training is that it can instil an innate and healthy scepticism that is not easily fooled by the latest claim to some extraordinary event having occurred. The rise of postmodernism with its New Age expressions in contemporary culture has created an atmosphere in which some people will apparently believe almost anything. A scientific education can act as a valuable corrective to this blurring between fact and fiction.

Some other points made by Hume in part 2 also have some validity. Competing miraculous claims made by different religions can be beamed around the world within hours. But the idea that reports of miracles are restricted to the uneducated or to people living outside Western cultures is certainly incorrect. Beliefs in alleged contemporary miracles flourish in the midst of secularized Westernized societies. The expectation, so prevalent a century ago, that such ideas would die out with the spread of education, has not materialized.

Nevertheless all the points that Hume summarizes in part 2 of his essay are relatively trivial compared with the central claim of part 1, echoed so vigorously by the *Nature* editorial 250 years later, that 'Miracles do not happen'. Can we be that sure?

Can the laws of nature be violated?

The term 'law of nature' was not used systematically in its modern sense until the early 18th century and was therefore a recent term in the era in which

Hume developed his arguments. As surveyed in chapter 4, there is compelling evidence to support the idea that the Christian belief in a lawgiving God nurtured the emergence of the modern scientific movement. God was the guarantor of the reproducible behaviour of matter in defined circumstances, and it was this that made science possible. The notion of 'laws of nature' had, in its earliest usage, theological overtones of God the lawgiver. These laws were 'out there' in the reality demonstrated by the properties of the physical world, waiting to be discovered by the investigator.[11]

Interestingly, perhaps due to his repudiation of its theological basis, Hume's concept of natural law was not typical of his time, since he believed that 'laws' reflect the ordering process of the human mind rather than any intrinsic properties of matter per se. Such a view was entirely consistent with Hume's argument that the connections between events which regularly occur are something that 'we feel in the mind' as the product of the 'imagination' due to the 'constant and regular conjunction' of causes and effects. So as the philosopher Antony Flew has pointed out, Hume was in a particularly weak position to argue that miracles are impossible because they violate the laws of nature, since for Hume laws implied no necessity. A view similar to that of Hume was put forward much later by Ernst Mach who maintained that the 'laws of nature' are nothing more than 'concise abridged descriptions' of reality. 'This is really all that natural laws are,' claimed Mach, useful summaries of empirical data that reflect the propensities of the human mind to catalogue phenomena in a tidy manner.[12]

Yet scientists have generally ignored the views of both Hume and Mach – in the realist tradition they have continued to insist that the laws described by science are not mere epiphenomena of tidy human minds but reflect properties that are intrinsic to the physical properties of matter. Nearly all scientists have therefore, knowingly or unknowingly, aligned themselves with the theologically understood tradition of 'scientific laws' as being rooted in the properties of the world that they investigate. Even though they may no longer believe in a lawgiving God, they are inheritors of a tradition established by theistic natural philosophers. Stephen Hawking is well within this tradition when he points out that 'It would be completely consistent with all we know to say that there was a Being who is responsible for the laws of physics.'[13]

Paul Davies has also drawn attention to the way in which the understanding that contemporary scientists have of 'the laws of nature' still has some remarkable resonances with the attributes of God as described by Christians.[14] Laws are, first, *universal* and apply 'everywhere in the universe and at all epochs of human history'. Second, they are *absolute*; whatever changes may occur in the observers, laws are unchanging. Third, laws are *eternal* in the sense that they are rooted in the mathematical structure of the universe. And finally they are *omnipotent* in the way that all natural phenomena lie within their scope. At times Davies expounds such an exalted view of 'the laws of nature' that it seems that it is the laws themselves that have the quality of the deity, whereas theists would see the laws having such qualities because they reflect the consistent creative actions of God the lawgiver.

It should also be emphasized that our contemporary understanding of the term 'laws of nature' is considerably different than it was in the early 18th century. As already discussed in chapter 8, a 'critical realist' view of 'scientific laws' sees them not as rules that the natural world obeys, like traffic laws, nor as entities waiting to be discovered, but as constructs of the scientific community expressing the pith of a large number of observations and experimental results that can be expressed as a limited number of broad generalizations. Such 'laws' can never be divorced from the theoretical presuppositions that underlie them, nor from the experimental contexts in which they have been developed. One day they will be modified to better approximations by new observations.

In contrast the science of Hume's time still remained strongly influenced by the Baconian notion that if only a sufficiently large number of observations could be made that were largely in accordance with each other, then one could proceed to infer some broad generalization or 'law' based on such an accumulation of facts. Although such an inductive process is by no means dead as a valid part of the scientific process, it has nevertheless been radically modified by the realization that a single piece of Popperian opposing evidence can call a scientific 'law' into question. However many white swans you observe, the theory that 'all swans are white' can readily be undermined by the observation of a single black swan. Laws are descriptive not prescriptive.

Hume's idea that a large accumulation of uniform human experience adds up to such a quantitative weight that no counter-evidence can possibly overthrow it, is therefore not a very useful one. If we believed his argument then we would never believe that we had been dealt a perfect bridge hand, since the odds against it are 1,635,013,559,600 to one (although this has in fact happened). The mere accumulation of further instances that things generally happen in the same way is no guarantee that they will not happen differently in the future under different circumstances and in a different context. One convincing well-attested counter-example can bring crashing to the ground a scientific theory built, until that moment, on an impressive edifice of 'uniform human experience'. Hume failed to realize that the 'wise and intelligent person' bases his or her beliefs on evidence rather than probability. Evidence is weighed not added. Evidence for repeatable phenomena is not necessarily greater than for events which have happened only once. This is why the cutting edge of so much contemporary science is characterized by the investigation of pieces of data that do not fit comfortably within currently held paradigms. 'Uniform human experience' is scientifically boring – the exceptions are much more interesting.

To preserve the pith of the older concept of 'law of nature', but at the same time take on board the insights of the more recent sociology and philosophy of science, some philosophers have attempted to make a distinction between 'laws of nature' and 'law-statements'.[15] 'Laws of nature' refer to the unchanging properties of the natural world, with an understanding of law such as that expounded by Davies, whereas 'law-statements' are the attempts made by the scientific community to describe those laws accurately. The former are unchanging, whereas the latter change as science advances. Had Hume placed his 'violation of the laws of nature' argument within the framework of the former understanding, with its prescriptive understanding of laws, then it might have had more punch. The concept of 'violation' only makes sense when a law is prescriptive, whereas the notion vaporizes when laws are merely descriptive. But at this stage it is difficult to take the discussion further without a prior examination of whether Hume's definition of a miracle, which we have accepted for the purpose of this initial critique, is in any case valid.

What is a miracle?

Hume has frequently been taken to task for missing out certain critical elements in his definition of miracles. Certainly he uses the term in a way which ignores aspects of its meaning that were well known and accepted in early-18th-century society. Hume's usage of the term was clearly self-serving to his argument, but also so successful that it is not uncommon to find even today books defending Christian miracles which, ironically, utilize Hume's definition.

In contemporary usage the term 'miracle' has splintered into a myriad different meanings in common speech. Newspapers commonly use the term to refer to very rare events. A headline in the paper speaks of 'Miracle town's fourth jackpot', referring to the fact that four winners from the town of Grimsby in England had won the national lottery. People who are saved from death in remarkable circumstances often refer to their experience as 'miraculous'. Richard Dawkins opines that 'events that we call miracles are not supernatural, but are part of the spectrum of more-or-less improbable natural events. A miracle, in other words, if it occurs at all, is a tremendous stroke of luck. Events don't fall neatly into natural events versus miracles.'[16]

Curiously, given Dawkins's antipathy for religion, the last sentence in this quote brings us closer to an understanding of the miraculous as espoused by the Bible. Although the biblical understanding of the term may be less widespread now than in Hume's day, it is nevertheless the one which, I think, can most readily be reconciled with contemporary views of scientific knowledge.

To unpack this understanding, an alternative definition of a miracle may be in order: 'A miracle is an unusual or extraordinary event brought about by a god within a significant historical–religious context.' Such a definition is much closer to the understanding of the term 'miracle' as it has been used down the centuries, and is important both in what it excludes as well as what it includes. First, it excludes Hume's idea that a miracle is defined as the 'violation of a law'. Such an idea is certainly alien to the Judeo-Christian tradition which underlies the biblical writings. There is, of course, no concept of scientific law per se in the Bible. Nevertheless ancient observers were perfectly aware that virgins do not give birth and that dead people do not rise from the dead. They were not stupid. The Bible's understanding of creation, as already noted in chapter 10, is of a God who not only generates order out of disorder 'in the beginning' but also actively sustains every aspect of that created order at every moment. In this view, there is nothing that scientists can describe which is not part of the nexus of the secondary causes that comprise God's actions. The Bible therefore makes little attempt to distinguish between the 'natural' and the 'supernatural' for the simple reason that the terms are alien to biblical thought – in fact the word 'supernatural' is not even mentioned in the Bible. The idea of 'supernature' in contrast to 'nature' is a more recent invention. As Augustine expressed it: 'Nature is what God does.' This does not mean that the biblical writers were not convinced that at various times and places unusual events occurred, only that they perceived all events without exception to be ultimately caused by God for particular purposes.

Imagine, for example that a well-known author has written forty-nine novels featuring the same central hero and with the same basic type of plot in each one. Each novel is distinctive enough so that the interest of the reader is maintained. Indeed, it is the familiarity with the characters and backcloth of the novel that provides half the fun – the challenge of the author is to take the familiar ingredients but then mix them in different ways to make a fresh and intriguing story. Finally the author comes to write novel number fifty. But this one is different. The same hero and ingredients are present, but they are woven into such a different kind of story that it stands out from all the others – perhaps it is the novel in which the author has finally decided to kill off the series by causing the hero to die under tragic circumstances. By definition it is novel fifty which is unique, and this is the one that the author's readership of millions remembers best even though they might have difficulty in recalling the difference in plot between novel number ten and number thirty-three. Novel number fifty is not distinctive because the author has changed but because the purposes of the author for novel number fifty were different from all the rest.

An intriguing example of this point is found in the biblical account of the crossing of the Reed Sea ('Red Sea' is a possible alternative translation – see below) by the Israelites.[17] Moses stretches out his hand over the sea 'and all that night the Lord drove the sea back with a strong east wind and turned it into dry land'. There is little doubt that the Israelites viewed their consequent rescue from the pursuing Egyptians in miraculous terms. But the text is explicit in providing what we might call a 'natural' explanation for the rescue. Our images of events at this point may become over-influenced by old Hollywood blockbusters or by somewhat newer Hollywood animations. A geographically more astute picture is provided by Professor Arie Issar of the Ben-Gurion University of the Negev who has carried out extensive research on the climatology and topology of this region.[18] Coming out of Egypt the Israelites meet the 'Sea of Reeds', the correct translation of the Masoretic Hebrew term *Yam Suph* (*Yam* means 'sea' or 'coast'; *Suph* means 'reeds': how this term began to be translated as 'Red Sea' remains obscure). This means that reeds grew along its shores, most likely fed by a source of fresh or brackish but not seawater, which in turn was fed by a rainfall estimated at 100 mm per year compared with the present annual rainfall of about 50 mm. 'Sea' in ancient Hebrew means any large body of water. This particular 'Sea' likely consisted of the huge swamps and lakes, locally called *sabkhas*, which at that time spread along the region through which the Suez Canal now passes. The swamps were surrounded by reeds. Issar suggests that as the people escaped through the labyrinth of *sabkhas*, the war carriages were coming after them and at the same time the *Khamseen*, a heavy dust storm blown by a strong east wind, 'made the sea dry land', most probably by means of a hardened crust that formed a layer of gypsum. This would have been sufficient to allow the fleeing Israelis to find a way through, 'with a wall of water on their right and on their left', whereas the heavy chariots of the Egyptians went straight down through the gypsum crust and were lost in the swamps. The Hebrew word 'wall' may be used as a metaphor for protection, and so refers not to waters heaped up on either side (à la Hollywood) but to the protecting effects of the surrounding *sabkhas*. Issar points out that the hot dry *Khamseen* from the east in this region is frequently followed by a low pressure heavy rainstorm from the north-west that floods the area. Stuck in the *sabkhas* with their chariots deep in mud, the narrative tells us that 'at daybreak the sea went back to its place'.

Since the Israelites knew the climate well, they were familiar with dust storms in general and no doubt with the *Khamseen* in particular. Nevertheless they had no hesitation in assigning their deliverance to God's direct action, albeit mediated by the 'natural' processes of climatic changes.[19] The narrative recounting the various plagues which the Egyptians experienced prior to the flight of the Israelites from Egypt also describes in some detail the succession of natural disasters which fell upon them – plagues of frogs, flies, locusts, extreme weather conditions and so forth, but equally they saw these events as God's 'miraculous signs'.[20]

In providing such examples (and there are many more) it should not be thought that all the biblical accounts of miracles have potential scientific explanations. Many do not. Everyone knows that water does not suddenly change into wine, nor thoroughly dead people return to life again, either now or in the first century.[21] The emergence of modern science has not made any difference to the way in which such claimed events are perceived. In fact a 1st-century rural Palestinian community, much more used to handling dead bodies than are most people in contemporary Western societies, would no doubt have been amused by the idea of rich 21st century cryofrozen Californians waiting for the day when their corpses could be revived. The idea of corpse revival belongs more to the 21st century than it does to the 1st century.

The Bible is by no means crammed full of miraculous accounts as people sometimes think who have not read it. The miracle accounts are largely restricted to the events surrounding the exodus of the people of Israel from Egypt, with a mere scattering of other reported miracles through the Old Testament, and then to those associated with the life of Jesus and the birth of the early church in the New Testament. It is possible to place the miracles on a spectrum, stretching at one end from those for which the Bible itself provides causal explanations (as in the crossing of the Reed Sea), through to those at the other end of the spectrum for which no scientific explanation can be imagined, even in principle (such as the resurrection of Jesus). Along the spectrum are located other claimed miracles which might, in principle, be amenable to scientific descriptions, but for which we simply do not have enough information to be sure. For example, some miracles of healing might be open to psychosomatic interpretation. Even the virgin birth of Jesus has received attention as an event that might, in principle, be amenable to a scientific explanation, due to recent advances and observations in our understanding of potential ways in which asexual reproduction might occur in humans.[22] The virgin birth debate provides a good example of the way in which a claimed miracle can move, in a single generation, from a status of 'absolutely no scientific explanation imaginable, even in principle' to the rather different status of 'a scientific explanation is at least imaginable, even though we can never know for sure due to the non-reproducibility of the event'.

The purpose in citing such examples is to underline the fact that biblical thought makes little distinction between remarkable events that, as we would say now, have scientific explanations and those, like water turning to wine, that defy any current scientific explanation. All are seen as reflecting the will and actions of God for particular people at particular times in particular contexts. What mainly draws attention to their status as miracles is not that they are necessarily events that have never happened before, or which may never happen again, but that they are unusual signs of God's actions in particular circumstances. Their designation as a miracle is not based on their law-defying properties but on the way in which they stand out as focused and particular instances of God's will expressed in a way made unusual by its timing or by its rarity (or occasionally uniqueness) as a phenomenon.

This understanding of the miraculous is illustrated very clearly by the biblical words and terms that the writers of the Hebrew and Greek texts have chosen to bring out the various nuances of 'wonders' or the 'miraculous'. Three words in particular are used most frequently. The Greek word *terata* and its Hebrew equivalent *mopheth*, translated as 'wonders', are frequently used to draw attention to events that are so remarkable that they are remembered.[23] The term focuses more on the amazement produced in the witnesses of the event rather than on the specific purpose of the event. The Greek word *dunameis*, from which we derive our word 'dynamite', is translated as 'acts of power' or 'mighty works' and emphasizes the biblical conception of miracles as the result of the operation of the power (*dunamis*) of God, who is perceived to be the source of all power. Whereas the word *terata* points to the impact the miracle made on the observer, *dunameis* points to its cause. The third word, which is the most critical of all in understanding how the Bible views miracles, is the Greek word *semeion* or 'sign'. This is the word that is particularly used in John's Gospel when describing the miracles of Jesus. Miracles are only meaningful in a particular context as they point to something beyond the event itself. A *semeion* emphasizes the ethical end and purpose of a miracle. The intention of a *semeion* is to reveal aspects of God's character – especially his power and love. As Monden comments: 'Miracles are set apart from natural happenings not by the fact that they demonstrate a manifestation of power, but rather because their unusual nature makes them better fitted to be signs.'[24]

The words *terata*, *dunameis* and *semeia* (plural, 'signs') are not the only words used by the New Testament to refer to the miraculous, but they are the most commonly used and are frequently mentioned together in the same breath.[25] Remarkably the word *terata* ('wonders') is always combined with one or the other, or both together, emphasizing the reluctance of the biblical text to dwell on the merely marvellous character of the miracles. In the Hebrew text of the Old Testament equivalent words are brought together to express the same sets of meanings, so that as Moses looks back to the exodus of the Israelites from Egypt, characterized by the plagues and crossing of the Reed Sea as discussed above, he reminds his people, 'With your own eyes you saw those great trials, those miraculous signs and great wonders.'[26] One of the miracle narratives in the life of Jesus provides a good example of the way in which the various threads of the New Testament's understanding of the miraculous are woven together in a single tapestry. A paralytic man is healed by Jesus (the narrative is in Mark 2:1–12). Everyone was amazed by the miracle (v. 12) – so the sense of *terata* is brought out, although the word itself not used. The miracle demonstrates God's power (v. 12), for at Christ's command the paralytic 'got up, took his mat and walked out in full view of them all', but it was also a *semeion*, for the whole purpose of the miracle was to demonstrate that 'the Son of Man has authority on earth to forgive sins' (v. 10).

Therefore in the Bible it is the *context* and *purpose* of the miracle that draws most attention – the 'significant historical–religious context' – an understanding in stark contrast to Hume's concept of miracles as isolated anomalies which violate the laws of nature. Miracles are made plausible by their coherence, by the way they fit into an overall picture or narrative. Of course such coherence is not sufficient alone to establish their veracity, but it is certainly necessary. In contrast, scientists who discover isolated anomalies in their data would do well to check their instruments for accuracy, or else to pursue the anomalies by further experimentation until they can be incorporated satisfactorily into a broader set of generalizations. Any other strategy is mere intellectual laziness. The PhD student who announces that his latest experiment defies the laws of physics and is therefore a miracle will not be treated sympathetically, although if the anomaly is reproducible, there is certainly room for excitement as it is precisely via such anomalies that scientific advances are likely to be made.

A key difference in emphasis between science and history is that science often, though not always, investigates phenomena that can be reproduced, provided the experimental conditions are carefully controlled. The 'not always' category includes sciences such as geology and evolutionary biology that construct historical sequences of events based on a broad range of data. Historical research, in contrast, analyses events that are unique in their context, their rationale and their outcomes. Military battles may have certain common themes running through all of them, nevertheless each one is unique in its historical context. Biblical claims to miracles draw our attention to this same vital ingredient of historical context. East winds may blow all night not that infrequently, even perhaps to the extent of affecting one's ability to traverse the Reed Sea, but an east wind that rescues you from imminent death to be carried out by an irate pursuing army has the kind of particularity that justifies its description as a 'sign and wonder', especially when it comes just after fervent prayer for deliverance.

The importance of the 'significant historical–religious context' for our definition of a miracle can be further illustrated by an imaginary contemporary account of a miracle.[27] Suppose that a woman called Mrs B has suffered from severe rheumatoid arthritis for a period of many years, during which time she has been treated by five different specialists but without success. The progress of the disease appears to be medically intractable and she is permanently in a wheelchair. The specialists have all kept impeccable medical records. Mrs B is unable to walk properly, make a fist or even grasp her husband's hand. Her pain is often unbearable. Mrs B then attends a religious gathering at which she is prayed for by its leader using the name of the god of that religion before a congregation of more than 500 people. Moments after the leader has prayed for her healing, Mrs B is in fact healed and walks from her wheelchair. Her pain has gone, she can make a fist, grasp her husband's hand and walk with ease. The next day Mrs B is examined by her five specialists who find to their amazement that the inflammation in her joints has suddenly subsided and that the degradation of her joint cartilage has been reversed. The panel of five continue to check Mrs B's health annually over the next ten years and there is no recurrence of the arthritis, so Mrs B's condition represents a cure and not merely a remission.

The reason for providing such an example is not, at present, to discuss whether such healings do in fact ever occur (see further on this below) but to draw attention to the importance of religious context and timing in the interpretation of such claimed miraculous events. Claimed miracles are not weird anomalies randomly scattered throughout the experience of a population, or through natural phenomena, but are restricted to particular contexts and happen for particular historical reasons.

It is for this reason that the *Nature* editorial, cited above, rather misses the mark when it expresses concern that if people – especially scientists – believe in miracles, then this will promote the acceptance of all kinds of weird and wonderful things, such as belief in 'all things paranormal, from ghosts to flying saucers'. First, the Bible's understanding of miracles has no need for the paranormal since, as we have noted, all events, without exception, from the very mundane to the very extraordinary, are perceived as being due to the continued will and actions of God. There is nothing paranormal about timely east winds blowing at the right moment.

Second, from a historical perspective, *Nature*'s editorial claim has already been tested by means of the beliefs of a previous generation and found not to be the case. The natural philosophers of 17th-century Europe were nearly all Christians who believed in a God who occasionally carried out miracles. Some may have believed that such miracles were confined to the biblical era, whereas others may have believed that God continued to carry out miracles very occasionally. But the general consensus of belief was in a miracle-working God. At the same time, however, it was precisely during this era that the concept of 'natural laws' began to emerge as reflections of the working of a lawgiving God. Far from belief in a miracle-working God stimulating belief in a plethora of miracles, the early natural philosophers were generally quite opposed to such a move, partly no doubt influenced by the opposition of the Reformation thinkers against the tendency of the medieval church to proliferate the 'miracles' associated with religious relics. The emphasis of the religious writings of the early natural philosophers is much more on God as law-provider, much less on the possibility of contemporary miracles, although the biblical miracles were often cited as evidence for the truth of Christianity, the precise point against which Hume was to react so strongly later on.

The third reason why the *Nature* editorial misses the mark is because it invokes a Humean concept of miracles that ignores historical and religious context. The world of ghost-busters is about as far from the highly theological framework of the biblical miracles as you can get. Fourth, I know many scientists who believe that the biblical miracles were real historical events but I cannot think of any who display the kind of gullible belief in flying saucers and the paranormal to which the *Nature* editorial alludes. Far from it – they tend to be a rather hard-nosed and sceptical bunch of individuals who have little time for weird and wonderful phenomena. The increase of belief in such things has much more to do with the popularity of New Age mysticism.

Science and miracles

The sceptic may wish to object at this point that we have redefined the miraculous in such a way as to make it slightly more acceptable than it was within a Humean definition – but nonetheless the core problem remains. Although some of the biblical miracles refer, no doubt, to events for which the biblical narrative itself provides an explanation, in many cases there is no obvious scientific explanation, even in principle. Water does not change into wine, nor do dead people return from the grave. As the *Nature* editorial suggests: 'As scientists, the signatories would not have given a favourable referee's opinion of such an account for a scientific journal. And far from science having "nothing to say" about miracles, the truth is quite the opposite. Miracles, which are inexplicable and irreproducible phenomena, do not occur – a definition by exclusion of the concept.'

Can claimed miracles be investigated using scientific methods? It all depends on the type of claim being made. If a statue of the Virgin Mary is claimed to bleed regularly at lunchtime every Friday, then at least there is a reproducible phenomenon that can be investigated using scientific techniques: if the red liquid does not contain haemoglobin then it is not blood. If the statue of a Hindu god regularly oozes milk at the precise time of the god's festival, then the appropriate controls and tests can readily be carried out. If there is a claimed miraculous healing, as in the example provided above, then it can be fully investigated by a team of doctors, provided medical records pertaining to the period prior to the claimed healing are available.

Contemporary claims to the miraculous such as these are relatively easy to investigate. Science can contribute not only procedural approaches and techniques to examine such claims but also a healthy dose of scepticism. But what about claims to miracles in the past? What, for example, about the New Testament accounts of the miraculous, in particular associated with the life of Jesus – claims concerning events that never normally occur, such as blind people suddenly receiving their sight, crippled people beginning to walk, Jesus commanding a storm to cease and it does so, Jesus rising from the dead, and so on. A common response has been to interpret such accounts within a purely symbolic or metaphorical framework. Turning water into wine then becomes a powerful metaphor for the way in which Jesus was inaugurating a new spiritual kingdom. The resurrection becomes a symbol of the way in which the spirit of Jesus lives on in the lives of his followers, just as the spirit of Shakespeare lives on through his writings. But it has to be admitted that this is a fudge. The gospel narratives leave us in no doubt that those who witnessed these events believed them to have actually happened. As a matter of fact, it is claimed, the tomb was empty and, what is more, the grave-clothes that had been tightly wound round the body of Jesus during the embalming process were lying undisturbed in the empty tomb.[28] The fact that in their context the miracles were presented by the gospel writers as *semeion*, signs, does not imply that they were *only* signs. Remarkable events can take place and they can be signs as well. That is the stance of the gospel writers.

It is difficult to see how science per se can be anything other than agnostic when considering such miraculous claims. Science is particularly good at investigating phenomena that are potentially reproducible and which can be investigated under controlled experimental conditions. Science is also quite able to build up a picture of historical chains of events to explain the present properties of the physical world, as in geology or evolutionary biology, since the present status of rocks and of animals provide the primary data from which the historical investigation can be launched. However, when the claim is of a unique and unusual historical event, then science has no investigatory tools to be useful in such circumstances, any more than science is of much use when investigating any other particular historical event that depends entirely on written eye-witness reports. The argument of the *Nature* editorial that 'the signatories would not have given a favourable referee's opinion' of miraculous accounts submitted to a scientific journal is therefore irrelevant, for the simple reason that historical claims are not published in scientific journals, and for the best of reasons. Science and history are distinct disciplines with their own distinct criteria for what counts as scientific or historical knowledge, respectively.

Despite Hume, science is in no position to rule miraculous claims out of court. Science can propose generalizations of increasing sophistication that incorporate a very broad spectrum of types of different data, but scientists remain observers of what in fact happens, of what is in fact the case. Scientists are meant to be empiricists not dogmatists. It is difficult to avoid the conclusion when reading Hume's short but pithy essay that his a priori argument simply begs the question. For if 'a miracle is a violation of the laws of nature', which have in turn been established by 'unalterable experience', then clearly there can be, by prior definition, no experience that anyone could have that would change such a conclusion. It is not for nothing that Hume's a priori argument has often been accused of circularity.[29] But in practice scientific endeavour shows no such signs of being a closed book in which we know ahead of time what we may or may not observe. What differing attitudes towards miraculous claims frequently reveal are not different beliefs about the scope and nature of scientific enquiry but about the underlying metaphysical assumptions that are brought to the discussion. The atheist who believes that the universe is essentially a closed system in which all matter 'obeys' deterministic laws is unlikely to be very open to the possibility that the material world occasionally behaves in an unexpected way. The *Nature* editorial expresses the view so well: 'Miracles, which are inexplicable and irreproducible phenomena, do not occur – a definition by exclusion of the concept.' In contrast, the theist who believes that there is a creator-God who is actively sustaining every aspect of the created order will not be surprised if God occasionally chooses to act in an unusual way in a particular historical context. This same theist will be hostile to the suggestion that God is profligate in bringing about such events, because it is the general consistency of God in creation which generates the possibility of the scientific enterprise itself and which thereby enables at least one type of miraculous event to be readily identified as such.

Ironically it is therefore the stance of the atheist that is likely to lead to a closed mind when it comes to the question of evidence for claimed miraculous events ('miracles do not occur by definition'). As Hume stated so clearly, even though the evidence in his own day for the alleged miracles of healing connected with the tomb of the François de Paris in France was extremely strong, nevertheless 'the absolute impossibility... of the events' was counted as a sufficient refutation for their actual occurrence. In contrast the theist can remain both cautious and sceptical, but still afford to keep an open mind about such matters and examine the evidence on its own merits, not eliminate it by appeals to prior metaphysical presuppositions. There seems to be little doubt that in this instance it is the stance of the theist that best exemplifies the general attitude which one hopes characterizes the scientific community as a whole, namely, an openness to the way the world actually is, rather than the attitude more typical of some forms of Greek rationalism, which already knew the answer before the investigation had even begun. The comments of Burns are interesting in this context, when he observes that Humean thought was actually alien to the British empirical tradition, being much closer to continental philosophical scepticism: 'Hume is much more to be regarded as the advocate in England of attitudes and approaches to philosophy which had been rejected by the leading empiricist scientists of the late 17th century than as the systematizer of the authentic latent tendencies of the English empiricist tradition.'[30]

In making this point it is not of course being suggested that theists are possessors of some kind of magical neutrality that makes them uniquely able to distinguish wheat from chaff when it comes to assessing miraculous claims. No individual is devoid of assumptions nor of expectations during the process of investigation, be it historical or scientific. There is no presupposition-free high-ground from which anyone can pontificate. Scientists are only too aware of the assumptions that they bring to their assessments of scientific theories. Sometimes their prejudices blind them to 'seeing' data that are contradictory to their favourite hunch, whereas data that support their position are eagerly seized upon. Such insights should encourage an attitude of critical and open enquiry.

The way in which scientists assess the 'big theories' of science may also help to elucidate the process whereby Christian theists view the miracles of, for example, the New Testament. These would not normally be assessed in isolation but would be seen in their historical context as supporting, illustrating and expounding the life and ministry of Jesus as a whole. So, even though the weight of evidence for any particular New Testament miracle might vary with respect to the evidence for another, the tendency of the theist would be to accept the miracles as a 'package deal': given that God is creator and that Jesus is portrayed as the Son of God, it is thereby not so surprising that the entry of God's Son into the world is accompanied by remarkable events that demonstrate God's control over the whole created order, illustrate his love, and reveal his purposes for the world in general and for humankind in particular. All of these events are associated with *semeion*, or signs, that embed the miraculous accounts into the overall aims and purposes of Christ's ministry. The miracles are as intrinsic to the New Testament account as natural selection is to Darwinian evolution. Rip them out and there is little of interest left of Jesus of Nazareth. That is why theists tend to accept the whole package of the New Testament account, or not at all, because it is the historical and theological account as a whole that makes sense to theists, just as the 'big theories' of science are appealing because they incorporate satisfactorily so many different bits of data. As Corduan comments: 'A crucial consideration is that beliefs about many matters of fact are embedded within larger worldviews, and evidence for miraculous events is evaluated in terms of broader conceptual schemes.'[31]

Non-theists sometimes express the concern that if miracles occur, such as the changing of water into wine, which run counter to all we know about the normal properties of matter, then disruptions would be introduced into the natural order that would render the scientific enterprise impossible due to our inability to know 'what nature might do next'. In addressing this concern it is worth emphasizing the rarity of the type of miracles that are being surveyed in this chapter. There has only ever been a single occasion when water was allegedly turned into wine and there has been only a single claimed case of a resurrection from the dead when the person involved (Jesus in this case) did not die again. Other claimed miracles involving events that do not conform to the normal properties of matter are equally rare. Such rare events are simply not detected nor collected as part of the data-gathering exercise that plays such a key role in the establishment of the broad generalizations that describe the properties of matter which can be labelled as 'laws of nature'. The number expressing the ratio between the 'normal event' ('water does not turn into wine') and the 'unusual event' ('water turns into wine') is so enormously high that for all intents and purposes there is no need to worry about the unusual events having any impact on the construction of scientific theories.

Can we know that miracles have occurred?

If science per se cannot help us very much with our enquiry as to whether miracles have occurred, such as those described in the Bible, is there a different line of approach that might be more fruitful? Are we left with two sets of people talking past each other because their prior metaphysical commitments cause them to lean in two quite different directions? It is beyond the scope of this book to examine the historical status of the biblical documents, or to delve with any depth into the important question of how sceptical (or not) we should be in our investigation of historical events. Nor do we have space to do justice to the moral and ethical criticisms that have been levelled against claimed miracles (such as 'Why doesn't God heal everybody?' and 'Why doesn't he eliminate all suffering?').

In the present context two preliminary points may be made. First, the scientific enterprise does not encourage an ultra-sceptical attitude towards the investigation of historical claims. There is a sense in which all empirically based scientific literature represents a series of historical reports written by witnesses of what took place under particular circumstances and conditions. As mentioned in chapter 8, it was the perceived trustworthiness of the gentlemen of the early modern scientific movement, such as Robert Boyle, that stimulated the progress of science since these represented a category of people who were already recognized by society as reliable witnesses and therefore likely to report the truth about the outcome of their experiments.[32] When Boyle wrote his *Sceptical Chymist* he invoked witnesses of unimpeachable reputation to testify to what they had seen. His experiments on mercury, published in 1675, were witnessed by Henry Oldenburg and by 'the noble and judicious' Lord Brouncker. The sceptic in the *Sceptical Chymist* plays the role of the examining magistrate.[33] The alarm and despondency with which the contemporary scientific community responds to claims of scientific fraud, still thankfully rare, underlines just how deeply the community still depends on scientists telling the truth about their observations. The scientific enterprise therefore encourages the notion that people can and do make observations that they report accurately. It is such reports, published as papers in the scientific literature, that act as the basis and launching pad for further scientific progress. Scientists see no need to practise a paranoiac form of suspicion in which people are thought to lie upon every possible occasion. In fact, no society could possibly survive for long based on such a supposition, let alone scientific practice. All societies operate on the assumption that most people tell the truth most of the time, and it is this assumption which also makes historical research feasible. The historian does not have to lapse into gullibility to maintain that it is safest to assume that someone is recounting the truth unless there are good historical grounds for thinking otherwise. Long ago Augustine made a similar point when he wrote:

> I began to realize that I believed countless things which I had never seen or which had taken place when I was not there to see – so many events in the history of the world, so many facts about places and towns which I had never seen, and so much that I believed on the word of friends or doctors or various other people. Unless we took these things on trust, we should accomplish absolutely nothing in this life.[34]

Interestingly there is a sizeable group of contemporary historians mounting a rigorous attack against the postmodernist notion that historians cannot establish the veracity of historical events 'beyond all reasonable doubt' but can only reconstruct history in a postmodernist mould according to their own favourite form of discourse. For example, Richard Evans, Professor of Modern History at the University of Cambridge, comments that:

> It is not true to say that historians are 'not too concerned about discrete facts'. On the contrary, whatever the criteria for the facts' selection, the vast majority of the historian's efforts are devoted to ascertaining them and establishing them as firmly as possible in the light of historical evidence... interpretations really can be tested and confirmed or falsified by an appeal to the evidence; and some of the time at least, it really is possible to prove that one side is right and the other is wrong.[35]

The attitudes of the scientific community resonate much better with this stance than with the postmodernist idea that the central role of the historian is merely to create historical meanings.

A second preliminary point that is worth making is that it seems reasonable that the moderately sceptical inquirer will wish to have more weighty evidence for the historicity of claimed miracles before believing that they happened than for events that are less out of the ordinary. It is expected that historians will utilize non-miraculous forms of explanation in their enquiries whenever possible, for the simple reason that the vast majority of historical data require nothing different. It is the rarity and unusual nature of the claimed miraculous event that demands the greater weight of evidence.

Antony Flew has suggested that it is actually impossible to know that miracles have taken place historically.[36] Flew's argument may be summarized by the following statements:

1. The believer in miracles investigates history in order to demonstrate the actuality of miracles.
2. Only if we assume that the regularities of the present were also true of the past can we hope to know anything historically.
3. In order to gain knowledge of the past, the critical historian must employ his present knowledge of what is possible/impossible, probable/improbable.
4. A miracle is a highly improbable, practically impossible, event.
5. Therefore, miracles cannot be established historically.

Points 1–3 are in principle non-controversial, although in his writings on point 3 Flew seems in danger of confusing the analogy between the present and the past as a *basis* for studying the past, with the *properties* of the past itself. This point has been illustrated by Geisler by drawing attention to the way in which the Search for Extra-Terrestrial Intelligence (SETI) programme has been established. SETI is based on the assumption that a single message from space will reveal the existence of intelligent life elsewhere in the universe. 'For even if the object of pursuit is the reception of only one message, nevertheless, the basis of knowing that it was produced by intelligence is the regular conjunction of intelligent beings with this kind of complex information. So, while knowledge of the past is based on analogies in the present, the object of this knowledge can be a singularity.'[37]

Still in the context of point 3, it should also be pointed out that historical enquiry may establish that certain perfectly normal and 'this-worldly' events are well supported by the evidence, and yet if the evidence taken as a whole is considered in its context, the only satisfactory conclusion may be that a miracle has occurred, based on an inference to the best explanation. It is not miracles per se that are investigated by the historian but rather the evidence that is used as a basis for the interpretation that a miracle has occurred. For example, the evidence for the bodily resurrection of Jesus involves no forms of evidence that are in principle disallowed by Flew's point 3 since the data under examination involves an empty tomb, grave-clothes lying in a heap, the recognition of the physical presence of a familiar person, and so forth, types of observation that are thoroughly familiar to the contemporary experience of the investigating historian. There is nothing particularly extraordinary about an empty tomb – it was in any case presumably empty before the body of Jesus was placed there. The type of evidence sifted by the historian in considering an alleged miracle is not therefore any different in principle from the type of evidence considered in any other historical enquiry.

The real problem with Flew's position, however, comes with his understanding of *why* a miracle is a 'practically impossible' event, as summarized in point 4. Flew maintains that when the evidence for miracles becomes so strong that we start to believe that the claimed event has actually occurred, then, since miracles are impossible, it cannot be a miracle at all but must have some natural explanation. Miracles are thus viewed by Flew as anomalies that are the result of unknown scientific laws, resulting in the argument that:

> Our sole ground for characterizing the reported occurrence as miraculous is at the same time a sufficient reason for calling it physically impossible. Contrariwise, if ever we became able to say that some account of the ostensibly miraculous was indeed veridical, we can say it only because we know that the occurrences reported were not miraculous at all.[38]

But this is a Humean question-begging argument if ever there was one! Flew tries to exclude by definition what the whole discussion is in fact about – whether miracles have actually happened. Of course if the miracle ceases to be a miracle, by definition, as soon as the evidence for it looks convincing, then the conclusion of point 5 is hardly surprising – of course miracles do not happen; how could they? Flew also fails to distinguish here between what is logically impossible and what is historically impossible. Married bachelors are impossible because the phrase implies a contradiction of terms. But historical possibility or impossibility ought to be defined in terms of historical evidence, not in terms of prior metaphysical commitments.

Rather than hedging critical enquiry around with all kinds of prior metaphysical commitments in the spirit of Hume and Flew, which make it difficult to examine evidence with an open mind, it is possible that the answer to the question: 'Can we know that miracles have occurred?' may emerge most fruitfully by using legal models as ways of evaluating whether or not it is reasonable to believe that a particular miracle has taken place.[39] The aim of legal reasoning is to establish beyond reasonable doubt that an event has or has not occurred. The legal profession has developed over centuries a set of meticulous criteria for distinguishing truth from error. These criteria are particularly relevant for investigating claimed miracles – since miraculous claims depend on the reliability (or otherwise) of witnesses, they involve claims about what in fact took place, and so specialize in the weighing of evidence, and they also include consideration of the counter-claims that the purported events did not occur. Hume himself expressed the point well when he stated that 'The ultimate standard, by which we determine all disputes, that may arise concerning them (i.e. judgments arising from testimony), is always derived from experience and testimony.'[40] More recently a law professor has commented: 'The advantage of a jurisprudential approach lies in the difficulty of jettisoning it: legal standards of evidence develop as essential means of resolving the most intractable disputes in society.'[41] Furthermore, it represents a type of reasoning that everyone in society is obliged to accept. We are all subject to the dictates of legal reasoning whether we like it or not. The critical consideration of evidence in legal reasoning as a methodological approach for investigating miracles also has the great advantage that it downplays the role of prior presuppositions when pursuing a critical enquiry. As already emphasized, to pretend that these play no role at all would be to exaggerate. But it is noticeable that the debate on miracles that Hume generated, and which philosophers like Flew have continued, has tended to get bogged down in circular arguments and question-begging prior commitments to philosophical positions that have excluded the possibility of miracles by means of prior definitions. Since the aim of legal procedures is to determine whether an event in fact occurred, irrespective of its intrinsic likelihood or unlikelihood, the rigour of legal reasoning provides a refreshing alternative to the sterility of such debates. And the gathering and critical assessment of data, the construction and testing of hypotheses, together with the final conclusions about what is in fact believed to be the case, are all past-times which are congenial to the scientific temperament. It is no accident that legal and scientific ways of thinking about things have much in common: both are directed towards the goal of establishing what happened, not the rather different goal of promoting what we think ought to have happened.[42]

Can miracles count as evidence for religious truths?

The main reason why Hume wrote his *Essay on Miracles* was to demonstrate that miracles could not be used as arguments for the historical claims of Christianity. As mentioned above, such an evidentialist role for miracles was popular among the natural philosophers of the 17th century and beyond. That the miracles of Jesus played, to some extent, such an evidentialist role in the context of the original generation of people who first witnessed them is not in doubt. In the very early preaching of the church, the apostle Peter proclaimed that 'Jesus of Nazareth was a man accredited by God to you by miracles, wonders and signs, which God did among you through him, as you yourselves know.'[43] Likewise the apostle Paul wrote robustly to the early church at Rome that Jesus 'was declared with power to be the Son of God, by his resurrection from the dead'.[44] Accounts about the miracles of Jesus were so widespread in 1st-century Palestine, then an occupied state within the Roman empire, that the Jewish leaders expressed concern that the Roman authorities would react unfavourably: 'Here is this man performing many miraculous signs. If we let him go on like this, everyone will believe in him, and then the Romans will come and take away both our temple and our nation.'[45] In another place John's Gospel also reports that 'while he [Jesus] was in Jerusalem at the Passover Feast, many people saw the miraculous signs he was doing and believed in his name'.[46] Nevertheless in the very next sentence John comments: 'But Jesus would not entrust himself to them, for he knew all men'. There is therefore an ambiguity about the evidentialist role of the miracles even in the context of the New Testament accounts themselves. The miracles of Jesus are portrayed as arousing wonder and drawing attention to Jesus as someone with divine powers, but at the same time Jesus shows no hesitation in criticizing those who remained in disbelief despite witnessing the miracles, or who thought that his miraculous powers might bring them personal gain. Miracles per se were no guarantee that belief would invariably follow: 'Even after Jesus had done all these miraculous signs in their presence, they still would not believe in him.'[47] Jesus also refused to perform miracles on request as if his mission was to provide entertainment for curious onlookers.[48] On one occasion Jesus even pointed out that if his listeners refused to listen to the prophets that God had already sent, such as Moses, then 'they will not be convinced even if someone rises from the dead'.[49]

There is therefore no support in the Bible for the idea that miracles provide some kind of knock-down proof for establishing the divinity of Jesus, even for those who witnessed his miracles for themselves. At best they could provide significant support for the claims of Jesus and the veracity of the message of the early church. At worst their *semeion* content could be completely missed and they could prove a distraction, playing a role only as entertainment, or for their curiosity value, or as a way of achieving personal wealth or power.

Of course when Peter stood up to preach to the people about the 'miracles, wonders and signs, which God did among you' he was able to add the important phrase 'as you yourselves know'. The miracles of Jesus were current knowledge with which his listeners were already familiar. Even though they may not each have witnessed a miracle individually, they nevertheless most probably had friends and neighbours who had witnessed such events. But we are now living nearly 2,000 years later in a different place in a different culture and we are dependent on the accurate transmission of eye-witness reports over the intervening years. Can the same miracles still play an evidentialist role under such changed circumstances?

One initial ground-clearing point is first necessary. Our definition of miracles has required that they represent 'an unusual or extraordinary event brought about by a God within a significant historical-religious context'. This raises a fairly obvious objection. If one does not believe in any kind of God anyway, then how is it possible to believe in a miracle according to this definition? Fair point. The sceptic may wish to point out that once you believe in a God who has the potential to perform miracles then you are already half way to believing in at least the possibility that a miraculous event may have occurred. Also a fair point. We cannot strictly argue from a belief in miracles to a belief in God because belief in miracles implies belief in God anyway. We are back to the concept of a 'package deal'.

Is there any way round this apparent circularity? I think there is.[50] For example, the atheist may become so impressed by the fine tuning of the physical laws of the universe, as discussed in the previous chapter, that s/he begins to establish the prior probability that the rational actions of God provide an inference to the best explanation for the existence of such a remarkable order. Given the probable existence of God, a probability derived on the basis of non-historical considerations, s/he may then surmise that it is possible that such a being might choose to produce a revelation that demonstrates his purposes for humankind, a revelation that might be confirmed by miracles. When a candidate revelation is then actually examined and found to fulfil the expectation that it be accompanied by well-attested miracles, this supports the claim that the revelation is authentic. This process therefore involves a kind of thought experiment in which the probability of God is mooted on grounds other than any evidence that miracles themselves may or may not provide, and is then kept open as a possibility while the evidence for the miraculous claims is being assessed.

Such a process of thought is familiar to any scientist active in research. There is the possibility that a complete set of data could be interpreted within a theory quite different from the one currently favoured by the research community. The distinctly different presuppositions of this rival theory are then floated in sophisticated thought experiments to determine whether the 'dataset' can be more satisfactorily explained by the new theory. This exercise may in itself cause the investigator to lean more towards the novel theory and, at the same time, may suggest critical experiments that will provide further data sufficient to decide clearly between the rival theories. If the results are decisive, the scientist will end up believing a different theory than before. This represents no sudden 'conversion' to the new theory but a gradual shift from one theory to another, in which 'what if?' thought experiments have played an important role.

An example that illustrates at least part of this process is provided by the acceptance of plate tectonic theory by geologists in the 1960s. By that time the evidence for continental drift was very strong despite the fact that no one could explain a dynamic theory of the forces responsible. The proposal of the mechanism of plate tectonics incorporated data that were already available and made it more believable as part of a larger story, as it could now be understood (at least in principle), how the movements of continents had actually occurred in relation to each other. This type of acceptance of data by its incorporation into a convincing theory is a familiar story in the history of science.

Thus even though belief in miracles per se can, in principle, provide no evidentialist support for belief in God, since the two are so linked together, the sceptical but open-minded investigator can nevertheless bring to their enquiry an openness to the possibility that God has brought about a miracle in particular historical circumstances and for particular purposes, and the pursuit of their enquiry may then eventually confirm or deny their starting assumptions.

The evidentialist role of the New Testament miracles may therefore lie not so much in the historical support, or otherwise, that exists for a particular isolated miracle, but in the way in which the miraculous element of the gospel narratives makes sense in the context of the overall claims made concerning the death, resurrection and overall mission of Jesus. The events themselves cannot be extracted out of the worldview and assumptions of the New Testament writers any more than the data supporting the idea that continents move can be extracted out of the conceptual framework provided by plate tectonics.

It must of course be admitted that the evidentialist role of the New Testament miracles cannot be as strong today as it was for those who were the original witnesses of the alleged events. When Luke was writing the opening words of his gospel he stated:

Many have undertaken to draw up an account of the things that have been fulfilled among us, just as they were handed down to us by those who from the first were eye-witnesses and servants of the word. Therefore, since I myself have carefully investigated everything from the beginning, it seemed good also to me to write an orderly account for you, most excellent Theophilus, so that you may know the certainty of the things you have been taught.[51]

The gospel of John ends with a similar reference to first-hand testimony:

This is the disciple who testifies to these things and who wrote them down. We know that his testimony is true.[52]

We cannot be in the same position as Luke and John, people who had personal opportunity to witness the miracles of Jesus and to sift the various narratives and question other eye-witnesses who were still alive at the time. For this reason some have suggested that the evidentialist role of historical miracles is zero – they cannot be utilized in any way, for example, to support the claims of Christian belief. My own view is that such an assessment is unnecessarily pessimistic. There is an intermediate position which suggests that while the New Testament miracles cannot count as evidence for us in the same way that they clearly did for the gospel writers as part of the justification for a belief in God, nevertheless they contribute to a cumulative case. This contribution is certainly much higher than zero.

In scientific rationalizing about theories a frequently used phrase is: 'These data are consistent with the theory that...'. It is the sort of phrase that everyone uses in the discussion section of their scientific papers in an attempt not to over-interpret their data, but at the same time to state firmly how the data are perceived to fit with a particular model. The kind of first-hand historical testimony that the gospel writers have bequeathed to us brings such a phrase to mind. What we have is not knock-down evidence but a cumulative weight of data, which, taken together, is consistent with the theory that Jesus really did have divine origins. In assessing the cumulative weight of evidence we can also, to some extent, picture ourselves in the position of those who contributed their eye-witness accounts which have been transmitted to us via the gospel records. If we had lived with someone for several years, then watched him die in a cruel way that ensured that he really was dead, then witnessed his well-wrapped body being placed in a sealed tomb guarded by soldiers whose task was to prevent body snatching, followed by the observation two days later that the tomb was empty and subsequent personal appearances of the resurrected Jesus, then what would we have concluded? Would we have believed the evidence of our senses or our prior metaphysical presuppositions?

The evidentialist role of miracles for the sceptical inquirer may vary considerably depending on the type of miracle in question. As already pointed out, the miracle accounts of the Bible vary from those at one end of the spectrum, for which the Bible itself provides physical explanations, to those at the other end of the spectrum, for which no scientific explanation is currently conceivable. Miraculous accounts in which a constellation of events occur at precisely the appropriate time for an event to occur (such as the exodus) are not necessarily devoid of evidentialist weight. The sceptic will point out that constellations of unlikely events happen quite frequently when we pool the experiences of large populations, and it is precisely these remarkable constellations that will be more likely to be noted and recorded in a nation's history. In response it can be pointed out that the constellation of events to which the Bible draws our attention were in the context of particular historical contexts, often in answer to prayer, and where the people of Israel (in the exodus context, for example) had been told by God that they would in fact be delivered. There is an element of prediction in the narrative for which the constellation of remarkable events became a fulfilment.

Yet it is probably the alleged miracles at the other end of the scale – those for which no scientific explanation appears possible – that have played the strongest evidentialist role as part of a cumulative body of evidence persuading the sceptic that, for example, Jesus really was of divine origin. For, if God is creator, and everything continues to exist by his will, and if the incarnation is true and Jesus really was God entering the world in human form, then it would not be unexpected that Jesus demonstrates his power and control over the created order in the same way that God does, even to the extent of reversing the very processes of death itself. This presumably explains why the alleged resurrection of Jesus from the dead has always proven to be pivotal in any discussion on this issue.

When Hume wrote his *Dialogues Concerning Natural Religion* he put some words into the lips of Philo, who concluded his assessment of the evidence for God's existence as follows:

> The most natural sentiment, which a well-disposed mind will feel on this
> occasion, is a longing desire and expectation, that Heaven would be
> pleased to dissipate, at least alleviate, this profound ignorance, by affording
> some more particular revelation to mankind, and making discoveries of
> the nature, attributes, and operations of the divine object of our Faith.[53]

Can we detect a certain wistfulness in Hume's words in this his final volume, published posthumously? If so, it seems ironic that his arguments against the evidentialist role of miracles may have excluded the very possibility that the 'most natural sentiment' that a 'well-disposed mind will feel' might be satisfied.

Do miracles happen today?

So far we have carefully skated round the issue of whether miracles still occur today, allowing Hume to set our agenda as to the nature of miracles and whether they have occurred historically. Personally I remain agnostic on the issue, but I cannot see why the possibility of contemporary miracles as defined above can be excluded in principle. If there is a creator-God who upholds the properties of matter that we investigate as scientists, then it is difficult to see why such a God could not choose to bring about an event or set of events of an unusual nature in a particular context and for a particular religious purpose. The unusual nature of the event could be recognized in the same way that we have discussed in the context of the biblical miracles, either as a constellation of remarkable circumstances through which God shows his plan or purposes for a particular individual or community, or due to the fact that the event itself does not fit with the normally expected behaviour of the physical world. Such events could be investigated by the same processes of legal reasoning that have already been suggested. The procedures involved would be greatly facilitated by the contemporary nature of the alleged miracle. Witnesses of the alleged event could be cross-examined, character references obtained, their trustworthiness (or otherwise) assessed and 'before' and 'after' reports obtained where relevant. For example, in the case outlined above of the theoretical healing of Mrs B who was cured of her rheumatoid arthritis, it is conceivable that all the necessary evidence and counter-evidence could be in place to make a sensible decision about the nature of the alleged event.

Given the definition of miracles utilized in this chapter, which in turn was derived from the miraculous accounts found in the Bible, there seems no reason to exclude an event as a miracle merely because there is a potential scientific explanation for what occurred. For example, let us suppose that a super-scientist had access to a complete analysis of Mrs B's body at the moment that she was being healed of her rheumatoid arthritis. It is conceivable that he might be able to describe what was happening within normal scientific terms, albeit referring to processes that were speeded up enormously compared with those that might normally pertain to a regression of arthritic disease. I cannot see why such a hypothetical thought experiment should count against Mrs B's claim that she had in fact been miraculously healed. Once we accept a biblical rather than a Humean definition of miracles, there will be no need to get bogged down in discussions of whether claimed miraculous events have potential or actual scientific explanations.

This will of course leave the demarcation boundary between the miraculous and the non-miraculous somewhat fuzzy. This will only matter for people for whom the confirmation of contemporary miracles is important for their faith. Personally it matters little whether contemporary miracles do or do not happen and the issue has no bearing on my own faith. For the theist who believes in a God who is actively sustaining every atom of the universe at every instant, it is clearly not impossible that God may choose to perform unusual events on occasion – but such a faith in God certainly does not demand or expect such events. It is the spirit of open-minded enquiry that hesitates before concluding that such events are impossible.

As to whether contemporary miracles have in fact occurred, it would clearly require a book at least as long as this one to investigate such a question thoroughly. However, it has to be said that the attitudes and actions of many so-called 'miracle-working preachers', particularly those of the American tele-evangelist brand, do not encourage confidence in their claimed healings.

A striking feature of the miracles of Jesus is their complete absence of hype and hysteria. Jesus speaks or gives a simple command and the miracle happens. The results were clear cut and there was no need for discussion among the onlookers as to whether a miracle had happened. They might disagree about its interpretation, but they could not disagree about the fact that it had happened. This is in marked contrast to the hype and hysteria that surround many contemporary claims to miraculous healing events. But the fact that most contemporary miraculous claims may be bogus cannot be taken to prove that no miraculous events occur at all under any circumstances. An open mind should not be closed merely by a large accumulation of counter-examples.

Some conclusions on miracles

It has been suggested in this chapter that the traditional Humean definition of miracles as 'violations of natural law', as expressed in the *Nature* editorial, is less plausible than a rival understanding of miracles that has been widely disseminated for many centuries and which finds its roots in the miracle narratives of the Bible. This understanding emphasizes not the violation of 'laws of nature', though this may be involved, but rather the purposeful and non-capricious actions of a God in bringing the miracle about within a significant historical–religious context. In this view God is the creator who actively sustains the whole created order and miracles are discernible as unusual actions of God. Some of the inadequacies of Hume's *Essay* on miracles have been surveyed, and it has been concluded that his prior metaphysical commitments led him to be unnecessarily closed to considering evidence for the miraculous in a way that contrasts with the scientific commitment to openness to evidence. Claims to miracles are embedded in a particular worldview, just as scientific data are embedded in particular scientific theories. Thus the assessment of miraculous claims cannot be made without considering them within their worldview context. This limits the contemporary evidentialist role of miracles, but they may be used as part of a cumulative case to support belief in God in a way analogous to the scientist who accepts a particular theory-plus-dataset as a complete 'package deal'. It is suggested that legal reasoning is a useful way of assessing the veracity of miraculous claims in both their historical and contemporary contexts.

Chapter 14

Science with a Human Face
The Humanizing of Science Within a Theistic Framework

Science has never encountered a barrier that it has not surmounted.
Peter Atkins

We are drowning in information, while starving for wisdom.
E.O. Wilson

Man is nothing else but that which he makes of himself.
Jean-Paul Sartre

Much as we might wish to believe otherwise, universal love and the welfare of the species as a whole are concepts which simply do not make evolutionary sense.
Richard Dawkins

We should put aside feelings based on the small, helpless, and – sometimes – cute appearance of human infants... laboratory rats are 'innocent' in exactly the same sense as the human infant... killing a disabled infant is not morally equivalent to killing a person. Very often it is not wrong at all.
Peter Singer

In the Introduction we began by alluding to the sense of threat that many feel when they contemplate the fruits of contemporary scientific research, particularly those involving the biological sciences. Frankenstein images are routinely fuelled by the media. Yet even if we lay these exaggerated images on one side, it is certainly the case that science is currently generating the ability to manipulate our own beings in ways that were unimaginable only a few decades ago. This is particularly the case for genetics, for the neurosciences and for reproductive technologies. The actual and potential applications of new research findings continue to draw attention to the fundamental question: 'What does it mean to be human?' How can we generate science with a human face, a science which is sensitive to human values and to natural human fears?

It has been argued during the course of this book that interactions between science and faith have been long and fruitful. As with members of any family, there have at times been quarrels and misunderstandings, but overall the interactions have been mutually beneficial. No single model will do justice to the richness of the historical data available, but instead there has been a myriad different kinds of interaction. Modern science was born in a theological womb. It occupies that womb no longer but still bears the unmistakable signs of its ancestry. Scientific and religious ways of thinking are not locked into watertight compartments but share similarities, particularly when it comes to assessing the 'big questions' of science and of religion, using inference to the best explanation as a common approach.

At the same time we have supported the stance taken early by the Royal Society at its inception, that the scientific community should focus on the goals which are achievable by science – the 'art of the soluble' – and not be distracted by metaphysical questions. The rationale behind such a stance is the same as for plumbers, airline pilots, doctors and accountants. The public wish is for professional groupings to carry out their roles in society in a professional way. We do not wish airline pilots to suffer a crisis in their views about the meaning of life at 30,000 feet, at least not in such a way that will endanger their passengers, any more than we wish our surgeon to dwell too much on the possible benefits of euthanasia as he holds the scalpel over us. Professional groupings should get on with doing what they are good at doing. Of course in their personal lives plumbers and airline pilots, as much as scientists, will have their own philosophical or religious convictions, and these will no doubt impinge on their professional working lives, but their primary responsibility is to make sure that pipes do not leak and that planes stay in the air at the right time. Similarly the primary responsibility of a scientist qua scientist is to do good science.

We have therefore displayed considerable hostility to those scientists who have tried to pretend that science can answer all our questions, a philosophy known as naturalism (or scientism in common parlance), as well as an antipathy to all attempts to laden scientific theories (like evolution) with metaphysical baggage that they are unable to sustain. On the other hand, we have been equally hostile to attempts by the religious to claim too much for natural theology, or to claim that biblical texts are a source for scientific theories. Science has been so successful that there is a constant temptation to utilize its intellectual kudos to support ideological positions that are not intrinsic to science itself. Theologians were guilty of such strategies during the heyday of natural theology and, like a mirror image of the natural theologians, a subset of scientists committed to naturalism are repeating the same mistake in our own day.

It is therefore definitely not the argument of this book that the church, or other religious bodies, should start interfering with the scientific community, e.g. by commenting on the contents of specific scientific theories. Likewise scientific organizations should distance themselves from the arrogant notion that 'science has all the answers'. The declaration by a group of thirteen leading scientific members of the US National Academy of Sciences, including its president, is exemplary in this respect: 'Religions and science answer different questions about the world. Whether there is a purpose to the universe or a purpose for human existence are not questions for science... No one way of knowing can provide all of the answers to the questions that humans ask.'[1] Professor John Ziman showed a similar level of commendable constraint during his 1995 Medawar lecture to the Royal Society, when he commented:

> Some scientists may find it difficult to accept that science should no longer claim that it can provide a universally applicable answer to every problem. I believe this position was always untenable, and that a retreat from it is one of the ways to defuse some of the current public hostility towards 'science'.[2]

A little more humility displayed by the scientific community to the general public along these kinds of lines would do much to restore the image of a 'science with a human face'.

An underlying assumption in this book, made explicit in several places, is that every human being is a philosopher, carrying around in their heads an accumulated worldview, or Paradigm with a capital 'P', which to a large degree influences the direction of their lives. These philosophical assumptions are invariably metaphysical in character, that is, they go well beyond anything that could be supported, even in principle, by scientific data. We have therefore expressed scepticism at the claim, to which a certain kind of scientist appears to be particularly prone, that their Paradigm occupies some lofty high-ground free of such metaphysical assumptions. In reality all worldviews are metaphysical rivals and can be assessed by the normal process of rational argument. Science itself does not represent a metaphysical worldview but is rather a series of procedures and techniques for obtaining reliable knowledge about the physical world.

The purpose of this final chapter is to sketch out in broad outline the way in which one of the metaphysical rivals, Christian theism, provides a Paradigm which undergirds 'science with a human face', a matrix within which human value can be sustained. We therefore pick up the discussion where we left it at the end of chapter 11, with the comment by James Rachels that 'God and nature are powerful allies; losing them does mean losing something.' In practice, what is lost? Or, putting the question more positively, what is gained for the practice of science and its applications in technology if we adopt a theistic framework? Even for those who do not themselves hold to such a worldview, it is hoped that the discussion that follows might at least represent a useful 'thought experiment' that could help in the assessment of conflicting Paradigms.

The value of scientific knowledge

Intellectual movements have endings as well as beginnings. Contemplating the demise of science in the current climate might seem implausible. A recent book suggesting that most of science was now known and that there was little left for scientists to do[3] did not meet with a very positive reception (especially from scientists, perhaps not surprisingly). Natural philosophers in the 17th century thought that the pace of discovery was so fast that there would be little left for them to do by the end of their century. We have already quoted the conclusion of Lord Kelvin's speech to the British Association for the Advancement of Science around 1900 ('There is nothing new to be discovered in physics now. All that remains is more and more precise measurement'), which was just a few years before Einstein published his remarkable insights. Such historical examples remind us that predicting the demise of science is a risky business. Certainly this is unlikely to occur due to the lack of fresh problems waiting to be resolved. Many such problems have not yet even been articulated because we do not yet know that they exist. Sequencing the human genome was not a challenge for Victorian scientists because they did not know that the genome existed.

The main threat to science is not therefore the possibility that scientists will soon run out of problems to solve. Instead the most significant onslaught on science which has occurred during the course of this past century has been the rocking of the epistemological assumptions on which the scientific enterprise itself has been built. We have already alluded to this chipping away at the philosophical underpinning of science in chapter 8 and concluded that the stance of 'critical realism' provides an appropriate middle way between the Scylla of naive realism and the Charybdis of systematic relativism. If, as in the postmodern view, science is merely a form of constructed knowledge valid only for a particular linguistic community and bearing no universal claim to assent, then scientists are clearly deceiving themselves when they imagine that they are making discoveries about the real world that anyone would be right to believe and wrong to disbelieve. But within such a framework it is difficult to know how to prevent sliding into a position in which scientific knowledge becomes trivialized.

If we had the possibility of interviewing early members of the Royal Society suddenly dragged into our TV studio from the 17th century, there is little doubt that they would find such notions bizarre. The reasons are not difficult to fathom. Since nature represents God's creative actions, they are assumed to be both reproducible and intelligible, created to be understood by humans and to serve their needs. Uncovering the actions of God in creation by natural philosophy generates one of the highest forms of human knowledge that can be attained, real insights into the creative actions of God that reveal his power and wisdom. Natural philosophy is one aspect of worship. Because it is no mere human construct, the scientific knowledge attained can never be trivial but represents descriptions, albeit partial, of the realities of God's working in the world.

A theistic Paradigm therefore provides science with solid epistemological foundations. Whereas the approach of critical realism maintains that our knowledge of the natural world is never exhaustive and is always filtered through human theories and instruments, nevertheless the scientific knowledge that we generate and the language we use to express it represent descriptions of God's actions. Such a stance dramatically increases the value of scientific knowledge as well as providing a powerful motive for getting the science right. The human brains that generate the language used in science are equally part of God's created order, and work rationally to elucidate the workings of an intelligible universe grounded upon elegant mathematical principles.

Talk of the end of science sounds implausible at present. Apart from anything else, science is thoroughly integrated into modern economies. The 'space capsule of science' speeds on, apparently no longer needing the 'launching rockets' provided by a theistic worldview. But the day may yet come when the trivialization of knowledge promoted by postmodernism undermines the motivation to investigate the physical world to such an extent that science will wither away in the absence of a solid metaphysical foundation. Within a theistic worldview, the scientific enterprise is intrinsically good because it provides insights into God's universe. A theistic Paradigm contributes to 'science with a human face' because it generates a science that is not arrogant but rather quietly confident that the knowledge wrested with so much expense and hard work from the created order is of real value and significance in the larger scheme of things.

Human value

A recurring theme in public perceptions of science is that it is dehumanizing. Some of this anxiety stems from the type of naive reductionism that we criticized in chapter 8. Scientists need to mind their language. It is very easy for them – especially when waxing lyrical over their latest discoveries about the brain or the genes – to give the impression that human thoughts are 'nothing but' neuronal impulses or that the purpose of human life is 'nothing but' the goal of passing on DNA to succeeding generations.

When I was a student at Oxford in the mid-1960s the biggest society in the university was the Humanist Society. The majority view was that Christian theism was outmoded. Nevertheless the majority opinion also maintained that the values based on human dignity which Christianity had underpinned over the centuries were worth keeping, and it was these that the Humanist Society intended to preserve. In the decades since the 1960s the Humanist Society has disappeared almost without trace and the extreme difficulty of building a rational basis for human dignity without an underpinning metaphysical framework has become increasingly apparent. If you start with a purely biological account of the individual human as the most important story that can be told about that person, then the rational maintenance of human value becomes problematic.

A controversial debate about infanticide has recently focused attention on how rival metaphysical worldviews generate very different understandings of human value. The debate is useful because it sheds light on how a given presupposition can lead inexorably, and in a highly rational manner, to a conclusion that many people find deeply abhorrent. I choose this example not because there is space here to do justice to such an important discussion in itself, but because it provides a clue as to how similar public debates may well go in the future when it comes to further questions, such as whether to clone humans, or genetically modify the human germ line, or generate human–monkey hybrids in order to carry out research on brain function and consciousness.

Peter Singer, an advocate of infanticide, is both accurate and explicit concerning the implications of rejecting a theistic framework for human value:

> If we go back to the origins of Western civilization, to Greek or Roman times, we find that membership of *Homo sapiens* was not sufficient to guarantee that one's life would be protected... Greeks and Romans killed deformed or weak infants by exposing them to the elements on a hilltop. Plato and Aristotle thought that the state should enforce the killing of deformed infants... The change in Western attitudes to infanticide since Roman times is, like the doctrine of the sanctity of human life of which it is a part, a product of Christianity. Perhaps it is now possible to think about these issues without assuming the Christian moral framework that has, for so long, prevented any fundamental reassessment.[4]

Infanticide was so common in the Graeco–Roman world that one contemporary historian, Polybius, writing in the 2nd century BC, concluded that it had contributed to the depopulation that had occurred in Greece at that time.[5] In Plato's description of the ideal state in *The Republic* infanticide is essential to maintain the quality of the citizens: 'The offspring of the inferior and any of those of the other sort who are born defective, they will properly dispose of in secret, so that no one will know what has become of them.'[6] In his *Politics* Aristotle also maintained that no deformed child should be allowed to live: 'As to exposing or rearing the children born let there be a law that no deformed child shall be reared.'[7] Plutarch described how in Sparta

> each offspring was not reared at the will of the father but was taken to a place where the elders officially examined the infant and if it was well-built and sturdy, they ordered the father to rear it... but if it was ill-born and deformed, they sent it to a chasm-like place at the foot of Mount Taygetus, in the conviction that the life of that which nature had not well equipped at the very beginning for health and strength, was of no advantage, either to itself or to the state.[8]

Singer is correct in his suggestion that infanticide declined due to the Christian insistence on the sanctity of life.[9] After the conversion of the Emperor Constantine to Christianity in AD 313, it was made a punishable offence in the Roman empire for a father to kill his child in 318, and in 331 Constantine decreed that those who raised exposed children could legally adopt them. In 374 infant exposure was made punishable by law. Already by the end of the 4th century AD Christian hospitals were being established in which there was a section called the *brephotropheion* set aside for orphaned children.

What, therefore, does Singer wish to put in place of the sanctity of life? Singer is a consequentialist, that is, he believes that ethical decisions should be based on an assessment of their overall consequences. His fundamental ethical starting point is the 'principle of equal consideration of interests', the belief that the interests of all human beings must be taken into account when assessing the consequences of our actions. This principle extends also, says Singer, to sentient animals, those animals who can suffer or be 'happy'. Only a being that can suffer can be said to 'have interests'. Human beings can be considered in two quite distinct ways – either as belonging to the species *Homo sapiens*, or by being a person. A person is a 'self-conscious or rational being' who can therefore act as an agent in making decisions. A person is capable of thwarted desires for the future. In addition Singer wishes to argue that primates, for example, are also self-conscious, at least to some extent, and should be included in the term 'person'. Therefore being a member of the species *Homo sapiens* is neither necessary nor sufficient for being a 'person'.

What are the conclusions of such a starting point? Adult primates are persons whereas newborn human infants are not since they are not yet self-conscious. It is not therefore intrinsically wrong to kill a newborn baby because the baby is not yet self-conscious whereas it would be wrong to kill animals who are supposed to be self-conscious. 'So it seems', writes Singer, 'that killing, say, a chimpanzee is worse than the killing of a human being who, because of a congenital intellectual disability, is not and never can be a person.' 'A week-old baby is not a rational and self-conscious being, and there are many nonhuman animals whose rationality, self-consciousness, awareness, capacity to feel, and so on, exceed that of a human baby a week or a month old... the life of a newborn baby is of less value to it than the life of a pig, a dog, or a chimpanzee is to the nonhuman animal.'[10] In the same passage Singer goes on to urge us, in words quoted at the head of this chapter, to put aside our feelings aroused by the sight of the small and helpless appearance of human infants. As people working out their ethical decisions by rational principles we should steel ourselves against such 'emotionally moving but strictly irrelevant aspects of the killing of a baby', for 'we can see that the grounds for not killing persons do not apply to newborn infants'.[11] Singer also remarks, surely correctly, that 'it would be difficult to say at what age children begin to see themselves as distinct entities existing over time', going on to speculate that even two and three year old children may not display such properties. 'If these conclusions seem too shocking to take seriously, it may be worth remembering that our present absolute protection of the lives of infants is a distinctively Christian attitude rather than a universal ethical value.'[12]

Of course Singer is not suggesting that healthy infants, wanted by their parents, should be killed, only those who are physically or mentally disabled in some way and who are for this reason not wanted by their parents. What happens to orphans who may be physically and mentally normal but who may be unwanted by everyone is not discussed. 'We should certainly put very strict conditions on permissible infanticide,' Singer writes, 'but these restrictions might owe more to the effects of infanticide on others than to the intrinsic wrongness of killing an infant.' Furthermore, it is more justified to kill the handicapped child if the parents are planning to replace it with another child who will (hopefully) not be handicapped, since the net consequence will be an increase in the net overall gain in human happiness. 'The decision to kill a newborn infant is no more – and no less – the prevention of the existence of an additional person than is a decision not to reproduce.'[13]

Peter Singer's reasons for his position appear impeccable. Given his philosophical starting point, it is difficult to see how any right-thinking person could conclude differently. Of course one could be picky about some of the practical detail. For example, what about the healthy newborn infant who is nevertheless unwanted by the parents, perhaps living in a society where there are too many mouths to feed already, so no one else wants to raise the baby either. Would infanticide be justified in such a case? After all, it would be very sad if a child was raised without really being wanted. Furthermore, if primates are at least quasi-conscious and are persons in a comparable way to humans, then should we not provide medical treatment for them? And maybe prenatal diagnosis besides? Any serious consequentialist who is concerned about the interests of non-human persons must surely be worried about the medical well-being of those many primates who yet remain in their natural habitats. Should we cut expenditure on human health to promote the health of animals deemed to be persons?

These questions are not intended to be merely whimsical but to press home the logic of Singer's position. What happens when we carry out a comparable assessment but now with reference to theism? Why is Christian theism, for example, so hostile to infanticide? There are two main interconnected reasons. First, each human life is seen as a gift from God towards which the human community has commitments and duties. These duties are particularly pressing when the individual is helpless and therefore entirely dependent on the human community for support. The love shown by the human community should reflect something of God's love for each individual, a love that operates independently of the person's physical status. The helpless newborn therefore has an intrinsic value that is independent of its biological status, reflecting God's love mediated by the commitment of the supportive human community. By being part of a moral community, the newborn cease to be the sole concern of the parents; they are no longer solely parental property.[14] The moral community acts as advocates on behalf of the weak.

Second, in Christian theism humans are made 'in the image of God'.[15] This expression is first introduced in the biblical text in the context of the responsibilities given to humankind to care for the earth and its biological diversity. In this scenario, humans are delegated by God to be his 'earth-keepers'. The 'image of God' is not therefore so much a static concept, referring to human reason, or free will, or other particular intrinsic human qualities, but rather to the dynamic relational status of humans to God, in particular regarding their delegated responsibilities. These moral responsibilities are given not just to a few individuals but to the whole of humankind. A severely disabled infant, for example, may never be able to contribute very much, if anything, individually to fulfilling these delegated responsibilities, but nevertheless is part of the human community that as a whole carries this moral obligation upon its shoulders. Bearing the 'image of God' is thus about relationship and solidarity, once again pointing not to the genetic perfection or blue eyes of the helpless infant but rather to its intrinsic worth as a member of this moral community. All humans are God's image-bearers in this sense and are our neighbours. Jesus says that we are to love our neighbour as ourselves.

Just as the consequentialist starting point is the beginning of a long discussion about the moral status of the helpless infant, so the framework provided by Christian theism is clearly only the beginning of a discussion, not its end. Hard decisions still have to be made, often involving the choice of the lesser of two evils. When is medical intervention over-intrusive and when is the continuation of treatment imperative? Debates on these difficult issues will continue.[16] Consequentialist arguments are certainly useful in such contexts. But the overall framework within which the debate is carried out makes an enormous difference. A theistic framework provides a powerful undergirding for the value of each human life. The hostility to infanticide from Christian theists in the 4th-century Roman empire, as also now from their counterparts in contemporary society, stems from a view of human value based on the creative activity of God, not on the biological properties displayed by individual humans.

It is not difficult to see how such considerations will continue to be highly relevant as the scientific community continues to delve into human biology. Let us imagine that we are starting with Singer's consequentialist framework as our only guide for bioethics. Let us also imagine that some years from now (perhaps not so many) a group of scientists propose that they should generate a series of human–monkey hybrids with some very specific scientific goals in mind. The hybrids could be generated by fertilizing human eggs with monkey DNA or vice versa. Most likely development would not proceed very far due to chromosomal incompatibility, but that would be part of the interest in the experiment. It would then be fascinating to see whether it could be possible to modify the chromosomes so that the fertilized ovum could be carried to term in a primate or human recipient. The result could be the birth of a genuine human–monkey hybrid with characteristics of both the starting species. Would there be consciousness? Or language? The new species generated could also give important clues about our evolutionary heritage, giving us the opportunity to study the properties of the 'missing links' that separate us from our primate ancestors. It would be difficult to turn down funding for such a project based on its scientific appeal and inherent interest.

How would a grant proposal for such a project fare based on a strictly Singerian framework for human value? The investigations on prenatal hybrids would present no ethical dilemmas since a hybrid would certainly be less conscious and aware than a human foetus, and therefore have no interests. Care would have to be taken to avoid inflicting pain on a hybrid fetus in late pregnancy just as for a human fetus. The hundreds of unsuccessful hybrids that would doubtless result from such experimentation, unsuccessful because they are malformed and fail to develop in a viable manner, could simply be aborted. Postnatally the hybrid infants would not be self-conscious (presumably) for some years so could be culled after suitable investigation, provided this caused no suffering. If infanticide is allowable in human infants then clearly it should be possible for hybrids also. But as the hybrids grew they would (presumably) become more self-aware, particularly of the possibilities of suffering, and so should be accorded protection like any other sentient being. It would also be in their interests to interbreed and establish themselves as a separate community. Might they be hostile towards the humans who had brought them into being? We have no way of knowing, and the utilitarian would be hard pressed to use this as an argument for not carrying out the experiment. After all, our scientific knowledge would be greatly enriched by funding such an enterprise. We might also understand more about ourselves and our own nature – equally about monkey being and its nature. A consequentialist would probably wish to put more weight on a definite outcome (growth in scientific knowledge) rather than a speculative outcome (the hybrids might attack us).

Most people would find such a scenario unsettling, to say the least, not to say illegal (fortunately), at least in some countries. But it is difficult to see why the project should be prevented on purely consequentialist grounds. No harm would be done to anyone and some scientific good might arise, which could be useful in human self-understanding.

This thought experiment highlights how frail is the defence of intrinsic human value once the undergirding theistic framework is removed. Countless other thought experiments could be suggested reflecting similar scenarios that are likely to become realities over the next few decades. Science will only maintain a 'human face' if there is a metaphysical system in place robust enough to provide a matrix within which intrinsic human value can be sustained.

Human justice

Discussions about the applications of science, and to a certain extent the scientific enterprise itself, can rarely proceed for very long without the issue of human justice receiving attention. Is it morally just that the benefits of genetic engineering are preferentially directed towards the profits of Western multinationals rather than towards the needs of hungry people in third world countries? Is it morally just that investment into cures for Western diseases is so much higher than for diseases prevalent in poorer countries? Is it morally just that opportunities to join the research community are so rare unless one belongs to the club of rich nations?

Intriguingly Peter Singer, our chosen foil for this chapter, makes a passionate plea to the rich to help the poor, defending the concept that a failure to provide aid to the absolute poor is morally equivalent to murder.[17] Sounding like an Old

Testament prophet, Singer urges us that 'the life-or-death needs of others must take priority', concluding that we all (in the richer nations) should tithe our income (i.e. donate 10 per cent) for the sake of the poor in other nations. We are clearly a long way here from Ruse's notion of a moral obligation to others which declines in proportion to our (supposed) genetic distance from them. For Singer, the tithe is 'by any reasonable standards... the minimum we ought to do, and we do wrong if we do less'. Such a position stems from his starting ethical principle of equality, which in practice means an equal consideration of interests, irrespective of the geographical location or cultural context of the persons in question.

The theist would clearly concur with an equal consideration of human interests as a valid ethical position to adopt. But there are two important problems. The first is that it is not clear what undergirds 'an equal consideration of interests'. The scientist has this nasty habit of asking 'why?' questions. Why should human beings be treated equally? The prevalence of systems of both caste and class in many cultures acts as a constant reminder of the forces pushing in the opposite direction to equality. And if we start with naturalistic presuppositions in which the biological account of human beings is given prominence, then it would seem quite reasonable to rank humans according to criteria such as reproductive fitness, genetic health, physical strength, and so forth. Why treat everyone equally when they are obviously not equal in these respects? Should not biological realities take priority? Second, as a matter of fact most people, including scientists, do not readily give up their successful careers in the richer nations in order to go and help people in less developed nations. I know, because I've done it. Even when people accept 'the equal consideration of interests' as a theoretical principle, it does not necessarily mean that they will do anything about it. A commitment to human justice is no mere academic exercise, but demands personal cost and involvement, otherwise it remains empty hand waving.

Theism provides a framework that provides both an intellectual basis and a powerful motivation to practice human justice, in particular to ensure that the benefits of science are not restricted to a small rich segment of the world's population. The intellectual basis comes from the fact that individuals, as outlined above, have an intrinsic value that is independent of their biological status, or whether or not they are wanted by their parents or society. If this basis is accepted, then justice is the natural *sequitur*. Once people are equals as a matter of fact, because all are created in the image of God, then it would be incoherent to treat them as anything other than the facts dictate. As God loves all, irrespective of race, colour, IQ or social status, so should we, with a practical love that involves justice – anything less fails to take seriously God's assignment of value to each and every person.

Why not try to retain the value system without the theism? The problem comes when people start thinking rationally according to their chosen Paradigms. If we are accidents of nature appearing as tiny specks in geological time in the midst of a vast and impersonal universe, why should we practise human value and human justice, particularly when our own lives are so short and we wish to live them to the full? Why not just accept that there are winners and losers in the roulette of life, and if people sufficiently far away from us not to cause us discomfort are among the losers, then why should we care? Human nature being what it is, the sustenance of concepts of human value and justice tends to decline as the metaphysical underpinnings are knocked away.

Care for the environment

Similar considerations are highly relevant to the question of how a long-term and consistent care for the environment can be nurtured. Public concern for the environment tends to be rather fickle, in general flourishing at times of economic plenty when financial survival is not the dominant daily concern of most people, or at times of perceived environmental crisis, or after the latest figures have been released on global warming, or after an oil tanker has broken up on the rocks of a beautiful piece of coastline.

Many justifications for environmental concern have been proposed, ranging from simple self interest, to 'Gaian' notions of the world as a giant self-regulating organism, to images of the earth as Mother, to pantheistic ideas of a divine universe, to 'deep ecology', to the Christian idea of a creator-God who is separate from the universe but active in sustaining it – and many other variations and pick-and-mix flavours beside. The main point to be made here is that these competing metaphysical Paradigms really do make a difference.

The kind of difference that we are talking about can be illustrated once again by reference to Singer. The person whose ethical starting point is the 'consideration of the interests of all sentient creatures' has a problem when it comes to the environment, for 'sentient creatures' comprise a rather small proportion of the total ecosystem. Singer is well aware of this problem, so introduces in parallel a further ethical principle to complement the first, 'the aesthetic of appreciation for wild places and unspoiled nature',[18] according to which we are supposed to care for and enjoy wilderness areas. Surely there is nothing wrong with that. But the two ethical principles taken together comprise only a weak justification for ecological concern, which in practice involves far more than sentient beings and the wilderness. Ironically, in light of Singer's concern for non-human persons, his position on the environment is markedly anthropocentric, since it is of course humans who possess aesthetic appreciation, and there is therefore no basis for the environment having some intrinsic value independent of human appreciation and desires.

In striking contrast, the Christian theistic Paradigm for environmental concern is rooted in the intrinsic value of creation, which in turn is based on the relationship between God and the created order. Paul insisted that 'He [Jesus] is the image of the invisible God, the firstborn over all creation. For by him... all things were created by him and *for him*'[19] [my italics]. Paul's theology in turn was based on the Jewish writings of the Old Testament where numerous passages tell us that God as creator delights in his creation for its own sake. We have already referred (in chapter 9) to the sevenfold repetition in Genesis 1 after each creative act that 'God saw that it was very good'. The affirmation bestowed intrinsic value. The created order was already declared to be good before humankind came on the scene. God is intimately involved in the enjoyment of his creation.[20] Such a Paradigm is theocentric rather than anthropocentric. In the twenty-four-hour clock thought experiment for the history of our planet (cf. chapter 10), the environment was loved and cared for during all of the twenty-four hours, not just the few seconds before midnight when humankind came on the scene.

The fact that the environment has intrinsic value within such a framework saves us from an overdose of utilitarianism on one hand, and from the narcissistic implications on the other of seeing the whole of nature, including humankind, as embodying divinity. The theistic framework per se will not help us decide precisely which species we should struggle to preserve, nor whether the preservation of this or that piece of wilderness is more important than the building of a hydroelectric dam which will bring benefits to thousands of people, but it does represent a very robust basis for our care for the environment, both now and in the future. The environmental decisions we make are important not only for their impact on the lives of future generations yet unborn, but because they are decisions about God's world. 'We dispute in the schools', wrote John Bulwer in 1653, 'whether, if it were possible for man to do so, it were lawful for him to destroy any one species of God's creatures, though it were but the species of toads and spiders, because this were taking away one link of God's chain, one note of his harmony.'[21] Environmental concern then as now is part of the normal language of theological discourse. A century before Bulwer, the Reformer Calvin wrote in 1554:

> The earth was given to man, with this condition, that he should occupy himself in its cultivation... The custody of the garden was given in charge to Adam, to show that we possess the things that God has committed to our hands, on the condition, that being content with a frugal and moderate use of them, we should take care of what shall remain... Let

everyone regard himself as the steward of God in all things which he possesses. Then will he neither conduct himself dissolutely, nor corrupt by abuse those things which God requires to be preserved.[22]

The terminology of stewardship sounds a bit old fashioned now (officers on cruise ships?), but it is a useful word since it conveys the idea of being put in charge of something that we have to look after and for which we should care. Implicit in the word is the idea of moral responsibility. The word 'stewardship' shares with the word 'ecology' a common Greek root for the word 'house' or 'household' (*oikos*), the steward being the one who looked after the household on behalf of his master, whereas 'ecology' literally means 'discoursing about the house'.[23] Stewardship therefore represents the practical outworking of ecology, and is close to the more commonly used language of management. But the problem with 'manager' terminology is that it can convey the anthropocentric notion that the earth belongs to us and we are its rightful managers. The language of stewardship includes the concept of management but conveys a different nuance, that we are tenants of a world that does not belong to us and we are to be held responsible for the way we look after it. This is God's world not ours.

The debate on the environment continues.[24] Many of the practical issues involved are highly complex. Science has an important role in informing the ethical debate.[25] A theistic framework provides a powerful rationale for caring for the environment, at the same time restraining human greed and arrogance.

Rebuilding the Matrix

In the Introduction we drew attention to the need to draw on all the resources we can lay our hands on if we are to maintain human justice, dignity and worth in the face of scientific disciplines, such as neuroscience and the new genetics, which increasingly lay bare our own biological constitution. We also alluded to the recent commentary in *Nature* that suggested that 'the scientific enterprise is full of experts on specialist areas but woefully short of people with a unified worldview'. What this book has maintained is that theism provides a unified worldview that does a remarkably effective job in providing a matrix for science in which the validity of scientific knowledge is justified and in which the fruits of scientific discoveries are channelled in ways that affirm human value, justice and care for the environment. We have also pointed out that this resonance between science and faith is no accident, but emerges from long and fruitful historical interactions between science and theism.

When data begin to accumulate that do not readily fit within the 'grand theories' of science, then the scientific community begins to cast around for better alternatives, new theories that absorb the new results and render them coherent. As in science, so in metaphysics: at present non-theistic frameworks are taking science in directions that are alien to its roots, contributing to the present widespread public misunderstanding of science and generating a feeling of malaise about the scientific enterprise. In contrast a theistic framework for science brings the enterprise back to its historical origins and provides a rational justification for maintaining both a high view of scientific knowledge and a solid basis for human values in the face of rapid scientific advances – which could so easily prove dehumanizing if abused. Rebuilding the matrix in the 21st century will be no easy task, but will be greatly facilitated by those who are prepared for a major Paradigm-shift in their understanding of the framework within which the scientific enterprise should be pursued.

Endnotes

Introduction

1. *Gallup International Association Report*, 2000.

2. E. Schrödinger, *What is Life?*, Cambridge: Cambridge University Press, 1944.

3. S. Ross, 'Scientist: The Story of a Word', *Annals of Science* **18**, 1962, pp. 65–85.

Chapter 1 (pp. 12–31)

1. Peter L. Berger and Thomas Luckmann, *The Social Construction of Reality*, Doubleday, 1966.

2. C. Barker, *Television, Globalization and Cultural Identities*, Milton Keynes: Open University Press, 1999, p. 30.

3. *Screen Digest*, February 1995.

4. D. Michie, *The Invisible Persuaders*, Bantam Press, 1998.

5. N. Abercrombie and A. Warde, *Contemporary British Society*, Polity Press, 1994, p. 421.

6. J. Lull, *Media, Communication, Culture*, Polity Press, 1995, p. 24.

7. D. Kellner, *Media Culture*, London: Routledge, 1995, p. 209.

8. Kellner, *Media Culture*, p. 58.

9. Kellner, *Media Culture*, p. 60.

10. G. Gerbner and L. Gross, cited in Lull, *Media, Communication, Culture*, p. 11.

11. Barker, *Television, Globalization and Cultural Identities*, p. 1.

12. C. Hoskins, S. McFadyen, A. Finn and A. Jackel, 'Film and Television Coproduction

– Evidence from Canadian European Experience', *European Journal of Communications* **10**, 1995, pp. 221–43.

13. Barry Barnes, *Scientific Knowledge and Sociological Theory*, London: Routledge and Kegan Paul, 1974.

14. P. Bourdieu, *The Logic of Practice*, Polity Press, 1990; P. Bourdieu, *The Field of Cultural Production*, Polity Press, 1993.

15. Thomas S. Kuhn, *The Structure of Scientific Revolutions*, 2nd edition, Chicago: University of Chicago Press, 1962.

16. Thomas S. Kuhn, 'Second Thoughts on Paradigms', in *The Essential Tension*, Chicago: University of Chicago Press, 1977.

17. A Kuhnian interpretation of this crisis in astronomy was made by S. Tremaine, Director of the Canadian Institute for Theoretical Astrophysics, at a symposium held at Princeton entitled 'Dark Matter in the Universe', 24–28 June 1985 (recorded in *Nature* **317**, 1985, pp. 670–71). For a further example of the way 'paradigm language' is being used by scientists see, for example, R.E. Vance, 'A Copernican Revolution? Doubts About the Danger Theory', *Journal of Immunology* **165**, 2000, pp. 1725–28.

18. J. Chiari, *Christopher Columbus*, New York: Gordian Press, 1979.

19. C. Jane (ed.), *Select Documents Illustrating the Four Voyages of Columbus*, 2 vols, London: Hakluyt Society, 1930–33, 1:xxii.

20. Cited in J.B. Russell, *Inventing the Flat Earth: Columbus and Modern Historians*, Praeger, 1991.

21. Russell, *Inventing the Flat Earth: Columbus and Modern Historians*, p. 24.

22. Russell, *Inventing the Flat Earth: Columbus and Modern Historians*, p. 14 and footnote 32.

23. Russell, *Inventing the Flat Earth: Columbus and Modern Historians*, pp. 52–54.

24. Russell, *Inventing the Flat Earth: Columbus and Modern Historians*, p. 38.

25. S. Jones, *The Language of the Genes*, Flamingo, 1993, p. 150.

26. Russell, *Inventing the Flat Earth: Columbus and Modern Historians*, p. 76.

27. R.D. Haynes, *From Faust to Strangelove: Representations of the Scientist in Western Literature*, Johns Hopkins University Press, 1994; J. Turney, *Frankenstein's Footsteps: Science, Genetics and Popular Culture*, Yale University Press, 1998.

28. *The Daily Mail*, 17 June 1999.

29. *Bild Zeitung*, 18 June 1999.

30. *Nature* **394**, 1998, p. 107.

31. J. Marston, 'A National Survey of Students' Opinions on Science and Faith', *Christians in Science*, conference paper, 27 September 1997. Further information about Christians in Science is at: http://www.cis.org.uk.

Chapter 2 (pp. 32–45)

1. Rather than give a barrage of footnotes for all the sources for this material on race, the general references for this section are as follows:

John R. Baker, *Race*, Oxford: OUP, 1974.
Melvyn Cherno (ed.), *The Contemporary World Since 1850*, vol. 4, McGraw Hill, 1967.
Stephen J. Gould, *Ever Since Darwin*, London: Penguin, 1980.
Stephen J. Gould, *The Mismeasure of Man*, New York: W.W. Norton and Company, 1981.
Stephen J. Gould, *The Panda's Thumb*, London: Penguin, 1983.
Howard E. Gruber, *Darwin on Man*, New York: E.P. Dutton and Company, 1974.
John S. Haller, *Outcasts from Evolution: Scientific Attitudes of Racial Inferiority, 1859–1900*, Chicago: University of Illinois Press, 1971.
Ashley Montagu, *The Idea of Race*, University of Nebraska Press, 1965.
P. Shipman, *The Evolution of Racism: Human Differences and the Use and Abuse of Science*, Simon & Schuster, 1994.

2. On 20 January 1832, Darwin wrote, in his *Beagle* diary, 'We began to enter today the port of the country [Tierra del Fuego] which is thickly inhabited... I shall never forget how savage and wild one group was. Four or five men suddenly appeared on a cliff near to us; they were absolutely naked and with long streaming hair. Springing from the ground and waving their arms around their heads, [they] sent forth most hideous yells. Their appearance was so strange, that it was scarcely like that of earthly inhabitants.' Despite this reaction, Darwin recorded plenty of evidence during his travels to demonstrate the essential unity of humankind and, much later, in his *Descent of Man* (1871), expressed the hope that, when both Monogenists and Polygenists accepted the principle of evolution, the dispute between them would 'die a silent and unobserved death'.

3. The demise of recapitulation is recounted in Stephen J. Gould, *Ontogeny and Philogeny*, Harvard University Press, 1977. Gould also describes how, soon after the collapse of recapitulation, the Dutch anatomist Louis Bolk proposed the opposite theory of neoteny ('holding onto youth'), the idea that 'juvenile traits of ancestors developed so slowly in descendants that they become adult features'. So, 'under recapitulation, adults should be like white children, but under neoteny white adults should be like black children'. Despite this reversal, Gould describes how Bolk still managed to extract a theory of white supremacy from his idea, claiming that 'the white race appears to be the most progressive, as being the most retarded'. The paradigm of racial inferiority was so strong that it could absorb both recapitulation and neoteny with relative ease (see also Gould, *Ever Since Darwin*, pp. 214–21; Gould, *The Mismeasure of Man*, pp. 119–22).

4. For example, *Progress of Race*, a study published in 1898 by Negroes Henry F.

Kletzing and William H. Crogman. The authors see the inevitability of the march of Anglo-Saxon civilization. New Zealanders, Tasmanians, Pacific Islanders and the Negroes of South Africa 'perished, not because of destructive wars and pestilence, but because they were unable to live in the environment of a 19th-century civilization... Their destruction was due not to a persecution which came to them from without, but to a lack of stamina within. Their extermination was due to the inexorable working out of a law as natural as the law of gravitation.'

5. R. Hernstein and C. Muray, *The Bell Curve: Intelligence and Class Structure in American Life*, The Free Press, 1994.

Chapter 3 (pp. 46–63)

1. O. Chadwick, *The Secularization of the European Mind in the Nineteeth Century*, Cambridge: CUP, 1975, pp. 18, 229, 264; J. Casanova, *Public Religions in the Modern World*, University of Chicago Press, 1994, pp. 12–14.

2. B.R. Wilson, *Religion in Secular Society*, London: Watts, 1966.

3. Quoted in Anthony Giddens, *Emile Durkheim: Selected Writings*, Cambridge: CUP, 1972, p. 245.

4. S. Bruce (ed.), *Religion and Modernization*, Oxford: Clarendon Press, 1992, p. 12.

5. Casanova, *Public Religions in the Modern World*, p. 3.

6. For example, P.L. Berger, *The Sacred Canopy*, New York: Anchor-Doubleday, 1967; *The Social Reality of Religion*, London: Penguin, 1973; *Facing Up to Modernity*, London: Penguin, 1979.

7. P.L. Berger, 'Secularism in Retreat', *National Interest* **46**, Winter 1996/7, p. 3.

8. R. Stark and R. Finke, *Acts of Faith: Explaining the Human Side of Religion*, University of California Press, 2000, p. 79.

9. Casanova, *Public Religions in the Modern World*, p. 19.

10. Cited by M. Goodridge, 'Ages of Faith: Romance or Reality?', *Sociological Review* **23**, 1975, pp. 381–96.

11. K. Thomas, *Religion and the Decline of Magic*, Weidenfeld & Nicolson, 1971.

12. Thomas, *Religion and the Decline of Magic*, pp. 171–72.

13. Thomas, *Religion and the Decline of Magic*, p. 159.

14. Thomas, *Religion and the Decline of Magic*, p. 164.

15. C.G. Brown, 'A Revisionist Approach to Religious Change', in S. Bruce (ed.), *Religion and Modernization*, Oxford: Clarendon Press, 1992, pp. 31–58.

16. L.J. Francis and P.W. Brierley, 'The Changing Face of the British Churches: 1975–1995', in D.G. Bromley (ed.) *Religion and the Social Order*, vol. 7, JAI Press Inc., 1997, pp. 159–84. It should be noted that measuring church adherence is a statistician's nightmare as only some denominations have an official church membership. In those cases where there is no membership list, sociologists use other markers of adherence such as regular attendance, financial commitment, etc. The references cited should be consulted for further information as to how patterns of religious commitment in society can be quantified.

17. Brown, 'A Revisionist Approach to Religious Change', pp. 46–47.

18. R. Finke, 'An Unsecular America', in S. Bruce (ed.), *Religion and Modernization*, Oxford: Clarendon Press, 1992, pp. 145–69.

19. Brown, 'A Revisionist Approach to Religious Change', p. 49; also see Finke, 'An Unsecular America'.

20. H. McLeod, 'Secular Cities? Berlin, London, and New York in the Later 19th and Early 20th Centuries', in S. Bruce (ed.),

Religion and Modernization, Oxford: Clarendon Press, 1992, pp. 59–89.

21. M. Abrams, D. Gerard and N. Timms (eds) *Values and Social Change in Britain*, Basingstoke: Macmillan, 1985.

22. A cottage industry continues to flourish comprising books either promoting or debunking the weird and the wonderful, including:
A. Aveni, *Behind the Crystal Ball: Magic and Science from Antiquity to the New Age*, Random House, 1996.
M. Gardner, *On the Wild Side*, Prometheus, 1992.
J. Randi, *An Encyclopedia of Claims, Frauds, and Hoaxes of the Occult and Supernatural*, St Martin's, 1995.
M. Shermer, *Why People Believe Weird Things: Pseudoscience, Superstition, and Other Confusions of our Time*, W.H. Freeman, 1997.

23. For a robust defence of the 'orthodox secularization model' see B.R. Wilson 'Reflections on a Many Sided Controversy', in S. Bruce (ed.), *Religion and Modernization*, Oxford: Clarendon Press, 1992, pp. 195–210.

24. McLeod, 'Secular Cities? Berlin, London, and New York in the Later 19th and Early 20th Centuries', p. 86.

25. Casanova, *Public Religions in the Modern World*, pp. 92–113.

26. Casanova, *Public Religions in the Modern World*, pp. 211–34.

27. For example, B. Appleyard, *Understanding the Present*, London: Picador, 1992. For a vigorous debunk of the notion, see Stark and Finke, *Acts of Faith*.

28. J. Brooke and G. Cantor, *Reconstructing Nature: The Engagement of Science and Religion*, Edinburgh: T & T Clark, 1998.

29. *Nature* **394**, 1998, p. 107.

30. McLeod, 'Secular Cities? Berlin, London, and New York in the Later 19th and Early 20th Centuries', p. 84.

31. M.C. Jacob, *The Newtonians and the English Revolution*, Ithica: Cornell University Press, 1976; M.C. Jacob, *The Radical Enlightenment: Pantheists, Freemasons and Republicans*, London: George Allen & Unwin, 1981.

32. McLeod, 'Secular Cities? Berlin, London, and New York in the Later 19th and Early 20th Centuries', pp. 83–84.

33. D.C. Dennett, *Darwin's Dangerous Idea: Evolution and the Meanings of Life*, Simon & Schuster, 1995. For further examples of the myriad ways in which science can be transformed to support different ideologies, see C.P. Tourney, *Conjuring Science: Scientific Symbols and Cultural Meanings in American Life*, Rutgers University Press, 1996.

34. O. Chadwick, *The Secularization of the European Mind in the Nineteenth Century*, Cambridge: CUP, 1975, p. 155.

35. O. Chadwick, *The Victorian Church*, part 2, London: Adam and Charles Black, 1970, pp. 15–23.

36. S. Budd, 'The Loss of Faith: Reasons for Unbelief Among Members of the Secular Movement in England, 1850–1950', *Past and Present*, **36**, 1967, pp. 106–25.

37. R. Stark and L. Jannaccone, *American Economic Review: Papers and Proceedings*, 1996, p. 436. Various 20th century interactions between science and religion in America have been surveyed by J. Gilbert, *Redeeming Culture: American Religion in an Age of Science*, University of Chicago Press, 1997.

38. C. Lemert, 'Science, Religion and Secularization', *Sociological Quarterly*, **20**, 1979, pp. 445–61.

39. J.H. Leuba, *The Belief in God and Immortality: A Psychological, Anthropological and Statistical Study*, Boston: Sherman, French & Co., 1916.

40. E.J. Larson and L.Witham, 'Scientists Are Still Keeping the Faith', *Nature* **386**, 1997, pp. 435–36.

41. *The Times*, 3rd April 1997; *The Daily Telegraph*, 3rd April 1997.

42. E.J. Larson and L.Witham, 'Leading Scientists Still Reject God', *Nature* **394**, 1998, p. 313.

43. D.R. Alexander, 'Theism and Science', *Nature* **378**, 1995, p. 433.

Chapter 4 (pp. 64–107)

1. D.C. Lindberg, *The Beginnings of Western Science*, University of Chicago Press, 1992, p. 355.

2. Brooke and Cantor, *Reconstructing Nature*, p. 8.

3. I have relied on a wide range of sources for this chapter. The following general works have been particularly useful:

J.H. Brooke, *Science and Religion: Some Historical Perspectives*, Cambridge: CUP, 1991.

Brooke and Cantor, *Reconstructing Nature*.

H. Butterfield, *The Origins of Modern Science*, London: G. Bell & Sons, 1957.

C. Chant and J. Fauvel (eds), *Darwin to Einstein: Historical Studies on Science and Belief*, Longman, 1980.

J.G. Crowther, *Founders of British Science*, London: The Cresset Press, 1960.

J. Dillenberger, *Protestant Thought and Natural Science*, Macmillan, 1983.

R.K. Faulkner, *Francis Bacon and the Project of Progress*, Rowman & Littlefield, 1993.

J.V. Field and F.A.J.L. James, *Renaissance and Revolution: Humanists, Scholars, Craftsmen and Natural Philosophers in Early Modern Europe*, Cambridge: CUP, 1993.

C.C. Gillispie, *The Edge of Objectivity*, Princeton, 1960.

D.C. Goodman (ed.), *Science and Religious Belief 1600–1900*, Milton Keynes: Open University Press, 1973.

A. Grafton, *New Worlds, Ancient Texts: The Power of Tradition and the Shock of Discovery*, Belknap Press/Harvard University Press, 1992.

A.R. Hall, *Isaac Newton, Adventurer in Thought*, Oxford: Basil Blackwell, 1992.

P. Harrison, *The Bible, Protestantism and the Rise of Natural Science*, Cambridge: CUP, 1998.

R. Hooykaas, *Religion and the Rise of Modern Science*, Edinburgh: Scottish Academic Press, 1972.

L. Jardine, *Ingenious Pursuits: Building the Scientific Revolution*, Doubleday, 1999.

H.F. Kearney, *Origins of the Scientific Revolution*, Longmans, 1964.

H.F. Kearney, *Science and Change 1500–1700*, London: World University Library/Weidenfeld & Nicolson, 1971.

A. Koestler, *The Sleepwalkers: A History of Man's Changing Vision of the Universe*, London: Penguin, 1964.

D.C. Lindberg and R.L. Numbers (eds), *God & Nature: Historical Essays on the Encounter Between Christianity and Science*, California: University of California Press, 1986.

D.C. Lindberg and R.S. Westman (eds), *Reappraisals of the Scientific Revolution*, Cambridge: CUP, 1990.

D.C. Lindberg, *The Beginnings of Western Science*, University of Chicago Press, 1992.

N. Livingstone (ed.), *Evangelicals and Science in Historical Perspective*, Oxford: OUP, 1999.

J. Losee, *A Historical Introduction to the Philosophy of Science*, Oxford: OUP, 1972.

J. Martin, *Francis Bacon, the State, and the Reform of Natural Philosophy*, Cambridge: CUP, 1992.

J.D. Moss, *Novelties in the Heavens: Rhetoric and Science in the Copernican Controversy*, University of Chicago Press, 1994.

Open University, *Science and Belief: From Copernicus to Darwin*, Blocks 1–6, Milton Keynes: Open University Press, 1974.

M. Osler, *Divine Will and the Mechanical Philosophy: Gassendi and Descartes on Contingency and Necessity in the Created World*, Cambridge: CUP, 1994.

M. Peltonen (ed.), *The Cambridge Companion to Bacon*, Cambridge: CUP, 1996.

J. Redwood, *European Science in the Seventeenth Century*, London: David & Charles, 1977.

C.A. Russell (ed.), *Science and Religious Belief: A Selection of Recent Historical Studies*, Milton Keynes: Open University Press, 1973.

C.A. Russell, *Cross-Currents: Interactions Between Science & Faith*, Leicester: IVP, 1985.

S. Shapin, *The Scientific Revolution*, University of Chicago Press, 1996.

Alan G.R. Smith, *Science and Society in the Sixteenth and Seventeenth Centuries*, London: Thames & Hudson, 1972.

B. Stephenson, *The Music of the Heavens: Kepler's Harmonic Astronomy*, Princeton University Press, 1994.

L. Stewart, *The Rise of Public Science: Rhetoric, Technology, and Natural Philosophy in Newtonian Britain, 1660–1750*, Cambridge: CUP, 1992.

K. Thomas, *Man and the Natural World: Changing Attitudes in England 1500–1800*, London: Penguin, 1983.

C. Webster, *The Great Instauration: Science, Medicine and Reform, 1626–1660*, Duckworth, 1975.

R.S. Westfall, *The Construction of Modern Science: Mechanisms and Mechanics*, Cambridge: CUP, 1977.

C. Wybrow, *The Bible, Baconianism, and Mastery Over Nature: The Old Testament and its Modern Misreading*, Lang, 1991.

4. R.J. Evans, *In Defence of History*, London: Granta Books, 1997, p. 120.

5. For a nuanced discussion of the vexed question of the continuity, or lack of it, between Greek, medieval and modern science, see Lindberg, *The Beginnings of Western Science*, pp. 360–68.

6. Lindberg, *The Beginnings of Western Science*, pp. 200–201.

7. Bacon, *Advancement of Learning*, book 3, chapter 4, p. 365.

8. Cited from Friedrich Klemm, 'A History of Western Technology', trans. D.W. Singer, MIT Press, 1964, pp. 21–22.

9. Hooykaas, *Religion and the Rise of Modern Science*, pp. 88–96.

10. Quoted in Crowther, *Founders of British Science*, p. 54.

11. See *Novum Organum*, 1, aph. 83; *De augmentis*, ll, c.2.

12. Tycho Brahe, *Astronomiae Instaurate Progmnasmata*, p. ii, chapter 3.

13. Cited in Harrison, *The Bible, Protestantism and the Rise of Natural Science*.

14. Harrison, *The Bible, Protestantism and the Rise of Natural Science*.

15. Harrison, *The Bible, Protestantism and the Rise of Natural Science*, p. 28.

16. Harrison, *The Bible, Protestantism and the Rise of Natural Science*, p. 74 and p. 77.

17. Harrison, *The Bible, Protestantism and the Rise of Natural Science*, p. 120.

18. Quoted in A. Koestler, *The Sleepwalkers*, p. 203.

19. John Wilkins, 'A Discourse Concerning a New Planet', 1640.

20. G.E.R. Lloyd, *Early Greek Science*, London: Chatto & Windus, 1970, p. 8.

21. B. Farrington, *Greek Science*, revised edition, London: Penguin, 1961, pp. 301–303.

22. Gillispie, *The Edge of Objectivity*, p. 75.

23. Lindberg, *The Beginnings of Western Science*, pp. 236–39.

24. See e.g. A.N. Whitehead, *Science & the Modern World*, London: Penguin, pp. 11–12.

25. All examples are from K.T. Hoppen, 'The Nature of the Early Royal Society', *British Journal for the History of Science* **9**, pp. 1–24 and 243–71.

26. See also G. Taubes, 'A Theory of Everything Takes Shape', *Science* **269**, 1995, pp. 1511–13; Paul Davies and Julian Brown (eds) *Superstrings: A Theory of Everything*, Cambridge: CUP, 1988.

Chapter 5 (pp. 108–39)

1. The Galileo publishing industry shows no sign of abating. Works which have been helpful in preparing this section include the following:

Brooke and Cantor, *Reconstructing Nature*.

G. De Santillana, *The Crime of Galileo*, Chicago, 1955.

S. Drake, *Galileo*, Oxford: OUP, 1980.

A. Fantoli, *Galileo, for Copernicanism and for the Church*, trans. G.V. Coyne, Vatican Observatory Publications, 1996.

R. Feldhay, *Galileo and the Church: Political Inquisition or Critical Dialogue?*, Cambridge: CUP, 1995.

M.A. Finocchiaro, *The Galileo Affair: A Documentary History*, University of California Press, 1989.

Galileo Galilei, 'Letter to the Grand Duchess Christina', 1615, in *Discoveries and Opinions of Galileo*, trans. with an introduction and notes by Stillman Drake, New York: Doubleday & Co. Inc., 1957.

Galileo Galilei, *Sidereus Nunclus or the Sideral Messenger*, trans. with introduction, conclusion and notes by Albert Van Helden, University of Chicago Press, 1989.

D.C. Goodman, 'Galileo and the Church', Unit 3 of *The Conflict Thesis and Cosmology*, Milton Keynes: Open University Press, 1974.

J.J. Langford, *Galileo, Science and the Church*, University of Michigan Press, 1992.

J. Losee, *A Historical Introduction to the Philosophy of Science*, Oxford: OUP, 1972.

P. Machamer (ed.) *The Cambridge Companion to Galileo*, Cambridge: CUP, 1998.

P. Redondi, *Galileo: Heretic*, trans. Raymond Rosenthal, Princeton University Press, 1987.

J. Reston, *Galileo: A Life*, London: Cassell, 1994.

M. Sharratt, *Galileo: Decisive Innovator*, Cambridge: CUP, 1996.

W.R. Shea, 'Galileo and the church', in D.C. Lindberg & R.L. Numbers (eds), *God and Nature: Historical Essays on the Encounter Between Christianity and Science*, University of California Press, 1986.

D. Sobel, *Galileo's Daughter*, London: Fourth Estate, 1999.

2. S. Drake, *Galileo*, Oxford: OUP, 1980, p. 64.

3. Galileo, 'Letter to the Grand Duchess Christina', p. 189.

4. Alan G.R. Smith, *Science and Society in the Sixteenth and Seventeenth Centuries*, London: Thames & Hudson, 1972, p. 97.

5. Richard S. Westfall, *The Construction of Modern Science: Mechanisms and Meanings*, Cambridge: CUP, 1977, p. 116.

6. Koestler, *The Sleepwalkers*, p. 362.

7. Hugh Kearney, *Science & Change 1500–1700*, World University Library/ Wiedenfeld & Nicolson, 1971, p. 104.

8. T.S. Kuhn, *The Copernican Revolution*, Harvard University Press, 1957, p. 196.

9. Further examples may be found in D.H. Kobe, 'Copernicus and Martin Luther: An Encounter Between Science and Religion', *American Journal of Physics* **66**, 1998, pp. 190–96.

10. Quoted in R. Hooykaas, *Religion and the Rise of Modern Science*, Edinburgh: Scottish Academic Press, 1972, p. 133.

11. Brooke and Cantor, *Reconstructing Nature*, p. 119.

12. Kobe, 'Copernicus and Martin Luther: An Encounter Between Science and Religion'.

13. Cited in W. Norlind, 'Copernicus and Luther: A Critical Study', *Isis* **44**, 1953, pp. 273–76.

14. James Atkinson, *Martin Luther and the Birth of Protestantism*, London: Penguin, 1968, p. 323–24.

15. Cited in Kobe, 'Copernicus and Martin Luther: An Encounter Between Science and Religion'.

16. Cited in Kobe, 'Copernicus and Martin Luther: An Encounter Between Science and Religion'.

17. G.J. Rheticus, *Treatise on Holy Scripture and the Motion of the Earth*, R. Hooykaas (ed.) and republished for the Royal Netherlands Academy by Amsterdam: North-Holland Publishing Co., 1984.

18. Quoted in Koestler, *The Sleepwalkers*, p. 250.

19. Kepler to Herwart von Hohenberg, 26 March 1598, *Gesammelte Werke* **13**, p. 193.

20. W.F. Farrar, *History of Interpretation*, London: Macmillan & Co., 1886, p. xviii.

21. Further details can be found in Edward Rosen, 'Calvin's Attitude Towards Copernicus', *Journal of the History of Ideas*, **21**, 1960, pp. 431–41.

22. J. Calvin, *Commentary on 1 Corinthians* 8.1.

23. J. Calvin, *Commentary on Genesis*, trans. John King, 2 vols, Edinburgh: Calvin Translation Society, 1847–50, 1:86–87 (the passage refers to Genesis 1:16).

24. See Robert S. Westman, 'The Copernicans and the Churches', in D.C. Lindberg & R.L. Numbers (eds), *God & Nature: Historical Essays on the Encounter Between Christianity and Science*, Berkeley: University of California Press, 1986.

25. Augustine, *De Genesi de literam*, ii:9.

26. Calvin, *Commentary on Genesis* 1:15.

27. Calvin, *Commentary on the Psalms* 136:7

28. John Wilkins, *Discourse Concerning a New Planet*, 1640.

29. Kepler, *Gesammelte Werke* 3.31

30. Quoted in *Science & Belief: From Copernicus to Darwin*, Block II, Units 4–5, Milton Keynes: Open University Press, 1974, p. 75.

31. William Foster, *A Sponge to Wipe Away the Weapon-Salve*, London, 1631.

32. René Descartes, *Passions of the Soul*, 1649.

33. Robert Boyle, 'A Free Inquiry into the Vulgarly Received Notion of Nature', in M.B. Hall (ed.), *Robert Boyle on Natural Philosophy*, Indiana University Press, 1965, pp. 150–53.

34. G.B. Deason, 'Reformation Theology and the Mechanistic Conception of Nature', in Lindberg and Numbers (eds), *God and Nature*, pp. 167–91.

35. Calvin, *Institutes of the Christian Religion* 1.16.2.

Chapter 6 (pp. 140–76)

1. C.A. Russell, *Cross-Currents, Interactions Between Science and Faith*, Leicester: IVP, 1985, p. 111.

2. M.C. Jacob, 'Christianity and the Newtonian Worldview', in D.C. Lindberg & R.L. Numbers (eds), *God and Nature: Historical Essays on the Encounter Between Christianity and Science*, University of California Press, 1986.

3. J. Toland, 'Christianity not Mysterious: Or, a Treatise Shewing, That there is nothing in the Gospel contrary to Reason, nor above it: And that no Christian Doctrine can be properly call'd a Mystery', 1696, p. 150.

4. P. Annet 'Supernaturals Examined', 1747, p. 44.

5. H. Butterfield, *The Origins of Modern Science*, London: G. Bell & Sons, 1957, p. 166.

6. In Voltaire, *Voltaire's Works*, Dingwall-Rock, New York, 1927.

7. D. Goodman, in *Scientific Progress and Religious Dissent*, Block 3, Units 6–8, Milton Keynes: Open University Press, 1974, p. 51.

8. C.C. Gillispie, *The Edge of Objectivity*, Princeton University Press, 1960, p. 154.

9. Condorcet, *Sketch for a Historical Picture of the Progress of the Human Kind*, trans. June Barraclough, Weidenfeld & Nicolson, 1955, p. 163.

10. Quoted by Roger Hahn, 'Laplace and the Mechanistic Universe' in Lindberg and Numbers, *God and Nature*, pp. 256–76.

11. See F.L. Holmes, *Lavoisier and the Chemistry of Life: An Exploration of Scientific Creativity*, University of Wisconsin Press, 1985, for a masterly exposition of Lavoisier's considerable achievements in the areas of chemistry and biochemistry.

12. Roger Hahn, 'Laplace's Religious Views', *Archives Internationales d'histoire des sciences* **8**, 1955, pp. 38–40; E. Whittaker, 'Laplace', *Mathematical Gazette*, **33**, 1949, pp. 1–12.

13. The details on Georges Cuvier have been largely obtained from D. Outram, *Georges Cuvier: Vocation, Science and Authority in Post-revolutionary France*, Manchester University Press, 1984. For further information on Cuvier and Lamarck see also the essays in C.A. Russell (ed.) *Science and Religious Belief: A Selection of Recent Historical Studies*, Milton Keynes: Open University Press, 1973.

14. Discussed by N. Coley, C. Lawless and G. Roberts in 'Nonconformity and the Growth of Technology' in *Science and Belief: from Copernicus to Darwin* Block 3, Units 6–8, Milton Keynes: Open University Press, 1974.

15. J. Priestley, *Autobiography*, with an Introduction by J. Lindsay, Adams & Dart, 1970, p. 76.

16. Quoted in B. Willey, *The 18th-Century Background*, London: Chatto & Windus, paperback edition 1980, p. 171–72.

17. Information on John Wesley has been obtained from:

R.E. Schofield, 'John Wesley and Science in 18th-Century England', *Isis* **44**, 1953, pp. 331–40.

J. Pollock, *John Wesley 1703–1791*, Hodder & Stoughton, 1989.

John Pudney, *John Wesley and His World*, Thames & Hudson, 1978.

C.A. Russell, *Science and Social Change 1700–1900*, Macmillan, 1983.

J.W. Haas, 'Eighteenth-Century Evangelical Responses to Science: John Wesley's Enduring Legacy, *Science & Christian Belief* **6**, 1994, pp. 83–102.

18. For further details see G. Cantor, *Michael Faraday: Sandemanian and Scientist*, Macmillan, 1991, from which much of the following material in this section has been obtained.

19. S.J. Gould, *Time's Arrow, Time's Cycle*, Cambridge, MA: Harvard University Press, 1987. For this section see also:

C.C. Gillispie, *Genesis and Geology*, Harvard University Press, 1951.

R. Hooykaas, *The Principle of Uniformity in Geology, Biology, and Theology*, Leiden: E.J. Brill, 1963.

J.R. Moore, *The Post-Darwinian Controversies: A Study of the Protestant Struggle to Come to Terms with Darwin in Great Britain and America, 1870–1900*, CUP, 1979.

R. Porter, 'Charles Lyell and the Principles of the History of Geology', *British Journal of the History of Science* **9**, 1976, pp. 91–103.

M.J.S. Rudwick, *The Meaning of Fossils*, Macdonald, London, 1972.

M.J.S. Rudwick, 'Caricature as a Source for the History of Science: De la Beche's anti-Lyellian sketches of 1831.' *Isis* **66**, 1975, pp. 534–60.

M. Rudwick, 'The Shape and Meaning of Earth History' in Lindberg & Numbers, *God and Nature*.

20. B. Rensberger, *How the World Works*, New York: William Morrow, 1986.

21. W.L. Stokes, *Essentials of Earth History*, Englewood Cliffs, NJ: Prentice-Hall, 1973, p. 37.

Chapter 7 (pp. 177–219)

1. The following sources have been used in this section on Darwinian evolution:

'The Crisis of Evolution', Block V, Units 12–14 of *Science & Belief: From Copernicus to Darwin*, Milton Keynes: Open University Press, 1974.

'The New Outlook for Science', Block 6, Units 15–16 of *Science & Belief: From Copernicus to Darwin*, Milton Keynes: Open University Press, 1974.

V. Blackmore and A. Page, *Evolution: The Great Debate*, Lion, 1989.

Brooke, *Science and Religion.*

F.B. Brown, 'The Evolution of Darwin's Theism', *Journal of the History of Biology* **19**, 1986, pp. 1–46.

O. Chadwick, 'Evolution & the Churches', in *The Victorian Church* part 2, Black, 1966, pp. 23–35.

C. Chant and J. Fauvel, *Darwin and Einstein: Historical Studies on Science & Belief*, Milton Keynes: Open University Press, 1980.

T. Cosslett, *Science and Religion in the Nineteenth Century*, Cambridge: CUP, 1984.

A. Desmond and J. Moore, *Darwin*, London: Michael Joseph, 1991.

J. Durant (ed.), *Darwinism and Divinity*, Oxford: Basil Blackwell, 1985.

C.L. Harris, *Evolution: Genesis and Revelations, with Readings from Empedocles to Wilson*, Albany: State University of New York Press, 1983.

J.V. Jensen, 'Return to the Wilberforce–Huxley Debate', *British Journal of the History of Science* **21**, 1988, pp. 161–79.

D. Livingstone, *Darwin's Forgotten Defenders*, Edinburgh: Scottish Academic Press, 1987.

N. Livingstone (ed.) *Evangelicals and Science in Historical Perspective*, Oxford: OUP, 1999.

J.R. Lucas, 'Wilberforce and Huxley: A Legendary Encounter', *The Historical Journal* **22**, 1979, pp. 313–30.

E. Mayr, *Towards a New Philosophy of Biology: Observations of an Evolutionist*, Harvard University Press, 1988.

J.R. Moore, *The Post-Darwinian Controversies: A Study of the Protestant Struggle to Come to Terms with Darwin in Great Britain and America, 1870–1900*, Cambridge: CUP, 1979.

R.L. Numbers, *The Creationists*, University of California Press, 1992.

D.R. Oldroyd, *Darwinian Impacts: An Introduction to the Darwinian Revolution*, 2nd edition, Milton Keynes: Open University Press, 1983.

D. Ospovat, *The Development of Darwin's Theory: Natural History, Natural Theology and Natural Selection, 1838–1859*, Cambridge: CUP, 1981.

A. Plantinga, *Warranted Christian Belief*, Oxford: OUP, 2000.

J. Rachels, *Created from Animals: The Moral Implications of Darwinism*, Oxford: OUP, 1990.

M. Ruse *The Darwinian Revolution: Science Red in Tooth and Claw*, University of Chicago Press, 1979.

J.A. Secord, *Victorian Sensation: The Extraordinary Publication, Reception, and Secret Authorship of Vestiges of the Natural History of Creation*, University of Chicago Press, 2000.

C.H. Smith (ed.), *Alfred Russel Wallace: An Anthology of His Shorter Writings*, Oxford: OUP, 1991.

2. M.A. Fay, 'Did Marx offer to dedicate *Capital* to Darwin? A reassessment of the evidence', *Journal of the History of Ideas* **39**, 1978, pp. 133–46.

3. The following references are relevant to this section:

R. Barton, 'An Influential Set of Chaps: The X-Club and Royal Society Politics 1864–85', *British Journal of the History of Science*, **23**, 1990, pp. 53–81.

Brooke, *Science and Religion.*

O. Chadwick, *The Victorian Church*, Oxford: OUP, 1970.

T. Cosslett, *Science and Religion in the 19th Century*, Cambridge: CUP, 1984.

Desmond and Moore, *Darwin*.

S. Gilley and A. Loades, 'Thomas Henry Huxley: The War between Science and Religion', *Journal of Religion* **61**, 1981, pp. 285–308.

A.J. Harrison, 'Scientific Naturalists and the Government of the Royal Society 1850–1900', PhD thesis, Department of the History of Science and Technology, Open University, 1988.

T.W. Heyck, *The Transformation of Intellectual Life in Victorian England*, London: Croom Helm, 1982.

J.V. Jensen, *Thomas Henry Huxley: Communicating for Science*, University of Delaware Press, 1991.

J. Laurent, 'Science, Society and Politics in Late-19th-Century England: A Further Look at Mechanics' Institutes', *Social Studies of Science* (SAGE, London) **14**, 1984, pp. 585–619.

Moore, *The Post-Darwinian Controversies*.

Oldroyd, *Darwinian Impacts*.

Plantinga, *Warranted Christian Belief*.

Rachels, *Created from Animals*.

C.A. Russell, 'The Conflict Metaphor and its Social Origins', *Science and Christian Belief* **1**, 1989, pp. 3–26.

Russell, *Science and Social Change 1700–1900*.

F.M. Turner, *Between Science & Religion: The Reaction to Victorian Scientific Naturalism in Late-Victorian England*, Yale University Press, 1974.

F.M. Turner, 'The Victorian Conflict between Science and Religion: A Professional Dimension', *Isis* **69**, 1978, pp. 356–76.

W.T. Van Dyck (ed.), *The Teaching of Huxley: A Compendium*, Beyrout, 1931.

4. For example, as noted in chapter 5, Calvin's famous 'quotation' denouncing Copernicus has no basis in fact (R. Hooykaas, 'Science and Reformation', *Journal of World History* **3**, 1956, pp. 4–139; E. Rosen, 'Calvin's attitude towards Copernicus', *Journal of the History of Ideas* **21**, 1960, p. 431), and neither does another passage from John Lightfoot about the

Earth's creation in 4004 BC (E.E. Daub 'Demythologizing White's Warfare of Science With Theology', *American Biology Teacher*, December 1978, pp. 553–56). Furthermore, White claimed that Simpson's use of chloroform for obstetric anaesthesia met with religious opposition, but this claim has also been refuted (A.D. Farr 'Religious Opposition to the Obstetric Anaesthesia – A Myth?' *Annals of Science* **40**, 1983, pp. 159–77).

Chapter 8 (pp. 220–88)

1. P.B. Medawar, *The Art of the Soluble*, London: Methuen, 1967, p. 132; see also D.L. Hull, *Science as a Process: An Evolutionary Account of the Social and Conceptual Development of Science*, University of Chicago Press, 1988.

2. S.W. Hawking, *A Brief History of Time*, Bantam Press, 1988.

3. Quoted in S. Weinberg, *Nature* **330**, 1987, pp. 433–37.

4. P.B. Medawar, *The Art of the Soluble*, London: Penguin, 1969.

5. See, for example, George Gale, 'Science and the Philosophers', *Nature* **312**, 1984, pp. 491–94.

6. I. Lakatos, 'Falsification and the Methodology of Scientific Research Programmes', in I. Lakatos and A. Musgrave (eds), *Criticism and the Growth of Knowledge*, Cambridge: CUP, 1970.

7. K. Popper, 'Natural Selection and the Emergence of Mind', *Dialectica* **32**, 1978, pp. 339–55.

8. Quoted in G. Holton, *Science and Antiscience*, Harvard University Press, 1993, p. 81.

9. T.S. Kuhn 'Logic of Discovery or Psychology of Research?', in Lakatos and Musgrave *Criticism and the Growth of Knowledge*, p. 13.

10. T.S. Kuhn, *The Structure of Scientific Revolutions*, University of Chicago Press, 1962.

11. The following references illustrate the debate between Popper and Kuhn from varying points of view:

Barry Barnes, *About Science*, Oxford: Basil Blackwell, 1985.

S.V. Barnes, 'On the Reception of Scientific Beliefs', in B. Barnes (ed.), *Sociology of Science: Selected Readings*, London: Penguin, 1972, pp. 269–91.

K.D. Knorr-Cetina and M. Mulkay (eds), *Science Observed*, Sage Publications, 1983.

H.M. Collins, *Changing Order: Replication and Induction in Scientific Practice*, Sage, 1985.

M.P. Hanen, M.J. Osler and R.G. Weyant (eds), *Science, Pseudoscience and Society*, Wilfrid Laurier University Press, 1979.

David Lyon, 'Valuing in Social Science: Post-Impiricism and Christian Responses', *Christian Scholars Review* **12**, 1983, pp. 324–38.

P. Medawar, *The Threat and the Glory: Reflections on Science and Scientists*, Oxford: OUP, 1990, pp. 91–101.

Michael Mulkay, *Science and Sociology of Knowledge*, London: George Allen & Unwin, 1979.

N.A. Notturno, 'The Popper/Kuhn Debate: Truth and Two Faces of Relativism', *Psychological Medicine* **14**, 1984, pp. 273–89.

Anthony O'Hear, 'Popper and the Philosophy of Science', *New Scientist*, 22 August 1985, pp. 43–45.

J.R. Ravetz, 'Criticisms of Science' in Ina Spieger-Rosing and Derek de Solla Price, *Science, Technology and Society*, London: Sage Publications, 1977, pp. 71–88.

Martin Rudwick, 'Senses of the Natural World and Senses of God: Another Look at the Historical Relation of Science and Religion', in A.R. Peacocke (ed.), *The Sciences and Theology in the 20th Century*, University of Notre Dame Press, 1981, pp. 241–61.

J. Taylor, 'Science, Christianity and the Postmodern Agenda', *Science & Christian Belief* **10**, 1998, pp. 163–78.

John Ziman, *Reliable Knowledge*, Cambridge: CUP, 1978.

12. I. Lakatos, 'History of science and its rational reconstructions', in *The Methodology of Scientific Research Programmes*, J. Worrall and G. Currie (eds), Cambridge: CUP, 1978, p. 112.

13. P. Feyarabend, *Against Method*, London: New Left Books, 1975.

14. Anon, 'The Sokal Affair Takes Transatlantic Turn', *Nature* **385**, 1997, p. 381; K. Gottfried and K.G. Wilson, 'Science as a Cultural Construct', *Nature* **386**, 1997, pp. 545–47; Anon, 'Campuses Ring to a Stormy Clash Over Truth and Reason', *Nature* **387**, 1997, pp. 331–35; P.A. Boghossian, 'What is Social Construction?', *The Times Literary Supplement*, 23 February 2001, pp. 6–8.

15. Quoted in L. Wolpert, *The Unnatural Nature of Science*, Faber & Faber, 1992, p. 99.

16. R. Trigg, *Rationality and Science: Can Science Explain Everything?*, Oxford: Blackwell, 1993, p. 66.

17. J.-F. Lyotard, *The Postmodern Condition: A Report on Knowledge*, trans. G. Bennington and B. Massumi, Manchester: Manchester University Press, 1985, p. 29.

18. R. Trigg, *Rationality and Science*, p. 117. See also Boghossian, 'What is Social Construction?', and A. Marwick, 'All Quiet on the Postmodern Front', *The Times Literary Supplement*, 23 February 2001, pp. 13–14.

19. M.B. Foster, 'The Christian Doctrine of Creation and the Rise of Modern Natural Science', *Mind* **43**, 1934, pp. 446–68 (reprinted in Russell, *Science and Religious Belief*).

20. H. Collins, *The Times Higher Education Supplement*, 30 September 1994, p. 18.

21. H. Collins, *Nature* **370**, 1994, p. 605.

22. S. Shapin, *A Social History of Truth: Civility and Science in 17th-Century England*, University of Chicago Press, 1994.

23. M.C. Banner, 'The justification of science and the rationality of religious belief', Oxford: Clarendon Press, 1990, pp. 126–30. See also P. Lipton, *Inference to the Best Explanation*, London: Routledge & Kegan Paul, 1991.

24. C. Darwin, *On the Origin of Species by Means of Natural Selection or the Preservation of Favoured Races in the Struggle for Life*, London: Penguin, 1968 (1st published 1859), p. 435.

25. Darwin, *On the Origin of Species*, p. 415.

26. Quoted in M. Longair, *Theoretical Concepts in Physics*, Cambridge: CUP, 1984, p. 7.

27. S. Weinberg, *Nature* **330**, 1987, pp. 433–37.

28. P. Davies, *The Mind of God*, New York: Simon & Schuster, 1992, p. 173.

29. P. Davies, *God and the New Physics*, Dent, 1983, p. ix.

30. A.R. Peacocke *Theology for a Scientific Age*, Oxford: Basil Blackwell, 1990, p. 82.

31. L. Wolpert *The Unnatural Nature of Science*, Faber & Faber, 1992, p. 7.

32. R. Dawkins, *Science & Christian Belief* **7**, 1995, pp. 45–50.

33. R. Dawkins, *The Selfish Gene*, 2nd edition, Oxford: OUP, 1989, p. 192.

34. Dawkins, *The Selfish Gene*, p. 193.

35. Wolpert *The Unnatural Nature of Science*.

36. Quoted in Wolpert *The Unnatural Nature of Science*, p. 60.

37. Quoted in Wolpert *The Unnatural Nature of Science*, p. 143.

38. Wolpert *The Unnatural Nature of Science*, p. 1.

39. For some striking examples of this statement see N.S. Hetherington, 'Just How Objective is Science?', *Nature* **306**, 1983, pp. 727–30.

40. B. Berber, 'Resistance by Scientists to Scientific Discovery', *Science* **134**, 1961, pp. 596–602.

41. T.S. Kuhn, *The Structure of Scientific Revolutions*, 2nd edition, Chicago: Chicago University Press, 1970, p. 84.

42. 1 Corinthians 15:14.

43. Matthew 28:11–15.

44. M. Ruse, 'From Belief to Unbelief – and Halfway Back', *Zygon* **29**, 1994, p. 31.

45. For a much fuller discussion of these points from varying points of view see:
M.C. Banner, *The Justification of Science and the Rationality of Religious Belief*, Oxford: Clarendon Press, 1990.
J. Hick, *Evil and the God of Love*, 2nd edition, London: Macmillan, 1977.
E.L. Schoen, *Religious Explanations: A Model From the Sciences*, Durham, NC: Duke University Press, 1985.
I am indebted to these authors for many of the points summarized in this section.

46. N. Nicolson (ed.) *The Letters of Virginia Woolf*, London: Hogarth Press, iii, 1977, p. 294.

47. Hick, *Evil and the God of Love*, p. 374.

48. Darwin, *On the Origin of Species*, p. 205.

49. Research News, *Science* **267**, 1995, pp. 1421–22. Also see J.B.C. Jackson and A.H. Cheetham, 'Phylogeny Reconstruction and the Tempo of Speciation in Cheilostome Bryozoa', *Paleobiology* **20**, 1994, p. 407.

50. J. Polkinghorne, *Science and Christian Belief*, SPCK, 1994, p. 41.

51. Cantor, *Michael Faraday*.

52. See Banner, *The Justification of Science and the Rationality of Religious Belief*, for a particularly fine example of this point.

53. S.J. Gould, *Bully for Brontosaurus: Reflections in Natural History*, Hutchinson

Radius, 1991, p. 430. Also published by London: Penguin, 1992.

54. R. Dawkins, 'The Ultraviolet Garden', Royal Institution Christmas Lecture No. 4, 1991.

55. E.O. Wilson, *Sociobiology: The New Synthesis*, Harvard University Press, 1975, p. 3.

56. R. Dawkins, *Unweaving the Rainbow*, London: Penguin, 1998, pp. ix-x.

57. F. Crick, *The Astonishing Hypothesis: The Scientific Search for the Soul*, Simon & Schuster, 1994, p. 3.

58. D.M. MacKay, *The Open Mind and Other Essays*, Leicester: IVP, 1988, p. 49.

59. D. Hume, *Dialogues Concerning Natural Religion*, edited and with a commentary by Nelson Pike, New York: Bobbs-Merrill, 1970, p. 22. Ironically Hume put this passage into the mouth of the theist, Cleanthes. In its context Hume is using the claims of Cleanthes to criticize the version of the design argument that tries to extrapolate from the nature of the world to the nature of the Deity.

60. Quoted in S. Rose, 'Reflections on Reductionism', *Trends in Biochemical Sciences* **13**, 1988, pp. 160–62.

61. S. Sutherland, 'Impoverished Minds', *Nature* **364**, 1993, p. 767.

62. N. Bohr, *Atomic Physics and Human Knowledge*, Wiley, 1958. See also A.P. French and P.J. Kennedy (eds) *Niels Bohr: A Centenary Volume*, Harvard University Press, 1985.

63. MacKay, *The Open Mind*, p. 35.

64. Peacocke *Theology for a Scientific Age*.

65. S. Weinberg, *Nature* **330**, 1987, pp. 433–37.

66. P. Atkins, 'Will Science Ever Fail?', *New Scientist*, 8 August 1992, pp. 32–35.

67. Wilson, *Sociobiology*, p. 296.

68. Jones, in the Introduction to *The Language of the Genes*, based on the 1991 Reith Lectures.

69. J. Polkinghorne, *Reason and Reality*, SPCK, 1991, p. 21. Polkinghorne has a very helpful discussion on 'models' in chapter 2 of this book entitled 'Rational Discourse'. Other useful discussions of 'models', considerably more extensive than that provided here, will be found in:

I.G. Barbour, *Myths, Models and Paradigms*, London: SCM Press, 1974.

I.G. Barbour, *Religion in an Age of Science*, London: SCM Press, 1991.

A.R. Peacocke, *Theology for a Scientific Age*, Oxford: Basil Blackwell, 1990.

A.R. Peacocke, *Intimations of Reality*, University of Notre Dame Press, 1984.

70. S. McFague, *Models of God*, Fortress Press, 1987, p. 33, quoted in Polkinghorne, *Reason and Reality*, p. 30.

71. Polkinghorne, *Reason and Reality*, p. 30.

Chapter 9 (pp. 289–329)

1. For example:
   P. Skelton (ed.), *Evolution*, Addison-Wesley & Open University, 1993.
   M. Ridley, *Evolution*, Oxford: Blackwell Scientific, 1993.
   D. Young, *The Discovery of Evolution*, Cambridge: CUP, 1992.
   S. Jones (ed.) *The Cambridge Encyclopedia of Human Evolution*, Cambridge: CUP, 1992.

2. Moore, *The Post-Darwinian Controversies*, p. 92.

3. G.M. Marsden in *Science and Creationism* A. Montagu (ed.), Oxford: Oxford University Press, 1984, p. 101.

4. The precise figures depend on how the question is phrased. In 1982 Gallup conducted a survey in the USA of beliefs concerning creationism. The sample consisted of 1,518 adults over the age of 18. Of those sampled, of whom nearly a fourth

were college graduates, 44 per cent believed that 'God created man pretty much in his present form at one time within the last 10,000 years.' Thirty eight per cent accepted theistic evolution and 9 per cent non-theistic evolution (9 per cent other categories). In a survey of undergraduates in three American states, published in *The Chronicle of Higher Education*, 19 November 1986, more than half said they were creationists.

5. Young, *The Discovery of Evolution*, p. 115.

6. Young, *The Discovery of Evolution*, p. 127.

7. Moore, *The Post-Darwinian Controversies*, p. 90.

8. Quoted in Montagu, *Science and Creationism*, p. 121.

9. The information cited on *The Fundamentals* is from Livingstone, *Darwin's Forgotten Defenders*, pp. 147–54; Marsden in Montagu, *Science and Creationism*, p. 102; Numbers in Lindberg and Numbers, *God and Nature*, pp. 392–94.

10. Quoted in Gould, *Bully for Brontosaurus*, p. 421.

11. The information concerning these two books cited here is from Gould, *Bully for Brontosaurus*, pp. 423f.

12. D.B. Paul and H.G. Spencer, 'The Hidden Science of Eugenics', *Nature* **374**, 1995, pp. 302–304.

13. Cited in Paul and Spencer, 'The Hidden Science of Eugenics'.

14. S.J. Holmes, *Studies in Evolution and Eugenics*, London: George Routledge & Sons, 1923, p. 62 and p. 72.

15. R. Pearl, *American Journal of Hygiene* **1**, 1921, pp. 664–65.

16. Paul and Spencer, 'The Hidden Science of Eugenics'.

17. D. Nelkin, *The Creation Controversy*, W.W. Norton, 1982, p. 33.

18. R.A. Eve and F.B. Harrold, *The Creationist Movement in Modern America*, Boston, MA: Twayne Publishers, 1991, p. 188.

19. G.M. Marsden, 'Literal Interpretations', *Nature* **360**, 1992, pp. 637–38.

20. R.L. Numbers, *The Creationists*, in Lindberg and Numbers, *God and Nature*, pp. 407–15.

21. Numbers, *The Creationists*, p. xi.

22. Nelkin, *The Creation Controversy*, p. 86.

23. Nelkin, *The Creation Controversy*, p. 20.

24. Quoted in Nelkin, *The Creation Controversy*, p. 173.

25. More detailed accounts of the creationist campaigns can be found in:
   T.M. Berra, *Evolution and the Myth of Creationism*, Stanford University Press, 1990.
   Montagu, *Science and Creationism*.
   Nelkin, *The Creation Controversy*.
   Numbers, in Lindberg and Numbers, *God and Nature*.
   R.L. Numbers, *Darwinism Comes to America*, Harvard University Press, 1998.
   M. Ruse (ed.) *But Is It Science? The Philosophical Question in the Creation/Evolution Controversy*, New York: Prometheus Books, 1988.
   I.L. Zabilka, *Scientific Malpractice: The Creation/Evolution Debate*, Bristol Books, 1992.

26. 'Kansas Kicks Evolution Out of the Classroom', *Nature* **400**, 1999, p. 701; the teaching of evolution was restored in 2001.

27. W.J. Bryan, *The Forum* **70**, July 1923, p. 1679.

28. H. Morris, *King of Creation*, San Diego: Christian Literature Press, 1980.

29. C. Matrisciana and R. Oakland, *The Evolution Conspiracy*, Harvest House Publishers, 1991, p. 15.

30. H. Spencer, *Progress: Its Law and Causes*, in *Essays: Scientific, Political and Speculative*, New York: Appleton, 1915, p. 35.

31. H.J. Muller, *Out of the Night*, New York, 1935. Quoted by J. Glover in *What Sort of People Should There Be?*, London: Penguin, 1984, p. 32.

32. J.D. Bernal, *The World, the Flesh and the Devil*, London: Cape, 1929, pp. 68–73.

33. H. Trevor-Roper (ed.), *Hitler's Table-Talk*, London: Weidenfeld & Nicolson, 1963.

34. R. Dawkins, in a speech at the Edinburgh Science Festival on 15 April 1992.

35. W. Dykeman and J.Stokeley, 'Scopes and Evolution – the Jury is Still Out', *New York Times Magazine*, 12 March 1971, pp. 72–76.

36. N.J. Segraves, *The Creation Report*, Creation-Science Research Center, San Diego, 1977, p. 17; 'Fifteen Years of Creationism', pp. 2–3.

37. Quoted in Numbers, *Darwinism Comes to America*, p. 396.

38. Nelkin, *The Creation Controversy*, p. 172.

39. *Congressional Record*, 9 April 1975, H2585–2587.

40. H.M. Morris, *Many Infallible Proofs: Practical and Useful Evidences of Christianity*, San Diego: Creation-Life, 1974, p. 249.

41. D.T. Gish, *Evolution: The Fossils Say No!*, San Diego: Creation-Life, 1972, p. 2.

42. See, for example, J.A. Endler, *Natural Selection in the Wild*, Monographs in population biology, Princeton University Press, 1986; 'Special News Report', *Science* **267**, 1995, pp. 30–33.

43. S.J. Gould, *Evolution as Fact and Theory*, Discover, May 1981.

44. Quoted in Ruse *But Is It Science?*, p. 35, note 27.

45. For some rare examples see Numbers, *The Creationists*, pp. 251–55

46. Quoted by Numbers, *The Creationists*, p. x.

47. Numbers, *The Creationists*, pp. 255–57.

48. Numbers, *The Creationists*, pp. 290–94.

49. R. Dawkins, 'A scientist's case against God', an edited version of Dr Dawkins' speech at the Edinburgh International Science Festival on 15 April 1992, published in *The Independent*, 20 April 1992.

50. R. Dawkins, *The Extended Phenotype*, Oxford: OUP, 1982, p. 181.

51. See, for example, Nehemiah 9:6; Job 9:1–10, 26:1–14; 36:26 – 41:34; Psalms 24:1–2; 36:6; 50:10–12; 77:16–20; 104:1–30; 148:7–8; Isaiah 45:7; Jeremiah 10:13; 51:16; Amos 4:13; Matthew 5:45; 6:25–34; Acts 17:24–25; Colossians 1:15–17; Hebrews 1:1–3.

52. A. Peacocke, *Theology For a Scientific Age*, enlarged edition, London: SCM Press, 1993, pp. 173–77.

53. A. Moore, *Science and Faith*, London: Kegan Paul, Trench & Co., 1889, p. 184.

54. A. Moore, 'The Christian Doctrine of God', in C. Gore (ed.) *Lux Mundi*, 12th edition, London: Murray, 1891, p. 73.

55. Origen, *First Principles*, book iv, chapter 3, trans. G.W. Butterworth, 1936.

56. Augustine, *The Literal Meaning of Genesis*, Vol. 1, trans. and annotated by J.H. Taylor, New York: Newman Press, 1982.

57. For translations of these accounts together with extensive notes see:
S. Dalley, *Myths From Mesopotamia*, Oxford: OUP, 1989.
A. Heidel, *The Gilgamesh Epic and Old Testament Parallels*, University of Chicago Press, 1946.
A. Heidel, *The Babylonian Genesis*, 2nd edition, University of Chicago Press, 1951.

58. G.J. Wenham, *Word Biblical Commentary*, Vol. 1, *Genesis 1–15*, Texas: Word Books, 1987. A much fuller discussion of the literary structure of Genesis is found in this commentary.

59. R. Hess, 'Genesis 1–2 and recent studies of ancient texts', *Science & Christian Belief* **7**, 1995, pp. 141–49.

60. Hess, 'Genesis 1–2 and recent studies of ancient texts'.

61. Heidel, *The Babylonian Genesis*, p. 132.

62. Dalley, *Myths From Mesopotamia*, pp. 9–35.

63. Dalley, *Myths From Mesopotamia*, p. 14

64. Heidel, *The Babylonian Genesis*, pp. 8–9.

65. Heidel, *The Babylonian Genesis*, p. 126.

66. Quoted in Heidel, *The Babylonian Genesis*, p. 89.

67. For a more detailed discussion of this point see Wenham, *Word Biblical Commentary, Vol. 1, Genesis 1–15*, pp. 11–15.

68. G.F. Hasel, 'The significance of the Cosmology in Genesis 1 in Relation to Ancient Near Eastern Parallels', *Andrews University Seminary Studies* **10**, 1972, pp. 1–20.

69. Wenham, *Word Biblical Commentary, Vol. 1, Genesis 1–15*, p. 21.

70. *The Times*, 25 October 1995.

71. Hess, 'Genesis 1–2 and recent studies of ancient texts'.

72. Wenham, *Word Biblical Commentary, Vol. 1, Genesis 1–15*, p. xlix.

Chapter 10 (pp. 330–59)

1. The hey-day of the creationist campaigns was in the 1980s, in the process spawning a massive literature. The list that follows represent a few examples of books written during that era, with some more recent examples, representing various viewpoints:
Blackmore and Page, *Evolution: The Great Debate*.
Derek Burke (ed.), *Creation and Evolution*, Leicester: IVP, 1985
N. Eldredge, *The Triumph of Evolution and the Failure of Creationism*, Macmillan, 2000.
A. Flew, *Darwinian Evolution*, Paladin, 1984.
Douglas J. Futuyama, *Science on Trial: The Case for Evolution*, New York: Pantheon Books, 1983.
S. Goldberg, *Seduced by Science*, New York University Press, 1999.
J. Haught, *God After Darwin*, Westview Press, 1999.
James Houston, *I Believe in the Creator*, London: Hodder & Stoughton, 1979.
Philip Kitcher, *Abusing Science: The Case Against Creationism*, Milton Keynes: Open University Press, 1983.
K. Miller, *Finding Darwin's God*, Cliff Street Books, 1999.
Mark Ridley, *The Problems of Evolution*, Oxford: OUP, 1985.

2. R. Dawkins, *The Blind Watchmaker*, Longman, 1986.

3. In *Charles Darwin and Thomas Henry Huxley: Autobiographies*, Gavin de Beer (ed.), London: OUP, 1974, p. 54.

4. T.H. Huxley, *Science and Hebrew Tradition: Essays by T.H. Huxley*, D. Appleton & Co., 1920, p. 47. This essay was based on Huxley's 'Lectures on Evolution' given in New York in 1876.

5. J. Houghton, *The Search For God: Can Science Help?*, Lion, 1995, p. 84–85.

6. Dawkins, *The Blind Watchmaker*, p. xi and p. 49.

7. J. Monod, *Chance and Necessity*, Collins, 1972, p. 110.

8. Quoted from a BBC broadcast talk, cited in D.J. Bartholomew, *God of Chance*, London: SCM Press, 1984, p. 16.

9. Rachels, *Created from Animals*, p. 124.

10. J.P. Hunter and J. Jernvall, 'The Hypocone as a Key Innovation in Mammalian Evolution', *Proceedings of the National Academy of Sciences USA* **92**, 1995, pp. 10718–22.

11. See, for example, Skelton, *Evolution*. On the topics in this section see also:
E.G. Nisbet and N.H. Sleep, 'The Habitat and Nature of Early Life', *Nature* **409**, 2001, pp. 1080–1091.
S.B. Carroll, 'Chance and Necessity: The Evolution of Morphological Complexity

and Diversity, *Nature* **409**, 2001, pp. 1102–1109.

R.D. Knight and L.F. Landweber, 'The Early Evolution of the Genetic Code', *Cell* **101**, 2000, pp. 569–72.

M. Pagel, 'Inferring the Historical Patterns of Biological Evolution', *Nature* **401**, 1999, pp. 877–84.

12. Dennett, *Darwin's Dangerous Idea*, p. 83.

13. Dawkins, *The Blind Watchmaker*, p. 50.

14. Dennett, *Darwin's Dangerous Idea*, p. 135.

15. C. Darwin, 1887, cited in Durant *Darwinism and Divinity*, p. 67.

16. K. Thomas, *Man and the Natural World: Changing Attitudes In England 1500–1800*, London: Penguin, 1983, p. 40.

17. Thomas, *Man and the Natural World*.

18. Thomas, *Mar. and the Natural World*, cited on p. 117.

19. *The Times*, 23 January 1996, p. 1. A civil case was brought by the police but losing the case cost the Metropolitan Police Commissioner £2,644.

20. Gould, *Bully for Brontosaurus*, pp. 338–39. Gould's essay entitled 'Kropotkin Was No Crackpot' in this volume, from which this quote was extracted, makes some useful points on 'Nature red in tooth and claw'.

21. Cited in Durant *Darwinism and Divinity*, p. 67.

22. H.J. Van Till, 'Basil, Augustine, and the doctrine of creation's functional integrity', *Science & Christian Belief* **8**, 1996, pp. 21–38.

23. I. Berlin, *The Hedgehog and the Fox*, Weidenfeld, London, 1967.

Chapter 11 (pp. 360–406)

1. For a wide variety of more nuanced definitions see, for example:

A.C. Danto 'Naturalism' in P. Edwards (ed.) *The Encyclopedia of Philosophy*, vol. 5, New York: Macmillan, 1967.

A. Plantinga 'Methodological Naturalism', paper presented at the conference 'Our knowledge of God, Christ, and nature', University of Notre Dame, April 1993.

W.B. Drees, *Religion, Science and Naturalism*, Cambridge: CUP, 1996.

2. M. Ruse, *Taking Darwin Seriously*, Oxford: Basil Blackwell, 1986.

3. C. Lumsden & E.O. Wilson, *Genes, Mind, and Culture*, Cambridge, MA: Harvard University Press, 1981.

4. T.J. Bouchard, D.T. Lykken, M. McGue, N.L. Segal and A. Tellegen, 'Sources of Human Psychological Differences: The Minnesota Study of Twins Reared Apart', *Science* **250**, 1990, pp. 223–28.

5. B. Devlin, M. Daniels and K. Roeder, 'The Heritability of IQ', *Nature* **388**, 1997, pp. 468–71; M. McGue, 'The Democracy of the Genes', *Nature* **388**, 1997, pp. 417–18.

6. Wilson, *Sociobiology*, p. 2.

7. E.O. Wilson, *Consilience: The Unity of Knowledge*, Abacus, 1998, p. 165. See also the critique of Evolutionary Psychology which appeared after the completion of this chapter: H. Rose and S.P.R. Rose (eds), *Alas, Poor Darwin: Arguments Against Evolutionary Psychology*, London: Jonathan Cape, 2000.

8. Wilson, *Sociobiology*; E.O. Wilson, *On Human Nature*, Harvard University Press, 1978.

9. D. Barash, *Sociobiology and Behavior*, New York: Elsevier, 1977.

10. Wilson, *Sociobiology*, p. 167.

11. D. Barash, *The Whisperings Within: Evolution and the Origins of Human Nature*, London: Penguin, 1979.

12. E.O. Wilson, *The New York Times Magazine*, 12 October 1975.

13. R. Thornhill and C.T. Palmer, *A Natural History of Rape: Biological Bases of Sexual*

Coercion, MIT Press, 2000. See the scathing review by J.A. Coyne and A. Berry in *Nature* **404**, 2000, pp. 121–22.

14. M.P. Ghiglieri, *The Dark Side of Man: Tracing the Origins of Male Violence*, Perseus, 1999. See the critical review by R.C. Lewontin in *Nature* **400**, 1999, pp. 728–29.

15. Lumsden and Wilson, *Genes, Mind, and Culture*.

16. Lumsden and Wilson, *Genes, Mind, and Culture*, p. ix, note 80.

17. Lumsden and Wilson, *Genes, Mind, and Culture*, p. 349.

18. C.J. Lumsden, *Ethology and Sociobiology* **10**, 1989, pp. 12–13.

19. P. Kitcher, *Vaulting Ambition: Sociobiology and the Quest for Human Nature*, Cambridge, MA: MIT Press, 1985, pp. 344–50.

20. For a sophisticated version of an evolutionary theory of cultural change and a more detailed discussion of the various sociobiological theories than my brief description can provide, see W.H. Durham, *Coevolution, Genes, Culture, and Human Diversity*, Stanford, CA: Stanford University Press, 1991.

21. B. Berlin and P. Kay, *Basic Color Terms: Their Universality and Evolution*, Berkeley and Los Angeles, California: University of California Press, 1969.

22. Berlin and Kay, *Basic Color Terms*, pp. 2–3. More recent research on the Berinmo tribe of Papua New Guinea suggests a much greater degree of linguistic influence on colour categorization, inconsistent with the existence of neurones which respond to all colour categories: J. Davidoff, I. Davies and D. Roberson, 'Colour Categories in a Stone-Age Tribe', *Nature* **398**, 1999, pp. 203–204.

23. R.H. Masland, *Science* **271**, 1996, pp. 616–17; V. Walsh, *Current Biology* **5**, 1995, 703–705; M. Neitz and J. Neitz, *Science* **267**, 1996, pp. 1013–16; S-K. Shyue, D. Hewet-Emmett, H.G. Sperling, D.M. Hunt, J.K. Bowmaker, J.D. Mollon and W-H. Li, *Science* **269**, 1995, pp. 1265–67; L. Stryer, *Proceedings of the National Academy of Sciences USA* **93**, 1996, pp. 557–59, and subsequent papers in colloquium entitled 'Vision: From Photon to Perception'.

24. S. Pinker, *The Language Instinct: The New Science of Language and Mind*, London: Penguin, 1994. For a different perspective see M. Tomasello, *The Cultural Origins of Human Cognition*, Harvard University Press, 1999.

25. I have drawn for this section particularly from Durham, *Coevolution, Genes, Culture, and Human Diversity*, pp. 289–360.

26. K. Hopkins, 'Brother–Sister Marriage in Roman Egypt', *Comparative Studies in Society and History* **22**, 1980, pp. 303–54.

27. P.L. van der Berghe, 'Human Inbreeding Avoidance: Culture in Nature', *Behavioural and Brain Sciences* **6**, 1983, pp. 91–123.

28. J. Shepher, *Incest: The Biosocial View*, London: Academic Press, 1983.

29. The results are summarized by Durham, *Coevolution, Genes, Culture, and Human Diversity*, pp. 311–13.

30. P. Bateson, *Nature* **295**, 1982, pp. 236–37; C. Packer, *Animal Behaviour* **27**, 1979, pp. 1–36; A. Pusey, *Animal Behaviour* **28**, 1980, pp. 543–52.

31. F. Livingstone, 'Cultural Causes of Genetic Change', in G. Barlow and J. Silverberg (eds), *Sociobiology: Beyond/Nature/Nurture?*, Washington, USA: American Association for the Advancement of Science, 1980, pp. 307–29.

32. C. Lumsden and E.O. Wilson, *Promethean Fire*, Harvard University Press, 1983, pp. 127–30.

33. Kitcher, *Vaulting Ambition*.

34. R.V. Burton, 'Folk Theory and the Incest Taboo'. *Ethos* **504**, 1973, pp. 504–16.

35. A fuller discussion of the points mentioned here can be found in Durham, *Coevolution, Genes, Culture, and Human Diversity*, chapter 6.

36. M. Kaffman, 'Sexual standards and behavior of the kibbutz adolescent', *American Journal of Orthopsychiatry* **47**, 1977, pp. 207–17. See also the fascinating interviews by Amia Lieblich with the members of one of the largest Kibbutz communities in Israel during the late 1970s in A. Lieblich, *Kibbutz Makom*, London: Andre Deutsch, 1982. Furthermore, the authors, who provided a detailed account of their findings on minor marriages in Taiwan, were extremely cautious about their interpretation: see A.P. Wolf and C. Huang, *Marriage and Adoption in China 1845–1945*, Stanford University Press, 1980.

37. M. Greenberg and R. Littlewood, 'Post-adoption Incest and Phenotypic Matching: Experience, Personal Meanings and Biosocial Implications'. *British Journal of Psychology* **68**, 1995, pp. 29–44.

38. Lumsden and Wilson, *Promethean Fire*, p. 30.

39. S.J. Gould, 'Sociobiology and Human Nature: A Postpanglossian Vision', in *Sociobiology Examined*, A. Montagu (ed.), Oxford: OUP, 1980, pp. 283–90.

40. J. Roughgarden, *Theory of Population Genetics and Evolutionary Ecology: An Introduction*, New York: Macmillan, 1979.

41. W.D. Hamilton, 'The Evolution of Altruistic Behaviour', *American Naturalist* **97**, 1963, pp. 354–56; W.D. Hamilton, 'The Genetic Evolution of Social Behaviour', *Journal of Theoretical Biology* **7**, 1964, 1–52; R.L. Trivers, 'The Evolution of Reciprocal Altruism', *Quarterly Review of Biology* **46**, 1971, pp. 35–57. Note, however, that more recent work has suggested that competition between relatives can counteract kin selection for altruism. For example, see S.A. West et al., 'Testing Hamilton's Rule with Competition Between Relatives', *Nature* **409**, 2001, pp. 510–13.

42. See, for example, L. Mealey, 'The Sociobiology of Sociopathy: An Integrated Evolutionary Model', *Behavioral and Brain Sciences* **18**, 1995, pp. 523–99, and references cited therein.

43. R. Axelrod, *The Evolution of Cooperation*, New York: Basic Books, 1984.

44. Mealey, 'The Sociobiology of Sociopathy', p. 524.

45. Ruse, *Taking Darwin Seriously*, p. 221.

46. Ruse, *Taking Darwin Seriously*, p. 255 and p. 272.

47. Wilson, *Consilience*, p. 157.

48. Ruse, *Taking Darwin Seriously*, p. 253.

49. Wilson, *On Human Nature*, 1978.

50. Wilson, *On Human Nature*, p. 119.

51. D.S. Wilson and E. Sober, 'Reintroducing Group Selection to the Human Behavior Sciences', *Behavioral and Brain Sciences* **17**, 1994, pp. 585–608, 1994.

52. Wilson and Sober, 'Re-introducing Group Selection to the Human Behavior Sciences', p. 605.

53. P. Hallie, 'From Cruelty to Goodness', in C. Sommers and F. Sommers (eds), *Vice and Virtue in Everyday Life*, New York: Harcourt Brace Jovanovich, 1989, pp. 9–24.

54. R.P. Busse, 'From Belief to Unbelief and Back to Belief: A Response to Michael Ruse', *Zygon* **29**, 1994, pp. 55–65.

55. D. Hume, *Treatise of Human Nature*, Oxford: Clarendon Press, 1978, p. 469.

56. Moore's 'naturalistic fallacy' is more clearly stated in a preface to the second draft of *Principia Ethica*, which was never published. However, Moore's preface is summarized in P.F. Strawson (ed.) *Studies in the Philosophy of Thought and Action*, London: Oxford Paperbacks, 1968. Other discussions of the fallacy are found in P. Foot (ed.), *Theories of Ethics*, Oxford: Oxford Readings in Philosophy, 1967.

57. Ruse, *Taking Darwin Seriously*, p. 242.

58. R. Grunberger, *Social History of the Third Reich*, Weidenfeld & Nicholson, 1971.

Grunberger tells how 300 occupants of professional chairs addressed a manifesto to the electorate, asking them to vote for Hitler in March 1933. 'Many academics who were by no means committed Nazis welcomed the national wave as regenerative and healthy in essence, despite such regrettable side-effects as Jew-baiting and storm-troop brutality.'

59. Ruse, *Taking Darwin Seriously*, p. 279.

60. Ruse, *Taking Darwin Seriously*, p. 244. This point is exacerbated rather than ameliorated by Ruse's more recent attempt to square the 'natural law' revealed by sociobiology with Christian morality: 'Doing things that are natural is not right simply because these things are natural, but because the natural is good as intended by God', see M. Ruse 'Can a Darwinian Be a Christian – Ethical Issues?' *Zygon* **35**, pp. 287–98 and 'Can a Darwinian Be a Christian – Sociobiological Issues?' *Zygon* **35**, 2000, 299–316. But the problem still remains: of that great diversity of behaviours which different people feel are natural (which include a good number that are distinctly non-Christian), which specific behaviours ought we to adopt?

61. Ruse, *Taking Darwin Seriously*, p. 239

62. Barash, *The Whisperings Within*, p. 167. For a robust and wide-ranging discussion on questions of intentionality and free will see Rose and Rose *Alas, Poor Darwin*.

63. Dawkins, *The Selfish Gene*, p. 3.

64. G.C. Williams, 'Huxley's Evolution and Ethics in Sociobiological Perspective', *Zygon* **23**, 1988, pp. 384–85.

65. Rachels, *Created from Animals*, p. 4.

66. Rachels, *Created from Animals*, p. 87.

67. *The Boston Globe*, 29 April 1994, p. 8.

68. Rachels, *Created from Animals*, pp. 197–98.

69. Rachels, *Created from Animals*, pp. 173–74.

70. Rachels, *Created from Animals*, pp. 204–205.

71. Rachels, *Created from Animals*, p. 205.

72. Quotations from Nietzsche are from R.J. Hollingdale (ed.), *A Nietzsche Reader*, Harmondsworth: Penguin, 1977.

73. J. Miller, *The Passion of Michel Foucault*, London: HarperCollins, 1993.

74. J. Coffey, 'Life After the Death of God? Michel Foucault and Postmodern Atheism', *Cambridge Papers*, November 1996.

75. Ruse, 'From Belief to Unbelief – and Halfway Back', p. 25.

76. R.N. Proctor, *Racial Hygiene: Medicine Under the Nazis*, Harvard University Press, 1988; B.Muller-Hill, *Murderous Science*, Oxford: OUP, 1988.

77. R.J. Lifton, *The Nazi Doctors: Medical Killing and the Psychology of Genocide*, Basic Books, 1986.

Chapter 12 (pp. 407–25)

1. J.D. Barrow and F.J. Tipler, *The Anthropic Cosmological Principle*, Oxford: OUP, 1988.

2. For example:
P.C.W. Davies, *The Mind of God*, London: Penguin, 1992.
Polkinghorne, *Reason & Reality*.
M. Rees, *Before the Beginning: Our Universe and Others*, Simon & Schuster, 1997.
J. Silk, *A Short History of the Universe*, Scientific American Library, 1994.
J. Leslie, *Universes*, London: Routledge, 1989.

3. Barrow and Tipler, *The Anthropic Cosmological Principle*, p. 15.

4. It has sometimes been suggested that the existence of intelligent beings in some other corner of the universe would posit dilemmas for religious belief on planet earth. John Davis argues that this is not necessarily the case in 'The Search for Extraterrestrial Intelligence and the Christian Doctrine of

Redemption', *Science & Christian Belief* **9**, 1997, pp. 21–34.

5. Barrow and Tipler, *The Anthropic Cosmological Principle*, p. 22.

6. B.J. Carr and M.J. Rees, 'The Anthropic Principle and the Structure of the Physical World', *Nature* **278**, 1979, pp. 605–12.

7. J. Gribbin and M. Rees, *The Stuff of the Universe*, London: Penguin, 1990, p. 247.

8. J. Doye, J. Hampton, P. Shellard, S. Walley and A. Wild, 'Evidence for Design in the Physical World?', *Christians in Science* Conference paper, 1996, p. 5.

9. Barrow and Tipler, *The Anthropic Cosmological Principle*, p. 385.

10. P.J.E. Peebles, 'Evolution of the cosmological constant', *Nature* **398**, 1999, pp. 25–26.

11. Barrow and Tipler, *The Anthropic Cosmological Principle*.

12. M. Rees, *Before the Beginning: Our Universe and Others*, Simon & Schuster, 1997.

13. C.F.A. Pantin, *Advances in Science* **8**, 1951, p. 138. See also I.T. Ramsey (ed.), *Biology and Personality*, Oxford: Blackwell, 1965, pp. 83–106.

14. Hawking, *A Brief History of Time*.

15. R.D. Holder, 'Fine-Tuning, Many Universes, and Design', *Science & Christian Belief* **13**, 2001, pp. 5–24.

16. Dennett, *Darwin's Dangerous Idea*.

17. Hawking, *A Brief History of Time*, p. 174.

18. W.L. Craig, 'Barrow and Tipler on the Anthropic Principle vs Divine Design', *British Journal of the Philosophy of Science* **38**, 1988, pp. 389–95.

19. The example in this paragraph is from P. Dowe, 'Response to Holder: Multiple Universe Explanations Are Not Explanations', *Science & Christian Belief* **11**, 1999, pp. 67–68.

20. Cited in Wilson, *Consilience*, p. 52.

21. S. Weinberg, *The First Three Minutes: A Modern View of the Origin of the Universe*, Glasgow: William Collins, 1977, p. 148.

22. S. Weinberg in interview with Margaret Wertheim, *Science & Spirit* **10**, 1999, pp. 20–22.

23. P. Davies, *The Cosmic Blueprint*, Heinemann, 1987, p. 203.

24. 'An Astronomer Sees the Light', interview with Fred Hoyle, *New Scientist*, 21 November 1983, p. 49.

Chapter 13 (pp. 426–57)

1. Letter to *The Times*, July 13, 1984, by Professor R.J. Berry FRSE, President of the Linnean Society, and Sir Robert Boyd CBE FRS, Professor Martin Bott FRS, Professor Denis P. Burkitt FRS, Sir Clifford Butler FRS, Professor John T. Houghton FRS, Professor D. Tyrrell FRS, Professor E.H. Andrews (Materials Science, London), Professor E.R. Dobbs (Physics, London), Professor J.B. Lloyd (Biochemistry, Keele), Professor M.A. Jeeves (Psychology, St Andrews), Professor C.A. Russell (History of Science, Open University), Professor D.C. Spanner (Plant Biophysics, London), Professor G.B. Wetherill (Statistics, Kent).

2. *Nature* **310**, 19 July 1984, p. 171. The first section of the editorial, which is not quoted here, is a summary of *The Times* letter.

3. For example, see:
F.J. Beckwith, *David Hume's Argument Against Miracles: A Critical Analysis*, University Press of America, 1989.
C. Brown, *Miracles and the Critical Mind*, W.B. Eerdmans, 1984.
R.M. Burns, *The Great Debate on Miracles: From Joseph Glanvill to David Hume*, Bucknell University Press, 1981.
A. Flew, *Hume's Philosophy of Belief*, Routledge & Kegan Paul, 1961.

J. Houston, *Reported Miracles: A Critique of Hume*, Cambridge: CUP, 1994.
M.P. Levine, *Hume and the Problem of Miracles: A Solution*, Kluwer Academic Publishers, 1989.

4. D. Hume, *Enquiries Concerning Human Understanding and Concerning the Principles of Morals*, L.A. Selby-Bigge (ed.), 3rd edition, with text and notes, Oxford: OUP, 1975.

5. A point argued at some length by Burns, *The Great Debate on Miracles*.

6. Thomas Sprat, *History of the Royal Society*, London, 1667, Facsimile reprint, St Louis, USA: Washington University Studies, 1958, p. 352.

7. Hume, *Enquiries Concerning Human Understanding*, p. 113.

8. Hume, *Enquiries Concerning Human Understanding*, p. 114.

9. Hume, *Enquiries Concerning Human Understanding*, p. 124.

10. There has been much scholarly discussion over the question of why, if miracles cannot happen, as Hume appears to be claiming in Part 1 of his essay, there should then be the necessity to add Part 2 which presented the standard deistic a posteriori arguments of the era to undermine the credibility of miracles accounts. If miracles cannot happen anyway, then what is the point in considering such arguments? The philosopher Antony Flew tried to smooth the ambiguity by suggesting that in Part 1 Hume was not really saying that miracles are impossible, only that they are very unlikely, making further arguments necessary in Part 2 (cf. Flew *Hume's Philosophy of Belief*). But a more convincing explanation has been put forward by Burns, who maintains that Hume originally wrote the essay in its Part 1 form only to demonstrate the absolute inconceivability of rational belief in miracles, but then reluctantly later came to the conclusion that his arguments would be taken more seriously if his claims were made rather more cautiously (see Burns, *The Great Debate on Miracles*, p. 154f.).

11. For a more detailed discussion of the varied uses of 'law' terminology in the history of science, see J.H. Brooke, 'Natural Law in the Natural Sciences', *Science & Christian Belief* **4**, 1992, pp. 83–103.

12. E. Mach, *Popular Scientific Lectures*, Chicago: Open Court Publishing, 1989.

13. S. Hawking, 'Letters to the Editor: Time and the Universe', *American Scientist* **73**, 1985, p. 12.

14. P. Davies, *The Mind of God: Science and the Search for Ultimate Meaning*, London: Penguin, 1992, pp. 72–92.

15. For example, D.M. Armstrong, *What is a Law of Nature?*, Cambridge: CUP, 1983, p. 8.

16. Dawkins, *The Blind Watchmaker*, p. 139.

17. Exodus 14:21. Whether the correct translation is 'Red Sea' or 'Sea of Reeds' is still debated by biblical scholars – there is evidence on both sides of the question – but the Hebrew text does state 'Sea of Reeds'.

18. A.S. Issar, 'La Bible et la Science – Font-elles Bon Menage?' *La Recherche*, January 1996, pp. 48–54 (English text kindly provided by Professor Issar).

19. See the Israelites' Song of Deliverance in Exodus 15. The early church clearly saw the crossing of the Reed Sea as a 'miraculous sign', cf. Acts 7:36.

20. Exodus 8:23. See also Psalm 106:21–22; 135:9; Jeremiah 32:20.

21. See John 2:1–11 and 20:1–18.

22. R.J. Berry, 'The Virgin Birth of Christ', *Science & Christian Belief* **8**, 1996, pp. 101–10.

23. For example *terata* in Acts 2:19, cf. *mopheth* used in Deuteronomy 29:3.

24. Cited by Brown, *Miracles and the Critical Mind*, p. 217.

25. For example as in 2 Corinthians 12:12; Hebrews 2:4; Acts 8:13, etc.

26. Deuteronomy 29:3.

27. This example is based on that found in Beckwith, *David Hume's Argument Against Miracles*, p. 96.

28. John 20:6–7.

29. I am aware that the idea that Hume propounds a circular argument is not supported by all commentators. For example, Beckwith suggests that Hume is not arguing for the uniformity of nature, but rather that 'our formulations of natural law, if they are to be considered lawful appraisals of our perceptions, must be based on uniform experience, or they cease to be natural law' (cf. Beckwith, *David Hume's Argument Against Miracles*, p. 28). Thus, according to David Norton, 'If our experience of X's has been "firm and unalterable" or "infallible", then we have, in Hume's scheme, a "proof" and are in a position to formulate a law of nature, or a summation of uniform experience. Correlatively, the moment we fail to have a proof, or perfect empirical support for any summation, we fail to have a law of nature.' In other words, if a miracle is by definition a violation of a natural law, but a violated law is really no law at all (because a natural law, by definition, is only such if based on uniform experience), then clearly miracles cannot happen. However, as Beckwith himself points out, this interpretation of Hume's position does not make his argument less of a tautology, for we may still ask the question 'Why must one accept that a natural law cannot be a natural law if it has been violated?', and if the answer is that 'natural law cannot be otherwise' then the question has been begged and Hume's argument remains essentially circular. Indeed, it is difficult to read Hume's Essay without receiving a strong impression of a circular argument – as soon as the possibility of a genuinely persuasive collection of evidence in favour of the miraculous is mooted, Hume pulls the rug by claiming that since miracles are impossible anyway the weight of evidence is insufficient to carry the day.

30. Burns, *The Great Debate on Miracles*, p. 32.

31. W. Corduan, 'Recognizing a Miracle', in R.D. Geivett & G.R. Habermas (eds), *In Defence of Miracles*, Apollos, 1997, p. 102.

32. S. Shapin, *A Social History of Truth: Civility and Science in 17th-Century England*, University of Chicago Press, 1994.

33. J.H. Brooke, 'Natural Law in the Natural Sciences', *Science & Christian Belief* **4**, 1992, pp. 83–103.

34. Augustine, *Confessions* VI.5, trans. R.S. Pine-Coffin, London: Penguin, 1961, p. 117.

35. R.J. Evans, *In Defence of History*, London: Granta Books, 1997, pp. 127 and 128.

36. A. Flew, *God: A Critical Enquiry*, 2nd edition, LaSalle, IL: Open Court, 1984, p. 140. The summary of Flew's argument is provided by Beckwith, *David Hume's Argument Against Miracles*, p. 94.

37. N.L. Geisler, *Miracles and the Modern Mind*, Baker, 1992, pp. 79–80.

38. A. Flew, 'Miracles' in P. Edwards (ed.), *Encyclopedia of Philosophy*, vol. 5, New York: Macmillan and the Free Press, 1967, p. 352.

39. cf. Beckwith, *David Hume's Argument Against Miracles*, pp. 122–33.

40. Hume, *Enquiries Concerning Human Understanding*, p. 112.

41. J.W. Montgomery, *Human Rights and Human Dignity*, Grand Rapids, MI: Zondervan, 1986, p. 134.

42. The argument is expanded in Beckwith, *David Hume's Argument Against Miracles*, pp. 122–33.

43. Acts 2:22

44. Romans 1:4.

45. John 11:48.

46. John 2:23.

47. John 12:37

48. For example Matthew 12:39–42; 16:1–4; Luke 11:29–32; John 6:30–33.

49. Luke 16:31.

50. See R. Swinburne, *Faith and Reason*, 1981, Oxford: Clarendon Press, p. 180, and R. Swinburne, *Revelation: From Metaphor to Analogy*, Oxford: Clarendon Press, 1992, chapter 5.

51. Luke 1:1–4.

52. John 21:24.

53. D. Hume, *Dialogues Concerning Natural Religion*, 1779, Indianapolis, IN: Bobbs-Merrill, 1947, p. 227.

Chapter 14 (pp. 458–73)

1. *Teaching About Evolution and the Nature of Science*, Washington, DC: National Academy Press, 1998, p. 58.

2. J. Ziman, 'Is Science Losing its Objectivity?', *Nature* **382**, 1996, pp. 751–54.

3. J. Horgan, *The End of Science*, Little, Brown, 1997.

4. P. Singer, *Practical Ethics*, 2nd edition, Cambridge: CUP, 1993, p. 88 and p. 173.

5. D.W. Amundsen, 'Medicine and the Birth of Defective Children: Approaches of the Ancient World', in R.C. McMillan, H.T. Engelhardt and S.F. Spicker (eds), *Euthanasia and the Newborn*, Dordrecht: D. Reidel, 1987, pp. 3–22.

6. Plato, *The Republic*, 460C.

7. Cited in Amundsen, 'Medicine and the Birth of Defective Children', p. 10.

8. Plutarch, *Life of Lycurgus*, quoted in Amundsen, 'Medicine and the Birth of Defective Children', p. 10.

9. See J. Wyatt, 'Application of Medical Technology to Paediatric Intensive Care', *Science & Christian Belief* **8**, 1996, pp. 3–20.

10. Singer, *Practical Ethics*, p. 169

11. Singer, *Practical Ethics*, p. 171.

12. Singer, *Practical Ethics*, p. 172.

13. H. Kuhse and P. Singer, *Should the Baby Live?* Oxford University Press, 1985, p. 134.

14. D. Gareth Jones, 'Infanticide: An Ethical Battlefield', *Science & Christian Belief*, **10**, 1998, pp. 3–19.

15. Genesis 1:26–28.

16. Further helpful discussion will be found in Refs 9 and 14.

17. Singer, *Practical Ethics*, see chapter 8, 'Rich and Poor', pp. 218–46.

18. Singer, *Practical Ethics*, p. 286.

19. Colossians 1:15–16.

20. For example, Psalm 104.

21. Cited in Thomas, *Man and the Natural World*, p. 278.

22. J. Calvin, *Commentary on Genesis*, 1554, trans. J. King, 1847, reprinted by Edinburgh: Banner of Truth Trust, 1965, p. 125.

23. C.A. Russell, *The Earth, Humanity and God*, UCL Press, 1994, p. 147.

24. I am well aware of the suggestion made by Lynn White Jr ('The historic roots of our ecological crisis', *Science* **155**, 1967, pp. 1204–1207) that Christianity had encouraged the exploitation of nature by promoting the notion of an arrogant dominion. It is now generally agreed that this claim is poorly supported by both historical and contemporary evidence. White's thesis has been widely discussed and there is not space to do it justice here. There is a large literature on the subject. For example, see:
J. Barr, 'Man and Nature: The Ecological Controversy and the Old Testament, *Bulletin of the John Ryland Library* **55**, 1972, pp. 9–32.
M.A. Jeeves and R.J. Berry, *Science, Life and Christian Belief*, Leicester: Apollos, 1998, pp. 222–25.
E.G. Nisbet, *Leaving Eden: To Protect and Manage the Earth*, Cambridge: CUP, 1991, pp. 90–92.
Russell, *The Earth, Humanity and God*, pp. 86–93.

25. Nisbet, *Leaving Eden*.

Index of Names

A

Agassiz, L. 36–37, 172, 191, 193–94, 201, 290, 293
Adelard of Bath 76
Ailly, P. d' 25
Alembert, J. le R. d' 148
Alexander of Macedon 73
Alexander the Great 75
Ampère, A.M. 218
Anaxagorus 70–71
Anaximander 67
Anaximenes 67
Anderson, C. 160
Annet, P. 143
Aquinas, T. 77–79, 116, 119, 138, 212
Archimedes 72, 80, 92
Archytas 92
Aristotle 24, 65, 68, 70–71, 73–79, 86, 89, 94, 96–99, 101–103, 110, 113–15, 117–18, 121, 126, 137, 165, 463–64
Arouet, F.M. *see* Voltaire
Artaud, A. 404
Ashurbanipal 321
Atkins, P. 57, 220, 279, 458
Atkinson, J. 127
Augustine of Hippo, St 12, 72, 76, 94, 119, 126, 131–32, 165–67, 173, 212, 320, 357, 426, 436, 447
Aurifaber, J. 126–27
Averroes, I.R. 76
Ayer, A.J. 231

B

Babbage, C. 210
Bach, J.S. 223
Bacon, F. 64, 85–88, 93, 98–101, 103–104, 106, 135, 148, 158, 162, 173, 191, 201, 231
Bacon, R. 81–82
Barash, D. 368–69
Barberini, M. *see* Urban VIII

Barnes, B. 18, 238
Barrow, J. 409–10, 418
Basil, St 357
Basso, S. 87
Becker, C. 218
Bede, the Venerable St 25
Beeckman, I. 93
Beethoven, L. 223, 253
Bellarmine, R.F.R., St 118–19, 122
Bentley, R. 138, 141
Berger, P. 46–47, 50
Berlin, B. 372–73
Berlin, I. 359
Bernal, J.D. 303
Berry, R.J. 428
Besant, A. 208
Bismarck, O.E.L. von, Prince 206
Bloor, D. 238
Bohr, N. 277
Bonaparte, N. 150
Bound, N. 52
Bourdieu, P. 20
Boyle, R. 64, 87–88, 92–94, 104, 133, 135–38, 140–42, 144, 147, 164, 244, 446
Brahms, J. 253, 275
Brahe, T. 80, 94, 97, 113–14
Brenner, S. 254
Broca, P. 32, 37–38
Brooke, J. 66, 125, 204
Brouncker, W. 447
Brune, J. de 130
Bruno, G. 116
Bryan, W.J. 295–99, 302–303, 305
Buckland, W. 172–73
Budd, S. 58
Buffon, G.-L. Leclerc, Comte de 166–67
Bulwer, J. 471
Buridan, J. 25, 102
Burnet, T. 165–67
Burns, R.M. 444–45
Burton, R. 378
Busk, G. 211
Busse, R. 390
Butler, L. 309
Butler, S. 108
Butterfield, H. 65, 145

C

Caccini, T. 117–18

Index of Subjects